Civil Disobediences

Poetics and Politics in Action

Civil
Disobediences

Poetics and Politics in Action

★ ★ ★ ★ ★ ★

EDITED BY ANNE WALDMAN & LISA BIRMAN

 COFFEE HOUSE PRESS

COVER + BOOK DESIGN Linda Koutsky
COVER PHOTO © Getty Images

Coffee House Press books are available to the trade through our primary distributor, Consortium Book Sales & Distribution, 1045 Westgate Drive, Saint Paul, MN 55114. For personal orders, catalogs, or other information, write to: Coffee House Press, 27 North Fourth Street, Suite 400, Minneapolis, MN 55401.

Coffee House Press is a nonprofit literary publishing house. Support from private foundations, corporate giving programs, government programs, and generous individuals help make the publication of our books possible. We gratefully acknowledge their support in detail in the back of this book. To you and our many readers across the country, we send our thanks for your continuing support.

LIBRARY OF CONGRESS CATALOGING-IN-PUBLICATION DATA
Civil disobediences : poetics and politics in action /
edited by Anne Waldman & Lisa Birman.
p. cm.
Includes bibliographical references.
ISBN 1-56689-158-2 (alk. paper)
1. American poetry—20th century—History and criticism.
2. Politics and literature—United States—History—20th century.
3. Political poetry. American—History and criticism.
4. Politics in literature.
I. Waldman, Anne
II. Birman, Lisa.
PS310.P6C585 2004   811'.509358—DC22
2004000683

FIRST EDITION │ FIRST PRINTING
1   3   5   7   9   10   8   6   4   2
PRINTED IN CANADA

Many people have helped us bring this book to completion—from remembering old manuscripts or lectures, to searching out and transcribing tapes, and providing supportive feedback. Thanks to Max Regan, David Gardner, Chris Fischbach, Ed Bowes, Anselm Hollo, Tara Blaine, Daron Mueller, Reed Bye, Traci Hales Vass, Peter Lamborn Wilson, Laura Wright, Todd McCarty, Randy Roark, Steve Dickison, Michael Smoler, Andrew Schelling, Stacy Elaine Dacheux, Andy Hoffman, Michelle Auerbach, Teresa Sparks, and Sean Hedden.

Thanks to the generosity of the authors and estates of authors published in *Civil Disobediences,* a portion of the proceeds of this book will be donated to the Naropa University Audio Archive Project. For more information about the project, please visit www.naropa.edu/audioarchive.

Civil
Disobediences

Poetics and Politics in Action

Contents

DHARMA POETICS

REVOLUTIONARY POETICS

GNOSIS & AESTHETICS

DOCUMENTS

Introduction

ANNE WALDMAN

Do we really want to expel poets from the Republic? Imagine Plato going through security at the Athens Airport, then arriving in the USA for a Modern Language Association convention. Would he be affronted? Amused? Would not the threat of censorship be worrisome? Would he appreciate the decor? If Henry David Thoreau were to travel, would he suffer humiliation and indignation? What might compare back then? Imagine your favorite radical literary heroes going through security: Lao Tze, Sappho, William Blake, Mary and Percy Shelley, Gertrude Stein, W. E. B. DuBois.

There is currently—and one feels this is not going to go away—a strange and disturbing "disjunct" or "rip" in our culture that calls for an articulate active response to the current repressive agenda where anyone who doesn't agree with current USA administration junta policies is "unpatriotic." It's as if people have given over control of their "destiny"—in fact, their "imaginations"—to a hopeless gray area of defeat and despair. When I get an e-mail that "someone is investigating your background" is it just a scam or something really creepy? When I hear little "dips" in the phone stream is it a malfunction or the U.S. Attorney General listening in? When I am harassed by the IRS am I being paranoid or just seriously targeted? And so on. Are "they" trying to drive "us" crazy? The point here is the irony of the artist's situation—and others have experienced similar aggressions—specifically in our presumed democratic American culture and how one needs to "act" to feel sane, human, alive, intelligent, effective. Is there still some power in the word, in a poetics that engages the spirit, that delights the intellect, that moves—in William Carlos Williams's phrase—the century a few inches forward?

This anthology answers an urgent call to a poetics of engagement, which includes inquiry, contemplation, lively investigation into history and fields of gnosis. It covers an enormous range of particulars—from a fascinating account of plant/animal symbiosis to a radical discussion of gender and identity politics. It is a "talking" book—composed in many cases elegantly on the tongue. Genres include talks, lectures, essays, manifestoes, colloquia, interviews, and documents such as site-specific histories, an essay on Buddhist poetics as well as urgent political statements meant for public dissemination. These texts are not necessarily "polished" or academic. They are refreshingly free of the jargon of critical theory and predictable received ideas. They are also delightfully intergenerational, reflecting the vital exchange between established writers and younger adepts. For the most part this collection is to be read as a poet-activist's handbook, balancing a rootedness in the act of writing poetry that includes reading and thinking about it, and understanding how the imaginative mind works in response to its own dreams, longings, and the "outside" world, with a sense of being able to take this knowledge out into the public arena, *into the streets* as it were. There is the intention here of making a difference, of words as actions, of keeping the world safe for poetry with wit and attendant wisdom. It is of major importance to anyone curious about why poetry can make things happen, and why poets have seemed to have more public relevance since the difficult political events of recent years. This book unequivocally implies that poets as thinkers, as "legislators of the race," exist to be heard.

Many of these discourses, lectures, and discussions took place at the Jack Kerouac School of Disembodied Poetics' legendary Summer Writing Program held annually on the spine of the North American Continent at Naropa University in Boulder, Colorado. Founded in the early seventies with inspiration from the poetics and politics of the Beat Literary Movement and the other "outrider" wings of the New American Poetry against a backdrop of the "crazy wisdom" lineage of Tibetan Buddhism, Naropa has continued to be a mecca and—in Hakim Bey's term—a "temporary autonomous zone" for serious writers and scholars and students since that time. The anthology attempts to convey the excitement and aspiration that arises in this unique educational community which is like no other "writing program" in the world.

Civil Disobediences is divided into six sections. The first section, "Talking Poetics," invites the reader to listen to personal commentary on the act of being a writer, on the struggle and commitment it involves, on the passion and individuality one needs to maintain perspective and function as a full citizen of the world outside the dominant mainstream of conformity and consumerism. The next section, "Ancestral Presences" includes scholarly tributes and invites the radical spirit of both ancient and recent "presences" into the mix. "Dharma Poetics" is a bow to the important influence of Buddhism on American poetics, while "Revolutionary Poetics" covers a spectrum of relevant subjects, including a salient history of money, which push to the heart of what Allen Ginsberg calls a "breakthrough" in one's own imagination and consciousness that can literally wake people up. The "Gnosis & Aesthetics" section advocates strongly on behalf of urgent issues of environment, gender, the mythic "Muse," and considerations of beauty and form in culture. Finally, "Documents" offers brief pieces composed for specific topical occasions. In many ways this book could be seen as a blueprint for future communities of cultural poet-activists, opposed to war, opposed to injustice, and ready to offer a language free of euphemism as an antidote to an in-the-pocket media's stranglehold on the imagination.

Henry David Thoreau wrote in "Civil Disobedience," from which this volume takes its title:

> A corporation of conscientious men is a corporation with a conscience. Law never made men a whit more just; and, by means of their respect for it, even the well-disposed are daily made the agents of injustice. A common and natural result of an undue respect for law is, that you may see a file of soldiers, colonel, captain, corporal, privates, powder-monkeys, and all, marching in admirable order over hill and dale to the wars, against their wills, ay, against their common sense and consciences, which makes it very steep marching indeed, and produces a palpitation of the heart. They have no doubt that it is a damnable business in which they are concerned; they are all peaceably inclined. Now, what are they? Men at all? or small movable forts and magazines, at the service of some unscrupulous man in power?

These are telling and cautionary words.

On a date that seems ancient history now, and in a "kinder, gentler" yet anxious and presciently *dangerous* time—January 20, 2001—a group of us attended the events of the Shadow Inauguration in Washington, DC's Stanton Park. We were there as poets-in-protest and specifically to support African Americans and others who had been disenfranchised at the polls in Florida and elsewhere. Before beginning a march on the Supreme Court Building, the large crowd (upward of 2,000 people) took an oath to uphold the Voting Rights Act of 1965. That law was established in order to reaffirm the right of African Americans to vote, a right that had clearly been hindered during the presidential election. We then proceeded to circle the building in spite of the taunts and banter from Bush supporters.

"Go back to Russia!"

"Get a job!"

"Get back to the back of the bus!"

This last ugly goad was a bracing reminder that the struggle for peace and social justice never ends and that one has to make a greater vow not to be discouraged from the activist path.

We were in an armed city. Then thousand members of law enforcement agencies were out in full gear. Our small cell of poets—Kristin Prevallet, Anselm Hollo, Alan Gilbert, Maggie Zurawski—and Catholic activist nun Maryanne Gleason kept steady with our stenciled signs in the cold rain. Kristin had invoked Voltaire's famous "Écrasez l'infâme!" ("down with infamy," "make war on the fanatics!" and in another version, "crush bigotry!")

Pondering the tragic events since that day, which have led to an even increasingly destabilized and globally warmed-up planet, and reflecting on all the marches, rallies, antiwar agitprop, a range of oppositional poetics activity both local and global, and poised now on the eve of the next decisive American election, one has to invoke once again the long view. *Never give in or up.* It's possible to build sanity into our daily lives, into our consciousness, as a spiritual and creative practice.

In this spirit, Lisa Birman and I offer this tome, which reflects a huge collective effort—as "civil"—polite, dignified, conscientious, decentralized thinking—"disobediences," poetic acts that need to be outside the strictures of repression, censorship, war, that are in disagreement with the going "capital" and the agendas of the rich and powerful cartels of the world. No one wants to be "dissed" on this planet, more people and life forms need to be heard from. Poets for countless centuries have had a pulse on the ebb and flow of the "polis" and can speak for the "tribe" and for other sentient beings. We invite you to join in this discourse.

The Jack Kerouac School of Dismebodied Poetics
March, 2004
Year of the Wood Monkey

★ ★ ★ ★ ★ ★

Talking Poetics

★ ★ ★ ★ ★ ★

In This Place Called America

SONIA SANCHEZ
July 3, 2003

★　　★　　★

Before I begin, I would like to call on living and ago resistors: Richard Moore, CLR James, Adam Clayton Powell, Geronimo, Geronimo Pratt, Toni Cade Bambara, Vincent Harding, Barbara Deming, Angela Davis, Elizabeth Catlett, Maurice Bishop, Maya Angelou, Nat Turner, Shirley Graham DuBois, Mr. Micheaux, Mumia, Ghandi, Gwendolyn Brooks, Amiri Baraka, Ed Bullins, Askia Touré, Allen Ginsberg, Dorothy Day, June Jordan, Ida Wells-Barnett, Ella Baker, Chris Hani, Oliver Tambo, Chavez, Odetta, Sweet Honey in the Rock, Du Bois, Fannie Lou Hamer, Victoria Gray, Sitting Bull, Sister Lolita Lebrón, Paul Robeson, Billy Avery, Jose Martí, Diop, David Walker, Margaret Walker, Alice Walker, Walter Rodney, Nkrumah, Sojourner Truth, William Wells Brown, John Brown, Sterling Brown, Dada and Mama Sisulu, Martin Delany, Mumia, Mandela, Viola Plummer, Ruby Doris, Ngugi wa Thiong'o, Nicky and James and Andy, Frantz Fanon, Robert Moses, Queen Mother Moore, Septima Clark, Bobby Sands, Patrick Hill, Toni Morrison, James Baldwin, Pam Africa, Ramona Africa, Langston Hughes, Mumia, Chinua Achebe, Dessalines, Toussaint, MLK, Malcolm, Malcolm (clicks her tongue) Malcolm (clicks), The Roots (clicks), Dead Prez (clicks), Aaron McGruder (clicks), Mos Def (clicks), Talib, Assata, Assata, 2Pac (clicks), Rakim (clicks), and all of us here . . . sitting here looking at each other (clicks) . . . ahhh . . .

I'd like to begin with a joke that my father told me when I was a little girl and I ignored it because I was too busy going outside to play. And who wants to listen to your father talk. But I had a chance again to hear my father tell this joke to my twins in a place called Philadelphia when I was in the kitchen cooking and I came and stood in the hallway and listened and thought to myself: we always have a second chance, sometimes, to listen to our parents. My father tells the joke about the first Black pilot in America which happened after World War II in a place called New York City. People went to La Guardia and got on the plane and the cockpit door was open. And as people got on they looked and saw this Black guy sitting there, you know, and they sat down. And at that time, the flight attendants were called stewardess . . . and all the lights went on.

"Stewardess . . . stewardess . . . is . . . that a Negro . . . in the cockpit?" And she says, "Well, just a minute, just a minute. Let me turn off the lights. Let me go talk to Captain Jack Jones and let him talk to you." And she goes in the cockpit and she says, "Jack, I told you to keep the door closed. Everyone has seen you now and there's a problem." And he says, "Oh, Janey, don't worry. I'll talk to everybody." So, he gets on the intercom and he says, "Good morning, ladies and gentlemen. My name is Captain Jack Jones. I am your pilot for our trip to L.A. today. But before I begin, let me tell you just a little bit of myself. I'm a graduate of Harvard University. I'm a graduate of Yale University. I'm a graduate of M.I.T. I'm a graduate of Oxford University. And then during World War II, I taught all the pilots how to fly. So, if you would just settle down and calm down, I will see if I can get this big motherfucker off the ground."

It's an amazing story and joke. So different from as I tell all my students when they say, "Did you see the comedy on *Apollo?*" And I say, "Yeah, they're always mocking each other. They're not telling jokes." And that's always a bone of contention during the semester as I bring the jokes to them.

But I was born in a place called Birmingham, Alabama. Some people call it "Bombingham." For years. Where many of the Black women were mothers, servants, and teachers. The men were mostly workers. A few well-trained conditioned ones were teachers like my father in Black schools. Or some worked in companies, like my grandfather, who worked at the American Cast Iron Pipe Company. As pipes came out, he tagged them with a number.

And my grandmother was a domestic housewife, mother, deaconess in the AME Zion Methodist Church. We lived within the shadow of segregation. Overt racism. In the shadow of Black folk at the mercy of everyone: schools, police, courts of law, government. And all of our experiences were shaped by these various forces.

I bring to you this short autobiographical statement because I believe the Caribbean writer George Lamming's definition of culture is very clear: "Culture is the means, whereby, people feed themselves and the ways in which they experience their existence . . . A dominant class, exclusively white, laid the foundation of a cultural force that would influence all our lives. It was the ideology of racism. A morality whose guiding light was the aristocracy of the skin. Black: a commodity for cheap labor. White was the symbol and source of authority."

In the South of my grandmother and grandfather and father stood a legalized institutionalized oppression that spoke to the imposed limitations of Black folk. Separate schools. Sitting in the back of the bus. Separate churches. Separate burial grounds. Cemeteries. Separate restaurants. Separate faces divided eyes viewing ourselves and the world. And fear was a constant companion for Black folk even if you were a privileged Black, like my father, because he was a schoolteacher, musician, and nightclub owner. Because a competent, relevant education was unavailable to most poor Blacks, just as today, for most poor people. If you had an education, you were a privileged Black and that made for real social stratification.

One of my missions, then, as a writer/educator has been to eradicate/erase the aura of the educated class while cherishing the creative power of learning. I want to say that again because it means so much to me. One of my missions, then, as a writer/educator has been to eradicate/erase the aura of the educated class while cherishing the creative power of learning. A task for the truly creative teacher, writer, worker, preacher, lawyer, human being. One of my missions has been to celebrate the red black gums, corn cob smoking, nodding, staring people who were never considered poetic but we gave them life, form, and beauty.

I always remember the first time I read Sterling Brown's poetry. A man who came out of the Harlem Renaissance. And I thought when I saw the people that he had created, that I knew those people but I had never come across those people in any books of poetry that I read. And I do understand fully and in no uncertain terms that is what you have to do. You have to paint those pictures about people who were never considered beautiful, but you give them form, life, and beauty.

In the North, where my family moved to the north of New York City. North of Harlem and East Harlem. Bodegas and barrios. The north of a first floor back apartment. The north of a bedroom with a window facing a brick wall. And a courtyard of garbage and smells and sounds of poor people's voices splintering the night. In the North of subtle racism, and oppression and open disrespect of a teacher walking into our classroom and stating to the boys: "I don't know why I'm going to try to teach you anything. Because you'll just end up in jail." And some of the young men fulfilled her predictions and ended up in prison. And she turned and looked at the young girls and said: "I don't know why I'm going to teach you anything. You're just going to end up having babies." And some of them did.

This teacher lived out what Carlos Fuentes said: "We only hurt others who are incapable of imagining themselves. Cruelty is caused by a failure of the imagination. The inability to assign the same feelings and values to another person that your harbor in yourself." So I help people to imagine me. My people. The women. The men. The children. All our beautiful and terrible selves. Just like them.

My struggle and the struggle of others for identity and liberation has influenced my imagination and the creativity of many writers. For, in this supposed "free North," I discovered schools that taught science in Black and Latino neighborhoods with no labs. I discovered tenements and no regular garbage pickup. I discovered corner store merchants who kept books on what you owed and purchased and dared your father or mother to speak up or disagree or you would be cut off the "loan line"—"the coming to the store and buying for credit" line. I discovered bars and liquor stores on our corners and storefront church sounds breaking the solemn Harlem air with the sounds of swinging jubilation and hope and despair. I discovered a little girl in love with books and writing . . .

. . . and no one cared.

And no one thought, years later, even at Hunter College, that writing was a possibility for someone Black and female. As my counselor stated at Hunter College: "You want to be a writer?" And she laughed. And she laughed. And she laughed. And she leaned back in her white hair and laughed. "No, there are no Negro writers," she said. "You must be realistic. We let you come here to Hunter College, you privileged ones. So you can be a social worker or a teacher or a nurse. A writer? That's not realistic." And she laughed. And laughed. Again.

And I accepted her analysis of life and others' analysis of life including my father's advice: "Get an education, girl. It'll help free you. Then get married and move to Long Island or Mount Vernon. Leave Harlem. The Harlem of Blacks. Yellow tan faces asking for equality, life, love. Freedom against great odds."

And then I heard the Southern thunder. I saw the bravery of Black students in the South. Saw them sitting in questioning others' authority over their lives. Then I heard new words. "Freedom now" words. "Boycott" words. Montgomery, Alabama words. Freedom Rider words. "Four Little Girls Massacred in a Church" words. "We Shall Overcome" words. SNCC words. Rosa Parks words. Sunday morning words and Martin Luther King words, which said: "We are on the move now. The burning of our churches will not deter us. We are on the move now. The bombing of our homes will not dissuade us. We are on the move now. The beating and killing of our clergymen and young people will not desert us. We are on the move now. We are moving on the land of freedom and are heard. Let us march on segregated housing until every ghetto of social and economic depression dissolves and negroes and whites live side by side in decent, safe, and sanitary housing. Let us march on segregated schools until every vestige of segregated and inferior education becomes a thing of the past and negroes and whites study side by side in the socially healing context of the classroom. Let us march on poverty until no American parent has to skip a meal so that their children may eat, until no starved man walks the streets of our cities and towns in search of jobs that do not exist." I heard,

"We must recognize that we can't solve our problems now until there is a radical redistribution of economic and political power. Integration must be seen not merely in aesthetic or in magic terms. It must be seen in political terms. Integration, in its true dimension, is shared power."

And then I joined New York CORE. Picketed television stations. Closed Woolworth stores for not hiring Blacks or feeding Blacks. Then, we in New York CORE threw a massive picket line around Harlem Hospital because the electrical plumbers' union was trying to build an extension to Harlem Hospital and we said, "No way. You must open up the unions to Blacks and Puerto Ricans here. In the richest city in the world." The union said no and the battle began. My father tells the story of hearing noises down below and he looked out from his balcony on 135th Street. And he got his binoculars and he saw us standing below on the ground standing arms outstretched joined at the spine with history chanting, "We shall not be moved." And policemen on horseback were heading for us and we stood our ground. And my father, grasping the situation, ran down his stairs to protect his daughter from the hooves of these policemen protecting the property of a city and city administrators. And as luck would have it, but there is no such thing as "luck," a Black police captain was being driven to work and saw the situation and drove his car up on the sidewalk and stopped this confrontation. That day, we who had been so close to death began to negotiate for the life of some Black or Puerto Rican men so they could work and become journeymen in a place called New York City. And one of the journeymen would be my brother, who became an electrician.

And then I heard the Northern morning thunder . . . Malcolm. And his voice set me out looking for myself into the Schomburgs of the world. And I found Robeson, Du Bois, Delany's *Blake: or; The Huts of America*. And I was no longer afraid of Malcolm because he was part of a continuum. He and Martin. And I found Toomer, Chestnutt, Wheatley, Langston Hughes, Douglass, McKay, Barnett, Spenser, Garvey, Brown, (Sterling, and William Wells) Brown, Arthur P. Davis, Margaret Walker, Gwendolyn Brooks. And he set my eyes overseas to Ngugi wa Thiong'o, Chinua Achebe, Nyerere, Nkrumah, Lumumba, Chairman Mao, C.L.R. James, Guillén, Neruda.

And I made an amazing discovery. When you go searching for your identity. When you write about yourself and your struggle. When you begin a journey of identity for liberation, you find yourself and others who have been vanished too or who have hidden their eyes from themselves. And as I helped found Black Studies in America and I taught Black Studies at San Francisco State College, I found for my two Japanese American students information about concentration camps.

Actually, as I was heading for class that day someone handed me something that they had found and said, "Sonia, we think this has to do about concentration camps." There's a rumor going around that Japanese people were put in concentration camps. Now, you have to remember that we're talking about '66 or '67, so you're not talking about the information we know now, right? So I went in with this thing, as most of you know I'm a bourgeois bag lady. I have all these bags that I carry around with me. So, I went in and I had it and then at the end of the class, I remembered it and I picked it up and said, "Oh, here," and I looked up directly at my two Japanese American students and said, "Hi, perhaps, you know something about this. There is some information, we think, that this is about concentration camps." And they got pissed. You know, you know how you get pissed at us sometimes, you students, you know, looking at me looking at you. They said, "I don't know anything about that!" And I said, "Well, would you just keep it? I think this is important." And . . . that's all I said and we made our circle. And in the circle they said very little. They just nodded their heads and I thought: whoops . . . have I made a mistake bringing something in that I really don't know anything about.

Well, they returned to school on Tuesday and they entered the room with such a quietness. And they said, "Can we say something?" And they began to talk and they said, "A very strange thing happened to us. We went home and we showed this to our parents. And an amazing thing happened; our parents told us that they had been in concentration camps." Isn't it amazing? The silence. The silence. The silence in this country. The silence. The silence in this country.

And they began to talk about that. And so, I thought as I looked at them later on when I went home and I thought, "That's their final there. They must interview their parents and others from this particular time. That is what you do when something like that comes up. This is important for them to interview."

And one of the young women went on to make an important seminal documentary on Japanese Americans and concentration camps. I was reading in Seattle. You know when someone comes walking toward you, you remember the walk. You remember the face. A little bit older. She walked up to me and I hugged her. I said, "Ah, concentration camps." And I said, "When I saw your name, after that, you know, I was utterly amazed and I just jumped up and down and said 'See, see, see . . . this thing does happen sometimes . . . something does happen!'" As I said to my students today, it does get better. You just have to work to make it better. You have to work to make it better.

And as I taught in the university setting, I discovered Native American poetry. I found the Long March. I started with African American literature.

Went on in my class to Native American poetry. I found the Long March, Wounded Knee, Sitting Bull, Geronimo, and every treaty made broken with Native Americans. I found Chief Seattle who said, "These shores will swarm with the invisible dead of my tribe. Be just and deal kindly with Indian people. For the dead are not powerless. Dead, did I say? There is no death; only a change of worlds."

I found Chinese men and women secreted in the creases of America building railroads, banging dynamite into mountains and exploding in western yellows. Dying alone, working the laundry rooms of America. Ironing white shirts with heavy irons. Asking my yellow skin, almond eye sister, "You Chinese? You Chinese?"

I found Chicanos portrayed as lazy and contented under movie sombreros. "Sí, señor. Sí, señor. I'll get up and do some work pretty soon. He, he, he, he. But, but, but, but I need a little siesta. Sí, señor. Sí, señor. Me not do too much work, you know. Ha, ha. Conchita, conchita. She do the work for me. He, he, he. Sí, señor."

I found concentration camps with Jews and Gypsies, and others stretched out along in a funeral plain moving in the rain of ash unraveling minds. I found Puerto Ricans alienated from their homeland. Found some asking for independence in the hallways of Congress. Found them not learning Spanish because their parents wanted them to be "good Americans." I met gays and lesbians coming out in the streets of America. Taking over San Francisco politics till "a strange illness" curtailed their action for a decade.

I found Bernard Haring, a great Roman Catholic teacher, who says, "We must stop the materialistic growth mania of more and more production and more and more markets for selling unnecessary, and even, damaging products. It is a sin against the generations to come. What shall we leave to them? Rubbish? Atomic weapons? Numerous enough to make the world uninhabitable. A poisoned atmosphere and polluted water?"

I found Bishop Camara, in Brazil, who said, "When I gave charity to the poor people, people call me, call me, call me saint. But when I ask why men and women are poor, they call me, call me, call me communist."

I found Martin Luther King saying, saying, saying, "We have got to camp in. Put our tents in front of the White House. The White House. The White House. We got to move. Make it known that until our problem is solved, America may have many, many days, but they will be full of trouble. There will be no rest. No rest. There will be no tranquility in this country until the nation comes to terms with our problem. There are forty million poor people here. And one day, we must ask the question, 'Why are there forty million poor people in America?' When we begin to ask that question, you are raising questions about the economic system.

About our broader distribution of wealth. When you ask that question, you begin to question the capitalistic economy. I am simply saying that, more and more we've got to begin to ask questions about the whole society. We are called upon to help the discouraged beggars and life's marketplace, but one day we must come to see that an edifice that produces beggars needs restructuring. It means that questions must be raised. Must be raised."

So, to be African . . . American. To be Black. To be African American. To be Black. To be Black. To be African American. To be Black. To be African-Americaaaaannn . . . in search of self, self, in America leads you on a journey to discovery of self where you find others hiding out also and you extend your hand, tentatively, and say, "You must be the brother. You must be the sister that Martin talked about in that beloved community. You must be the sister/the brother they never told me about. Nihow. Hotep. Alafia. Shalom. Hola. Salaamaleikum. Bonjour. Hey, how you be?" My brother and sister looking at me on this hot afternoon in a place called Boulder.

And I just wanted to share some of that and talk about a couple other things: what it's meant to be this woman . . . trying to write in this country . . . trying to use this language . . . which is just a symbol, you know . . . of our thoughts, of the thoughts of a people. Trying to extend this language beyond what it was to grow up Black in a place called America. And I've said on many occasions, and you've heard me say this too, that when I began that search it happened in a classroom. It happened because even though a class was called Black Studies everybody came. And I couldn't limit myself at some particular poet, so I had to stretch myself. Stretch my heart.

Stretch my hands. I had to connect to people that I knew had enslaved us. I had to connect to people who had made my father feel like a "boy." My father who really never knew freedom and was always full of fear.

And so, one of the things, one of the people who really influenced me a great deal was my grandmother, Mama Driver, in a place called Alabama. I was a terrible little girl, you know, when I was growing up. I was always in trouble. I don't know what it was about. And I lived in a house of women. It was my grandmother and in the South she had these children, but, you know, they were old enough and we called them "aunties." She had so many children that the oldest ended up being called aunts, in this house with my grandmother and these three aunts and my sister and myself. My sister was what you would call a perfect child. She was always very pretty; looked just like my mother. So I remember, sitting, playing with her. Every now and then, she wanted to play with dolls and I hated dolls, but it was a rainy day so I had to play dolls with her. You know, they would tell me, "You have to play dolls sometimes. After all, you're a little girl, Sonia." So, we're playing these stupid dolls, you know, and all these women were cooking on a Saturday snapping beans and whatever. And one of the women looked up and said, "Ahhh, Pat . . . ahhh, Patricia . . . She is so beautiful. She looks just like her mother." My sister heard it and she raised her head to be appreciated, you know, this praise. And they all gave it to her and she lowered her head and kept playing with the stupid little dolls. And then, one of the women said, "And Sonia . . . " and I raised my head to be appreciated by all these women. And there was this silence and I raised my head and looked back at my grandmother who looked up and said, "Ahhh Sonia . . . ah, yeah . . . she's smart . . . She looks just like her daddy, but she's smart."

And it's amazing how in one day, people can form or deform or reform you, in a sense. Because from that day on, I spent my whole life doing that. And my sister spent her whole life being beautiful. And when you get older, beauty disappears, people, you know. And I kept telling her for years, "But you're smart. But you're smart. But you're smart. But you're smart. But you're smart." But it's so much easier to have people to take care of you when you're beautiful, you know that? When we would go outside my sister would go outside and stand. She didn't play. She stood, you know.

I'm serious. She stood, you know. And she'd move around or wherever. And whatever she had on when she came back into the house, she looked just the way she went out. No dirt. No dirt. No dirt. No play whatever. When I went outside, I ran and I left her and Sylvia and all those kids who just stood there and just looked pretty. And I ran with the boys which meant we climbed trees, you know. We jumped over embankments, you know. We went out of the neighborhood. We ran across traffic and almost got killed, but no one knew that. And we came back in and I was ragged. And the pigtails and ribbons: out. And my aunts nipped me at the door and let Pat in and they would say, "Enter in, Pat." And they stopped me at the door crossed their arms and said, "Tsk, tsk, tsk . . . You're just never going to grow up to be a lady." And years later, I thought, "That's good," you know.

But then I was intimidated, you know, and I went, "Aww . . . aww . . . aww." I mean, the level I was on is that one day one of the little boys came in the house and said, "The person who jumps out the second story window will be leader forever."

And I really thought that was hip, you know. So, he came running in the house, up the steps. And I looked out, and it was high, but we had this big tree outside the window. And I figured, if you jumped far enough, you could hit the tree and slide down.

But as I got to the window, they ran down the steps calling to my grandmother, "Sonia's jumping out the window. She's going to kill herself." And by the time they all rushed out the front door and the back door, I was sliding down and I hit that ground really hard, and my knees were all scraped and scratched up and whatever. And my aunts came with their eternal arms folded, you know, said, "Tsk, tsk, tsk." And my grandmother, who was in the kitchen said, "Girl, you okay?" I said, "Uh-huh." "Okay, get up and go play." And she turned to them and said, "Leave that girl alone. She's going to stumble on gentleness one of these days."

I'm not sure . . . that I have stumbled on gentleness . . . but what I have stumbled on in this country is a battle for us all to be human. And when I first started to write, we didn't know that we had been enslaved. No one taught us that in those southern schools. No one taught us in the junior high schools of New York City. In the high schools in New York City and Hunter College in New York and NYU of New York. But I picked it up along the way. But no one taught it formally, you know. I had to go find it myself. And when I stumbled into a library and I found it, I came up. I raised my head. There was fire all over my body. And someone asked me in a long interview, "So why did you curse everybody out?" I said, "Well, I cursed everybody out. America. Newspapers. My daddy, you know. Everybody. Because I was angry. How could you keep something so hidden from all of us?" And I was annoyed at my father because why didn't he tell us? Why didn't they tell us what that was all about? Why do we have to stumble on this thing?

And so, of course, we came out cursing everybody. Investigating this country, you know, calling people names. Saying simply that "yeah, here we is" on this earth trying to work. Trying to move. But, you know, in that same interview, the young woman says, "But you write so differently today." I said, "You know, what does it . . . tell me, if I should still be writing the way I wrote in the sixties. What kind of growth would I have had? You know, just as you don't look the way you looked when you were ten, right?" And you don't write the way you write when you were indeed eighteen, nineteen, and twenty, people. You know, you grow and you travel. You look up and you say simply, if I kept calling America names, then I would have been fixated there. You did it and you moved on beyond it and began to talk about other kinds of things that were happening and are happening in this country called America.

And that's what many of us did. And we began that long, long study period. I lived in the Schomburg. I don't know if I told this story here about trying to get a job and ending up at the Schomburg. You know, I got out of Hunter at nineteen, but I was going to teach because my father said, "You must teach. You must teach. That's the only job you have."

So, you take an exam to teach. But it takes time before you get that job, so I needed a job in the summertime because I had no money. So, I answered an ad in the *New York Times.* "Write x y w z . . . five four six," you know. What they were looking for was a writer for their company and they said, "Send sample." So, I sent a sample of my writing and my cv. I got a telegram. They don't send telegrams any more. I got a telegram on a Saturday: "Report to work on Monday."

Well, I went around the house . . . I picked up the telegram and told my father. Got in his face. " See, you can get a job writing," you know. And my father said, "Girl, you better wait till you get that job teaching, OK?" I said, "No, no, no. You see this? I am showing up." So I got dressed up. I had a blue suit on and blue heels on and a blue hat on and blue purse and white gloves. And I went down for my job, people, and I did not show up for CP time. They said, "Nine o'clock." I was there at eight-thirty, standing at the door. And in comes the secretary and she says, "Yes?" And I took out the telegram and I was just all smiles and she looked at me. No smile. And she opened the door, came in, sat down at eight thirty-five. Eight-forty.

And then, there must've been another way to get into that building because all of a sudden there's a head that came to the door, and I smiled. And another head came to the door, and I smiled. And a third came. And then about ten minutes till nine, a guy walked out and said, "I'm so sorry, but the job's been taken." And I said, "What?" and I looked at my watch and it is not nine o'clock. It is now ten minutes till nine. I took out the telegram. It was for this company. I said, "See?" And he looked at it and he looked at me and said, "Oh yes, we sent that, but the job's taken." I said, "Well, who has come in here that I have not seen?" Right? So, the guy . . . he just left me. I was still asking the question when he turned and left. The secretary looked up and put her head down. She wouldn't look up. And I said to his back, "That's all right. I'm going to report you to the Urban League."

I'm laughing because the Urban League had no power at all, right? "I'm going to report you to the Urban League about this kind of discrimination." And the guy kept walking, you know. I walked out and took my hat off, people, you know. I got on the train. I'm from New York, people. I got on the train. I knew I had to get off at 72nd or 96th to stay on the West side to get off to walk to the Urban League there at 125th Street and 8th Avenue and St. Nicholas onto 8th. But I was sitting there, I stayed. And all of a sudden I realized this train was doing all kinds of things and I looked and I was on the East side, right? 116th Street, 125th and I went "Oh, oh, oh . . . " I just . . . you know, how you just start to cry? People getting on and looking at you, and you're just crying. And I dried my eyes and I got off at 135th Street.

Zoom. Getting ready to cross 135th Street and lo and behold there's this building about a third into the block and it said "Schomburg." And there's this guy standing outside smoking. I said, "Schomburg? What's a Schomburg? What does that mean?" He said, "Ah, lady . . . this is the Schomburg Library." And I said, "How can it be a library? I thought I had been in all the libraries, I thought I had, in New York City. I've never been inside this library." He said, "Go inside. Ms. Hutson will tell you about that." So, I walked in.

And for those of you who ever been to the Schomburg. Anyone ever been to the Schomburg now? The new one faces Harlem Hospital. The old one was in the block, and the theater is now part of that. The old one was really little, little, little. And you walked in and there was this long, long table and all these scholars were sitting there. And you walked in and they never looked up. There were just all these books, I mean, just stacked up. And there was a glass door. And I knocked on the door and the curator at that time was a woman by the name of Ms. Hutson. And she always told my students this story because we used to take bus rides wherever I was teaching. Wherever I was teaching, every semester we made a trip to the Schomburg to do research. And I said, "Hello?" And I told her my name and said "hello" and I said, "What kind of library is this?" And she said, "Oh, my dear . . . "

This is how she spoke, actually. "Oh, my dear, this is a library that has books only by or about Black people." And I said with my nineteen-year-old smartness, "There must not be many books in here."

She never let me forget that.

Every time I brought a class, she told that story and I would back up to the back. And all my students finally had something on me. They would turn, look, and smile. Never let me forget that. And she said, "Well, why don't you sit down. I will bring you some books." And so, I literally had to insinuate myself into that table because none of the men moved. I mean, they did not move, you know what I mean. She had to help me push the chair in and they haven't looked up. They haven't moved at all. And she moved their books over a little bit and she said, "I'm going to bring you some books." She brought me three books. Oh, oh, oh . . . *Souls of Black Folk*, *Up from Slavery*, and on top was *Their Eyes Were Watching God*. And so, I sat there and opened *Their Eyes Were Watching God*. And I was thrown back a little bit with the language. You know, speaking in that Black English there, because the ear was not in tune to that. But I got through that, and I read about a third and I inched out and I went and knocked on the door.

And I said, "What's your name again?" And she said, "Ms. Hutson." I said, "How could I be an educated woman and not even have read this one book?" She said, "Yes, dear. Now go sit down and keep reading."

I went back, and the men have never looked up still, right? They have not looked up and I started to cry. Two-thirds through, I started to . . . I put my head down. They have never looked up. I got up and knocked on the door again.

I said, "No, no, no, no . . . you're not hearing the question." I said, "How can a city educate us?" Right? She said, "I know, dear. That's why we're here." Blah, blah, blah. And as I started to sit down, one of the men raised his head and said, "Ms. Hutson, either you have this woman sit still or she has to leave. She's bothering us."

And I sat still for weeks, people. I never went looking for a job again. For the rest of the summer, my job was to learn to read all those books in that Schomburg. By golly, by gee. And by the time someone had started something called Black Studies someone said, "You know, who can teach a Black Lit class?" And they said, "You know, that Sanchez. She's always talking about those Black books."

You know, whenever I did go out, I went to Ms. Hutson. Because you know that a lot of these books were not in print, people. I said, "Ms. Hutson, what do I do? I don't have a lot of these books. I couldn't buy these books by myself." And she said, "Don't worry, we'll get you those books." And she did. So, when we went out there to teach, we mimeoed. I wanted to say xerox, but there was no xerox, people. We mimeoed, and our hands were forever blue and purple. You know, it seemed as if it was forever blue and purple because we mimeoed sections like DuBois' *Souls of Black Folk,* we took certain chapters out of there. And one of the most amazing ones . . . how many have read *Souls of Black Folk?*

Read it . . . Read it this summer. This is the centennial of *Souls of Black Folk.* It was published in 1903 and this is 2003. DuBois was the most important scholar in this country and he was not read. Taken out of the curriculum. You know why? Because they always said he was "Red." That he was a communist. When I started to teach, he was one of the people I taught.

Did I tell you about the FBI coming and knocking on my door? Ohh . . . This is part of how I decided to stay and keep being a writer, people. Because there were many points when my father would call and say, "Why don't you come home? Why don't you come home and just get a job teaching? You know, just teaching. And leave that stuff."

You must read the story "The Coming of John" in *Souls of Black Folk.* It is a short story that talks about the double consciousness in America. There's a Black John and a White John, you know, and what happens when we don't understand the meaning of these two. And we keep them apart, in a sense. Anyway, I taught Langston Hughes, *Souls of Black Folk,* I taught Marcus Garvey. I taught Paul Robeson's *Here I Stand,* people. And some other books. Poets, whatever, from the Harlem Renaissance.

I was in my house on my off-day and there was a knock at the door. I opened the door and there was my landlord and two men. And my landlord said, "Ms. Sanchez . . . Professor Sanchez, these men want to see you. They say they're from the FBI." And I said, "Oh gosh . . . " I lived two blocks from Haight-Ashbury, so I figured something was going on. And I said, "Oh gosh, what happened?" Right? And the guy took out his badge and pointed it and said, "I'm from the FBI!" And I said, "Yes?" And the other one was still as stagnant water. Didn't move. His eyes didn't move, people. He just stood there. And I said, "Yes?" He said, "You're out there teaching DuBois!" He didn't say DuBois the way we say DuBois. He said, "DuBois! Hughes, Garvey, Robeson!" And I said, "Yes." Now, look how naive I am. And I say, "Yes, it's Black Literature."

Well, it is Black Literature, people. However, that's not what they were seeing. They were seeing that we were introducing in the curriculum people that they had banned in America. No one taught DuBois. No one taught Robeson. No one taught Garvey. Maybe some few radicals might at some point might have taught some Langston Hughes in a class. That's what they were saying. And how dare you resurrect these people that we have successfully banned from these schools. This is 1967, people. I said again, "No." You know, "hold it." I said, "You cannot teach the first semester of Black Literature without including . . . " Huh, listen to what I'm saying. Hughes, right? DuBois. Garvey. If you're going to talk about the Harlem Renaissance, you've got to include Garvey. You know what I'm saying? And I went on. And this fellow looked at me, like, "Duh, are you kidding? Don't you get it?" You know, and I'm standing there trying to get it. Why are they so angry at me?

The landlord leaves, by the way. My Japanese American landlord said, "Bye." And I'm trying to figure this out and the FBI man was furious. Just furious that in some miraculous way these young people starting something called "Black Studies" had the sense enough to go back and rescue these people who had been obscured here. Now, it sounds strange to you in 2003, you see. But that's what happened at that point. So, I'm standing thinking, "OK, this must be over with. I'm going to close the door."

And I had a dog. A Samoyed. I don't know if you know Samoyeds, but they're the most intelligent animals on the planet Earth, right? And my landlord had given me this dog because he thought I needed someone to protect me. And I was just getting accustomed to this dog. I had this dog no more than one week. And I used to slam my door and put the chair against the door because I thought he was just going to come in and just devour me every night, right? He was that big. And every night, he had pushed the door open and he was right by my bed. And I would wake up in the morning and say in a very bravado style, "Get away from me, dog! What are you doing by my bed. Go outside or wherever." This dog with these big feet. All you heard were the big feet. And he came and sat right next to me and looked up at this man. And I turned, you know, I'm still getting accustomed to this dog. We named the dog Snow, we fed him well. He was in a vegetarian house too. It was hard for that dog, I'm sure. And he's looking up like this and the man said again, "I said you're teaching DuBois! DuBois! DuBois!" And my dog leaped for him . . . and I said, "Snow, Snow, Snow." And he said, "Call off your dog, lady!" And Snow sat down, but he never kept his eyes off that guy. And then I said, "Well, OK, I think we're finished for today, aren't we? I thank you for this visit." And I slammed the door and as I walked down the hall with Snow I had a new appreciation of that dog. I said, "I'm going out to buy you some meat today!"

It was an amazing moment. And then I called back East and I got on the telephone to Ms. Hutson and she said, "Oh, my dear. Oh, my dear. Don't you understand? Once you start teaching these people, didn't I tell you, that people will get upset about it." And I said, "Now, you tell me." Ha, ha.

But seriously, it was from that moment on that I began to understand how to teach literature. I used to teach that literature quite often by themes. Then I realized, you cannot teach our literature unless you do the economics of it. The sociology of it. You do all of that, you see, and then you are truly doing the literature here in this place called America. You are truly then teaching at that point what this is really all about. And that was just part of that experience there. You know a man by the name of Hayakawa became president of San Francisco State College (he became a senator from California years later under Reagan's presidency). He went on television and went on the news and he said to the Japanese American community, "I want you to help me come up against these radicals out here on this campus. I'm appealing to my community." And the next day, a very stately Japanese American responded and said, "Oh, we didn't know that President Hayakawa thought he was part of our community." Ha, ha, ha. I loved it. I kept that for years and years that response. An amazing response.

But certainly, there was the structure there. A woman by the name of Kay Boyle, who was my dear friend, became chairperson of our department, the English Department. This woman, who was my mentor and a person who guided me, called me and said, "Sonia, they're going to fire you tomorrow. You should resign." And I resigned, so I wouldn't get fired, you know. And I called my father and told him I might need some money and he said, "I told you. I told you. I told you. I told you. You need to stop with that stuff and just come home, Sonia, and get a nice job teaching." You know, and not saying anything about anything because he says to me at that time, "It doesn't pay to do that. Nothing changes, ever."

That was my father in the 1960s. And I said, "Dad, dad, dad . . . we're going to make sure things change. I refuse to let things stay the same. I refuse . . . ", and it was a harsh thing that I said, "I refuse to keep turning out men like you." I said that to my father. I regret it. I regret it. I regret it to this day.

But I will read a poem to my father from that time to let you hear something. Because my father was indeed this ladies' man. Had plenty of women, you know. And I would write a poem in the 1960s called "A Poem for My Father." Now, listen to this, and when I read on Saturday, I will read you a poem . . . a section to my father from *Does Your House Have Lions?* If you live long enough, it is possible to get reconnected to a parent.

[Reads]

A Poem for My Father

how sad it must be
to love so many women
to need so many black
perfumed bodies weeping
underneath you.
when i remember all those nights
i filled my mind with
long wars between short
sided trojans & greeks
while you slapped some
wide hips about in
your pvt dungeon,
when i remember your
deformity i want to
do something about your
makeshift manhood.
i guess
that is why
on meeting your sixth
wife, i cross myself
with her confessionals.

That's a poem I did for my father in the sixties. And so, you know, it's not a nice poem. It's like I'm saying, "Look, look, look, man." You know, all those women that even I had to experience some of them, right? You know, like, "Whoa!" And I wrote that poem for him.

And then, years later, when I'm getting ready to write a book about my brother and then about my father and the whole family. I say to my father, "I'm writing a book about Wilson." And he says, "Well . . . " He says a couple things. He says, "Well, you can't write a book about your brother unless you write about me also." And I looked at him and said, "Uh-huh." And then he said, "And I hope when you write about me this time you get me right." And I really said, "Uh-huh" at that point, you know. Like "uh, ha, ha, ha."

But when we came through and left California, I went to a place called the University of Pittsburgh because we were beginning Black Studies in other places. Heading home, by the way. Heading back to New York because I was ready for New York. I was ready to go home. I had married a man by the name of Etheridge Knight who was a poet also and we were together, only, actually, one year because he couldn't come out of drugs. Now, some people say simply that, you know, you hold onto people, and at some point you do, but people have to come out of drugs. They've got to be willing to not kill people with drugs, you know. Not kill children with drugs also. And so I raised up and went to Pittsburgh and he followed and we got a position for him there in Pittsburgh.

But I remember walking, one day, into the bank to ask for a reading on my account and the woman said, "Oh, Ms. Sanchez . . . you have five dollars in your account." And I said, "How is that possible? I just put a check in." And she said, "Well, here . . . I can," you know. And I realized what that was about, when a person is involved, indeed involved, with drugs the way he was at that time with no controls, everything went. Televisions went, bicycles went. Anything, typewriters went at that time. Typewriters . . . that's what you use. I think that's one of the reasons why I still do everything longhand. At some point, I had to do things longhand.

And that is very real, but then Etheridge was dying in a place called Indianapolis. I'd flown out to the University of California–Irvine and there's a flight that leaves L.A. that comes directly to Indianapolis and then it goes on to Philadelphia. I got off that flight and I had contacted his mother, Mama Knight, and told her I was coming in. I had been talking to him all along because we were very close at that time. And I went to see him. He couldn't talk anymore. The cancer had moved so that he could not hold a conversation anymore, so sometimes his sister would dial the phone and I would just talk to him and tell him what I was doing. Where I was. How crazy things were. How crazy the country was, still.

And I walked in, I got there about six o'clock in the morning and he was asleep. And I sat by the couch. He was not sleeping in the bed. He was on the couch and his mother was there. And his girlfriend was there and we were talking and then he woke up. And he had a gown on and he got so self-conscious that he had people help him up, he wanted to have a robe. He wanted to look just a certain way. And I talked to him and said I had been in Orange County, you know, Reagan Country . . . and what that reading had been about. And I talked about heading up to Columbia that night, but I had detoured to stay there until three or four o'clock.

And then, finally, I asked some of the people to leave the room. His mother knew and I finally turned and asked the other young woman to leave the room. And I whispered into his ears . . .

. . . and I asked his forgiveness. And then I said, "I forgive you." And then I asked for his forgiveness again. And I said, "I forgive you." And I asked his forgiveness and I said, "I forgive you. My friend, my husband, my comrade. One who is greeting death before me and do it gently." And then he went off to sleep again. And I left. And he was dead, two days later. And I did not go to the funeral because there were so many ex-girlfriends and ex-people there. And there were so many people who took sides in that relationship. So, I called his mom and sent flowers. She said, "I know you're not coming." I said, "No, I'm not coming. I can't come into that." And I hugged her over the phone and said "beso" and went about my business that day.

But the people that we meet, for you young writers, who touch us so. The people we meet who help make us human in special ways. Those are important people to us. Someone asked me in a long interview: "Have you ever stopped writing?" And I said a very strange thing. I said, "No." And then she said, "Well, Ms. Sanchez . . . " And you know I love some of these young writers who come in interviewing you. They're so together. They are so astringent. They're just so, like, upright. "Well . . . you didn't have a book for seven years, Ms. Sanchez." *Whoa!*

I said, "You're right, you're so right. I was writing, however. I just had not organized a book, right. I didn't have the strength to organize a book. You're right. I didn't have a book. You're right." And then I said, "I did four straight books," because they were already in my journals, if you understand what I'm saying. They were already there. I just had to pull them together. But I had not realized in the living that I was doing at that time, and the struggling I was doing at that time with family, that I had not produced a book. And I was accustomed to producing a book, as she said, every three or four years. There was a book I had done in my head I just hadn't put it on paper and gotten it to an editor as yet. But all that time, I was writing.

And as I said in my writing class one day . . . you know how people say, "Oh, Sonia . . . " A student walked into my class and says, "Well, you know, I love to write, but I only write when I'm in love." I said, "We're in trouble . . . "

"Because, eventually, you will fall out of love, you know, and then we'll have a little stasis on our hands. So, get rid of that." I said, "We will start you writing as you come into this workshop. Begin you, via free association exercises, and keep you going. And we want you to write every night, every night, every night in a journal. Nothing, you know, superb sometimes, but the point is to keep up that whole thing called writing. To keep it going."

Last night, I woke up, you know. And I was full, but I dealt with that. But I had realized that I had gone to sleep without writing in my journal. And I pulled that little sucker. You know what I mean? And sat down and wrote about what had happened last night. Here, in this room. And the amazing things that students did in this room, you know. The reverent motion and movements in here were so important. The fucks and the non-fucks that went on in here, you know. And the love that went on in this room. And the collaboration that went on in this room also. And people getting up saying, "I'm willing to share this with you." And that's what I wrote about and it was such a pleasant, pleasant moment. What we saw last night. You know, what we saw. People saying, "I'm willing to get up on the stage and share my work with you. It might not even be finished, but I'm willing to share it with you. It might not be complete, but I'm willing to share with you. It might even have offended you a little bit, but I'm willing to share it with you. I'm willing to throw it out to the universe, you see, and you can throw it back at me with, via a conversation, via another poem, also." That was so amazing and I enjoyed it so very much. I look forward to the other readings that will happen here also at this place.

Let me wind down a little bit because I think I'm carrying it over. I just want to say at some point that, you know, you don't start off at this point. I started off at a point that was southern and New York. I started off at a point that said, "I am here writing this poetry for my people." And then I looked in audiences and saw my people were always, from the very beginning, young students. Black, white, green, purple, blue, you know. And so I had to extend that conversation in a very real sense. My people in the classroom have always been, you know, people. Sometimes on the edge.

I taught at Tyler School of Art and always at the end of my class we make a circle where we touch. Those who teach should always do that if you would. Get in a circle. Make people say things to each other. Sometimes apologies. Sometimes perhaps from the way they said things, but say things to each other and touch each other. And there was this very, outrageously dressed, gay young man. And it was an art school, so, to me, I thought he would be OK. You know what I'm saying? And no one picked up his hand. So, I grabbed his hand and told one of the females to grab his hand. And we went around the circle and when he spoke everybody was looking down like this. And three weeks, people, when they heard his work and his writing, everybody looked up. It was an amazing moment for them, you know? Everybody wanted to grab his hand and say, "Oh yeah, John . . . that was some . . . that was some poem that you wrote . . . " You know, you got to be there in a place.

And I remember just because I'm saying to all of you when you teach you learn so much. And so, the next time I went to a reading, when I called out resisters, living and ago resisters, when I called out a litany of something, I said, "Gays . . . " And half the audience walked out on me. With their eyes. Their bodies.

I'm telling the truth. And I looked up and I got very nervous, you know? I said, "Wow . . . what happened?" You know? "Q & A!" "Well, ahh . . . Sister Sonia . . . how can you put gays and lesbians on a line of . . . of, of, of Blacks . . . " I'm serious! And I said, "Well, are they not human too? Like we are? And are there not Blacks that are gays and lesbians? Huh?" "Oh, ah . . . ah . . . but not in Africa!"

I mean, this thing went waaaaay out! And I'm up here saying, "Whoa, whoa, whoa . . . what have I done," you know. But I knew it was right, people, stay with me. I moved to a poet there. I'm not a revisionist like everybody else when people talked about gays and they went: "ha, ha" and I went "ha, ha, ha, ha, ha." Because that's what you do. You follow what people do. You hear what I'm saying? When people make jokes about dumb Poles, you know, I went, "ha, ha, ha, ha . . . " But then it reached the point where I wouldn't go there and people would say, "I don't know . . . you can't . . . don't tell jokes around Sonia. You can't tell jokes about people around Sonia," you know. I said, "I love jokes. Let me tell you a joke." And I would tell a joke similar to what I'd told and everybody fell out laughing. But I don't like jokes that demean, right? I can't listen to jokes like that. And these little parties you find yourself, like sometimes, standing alone, eating by yourself.

I studied with Louise Bogan in a place called New York University. I walked into her class at NYU because I had been to a number of workshops in New York City. I raised my hand to say something; nobody responded because it was all white males. I was the only female and the only Black. And after a couple of times, a couple of weeks, I left. I mean, I just left. Then I tried another workshop the next semester, right? I got in there and looked . . . I was the only Black, the only female. And I didn't say anything right away. I figured I'll wait till several weeks had passed before I said anything. And I would say something, silence. Nobody responded. The teacher, the poet didn't respond. After that class, I left.

So, when I went to Bogan's class at NYU, I sat right by the door. I did. There were about forty-five people there. Forty-five people. There were three women. Three women out of forty-five. I was the third woman. Three women. You've got to hear that. Three women. And I'm sitting there and she spoke in a very aristocratic voice. "Well, here we are. . . . And why do you want to study . . . poetry?" You know, and I'm thinking "Oh, this is really going to be tough." You know what I mean? So then, she asks,

"Does anyone have a poem?" It was the first night. It was like asking an alcoholic if he had a bottle someplace, you know?

Because we went in pockets, purses, whatever. And I said to myself, "Get it over with fast! Right away!" She had called you to come to the front, so I came up front and started reading this poem. And I looked at her because I said, "Well, we'll see what happens here . . . " and she says, "Well, let me tell you about that poem." And I stayed. I stayed. And I stayed. And at some point we had to choose a form and I was reading the haiku at that point. And this is, we're talking now, people, about the late fifties at this point. And I was so intrigued by this form. At that time, there was a limited discussion about it, you know, because it was all about the three lines, right? You know, that was that limited discussion: five, seven, five, you know, the haiku form. So, I was all into that, but that's what I did my final on, what I did at the end; all of these haiku. And a guy by the name of Fred Stern, at the end of the semester, said, "You, you, you, you, you, and you . . . let's continue to meet. Let's meet in the Village." And we did. And for the next three years, every Wednesday, you had to bring a poem. That's all you had to bring was a poem.

But during that workshop with Bogan, I published for the first time, I think, in the *New England Review* and I brought in wine. Bottles of wine into NYU at night. And we celebrated that. And I asked Bogan, I only had one interview with her, I went to ask her, "Do I have any talent, Ms. Bogan?" And she said, "Why do you want to know that, Sonia?" You know, I'm looking, I'm holding on. I said, "Well, umm . . . sometimes I wonder if this is worthwhile doing." And she said, "Well, many people have talent, Sonia. But what are you going to do with it?" And I said, "Um-hmmm. I think I can figure that one out myself a little bit." And we met in the Village for three years and during that time I was beginning to publish in the small magazines. I went the small magazine route, people. You know, no one came to me asking me for a big book contract, OK? I did the *Minnesota Review, Trans-Atlantic Review,* all those reviews. OK? *The Mass Review,* you know.

I was telling my class because Bogan made us do that. The second day, the second week of class she made us get a notebook and fill out on pages the name of the publication, the date sent, and if returned the date returned. And she insisted that we send out only three poems. We went to the bookstore and libraries and figured out the ones for the kind of poetry we wrote. And it's a good thing to do, people, because from the very beginning, we were sending work out. And I went and mailed some poetry on a Tuesday. By the time I got back home, it was returned with just "The Editors."

And then I remember one day after I had been doing that, well, after I had published in *New England,* but later on with the workshop in the Village.

I'd finally sent to the *Paris Review* and I got a letter from George Garrett that said: "We would have published it this time, but we had nothing but poetry. Please send some more work to us, Sonia." That was the struggle we went through. That was a hard struggle, people. It was not like a struggle where all of the sudden, here it is, some miracle happened, you know. But it was that struggle of going through those small magazines just in that fashion. Sending out, waiting, getting rejected, whatever. And during the time, if you're in a workshop, however, and I say this to people sometimes, you have to learn to get out of workshops. And I had to learn to get out of that workshop, after three years, because I had moved to a point where every time I brought in something I had published there was stillness in that room. You know, because no one else was publishing at that time. And that was a hard thing, so I stopped doing that.

But one night we left the workshop, one Wednesday night, and we went to the Five Spot. And we walked inside the Five Spot and there was a man called LeRoi Jones [Amiri Baraka], at the time, sitting right near the door, hat sitting acey-deucey, gold tip cigarettes in his mouth, drinking a boilermaker, and writing a review of jazz. And we all went by, you know, filing in and his voice said, "Hey Sanchez." And I jumped. I'm an ex-stutterer, people. I turned, "I,I,I,I . . . yes?" Because we knew who he was when we came in. That was LeRoi Jones. He said, "I'm editing an anthology coming out of Paris. Send me some of your work." I went, "Umm-hmm."

And we sat down to listen to the music and they said, "Ohhh, Sonia . . . " And I said, "Naaaww, he doesn't want my work. Are you kidding? Noooo!" I ignored it, right?

Well, about one month later, we were coming in to hear some music and he's sitting there and I kept going because I didn't know he had seen me. And he said, "Hey Sanchez . . . huh . . . you don't want to be in the anthology, huh?" And I turned and said, "Were you serious?" No stuttering. "Were you serious?" He said, "Of course, I was serious." I said, "Thank you." I said good-bye to my friends, right?

I got in my little vw. I had this little vw. Went up the highway. For those of you who know New York, being at the Five Spot, I was home up on Riverside Drive at 146th Street in five, ten minutes. I pulled out my little typewriter, I sat down and typed up these poems, put the typewriter back up, came back out that night, got back in that car, took it downtown to the main post office, and dropped it. And about two weeks later, I get this note from Baraka saying, "Dear Sonia Sanchez, Yeah." That was all.

Just "Yeah," you know. So I had to call this in, "Well, did that 'yeah,' did that 'yeah' mean you took it? Or did that 'yeah' mean, 'Thanks for sending it or whatever?'" Anyway . . . at that point that's how I got to know a man by the name of Amiri Baraka and was privy to a lot of his early plays, you know. And along the association of friendship with him. With real differences along the way, people. I remember going through Pittsburgh. I stopped by his house and Baraka was a cultural nationalist at that point. And people bowed down to him, you know. So, I walked into the office and people were waiting for me to bow and I say, "Hey, man, how you doing?" Right? Everybody looked kind of funny, you know. And I sat down and started talking to him about going to Pittsburgh and how hard it was, at this point trying to make a living right now, coming out of San Francisco State. But I'm just saying, those are just interesting points along the way. He and Amiri are still by dearest friens.

You can disagree with people, but you can stay friends with people. You can like their work, you know. And you can wait sometimes for people to move to other arenas. We don't have to damage people and we don't have to destroy people with our hands and our hearts and our mouths. I want to thank you for coming out. I hope I helped some. Thank you, I really enjoyed it.

Workshop

TED BERRIGAN
July 24, 1978

* * *

TED BERRIGAN: If you write poems, and you're an aspiring poet, that is, you aspire to be a poet—a poet is just someone who writes: you could be a bad poet, but you're still a poet. You may never write any good poems. You're still a poet if you write poems. There's no magical, mystical meaning to the word "poet." But being a student in a poetry workshop is another thing entirely. There, you can get messages about being a poet from each other, from your teacher as well.

What poets do to get to be poets and to stay poets, get to be good poets and stay good poets, is they read lots of books all the time. And they write lots of poems all the time. And if you don't do both of those, you're not going to make it. And it's as simple as that, really. Nobody doesn't read any books and writes good poems—nobody! Nobody ever has, and nobody ever will.

Q: What about Russell Edson?

TB: Who? Russell Edson reads millions of books! You don't think he invented that form, do you? So he says; I say he does. I read his work.

ALICE NOTLEY: That's a typical lie—

TB: Yeah, poets like to say that—

AN: A typical poet's lie.

TB: It's very common to hear it said that Allen Ginsberg doesn't read. Allen doesn't really read too much, as a matter of fact. He only reads about a hundred pages a day. I consider him horribly deficient in that respect.

Q: Somebody said Ashbery didn't read much.

TB: Well, you guys should read a few books and then read John Ashbery's poems and see if you can't tell that he's read a few books. I mean, it's as simple as that, really. John Ashbery, he went to Harvard, man, and they make you read a few books there. Maybe he doesn't read any books anymore, that's probably why his poems are no good anymore . . . you know, to exaggerate slightly. Whereas most of you don't read enough, and it's very evident in your works. It doesn't keep you from writing good lines and having good things in your works, but it keeps you from having an ongoing and developing sense of how to have your poems have some shape to them. Some tangible shape that one can feel when they're reading them.

Without that shape, poems are just these lists of lines. And there is a reason why any group of words is on a line and other words are on the next line. And you don't usually know those reasons, you can just feel them. When you can't feel them, then everything seems a little peculiar.

Also, you see, there are a lot of bad poems in the world; in books, too. And it's very hard to know if anybody that's alive is any good. Although you can rest assured that everybody that's dead that everybody says is a great poet *is* a great poet. They may not be very interesting at the time: lots of really good poets write poems about what it's like to be fifty years old, and lots of people that are not fifty years old are not too interested in what it feels like to be fifty years old. But, in the end, it doesn't matter what the poems are about. You don't have to read any certain poets now. You can read anybody now, but you have to read somebody. And so you have to keep looking. I mean, the best poets for you to read might be in little mimeograph magazines, or they might be in the Modern Library Classics. But you have to read them, in some way.

Also, just by way of advice, most of you better read a few biographies of dead poets and find out what that life is like. You'll find that most of these biographies are very similar and appalling—as a whole, but I mean, everybody's life is appalling. You're born, and you grow up, and as you're growing up, things never quite happen in the right way, and you never get enough of everything, and then suddenly you're a little bit older and you're getting too much of everything, and then you're quite a bit older and everything hurts a little. Then, alas, you die—often quite painfully, although it's much more painful to those around you than it is to you. Because they think you're in pain, and they feel guilty, and *bye-bye*.

But you do die, and sometimes—if you're John Keats, you die pretty young, and if you're Ezra Pound, you die pretty old, but it's fairly much the same. But if you read these biographies of poets, you'll find that just as many good things happen in lives of poets as happen to other people. And just as many bad things, but at least you'll get some sense of what poets' lives are usually like. You'll not get a sense of what a poet is like from reading the works of Gurdjieff or someone like that. Gurdjieff was a good storyteller. Although you can't tell too much about what his life was like from reading his stories, or any person like that.

You should read the Gospels, and you should read the works of Chögyam Trungpa, but they won't tell you too much about being a poet.

They might tell you a lot of other really useful things. No doubt they will. Any book can tell you lots of useful things anyway.

Being a poet is twenty-four hours a day, and the nice thing about it is that it doesn't need to interfere with you being a person. But it is twenty-four hours a day. You mustn't complicate your life with things like psychodramas, nervous breakdowns, and things like that, if you're trying to be a poet. You can have all those things, but you shouldn't let them get in the way of yourself being a poet, and poets don't let those things get in the way. A poet might die of hideous drink and horrible diseases when they're forty or thirty-five, but that would have happened to them anyway, because that's what they were like. Nevertheless, they wrote a lot of good poems, which made their lives a lot better than they would have been if they'd just been this boring person that died of hideous drink and—you know.

Actually, everybody that doesn't write poetry is pretty boring. It's true. Trungpa writes poetry, and Allen writes poetry, and neither one of those guys is boring to me all the time. My mother writes poetry. Her poetry is pretty boring, but she's not boring.

Poetry is where you tell the world what you're like, where you show the world what you're like. The world will not pay much attention, unless you get famous, and if you get famous, you can get your picture on the front page of the *Rocky Mountain News,* like Allen did today. He looked pretty good, too. He looked a lot better than he does in person.

I read all the poems that have been handed in to me, and I'll give them back today, and I'll be happy to take any more poems from anyone. When I give you back these poems, try to understand that the more I wrote on them, the more interested I was. However, everything I wrote on them might be horrible, but it's still to your credit that I was interested. I just react straightforward. I did read all the poems. Some I wrote on, some I didn't. I think I wrote on some poems by every person.

I want to say a few general things about that. The most basic and most general thing is that you guys got to get your act together a little more. Why should you give a workshop teacher six pages of illegible handwriting? I can't handle it that way. One person gave me about four or five pages of work that looked pretty good. What I could read of them seemed pretty good. And, I think, with a magnifying glass, and a lot of patience, and about a week to do it, I could have read them all. But I didn't. And I made a note on there that said: *These look pretty good; why don't you get somebody to type them?*

But you don't have to type your works. You can write them on napkins and do anything you want, but if you're going to show them to anybody other than your lover or your mother, you better get them to where they're a little more legible. I don't think anybody should write poems by hand unless they have beautiful and legible handwriting, or possibly even just legible. Beauty is no good when it can't be read, if it's a poem. I think that all your poems should be typed. You have to see how they would look if they were printed, so you can make some changes, if you want to. I don't mind if they're not typed. If they're legible, I'll read them anyway. I just think you should do that. I also think you should put them in folders, and you should not write things on the top like "North American Cereal Surprise" or "Twenty-One Lines." You shouldn't write anything on the page that you don't want to be read as part of the work. You should write the title of the poem and your name. Your name is not necessary, but it's just a couple of words, and names are often pretty interesting words, so it's pretty good at the bottom of a poem. You're making something, and you're making it with a piece of paper. You should have some sense of that. It will make your poems better if you do have some sense of that.

OK. The final thing about that is, try to make your poems more show than tell. Try to lean a little lightly on the wisdom and how much you know. No particular human emotion makes you know more than you know. Pain does not make you smarter, neither does pleasure. They might help. I mean, the fact that you just suffered a hideous painful situation does not mean that you can then talk about it in a way that will be really interesting, informative, and illuminating to everyone else. However, you can make something out of what happened to you that will be all those things.

Try to imagine that you're a little bit like a painter or carpenter. And any time you're going to express yourself, you're making a chair. You try to make it so other people can sit in it. Even though you've had a horribly trying experience in which your lover refused you forever, and your parents died, and your children said they hated you, you still have to make that chair comfortable enough to sit in, and attractive enough to look at, and strong enough to stand on its legs, and have it be beautiful in some way. Somehow, it can still show all that happened to you, I think. The ability of human beings to make something strong and beautiful and marvelous out of dark things that happen is what makes people be human beings. Dogs can't do that. Maybe they can, in the dog world, but they can't do it in any way that we humans can see it, except very briefly or momentarily. Maybe they don't want us to see it, which is an idea I would like to entertain. I think that probably is the truth.

When you write poems in which the main character is someone named "I," you have to create that character in the poems. You have to show what that character is like. It is not interesting at all what the person who wrote the poem—the name at the bottom of the page—is saying, except inasmuch as that person is created within the poem. When you're writing the poem, you're writing about experiences you've already had, even if you only had them an hour before; and so, you're no longer that person. You have to remember that it's your duty to make a person in there. The first thing that should be registering while one is reading poems is, who is speaking here, and what kind of person this is.

Back about eighteen years ago, I sat in on a class by Amiri Baraka, who was then LeRoi Jones. It was a class on John Ashbery, and he passed out one of John's typical poems at that time, which said things like the clock . . . lunch . . . dog . . . foot . . . is . . . wet, and things like that. And he said, "What kind of person do you think wrote this poem?" And that was so much easier than trying to think of what this poem said. And then, once figuring out, though, in some ways, what kind of person wrote this poem, I had a lot clearer take on what it might be saying, and to whom it might be speaking.

Men write poems from their female self, and women from their male self, and it's nice to notice that sometimes when they are doing that, they don't always know they're doing that even, but their poem knows. You should be getting an incredible amount of information from poems, but should not be being told that information by the voice speaking in the poems. That person speaking in the poems is a liar. They're hurt or they're feeling wonderful, so you can't trust anything they say. People that are feeling wonderful will tell you that God is love, which is not much help when you've stepped on a tack or something. On the other hand, people who've just stepped on a tack will tell you that life is shit, which you frankly don't believe very well when you've just had a milkshake. If you want to say that God is love, you should throw in a few milkshakes at least, so one will understand where you got this feeling. Dig it, right. . . .

Many of you, I think, should go through your poems and find all the best parts and put them all together and make a couple of other poems. I mean, that's really how people write poems. It's very hard to sit down and write a poem. A machine could do it much better because it wouldn't get distracted, but there are no machines that know how to write poems, unfortunately. They only know how to write things that look like poems and sound like poems, but they're not really poems, because machines don't have feelings that are translatable into human terms. Art is all about feeling.

Yeah . . . it's all you, writing. So, you write five poems, that's you. There is an ongoing you, your soul as it were, or whatever name you prefer to call it. Your spirit, your psyche, your other, whatever. You can trust that what you write that comes across with feeling and honesty, is real. The act of sitting down and writing a poem that takes from five past three till three twenty-nine . . . the integrity of the feelings and the beauty of the poem do not depend upon the fact that nothing that was put in was written earlier than five past three or later than twenty-nine past three. If you say something good about the way you feel at a certain time, which is a kind of feeling that you have reasonably often, and if you said it three months ago, and in the poem you're writing now that feeling comes in, you can put in the same thing you said three months ago, especially if it was in a poem that didn't work. That's why you should never throw away any poems, you should always keep everything, because you might have some good parts in them, and you can use them.

And finally . . . assignments are like that, assignments are terrific to do, that's how poets write anyway, mostly, because they give themselves assignments to do. Lots of times when you do an assignment, only a part of it will be any good. You'll get everything that you'll—the excitement of doing the assignment, and the fact of writing, had to give to you, maybe two thirds of the way through, and the rest of poem will be lame. That's fine. That's perfectly all right. You hand in the assignment as it was called for. But you might have a good poem by cutting out the final third. Don't be afraid to do that, or to cut out the first third, or whatever. If you have a twenty-line poem with a few things in there that are not very good, try just taking those things out, and leave everything else the way they are, and close up the spaces—a little mystery never hurt anything. People do not talk in uninterrupted sentences all the time, unless they're sitting here, and this is a shtick, too. I can write poems like this, too, but I get a little giddy.

Poets, especially poets that are still taking workshops, should write a lot. You should write at least three poems a day . . . and if you don't, you're being hideously deficient. You're not supposed to write three good poems a day, I mean, if you write three good poems a day for about three days, come and see me and I'll make you a fortune. But you should write a lot. I mean, what the hell are you here for?

Larry Fagin and I contrived this plan where we would go and interview all the students and all the staff members—the poets—and find out how many poems each person had written in the last three months. Then we wouldn't do anything with it. We'd know something, and we'd die laughing. . . . Yeah, but you should write all the time, every minute. You're not here to be these students, you know, or to have fun, or go to the New York Deli, or to go up into the mountains and have giant orgies, and things like that. You should do all those things, but you should just sneak off for a few minutes every now and then and write a poem.

All this life here that's going on is just grist for your poems. You only exist to write these poems. You're only having these lives so you can write these poems. Life is not important, only these poems are. Take that with a grain of salt, but it's true, in a way. It's necessary to believe that when you're writing these poems. Not the rest of the time, you can't be this poet when you're having this orgy, I mean, you won't get any extra points for it, and it won't make your milkshake taste better. But the milkshake and the orgy will make your poems be interesting, and likewise so will going out to the store to buy the paper or buy the groceries. In fact, I recommend buying the paper and reading it much more than having an orgy, because if you just buy the paper and read it, you'll have a lot of energy left over to write these poems.

I'd like to repeat about a hundred times this business about writing a lot of poems. I mean, you have to get with it, come on, work! What the hell—it's a short life, and because everything is Maya, therefore you must get your ass to work. And you have to understand that; it's one of the basic truths that is often forgotten to be stated by these guys that are working their ass off, like Trungpa, founding schools and doing everything, and they're doing it because everything is Maya, and they think everybody should be enlightened, and understand that all desire is a no-no, and one should just be calm—right—and so, they're doing everything every minute—right—and that's what you should do too. It'll keep you busy, and it'll keep idle hands out of the devil's workshop. It'll keep you out of trouble. It won't make your life any better, but it will give you something to do some of the time.

Q: What do you think of nonworking poets, like Corso, maybe Villon, or Peter Orlovsky?

TB: They just do . . . a little? What do you mean? You mean they don't write a lot?

I just finished editing a book of poems by Peter Orlovsky, poems of the last twenty years, and I took it from journals written over those years, and there were about ten thousand pages of those journals. And this book is only a hundred and fifty pages long, and it could have been three hundred pages long. And when that book gets published, there should be another book, and then there should be about five books of journals, because they're all brilliant.

Q: Well, I was thinking specifically about Gregory, because it doesn't seem to work . . . the poems aren't very sharp poems . . .

AN: I see him through the window every day at his typewriter.

TB: I estimate that in the years that I've known Gregory, which has been since about 1963, that, ah . . . I mean, I myself have written—Jesus, since 1963—from 1963 to 1970, I probably averaged about three hundred poems a year. At least three hundred pages a year. Not too many of them were all that good, but that's beside the point. And from then on, somewhat less, at least one hundred and fifty a year. I figure that Gregory, to my knowledge, has written at least twice as much as I have. I mean, I've seen these things. Gregory has suitcases full of works that he leaves in lockers in bus stations. It's the fact that he doesn't have them around. It's true. We live here, and he lives over there, and every time we go by his house during the day, when nobody else is around, he's sitting at the typewriter. I asked him the other day, I said, "What are you doing?" He said, "Piling up the pages."

Believe me, these guys write. They don't know how to do anything else. Not everybody can be Allen Ginsberg. If you can, that's great. It's great for all of us. Not everybody would want to be Allen Ginsberg, it's not all that great for him a lot of the time, but it's great for us.

There are no poets who write little. There are plenty of poets who publish little. Some poets will write five hundred versions of one eight-line poem before they publish it. That's OK, that's just their method. I'm just telling you that poets write all the time. They can't help it. They make things up in their head and forget to write them down. They just do it all the time. A car goes by, and the poet doesn't notice what kind of car it is, he just thinks to himself *a car goes by*. He doesn't even think a car went by. I say he, because I'm a he, but, I mean, it's all poets. A car goes by, and you wonder if you can use that line. Maybe you can . . . put it in the back of your mind.

In the back of your mind is this little room, and in that little room is this guy, and that guy, if you read lots of poems all the time, that guy will learn everything about poetry, about form, and shape, and when you make your poems, that guy will take care of all the technical details. All you have to do is write those poems. But that guy, you got to feed that guy plenty of material all the time, or else that guy will start raising a giant ruckus in the back of your head, and you'll think you're going crazy. It's only because you're not keeping that guy busy, you know. And that's true—believe me. And if you're a man, that guy is probably a woman who will really cause you a lot of trouble. I don't know . . . I never go in that room. I don't know what manner of creature's in there. I don't want to go in there, because that's my guy. I mean, if I go in there, he might be dead or something, and then I'll be in trouble, because I think he's still alive.

I read other people's poems, and I see they're doing these really brilliant things, and I know they don't know how to do those things. They're just these dumb clucks. I mean, Allen Ginsberg—you got to be kidding. That guy . . . I mean, Jesus, if that guy can do those things he does with his poems, I can't believe it. But he keeps his guy busy.

Some people don't write poems very much, and then they write a few poems, and once in a while their guy gets so excited because he hasn't had anything to do for so long that he cranks out about three good poems for them. But nothing happens any longer. Then that guy turns out about five hundred bad poems for them for the next two years. But there will be three good poems.

Philip Whalen—I turned to Philip Whalen and I said, man, in this poem you had three sections, and they were rectangles, and at the end they turned into circles, and in the middle there was a giant jet of green light going up in the air. I said, "How did you do that?" He said, "I didn't do anything like that." He's right, he didn't do anything like that, he just wrote this poem. The poem did something like that.

OK. When I see that his poem did something like that, I think, ah, great, I'd like to do something like that. So I think all about him doing something like that. Then, the next time I write a poem, though, I forget I want to do something like that—how can I remember that when I'm writing this poem? But that guy remembers. Then I read my poem, and it has three rectangles that turn into circles, the green light goes up, and I have to throw it away, because it sounds just like Philip Whalen. But then I take that green light and make it be blue, and I throw out one rectangle and put in a triangle, and then you say: "Here's a brilliant poem with a new variation on a theme by Philip Whalen that takes it far into uncharted territory that Philip Whalen was too ignorant to go into." Right. That's how you be a critic, you have thoughts like that.

Actually, I thought of another thing I was going to say. I thought of all these things last night, I thought of lots of them, but I only remember the ones I thought would be fun to say. When you're playing this teacher, you have to be this wisdom-oracular figure who's also totally engaging, electric, and so on, so I only try to say things like that. But, if you write a good line and that's all you can think of, that might be good enough. Just put that on the page. Maybe it will be a poem. If you write a good line and put it on the page, don't be afraid to just have it be like that. Don't gussy it all up and repeat all the words six times each and make some wonderful shape. That's silly. If the line's good, that just gets in the way. If you write a line that's no good, you can try that. It doesn't work, though. It's very hard to write lines that are no good. Lines that are no good are almost good, but lines that are only half-good are terrible.

You should be wary of tricky or fancy arrangements on the page, unless you have a feel for that. You have to be good at it, you know. John Giorno does that, for example, he's remarkably good at it. I love to look at his poems on the page—I never read them because I don't want to read all that repetition. But I love to hear him read them. Maybe I would read them if I could never hear him read them, but thank God I can. But I can see the poems are good when I see them on the page.

You can rest assured that if your poems aren't very readable, most people won't read them. Other professionals will, but that will only earn you respect of other professionals. Also young ambitious people will. But by the time they all get to loving those works, you'll have moved on to a more accessible place, and then they'll hate you and put you down for being reactionary.

It used to be that Bernadette Mayer and Clark Coolidge were the great avant-garde poets of America. Now they're not so avant-garde anymore, and they're just these mainstream poets—which is a very nice thing to be . . . but it's disappointing. Some friends of mine are preparing to blacklist Bernadette from the ranks of the avant-garde because her poems can be read now. It upsets my friends who have to blacklist Bernadette because they like her, and they like her earlier works. It doesn't upset Bernadette, but it puzzles her a little. But I think it's wonderful, either way.

The main point is that you have to make your poems be as readable as you can make them and still have them be integral to what it is you're trying to say. If you don't know what you're trying to say, and you have a lot to say, then you'll have to get things down on the page and pay the most attention to not saying anything you don't want to say. And therefore your poems may be very difficult to read, but they'll be true, and they'll be honest, and they may even be beautiful, and that's good enough. Your poems don't have to be intelligible, and they don't have to be easy to read. They just have to be true. And they have to be beautiful. If they're true, they're liable to be beautiful, because if they're beautiful, they're not necessarily liable to be true . . . the philosophers in the history of philosophy are still working on that one. It's very likely that the beautiful is true, but it's possible that it's not always true. I don't know. Maybe it just doesn't stay true, but the true is nearly always beautiful, to somebody, in any case. Sometimes it's a pretty peculiar kind of beauty— I mean, a true scorpion, or a true cockroach—but nevertheless, you have to get into a certain state to see how that kind of true can be beautiful, but it is.

If you feel a lot, and are bursting with a lot, and have the desire to write, and have no idea really what to say about your feelings and how to begin—then your job is not to get them wrong. Do not betray them. You have to be true, and you owe everything to your feelings, and you have to make sure you get them right. And the only way you can get them right, if you don't know how to put them into words, is to get the words down that fit the feelings, and not worry too much about what they say, as long as they don't say anything that is untrue. Then you're liable to come up with giant early Clark Coolidge works, or something like that, but they'll be good works, and they'll be terrific, and they'll also have you be on your way. But in the end, the final aspiration is to write works as wonderful as Shakespeare or as Homer.

You do want to write poems that everybody will be reading for five hundred years, but you don't have to worry about it. If they're good, everyone will be reading them for five hundred years, and it's all right to mention your dog's name or your friends' names, because in five hundred years people will find that just as interesting as the names of Zeus and those jerks that are in Dante's Inferno—all of them are just these insane dagos that get sent to the inferno for being these bad guys, you know . . . Or the incredible Irish mythology: guys that cut off their hands and throw them onto the shore—great guys, you know. Change their names to George, or something.

All right, this poem of mine is called "Wrong Train." I'll read it to you. It was part of a sequence of six poems—I don't know what a sequence is—it's one poem of six—either six or seven poems—that were all written at the same time. Simultaneously, in fact. I had this device with seven pens on it, and there were these seven pieces of paper . . . that's almost how it happened. They're only together because they were written at the same time, and they kind of look alike.

Wrong Train

Here comes the man! He's talking a lot
I'm sitting, by myself. I've got
A ticket to ride. Outside is, "Out to Lunch."
It's no great pleasure, being on the make.
Well, who is? Or, well everyone is, tho.
"I'm laying there, & some guy comes up
& hits me with a billyclub!" A fat guy
Says. Shut up. & like that we cross a river
Into the Afterlife. Everything goes on as before
But never does any single experience make total use
Of you. You are always slightly ahead,
Slightly behind. It merely baffles, it doesn't hurt.
It's total pain & it breaks your heart
In a less than interesting way. Every day
Is payday. Never enough pay. A deja-vu
That lasts. It's no big thing, anyway.
A lukewarm greasy hamburger, ice-cold pepsi
        that hurts your teeth.

Now. I wrote a long poem, I took a ride on the train. It took four hours to get where I was going, and I had a little book, something like this, only a little smaller with a lot of blank pages. I thought I would fill up that book—I gave myself an assignment. As usual, I didn't have anything to say, but I was on this train, so I said, "Here I am on this train," and that was the beginning. Lo and behold, here came the conductor. I thought of this brilliant phrase I'd heard on the street, which was "Here comes the man." I think I made up "He's talking a lot." "I'm sitting" is a fairly simple observation, but "by myself"—I mean, this is all very funny, but it's all true—"by myself" is derived from a song that Fred Astaire sang in a movie called *Bandwagon,* which says, "I'll go my way by myself." It has a particular feeling about being alone and sort of slightly jaunty. "I've got a ticket to ride," that's the name of a song.

But the point is that I wrote in this book, and I filled up the whole book, and I had a work about thirty pages long, and at the time, or later, a few weeks later, I didn't think the work was really any good. It wasn't very good, and I didn't think it really held up. I was very happy to have written it, but I remembered that there were things in it that seemed very true, that seemed right when I wrote it. And so I looked through to see what there was, and I found that things simply—all these things right here—and I found them about up to halfway through, but by the time I got halfway through, this poem was finished. And I didn't write them in this sequence, but when I extracted them from the work, they went into this sequence.

These things all did happen. A fat guy did say that, and the conductor did come for my ticket, and the other things are just thoughts, except we did cross a river, only we didn't go into the afterlife. And I did have a lukewarm greasy hamburger and an ice-cold Pepsi that hurt my teeth. But meanwhile I had all these other thoughts, and why this poem is called "Wrong Train" is because I don't think you should write poems about this kind of subject matter. It's my thought. I mean, I think it's totally boring to write poems about how hideous life is, because life is hideous, and so—so what? That's only in general—I mean, that's only in the extreme, but the particulars vary so much. If you didn't have a memory, you would never know that life is hideous. Dogs do not know their lives are hideous. If they did, what would they do? They can't shoot themselves, but they would do something. They would bite themselves to death, but they don't, and we shouldn't either, because dogs are not smarter than we are. What do you want to say?

Q: I don't want to interrupt your flow—

TB: Please do, I mean, this flow is a total device which I use.

Q: I'm interested in everything you're saying, but—I don't know. I mean, I go down to this other class, and there's this whole other stance that's also entertaining—

TB: Dig it. Right. That proves what I'm saying, exactly.

Q: What I'm wondering is if you could comment on some of the material from the other class.

TB: Well, ask those guys how much they'll pay.

Q: Well, what they're saying is, write when writing happens, and—it's an Objectivist trip—

TB: Wait a minute, I followed the "write when writing happens," but what did you say after that?

Q: Well, a whole bunch of other stuff—

TB: Yeah, I don't follow what "an Objectivist trip" is.

Q: Well, I don't know how—

TB: Train trip, maybe?

Q: —to say it as efficiently as possible, what I'm getting at. I'm probably more out there than I've put in, but the impression I'm getting is that the aesthetic that is being offered or considered or reinforced is to sit, and to let the experience itself orchestrate the poem, so that you're not really doing a whole lot. You're simply noting it, and "this life is hideous," there's nothing about that, you simply don't even think. There's not any attempts to make anything beautiful, and there's not any opinions on writing a lot. I mean, their opinions, to a certain extent, seem to be running a little counter to what's going on down here.

TB: Well, those gentlemen are a lot more noble than I am myself. I mean, I am ambitious, and I aspire to the beautiful, and I think that I can help a little. . . . No, no, I hear what you're saying. It's just that some of it doesn't quite make sense. I mean, "to sit"—and I'm assuming by that you mean sit and write—is to sit and write and to let experience orchestrate the writing? I don't understand what that means. I mean, nobody's going to write it for you. You know, it's just you, you've got to choose the words. Now, you can just know it, but when you're sitting and writing, you're only looking at a paper and pencil or typewriter. So, what—so, you must be looking into your mind, and you see things. But in your mind there's also thoughts, and you can see those, and they take the form of words, and so, you see words, and so—can you put those in the poem? Certainly. And if one of those thoughts is that life is hideous, can you put that in? Yeah, because hideous is a funny word, and has a lot of energy in it, so you get both things at once: that life is hideous, and that you just said something funny. I mean, you can put anything in your poem, right? That you see? Certainly. I say that, too. Let life and experience orchestrate the reality of your poems. Do not interrupt your poems with your idiotic ego. I agree. However, my ego is not idiotic. My ego is sensational, especially when I'm writing poems. I mean—I agree, if you're going to point the arrow at the target, don't fool around, shoot the arrow into the bull's-eye. Away with everything else. Try it. If you can sit down and get that straight in your head, then do it. You can, though, maybe even for the first three times, then you can't do it anymore for a long time.

I'm talking to you guys, you know. I don't talk like this to other poets that are friends of mine, that I've known for a long time. I show them my poem, they say, "That's nice. I like the use of 'of' in the third line." I feel pleased. I said to Dick Gallup, "You got any new poems?" He says, "Yeah." I say, "Great." Then I get to read them some time.

But I'm trying to talk to you about how to think about what to do. I don't like aesthetics that tell you not to do much. Get your ass to work, is what I think one should do. We are Americans, right? We have to work—let's discover, be pioneers, go to the moon. It's a good idea to go to the moon. Everybody says it's not, now—because they didn't find any money there, that's why. It was a good idea because there wasn't any money there. Send all the money there! Good idea! Money is bad, send it all to the moon.

The world is big enough to entertain all aesthetics. I think they are all interchangeable, like diseases. They're communicable. Aesthetics will not help you write poems. I'm not trying to give you any aesthetics, I'm trying to tell you to get to work. I'm trying to make it sound like it's fun. I'm saying, simply, that if you want to be a poet, you have to write a lot of poems. A lot of poems! And in order to write good poems, in order to write any poems, anything that even is a poem, you're going to have to read a lot of poems, so you can see what a poem is, and I'm trying to tell you that when you're reading all these poems, please do not worry too much about anything, because you just *read* them. If you have any thoughts, well, they might be good thoughts—one of the reasons why we think is because we can think, because thoughts are good, many times. There is a sensual pleasure that brain cells derive from having thoughts, even though thoughts are baffling and frustrating, and there's negative pleasure which can result in frustration and pain.

I think the aesthetic you're talking about—and I myself am not too interested in bringing in names, here—is very good for poets. It's what all poets try to do. I mean, I'm a kindergarten teacher myself. I don't know anything. I've never been to the enlightened place. I'll tell you what to do while you're waiting for the bus. When the bus comes, you're on your own. You're going to have to drive that bus, you might even be that bus, you'll also be all the passengers, and then you're going to run into yourself coming the other way. But you'll take care of that.

My Buddhist philosophy is that the bodhisattvas are all hoaxing you, and that that's the highest step, and that is known, therefore there might not be anything beyond that. The bodhisattvas will help you because they can't think of anything else to do. However, you have to entice the bodhisattvas, seduce them into being helpful to you—to show them that they're needed. I could go on in that way . . .

You're not going to write good poems unless you write a lot of poems, and you're not going to write a lot of poems unless you write anything. That's what I'm telling you. Write anything, and I suggest that you write it well, and the best way to write well is to not try to write well, but to just write. Almost every line that I've read by anybody when they were trying to write well was truly horrible, simply because most people hadn't read enough poems and didn't know really how to tell a good line from a bad one. The most fatal thing for a poet to do is to be poetic. It's also utterly unnecessary. So, you have to work that one out, too.

The only thing about this poem, however, and why I wanted to read it, and why I wanted to talk about it, is because I made it out of sitting down for four hours and writing lots and lots of things, and then taking not all the best things out, but all the things that went on one kind of line and made a couple of turns. This poem is all revelation, and it's all epiphany, in a way, but it doesn't help. I'm suggesting that rather than writing a poem and writing it over fifty times, you write long long poems, and make them into short poems, not by taking out the bad parts. "I've got a ticket to ride" is not an inspired, gorgeous line, but put in the right place it carries a certain amount of energy. "God" is a really terrific word. It's very American, and therefore accurate.

One good way to get everything out that's inside you is to write for about four hours, then go and see what you have, and make it be a good poem. In this case, you can follow the Allen Ginsberg method of taking almost everything out, though I generally prefer the other method, which is: when your poems don't work, put a lot more in. I like the idea of giving. I also like the idea of receiving.

Transcribed by Todd McCarty.
Edited by Anselm Hollo.

"A Little Endarkenment: and in my poetry you find me"

ROBERT DUNCAN

Interviewed by Anne Waldman and John Oughton
June 21, 1978

★   ★   ★

ANNE WALDMAN: So what about obedience?

ROBERT DUNCAN: Obedience is the obedience to what's going on in the poem that we have and that one is just fine. Meanwhile, our whole life obedience I also talked about, that I wouldn't let a poem, for all of how wonderful it is as it comes in there, come in and interrupt if part of my obedience, is in household or something that I obey. But I obey it.

AW: Household?

RD: My household. But I obey it because it's not laid on top of me, it doesn't come at all, as in that Burroughs thing, "lean, lean, lean." [William Burroughs gave a reading the night of July 19, including a piece with this phrase.] It never leans on me. What it is, is more genuinely me than I most of the time can be without it. And that household can tell me more about the poem because the poem can promise us all these pictures that we get of being a power or something. I hated it when my mother laid on it "That's not really you" but there is another feeling we've got in us. I'm really talking now. That's a wonderful feeling. OK, now we have enough confidence. We haven't started talking about confidence. But as we were talking earlier because we're aware that you begin and you're obedient to a poem that begins. A poem can do various things and what if the poem comes forward and the poem is a big monster wipe-out that promises you that you'll be addressing thousands and that you're going to be about bigger than Shakespeare when you finish and I don't mean it's fake. What if it's real!

JOHN OUGHTON: Like Aleister Crowley.

RD: All right. Look at Shakespeare, how gracefully he retires from the very stage we make him famous for. Aleister Crowley is not Goethe or Shakespeare.

JO: I was thinking more of his following the messages in his poetry no matter what.

RD: Oh right, onward and upward, right, right. Oк, that's not what I'm talking about when I talk about this feeling. There's something awfully simple I am, that's what I mean.

AW: But some people you see will have the other interpretations for "lean, lean, lean." It's something different for everyone. A lot of people would not be as comfortable as you in the household, for example.

RD: "Lean," no, but I wouldn't be in the household if it leaned. I'd be out of it, I mean my life instinct would tell me to get out of it.

AW: I was just continuing to wonder about this obedience.

RD: I'm in error, in the first place there's two of us in the household and we take care of each other and we have various reciprocities. There's just every allowance in every direction, that I can be absorbed in a poem for some days. There are whole areas in my poetry that I have not allowed it to take me into, or to do and it is mine in that sense, so my poems cooperate with me. But I stop poems when I can see I'm not willing to cooperate with you now, poetry, with what you've got going. I'm not going in the direction you're going. Words. I don't obey them in that sense. I obey them, and mostly it is wonderful how words are appropriate, but they can be wrong.

AW: But what if you had a teacher? Could you do that with say a heavy Vajra master? [Vajra—the "diamond energy" path of Buddhism, which has to do with drastically cutting ego-trips and obstacles of all kinds. Many Tibetan lamas are Vajra masters.]

RD: Well, let's just say you're taking a course, and you get a grade at the end. No you can't, you get a flunking grade, and most teachers get angry when you walk in and walk out. But I wouldn't want that teaching situation. I'm talking about the students for credit here [the majority of the students were taking Duncan's class on a noncredit basis], all I'm going to be able to say at the end is, "Oh, I've never met them." It's a lovely, charming remark, but they may be ascended masters, they may show up and hand me a wonder poem or something, but they haven't been there.

JO: Maybe they're invisible students.

RD: Maybe they're invisible, and that would be extraordinary.

AW: I'm just wondering about your own sense of obedience to the poem, or to love, or to a . . .

RD: Remembrance maybe, or more important, a recalling. But I do think that I obey a poem, I work with everything that comes. I begin to talk about correcting.

AW: You don't reject?

RD: We started talking about correcting, and since that really is the thing I feel, I don't feel that just as any arbitrary way, I feel that that's my responsibility to work with everything that comes. I don't think everybody should, but of course that's what I'm demonstrating, because that's the way that I work.

JO: You said today that your poems sometimes take you into very heavy places, you know, violent or whatever, I don't know. Now where do you distinguish between that and the areas you won't let your poetry take you to?

RD: It's not where the poem's going to take me, it can take me to hell or anywhere. But if the poem starts being one of those . . . if the poem starts building me a throne, and I'll even sit on a pretend throne in the poem. I'm a great vanisher of thrones. In "The Venice Poem" I announce that I'm a cross-eyed king of a thousand lines, I mean I can place that king thing because it's important to me. I talked in the class about how if all of Christendom had gone into the imagination and returns to us as imaginary, not as posited in the real when we've got Dante. That's why it enters poetry. I wonder if in the great Hindu epics that the whole world hadn't gone into the imagination, and I wonder if people who tried to put that on top of themselves can't anymore because it really is imaginary, it's got the freedom of the imagination. We can read it as fairy tale.

JO: But you can't live the *Upanishads*.

RD: No, it's a fairy tale. I mean it's entered the world of the fairy tales and it may have been read, it must have been. We realize that the wars and everything went on, but it all passes into imagination, and see it revealed in another way. And religions are hostile to imagination because they want real things to happen and real powers, then they have to prove their powers. I'm meeting with this mathematics class, $2 \times 2 = 4$. They're hung up on their proofs. And I asked well why can't they just imagine, I mean why bother, why is it important to prove the equation. They all just look at me, I mean that's just ruled out, you're supposed to prove everything. But that is the nature of power in the actual word, in the imagination we realize that I have only the power I have, but in life I'll prove it, and I'll ask you to go up there and put a mark on the wall to see if I have some local power. Then I'll worry that you may have done that because you wanted to, or you may have done it because you like me, or you may have done it for the wrong reasons, or make a situation which is painful and now you'll get up and make a mark and so forth. Well, I won't know if I have power, because in the imagination not only would you have it instantly but you'd also know you didn't. Anyone telling a story knows what kind of power everyone in the story has and they know how grievous it is when someone is locked in this box of having to prove something. So that we'd be back in the poem. What if the poem proposed something that you had to prove you were? Aleister Crowley [Crowley led a disastrous climbing expedition on Kanchenjunga Mountain in the Himalayas], the one very real thing that you come across in his life is that he had mountain terror: the point when all the party was lost and he was left. Now, in the descriptions of mountain terror it's supposed to be one of the greatest, most tremendous, really shaking experiences one has at all. I think he kept trying to get back to it. So he wanted black magic and anything that would get into like terror, because it was intolerable not to come across, and of course there was no such thing. You can't make a mountain give you terror, that's being so entirely in that moment and you certainly can't make the human community, and he actually becomes a pitiful old man saved only by humor, by fragments of poetry, and so forth, yet for all of them he had contempt because none of them would give him the sense of terror and possible violation he had because he had betrayed the people he took up there. So he practices betrayals and so forth, well, good and evil don't signify here at all. I do think there's an evil in poetry, that's the thing here. I think there was an evil for Jack, for Spicer, who was a great and beautiful poet and who fed himself into return to the field of the poem, was in greater and greater suffering, terror that there wouldn't be poem again, and who lived in one psychodrama in which he'd fall in love with somebody and curse them out of his falling in love. And whether that was a fragmentary, whether that was an early psychodrama out of which he got a poem, he repeated it over and over again and finally anyone could know he was feeding a poem by falling in love. I mean what a misuse of experience, that none of us are that skilled.

AW: What was he threatened by? Why would the imagination be a threat to him?

RD: No, I think that he's returning, you see, I don't know that it's a threat. In Spicer's case certain elements that he didn't want to be imaginary, that's true. He didn't want those angels from outside to become.

AW: Wasn't that one of his rules, don't let the angels come in?

RD: Well, he said something marvelous about them, he said it didn't signify whether they were Martians or from the unconscious because they were from outside the poem. And today, in class, I said it comes from inside and then I finished and I realized, no Jack was right, it does come from outside. After all it's just as much outside, after all I have to write the board on the word, like the word on the board. And if I've heard Helen Luster give me a line, I turn to myself and say give me a line, is that any different? It goes into this thing. So it is outside every time it lands, there is no outside-inside, that is like I was very clear on the subject-object thing at that point but suddenly I came to where does it come from, I wanted to say it comes from here. But Jack pointed out that here is strange and outside the poem when it comes there.

AW: Well, he reportedly had so much doctrine.

RD: Yes, but doctrine got more and more closed. But what I'm talking about, about the evil of the poem, I think that he made the poem so paramount that he really did go through a kind of ritual that people had to cooperate in and suffer through, but I think that that's incidental, although none of us feels good if we're falling in love and get used for somebody's strange little formula since it's often, at least it felt like, a state that both parties had to do something about. But Jack really did go—I mean I can think that . . . bewildered Fitzgerald with Jack had just run through this and the poem would be a curse against this thing, against embodied love.

AW: Fitzgerald, you mean?

RD: Russ Fitzgerald, who was one of the early ones that actually lived with Jack, not many of them lived with Jack. Jack actually had an intense enough feeling about what the other person was like to be doing a lot of this in his head.

AW: So what's religion?

RD: Religion?

AW: Yeah, what's religion's problem with the imagination?

RD: Well, Jane Harrison may be right that it comes from yoke, I'm not sure.

AW: Yoke?

RD: From yoke. Religion has a wide range. In Greece, for instance, in the cults of Greece previous to the Hellenistic period, if you were going to go to the Aesculapian temple and dream, there's a kind of dream medicine, not only a cure but [you] receive a real Aesculapian dream. You went through a series of things, you didn't eat or drink the day you were going to dream, and in the previous period you ate only vegetables.

AW: Were you thinking of a natural medicine?

RD: No, no, you dream, it's dream medicine, not medicine medicine. There were medicine medicines. The dream interpreters might have given you a medicine learned from a dream, but actually they had various dream people. After you'd had the dream and then when you told it, the one who was into medicine would give you what we'd call medicine, but there were other things, other people would say, "Ah yes, but also this dream says you should do so and so," so you carry it through. But no Greek had a subscription that was binding beyond you were going to go to the temple, unless you were a priest or a priestess in the temple. And I think that often when we're talking about religion, you're talking either about those who go in as lay members, now they're usually not under such heavy stuff. But the ones who go there to be priests or priestesses have always been totally subscribed to the god, goddess, or set of beliefs and so forth. And yet these were co-existing temples. The ones in the inner rites. And the same was true of the Jewish cult. But in the Jewish cult it expanded and became a total racial tribal subscription so they're all under the law and then they all could be damned for not following the law and everything, so it looks like everyone was in one of those cults but not Greek. The only Greeks who thought near that were Pythagoreans who when they entered the Pythagorean cult—that was obvious to the other Greeks—they never ate beans. They all believed in reincarnation, they took the . . . because the code of beliefs is another character of religion. And the poets—what if the Black Mountain School had been a code of beliefs?

AW: Oh, my god.

RD: And it wasn't, I mean it was perfectly evident there was no code of beliefs and yet everyone read out because it itself advanced. There was a thing called *Black Mountain Review,* so it labeled itself practically Black Mountain by that time, and then school gets to be like a school of fish.

AW: And now it seems to be.

RD: Like a school of fish. But out of it comes a code of beliefs and particularly a code of hero-worship, so that you can't think of various ways about Charles [Olson]. I get to be a heretic because I was writing before Charles started writing but that doesn't sound good in Black Mountain ears when I'm talking about what might be right or wrong. There are people who find it impossible to love and at the same time to know lots of things about the person they love and to be critical and so forth. So, all of a sudden they're enemies and they get angry when they're talked about. One thing Freud said to H.D. when she went to have her sessions with him, he said, "Never defend me, because if you defend me you will find that you're the one. That this is your repressed criticism of me," this is what you're failing to see, it's what you're defending against, that's the only thing. So all religions are built in the "Thou shalt not think, think about me."

AW: So what of the Jack Kerouac School of Disembodied Poetics being based at Naropa Institute, which has Tibetan Buddhism, or let's say, American Tibetan Buddhism giving the space, giving the poets a psychological space?

RD: Well yes, and more than that they bring us a place to move in. Now for instance I am not Buddhist. Now I felt really called here. I made negative jokes about it, I said I'm paying my blackmail to Anne and Allen. I wouldn't be called to some place if they're not part of my real poetry world and my real poetry world is real to me. It's not a part of a literary setup. It somewhat looks like, were we a clique? It looks like it but there are too many people in it to be a clique, but on the other hand I wouldn't feel called even when . . .

AW: Something like the Iowa Writers' Workshop.

RD: Right, right, I don't feel called, hog-called, I'm not a hog.

AW: [laughter]

JO: Sooeee.

RD: Right, right. I'm not sure, maybe I am. I'll come bouncing up the hills but not thinking I'm going to find that classroom is filled with people who have been just giving me really magic stuff. OK. But I also said that this is the only time because I could see that, surrounded and associated with this constant presence of any kind of Buddhist order. I'm very friendly with the Zen Center and they don't have any lien on me at all except that, for instance, they have a VIP weekend or a couple of them that they have at Tassajara. Roshi Baker said, "I'd like to invite all the guests for this VIP, the ones you want." Would this be like your real Zen? Well, real Zen proves to be real Tao, I couldn't think of nobody. I mean look, I've got a blank mind and then they start "lean, lean, lean." They're phoning saying, "Where's this list? Where's this list of people?" Then I'm running down, running through people, like an awful birthday party. "Robert, you're going to have a birthday party, where's your birthday party list?" Who have I left off the list? I don't have anyone on the list yet. Am I going to invite you? I haven't invited anyone. Have I already invited too many? And so forth, and I find that, and actually they weren't doing all that [much] leaning, so the question of leaning is what you feel, isn't it? It's not that someone leans. It's a magic that you feel leaned on, you read it that way.

Then if they can't deal with it, then we see something else. But actually, then the Zen Center said, "Oh well, if that's the way." It's like Roshi, Richard Baker, we sit around. The great joke is that he never gets off on time; he's always saying, "I want you to go back with us," and I say, "You mean at nine, at ten o'clock tonight, Roshi, tomorrow? I did want to get back." "OH, no, no, we're going right away," and then soon there'll be four or five of us sitting around cursing ourselves out because we're waiting on this. Built into Zen is this kind of freakish behavior in a way, like poetry. In poetry we can say we've got temperament, can't we? We expect to have strange things happen.

JO: You can't hit the reader over the head with a stick at some point.

RD: Well, the nice thing about poetry is that it's in a book and a reader gets to close it when a reader doesn't want to read it. That's our one great noble courtesy and since we read, now we read in big auditoriums. I'm certainly never bugged if someone gets up and moves out. But Charles [Olson], for instance, was coming on like he was a superpower. First Borregaard—this is that long spiel of Charles's—and first Borregaard gets up after the fourth or fifth time Charles has . . .

AW: Ebbe Borregaard.

RD: Ebbe Borregaard. About the fourth or fifth time that Charles says, "We've had enough of beauty." And I'm muttering, "Cripes, you've never seen anything beautiful in your whole life, you silly old man." In a world that hasn't got any beauty around he's saying "NO MORE BEAUTY" and we're sitting in the ugliest auditorium you could ever see, with *ugly* chairs all around and *ugly* everything and an *ugly* occasion and I'm thinking like, like, like the monkey in the tree, how do I get out of it when this king of beasts is calling us all into order. When Ebbe gets up and walks out, Charles doesn't dare say a thing. Here's this big, tall, blond, cool cat walking out. If he'd called on Ebbe, Ebbe would just have turned around and said, "Oh shit" and walked out the door, and he didn't want to hear that. And then a little old lady who thinks, "Oh god" there's going to be a space for her to get out. Unfortunately, Ebbe is already out the door and she starts out and Charles turns and roars at her. Then I thought this is not a test of powers, because I don't believe in a test of powers at all, because I thought, "Will I bring a big whammy?" Charles felt my flunking out as if I'd brought a whammy. Then I realized, it's not a whammy, we all have to pee, so I said "Charles, can we have our break to go pee?" And then I just never came back from the break to go pee. He felt like it was a whammy, but the alternative in my mind, that's another thing. So we're just talking about poetry.

JO: Poetry orders?

RD: Poetry, people with poetry orders. And the great offense, if you were to go "Uhhh" and yawn in the middle of a Duncan poem, right, I mean we're scared by it so it's a big offense. We come on we've got everything out there, the real stuff or the poem stuff or whatever. My whole sense of it is to find, why can't we go pee and not answer to it, get right out from under it. When Eshleman's magazine, *Caterpillar,* interested me but I saw in it he had a thing in which he was reading the Black Mountain group as a royal family. But I'm partly responsible for all those figures of kings and princes because my poems are filled with them in order to move them around, move them off their ass. But anyway, he sees this straight down and he says, "How come Creeley gets in instead of him?" And I looked at it and I thought not only do I feel like I'm not read and he's trying on the robes which were made to be not there—to be invisible robes. And all I did was never contribute again, all I did was never write to Eshleman again. That was no punishment. As a matter of fact I continued to read the magazine. I was interested in the magazine. I just backed out, I just disappeared from the scene. I avoided it. So avoidance is a power in itself.

AW: Does that mean that order . . .

RD: It's a very strange order. I mean actually that we are sensitive, that's what the person who gets up and leaves in a sense avoids. And yet how simple—all of us should have removed ourselves from scenes that we suffered through. And yet there are other things that we suffer through, with great reason. There can be courses that you can think, "Oh god, why do I have to go today? Why do I have to do my sitting-up exercises?" And so forth—I know why. It's a different matter, isn't it?

AW: Isn't that like religion sometimes?

RD: Well, it could be for religion, I mean there must be people for whom in their religion it's central. They're not the ones who've got the question we're raising.

AW: Right, that's true.

RD: We're not talking about religion as such, we're talking about religion when it's very easy. There are people who love the poem no matter what comes, what's going on, almost. But when we begin to be aware of where the poem goes, in its disorder, when it starts being as if it ought to be there for everybody. Someone like Jonathan Williams blaming America for not supporting the poet, and finally you end up picketing the football stadium because they're not at McClure's play. I mean, if you can see the absurdity— or the other way around, picketing McClure's play because they're not at the football game.

JO: For the work and dedication that you put in as a poet, do you not feel that society owes you anything, even if it's reading you occasionally?

RD: I rip off everything that they have ever extended to me but I sure don't feel they owe me a thing. Not at all. I'd love to cash in on my readers but they don't owe something. Remember, remember the work, *work* is something you do and more than that. If you thought about payment! Well, we just had today the real source that it's all coming from and going back to is that sound up there that was put at the top of the board [Om] . . . Now, that's the circuit. What the poet does rightly have to aim at is how to make the time and space in which they can work. And since the society doesn't offer it—it offers it in peculiar ways, if you can find a way to find that time and space. Poets are very cunning about it. Shakespeare. In Shakespeare's day the stage was there and they all wrote for the stage. Then they're all Protestant ministers, for almost the next two centuries. They could always get a little parish someplace and give their sermons. And in our period, the thing they buy at all for the arts is terribly destructive because what they buy is a personality up front. You make it in the movies or TV just as far as you're a personality, so poets build personalities all over the place out front in order to move around and buy, that way, the space and time. That's our star system. Well, it's very destructive of our energies, and especially it can be destructive of the person we are. I think personality is sort of a growth out from, and uses some of, the central person energies in order to make this front thing. When I extend my personality and the imaginary me, I build in prefaces, and legends, associations. And that's in general the way we do it. So that our readers for instance begin to have us as stars just about the time they're reading us. And yet that's very hard on the reader. My real imaginary reader is someone who knows nothing of all that.

AW: Ideal reader.

RD: Ideal reader, who picks up the book anonymous in a secondhand shelf and starts reading poetry, poems of whom he knows not. Because the one who suffers most under this is that the reader is drawn into the glamour and hardly gets a real experience of reading a poem, which is how much it means to ourselves. So I try in my prefaces to sort of build in a picture in which the reader knows, begins to know that I am handing it across. But the money thing is not "owes." No, no, we use our cunning, we do what anybody else does, we try to make that space for it to happen.

ROB FROMME: Could you talk about the nature and astrological circumstances of your birth?

RD: Well, I was born in a working-class family. My father was listed as a day-laborer as late as I last found a listing for him, which would be about ten or fifteen years ago. My mother died in childbirth and I was adopted at about the age of six months, into a WASP theosophical-hermetic brotherhood-type family. Both my father and my mother were in a Hermetic Brotherhood and her mother was an elder in the brotherhood. So, the character of hermeticism as a religion—this is American hermeticism coming after Blavatsky and theosophy and so forth but its character always has been like the character of Gnostic communities and so forth, that it's composite and not integrated, that it carries contraries, and that it allows for areas of confusion and a lot of fantasy. A lot of fantasy—mixtures of *idées fixes*—and fantasy I was very used to by the time I grew up. So parents in my household, instead of like Joyce's where they were quarreling about Parnell, would be having violent quarrels about who wrote Shakespeare. All this is trivia, but whether Atlanteans flew in astral projection or whether they flew in machines. There were fierce scenes, within one family. You can't check up on this, but they'd all check up on this back in the Akashic Record and the Akashic Records are like—that's the *Encyclopedia Britannica* of the astral world—so everyone can go there and get a different message. Every time they wanted to have a family thing, wingding, and then when my oldest cousins were old enough they had their great breakings away, mostly over astrology, or over the Shakespeare thing, both of which I found atrocious. To read Shakespeare, and then have a family diddling around, working cryptograms out of it and thinking the real thing to worry about was written—and especially if you'd read Bacon—to think that he wrote Shakespeare. You want to know how come Shakespeare wrote Bacon, not how come Bacon. If you could write Shakespeare, would you ever want to write Bacon?

JO: There's a big book by Ignatius Donnelly, all those ciphers from lines of Shakespeare.

RD: Oh, yeah. All that was that my father was an architect and loved things working with numbers, would work cryptograms and codes all over the place. And astrology was used in a fundamentalist way. I was adopted by astrology, and the family did make decisions, all important life decisions were made by astrology. Astounding ones, like "you have to move now" like in 1927 or 1928 and buy an architectural practice in Bakersfield. He was told at the brotherhood level he had to go back to his beginnings and the place where he decided to be an architect. His father in turn—this is my adopted father—had been a railroad engineer, you know, driving a railroad train, and he was working in the roundhouse in Bakersfield when he decided as a boy to take the exams and enter architectural school in 1905 or 1906, a graduate program or whatever. So he really had determination; he was the only one in his whole family who ever went to college at all. He simply boned up in the summer and did it. Ok, he bought a practice in Bakersfield, so my adolescent years were in Bakersfield. It was a town of about 40,000 at the end of the railroads there. My father was the first period, from one to six months. I do know of that now, I was named after that father. My name was Edward Howard Duncan and that's how I could look him up since. Ok, and there were two older—I had two sisters, one was twelve and one eighteen or something like that—and the eighteen-year-old took care of me. As I read it, if that was the family, they didn't want to let me go, since I was named after my father. To let a boy baby go when you have two girls was a very heavy trip for a working-class. Again, he had to be a WASP, by the way, because my theosophical parents would not have adopted a baby, merely because it was a white Anglo. It would have to be a Saxon and also have to be Protestant. They wouldn't take a baby of another religion. The court judged me to be in a state of imminent starvation, so my parents had me within a day of seeing me. They simply took the baby before the court, and the court decided instantly. I think, you know, even then you had to go through [adoption procedures]. My sister was four months between the time the adoption closed, but the adoption was closed immediately on me. There was no question at all about it. [In] my poetry more and more powerful figures of hunger, thirst, and intense being deserted or alone and so forth [enter]. So that's a very formative period in this one-to-six and I have a very flash reaction toward big-sisterism and I think it may come out of what you feel if you're a baby being babied by a big sister who didn't really get the food they're supposed to at the time, and left you, both neglected and whatever. I was born in 1919, so I grew up through the 1920s and my parents were a combination of this Masonic, hermetic religion which was already not a public religion although it had a temple. But it did, and it had classes. That would be interesting in relation to what do you do in obedience. Its main trouble is that it's intellectual. You go by grade. So in this it would be like the Buddhist schools here, wouldn't it, or do they have grades in Buddhist schools? Well, Buddhism doesn't have grades.

AW: Well, there are levels of practice.

RD: Levels of practice, ok, that would be similar.

JO: And vows you take.

AW: Vows you take, through the Hinayana, Mahayana, Vajrayana . . .

RD: All right then, yes, they had this. They had vows and they had initiations. And my father was a high-degree Mason and so everywhere was this business of hierarchies. Actually after I graduated from high school I didn't want to graduate from nothing, and if I could have figured out earlier than high school I would have failed. I would have gotten out from grad-uating [from] high school. So I really read life, "I'm not going to graduate, I'm not going to be . . ." So I immediately turn away if someone says, "I'm going to spiritually improve you, here's a little enlightenment." I say, "No, no, I'll take a little endarkenment and in my poetry you find me." I'm very different from Blake in my poetry, absolutely the antithesis of Blake who wants it light. You find me no, *sfumato*, mixture, color. I love Blake so I'm not phobic toward the light kids, you know. I love Rembrandt with his dark, deep study of the dark. Of course Freud was lovely because not only do we finally have an asshole but finally shit. And so is Joyce, and not only was it part of life, it was a meaningful part of life. That was one of the things I think we most importantly bring forward today, is the complete-ness of existence, admitting the completeness of what we are. My parents' religion, like Neo-Platonist religions, was all to sublimate, to move up, and I love sublimation. I have no trouble when the Freudians say, "That's just sublimated." I say, "Hooey, I mean I just told you I have an asshole and I also have a sublimation so don't tell me I borrowed for one from the other." No way. There are many things I carried forward from that family. As above, so below, obviously. I mean the Freudian as above, so below fas-cinates me, carried forward there. There were also Christian Cabalists because both Masonry and Hermeticism . . . Hellenistic Hermeticism had already got shades of the fact that very early stages of the Cabala are devel-oping. But once you've come past the Renaissance, there everything's together, one great big melting pot. And I tend to bring forward all the things that I find fascinating and try to find a way of having them so that they don't form subscriptions. My mother, when she was dying, died in fear of the Dweller on the Threshold. Now, I mean, this is a religion. She never went beyond the first grade because it's an intellectual religion, so it doesn't leave any place for someone who doesn't go through all sorts of intellectual monkey tricks. My father, my mother's oldest sister, my grandmother were all intellectuals, and I was fascinated. Yet I didn't do the magic square. I said "Do a magic square"—no one did it, but I especially didn't do it. [RD had suggested to his class that they make a "magic square" of the words in Helen Luster's line.] I tried to say I'll force myself to do it because that's what they did all the time. I don't mean that it had magic, that I don't mind. So I guess I have a bent about not developing cer-tain qualities, certain kinds of possibilities of mine that I've seen. Not admirably, but I certainly have seen people caught out this way. This sci-ence group here, the mathematicians [RD refers to two members of Naropa's '78 Summer Science faculty, and a course on the nature of math-ematical knowledge and proof]. I've had dinner with Charlotte Linde and [Joseph] Goguen. And Goguen was expressing this business of being caught out, being taught the trance state in which the mathematics arrives and then being isolated with this mathematics, not knowing how that relates to this whole thing. But my response was also—Yes, and yet in poetry I obviously have trance states. You see, I entered—poetry we enter. We choose our own masters, by the way, in poetry, because we don't meet them personally. We choose them in texts, although I had sessions with Ezra Pound and sessions with H.D. They weren't these kind of sessions we're having today. And that's the only kind of session. Mostly poets don't study with masters, painters do. They go to their studio, they grind the paints. Painting has a whole order which would be exactly like the acolyte-master-discipline thing. That's what Renaissance painting came from, but even Renaissance poets had no poets. Dante met with Cavalcanti and met with Ficino and so forth. They were a group, like we are, sitting around, and they talked about love. There was no doctrine. And they imagined what do those poems mean and poems, I think—the characteristics of poetry—it would be very hard to get a doctrine from it. My last session with Charles, I said, "Isn't it wonderful that from the beginning you would think that you were laying down a dogma. Maybe only *you and I* are interested in what composition by field is. All the time you must have realized one thing you didn't need was a secondhand Charles Olson." He beamed, he said, "We've been on a great adventure." And that's something . . . that's like Robin Hood Duncan. And this of course, in the imagination all these things can be re-posited. And in the meantime this was a man who was not on a great adventure when he was standing up on a platform trying to say, "Well, here we are. We're a big power and we're going to have some poetry politics." His fantasy is imagination, and suddenly he wanted to make it realer than imagination. That's what I mean about that imagination, in that essay on "Occult Matters." On Blavatsky I talk about the fact that although she could work marvelous tricks and produce all sorts of magic effects, she wanted it to be *real.* She wanted to come down on things. Her head was more marvelous than anything she could have done. She writes to, I think it's Sinnett [Alfred Percy Sinnett, 1840–1921, Anglo-Indian theosophist], "Can you bring back a real magician from Egypt?" And while we can hear rumors of real magicians in Egypt, I'm sure they couldn't have brought anything that compared with Madame Blavatsky when she was going on. Not at all. But she wanted it real. When religions don't want to be real in that sense they're doing all right. They're doing fine, because it's a whole realm, like theater and everything else. And yet it's not theater, you go into it in a different way. But we're still talking about what about the coexistence of poetry and the misunderstandings between a poetry and a religion. Burckhardt [Jacob Burckhardt, 19th-century Swiss historian, *Civilization of the Renaissance in Italy* (1937)] says there's a fundamental misunderstanding between poetry and religion. Poets think that religion gives them a great subject matter, wonderful. And religion thinks, "Gee, they're really a jazzy way to get our message across." And so between these two people there must be a larger misunderstanding than you can imagine, of any kind, between the two groups.

AW: But poets don't come here for the subject matter, I don't think.

RD: Yeah, I know. But they could. When I say that Christendom enters the imagination in Dante, the whole subject matter is there.

AW: Of course.

RD: Aquinas is sitting there, and meanwhile I'm not reading Aquinas. Aquinas has written, wait a minute now, I'm blabbering on in philosophy. But Aquinas is where it has to be real, in medieval law. There are no laws in poetry.

AW: No laws.

RD: Well, are there? Can you think of a law?

JO: I was just wondering if anyone has asked Anne to write a Buddhist poem, you know, to say, "If you could get a little Vajra into that poem it would really help the movement." Does anyone do that?

AW: Not quite. [laughs] Not yet.

RD: There's no reason why certain terms couldn't be there. I'm disturbed by Joanne Kyger, for instance. Actually the Buddhism isn't part of the poem, it isn't part of the imagination. And so you get a little homily in the middle of the thing. And poets have homilies of different kinds. I just call, I call this whole . . .

AW: Speeches.

RD: . . . I call this whole department Mother's Day Message, you know. How many poets write "To My Wife" and you wonder, what did they do to her that day, that they want to give a guarantee again in a poem, Mother's Day Cards, or "My Country 'Tis of Thee." I mean it's all of that level. And yet it could be. Certainly we can have powerful feelings of country, powerful feelings of religion and so forth. In my poetry the religions that appear, like the Christ and so forth, are because I don't have a subscription, so I get to move them around. Michael Davidson said he was always puzzled, what were the movements of Christ in there until he had a new second-born Christian in one of his classes and the new second-born seizes a Duncan poem. Try to think of yourselves as a second-born, you've just got the message and the line is reading like it belongs to the message, and then try to go to the next appearance of the same figure and you'll find yourself absolutely freaked out-of-doors. And yet Christ is a very important person of the poem. I began to talk about persons that come forward in the poem, like the Master of Rhyme. We can't explain them. We don't think them up. And I was puzzled indeed why this Christ—and the ugliest thing that comes romping over the mountains is Christ, and next to that, Jesus. We say Jesus because it's just about caught us, meanwhile I have even a subscription to Jesus in the middle of a poem. So does Spicer. Astounding. And I stared—when the subscription comes, I wanted deeper into it. Oκ, but a poem has to do with feeling that emerges in language, where it does, and so forth, and in the vast tapestry of things it all belongs. So does Buddhism, is what I'm saying. And so do all the realms, the Buddhist realms, by the way, oh, and Hindu. The only reason I sort of resist the Hindu is that it's so vast, I keep thinking could I possibly if I got moving in there? And what it opens up is such a glory of constantly moving and nowhere are you stuck in it. I mean if you are on the way you're stuck because you've got to go a particular way. But it's a glorious huge picture, and that movement in poetry is what we in the West [call an] adventure.

AW: Adventures in Buddhism.

RD: I think of it as on the way to a world consciousness, and while we bring ourselves into it, we come into it in these other realms, and so . . . talking with you I think this morning I had a strong feeling that there's a meaning to this coexistence. Not the one that Allen's seeing self-consciously to the coexistence of the Disembodied Kerouac School and a Tantric, and highly authoritarian order, compared with Zen or something. I mean Zen is not big. But the real significance is that isn't it interesting indeed that a lama from a kind of mind you would think is antithetical to the American mind, comes *here* in order to exist. He's already come somewhere, and that around this it comes up to a school of poetry which is really one of the most open and un-cratic. I mean how do you find the -cratic? It's a goofball if they're going to write secondhand "Howl"s. I mean . . . and that isn't the way Allen shapes it. That isn't the way people teaching here cluster together—you've got an Allen Ginsberg and so forth. I read the crisis that happened with [W. S.] Merwin. The most interesting thing in it is that his holiness Rinpoche doesn't get to be everywhere in the canvas the same figure. He moves.

AW: Trungpa?

RD: Yeah, Trungpa, you've got a huge canvas and we're moving through realms and realms and realms and realms and we take a figure from this realm that in the Tibetan realm is the center of the whole thing, and we move it down here and we get to Boulder, Colorado, and he's just one along with the Rolfing Center. I took the Freebie ride around and the end of it starts at a Rolfing Center. So he's just a cult here, but just a cult is very American. It's Oz. If you read any Oz book you'll meet, you'll meet exactly the scene that took place in . . . Oh god, Blue Monday is even worse. I'm thinking of the poet Percy Veere and Dorothy are captured on Blue Monday Mountain and they have to wash clothes. I mean Blue Monday Mountain has a very hard regime. And they keep spotting away to run away.

AW: Is that the name of a soap?

RD : Yeah, right, Blue Monday. But Oz books are filled with sultans and little tyrants. Tyrants, tyrants are part of American life really. It's almost how to kick around IT&T, you know. I mean, IT&T's a heavier picture, isn't it? We've got to coexist with that but, so that you have the two changing potentially, have to be changing. And his holiness and so forth looks more and more ridiculous.

AW: I think they call him his Highness.

RD: His Highness? Oh.

AW: Karmapa is his Holiness.

RD: Oh, who's Karmapa? Where is his Holiness?

AW: Karmapa is Trungpa's boss. He's the head of the whole Kagyu lineage.

JO: Right below the Dalai Lama, along with a couple of other guys . . .

AW: No, they're parallel actually. The Dalai Lama and Dudjom Rinpoche are equal in that they are the heads of their particular sects.

RD: OK, for instance, certainly you can see that this order is more exposed than the Vatican.

AW: How so?

RD: We aren't about to be sitting in the front of the Vatican as coexisting with the Vatican and zapping it out, and failing to kiss the Cardinal's shoe.

AW: [laughter]

RD: And, and, messing up how you address the Pope and so forth.

JO: Maybe that's because the Pope ain't no poet, whereas on the other hand Trungpa's been writing.

RD: Popes have been great patrons in the [past].

JO: Some popes have been.

RD: Yes. No, there's nothing but it. I'm just saying we aren't sitting there. No, it'd be very hard to put the Pope together with a picture of the kind of scurvy poetry we all are, so something has happened here that this order gets around the kind of scurvy poetry we are. Something of a real spiritual happening has taken place. I took Renaissance and Medieval studies in a way that would have brushed my teeth almost to have been doing my poetry in the Vatican. I mean, I think I even understood the protocol, and poets have never been bugged by protocol. Although mostly poetry's a heresy.

AW: Well, pretend they are.

RD: Actually, that's where we are again. Poetry carries very powerful heresies toward powers, toward the powers of this world. So this is a little power that can coexist with it and constantly bounce off it. We love to bounce off the powers that exist.

AW: Well, that's a good instructor. I also don't know why it's here. You know it's something out of my control.

RD: But then is it to be here forever? I mean, I know that I'm not to be here forever, that gives me a great . . .

AW: No, I don't think so. Allen might be here forever.

RD: I am sorry I'm not teaching for five weeks, but no way could I even have volunteered that. This is painful enough for Jess, for me to be away as long as this, and I would have not taken it if I had not felt a calling. I barely talked about the word in the first session, saying I had a calling to do poetry, but I hadn't felt a calling. Actually I wouldn't have let Anne and Allen blackmail me. They don't have all that heavy stuff.

AW: We don't have too much on you.

RD: Oh yeah, but negatively I just say I was called to pay my poetry dues so I wouldn't be a baddie. They don't read people out as bad when they don't turn up here so that's all right. And Boulder is a very, very interestingly charged town.

AW: I think it's an illusory town, it's a bubble town.

RD: Yes, it is. It's like San Francisco, it doesn't exist in this world and that's great, that's great, that's just marvelous, it's like the world center of Rolfing.

AW: It may not last very long.

RD: I mean all imaginary things can center here.

AW: It's a fantasy town, like Hollywood used to be.

RD: Well, right, that's exactly how Hollywood should be.

AW: And also we're on the spine.

RD: Probably Hollywood is just around the corner and I didn't notice it.

JO: There are more poets in this town than there are factory workers, I think right now that's the case.

RD: Well, that's a very healthy condition, right.

AW: And some of our poets are even factory workers, like Jack Collom.

ALL: [laughter]

AW: But there's something. We're on this spine, you know, of this continent, the mountain spine which goes clear down to Central and South America, and actually there have been predictions in the past about this being a real energy center.

JO: Power spot.

AW: Power spot, and the negative ions. I feel very different here compared to how I feel in Manhattan.

RD: Oh yeah, well I feel differently here from what I would in San Francisco.

AW: And I remember Trungpa originally saying, "Come to the mountains." He was doing this in 1974 with me and Diane di Prima and Allen. "This is the new seat of poetry, come to the Rocky Mountains, very beautiful!"

ALL: [laughter]

RD: What is the relation of this order to Milarepa?

AW: Definitely a connection. Kagyu lineage is Milarepa.

RD: So is someone in the line supposed to be an avatar of Milarepa?

AW: It's possible, yeah.

JO: I just wonder because I can't see it. I look at Trungpa's poetry and wonder what in the world that's doing and think, "Gee, is this what Milarepa's supposed to be doing this generation?"

AW: There's probably some more direct lineage.

RD: Reincarnation?

AW: Reincarnation. Or maybe there's multiple incarnations. There can be a hundred Milarepas.

RD: But we tell Milarepa by the emergence of the poetry, not by the man.

ALL: [laughter]

JO: Each of those Milarepas writes one-hundredth as well as the original.

RD: Yes, right, and finally we get a Milarepa.

AW: I think that was an inducement to Allen. If there hadn't been a Milarepa in this lineage . . .

RD: Yes. He wouldn't have been that induced? I still don't get from Allen's poetry. His poetry seems to be about the way a poet picks up a thing like Buddhism. It is not . . .

AW: To display.

RD: Yes. I do see that Buddhism means something and Allen's trying to find the meaning, and what he's doing when he protests and what it is when he comes before the powers of the world.

AW: Energy, just energy.

RD: Allen comes before them with absolutely no distortion of person. He does meditation, I mean but would he get together with his body, would he get together? That's what he's not doing. So even meditation must be a drive against it all because what I see in Allen is everything intent forward and no coming into the body.

AW: Allen, the Vajrayana, you see, in Tantra, the whole notion is working with energies, converting any negative energies into positive ones: transmutation. So I think Allen is incredibly energetic in so many directions, and his body can't take it all the time.

RD: Yeah, but whatever's happening, his energies are eating up his body and that seems to be . . . It's funny, we say "my body," that "my" is the most peculiar thing in the world. Who is this? I mean, my brain, my hand, the whole thing, I find that in Hindu wondering, in Buddhism wondering too. I guess he wasn't centered so he goes to meditation, yeah, but I think I'd just get with the body, try to fall back on it, in my whole sense of it. . . . We didn't get to the astrology thing you asked about, moon and sun. My sun is in Capricorn and my moon is in Pisces. But my poetic relations to moon and sun I find much more important because I don't check them out as astrology. There are certainly some things I'm convinced about. We'll start with the zodiac, with the fact that we read the zodiac. And we all know that with the precession of the equinoxes, actually the sun is in Sagittarius, not Capricorn, in January, when I was born, in the early part of January. But most of that zodiac, the readings of that zodiac, don't come from the sun or moon, they come from the earth. I mean they don't come from the sun in relation to the outer stars. That's where we're reading the Sagittarius, not the signs. They come from the relation of the sun to the earth. If you are born in the depth of winter, and that's where the sun is in relation to the earth, regardless of that outer star thing, then most of what you read belongs, then, to that fact. That you're born in the dark of winter, that you're born in spring, say that your first six months are the rise of the sun until it's in full, or that the first six months, because the child's in the presence of that light and the lengthening and shortening of shadows, and more than that, the total change of the human community as it goes up to summer, and that part is permanent. We would never precede it or anything, we'd be in happy hooligan land if we changed readings, made those readings attach to the Sagittarius or attach to the Capricorn.

Moonwise, I can't dream that we're not immediate to the moon, because we're mostly water. The pull of the moon on every body of the kind we are is tremendous. Not only do we watch the sea respond, but we happen to be little walking seas. And so, in tune with this, if we refer to the moon, they can land on it, it can prove to be real estate or whatever, but it is always the moon we are talking about. And so moonlight and every bit of this, all its phases of light we feel and we recognize right away as a language of our real consciousness and so being intuitive we're in full moon, which has at top full moon. We don't miss full moon. I had a period when I was learning stars and watching stars. That's the other thing that I find absolutely wonderful, when I commune with the stars. And part of communing is coming to know the constellations, and then coming to know key stars. And you do feel recognitions and closenesses to stars, almost like you do to individual animals, or individual people. So I don't read why they're there by some formula. I make my romance immediately, and not because the star's big or little. As a child I can remember when stars . . . particularly in intersolar space where the set of planets was present and was felt as what probably . . . I mean what I felt as a child was the music of the spheres my parents talked about. Which seemed to me the music of the planets and the sun and they appeared to me as a music and I've got times in my poetry where that's come forward, and as a matter of fact has been very well spoken in the poetry, always throwing to me that that gets there better than I can say it, but that has happened in dreams.

And, ah, then one time, the first time that I fell in love with somebody after I had been living with Jess. It was not long after, four years or something like that and I was sort of in an agony. I would have to sleep with him in order to lift it and at the same time I've never been away from home, I would have to, so I was really quite torn. I sat down with Jess and said, "Well, I have to do this." At the moment of coming I found myself in that same interstellar space. At first it was as if I were falling, and then sort of free-fall and actually this is at the second because when all of this is finished it took no time at all, you're still in the same come, exactly the same come. And then, painfully, I was making my way back along the streets that I had walked to go to this guy's house, back and up the stairs, and then I realized I *have* to know the number of stairs, I've never counted them, I have to know the number. We're on number. And then to the bedroom, where I saw Jess crying, and was there, carried through. And then it was done, and I was back, and there was no time, so I know all about that no time. And I'd actually done what I had to do, I mean not just there, I was there, but he knew I was there. Although painful or not, I never had to do that again. But I had to do it—not just for us—*I* had to do it. So there are types of little orders I obey. I mean there was only one thing I had to do, I had to do it, nobody laid it on me at all or something else. It was just what you had to do at that point. So there was a very funny space feeling there, I do know something about interstellar space. Just exactly the black, there's no light sort of thing. And also suddenly, with no transition, coming, but I fell into it in just the point when the spurt of semen rises, just the no-time in which you actually are united with something. And at this point I was not just united, but I was there and made that magic trip. That magic trip appears in a poem again, where I name that I had declined. So one thing that interests me: there are many very important experiences in my life that have never come forward in poems. And there are things that come forward in poems that I would never have dreamt were essential experiences until they appeared in a poem. And sometimes, and it always disturbs me, when something that I felt was a powerful personal secret appears in a poem and is necessary to go in the community and then of course one tells. So, there's a star of a movie in its own.

And moon has definite moon angels. I've had moon actual presences, moon columns of light, columns of moonlight, and in them, presences that have forced me to do things, told me to do things and so forth. These were more ancestral because they were my mother, H.D., some other women in the chords, human angels . . .

AW: These aren't actual dreams?

RD: That was a dream. That's a dream. That's a dream. I've had some moonlight, moonlighting him, with moonlight. So that has its special moods as I guess it has for everybody and transformations.

JO: How do you feel about your place in the Whitman-Pound lineage, tradition of poetry? I'm thinking mostly in terms of anyone who's carrying on from your discoveries, who's sort of forging ahead in terms of new technique from your work specifically.

RD: I think of myself as close in spirit to Whitman and Pound and so their language speaks for me and I tend to write like that frequently. I really don't think of myself, nor do I think of them as "forging ahead" or something. My experience about poets is discovering a company. Growing up in that WASP family, I really didn't have much company, I felt insane much of the time. And then, a teacher in high school, ah, Miss Edna Keogh, I still know and see, opened up to me Lawrence and Pound, not Pound, no, D. H. Lawrence and Virginia Woolf, and suddenly there were spirits I could really commune, feel I had a company. I didn't care that I wouldn't know them. I understood that, yes, probably I will never meet these people but I understood. I love to read, anyway. But it never dawned on me that what I loved in reading was that all the time I felt suddenly companied. I didn't have to talk to them but they were making it clear that I could have, because they were extensions. So I feel them as extensions, is my feeling. Sometimes poets have written poems . . . Well, LeRoi Jones [Amiri Baraka] is coming here and he wrote a poem on dancing responsive to my poem "The Dance." I almost burst into tears because I didn't know him. I had never met him. It was so close to me and I felt, "Oh my . . . " I mean I'd found a like soul. A very early thing, I said I write for those alike in soul. Yes, I feel close to Whitman and to, ah, Pound as if there was some kind of spiritual company in that. And with Emily Dickinson, she seems awesome. I mean, I tremble. I spoke of some other poems and things where I found myself trembling in Wordsworth, I'm not sure. I don't feel the kind of company with Wordsworth because it is awesome, because it seems too grand. Shakespeare I love more and more. But Shakespeare seems to have so indwelt on imagining who any of us readers were going to be that we all discover ourselves in him. That's why everybody thinks someone else wrote him. Because almost anyone who gets into him finds that he was really writing for you, whoever you are. That's way out. That's unbelievable. I felt, "Yeah, well, OK then, what are we answering to? I also would like to be that open, I also would like to be for everybody." Then you don't have to feel that they have to pay you, do you? I mean, Shakespeare doesn't feel, "Lorenzoni has to pay me for the misery I went through." God even Macbeth, if he could have read, could have read it and not been insulted at all, by the play. We would all try to injure Hitler. We'd all try to. That doesn't even signify. We'd all try to injure Nixon. Shakespeare does not try to injure Macbeth. I think this is a miracle of displaying what it can mean, that you can see what a person is and not want to injure them. And not want to add a little kick.

JO: Just portray them as they are?

RD: Well, when Dante's going through hell with Virgil, when they get to the circle of lawyers and the ones who lie, and Dante suddenly wants to give one of them a shove back into the shit they're in, and Virgil says, "Look, ah, you're now taking on the character of this place." Everywhere else Dante also doesn't injure. And suddenly he wants to injure, and he embodies it in the poem and tell us something wonderful at that point. Because his guide, the spirit guide, Virgil says, "All right, Buddy, if you want to injure, this is your circle, and I will leave you. You're not making the trip you said you were in." Oĸ.

AW: What about the younger poets?

RD: Younger poets? I've had several times when surprising books have seemed very close to me. One recent one is Michael Davidson's, where I actually wrote on. Oh, Jess wanted to do a cover. How did we contrive it? Yes, Jess was thrilled by the book too, and very close to it, and so he did a cover. Then they printed it, and the printer printed it in colors when it should have been in black and white. So I said, "Fine, the solution is we'll make a jacket for it and I will write on the jacket." I was thrilled by the book. But it was also because the book was very close. The things that, ah, where I feel close indeed to poetry I guess is to a poetry that embodies a very human and personal love situation, in a very immediate way. I think that's the thing that's most essential to me. To make me feel close to it. I understand Whitman that way although his kind of love is not at all. Since he was one person after another after another, so it isn't even that, it's the person . . . the immediacy, personal immediacy, that kind of present time. Well of my contemporaries, Denise Levertov—and I have terrible quarrels with other poems of hers—she's written poems that I gaze into over and over again. Immense closeness is felt, and a puzzling one. Because she's a moralist, and I don't like moralism. And so forth, lots of things. So, so, it isn't that you get along with them all the time, that's the story on that. There's such a richness but I'll take you're one going back to the ones that mean something *very* personal to me. And that would mean some poems of Denise's. H.D.'s poems were a great revelation and the *late* poems of William Carlos Williams, I cannot separate them at all from the human condition. I can't think of them as whether they're great poetry or what kind of poetry because they seem to be just purely, just immediately the voice.

JO: Do you still read Yeats?

RD: Oh yes, I read Yeats. But Yeats seems to me an artist, and I understand Yeats most on artists and mysteries. And I love arts and mysteries. I read Yeats over and over and over again. And his prose I love. I don't feel the closeness to Yeats. I feel close to Pound because I'm a mixed-up person like Pound, perhaps. I mean, this is a personal thing.

AW: What about Stein?

RD: [fake Southern accent] You're referring to my mother. Yes, there are times when Stein is certainly in. The "Valentine for Sherwood Anderson" is a lovely little love poem to Alice, and "Lifting Belly" I love. It's just a glorious, glorious poem. Yeah, she would be one of those. Not only is she a writer that is absolutely liberating to go to and learn to let language move that way, and get the sort of thing we were doing where you let "turbine" talk, instead of you trying to move it around. That's just great. But she does have also the crossover where I feel the same. I'm not a person with only ten poets to mention, so we've got too long a list to be going to. I could only take the poets that came immediately to mind.

Transcribed and edited by John Oughton and Anne Waldman,
July/August, 1978.
Naropa student Robert Fromme also was in attendance.

Irreparables, I: an essay-ode

ROBIN BLASER
July 11, 1995

* * *

ROBIN BLASER: This talk is really a kind of compilation . . . it's a combination of things, I try to summarize where I'm working now both poetically and in terms of essays. But these are working in a particular range, and part of this was a presentation for The Kootenay School of Writing, the anniversary of their tenth year. The Kootenay School is, well, those are our "language writers," to use that overused and misunderstood phrase, and marvelous poets. And to it, I've added a lot of other things. . . . So it might be a little bit haphazard. But I've always liked the haphazard. . . .

So, I open up with just a little thematic that informs a lot of this "stuff" in simply a note: *If god, self, history, and book are convenient names for the paradigms of our thought, then when one of them shifts, all the others tremble, because shifty pronouns begin shifting.* Now, this poem is not by me and most of you will know it, but I have titled it "Rigging":

Rigging

> My soul is an enchanted boat,
> Which like a sleeping swan, doth float
> Upon the silver waves of thy sweet singing;
> And thine doth like an angel sit
> Beside a helm conducting it,
> Whilst all the winds with melody are ringing.
> It seems to float ever, for ever,
> Upon that many-winding river,
> Between mountains, woods, abysses,
> A paradise of wildernesses!
> Till, like one in slumber bound,
> Borne to the ocean, I float down, around,
> Into a sea profound, of ever-spreading sound . . .

It is of course Shelley, from the *Prometheus Unbound,* Act II. A marvelous moment, and it's Asia speaking. And what I am after in particular is the phrase, "a paradise of wildernesses." So, to go along with that is another one I've called "Shipped Shape," a tiny poem:

Shipped Shape

is it a boat?   open   little rigging
this soul's enchantment

becoming larger   fully rigged   is it
       a ship
       shape?
             this soul's territory

And, another little poem that is true to the . . . I have a series called "The Truth Is Laughter," and this one is 19:

The Truth Is Laughter 19

I sent out invitations to an original party
asking everyone, women and men alike,
to come dressed as Adam—RSVP,
of course—
          they all sent regrets,
no such disguise could be found in the shops

I've shaken loose a bit, so there we are. I'd like to open up with some lines from the Middle Ages. It's out of the period of the troubadours and it is a riddle dialogue. And the two figures speaking in it, one is called Pippin, who is obviously a student, and the other takes the name of Albinus. And Albinus is really Alcuin, who is the great figure of Charlemagne's court, who set up the educational system around the year 800 AD. And the two are talking about very serious matters in this dialogue. Pippin says: "What is a word?" Albinus answers: "A betrayer of the spirit." Now, I'm not going to give the names each time. Just remember the answerer is Albinus and the questioner is Pippin.

[Pippin:] *What is a word?*
[Albinus:] A betrayer of the spirit.
Who produces words? The tongue.
What is the tongue? A scourge of the air.
What is air? The guardian of life.
What is life? Joyful for the blessed. Sadness for the wretched.

The expectation of death.

What is death? An inevitable event. An uncertain pilgrimage.

Tears for the living. The establishment of one's will. The thief of man.

What is man? The servant of death. A transient traveler. A guest of Space.

What is man like? An apple.

How is he situated? Like a lantern in the wind.

Where is he placed? Within six walls.

What are they? Up, down, before, behind, right, left. Six walls.

And, the one that delights me most, it's number 84 in the sequence of this marvelous, riddle dialogue from the troubadours: "What is faith?" The answer: "A certainty of an unknown and miraculous thing." You know, they were rather smart in "the old days."

Well, as a poem this stuff is *pro-em,* to be really fancy for—it's "a song that comes before." Let me begin from my favorite habitation: two or three quotations, super-inscriptions for us today. That is to say, with "that which is written or engraved on the surface outside or above something else," a super-inscription. I found this in Umberto Eco's *The Limits of Interpretation.* A story told by John Wilkins, in his book *Mercury; or, The Secret and Swift Messenger* (1641). Now the English is a bit archaic, but that, for me, does nothing but charm me. This is the story told:

> How strange a thing this Art of Writing did seem at its first Invention, we may guess by the late discovered Americans, who were amazed to see Men converse with Books, and could scarce make themselves to believe that a Paper could speak. . . .
>
> There is a pretty Relation to this Purpose, concerning an Indian Slave; who being sent by his Master with a Basket of Figs and a Letter, did by the Way eat up a great Part of his Carriage [the figs], conveying the Remainder unto the Person to whom he was directed; who when he had read the Letter, and not finding the Quantity of Figs answerable to what was spoken of, he accuses the Slave of eating them, telling him what the Letter said against him. But the Indian (notwithstanding this Proof) did confidently abjure the Fact, cursing the Paper, as being a false and lying Witness.
>
> After this, being sent again with the like Carriage [the figs], and a Letter expressing the just Number of Figs that were to be delivered, he did again, according to his former Practice, devour a great Part of them by the Way; but before he meddled with any [of the figs], (to prevent all following Accusations) he first took the Letter and hid that under a great Stone, assuring himself, that if it [the letter] did not see him eating the Figs, it could

never tell of him; but being now more strongly accused than before, he confesses the Fault, admiring the Divinity of the Paper, and for the future does promise his best Fidelity in every Employment.

I think the moral is clear. And we live in that condition: *disclosure* and *concealment*. *Presence* as human activity, not as an irreparable tear in Being or in God—as the content of the word "god," taken out of the dictionary, has come to be summarized in the words "being" and "presence." And so, *God* is poignantly absence. Wilkins's title is lovely: *Mercury . . .* , the Latin name for the god Hermes; mercurial language; Hermes of the labyrinth; actinic, *actino-,* meaning "language emitting rays and radiated structures"; *actino-,* chemistry, zoological, "radiated structures"; language with the qualities of liquid mercury; mercury vapor lamp. . . . Not to be confused by contemporary theory that would defer the radiated structure.

And, from Giorgio Agamben, whose work in *Infancy and History . . .* this Italian philosopher contemporary is of extraordinary importance to me, a recognition of him that came something like a year ago this January. And then I was to find that Norma Cole, who is present, has a very clear and strong relationship to Giorgio Agamben and his work, as does Michael Palmer. And now we even have translators working to do more than the four books I'm going to name that are in English. *Infancy and History*—and the point here is to note, we take infancy to mean "a child or the condition of childhood," when the word itself means "not speaking." *In-fans,* not speaking—and the subject of the book is the nonspeaking at that boundary wherein it would meet all the problematic of speaking of language. Another book is called *Stanzas* and a third, *Language and Death,* which takes up perhaps the most extraordinary relationship that young, middle, and old face in writing—that, constantly, language moves toward that boundary.

In my workshop we were talking briefly about how, if one notices, youth will write poems about death, you know. And a seventeen-year-old writing poems to me about death, you want to kick him in the ass! But on the other hand, the truth is that's where it's going, and somehow the youth manage to get there. And then, a book of astonishing use for me, as a poet, is a book called *The Coming Community.* Now, these inform me and draw me to use—and I will be doing so as I talk on—the use of the word "irreparable" and of the word "whatever." *Whatever* is almost my favorite word these days. You know, wherever I go I've wound up in whatever. That's where *my* poetry is going. And I intend to keep going in that direction, because it is the continuing song of *The Holy Forest.*

Now I have four brief quotations from Giorgio Agamben, and so I'll move those along:

After having transformed the work into a commodity, the artist now puts on the inhuman mask of the commodity and abandons the traditional image of the human.

"What reactionary critics . . ."—and I've inserted here the remark, and this is a key, to the fact that certain aspects of contemporary theory play into the hands of the most reactionary. Since I am particularly interested, well-read, concerned with contemporary theory, I put that out as an admonition—that it plays into the hands of the most reactionary. And, as a consequence leaves the community that is the matter of writing. Which is to say, we write of what we share. What we share is first our singularity and, secondly, the relations that singularity reaches for. It's as simple as that, and your energy can get mighty fancy. You can learn Greek, you can learn Sanskrit, that Andrew Schelling does for us, and on and on. These are *energies* that go there. They are *not* elitisms. So, all right, there goes the first tantrum. [laughter] Let's go back to the second one. . . . Or no, let's go on to Agamben and stop the tantrums.

> What reactionary critics of modern art forget when they reproach it with dehumanization is that during the great periods of art, the artistic center of gravity has never been in the human sphere.

Hold on to that. Let's take Agamben's footnote: "What reactionary critics of modern art forget when they reproach it with dehumanization is that during the great periods of art, the artistic center of gravity has never been in the human sphere." I think you could take this and simplify it into never in[to] the human sphere as a reduction, as a limit. The fault with, say, Socialist Realism is/was that it simply forgot there were worlds and that there were relations that belonged to singularity, and to the absolute beauty of singularity and its movements outward. I do not mean to say that Agamben would approve my annotation, but this will at least clarify this for the moment. Agamben's footnote here is: "The polemic of modern art is not directed against man"—and this is a very, very important point—"but against his ideological counterfeiting."

A phrase, an unforgettable phrase: *ideological counterfeiting*. It is not anti-human, but *anti-humanistic*. That involves us in one of the most complex patterns of *modern* art, and then this continues into extraordinary adventures in what is called postmodern art. Now, a third quotation from Agamben:

> What is new about modern poetry is that, confronted with a world that glorifies man so much the more it reduces him[/her] to an object, modern

poetry unmasks the humanitarian ideology by making rigorously its own the boutade [its own outburst] that Balzac puts in George Brummel's mouth [quoting Brummel]: "Nothing less resembles man than man."

All right. Quote again:

> Whatever the name given to the object of its search, the quest of modern poetry points in the direction of that disturbing region where there are no longer either men or gods, where there is but a presence, rising incomprehensibly over itself like a primitive idol, at once sacred and miserable, enchanting and terrifying, a presence that possesses at once the fixed materiality of a dead body and the phantomatic elusiveness of a living one. Fetish or grail, site of an epiphany or a disappearance, it reveals and once again dissolves itself in its own simulacrum of words until the program of alienation and knowledge, of redemption and dispossession, entrusted to poetry over a century ago by its first lucid devotees, [will be] accomplished.

And I would only annotate further, that "open form" is the becoming of open work. The mind of the field, the mind's field, to pun, dangerously. Thus, an *endemic*. From Greek, the word endemic, from Greek, *en-, in-,* "to," plus the word *demos,* from "people." *Endemic,* what is in people, belonging to people. And *epidemic,* from Greek, *epi,* "upon," plus the word *demos,* "people," what is laid upon people. The *demo-cratic*—so much presently endangered, the democratic—from Greek *demos,* "people," plus *krateo,* "the rule." So new, democracy, so un-understood, now that capitalism has inherited "the end of history" (you may all go to bed with Fukuyama if you wish to; I give up my homo-Eros if I have to do that!) and other numerous superstitions. So, the words *endemic,* an endemic, an epidemic, a democratic, are not transparent to whatever we are, at least they were not initially so transparent. Transparency in language is an assumption made, that when one oneself *owns the language,* looks through it clearly into some "grids of meaning," to use Foucault's vocabulary, that we are *certain of.* . . . And that transparency may well be a trap, because you may have looked through a window into a horror you didn't recognize, even if it looked a little like yourself.

Then I found in Agamben this poem by Giorgio Caproni—*è morto a Roma,* 22 January 1990—this marvelous Italian poet. The only way I've come upon him is by way of Giorgio Agamben. We now have a translator, Pasquale Verdicchio, among us who is translating Caproni, to my delight. A small book came out in Montréal, and you may get that, and there will be further pieces coming out from him. But this little poem, and I'm going to try to remember to repeat it. Because I love it. Agamben gave it to me, and he gives it there in both Italian and English, and we'll just leave it with the translation. Well, I might read it twice now, but I want to repeat it at the end of whatever I get, because I won't get where I think I'm going to get anyway. So, we'll just do whatever I please, if you don't mind.

The poem is called "Ritorno," and I hope some of you would think of Pound's "Return," that wonderful thing, the poem "Return," which is actually return of the gods and, oh my, what a situation. This one, though, is "Ritorno," return:

> I returned there
> where I had never been.
> Nothing has changed from how it was not.
> On the table (on the checkered
> tablecloth) half-full
> I found the glass
> which was never filled. All
> has remained just as
> I never left it.

Now, if I have a belief, this is it. May I read it again? Because the reverse is *ritorno*. What a marvelous sense, that you would keep a return. And it's just simply a most natural experience. [reads poem again] A little stunner. Worth looking further into. Into *him*. I wrote—I was desperate because we couldn't get it. . . . As I tried to explain to Giorgio Agamben, I mean, he didn't understand the idiom, because I said, "Well, I can manage Italian, but I have to beat my head on the dictionary." Well, I had to explain, embarrassingly explain what it meant to beat your head on a dictionary. Which was a hit, it was all right. So then I cabled, faxed actually, Stan Persky in Berlin, and I said, "Well, over here there's nothing like this. I can't locate anything in San Francisco at this point. Would you see if there's an Italian bookshop in Berlin? I want the collected poems of Caproni." And sure enough they came through. Gorgeous little book, in fact, the *Poesie 1932–1986*. And they're published by Garzanti, under the sign of the elephants of poetry, which I really rather like also.

This little run now is called "thinking of/about irreparables." I really mean this as a fundamental kind of honesty from my own work, but I also think we need to look into the *irreparables*. *Whatever* beliefs . . . (and I wish to respect beliefs, they belong to singularities) whatever beliefs, those beliefs must not cover over the fact that we live among irreparables, things that are *not reparable*. And so, I'm going to play games with those words for a few minutes.

This is not a sad story. Now, that's where you begin, with irreparables. The first line of whatever I wish to say is, "This is not a sad story." OK, as I told Tom McGauley when, in companionship, he phoned recently wondering how I was managing *whatever* I was up to, his laughter was exactly what I wished my first line could play for you now. What word is there for laughter *with,* not *at,* this whatever that entangles and embraces us? What word would sub in with laughter, entangle and embrace us? And then a letter from Jery Zaslove arrived not long after that, hoping I would talk more in this talk—he'd heard I was going to talk about irreparables, so he hoped I would talk more about *reparation.* Thus joining me out of the profundity of his own work, I quote him: "on the way modernism faces the problem of loss, the loss of loss, the loss of the book, the loss of eternity, the loss of a number of specific what are now called *tropes."*

For me, the magnificent task of modernism is the reception/rejection of, the acceptance/disavowal of, the obedience/disobedience to our *uncovered materiality* in all the arts. Poignant and close to home in our experience of the materiality of language and its creative. . . . And I stop over the word *creative.* It's Greek, from Greek *kreas,* and it means "flesh." The creative is *flesh.* It is also probably the very process of the universe, but that would be pretentious of me to say. The creative, *creatine,* "a white crystalline nitrogenous substance, $C_4H_7N_3O$, found in the muscles of vertebrates, and the brain, blood," etc. Nitrogen belongs to all living tissues. So, to keep language close to the chemistry from which it comes, *mind's fire in rhyme, enjoined embodiment in rhythm.* The word *trope,* from Greek *tropos,* meaning "a turn," a turn in the language which occurs as a change in meaning, or rather the changing-*ness* of meaning.

Have you ever gone through, say, an art gallery and listened to "What does it mean?" Well, it's a very interesting question, and should not be treated with any disrespect. The problem with it is, "what does it mean?" proposes that there is a meaning! I know of no modern art that has a meaning. But the changing-ness of meaning may often be its central concern. The specificity of, say, a metaphor—which is a trope—may be lost, but it remains an instance of polysemy, of many-meaning. On the other hand, in slippage of meaning, frequent in the condition of polysemy, we get multiplicity of meaning. The signifying function may well become opaque. For thought, whether poetic or not, does not begin in clarity. *Claritas* is the great crystal of which Pound asked "who will pick it up?" Certainly not himself. For me, the central figure in my working definition of postmodernism is that it is nothing more than and certainly nothing less than the correction of modernism . . . politically, socially. Particularly politically and socially. That would of course include sexism, racisms, and so forth.

For all my debts to Pound's immense musicality of form and content, he would not pick up the great crystal. In fact, in his own honesty, leaves it "who will pick it up?" (in the question). Certainly *loss* is the perfect word for the initial sense of this ongoing changing-ness of meaning, human and cosmic. The word *loss* is a back-formation, from the past participle of "to lose," "lost," "being lost." Central to this is the sense of not continuing, which brings our language round, turns it to *death,* where our language has hovered all the time.

The *loss of loss* is perhaps the most terrible, because it is loose, unbound, set free into *whatever* of experience, having passed from Holy Ghost to "Lowghost" (Spicer) to *wild-logos.* Now, I perhaps make an effort to enter upon the theme of the week, "wild form," where in philosophy I found—and this is Merleau-Ponty—where there I found a curiously suggestive term, *wild-logos.* And I hold it, it comes up in my poetry, I return to it over and over again, the notion of a wild logos. A logic that deals with wildness, a logic that never is able to stop for its wildness, that is un-linear and so forth. Now, curiously, for me this is suggestive of what we have called the sublime—that which speaks, in Hannah Arendt's marvelous definition of it, *with a human voice* that is never so simply "hers" or "his." Wherein, nevertheless, both of them, man/woman, woman/man, are musical as trumpeter swans.

Once years ago, during a walk around North Beach, I was taken to task by Robert Duncan for probing the difficulty of holding *experience,* just plain undressed experience, in our poetry. This was attendant upon our shared admiration of William Carlos Williams's "realism" and Creeley's exact and beautiful "nowness." A *real* and a *now* larger than any I myself had found language for. And, I will be impertinent enough to say, larger than the West Coast had yet found language for—it did, in particular, for all the poets named. Duncan that day cared to understand experience (the word *experience,* which actually is what we should just do with *experiment*—take it out of its abstraction and just simply say it, we're talking about *experience,* and that's all there is to it; *whatever* that is, including a sense of test and trial) as somehow reductive in relation to imagination. Now, this is the problem. And it was Duncan, it was a very real quarrel and he somehow was either admonishing me or swatting me, I don't know which. It doesn't much matter these days. But it was, that if you were too insistent upon what you had experienced, *then* what happens to imagination? Well, I think it's a real question, and I think that every writer comes into that range, and I think Duncan was actually right. I didn't think so then, I was furious. But on the other hand the imagination, now then, *that* becomes another activity that we will either return to or won't, whatever happens.

That glamorous word *imagination,* whose etymology is just plain fuzzy. They really don't know how the word got together. It is an activity of *image,* quite clearly. But to go through it, there is not an etymology that is respectable. It is said to be from the root of *imitare,* "to imitate." Now this is not true, and it is very, very bad etymology. You'll find it in the dictionary. And just put a stop to it! Didn't you ever open your dictionary and draw a line through the definition? It was totally wrong. Yeah, well you should. That's when you mark books up. This is—*imitation*—where's this coming from? Plato! It's from the *Republic!* What other imagination does Plato allow us at that point? He had an imagination beyond himself, that we know. So, "to imitate," which stretches a bit, even in terms of the sound of the word *imagination,* shifts of continents—of consonants—over centuries, and suggests a first meeting with Plato before the dictionary was itself compiled. But then, that gets in there anyway.

The experience of reading Greek, for example, and the people who have gone at that job. And trying to read Homer, you find out the view of language that there's one *behind us*—that it's *total,* that it's *there,* and so all the languages, especially the family of Indo-European languages, may enter the dictionary by *direct* equivalences—simply doesn't work. There is no such language behind us, number one. There are structures behind our languages, so that we may identify the families. But in the Greek example, which is the one I had the good fortune to experience, you move in the dictionary from the Greek word to an abstract, kind of like an explanation of it. And so you're losing—in Plato, when Achilles raises his spear, it says clearly that his breast let him do that. He doesn't stand there raising his spear. Well, you try to translate it that way, you'll get in a lot of trouble with those terrible translations.

So anyway, there we are, and between Duncan and me there ensued a kerfuffle. That's a wonderful word itself, a word that originally meant "an amorous embrace." Can you imagine, *kerfuffle* meant an amorous embrace? Now turned, Gaelic *ker,* "to turn about," into "a violent effort," a fuss, a fuffle (Scots). Both of us, I now think, having entered upon unmapped territory. But a map cannot be territory. This is one of my obsessions, as I was telling my workshop. *A map cannot be territory,* and in terms of what I am trying to talk about in the irreparables, I'm arguing *we are in territory.* Spicer and I discovered, something like forty-five years ago, in a book by Alfred Korzybski called *Science and Sanity*—it was a very fashionable book then, and it is still actually a very good book—we found the phrase "map is not territory." It delighted us so much it turns up in Spicer's poems, where I think he turns it around: "territory is not map." That turns around perfectly. That's the point! And it also tells you what a map is—it's *not* territory—twice over. Ok.

So, territory of the mind's and body's quarrel with the *invisible meta-physics* (a considered redundancy in this term, "invisible metaphysics") of traditional sureties, so to enter upon *imagy tokens*. That's my phrase for our condition, we enter upon imagy tokens. And that would be my best definition of imagination. Now, *reparable* . . .

AUDIENCE: "Imagy" or "imagery"?

RB: *Imagy*, I-M-A-G-Y. I like the camp of it, if you want to know the truth. Anyway, *reparable*, "a quality among things, whether thought or sensible." To the word *quality*, from Latin *qualitas*, meaning "how constituted," or "constituted as," now add the complexity of the word *constituted*, in trying to understand what would be reparable, "a quality among things, whether thought or sensible." A quality—the reparable is a quality. All right, now we've got the trouble of what is constituted, from Latin *constituere*, "to place." How odd, the further complexity of all those words holding the Indo-European stem, *sta*. Just go through your own head and check out all the words in which you've got a "st"—Check it out: institutes, *st*and, and so on. All those words that have to do with *place*. As in our word stand, "to place," from Latin and Greek *plateia*, the word place, "a street, an area." Or a statue, a *statua*, "to stand." *Reparation*, "a condition possible or given among things." The word *condition*, from Latin *condicio*, means "agreement." The word *agreement*, from Old French, "to or at," plus *gré*, "will"—it means "will, or pleasures"—so you're supposed to be getting this as a pleasure, from Latin *gratum*, etc. We swim among the constitution of words, their materiality, whether or not we consider them as sacred, behind us, as *forevers*, or as *transparencies of permanence*, or as *ownerships*. They are *chemical*, older and other than ourselves, always challenging our stillness.

Reparability, the "could be" of it, the potential, latent. *Reparableness*, the noun of it, its name. *Reparably*, the possible adverb of it, in the face of, in the mirror of the *ir*'s. Now the *ir*'s, you know that ghastly term *irregardless?* That is very American. And there you have it, you know, irregardless. Ah, yeah, I like the word. I'm going to put it in a poem one day, with great pleasure. But, in the meantime we've got the *ir*'s. Do I have in mind the *er*'s, interjections? Do I have in mind *Ur* of the Chaldees, home of Abraham and the name of the father of one of King David's valiants? Do I have in mind the German prefix *ur-*, designating a primeval, Latin *primum* plus *aevum*, "age, or originary condition," from Latin *orior, origo*, "I rise, become visible"? Yes, I do, and all prefixes *ir*.

The irreparable, irreparability, irreparableness, irreparably . . . I can only coin the word *irreparation*, so gaining an odd sense of things. Reparable and irreparable, and vice versa, the curious poetics of relations being reversed in the mirror of . . . Both reparable and irreparable, if we use these words, return to Latin *re-* plus *repare*, "to make ready," so "to make ready again," that is, to *prepare*. And what I'm after here is that, if we want to find the *reparable* (I don't think you can very well find it if you've got a car), that you can't very well find what's reparable if you haven't gotten what's irreparable. And in our culture, you'd better look for the irreparable before you try to make it reparable. It's just an old rule from Will Rogers, from my childhood. *Re-repare* . . . But the lovely thing is, that when one looks at what it means to *repair,* to be *reparable,* one is "making ready," one is *preparing.* And one of the grand things about the problem of the irreparables is to be prepared for them. To prepare, thus *repair*—we've got that wonderful word repair, from *reparare,* "to prepare again." In English we hear it as two verbs, to repair: the intransitive "I repair to, I betake myself." This verb comes from Old French and Latin, and so on, *repatriare,* "to return to one's country, to repatriate" . . . most difficult in the mirror of the irreparable, and a different verb than we have from *repair* as a transitive verb. Transitive, again, through the same source from Latin as we've seen, "to prepare." We are not, it should be noted, making amends for wrong in *reparation.*

I do not think I stretch unduly the words reparable and irreparable to say: *reparable* is to prepare in consciousness, in poesis, in feeling. The reparable is to prepare. . . . The *irreparable* is to be, if we are not careful, unprepared, say, in consciousness, in poesis, in feeling. I am trying to say to you here—have you ever noticed how difficult it is to use the word *we* these days? I've asked myself what I could do to earn the right to say *we.* I address 'you'—that means I'm fond of you, when I put those little marks on. "Scare marks" mean I'm fond of you, ok? I address 'you' sometimes with scare marks, those single quotation marks, to indicate a beloved, a stranger, a community I might belong to. I am trying to say to 'you' here, that there are depths in words by which we come toward our materiality, in language, out of a timeless, sacred language that is behind us, *al sacer,* is "sacrifice," putting the make, *facere,* on the human and the cosmic, which I am calling the *whatever.* The human and the cosmic *against the sacrifice.* One of our greatest authors to correct the tradition of sacrifice within the sacred is William Blake. . . .

Coming toward *our materiality in language,* without the intention of *any* nihilism—'we' (even with a few pimples of nihilism, due to a bad diet of course) are surely beyond nihilism, as Nietzsche, carefully read, was also. Very poor reading of Nietzsche to leave him in nihilism. . . . Coming toward our materiality in language, we enter upon *surfaces of the metaphysical depths.* Here, the Language poets are especially bold and courageous in the community of poesis. Or, to adapt Charles Bernstein's term, in the community of *a* poetics. Coming to the *surfaces. Sur-* is a prefix out of Latin *super,* meaning "over and above," and *face* from surface is an inheritance out of Latin *facare,* "to make a form, a shape," a surface . . . *to make over the surface* would be the proposal. There is a wonderful legal term here to name the dangerousness of surfaces: the *superficiary,* or -ficiary? [pronounced with hard Latin *c*]—you might, to keep the real Latin sound going—"one who holds rights only to the surface." Superficiary is the guy or gal who's only got rights to the surface. Say, a man or a woman whose house is on somebody else's land. Say, an uneasy renter. But we've been for a long time on somebody else's land, and haven't got off it! The laws are yet to be found.

Sur-face is remedial, an over-making, a making over. And that is what I would wish the surface to be understood as, at least in my own works. This astonishment, that *surface is depth* and depth surface in poesis. That Anglo-Saxon word *deop,* that speaks to "great extension downward, into things," *depth,* "among things," becoming a *dip,* Old English, into *liquid meaning* (trope) under and over the *surface* (trope). 'We' do not "fall into" history. . . . I've used that trope before, heedless of the theistic, even angelic, human nature the word *fall* presupposes. 'We' become historical, the surface tension of what was once called being, and is now *complexity,* "entwined with, wrapped around," a sense of time that is the life of space—with political, social, and belief consequences. *Astonishment,* inherited from Latin *ex-,* the as-, astonishment is *ex-,* "out of," *tonnare,* "to thunder." So, astonishment is to find out something that came out of thunder. And here (I'll skip over it, but I was going to read you one of the examples) is the hundred-letter name of God, in Joyce's *Finnegans Wake.* It is simply stunning, and it happens tens of times over in *Finnegans Wake:* "bababadalgharagh . . . " I'm not going to do it all, unless I sit here and concentrate, but when he finishes this name of God—

AUDIENCE: Read it!

RB: All right, all I wanted was an invitation!

bababadalgharaghtakamminarronnkonnbronntonnerronntuonnthun-ntrovarrhounawnskawntoohoohoordenenthurnuk!

God just spoke. ". . . of a once wallstrait oldparr is retaled early in bed and later on life down through all christian minstrelsy." They're wonderful. Anyway, *this is not a sad story*. That must be clear by now.

I think of what I'm doing here today as an essay-ode. An *essay* is always an attempt, a try, really a verb first, "to essay," a noun afterwards, very close to assay, though, in French *essayer de l'or,* which would be "o gold the ode sings" in a very careless translation of *essayer de l'or.* The word *ode* means song: as in *ge*-ode, like the earth, but lit crystals on the inside, a geode. And an *electrode,* "path-way." You will all know how an ode works, usually a celebration by way of *strophe*—"a turn, a twist"—*antistrophe,* another turn, as answer. An *epode,* "to sing after." In Pindar's Seventh Olympic Hymn, which I've translated and kept in *The Holy Forest* (it celebrates the winning of a boxing match in 464 BC by Diagoras—wonderful poem!—Pindar is a wonderful poet, as Duncan has showed us already), the final epode closes in that ode with the love of the gods. I quote from my own translation:

> ...the city   holds the beauty   of the flower-bringer
> Thalia   .   but in a moment,   the winds hit   and turn
>
>   bound for

The lovely thing about that ode, and Pindar's odes in general, is that they go at the contrariety. Celebrate your punch, and that you knocked the bastard out. But you better watch out because from the Greek point of view, of course, to *win*—and it still goes on in our interest of sports—it's beyond human limit, those wins. These give you at least some relation to what the Greeks called heroes. The heroes gave you some notion of what it meant not to be stuck in your limit, and so you could be, in some sense, close to the gods. As a consequence, you celebrated the sports near the temples, at Delphi. But Pindar, in the ode, keeps trying to tell not only the genealogy of Diagoras—the grandeur of his family, the grandeur of his win—but warns him, the winds may change. It's a marvelous poem when read, and you know the academic view until very recently was that a Pindaric ode didn't believe anything it said, it just simply decorated everything with mythology. Well, you know where that came from— the New Criticism.

All right, so where are we? So, a celebration of *change, chance,* my ode-song-essay. Chance in which 'we' dance to find 'our' composition. I think it necessary to look at the other side of the century, 'our' century, if I may adapt the title of Douglas Messerli's anthology of the new poetry, as well as to look at the other side of our cultural unconscious, usually called *cultural forgetting.* Here the poet, if she or he is lucky, comes into conversation with philosophy and theory—and with theorists, lacking sufficient philosophy or poetry. Very interesting to read Derrida with no French, when you can't get a single joke. Well, you've lost the point!

Ok? Poetry and philosophy both become *matter* only if they are experienced. Thus, you work out your own definition of experience. I grab from Merleau-Ponty the notion that I've already mentioned, that we need not, should not confuse philosophy and poetry, but that since the collapse of totalitarian ambitions in thought, philosophy and poetry *share* something. So they converse much more easily, much more informally. They share an operative sense of language. The word *totalitarian,* which we have as a political term, with all the disaster of our century, over and over again, the original use of it was that ambition of philosophy to give a total system. So, the totalitarian was that thought that gave you *wholeness* and *totality.* And when 'we' enter upon this, and in this *conversation,* 'we' have instead not a systematic language headed for wholenesses and totalities (there are still philosophers who have such ambition) but, instead, to *sharing.* "Things shared" is an operative sense of language . . . "to work," to compose an *opera,* "a work," pains and work.

The conversation is not the work of any one poet, but of a community. I was so pleased with David Bromige, who sent me a letter that I didn't have time to reply to before I came. But what he'd been interested in, at the Vancouver conference, was that it was not organized as a hierarchy. And when I found him here, I immediately said, "Oh good, I'm so glad to hear that—because hierarchies have been the bane of my life!" And they have. They've been the bane of my life in family terms, the bane of my life in poetry, the bane of my life in thought, the bane of my life in the academic world, too. OK, the conversation is not the work of any one poet, but of a community, a *lack. The community is a lack.* And he or she in such conversation must be armored against petty bourgeois charges of elitism . . . (here comes another tantrum!). It is rather a matter of how one arranges her or his *energies.* Nor is this a matter of mere aesthetics. The conversation proposes that the autonomy of art, a brief phantasm of our understanding of it, has died in its own incestuous embrace. The conversation enters upon *open form,* which I ponder.

So, Lyotard's reflection—and this is from the philosophy of *The Postmodern Condition,* a very useful final chapter. There's also other useful stuff in there on this business of the sublime that some of you have talked with me about, where he puts modernism as being inside the Kantian sublime. And I'm trying to say *we're inside the sublime,* which really changes our relation to whatever we call the sublime: "that which overwhelms, is uncanny, is larger than ourselves." And of course an obsession with me is that I think we all work, as writers, with wanting, desiring, or having received a *cosmology,* that big fancy work, that we now have to change to *cosmogony.* So that we're absolutely playing with the way in which *we make it,* more Hesiodic than ultimately Papal—

BOBBIE LOUISE HAWKINS: Could you make that distinction clear, between cosmology and cosmogony?

RB: Well, *cosmology* would be the word *cosmos.* Snazzy word, but we have so much trouble with the word *world,* because every government wants to claim it. And right now we're in the American world—all around the world—and everybody knows that isn't true. So, the word *world* got very slippery, very much a matter of slippage. So *cosmos* seemed a very good one, and the word cosmos is fascinating, because it's a very, very old Greek word, and way back in it, it also meant *rhythm*. It also meant something *alive*. You see, my contribution to the panel yesterday was that I wanted to put in my own favorite phrase, which is *form is alive*. And that changes your relation . . . as soon as you know form is alive, then your relation to content has changed. You also know that Williams was perfectly right. If you have to wander around looking for content you're in trouble. Because *everything* is! But the *form* is alive. So—and *cosmogony* is "to take it down into," which it's part of, "the earth," and it becomes a cosmos as it is being made by *fuses,* by physical forces. And this is what the poet Hesiod describes in his cosmos, in the great *Theogony*. It's a *cosmo-gony*. And I do that because I like very much having the sense that we're very *aware* that we have something to do with what we have accepted that isn't *true* of the world we're in. Yet my prejudice is that nobody writes easily without a cosmology. That would usually mean *God*. And we have all kinds of very elegant corrections of the Western tradition now, including the Buddhism which is so present here at Naropa. Yeats was right, you know. The wonderful thing about Buddha was that he refused to become God. That's what Yeats said. That was Yeats's fascination, in that mess that a thinker like Yeats got himself into. A terrific mess. I mean, I admire that man.

O K, the Lyotard: "We have paid . . ." And this, I really—I want to get to the *imagination of person* inside this problem of imagination, and so on. And I'll do some cutting and just hope to hell that *whatever* is . . . not just out of, well, control. But it's wild, I'll tell you that!

Lyotard, from the philosophy of *The Postmodern Condition*: "We have paid a high enough price for the nostalgia of the whole and the one . . ." And if you think that isn't important, watch what's going on with this vicious resurgence of religions, the nostalgias of wholeness and one—"for the reconciliation . . ." We've paid a high price for the reconciliation

> of the concept and the sensible, of the transparent and the communicable experience. Under the general demand for slackening and for appeasement, we can hear the mutterings of the desire for a return of terror, for the realization of the fantasy to seize reality. The answer is: Let us wage a war on totality; let us be witnesses. . . .

Now, the book, there are lots of things haywire with this particular book of Lyotard's, from my point of view. But, I mean you—my respect for a man who sees that clearly, the problem of retrenchment, the return of something that is dangerous and frightening, and that has so endangered

. . . the greatest democracy in the world, the American democracy, is, I think, something that our poetry must attend as one learns how. We are in danger of winding up in Francis Fukuyama's "end of history." Where do you suppose he picked that up? He's taking it out of Hegel, and it's the whole philosophical principle that there may be an end of history and all this stuff. And in one instance you get the end of history in spirit, and in the other instance, you turn it around backwards and you get the end of history in matter. And both ways, we've tried them both, and look what we got. We got *terror*. And *Time* magazine said that—"Oh my! Hegel has recently been discovered." They didn't think he was well-known. This went on and on and on and on. . . . So, where do you suppose that Fukuyama picked that up? Now, I have read Fukuyama's book. I mean I've tried. I have to be honest with my scholarship, so I did. I thought, well, maybe there's more to this guy. There isn't. Without Hegel's vast intellectual effort, there is *not*. Taking us into a hypocrisy, untouched by social justice . . .

I have a section here on the issue of Marx. I've proposed to gather . . . now, this is my celebration of the fall of the wall, the Berlin Wall. My celebration was to go back, and with a group, because I believe absolutely in the conversation and dialogue of scholarship, of reading and so on . . . that we will be joining, a small group of us, rereading Marx. Because my interest in this is not only "can poetry do something with this?" that certainly Marxism was not able to do. Marxism as a practice that moved *from* Marx. I've also been very cranky over many years about *Marx had no linguistics*. This is 19th century, you've got to remember this. Marx is 19th century mind. He had no linguistics, he thought of language as a matter of ideas. And what are ideas for? They are to push reality around. One problem! Another problem was, no psychology. Now, look—what happened in modern Russia? In the midst of great difficulty with those awful things on genetics by Lysenko and all that, that ideological verbiage, you still had psychologists of great distinction popping out, great linguists popping out. Olson was right. When extremes get so extreme, there are minds that pop out like violets. They come like violets, out of the cultural asshole (if I may use a Boschian image; Hieronymous Bosch would approve of that image) in order to make up for it.

Now, what do we have left that we would be interested in Marx, apart from the fact that he is a splendid thinker, and a good writer? *A vision of social justice*. I will just give this quotation on Marx, again from Giorgio Agamben, this is from the book *Infancy and History:* "Marx abolishes the metaphysical distinction between animal and *ratio*" (between animal and reason). See now, I said *social justice,* and watch the moves now, because this—"Marx abolishes . . ." Why do you go back and read that? Because it did, in good thinking, abolish the metaphysical distinction between animal and ratio, between nature and culture, between matter and form, in order to state that within praxis [the practice of our lives] animality is humanity, nature is culture, matter is form. If this is true, the relationship between structure and superstructure can neither be one of causal determination . . .

—built in! If Agamben (and Agamben is a great thinker) . . . the "causal determination" that the ideologies presume is already *built in* to the thought? It's worth looking into. It may even have poetry in it, if you look for it.

. . . can neither be one of causal determination nor one of dialectical mediation, but one of direct correspondence.

The move from *dialectic* to *correspondence* is one that every poet has to think about in his own or her own terms. Because the word dialectic belongs to the relationship of *negatives,* that is of propositions and their negation and resolution. It's a logical structure, a long history from Socrates. It does not, as Blake told us long ago, exist in human experience. *Negatives do not exist.* Allen [Ginsberg] will know the two great passages on that. One in *Milton* and one in *Jerusalem.*

Oκ, these are bare notes of the territory in which possible composition works *against linear time,* against the apocalypse at the end of which we, phantasms that we are, come into our divine nature. In Agamben's words, "the inability of man, who is lost in time, to take possession of his own historical nature." And, I add, *irreparably* at a loss in the now, where her/his responsibility lies, a territory without a map. Here Benjamin and Zukofsky become companions, more than in any poem, I understand. Agamben:

One of the most urgent tasks for contemporary thought is without doubt to redefine the concept of the transcendental in terms of its relation to language. . . . Idem. The original cohesion of poetry and politics in our culture was sanctioned from the very start by the fact that Aristotle's treatment of music is contained in the *Politics* [the book the *Politics]* and that Plato's themes of poetry and art are to be found in the *Republic* [a book about politics]; it is therefore a matter beyond dispute [that, the original cohesion of poetry and politics]. The question is not so much whether poetry has any bearing on politics, but whether politics remains equal to its original cohesion with poetry.

May I repeat that last line? Because I'm moving to try to find a way to do some speaking, politically, in poetry. And I don't want to fuck my poems. So, essentially . . .

> The question is not so much whether poetry has any bearing on politics, but whether politics remains equal to its original cohesion with poetry.

Now, I think that's very important. I had told one or two of you—and I'll throw it in now as a kind of explanation, this, the Mallarmé thing—and I'm sorry that there were few who were talking about it. And I was saying that this sense of the *imagination of person* was very much implicated in this territory. And this territory can be so wild that there can be a loss of self. There are all kinds—and in fact you even begin, even the sense of what a person *is* begins to shift. But, first of all, I wanted to feed this in. I said, if we wanted to track the disturbance, of the relation, say, to the cosmos, if you wanted to track the disturbance of what the person is in relation to his or her language, you could move back to Baudelaire. And there are magnificent examples of this in the literature. There are other places we can go to, but just to sketch you an outline, the one to whom almost all of this postmodern theory is indebted is Mallarmé.

Now, very similar experiences have occurred in American poetry. Jack Spicer is one of the very great examples of this experience of the 'I' shifting in relation to whatever it is the language may define. So you begin to lose definitions. The self begins to be disturbed. Now, I just wanted to throw in this great passage with the . . . it's a letter to Henri Cazalis, if you want to look it up in a volume of letters by Mallarmé, but it is famous and important for the business that Mallarmé went through in incredible crisis—mental, emotional, and so on. It was a quarrel with God. And he left a record of it. We see it in the poetry. We see the disturbed syntax. We see the splaying of imagery. We see all kinds of things going on that amount to the materiality of Mallarmé's work, as opposed to the spirituality which he described in Hegelian terms at times, but also in occultist terms and so on. The fascination for the writer's problem is actually in that very materiality of disturbed syntax, the way in which images move and suggest and all that. Well, here is a brief description of what he went through: "—you can see," he writes to Henri Cazalis,

> —you can see I am unable to distract myself. But this was even more the case a few months ago, firstly in my terrible struggle with that old and evil plumage, which is now, happily, vanquished [1867]: God. But as that struggle had taken place on his bony wing which, in death throes more vigorous than I would have suspected him capable of, had carried me into the Shadows, I fell victorious, desperately and infinitely,—

I mean, the movement of this is exact. This is several years of a depression, as we would call it, in Mallarmé's life, and it questioned every move of the writing.

> —until at last [he writes] I saw myself again in my Venetian mirror, such as
> I was when I forgot myself several months before.

Now, he had a Venetian mirror, which simply means that he has a beautiful Venetian frame, maybe the mirrored glass itself came from Venice, but he really had one. So, that one extraordinary disturbance of the self. The *imagination of person,* the first spot that I find it most disturbed is in Poe. It's the figure, the wonderful story about the figure that's all made of bottles, his arms are bottles and he keeps banging the poor poet, or Poe or whoever he is. It's an absolutely marvelous story. But, he's got a sense of something out there that no longer has strictly a human shape.

The imagination of person, to me that's a Robert Creeley theme. An important one, and one that has haunted me out of Robert Creeley. I think I will close with Avital Ronell, her book *Finitude's Score.* And I'll leave it with this:

> As the millennium comes to an end, and the twentieth century scarifies our fragile memory, very little will stand out in terms of epochal splendor. If anything, humanity will have exhausted the heroic mythemes on which so much has been staked. Humanity (a term which acquired the prestige of its contemporary usage at the Nuremberg trials) will certainly have to rethink the projects and projections that have, despite everything, traced out a history of indecency—a history which compromises the very possibility of a thinking of futurity. In its fading moments, even as it signals change, the last century [ours] will have been dominated in the end by a diction of deficit: deficiency, whether immuno or projected outwardly and marked by complementary economies, no longer carries the bounce of lack or the sure fire of nihilism but says, more simply, that we have been depleted. This depletion has to do with a relation to the outside—a *national* deficit, for example—but it also controls a low-energy intensity that involves everyone. It seems as though all accounts of savings and saviors are understood to be depleted. Exhausted with the failure of models, identities, leaders, promise, so-called breakthroughs, vampirized by figures of exigence or ecstasy, the last century sees itself as standing out, if only in the sense that there is an outstanding debt to be paid—but to whom? to what?

In case you're thinking, Well, Avital, fuck her, she just lives inside her own head, this work reveals a growing concern over the finite figures that comprise our shared experience. As long as there is something like experience, it is not entirely mine. Nonetheless, if there is a growing sense that the writer is inhabiting an inside that is out of it, this condition cannot simply be debited to the account of the solitary worker but is rather a symptom pointing to *the vanishing of the experienceability of the world*—assuming that, after all is said and done, one can still say 'world.'

Thank you.

Edited by Steve Dickison, with thanks to Robin Blaser.
(Initial transcription from audiotape recording by Michael Smoler.)

The Poetics of Disobedience

ALICE NOTLEY
June 15, 1998

★ ★ ★

For a long time I've seen my job as bound up with the necessity of non-compliance with pressures, dictates, atmospheres of, variously, poetic factions, society at large, my own past practices as well. For a long time—well in fact since the beginning, since I learned how to be a poet inside the more rebellious more outlawish wing of poetry; though learning itself meant a kind of obedience, so like most words the Dis word, the Dis form, cannot be worshipped either—and that would be an obedience anyway. I've spoken in other places of the problems, too, of subjects that hadn't been broached much in poetry and of how it seemed one had to disobey the past and the practices of literary males in order to talk about what was going on most literarily around one, the pregnant body, and babies for example. There were no babies in poetry then. How could that have been? What are we leaving out now? Usually what's exactly in front of the eyes ears nose and mouth, in front of the mind, but it seems as if one must disobey everyone else in order to see at all. This is a persistent feeling in a poet, but staying alert to all the ways one is coerced into denying experience, sense, and reason is a huge task. I recently completed a very long poem called *Disobedience* but I didn't realize that disobeying was what I was doing, what perhaps I'd always been doing until the beginning of the end of it, though the tone throughout was one of rejection of everything I was supposed to be or to affirm, *all* the poetries all the groups the clothes the gangs the governments the feelings and reasons.

I seem to start with my poem *The Descent Of Alette* these days, whatever it is that I am now seems to start there. It was for me an immense act of rebellion against dominant social forces, against the fragmented forms of modern poetry, against the way a poem was supposed to look according to both past and contemporary practice. It begins in pieces and ends whole, narrated by an I who doesn't know her name and whose name when she finds it means appendage of a male name; her important name is I. I stand with this, and with the urgency that saying I creates, a facing up to sheer presence, death, and responsibility, the potential for blowing away all the gauze. In two subsequent narrative poem/proses, *Close to me . . . & Closer (The Language of Heaven)* and *Désamère* I felt myself pushing against ideas of reality as solely what's visible and in what shapes and colors it's said to be visible, against the idea that religion is solely an organized affair, against the pervasive idea that one must not protest what everyone else has named the Actual—how can you fight Reality?—against the psychology of belonging, of aiding and abetting. *Désamère* especially is about not wanting to belong and the process of ceasing to belong to the extent that's possible. All three of those works are characterized by emphatic though variable metrical patterns, in the prose as well as the poetry parts; two are very quirky as to physical presentation; all three have narratives that tend to the fabular.

In my book, *Mysteries of Small Houses,* I was firstly trying to realize the first person singular as fully and nakedly as possible, saying "I" in such a way as to make myself really nervous, really blowing away the gauze and making myself too scared of life and death to care what anyone thought of me or what I was going to say. Saying I in that way I tried to trace that I's path through my past. In a more subsidiary way I decided to go against my own sense that certain styles and forms I'd participated in formerly might be used up, that autobiography was, that the personal-sounding I (as opposed to the fictional I) might be, against the rumor that there's no self, though I've never understood that word very well and how people use it now in any of the camps that use it pro or con—I guess I partly wrote *Mysteries* in order to understand it better. I came to the conclusion, in the final poem of the book, that self means "I" and also means "poverty," it's what one strips down to, who you are when you've stripped down.

It's possible that my biggest act of disobedience has consistently, since I was an adolescent, been against the idea that all truth comes from books, really other people's books. I hate the fact that whatever I say or write, someone reading or listening will try to find something out of their reading I "sound like." "You sound just like . . . ," "you remind me of . . ." "have you read . . . ?" I read all the time and I often believe what I read while I'm reading it, especially if it's some trashy story; intense involvement in theories as well as stories seems difficult without temporary belief, but then it burns out. I've been trying to train myself for thirty or forty years not to believe anything anyone tells me. Not believing, then, became the crux of *Disobedience,* which is my most recent completed book. Not believing and telling the truth as it comes up. One of the main elements in the poem is an ongoing fantasy in which the I, who is pretty much I, keeps company and converses with a man very much like the actor Robert Mitchum and that of course is not strictly believable. On the other hand it's fun, and it stands for something, a sort of truth, about how we do have stories going on in our consciousness and unconsciousness all the time and about how we're always talking to some "you" mentally. I wouldn't expect you to take this book as the truth, I would expect you to go with it, given that you like to read. I find the act of reading puzzling at the moment, since in a book I've been working on since *Disobedience* I ask the reader to read despite the fact that I'm not really entertaining the reader or being clear in any of the traditional ways I can think of. I think books may imply a readership that simply likes to read, which may sound obvious but it's something I myself have only just thought of. But back to *Disobedience*. It asks the reader to read a lot of pages, about 230 A4 pages in verse, but it's fairly easy to read and it makes a lot of jokes. It's very feminist but men seem to enjoy it a lot, it possibly contains a rather virile approach to things riding roughshod and shooting at every little duck that seems to pop up. As I implied earlier, *Disobedience* didn't exactly set out to be disobedient; it set out actually to try to do the kinds of things I'd previously done in different poems all in the same poem, that is tell a story, interact with the so-called visible or phenomenal, the despised daily, and explore the unconscious. But it got more and more pissed off as it confronted the political from an international vantage, dealt with being a woman in France, with turning fifty and being a poet and thus seemingly despised or at least ignored. The title popped up in a dream, a real dream I had toward the end of writing the work, in connection with a comic poet I know: it was the title of his book in the dream and I realized later that there was probably nothing more disobedient than being a comic poet, since no one's ever sure if that's good enough, particularly the academy unless you've been dead since the 14th century or unless you've also written a lot of tragedies. I myself wouldn't want the limitation of being only one kind of poet, but I realize this comic business is something to think about. But more and more as I wrote *Disobedience* I discovered I couldn't go along with the government or governments, with radicals and certainly not with conservatives or centrists, with radical poetics and certainly not with other poetics, with other women's feminisms, with any fucking thing at all; belonging to any of it was not only an infringement on my liberty but a veil over clear thinking. It's necessary to maintain a state of disobedience against . . . everything. One must remain somehow, though how, open to any subject or form in principle, open to the possibility of liking, open to the possibility of using. I try to maintain no continuous restrictions in my poetics except with regard to particular works, since writing at all means making some sort of choices. But NO DOCTRINES. Rather I tend to maintain a sense that a particular form or set of rules at a certain point might serve me for a while. Like many writers I feel ambivalent about words, I know they don't work, I know they aren't it. I don't in the least feel that everything is language. I have a sense that there has been language from the beginning, that it isn't fundamentally an invention. These are contradictory positions but positions are just words. I don't believe that the best poems are just words, I think they're the same as reality; I tend to think reality is poetry, and that that isn't words. But words are one way to get at reality/poetry, what we're in all the time. I think words are among us and everything else, mingling, fusing with, backing off from us and everything else.

Since *Disobedience,* I've been working on this other thing which isn't as friendly as *Dis* is, though it isn't meant to be unfriendly. It's just hard to read, in that you have to decide to sit down and read it word by word giving each word the rhythm and weight it requires. That sounds like poetry but this one tends to be in long blowy sentences all down the page. I am going at several ideas at once: one is that the world is intensely telepathic, infused with the past and continual thought of all the living and all the dead. I started out with that idea and with the idea of a Byzantine church as a sort of head, mine, full of icons and mosaics on ever-expanding and shifting walls. But the church or head got bigger and bigger and more and more full of images and words until it expanded into a city. So at the moment, on page one hundred and something, I'm dealing with the idea that there are two cities or worlds at the same time, an ideal crystalline one and the supposedly real one. Generally I'm neither all the way in one nor the other, though sometimes it seems as if I'm nowhere near the crystal one and its reasonable opulence so I start beating hard at all the doors I can find in my mind. Then sometimes it seems as if the supposedly real world just isn't there or here at all though I know if I stop typing and go outside it will get me. This work is also very disobedient, in a way it picks up where *Disobedience* left off; but it doesn't lecture as much or shake its fist so, is less interested in the so-called real than in denying its existence in favor of the real real. You can't fly unless you're not on the ground and this one really flies sometimes.

I think I conceive of myself as disobeying my readership a lot. I began the new work in fact denying their existence; it seemed to me I needed most at this point to work on my own existence so I couldn't afford to cater to them if they got in the way of my finding out things. But this is a work of mine, it should be published sometime. I'm now in a predicament I can't get out of, a form I can't manage for the reader, which just keeps leading me on and leading me on. It's predicated on leaving in as much mind fuzz as possible, that is being open to all that is out there in all telepathy—not a very organizable entity, *the* entity. Too wordy too long; and I've allowed in a lot of notions from my dreams again, have allowed odd images to take on the weight of truth; and I'm stubbornly involved again in what you might call mystical conceptions, but aren't those a no-no? except in icky New Age territory, yuck. The reader likes you to tell

　　　　　　　　　　　　　　　　　　　CIVIL DISOBEDIENCES

her/him what she/he already knows in a familiar form whether in main-streamese or avant-gardese, but then there is the individual reader who is often not like that at all, who prefers poems to talking about them and has strange individual experiences with them. That's a very scary idea. It's possible that the reader, or maybe the ideal reader, is a very disobedient person a head/church/city entity her/himself full of soaring icons and the words of all the living and all the dead, who sees and listens to it all and never lets on that there's all this beautiful almost undifferentiation inside, everything equal and almost undemarcated in the light of fundamental justice. And poker-faced puts up with the outer forms. As I do a lot of the time but not so much when I'm writing.

Written for a Conference on Contemporary American and English Poetics,
held at King's College London, Centre for American Studies,
on February 28, 1998. Presented at Naropa University June 15, 1998.

On Translation

ANSELM HOLLO AND KAI NIEMINEN
July 2, 1998

⋆ ⋆ ⋆

ANSELM HOLLO: Since not all of you have taken Kai's translation workshop this week nor taken my translation workshop during the year, I guess I have to somewhat boringly start out by your basic definitions, or maybe they're more opinions than definitions, of translation that currently exist. It's obviously an area that is of great interest to linguistic theory, to modern linguistics, since it deals with language and languages, plural. So, linguistic theory—I'm reading here a summary provided by dear friend and fellow translator Joe Richey some years ago in his magazine the *Underground Rain Forest* which was a translation issue, and I found it very useful because it's sort of compact.

> "Linguistic theory bears decisively on the question of whether or not translation, particularly between different languages" [and that's an interesting point because there is translation within the same language as well], "whether translation is in fact possible. In the philosophy of language two radically opposed views can be, and have been, asserted. One declares that the underlying structure of language is universal and common to all men, women, and children. Dissimilarities between human tongues are essentially of the surface. Translation is realizable precisely because those deep seated universals, genetic, historical, social, from which all grammars derive, can be located and recognized as operative in every human idiom, however singular or bizarre its superficial forms. No language has been found to lack a first and second person singular pronoun. The distinction between I, thou, and he exists in every human idiom. Every language has a class of proper names. A type of clause in which a subject is talked about or modified in some manner is also observable in every linguistic system. So, in this view to translate is to descend beneath the exterior disparities of two languages in order to bring into vital play their analogies and the final depths and common principles of being." [It gets a little lofty here.] "Here, this universalist position touches closely on the mystical intuition or assumption of a lost primal or paradigmatic speech."

So in a way the Tower of Babel comes into play here again. But it's actually still a respectable view, I think the most prominent exponent over the last decades of it, although he has modified his views on it going along, is Noam Chomsky, otherwise an important political American thinker. He talks about deep structures, he calls these universals "deep structures" in language. And one may assume that they're there. On the other hand I don't know how much good it does. Because the reply to this, the counter theory, the contrary view holds that universal deep structures are either fathomless to logical and psychological investigation, or of an order so abstract, so generalized as to be well nigh trivial. Arthur Sze just mentioned Lao Tzu's view or that view that some of the younger Chinese poets seem to be returning to, in other words, which is also identical with the Wittgensteinian (Ludwig Wittgenstein, great Austrian philosopher of language) view that language is in a sense finite, that there are things that no language should even try to deal with because it cannot deal with them. Maybe those universal deep structures could be identified with, say, religion and religious belief, which is also fathomless to logical and psychological investigation. Those tools don't work in that area. So, to go on with the contrary view—

> "that all human beings use language in some form, that all languages of which we have apprehension are able to name perceived objects or to signify action, these are undoubtful truths. But, being of the class, example 'all members of this species require oxygen to sustain life,' they do not illuminate, except in the most abstract formal sense, the actual workings of human speech. These workings are so diverse, they manifest so bewilderingly complicated a history of centrifugal development, they pose such stubborn questions as to economic and social function, that universalist models are at best irrelevant, and at worst misleading. This extreme monodist position leads logically to the belief that real translation is impossible. What passes for translation is a convention of approximate analogies, a rough cast similitude just tolerable when the two relevant languages or cultures are cognate, but altogether spurious when remote tongues and far removed sensibilities are in question."

So, Ok. These are two extremes, in other words, and obviously as in most such considerations the possible truth lies somewhere in the middle. These are two viewpoints, if you put them on an arc, you can probably put a hundred seventy-eight other viewpoints on that arc in between those two. So, it's true that "real" translation, if we take real translation to mean—as in, say, basic arithmetic, we translate one plus one into the word "two"—that's real translation. You don't argue with that, given the parameters of arithmetic, that's unarguably a real translation. Any addition can be expressed either as many little numerals or just one little cluster of numerals. But obviously there are ways of getting close to the original, there are ways of getting something in the target language, i.e. your own language, the one that you're translating into, something that stands up in the universe as a work in its own right, whether it's a poem or a novel or a short story or a play. Think of the Bible, for instance, a book that many people regard as "the book," and there are many translations. In terms of beauty, the most delightful English translation is still the King James version. It's inaccurate, it makes mistakes. The scholarly, more recent—there's a wonderful edition that has about four translations of the books of the Bible in parallel columns. So if you want to get closer to what those old desert dwellers who thought of one god as being more convenient than many interesting, delightful, playful gods, to what they thought and wrote and experienced, then maybe you should read that edition, you should read those four columns, read across the page. And then there is something known as a version, which is essentially what Ezra Pound, who gave us classical Chinese poetry, gave the anglophone (I think anglophone is an English word, someone just said they didn't know whether it was an English word, I think it's an English word, it's in every goddamn MLA publication, they talk about anglophone this and anglophone that—I guess francophone was there first) . . . [Pound gave the] first great very influential anglophone versions of classical Chinese poetry. They are not—they've been picked apart by scholars endlessly—they are not accurate, they're slanted, their tone is not very similar to the original, but they're terrific poems. *Cathay,* that collection. You just need to look at that next to Arthur Waley, who was a contemporary who was a scholar, next to his translations, they're pretty damn good too, but they don't take off. Pound created poems that are part of the anglophone canon forever and they're Chinese poems, they're Chinese poems that Pound translated. And the same could be said obviously for a number of—you could say Shakespeare translated Italian popular tales and so forth into English in his plays, [such as] *Romeo and Juliet.* Versions. And contemporary poets—Robert Lowell called his versions imitations, he was even being more modest about it in a way.

So there's all that you can do and the product in the case of poetry which is I guess what we're going to try to limit ourselves to here, in the case of poetry it is a question of writing a poem in your target language, in a sense *over* the original, so that it almost totally obscures and in a sense obliterates the original. But we have this other thing now, and it's for those people—it's not only for those people who can't read, say, Dante, in the original, they might still find it interesting for its own merits and possibly for those inaccuracies and divergences from Dante's literal meaning.

So, I'll just read three more short statements on translation and then

I'll pass the mic to Kai here. The first one is from Octavio Paz, who just passed away recently, great, great Mexican poet and critic and essayist and thinker.

> Every text is unique and at the same time it is the translation of another text. No text is entirely original because language itself in its essence is already a translation, firstly of the nonverbal world, and secondly, since every sign and every phrase is the translation of another sign and another phrase. However this argument can be turned around without losing any of its validity. All texts are original because every translation is distinctive. Every translation up to a certain point is an invention, and as such it constitutes a unique text.

And here, he obviously talks about creative translation. Because translation of a Japanese instruction manual for a hair dryer does not really require any powers of invention, although sometimes when you read those instructions you think that the person doing it really thought it might require some invention. Jacques Derrida, still with us, says

> Difference is never pure. No more so is translation. And for the notion of translation we would have to substitute the notion of transformation: regulated transformation of one language by another, of one text by another. We will never have and, in fact, have never had to do with some transport of pure signifieds from one language to another or within one and the same language, that the signifying instrument would leave virgin and untouched.

That's a very nice quote, actually, I'd never realized the sort of phallic element in it. I guess reading Derrida makes one very conscious of that. And the last one is from the de Campos brothers, two presently I think it's ok to call them ancient because they are, I think they're both in their nineties. Geraldo and Augusto de Campos of Brazil have used Derrida to develop something like a postmodern and non-Eurocentric approach to translation. They refuse any sort of preordained original, but instead view translation as a form of transgression. And come up with their own terms, one of which is translation as a form of cannibalism. Yet this term is not to be understood as another form of merely possessing the original, but as a liberating form, one which eats, digests, and frees oneself from the original. Cannibalism is to be understood not in the Western sense, i.e. that of capturing, dismembering, mutilating, and devouring, but in a sense which shows respect, i.e. as a symbolic act of taking back out of love, of absorbing the virtues of a body through a transfusion of blood.

Translation is seen as an empowering act, a nourishing act, an act of affirmative play, which sees translation as a life force that ensures a literary text's survival. And it is true that we have a great number of literary texts that would not have survived if they had not been translated. If we take the gospels as a literary text, which I think one may well take them, a lot of the original Aramaic has not survived, we have the Hebrew translation, then we have the Greek translation, and then we have the translations into all the other languages. So, I thought that might sort of clear the ground. We're talking literary translation, and the most, in a way, dangerous and difficult, but also most fun and least lucrative form of literary translation, the translation of poetry.

KAI NIEMINEN: Thank you, Anselm. You and Octavio Paz said many things that I was prepared to say. Actually I can rephrase them. Now that you took care of the theoretical part I can take an untheoretical aspect to the picture. I will start with some kind of theses or some kind of premises with which I will try to describe my own approach to translating in general and translating poetry in particular. One of the things that is important to me is that whether I write my own poetry or I translate others' poetry, is that there is always something that I or let's say the writer wants to say. There is always "asia" as we say in Finnish, there is matter. So, the translators' and the poets' job is to put this matter into words as well as possible so that others would get the meaning, catch that matter, that it would go home. This is one of the theses. The other one is my approach, and I'm not saying that this would be the one and only correct approach, and I'm not saying that it's my only approach. But one approach that is very much the basis of my work is that I believe that there is a proto-poetry within each thinking human being (and maybe in animals, I'm sure there is in animals too), there is a language of poetry with which we are communicating with ourselves. It's the language that we maybe use when we dream, the language that when we awaken from a dream makes it very difficult for us to explain to ourselves, in words, the dream. But certainly while we are dreaming it seems very logical, we are communicating with ourselves in a perfect way while dreaming, and after we are awake we must recognize the dream. So then, the original language of poetry in this sense would be the language of cognition, the thing that comes before the words, before the universal words, before the public words. So there is a private language that is needed to be translated even to ourselves in order to speak about other people. And if we take this as the starting point of poetry, this proto-poetry, I have this belief that all the poets in the world, in this sense, speak the same language. And translation is only putting them, connecting these languages to universal language, which is the native language. Universal language is divided into natural languages, into the native languages, into the different language families and so on. But at least for me it's a tremendous delight to read poetry in my own language and find out from below or behind those words written in Finnish, to find out the personal language of the poet and find out how he translated it into the Finnish that I read. Reading it I retranslate it into my personal language. And I not only feel, I share the poem with the author. And it's also not only sharing, it's dialogue, I'm in constant dialogue with the poem, with the poet, with the author. Or maybe I'm merged into the poem. All this is a continuous process where I become the poem, the poem becomes me, I become the author, the author becomes me. It's a delightful process. And there is actually nothing, [there are] no problems concerning the languages that I am reading, I mean if I can read Japanese, English, German, Swedish, and Finnish. The words on the paper are only a tool, they are only a medium, they are only something that is meant to help me get to the original language, to the original poem.

Estonian poet and essayist Jaan Kaplinski has put this in slightly different words. But I feel that his meaning is very near to my feeling. He is talking about the unnecessary dividing of literature into prose and poetry. He says that the division goes between everyday language and the language of poetry. So it has nothing to do with how you write, how you put the things on the paper, if it's right-justified or not. Because what seems to be printed as prose might in reality be poetry, very fine poetry. And what seems to be poetry, by the way of printing, might just be everyday language, blabbering, that is not having any matter, that is not having anything to say to us. And Kaplinski says also that in this sense poetry is the meta-language of everyday language. And he says since poetry is the meta-language it is not possible to define poetry with everyday language. Poetry as the meta-language can only define itself in its own language. If I talked about poetry as a proto-language and Kaplinski is talking about it as the meta-language, it seems contradictory, but I don't disagree with Jaan Kaplinski at all. As a poet, writing my own poetry in Finnish, I am, as I said, translating my own experiences, my sensations, my mind contents to the universal language in order, in this explicit order, to make the others understand it. If I wouldn't care to make the others understand it, then I wouldn't—

AH: Which others?

KN: The ones that—This is a very important question. This means also that I deem it necessary that I share my mind contents with the people whom I have around me whom I appreciate and whom I want to appreciate me. So it's in a way a narcissistic process of course, writing poetry is, otherwise why should I take the trouble? If I would be self-satisfied with my poetry I wouldn't need to write it down, I would just dream it.

But what I was saying about this proto-poetry, it's not only words on paper or words on air, sound waves in air, it's also self-communication. So, it can also be translated into music, it can be translated into paintings, everyone might have his or her own way of translating the matter that's important. But now we are talking about the poetry that is written or spoken, that is words, that is ideas put in words. And it has, as has been said here before, not only this aspect of having a communicative function, it has also a magical function. In this sense I would like to compare it with music, because reading or listening to poetry can lead to a similar experience as does listening to music. Which is that (at least for me it often does this) which is that I get so absorbed while reading or listening I fully understand every word. I lose the sense of time, I am one with the piece of art, the work that I'm reading or listening to. And five minutes after, I don't remember anything about what I heard or what I read; it's just going somewhere deep into my mind and merging there with the things that are already there. It's a process that is like breathing. We all forget that we are breathing all the time. We don't know actually how we breathe. So when I get back to that text or when I hear that music again, I immediately recognize it. And when I recognize it, I have gained something more than at the first time, because I have been living with that knowledge, that hidden knowledge hidden inside me, about that poem, about that poetry. I have been living and using it, I may have been cultivating it. Maybe I have been plundering it. Maybe I have just used it for digging a hole in the earth or whatever. In that sense this kind of translation is done every time we appreciate a work of art, whatever kind of art. Whatever kind of poetry the piece of art is containing, we are translating it, as I think Octavio Paz was also saying in the citation.

The thing that I called magic, the magical aspect is of course that by naming things we aim to own them, we aim to rule, to have command over them. And by using them, by using names, we also fix the things. We don't dare to see the real ambiguity of things, so we must fix them for our own purposes, and translation is one way of ruling the world. Because translations are in nature more unambiguous than the originals. That's unavoidable. The translation is an interpretation, it is like in quantum physics, you either know where the thing is or you—how does it go in English?

AH: Oh, you mean the Heisenberg thing? There's two parts to that. You never know exactly where any particle is at any given time, and plus your being there affects that—but you still can't know it. You know you're part of it, but how your presence affects it is also unknowable.

KN: Yes, and the lovely Heisenberg principle doesn't work with translation (as well as it should, I mean) because in translation you must fix some things better than they are fixed in the original. At least, translating into languages that are precise by nature. I've been telling my students about an interesting thing, that the Chinese tend to be easier to translate into English and the Japanese tend to be easier to translate into Finnish. Because Chinese and English are almost monosyllabic languages nowadays. And in Chinese, as in English, the same form of a word can act as a verb or a noun—like in Chinese it's just the place of the word in the sentence that makes, at least in classical Chinese, that fixes if it's an adjective or a noun or a verb. Actually there is not such a distinction between adjectives and verbs in some languages as our languages have. Whereas Japanese, as a polysyllabic language and an agglutinative language, like Finnish, can be more ambiguous because you can hide the subject, you can be more elliptical. You don't need to show your face in every sentence, so to say. Which is also of course good for the politicians, those languages can be used seemingly very definitely and actually saying nothing.

So I believe, after what Anselm said and what I've been trying to say, we agree that it is possible to translate things. Because we all know that we are communicating with each other, and if everything needs to be translated, we have just proved that we have translated, so it is possible. Translation has also something to do with such delightful things as association of words and things. A translator must find, of many synonyms, a word that would lead to the nearest possible associations similar to the original language. The words are not one to one. But also the fact that translation is not translating words, it's translating concepts, translating ideas, leads to the idea that word-for-word translation is not actual translation, at least it's not translating literature or poetry. The associative technique is one key to translation. You can actually use whatever—it's allowed to use whatever trick you can find to achieve the goal of making the reader have the same idea, the same kind of association, that the original has, the reader of the translation to recognize the cognition of the original author. This I think is important.

I am familiar with many theories of translation. Translation theories very often are conflicting, which is a very good thing because they make you think for yourself. You can't have an authority who would say that this is the only right way to translate. But then I do have one homemade theory of translation,

AH: Ah! let's hear it—

KN: and it is the practical theory that I try to fulfill. It is that I try to become the author, the original author, I try to get into his or her body, so to say. It's easier if he is dead—so I can kind of become his or her imma-terial body. And then I try to live what has been written, lived or experi-enced, I try to assimilate that situation; and then I try or not only try, I will write the work in the way that he or she would have written if she or he had used the Finnish language. So, it's so simple: simply said, I mean. I guess that is kind of summarizing many of the translation theories.

AH: I think the first person who I ever heard that from—we don't own anything do we?—was Paul Blackburn, a wonderful American translator from the French and the Spanish, who said "it is rather like being an actor, isn't it?" He was working with 13th-century Provençal lyrical poetry, so he was somehow able to, living right above McSorley's Wonderful Saloon in New York, he was able to somehow transport himself back to early medieval France. And as the results show, was very successful with that, at some cost to himself, I think. He died way too young. There's this book recently published called *Performing Without a Stage: The Art of Literary Translation*. Which basically just says that. It looks at literary translation as a performance. And it is a performance of the other author as well as the author of the translation. They're both there. And their outlines merge and shift and come back together again.

Another idea that we had, talking with Kai, was also connected to what Peter Lamborn Wilson was talking about, was it only yesterday? (Time really stretches or contracts—does both probably—during these summers.) In any case, *boundaries*—and why translation is also a hermetic art. Hermes the traveler, Hermes the crosser and also at the same time the marker of boundaries. It's an interesting fact that in all of history, the examples we know best are those from Europe, groups of people that are relatively small but share a language, have, as we say, a language, who live on the borders, in areas that are being contested by larger groups who speak different languages, by the very virtue of their historical situ-ation, have been familiar for many thousands of years with the idea of translation, with the ability to command more than their own lan-guage. In a sense, in order to preserve it, in fact. Because the Alsatians could have decided a long time ago that since they were now becoming, at one point in the 19th century they were becoming Germans, just for-get about French, you know, speak German. And then again, when the French took them back, well, we can't forget—. The Finns are a partic-ularly interesting example, actually, because they were constantly, they were fought over for almost a thousand years, by two much bigger lin-guistic groups: to the west, the Scandinavians, Swedes (Swedes, Norwegians, Danes—all the same—I'm not saying that these aren't separate literatures, but it is basically the same language)—and to the east, the Slavs, the Russians. And Finland didn't really gain any kind of definite political autonomy until this century. And yet, it was able to hang onto its language, from—the first printed Finnish text was a translation of the Gospels in Luther's day, by a man called Michael Agricola, Michael the peasant, who went to Wittenberg and studied with Luther and wrote this truly amazing Finnish, which is a lot more interesting than much of the presently written Finnish actually. Then there was a long hiatus, because it was felt by the various colonial powers, whether Swedish or Russian, that these benighted peasants really—well, give them a Bible, that's OK, they should go to church and be good, upstanding people, but they don't really have a literature, do they. So to get something published in Finnish, that took another couple of hundred years. Kai, would you like to say something about that? Because it has some interesting bearing. My homemade theory about survival of small languages, I mean we're losing languages every day, like we're losing natural species, and I think we're losing them because they don't have writing. If they never made it into writing and don't have a literature, they will be gone. There's an exception on this continent that I know of, which is the Cherokee, where actually someone indeed invented an alphabet for them, and there were books in Cherokee printed in the 19th century, but I haven't seen any recently and I don't think that's an active situation anymore.

KN: When Finland gained its independence, that's the first time that borders were fixed. And that means there were constant wars between Russia and Sweden, so one part of Finland would be under Russian regime, while another part would be under Swedish regime, and then again the eastern border would go further east and so there would be intermarriages across the border, there would be bilingual people speaking both the Karelian language or Finnish language and the Russian language, and on the other border people speaking both Finnish and Swedish. Actually, in Lapland there are the Sami people who have their own languages, there are at least four or five different Sami languages plus some dialects. The Sami people are very interesting—

AH: Lapps, we used to call them; the Sami is correct.

KN: Sami is their own name for them. I have friends up there, living at a point where the three countries' border is very near—Sweden, Finland, and Norway, are very near each other at that point. And I was asking my friend, whose mother tongue is Sami, is Lapp, which language does he use when he meets his Norwegian cousins, I asked is it Swedish or Norwegian. He said: is there some name for that—I'm just talking our language, or their language, because he knows Finnish and Sami and then this

Scandinavian, and actually the Scandinavian language in that area is a mixture of Swedish and Norwegian with a Finnish pronunciation.

AH: It's a Creole, I think it's called technically. How did the Lapps, how were they able to hang onto their language? I'm just realizing that my homemade theory is somewhat collapsing because there never were that many of them either. Maybe there's some kind of critical mass, you need a certain number of people. So if the number of speakers declines below a certain point the language is gone.

KN: And also you had movement all the time. They were not fixed to a place where they would be overrun by somebody. They were kind of running away—

AH: Oh, I see. So you mustn't get tucked away somewhere where in order to get out you . . . This country tried to force the Native Americans to abandon their languages. Kids were beaten for speaking their native languages in schools in the 19th century.

KN: So were the Sami, the Lapps. In this century, actually, they were forbidden to speak Lapp at school and the language had very bad times. But now it's taught again at school, and you have a right, not only a right, there are some communities where it must be the first language at school. But it's only recent.

AH: Slow business, isn't it?

KN: It had to do with religion also, because the Bible and the hymnbook were translated into Lappish quite early. Laestadius did great work with that, so that he kind of established that also as a written language.

AH: Well I think maybe now, since we can go on babbling like this forever, translation is Babble! Tower of Babel. Translation is boundless, it doesn't have any boundaries as a subject. We would like to invent, yeah, we'd like to "invent" questions from the audience.

Q: I think this is mostly addressed to Kai about, in terms of proto-language, and wondering how much the language that we use affects that proto-language in reverse. I understand the idea of thought and of cognition and translating that then into words, language that we communicate to others with, but how much is it the reverse? How much does that, the way we communicate things, affect the way we even have any cognition of them?

KN: It must have a tremendous effect, I am sure, because as soon as we start the thinking process, as soon as we cognize the cognition, we start doing it with words, with language, with native language, so the language is forming our mind very much. We might even not see things that are there if we don't have a word for them in our language. We might even not have emotions that would be possible for us to have if we wouldn't have words for those emotions. So that the language is ruling us, we are quite helpless under the pressure of language.

AH: But how does that fit in? That makes it sort of into a chicken or egg problem, doesn't it. How are we then able, as you proposed, for instance, in our dreams, where does that language—how do we recognize things in dreams? If we recognize them only by means of everyday language?

KN: We don't recognize them always, that's the problem. Why, when we wake up—

AH: That's good. This is going to be nothing but confusion . . .

Q: And then to follow up with that, I've never come across concepts written down that I don't have experience for because I don't have language for them. Is that something that's the case when you're translating in your languages?

KN: The experiences that are needed, the translator must get from sources, reading books, getting into that period, getting into that environment, reading as much as possible of the author, if possible, I always like to read the diary of the author if available. The Japanese very often, luckily, have it. Letters from the author, for example Basho's letters are wonderful, wonderfully simple things. He is thanking his friends for presents, or telling them where he is going. You can follow his everyday life. Then you start understanding the things without experiencing them yourself, you just kind of, you can buy those experiences with lots of time and work.

AH: That's like the actor studying for his role in a way, trying to find out everything possible about this character. But I think when you say that you've never come across a concept in English that you didn't immediately understand, I don't believe you. Because that means that you've read nothing written before, say, 1880. Because, you know, language changes. Concepts change too. If you're reading Francis Bacon, who was a very lucid writer, you'll have to translate in a sense to figure out what it is he's saying.

Q: So on that same basis, mine is going to be culturally oriented, is then the goal in translation to bring the essence of that other person's experience and culture, but actually market it more toward your target language, so that it's the essence that's captured, more so than worrying about the verbatim translation?

AH: There goes that word "market" again. I don't think marketing really is what you're trying to say. But that's a good question. Because everybody always trots out dear old, poor old Walter Benjamin in this context, who wrote a pretty wonderful essay actually, he was a translator into German of Baudelaire. He said that translation—you don't want to do what previous centuries (he was early 20th century), what previous centuries did without giving it a second thought, which was to basically translate everything, including names. That's how come Jesus' younger brother's name is James, for god's sake—it was probably Yakub, but it's now James, it's the letter of James. And so on and so forth. The English did it throughout. They translated the names of cities—Köln is Cologne. This was done throughout the ages, we tried to—I guess not with the classics, with the *Iliad* and the *Odyssey* there was some kind of restraint exercised because they were venerated, but certainly anything contemporary was immediately anglicized. So that's not what we do anymore. Benjamin says you have to leave a little strangeness in there. You don't want it to be—if the characters in a novel are peasants in Southern France, first of all you don't change Jean to Joe or John, and secondly you don't want to make Jean sound like some guy from Iowa. You leave a little French in there, in the English that you're translating it into. It's a tightrope in a funny way. Because you don't also want to—unless you're a scholarly translator and you sort of almost believe, it's curious that some of the most sophisticated academic people who translate really actually still believe in what Kai calls word-for-word translation, and create these very dull cribs, essentially, that they then publish as translations. But they're not writers, that's the problem. I think the best translator of a creative writer is another creative writer.

KN: I think there's also in this point the need to think, what are we trying to gain with the translations. Is it like, they have this huge international, global, cultural heritage. So by translating are we trying to take a part of it to ourselves, or are we going out to the world with translations, to travel, to kind of be on the road in this global culture. I guess that's what *we* do, we use these translations as maps or passports to this traveling and not as means of grabbing something for our exclusive property.

AH: There's an interesting footnote to this which I just remembered. One reason we are lucky to have Kai here this summer is that the Republic of Finland does have something called a Ministry of Culture (unheard of in this context here), which has various branches or agencies under it, and one of them is the Finnish Literature Society, and the Finnish Literature Information Service, which actually tries to, in some kind of one might say quixotic way, spread some knowledge of past and present Finnish literature abroad. All the Scandinavian countries do have agencies like this, so does France, so does Germany. I think the anglophones, those bloody old imperialists, are the most retrograde in that sense. They don't need to, because Hollywood and TV and the media take care of that for them. The

United States certainly is very actively exporting its popular culture. And since the United States does not believe that it has a high culture—which I think is a big mistake, because it does—no attention to its dissemination is paid. So we've no money. The NEA is probably some kind of little vestigial appendix thing that will soon be removed. But in any case we have to thank the Finnish Literature Society and its director Marja-Leena Rautalin for, since Naropa is so very poor, for financing Kai's and Elina's [Kai's wife's] trip over here. [applause] Don't lose the tape.

KN: I'll tell this to Marja-Leena, I'll confirm it.

LAURA WRIGHT: I think I have more of a series of ideas that maybe you can translate into questions and then answer. Or they can just sit. The first thought is that translation is entirely impossible in the same way that language is entirely impossible and the only things worth doing are those that are entirely impossible. And the second is an anecdote which I'm sorry Anselm already knows, but it was an argument I had with a dear friend of mine who initially said, well soon computers will be able to do what you are doing when you translate, and you can just type in the text and Michaux will come out in beautiful English for you. So I was trying to explain why this wouldn't ever work, and he ended up saying what I was doing was immoral, because there cannot be a precise translation, there's not a literal this word means that word. And I started just now thinking of this in terms of technical language or some sense of mathematics versus language as those of us who sort of live in language in a different way use language, in that if I'm going to give you directions to build a house, right better mean right, left better mean left, measurement better be measurement, up and down and everything really should mean something. But if I'm going to write a poem I think it'd be dreadfully boring if it were nothing but a blueprint.

AH: I guess, well, the impossible part is self-evident, that's a nice aphorism. Obviously we have, the human species has operated on that basis for a long long time. We will always try to do the impossible. And only the impossible is interesting. But, the second part—well, sure. I think it also depends in part upon whether a person is a reader and thus has a more sophisticated understanding of what language can do. Which is, in fact, what Pound called phanopoeia, the casting of images on the mind. Studies have been made where kids who have not been read to, and who have not really ever read anything except what they were forced to read in school, and who have grown up watching television, are in fact incapable, if they have not managed to create this casting of images upon their mind, from a written page, before the age of ten, they won't ever be able to do it. So we have a few generations now of people who, literally, their only use for reading is instructions, how to do something or how to avoid something. Paladin books, you know. That's a Boulder in-joke: they publish books on how to most efficiently kill people and stuff. With absolutely no literary merit, unlike, say John Le Carré who can be said to be doing the same, but it has literary merit. I think that's basically your answer. I don't know, one could obviously perhaps try to persuade your friend to read a little linguistics, for instance, that might be helpful. In other words to see that language is really a far more complicated construct than that. And I think even if you built a house, sure a right angle is a right angle, but on the other hand, as soon as it comes to any decisions as to what shape it's going to be and so forth you do have to look back into the language of building or architecture. That's a language that has evolved over millennia. There are analogs to this, obviously, some people can't look at pictures unless they know exactly what the picture "represents." You know, that's a doggie, oh good. I don't know. That's all I can think of.

KN: And only that—what we were talking about with Anselm also during lunch was that we must not forget that there are texts, there are poems that never were meant to be translated. They are kind of inside jokes of the language, or they are experiments of the language that they are written in. They are not impossible or not possible to translate, because they are not meant to be translated. But then again there are books like *Tristram Shandy* that has just now been translated by Kersti Juva into Finnish, Pentti Saarikoski translated Joyce's *Ulysses,* so it was possible.

AH: It's a wonderful translation. The first edition, I think all the editions still have his foreword—he died in '83. But he says, this is going to be full of—he says in the introduction, I'm paraphrasing, I'm sure there will be lots of instances in this text that will be considered mistakes. (You can't not make those kinds of mistakes translating even the simplest text, but in a book like *Ulysses* obviously the chances of making mistakes are multiplied tremendously.) So, please, if you find one send it in to the publisher! And we will evaluate it and if you're right about this, we will correct the next edition. And I think it's been done, I don't know how many editions it's gone into—but, you know, it's a slow process.

From the Gone World

LAWRENCE FERLINGHETTI
July 4, 1998

★   ★   ★

LAWRENCE FERLINGHETTI: I started out writing poems years ago that you didn't need to have any literary education to understand. In other words, they had a public surface which anyone can get. A sensual, visual surface which is totally available. The poem shouldn't have to be explained. If someone asked me to, that's another thing. Quite often the newspaper reporters say, well, what does that mean?

If the poem has to be explained, it is a failure. So I refused to explain it. But, I would read it again. And then, if he or she still doesn't understand it, well, then I know I am a total failure and so does he.

I wanted to mention that at the end of the colloquium yesterday the subject of the National Endowment for the Arts came up and various people gave their views on the NEA and Anne Waldman asked me to say something because City Lights [the press and the bookstore] had never taken grants. Michael McClure told me, "Well, that's the purist position. You can afford to refuse the grants." And so the sentence I forgot to wind up with last night was: well then, freedom is something you have to be able to afford? Thought so!

I'll leave it at that.

What else should we talk about?

You know another thing that came up yesterday was that one student got up and said, I've heard enough about process. I really liked that because it seems to me that all over the country, and in literary criticism, it's all about process. I hope that's not the case here. I think in painting, in visual arts, it's the same thing, in poetry they talk about craft, in painting they talk about process. There's all kinds of learned articles in the art magazines about process and the artists that are doing process and their performance art is process, the installations are really process art, and where's the content? So you have this and that—heaps of this or that—on gallery floors and you put an inscrutable title on the wall and that's it. And it's supposed to be profound. I think it should be much more. There should be courses on what the poem should be *about*. There should be courses on the *content* of poetry, what the content of poetry should be. I gave a lecture at Michael McClure's invitation at the California College of Arts and

Crafts a few years ago and the name of my so-called lecture was called, "Why Don't You Paint Something Important?"

According to Michael, the students were up all night debating that because they had never heard of such a thing, "something . . . important?" "What about this pile of rags on the middle of the floor in the shape of a . . . whatever? Well, what do you think about that?"

This is supposed to be a rap session. Not just me.

ANNE WALDMAN: Well, I guess The New Age has brought this word "important" to the fore because it validates everything leading up to the fruition, the art work, the object. So, [it's] an attempt to make you feel better about your life in some way. And in our context here we're fighting the good fight against that kind of, call it New Age Speech. I was listening to a few things yesterday, even the word "intensive" is used a lot as a noun you might have noticed. The Naropa catalog is riddled [with] "intensives" for this event or the other, but, also "dialoguing," "processing," "workshoping." I think our poetics students, much to their credit, have one really astute kind of ear for that phoney stuff. It masks the real work, so to speak. But, on the other hand, and certainly in my classes, we talk about how there isn't that much new under the sun in terms of content. So of course it's *how* you do it. How you work with your content. But, then there's also political issues in terms of, what are you really talking about? Is your work alleviating the suffering of others? Is it helping advance the century forward a few inches in Williams's sense? So these come up a lot.

I think in terms of Pound's little breakdown of the *logopoeia, phanopoeia,* and *melopoeia*. The *logopoeia* is the dance of the intellect, and, clearly—more of that is needed but, I get bored when a poem is so subject-matter-based that you can wrap it up and say that this is a poem about a dead seagull on the Southampton beach or the angst over buying—what do they call it? Those kind of tomatoes? Hydroponic. There was a poem in the *New Yorker* last week—terrific angst over buying hydroponic tomatoes.

LF: Are there more opaque images of the seagull? Well, the trouble is a lot of my poetry commits the sin of too much clarity. It's more fashionable to have an opaque poem which, therefore, must have a lot more depth to it because you can't see through it—an eighth type of ambiguity created by the poet unintentionally.

Just to get a little reaction I'd like to play the devil's advocate and suggest that maybe poetry writing classes are the worst thing in the world for a poet.

I've always stayed away from them. I don't teach them. I never went to them. But, I think this is a very snobbish point of view. If you go out in the great waste of middle America there's a poet in every one of those little towns. You can go to Winesburg, Ohio—there's a poet. Or you can go to anywhere and you'll find some subterranean poet or artist trying to survive. He finds a couple of other people and they start having meetings and, then they have a little weekly poetry meeting. I think it's very useful—anywhere outside of the great urban centers. It's a very valuable thing for creating a sense of community for people who are basically artists or poets and have no one to talk to. But besides that, I think the form of the poem is dictated by the content. So too in poetry writing classes it seems to me. I've never taught, so I'm not giving this a fair shot, but can you imagine Shelley giving a poetry writing class?

And going to one?

What does anyone think about that?

LISA BIRMAN: I think you just summed up what I wanted to say about process. If someone doesn't get the poem when you read the poem, you can read the poem again. Or they can read the poem again. But, if you have to explain to them what you were attempting to do, and what you were engaged in when you were writing this poem, that's no longer the poem. Maybe it's footnotes, maybe it's interesting background material. But it's not the poem.

LF: Well, those that came to my reading last night might have noted that there was hardly any comment between the poems.

Q: That's actually what I want to bring up. I heard Allen Ginsberg say while he was being questioned about a poem, and I think it was Gregory Corso asking the questions, and Gregory was saying, "I'd really like you to say something special about the state we're in today," and Allen said, "Let the poetry speak." I thought that was really good. I write straightforwardly and simply, and it seems like you do too, but there's so much poetry that I hear and that I read that I don't understand. It seems like sometimes the poem has a point or it should have a point. I don't know. If it does have a point it is obscured. If poetry is a form of communication, why deliberately obscure the message, or the image? You know what I mean?

LF: You're right on.

Q: And that's a big thing. So I thought we'd be straightforward. Let the poem stand by itself. Maybe I should have read a different poem? I'd like to get your comments more on that if I could. That would be great.

LF: Well, I coined this term, "public surface," years ago and I said earlier today, the poem has to have this public surface anyone can get, but, if it's going to go beyond literary journalism, then it has to have other surfaces or other levels of meaning so that someone who's got a literary education can get a whole, totally different level of meaning out of the poem and still have a subversive or subjective level of meaning. Otherwise, it's just on a public surface and you might as well be a stand-up comedian, right?

Q: I wanted to address the matter of the futility or utility of the writing classes and the poetry classes because it always upsets me when I hear people entirely dismiss the value of taking classes in writing or poetry. I just graduated from Barnard where I spent four years studying to be a creative writing major. I learned so much and studied under great writers like Mary Gordon, Allen Ginsberg, and Kenneth Koch. Taking writing courses, studying great writers, and learning to read extremely closely is so valuable and benefits your own writing so much. But, what it seems is happening, is that people look at a symposium where people are drinking and where there are writers talking in this thriving manor and [see] everybody being so excited and feeding off one another's ideas. That, to me, is parallel to the classroom. It's just that maybe your chairs aren't velvet and there aren't broken wine bottles lying around. It's still learning. You're still benefiting from great minds. I think it's invaluable. I think you have to appreciate the value of studying writing and studying poetry as much as possible. Have you felt that?

LF: That's very valuable. I agree with you. But, I'd like to mention that the great libraries in this country is where this used to happen. And the conversations of the ages between, for instance, Greek philosophers and great 19th-century poets—I mean that eternal conversation still goes on in libraries. And I question whether you can't learn more just going to the library every day for eight hours. But nobody wants to do that anymore now. In fact, I'm really shocked by that. The other day the University of California at Berkeley announced that it was going to put its whole stock on computer. The book won't be available on the open shelves the way it has been in the main student library at UC-Berkeley. You will have to do it on a computer. Two years ago, a San Francisco librarian was fired—it was a huge hullabaloo—after he had junked thousands and thousands of books from the San Francisco Public Library without letting anyone know that they were available for anyone to take. There was a huge article in the *New Yorker* about it when he was fired. The electronic revolution that is going on is in its early stages and—as in the early stages of the industrial revolution—a few facts surface like the facts about the library switching to computers or it comes to surface every once in a while in the newspaper, but meanwhile, the whole century is going down the funnel. The old culture, the traditional culture, is disappearing so fast it's unbelievable. In ten years it could be all gone the way things are going now.

Q: This is back to the publishing end of things. As a poet publisher, I started my press about seven years ago influenced by you. I mean I had *Pictures of* *the Gone World* in one hand and the first chapbooks we were doing in the other to see how to do a title page and how to do a copyright page and [see how] all of that stuff works. And I have just a couple of questions on the poet/publisher side. I guess Anne can talk about this as well [from her experience in small press publishing] back in the late sixties and early seventies. Two things: one about publishing your own work and reconciling the idea of publishing your own work, and, also, reconciling that you're still a poet, and making sure you're still active as a poet, and that people know you as a poet. I guess I'm really hearkening back more toward the fifties than to now.

LF: When I go on the road it's usually as a poet and I leave my publisher's hat behind. Generally we don't consider it a business. A bookstore such as ours is a way of life and the publishing was never done to earn money. So you might notice I never carry bookstore or publishing propaganda catalogs with me and leave them on the table for people to pick up. I make it solely as a poet. I'm running into this crossover problem with painting. Because I was going to art school when I was on the GI Bill in France—a hundred and thirty-five years ago—and I've been drawing from the model all those years. I never exhibited. I've been painting since the fifties, oil on canvas, yet I didn't start exhibiting until the eighties. Immediately, I get, "Oh, he's the poet who also paints."

"He also paints? Oh, I didn't know that."

I'm still running into that. So I want the painting to make it on its own. I had a big show in Rome—a painting show at the Palazzo della Expedicione in the Via Nazionale in Rome two years ago—and I insisted they not have a lot of essays in there relating me to poetry. It's very hard to avoid that in this country. It seems like everyone is in their pigeonhole. "Oh, well you're a poet. Stay. You're not supposed to do all these other arts." In Europe it's quite usual for the poets also to be painters or the painters also to be poets. Like Hans Arp. He wrote poetry. The French Surrealists. They wrote poetry, but they also painted. And this is quite usual in France and Italy. I noticed that some in Prague. In Europe it seems that if you were a man of letters you were considered an artist and not just a poet or not just a novelist. You weren't kept in one pigeonhole. Anyone who presumed to think he was going to make a career of this, "to be a man of letters"—and not just a professor—was naturally assumed to know one other language, probably two. And I've been to quite a lot of international poetry conferences and quite often everyone has to end up speaking English because the Americans don't know any other language. Allen Ginsberg was a big exception. He could make himself quite well understood in French and especially in Spanish and a little bit in Italian.

I remember the first trip we took out of this country as poets. It was in 1959. We were invited to Chile. The University of Concepción. Allen stayed up all night translating Chilean poets into English. He spoke in taxi cab Spanish. The next day he read "Howl" in Spanish—the third day after he arrived—because he'd been to Mexico before. We were invited by the Communist Party. This was in the fifties when McCarthy and the Un-American Activities Committee were going around staging hearings. McCarthy's favorite question was: "Are you now, or have you ever been a member of the Communist Party?" Which us anarchists thought was a pretty absurd question because the anarchists are 180 degrees opposed to Communism. Anyway, we were invited by the Communist Party but we didn't know it. The way it happened was that Fernando Allegría who was a Spanish professor, at that time, at the University of California-Berkeley, now he's at Stanford—had a brother in the Communist Party in Chile. And his brother was the one that invited us and we only found out later. There was a coal mining town on the coast called Lota. They have undersea coal mines there. And there was a strike of the coal mines when we were there. So the Communist Party organized a busload of us poets from countries all over to come down to Lota and see the desolate conditions of the miners and then be interviewed by the press. It was really shocking. The miners came out of the ground in elevators after twelve hours underground where they had walked three miles under sea to the mine head. They came up covered and totally black with coal and dust. Then, the press shoved microphones in our faces and asked what we thought of that. And it should be a total setup, but, it was the truth and I think we made a lot of strong statements on the subject. I remember the Santiago paper interviewed me and asked all these literary questions on process and other serious literary questions. For every question I answered, "The faces of the miners in the coal mines at Lota." It didn't matter what the question was. Allen did a similar type of interview with a different type of answer.

Q: You said that if a poem cannot be understood it is defeated and that if it should be explained it is a failure. I have a problem with that—I can understand it if they're using these huge words, these scientific words, or creating something that's out of context. But, a lot of times I am not forced to explain my poetry but, to clarify it. A lot of people don't exactly live in suburbia or in Americana. In that context people are always separate. I have a different view of what reality is for them in America. Just like today on Independence Day. Is this Independence Day? Or, is this Independence Day for my people? I mean, what does it mean? I clarify my work because it comes from mythological sources. It comes from a different place, but it's in the same place. Sometimes, I think it's not such a failure. It's just that everybody belongs to this monolingual oneness that America has become. It's become this one language. It's almost imperialistic in a way that only sees things in one way. But, there are plenty of ways to actually see reality. There are plenty of ways to describe reality to other peoples. Another question too, I think that City Lights has been publishing Guillermo Gómez-Peña? That's a wonderful step. I think you're also printing Ward Churchill. I guess I have to thank you for doing that because I'm not sure who else would.

And about the NEA grant, I go to the Institute of Native American Arts. When the NEA was cut, for the first time, our school was affected directly. I could say that a lot of the writers and a lot of the artists and the people who are on the forefront of the Native American art movement, the Native American renaissance in writing, do have a direct tie to the Institute of Native American Arts. If it wasn't there where would we all be? Our voices would not be heard. We'd probably still be on the reservation searching and searching and in the galleries of Gallup, New Mexico. There's really no extreme sometimes. In certain ways I think America has just become so specialized. I mean I paint and I write poetry and I take photographs. I want a full life. Sometimes people get so specialized. Why?

LF: The best, most interesting, writing nowadays is coming out of the third world or from women writers, it seems to me. And the books coming from third-world authors now are the ones that have the most to say.

AW: First world. First-world writers.

That was a good comment, talking about the importance of the support that creates something like the Institute of American Indian Arts. There are very different perspectives. Would that there was some kind of wisdom body that could determine how money was spent. I often go through this. We don't get outright government money here, but students are on government loans and this kind of thing. People have gotten NEA grants and had to work that out. Whether they can actually sign those—what did we call it the other day? Grievances? But, in any case, would that there was some kind of wisdom body that could somehow say where tax money could go. Obviously that would be something to work on. I think there should be some inspiration—maybe you can carry the torch in terms of thinking about ways to publish, and inroads there and, certainly, the IAIA magazines. Writing from there gets around and is noted. I think there's more and more of a voice but, it's so much up to individuals and likewise, this place has to struggle too. I remember, seven years ago, we almost closed this school. Everybody went the extra mile. Of course you have the talent and the intelligence to be reading, and studying, and so on, but, it's this other—it seems more interesting, I mean there were certain struggles that Lawrence seemed to have that accomplished things and set ways for us or precedents for us. The context is different now. It's a different kind of struggle. It's much harder [these days] to go to New York or to go to California and find a community to survive. Artists have to struggle so hard just to keep it together. You aren't going to get this kind of richness, at least for a time. I'm constantly telling people to start their own things rather than thinking that they'll go and work in some tenure track in a university and that [that] would be some fruition of getting an MFA degree. I mean that seems counterproductive to what this is about anyway.

RACHEL LEVITSKY: One of the things that I noticed a lot this week is the lament that there is no audience for poetry in America and that part of it would be because so many kids grow up just being plopped down in front of the TV instead of being handed a book. One of the things that I've been trying to figure out over and over, and maybe people here can help me, is: how do we get people out from behind their TVs and their computers and into reading poetry? Instead of complaining how there is no audience, how do we recreate the audience?

LF: Well to take another tack on it, you said there's no audience for poetry on TV, or in mass media in general, but, maybe if you wrote on subjects that were important enough, and vital enough—and, absolutely, the most important subjects to the general public—then it would be on TV.

RL: I'm not saying, put it on TV. It's how do we get people away from watching TV and back into finding—

AW: We had an Unplugged Month about three years ago. It started in Berkeley. Everybody unplugged their TVs for a month, primarily writers and artists.

RL: I live in Northern California now, but I never heard anything about that. It doesn't seem to get out there, so that everybody in America is finding out about it. It's more like, mostly aspiring poets are the ones who read poetry instead of the general population.

LF: Well I know that there are an enormous amount of people reading poetry. Now that we have computers at the bookstore we can keep track of how much poetry comes in the store and goes out: enormous quantities every month—it's really astounding.

The whole question is that we're still talking about community and the community in this country is—the largest community [at least]—is on TV and so you know the TV anchor better than you know your father. You've heard him speak more than you've heard your father speak.

So, you have this floating in the air waves around the country. I feel one great hold-out is FM radio. I think here in Boulder you have a fine example in David Barsamian and alternative radio. What intellectual life that exists on the national level now is on FM radio. There's been huge battles in Pacifica Radio the last few years and it looked like KPFA Berkeley—which didn't have an intellectual program after 7 p.m. at night for the last ten years—was contributing to the dumbing down of America. And now, we've heard it from the head of the national board of Pacifica Radio, who was recently fired, that it had taken a turn back, and now we'd have intellectual programs in the evenings. There's lots of FM stations that are really the life of the mind, I find. These days you just don't get it on television.

To end up this discussion I wanted to bring up something that's really at the heart of the Naropa poetics program. About a couple of months ago I did an article with the *Paris Review* which hasn't come out yet. I might have been totally wrong, or too simplistic on this, but I characterized Allen Ginsberg's school of poetry as "the graph of consciousness school of poetry."

AW: That's good. That's the slogan we've been looking for. Thank You.

LF: Someone had said, well, Allen wrote and talked about his process. Well, Allen was a great teacher. He was essentially a great teacher and I think he always wanted to be a professor at Columbia—but he made it to City College. He was a great teacher, no doubt about it. And he had a fascinating and genius mind. He had, really, a pack rat mind. When I went to Australia with him he would just take down—write in his notebooks—everything in sight. I mean the type of tree along the highway, what kind of dog was scurrying down the street. He would get in conversations with total strangers and he'd be totally wrapped up in them and you'd wonder what in the world he could be talking about. It was like Allen was siphoning up the guy's brains. He siphoned everybody up sort of like Picasso siphoning up Braque. But, going back to the idea of Allen's theory of his poetics. The graph of consciousness is transcribing onto a tape recorder or onto paper exactly what comes into your mind at any moment with as little possible interference or editing by the conscious mind while you're doing it. You get as direct a transcription of consciousness as you can get. In the *Paris Review* article I think I, maybe erroneously, mentioned that the Naropa Institute is the place where the Ginsberg school of poetics was taught. Is it true that this really is the basis of the poetics program here?

AW: I wouldn't say that entirely. We talk about the "mind grammar" of Gertrude Stein—it's honored and part of the ground for what's come along, but we really respect the poetics and praxis of the individual writers that we bring in here as faculty. There's no one party line in terms of curriculum. Anselm Hollo might build work differently from how Allen did. There's certainly Allen's "mind breath." His writing slogans. "Snapshot poetics" is something that's included, or the way he would talk about projective verse or, "no ideas but in things," from Williams, but these ideas are very particularized rather than generalized as some overriding theme or agenda. It's trusting, as you say, the consciousness, and certainly the proletarian spirit and what you, Lawrence, represent being such a great populist poet. And ultimately it's the sense of writing to alleviate suffering or why do we do this? What's the work?

LF: Allen certainly did that.

AW: And that's very much a tenet of this school which is why there is so much emphasis on community. What you find is a very noncompetitive environment here. That was also something Allen promoted. So, beyond the writing, the ideas of poetics, is how to be a human being in the world. How to benefit others and how to work together in a noncompetitive way. Those are the real values that we all share aside from just differences in poetics. We talk about it being an "outrider school." So, *outside* the more academic mainstream. Or, outside the literary mafias of New York and California, and that sort of thing.

LF: Kenneth Rexroth used to talk about that. That's why he went to San Francisco from back East. The graph of consciousness technique for poetry is very good when you have a genius consciousness like Allen's that is being recorded. But, then when you have thousands of students using it, not every one has a very unique, or prophetic, or genius consciousness and you're liable to get some very boring poetry. If the mind is comely everything that comes out of the mind will be comely. Well, if the mind is boring, everything that comes out of the mind is going to be boring, too. But, I find in this *Paris Review* they were identifying me with the Beats—and I kept insisting—there was this pigeonhole thing again. I was not one of the original Beats. I got associated with the Beats by publishing them and my poetics is entirely different. I mean, I don't believe in "no ideas but in things." I think that's kind of a mindless statement or point of view. I mean things are *dead*. Right? Another thing I don't really agree with is "first thought, best thought."

AW: No, it's "first thought worst thought."

LF: In my poetics, quite often, the second thought is better.

AW: I think these are really good points that you're making, about the vitality of Allen's poetics but—the last thing we want is people writing imitations of Allen Ginsberg.

Q: Seeing Ginsberg two years ago, and seeing his scholarship, and his devotion to ongoing learning I think is so much a part of it. If you're going to be recording your consciousness you'd better be willing to continue to learn and to read and that I think is a gap in some of the writing that comes out of many programs. I think there isn't as much reading as writers—with the attention of a writer.

LF: Yeah, in other words, not just, find your own voice, but, find your own mind.

AFTERTHOUGHTS:

After the above conversation at Naropa, I have had a few critical second thoughts.

One is that if you strive toward the Buddhist state of "empty mind" you may find your own mind but end up with a mind that is *too* empty.

Another second thought I have had is that "first thought, best thought" is an invaluable practice for *poetic* thinking, for intuitive perception. The phrase that pops into mind, raw, untamed and uncensored, is the very soul of poetry, and if you do not seize it at once you may never be able to retrieve it. This primitive, unprompted perception is *the* most indispensible element in poetry. (Thus, for instance, did Gregory Corso spout his mad mouthfuls of primal speech, and thus did Allen Ginsberg come up with so many spontaneous and astounding piths of poetry.)

On the other hand, thinking twice is extremely valuable in *critical* thinking, and second thought may indeed prove to be best thought, in this rethinking.

March, 2004

Panel on Personal Geography

ROBIN BLASER, ROBERT CREELEY, BOBBIE LOUISE HAWKINS, AND MICHAEL ONDAATJE
June 17, 1999

✷   ✷   ✷

BOBBIE LOUISE HAWKINS: This is a very exciting event. The three persons, other than myself, that you see at this table are three of the most wonderful people in the world. In wanting to arrive at something for this panel that couldn't be called a theme, which in fact would not instantly preclude the possibility of human behavior on the part of these people, we managed to come up with "personal geography," or put it "geography both personal and literary." All of us have traveled extensively and it has informed our writing as well, obviously, as our lives. Robin, would you like to begin?

ROBIN BLASER: This is my country. I was born in Denver, Colorado in 1925. I was hidden here by the Sacred Heart nuns who are Jesuit sisters of the Jesuit society. Smart and dangerous people. For five months I was a little Jesuit. I then left Denver only to return when Naropa invited me. After that I am in Idaho. There is a Blaser, Idaho. And I suggest that you go look at it, it's by the Pont Neuf River. If you look in the *Rand McNally Atlas,* you'll find it listed with no population. There are two shacks there at some distance apart, humming with machinery of some kind. Probably, I suppose to change tracks or something, because it is a railroad that runs right there by the river. One is called East Blaser and the other one, West Blaser. It is not far from Bancroft, Idaho, named for the wonderful historian, and that place is nearly a ghost town. But there is a graveyard there in which my great-great-grandmother and my grandmother are buried. All of this is in my poetry somewhere. You know, the pioneers. So this is my country. And we lived in places during the Depression. 1925 goes directly into the depths of Depression. My grandmother worked as a telegrapher on the railroad for Union Pacific. So we lived by the railroad very, very often, in fact between the tracks sometimes where she used to, as a telegrapher, send the messages by Morse code. They don't do that anymore. There were hoops made out of bamboo—bent bamboo—which would hold the messages out to the train as the steam engines blast by. Me holding her skirts. I was not exactly welcomed by my father. It took him five months to come to terms with me and so I was often sent off to my grandmother.

Now, Orchard, Idaho is an interesting place to go. There is nothing there except a water tower, which amazed me because it dripped. Can you imagine in the middle of a sage brush desert there would be frogs. And I have still not answered in my poetry where the frogs came from. So, you see this is my country. When I had a so-called nervous breakdown, which was at fourteen and I'm certain it was sexually centered, they sent me off to a sheep ranch in Wyoming where I thoroughly enjoyed being with the cowboys who were very kind to me and they decided that I should wrangle the cows. Now I was very good at that. No one told me until after I had left that the horse did it. It was a wrangling horse that knew exactly how to bring the cows home and they wouldn't have needed me at all. It was my first experience of a kind of genius. Wrangling the cows.

I could ride a horse. I was rather good. My father kept palominos in late years and then he got lazy and fed them sugar. So we had fat palominos and they're not particularly good to ride. This was in Twin Falls which is right on the Snake River on Martin's Canyon. If you can imagine that. And there's a second canyon that goes around it, Roxbury Canyon, and so the canyon is a wonderful one. Now as to when did I become a writer? I was writing even then and nearly always. My mother fixed them up. So they're really poems by the two of us published in the local paper, the *Twin Falls Tribune* it was then called. And she was better at writing than I was. I remember when I wrote "The Barn Story," it was the barn talking when Christ was born.

I was a reader all the time. There's one thing—when you're not the welcomed child, you learn to read early. It's very good for you. And then you spend all your time reading. And then they think you're a good boy. I was not a good boy in any sense. But I would do my music lessons like nobody's business, years and years and years of it. And all of this, I'm trying to say, all of this becomes grounds for the sense of measure, and the language. What I find kind of fascinating, I don't know about all of you, but there we were, not in the 20th century, except for the Depression. Never got there. I was trying to go there and I was not going to go far with carefully rhymed little poems and being a very good little Catholic boy even though I was considered a bastard. And the writing would probably have stopped except for winding up in 1945 in Berkeley. There was a lot of drama. So anyway this is all training for writing. Very seriously.

Well I went to Northwestern. I received my little fellowship in Chicago, Evanston. And then finally the College of Idaho. That's in Caldwell, Idaho. And the dean called my mother and said, "He sticks out like a sore thumb. Send him someplace else." I don't know what that meant and I like to guess. Anyway I went to Berkeley. There I ran into many, many marvelous people. I have trouble with those histories of Berkeley, San Francisco Renaissance. The term *Renaissance* comes from

Rexroth naming the Berkeley Renaissance. Then it was picked up by Ferlinghetti who termed it the San Francisco Renaissance from that term. Berkeley is a university that is a town of its own. As a consequence, I have the experience of the university as a commuter. This is a very different thing. What they did in Buffalo, New York was, they had Buffalo downtown, this wonderful place downtown, then they had the student riots and they decided to get an architect and fix it so you could never gather anyplace and they moved it seventeen miles out of town. And there it is seventeen miles out of town, dour brick. It is a dour kind of brick. And anyway I get to Berkeley, San Francisco and then this was of course the meeting among all those wonderful people in a university town, where you lived in the university itself. There are, we call them, using German to be funny, *ewiger Student*, these are students who never leave. Robert Duncan's Greek tutor, and my Greek tutor, was a girl from Puerto Rico who didn't like anybody to know that. She was Spanish, she had superb Greek, but she couldn't pass astronomy. So I went in and took the astronomy test and got caught. Well fortunately they didn't expel me. I don't know why. But anyway, she never got a degree of any kind, and we both had this high-level classicist bravado community to be remembered forever. Well that's where the writing began. There was a group called the Writers' Conference where we all met. And this went very well. Duncan's *Venice Poem* was given there and some of my very early tentative stuff was given there and Jack Spicer's beginnings, these wonderful early poems that came out in a little volume called *One Night Stand*. All of this. And Robert Duncan was seven years older and he'd been in New York and you know what New York does to you. Well, he had all the sophistication in the world. He'd run into the surrealists, he got it all. It just began to flow. William Carlos Williams's *Paterson* was just appearing. The *Four Quartets* of Eliot just appearing. All this stuff. And we met in groups, Jack and Duncan and I would read these out loud. And so on and so forth. Duncan set up a thing at his place Strathmorton, which was an old house where they all rented a place because you couldn't study 20th-century poetry properly at all in Berkeley. It was all set up there. We read *Finnegans Wake* together. It took forty people to get through a few pages. So the writing then begins at this point. The challenge began with Wallace Stevens for most of us and then it moves forward and you begin to try to write. And you begin to try to be in the 20th century, or at least I do. Duncan was already in the 20th century. I don't think Jack was in the same sense at all. He didn't know the writing. He didn't know the writers. And all of it had to flow in. And it becomes like a, what Olson called, time is the life of space—you suddenly realize that your whole space became alive as the time was spent on this stuff. All the time has been on this stuff.

The only piece that's kept from this period is in *The Holy Forest,* inside a poem called "Lake of Souls." And it's called "Christ in Heaven Dancing." You see there already a little problem with Western myths going on in my young and uninformed mind. I stuck it in there because I sort of like it still. And it was reviewed in the university magazine and the reviewer, Keith Jones, now a union leader in California, he reviewed it with great pleasure and the student newspaper made fun of it all and said, "Keith Jones dance with me." They were picking up on it. So there. That's the story of the first poem I want anybody to know about.

MICHAEL ONDAATJE: I also wanted to be a cowboy. And the problem was I was born and lived in Sri Lanka, which didn't have too many cowboys. But there was a rumor of cowboys. And in the back of *Billy the Kid* there's a photograph of what looks like an eight-year-old boy wearing a very dashing cowboy outfit with emeralds on the belt and stuff like that, which was me.

What's very interesting about how one becomes a writer, or how one becomes anything, is how there's this kind of leapfrogging thing that happens when you grow up in one place and your real brothers and sisters are five thousand miles away. And maybe your ideal teachers as well. I think that's what happened with me. One has to travel to find your home. I was in Sri Lanka a few years ago and there's a wonderful dancer there named Chitrasena, he's now about eighty. And he really revolutionized dance in Sri Lanka. He had turned it from performances done by foreigners to much more local, regional dance. I asked him what was his biggest influence, what made him a dancer. And he said it was reading the autobiography of Isadora Duncan. And I thought—this is the most amazing thing. Here's a dancer who had never seen her dance, but somehow through a book he had witnessed a possibility of what he could do. And I think this is so common in us as writers. This happens for any kind of artist, with any art form. I think geography is quite surreal, just as history is.

So I was born in Sri Lanka. I lived there until I was eleven. I had no idea I wanted to be a writer until I was about nineteen. The idea seemed to be impossible. It wasn't even an idea in my head, or a desire. I didn't know what I wanted to be. I went to school in England when I was about eleven, which was sort of a tradition. If you were middle class in Sri Lanka you went off to England and you came back and you took over the family law firm. And I think our generation is the first one that didn't really go back. So I went to school in England, which I didn't like at all but when I was about eighteen came to Canada. And it was there really that I finally discovered English at university and writing, mainly because I had a wonderful teacher who would read Robert Browning at the drop of a hat— just read it and perform it for you. So all his students wanted to be Robert

Browning, wanted to write dramatic monologues and I think that's when I started writing, at that point. That's what happened to me.

It seems to me that this is similar to the way that dancer and Isadora Duncan connected up. What is most interesting and most moving is this dialogue that happens in these leaps across geography. And not just in terms of geography, but also history. I was at the Sackler Gallery in Washington and I saw a sort of bamboo drawing that had been done many years ago. It had been based on a stone carving that had been done three hundred years earlier and had been shattered by a foreign Emperor. And this artist had gone there, and for a year he stood there and did his version of this broken stone. So that kind of dialogue between generations, with more than three hundred years between people, fifty years apart, twenty years apart, is the most moving thing in terms of what the geography is.

ROBERT CREELEY: Two weeks ago in New York I met a curiously engaging man who was head of a financial services organization in New York. Apparently he had been hired by Buffalo's city government to do a report on that city's situation. He told me that after finishing their review, they had come to the conclusion: "There's only one thing wrong with Buffalo. It's in the wrong place!" He said that actually it's not part of New York at all. It would be much more aptly joined to Canada—or to Ohio and the Middle West, which was really its defining company. As things were, it was at the farthest possible reach from its active financial funding center, New York itself. So he thought if one could just move it down to some place like Poughkeepsie, its troubles would be over.

So there one was and is, in Buffalo, myself since 1966, in some particularly continuing manner. Tonight the Buffalo Sabres are playing in the fifth game of their playoffs with the Dallas Stars, who wiped out Colorado a few weeks ago. It isn't just "Jack, the Giant Killer," but Buffalo's economy is so defined by that game. For instance, the payroll of the Buffalo Sabres is about one-twentieth of that of the Dallas Stars. And that example is seemingly endless. Buffalo is that kind of place. In the city now, on every street corner, there's some terrific public insistence, Go *Sabres!* The place is in a beautifully manic mood. The last game was just wonderful in its heroic determination and tender civic pride. So that is a fact of being somewhere, living somewhere, in a place with others.

I taught a seminar, like they say, this spring. It had a curious title: "Poetry as Public." It used just four texts. One was Eric Havelock's *The Muse Learns to Write,* which gives a quick, succinct, and beautifully demonstrated sense of the shift from an oral tradition to a literary tradition. An extraordinarily sweet book. The author is eighty-five at the time he's writing it and he's waited all those years before summarizing his opinions. He feels they would have made an awful mess in the whole field of classical studies, had he published them earlier, just that they were divergent and provocative, as one says. But he now recognizes that he's beyond such argument and so he writes this terrific beautiful book. And in it he says such simply *clarifying* things! He asks the reader, for example, to think of what happens when one asks "what it means . . ." Someone is saying something. And then some other, like Socrates, says, "What do you mean by that?" The first was talking but suddenly there's this peculiar displacing "objectivity"—specious, ugly, and distracting, with no pertinence whatsoever. What you mean by what you mean?

I think why I held to poetry as a veritable lifeline is that in poetry "meaning what you mean" is what you're meaning. There's no other "meaning" but "what you mean." Which goes for everyone else as well, happily enough.

Also in the same course we finished up with "The House That Jack Built," which is, I must say, a beautiful poem. At that point everybody was bringing in lots of Jack Spicer's work, it became really extraordinary. It all became so specific, reading what Jack was saying and following the ways he was thinking. The presumption, of course, concerning poetry, is that one somehow owns that which one makes. But poets, I'd hope, would rarely share such an assumption. I remember Robert Duncan saying years ago, a poem that satisfies one's imagination gives a great feeling of elation. "Here, I've written this poem!" But after a very short time indeed that fact's not a remarkably interesting thing, at least not the "hey, I can write a poem" part. Poems in themselves are what is interesting, not that I, you, or someone else is writing them. So, coincidently, just at the end of this business in Buffalo it happened that we got to my part of the scene. Charlie Keil, a very brilliant old-time person particularly involved with musical instruments and cultures from all over the world, put it very simply: "Music is *not* a noun."

RB: Great!

RC: And I thought, poetry isn't a noun either, come to think of it. It certainly doesn't become a noun, it isn't a thing, it's an activity. So that, as Christopher Small would say of music, it's not music, it's *musicking*. It's the act of musicking. That really made great sense to me. The confusions I've had even with the word, "music," suddenly became quite clear. But it had equally to do with how is it that we have thousands of people making poems, writing poems, but very damn few reading them. *Making* them is a great deal more fun than watching someone else do it, or then trying to figure what they've done. *We're* doing something, not producing objects of discrete order. Again, it tied in with that sense of writing one poem all one's life, as Whitman, much like Turner, who kept painting on a canvas even after it was hung in a museum, or Duncan, or any of us for that matter. It's something we're *doing*. This was to me the wonder. And again in my own thinking, or life, or Habit, it's almost impossible for me to secure any sense of what it is or has to be. As we're talking or thinking about it, it's always amazing to me how ranging and diverse the sense of possibility is, which it actually permits. As I said, no one reads poems anymore. Well, no one ever did in the manner presumed, and no one ever had a particular object he or she had fixed as "poetry," It's forever what is being heard or read or remembered. It's always part of something more. It's always an activity rather than a "subject" that can be secured. I think in that way, it's "doing something."

Again, thinking of place, as Michael was talking about it and Robin also, I was the youngest in my family and my father died when I was about five. He had been married once before, so I had two half-brothers, Tom and Phil, from that previous marriage, whom I never really knew except in a very minor way. So I had a sense always of being in a curious "displaced" place. I grew up in the country but my father's actual life was in the city.

A few years ago, my sister Helen and I went to see the house, which I would have come back to as a baby, on Mount Auburn Street in Watertown, Massachusetts. My sister's memory was incredible. In her mid-seventies she could still remember the license plate of the car and the phone number of the house back to about 1922 or '23. And she talked her way into our old house, charming the present occupant, showing her where this had been, where that. And as we're coming away—we're now wanting to go over to Belmont, where my grandfather's, my father's father's, farm had been—and I suddenly see a street sign saying "Common Street" and I remember the poem I have called "I" that goes:

> His house was numbered 375
> Common St . . .

So I just on impulse turned left on Common Street and, sure enough, it took me right over to Belmont and put me right on the backside of where my grandfather's farm must have been.

Still it was a world that I never actually found a place in. If I *go home*, I go to my mother's family, although I never was there either, except in the aforesaid displacement, as we were all by then living in Massachusetts. Nonetheless the real home that I have as an emotional or social person is probably Maine, where my wife says they can understand my jokes. I don't even have to think about it. I just feel completely at ease there.

I suppose what I'm trying in a curious way to say is that I'm fascinated by the way that particularly Americans, I was thinking of Maine specifically, how we have, it seems, to invent the whole condition as though one had to play baseball with no clue that there's some kind of a ball you use and some kind of a bat. That is, with no particular tradition or information, one contrives to make the thing out of whole cloth. I feel as though I've done that. And I've felt that that was what I seemed to have to offer. This curiously homemade act.

But I loved it that poetry, of all the things one could humanly do, seemed to have the most capability or flexibility; it seemed the most provident and securing of such need. "How to get said what must be said . . ." Those words that "came to me, based solely on air," as Williams writes in age. Or Allen Ginsberg's "some of my time now given to nothingness"— this aspect, or this fact, of being, of poetry as act.

RB: Amen. I was just picking up on "making it out of whole cloth." This is a wonderful term. I was whispering to Bob what Duncan would say about the West Coast—that we made it out of whole cloth. That there was nothing to go on. That relates to my sense—you're not in the 20th century, so what are you going to do? Maybe you're writing wonderful things in that manner of Shelley, but it's not whatever this whole cloth thing is, when it is your own activity. In fact, I think that relates to Spicer's sense of dictation that you didn't own the language that you didn't own the poem and certainly there's not an ownership in activity. As it's in life.

BLH: When I was living in Japan there was a sense in Japanese painting that if the painting was imperfect enough you could sign it. But the point is, the painting was in fact a manifested thing of its own. You no longer had the right to sign it because then it was its own and you had simply allowed it to arrive.

RC: I very much believe that. I remember one time, William Carlos Williams said there was a poem of mine that he liked, "The Rose," that he felt was remarkable in what it accomplished, but then he said, of course, we know when something like this happens, the person writing is not responsible. For me that's the point. One knows when one gets "there," so to speak, it's no longer a "me" thinking, "I will do this or that."

Again, I was always in some way embarrassed that what for people was most effective, let's say, in my own poems was that which took the least possible effort. If and as it really worked, there wasn't any effort at all. I didn't have to revise. I didn't have to do anything. All I seemed to have to do was just write it down. I don't know why that's the case and I don't care. It's a little late for that.

MO: Going back to that cloth issue, leaping from geography to geography, I just finished the biography of Truffaut, and then I read *Easy Riders, Raging Bulls,* which is about the American movie industry in the sixties and seventies. You can't believe these people come from the same planet. No one would want to pick up the collected letters of Steven Spielberg, or anything like that. But Truffaut at fifteen, wrote three or four letters a day, read two or three books a week and saw two movies a day and had a job and went to a jail and had syphilis by the time he was eighteen. So there was a full life going on, which I don't think you can say of some American directors. You can see that great gap there is between one kind of civilization and another one. It seemed to me an example of different kinds of effects of geography.

BLH: You know this topic came about because Bob and I were talking about what we could do this afternoon. Every time I'd bring up something he'd say, "Oh, no," and I said, "Well what do you think would be interesting?" And he said, "If we talked about geography we could find out why Michael ended up in Canada." How did he get from Sri Lanka to Canada and what was the drive? And what did you mean by that Michael?

MO: My brother had come to Canada before me and said, "Well, come here, this is a great place." It was something as simple as that. So I came to Canada. There wasn't any kind of vision that I should go west. As I said I couldn't imagine being a writer in England and Sri Lanka. In Sri Lanka there was an amazing oral tradition, but there were very few books about the place. So when I was writing *Running in the Family,* one of the things I wanted to do was to try and translate some of the verbal stories into my book to give it that sense. I've been working on a book now that's set in Sri Lanka and it's been very difficult because it is about a community that has nothing to do with the community that I grew up in. So it's much more tentative, much more research. Trying to write about a place you grew up in but about a community you were not really a part of. It's been very difficult.

BLH: Some time back I was loaned a book by Jack Greene which he said belonged to Lisa Trank, but which he was intent on having me read. And they very decently then gave it to me. What's the name of that guy? William Calvin. And what's the name of the book? *Cerebral Symphony.* In that book there's a description of a one-celled organism that lives its life by flopping. It flops and it flops and it flops and then there's an atmosphere of sustenance. And when it arrives at sustenance it stays there until there is no feeling of sustenance, at which point it flops and that's its major description. It flops into what it needs and then it stays there until it's used up and then it flops some more. And as I read that I thought—that's the way I've lived my life. It's like that line of Michael's, you move to find your home, you move to arrive at your home. You move to sustenance. And I mean within a situation like this where people in the tent here are really hoping that people are going to tell them how to write so they can finally just get on with it. I think that what you will find is going to happen here is that people are more and more going to say that what you're doing is the job description and that the insecurities and the flop of it are pretty much what you're now dedicated to as a lifestyle. So that if you have any question of why your parents have questions, that just may be it. They think when you're flopping you're just flopping.

RB: Well, I could say that the only problem with flopping is there are a lot of obstacles. This is leading me to ask Michael . . . One wonderful day a postcard arrived from Michael and it was Ganesh from some place in Sri Lanka. Wasn't it a chalk Ganesh on a tree trunk? And there were offerings in front of it. Well it set me off to find out exactly what Ganesh would mean. And my own sense is the guardianship of Ganesh—now thank you, Michael, very much—Ganesh is the guardian of all obstacles so that one needs in terms of writing at any rate, it's a constant journey through obstacles, in my sense. And I mean by that even the fundamental musicality of the language. That one has to pick it up and it's an awfully good idea I think to be in touch with the musicians. And so on and the little companions, or big companions or whatever. And if you do have a cliché it's there because you know it's a cliché and you value the cliché of it. So I would ask as a writer, if you don't mind, or a flopper, that I have my Ganesh. I gave my friend David one I very particularly like. It's a Ganesh who is a child with the elephant trunk—Michael would be best to describe Ganesh. He's playing with a ball and running. So he's stretched out, the ball caught in the elephant trunk of this wonderful spirit, guardianship of the thing. You keep it in your office with you, don't you? David's a social worker where there's lots of floppers and flops. Would you mind saying something about the wonder of Ganesh?

MO: I don't know much more than the fact that he's the guardian of the obstacles. I did see a great Ganesh recently in Washington. They have a Goddess show, which is a remarkable show and one of them in that show was a Ganesh being suckled by his mother, which I've never seen before. It was very sweet.

A friend of mine is an architect in Sri Lanka. He said that eighty percent of all architecture is loitering and I think that for me as a writer I feel that loitering is a very central necessity, especially starting something. It's a sense of just hanging around and picking up doors and going to another house. One of the things about architecture in Sri Lanka is there is no *then* and *now*. Everything is present.

BLH: When I first married and went to Denmark I was living in a house that had English-language books and magazines because my first husband's brother-in-law was teaching English at the university and one of the things which I found there to my delight was a copy of the *Harvard Wake,* which was called "the E. E. Cummings number." And I adored E. E. Cummings—he's one of the poets I memorized extensively and another one was D. H. Lawrence. So I was capable of quoting a lot of D. H. Lawrence and E. E. Cummings, and so I got to read not only the E. E. Cummings but there was an unpublished poem in there by D. H. Lawrence. Years went by and when I met Robert Creeley it turned out that he and two friends of his, Race Newton and Buddy Berlin, published that particular issue of the *Harvard Wake.* Which brings me to the sense that within all this business of traveling you also arrive at the friends who matter to you for the rest of your life and those two friends were in Albuquerque, New Mexico, which is why you came to Albuquerque, New Mexico, isn't it?

RC: Yes, yes it is.

BLH: You told me once that when you were at Harvard, Kenneth Koch invited you up to his room to drink "a bit of sherry" and to listen to him read you a poem of his. How did he create this event? Why did he think you'd want to hear it?

RC: We were sympathetic to one another as aspiring writers. He was a very shy and he had an extraordinary stutter. He'd typed these five or six poems immaculately on this bond "onion skin" paper and he sat me down with them and he poured me a little glass of sherry and he then retired. He went out of the room for a discreet period while I mused on his poetry, and then he returned, and I said, "Oh, those are very interesting." We actually became very particular friends in a curious way.

Thinking of that time, there was another friend, Jacob Leed. He's writing now an interesting memoir of his growing up and of his time at college, in which part he recalls me in a way that is interesting to me because I had no objective sense of who I was then at all. He remembers that unlike himself and other friends I took everything not so much personally but particularly. I didn't seem to follow the disposition of the class or the teacher, or any qualifying attitude. It wasn't that I was protesting. But until I came to be able myself to think, "This is interesting," I didn't accept any relation to it on faith, so to speak. So that I took things much more seriously, much more energetically, than possibly others. We all used to sit and drink beer for hours and we'd end up yelling into the night. Jake also remembers the curious displacement of the gang when I suddenly stopped college entirely. I was thrown out. But I made no effort to return.

It was certainly not easy, as you, Bobbie, will remember in Albuquerque, being thirty plus and having no viable degree. It's hardly a recommendation. Carl Rakosi here once at Naropa, just before we were to head out for our respective workshops, said in a kind of thoughtful musing, "Well, the last thing they need is encouragement." In an old-fashioned sense it's absolutely true. It's nice to get encouragement but I can recall years and years of plugging along without it—or much else to make clear what I was up to. My mother would say, "I'd like to think Bob could get a job if he had to."

"Poet" is not a very simply defined occupation. You can check it out in the *Encyclopedia Britannica.* There's an interesting discussion there on whether it constitutes a profession at all. The numbers of persons supporting themselves through the exercise of poetry as a profession are small indeed. Finally, if you look in the dictionary, it says, "A poet writes poetry" and "poetry is what a poet writes." It's a completely circular definition.

RB: I love it! I love it!

RC: I love that. Years ago someone said after somebody else's reading, "That next to last poem you read, was that a real poem or did you just make it up yourself?" You might consider that, friends and neighbors. That's the question to ask yourselves. "Is that a real poem or did I just make it up myself?" What *is* a real poem? Bang!

★ ★ ★ ★ ★ ★

Ancestral Presences

★ ★ ★ ★ ★ ★

Symbiosis

PETER WARSHALL
June 13, 2003

This is a presentation of the Maniacal Naturalist Society, of which we have two fine members here, Jane Wodening and Jack Collom, and they're all for people who think that all beings are equally evolved. The 3.8-billion-year-old bacteria or the 5-million-year-old human beings are equally evolved. There's no more hierarchy where you have more consciousness than I do, you have more intelligence than I do, you have more reason to be existent than I do, we are an incredible minority and in fact the Maniacal Naturalist Society does not exist. But I am really happy to have both members here of our nonexistent society.

There's going to be a lot of information I'm going to lay on you. I've never done this talk before and there's going to be a lot of dates like billions of years and billions of that and don't kind of worry about it. I mean don't start taking notes on it. The reason I'm doing this talk is because this week is about alternate communities and I'm going to give a really different alternate view of community because it's going to be a 4.6-billion-year view of the whole earth.

The tradition I'm talking in is the tradition of people I've known in Africa, especially in the mid-sixties when I was with Kum Bushmen, near Botswana. It's the hunter-gatherer tradition of sitting around at night, and sometimes there's a fire, hopefully there's enough wood for a fire, and just telling the day's events. So you're just talking through the day's events, they're just kind of "just so stories," like Kipling's stories. In this case we're going to be sitting around the sun, and the stories will be about the suchness of the planet.

There's no metaphysical language involved. You're just trying to tease out the truths that are always true by looking and living with other beings on the planet. And it's especially against "truth by repetition" truth, which seems to be the most prominent kind of truth in America right now. If you say it enough times it's got to be true.

The story really has three heroines. It's going to start with Beatrix Potter, move on to Lynn Margulis, and end up with Gaia, the Earth Goddess. And the theme is symbiosis. Symbiosis literally means "together living." It's really about biological companionship, other ways of translating it would be living embracing lives, or in-contact beings, or inside-each-other creatures, or at the same time going along with sentient existence. It is the story of existential interdependence. By that I mean if any one of the two life forms or three life forms that live together disappears, the other is gone also. It's not functional stuff like most marriages where you can leave it and find another husband or wife, or another partner. If one of you separate, both are gone. It's an existential interdependence.

Symbiosis, like courtship and mating, brings previously evolved beings together in new partnerships. It's about self-propelling creativity on the planet. And that's really the planet's view, when you bring disparate beings together you have a kind of creativity that propels itself more and more.

As part of the Maniacal Naturalist Society I have to give one little background. And that's about our only character, which is life itself. And let me say that it's weird that people don't really think about what life is. So here's the Maniacal Naturalist view of it. Life is a local phenomenon in the multiverse. If you say, "Praised be God, King of the Universe," that's not part of the Maniacal Naturalist Society. We don't even know that there's only one universe. As far as we know universes could be next to universes could be next to universes in a kind of eternal boundless foam. Like big bubbles and each universe could have a different gravity, could have a different speed of light, could have a different Avogadro's number, could have a different number of elements. And so it's the multiverse and we are a very local phenomenon in that multiverse. Life is made of star-stuff. About 4.6 billion years ago a supernova blew up and the pieces of that supernova are the pieces we are made of. So we are remnants of the supernova.

Life is also the present expression of a historical and past chemistry. Basically there's a great novel by Philip K. Dick in which human beings walk around like leaky canteens and that's what we are, we're watery beings that were slightly enclosed and we leak all the time all this water. We're kind of permeable castles of space-time. We also leak a lot of heat. So life in this way fights to maintain its heat at a constant level. And only by maintaining its heat at a constant level, which was sometimes called metabolism or the fire of life, can we also sustain creation. If we're too cold, creation is dead, if we're too hot, creation burns up. So life struggles to maintain its own integrity in terms of both heat and water.

And finally life is more sensitive and more intricate and baroque in its manner of connecting, configuring, composing creations. Those are the three C's of life, connecting, configuring, and composing. And it's more so than all the nonlife chemistry that existed before it.

If we look at life as a community, it is many beings living together. For about 3.8 billion years there have been merger manias going on. These are very fallible attractions. They're kind of like love in that some are for mere moments and some have lasted quite a long time, a couple billion years. But they're always fallible, as this story is going to be, because they are composed of other beings.

Finally, life on this planet has been exuberant as well as intricate. We all know the poem that begins "God be praised for dappled things / things of different color. . ." The Gerard Manley Hopkins poem. It's the greatest poem ever written to biodiversity, actually. And so what I'm going to do is give you what's happened to Gerard Manley Hopkins. He's become "believe it or not" stories. *The Guinness Book of World Records.* All the weird bestiaries. All the field guides and scientific monographs about animals and plants and lichen. And so I'm actually going to tell you those stories.

And so finally life is ultimately, now, at this moment, an expression of light. Of solar radiation. As we used to say in the Maniacal Naturalist Society, "of de-light." So you've gotten the character. It's local, it's star-stuff, it's historic, it's water, it leaks, it's sensitive, it's intricate, it is an evolving composite of critters, and it's exuberant.

It hasn't been easy for humans to accept this truth. The story really begins in 1850 with Alfred Lord Tennyson, when one of his close friends, a young poet friend of his, Arthur Hallam, committed suicide. And somehow Arthur Hallam had been reading about evolution and when he died Alfred Lord Tennyson wrote, one of the more famous poems, called "In Memoriam," which really was worried about the cruelty that life or nature has.

> Are God and Nature then at strife,
> That Nature lends such evil dreams?
> So careful of the type she seems,
> [the word *type* in here means species, group of animals, and again this is written for Arthur]
> So careless of the single life;
>
> That I, considering everywhere
> Her secret meaning in her deeds,
> And finding that of fifty seeds
> She often brings but one to bear,
>
> . . . .
>
> "So careful of the type?" but no.
> From scarped cliff and quarried stone
> She cries, "A thousand types are gone:
> I care for nothing, all shall go.
>
> . . . .

Man, her last work, who seem'd so fair,
Such splendid purpose in his eyes,
Who roll'd the psalm to wintry skies,
Who built him fanes of fruitless prayer,

Who trusted God was love indeed
And love Creation's final law—
Tho' Nature, red in tooth and claw
With ravine, shriek'd against his creed—

And that became the phrase that still goes on about Darwin's attitude about nature. "Tho' Nature, red in tooth and claw / With ravine, shriek'd against his creed." Against love and against the creation of love.

So is that story true? Did Tennyson get it right? Well, this is the story about the reverse plot which says that many discrete loves, many discrete attractions that punctuated moments, created a diversity that boggles the mind. And the moments I'm going to show you today created magnificent new forms of living.

The struggle to bring symbiosis as the central tenet of poetics and ethics away from Mr. Tennyson starts with my Joan of Arc, my Beatrix, not Dante's, which is Beatrix Potter. She was born in a pompous and prejudiced Victorian society. Because she was a girl she was not sent to school. And she snuck out of her house with a little pad and went to the Natural History Museum in London, which was right in her neighborhood. She drew everything. She became shyer, she became more retiring. She drew the gills of mushrooms, the gills of fish, she drew anything she could draw in that museum. And then she was given a watercolor set and started to do it all over again, this time in watercolors.

In the summers she was taken up to the Lake District and she met a postman and the postman was in love with fungus and mosses. And they became the greatest friends. And so she showed her pictures to the postman, who criticized her and told her how she could make better pictures of fungi and mushrooms, and her uncle noticed that she really loved natural history. Her uncle was Sir Henry Roscoe, one of the great chemists of England at that time, and gave her for her birthday a microscope. She started to do even more drawings. And she confirmed a suggestion by a very ridiculed and weird Swiss botanist that lichen was not a lowly plant but instead a fusion of two fully evolved beings, an algae and a fungus that had merged into a third being.

After she found out that this was actually two distinct beings fused together, Sir Henry said she should give this as a paper at the Linnaean Society, which is where Darwin had given his paper. There was one small problem, women were barred from the Linnaean Society, and they were even barred from open meetings, they couldn't even go and listen. Well Sir Henry, this is a real Dickensian story, this is the period of Dickens, and Sir Henry Roscoe says, "I will go and give the paper myself and they can't say no because I've been knighted." So he won the right to give her paper, and oddly the proceedings of the time he gave that paper completely disappeared and no one has any record of what was said. But Beatrix in her journal, which has become encrypted, so that the Victorian scientific community can't read it, discusses what Sir Henry had told her, which is that most people in the audience went "tut-tut," and smirked, and said that lichen could not possibly be two different creatures because, and this reflects Gay Liberation and you've heard it before, "Lichen was an unnatural union, and therefore couldn't possibly exist."

Well, Sir Henry, the good uncle, would not give up and took her beautiful drawings, and I couldn't get any pictures of them, which is in itself interesting, to the Royal Gardens at Kew, where the head of the Royal Gardens had another great Dickensian name, W. H. Thistleton Dire. The dire thistles in great quantity. Well, he took Beatrix over there, and Beatrix writes in her journal, again this is where we get all this information, she was a very good journal keeper. She was suspicious that anything good was going to happen because all the women who worked in Kew were either required not to wear dresses, not to wear blouses, but only to wear knickerbockers. And every woman was required to wear the same knickerbocker. And so she writes that she thinks this isn't going to work out. Well, she goes in and W. H. Thistleton Dire is puffing cigarettes and won't even look at her. And he won't look at the portfolio. And he talks looking straight at her uncle, and boasts that his hyacinths are more beautiful than the hyacinths you can find in Holland, and doesn't that prove that the Royal Gardens are better than any other place. And finally her uncle points to the beautiful drawings she does and he says, "Well, maybe Cambridge would like to look at this." And he never opens it. Well, she leaves, and she writes in her journal that this will be the end of her encounter with grown-up science. And that's what she calls it. And she leaves that and moves finally to the Lake Country where instead we get Peter Rabbit.

So she ends up in the Lake Country writing about Peter Rabbit and Jemima Puddleduck and Squirrel Nutkin, and they took the place of her becoming a famous lichenologist. Finally in 1929, H. G. Wells and Julian Huxley get together and write a book called *The Science of Life,* where they cite Beatrix Potter and agree with her that indeed this isn't a lowly plant, on a lower echelon of the chain of being, but is actually a fusion of two. This is the triumph of symbiosis, led by her. Although it took until 1967 when William Findlay, another guy, big scientist, finally took her paintings and drawings, which again I could not get a hold of, but seventy years after being rejected by the Kew Gardens, publishes *The Lichens of England* with her drawings in it. One hundred years later, in 1997, the Linnaean Society issued a formal apology. It's really not so bad if you consider how long it took the Vatican to apologize to Galileo for his house arrest. So the Linnaean society might be liberal from that point of view.

What was interesting is that when she did her drawings for her children's books she put lichens on all the trees, but because it was so controversial, this unnatural union she was talking about, all of her printers took the lichens off the trees. There has never been a republication of *Peter Rabbit* with the lichens on it. There is only one picture I could find which has shreds of lichens in the corners and lying around that they allowed to be left in any of her twenty-four stories that she ever wrote.

I'm just trying to give you a feeling for how resistant people were to the intimate love of the algae and the fungus. The fungus envelops the algae, or sometimes green bacteria, and keeps it hydrated. Fungi are really great at holding water in, unlike us more evolved beings, we leak our water. It also helps shield it from ultraviolet light which would otherwise break apart and bust up the algae or the green bacteria inside. And this fungus is so sensitive that it crawls all over the trees till it finds the right algae. And it tests the algae, it touches the algae. Sometimes even entering into the algae a little bit to make sure it's the right species. And if it's not it says "No, no, I've had this affair before," and goes on and the fungus keeps crawling the tree until it finds the right algae.

The algae supplies the fungus with sugar, to get high, because fungi can't make sugars. And it does that of course, by trapping light and converting water and CO_2 into sugar. So close is this turn-on of each other that if you separated out the algae and the fungus you'd have a green blob and a brownish blob with no form at all. The two come together and create new forms. This has occurred not once, but 15,000 times on the planet. Now remember that these are not species, these are two different creatures. Only 300 of the 15,000 fungi have had their bacteria and algae identified. So there's a little bit of work to be done there.

The interesting part about this symbiosis, this living together, is it protected itself all over the planet. Here we're looking at watermelon snow, pink snow, in the Antarctic. Here again the fungi is protecting the green bacteria, which are hidden under the red bacteria, from being blown up by UV and from getting too cold by creating a warm water blanket around it, the red part is the bacteria living inside the fungus. What's interesting is that this is the way that plants gained a hold on the earth. I'm going to quote Lynn Margulis here, who is kind of the inventor and modern heir of Beatrix Potter, and she says, "Symbiogenesis was the moon that pulled the tide of life from the oceanic depths to dry land and up into the air." Really for a scientist, that's a pretty nice sentence. And what happened is that out of the sea came these two creatures together, not separate, and they started to cover the earth. And they kept the ocean with them inside. The salinity of a fungus is about the salinity of the ocean. You may know also that the salinity of our eyeball is about the same salinity as the ocean. We keep the ocean in our eye because that's where we first receive light and so we already developed the filtering mechanism, the apparatus to deal with light in the ocean. So when you came out of the ocean you just kept the ocean inside your eyeball.

Well, the fungus did the same thing and it created this net, this huge net across the planet. I mean this is the first real World Wide Web. And this web of animated water, for instance just one was discovered in Michigan, to give you an idea of this web of fungus, and it is the same fungus and covers thirty-one miles. It's the biggest creature on the planet. Not the blue whale or the elephant or anything like that but this fungal mat, and they took DNA from one end to the other to make sure it was the same critter. And so, we see as this is happening we have this one first symbiosis that is creating more life on the planet and beginning to infect the planet and become a great Gaian physiology, which I'll get to. I want to say that this is for me as part of the Maniacal Natural History Society Commentary, really worked up with Kafka, who wrote that the real sin of human beings was not that they ate an apple from the tree of knowledge, but that they ignored an apple from the tree of life. And had they eaten an apple from the tree of life they would have gotten immortality, which would have given them lots of time to think about and learn things.

But he didn't look underneath the ocean, he didn't look underneath the trees. And if you looked underneath it, the tree of life and the tree of knowledge are connected by a mycorrhizal mat, by a mat of fungi, that connect all trees together, in fact without it they wouldn't live. If you hurt one tree it communicates to the next tree so that it can prepare for an attack of insects. If you break the connection by just taking a bulldozer between two trees, both trees go into stress mode because they're no longer in communication.

The fungal mat actually connects those trees, and what you have is not the image of all the Abrahamic religions, that things come out as the tree of life, with branches that go further and further apart with humans over here and elephants and frogs over there, but you actually have the image that symbiosis teaches, that life is a braided river. That things come apart, like an algae and a fungus and then come back together again. And then they spread out and come back together again. So the whole imagery of symbiosis is contrary to the prevailing religions all over the world in not thinking of life as a tree but more or less as a braided river.

So what I'm saying here is that this symbiosis is not just something to throw away or not think about. The Kafka, by the way, is in *Parables and Paradoxes,* which is one of the great books of all times, where he goes through the Bible and re-does almost every story in it.

The fungus lives inside the root of a tree, too. The fungus does the same thing, it provides a moist environment around the root. It actually breaks down some of the soil particles, takes phosphorus and calcium, the minerals you need, and gives it to the plant. The plant pumps out all these sugars and sends it down to the fungus. And together, if they are one organism or two, or however you want to look at it, that's how they feed each other. Over the billions of years, the fungus has turned into a kind of nerve net for forests so that the forests are completely communicating between the trees.

In Act II of this we leave Beatrix and enter Lynn Margulis. Lynn Margulis is one of those geniuses who at seventeen almost graduated college, at nineteen she married the astronomer Carl Sagan, who talks about billions and billions of galaxies. She's the only mother I know who writes almost all of her books with her son. I mean it's a remarkable relationship that you can go through and write a whole book with your son, and not only that, but they've written six books together. So her son, Dorian Sagan, you'll always see as the second author on Lynn's books. He kind of provides a strange New Age hippie overtone to this very scientific writing. She lives on the same farm that Emily Dickinson was born on, within a couple of hundred feet of Emily Dickinson's house. She has memorized literally two to three hundred poems of Emily Dickinson's, which also infuses her work. She is probably one of the most controversial woman scientists in the world and probably deserved a Nobel Prize, but like Beatrix has been frowned upon. And I'm going to tell her story. Lynn's a good friend, so this is also an homage to Lynn.

About 3.8 billion years ago the planet was really chthonian: sulfuric fumes were coming out, it was overly hot, it was over-radiated by UV light that kept on battering everything that tried to be life, it was fermenting these "when shall we three meet again" Macbethian beginnings, all the waters were too acidic. And in the middle of that, came the staff of life, and that's the word "bacteria." *Bacteria* means "staff," it's the Greek word for staff, also the word baculum comes from it, which is the little staff that monkeys have in their cocks so that they can get hard-ons, flip their cocks any time they want. So baculum, bacteria, they all mean little short hard things. What we're trying to say here is that the staff of life is not bread, but bacteria. And these bacteria were pretty amazing. What you're looking at there, the line down the center is DNA. The little squiggles coming off it is RNA, and they were loose in the cells of bacteria, which were single-celled. They had no nucleus, they just had RNA and DNA all over the place. There were no distinctions. They had no idea what sex was about. Here is the closest to what you could call sex in a bacteria, where the bacteria on the top has sent down little channels to the two bacteria on the bottom. They've been attacked by a virus. So what the bacteria on the top is doing is giving them new genetic material, hopefully the right genetic material so they can fight the virus.

So all of them get together, and you could have literally hundreds of millions of bacteria exchanging genes back and forth. In fact you don't even have to do it between them. If bacteria dies and the DNA gets into the water, another bacteria could come over and just absorb it through their skin. So this is another big kind of genetic soup that spread all over the planet. The more people tried to study bacteria the less and less they were able to distinguish them, so for instance when you take antibiotics one of the main problems is that the more antibiotics you give the more these little bacteria go around and exchange genes with each other until they can fight that antibiotic, so an antibiotic now only lasts for four to five years and you've got to find another one. The genes just get exchanged again and it goes on and on.

Notice everything here is being done laterally. It's not being done through what we call generational time. It's not even clear if it's not one big microcosmos all over the planet that way. But something happened that was really interesting. A kind of bacteria that had a tail on it invaded the other bacteria to try and eat it out and it infected it. These are known as spirochetes. *Spiro* means "coils" or "whirls" and *chetes* means "long-haired." Like a Medusa's rope-ness. Lots of Medusa snaky things. And in fact it's a speedster little bacteria and it goes around snake-like in its corkscrew shape and it likes viscous places. We're still in the chthonian time, there's no oxygen around. It likes slime, it likes mucus, it likes really gooey muds. This creature goes into one of those bacteria and it gets stuck in the cell wall. It does this 100 times and both of them die or both of them get along or both of them don't but when they finally reach this truce we have a new animal, not an animal created by natural selection, not an animal created by mutations, we have an animal created by fusion. These animals have this new tail on it, and that tail comes in nine little circuits around it and two in the middle, which is its characteristic. And what's weird about it is that it gives mobility to animals that just had that one flagellum and weren't running around. It's a beautiful word, it's called *undulipodia* which means "a wave foot" or "a watery foot." So we're looking at undulipodia and what did this lead to. Whenever we have reproduction we go back to the bacterial microcosmos. Sperm's tails are the same, they're undulipodia. If you go into the fallopian tube and you're trying to get the egg to come down into the womb, you'll see all these little tails wagging around in the fallopian tube and they're called cilia. What are they? Undulipodium. If you look in the ear, and you know the ear is made up of a little liquid to tell you if you're standing straight or not, well, every time you bend, what is the water pushing? It's pushing the spirochete ancestors. If you go into your brain and look at all the nerve cells, what are they? The tail has extended out and become the neuron with the end of the tail being a little feeler and the other head of the tail becoming a nerve cell.

Again all of this came from that fusion. We are literally hard-wired in our sensitivity by this particular moment in evolution. One of the great proofs of this that is still controversial, but Lynn and I like it a lot, is that syphilis, which is a sexually transmitted disease and happens in a great deal of mucus, and so it is a favorite of the spirochetes, is caused by a spirochete. There are three stages of syphilis, I'm not going to go through all that, but in the third stage what happens is that the body begins to devolve. It loses its evolutionary integrity and it no longer can distinguish between the spirochete that came in and caused syphilis and your own nerve cells which are the inheritors and ancestors of the spirochetes. And the body begins to replace nerve cells. Every time one dies it moves in this new syphilis spirochete. And that's why people go crazy at the end of syphilis. That's why the king went nuts. Because in your brain and in your body one spirochete is simply replacing another. So that's the devolution of this first fusion.

The way we found this out is that the tail in the sperm or the tail in the cilia in the throat has its own separate DNA. Not the DNA of your own body. It has the remnants of the DNA of its original ancestors stuck right at the point where the head went through the cell membrane. Lynn is just brilliant.

If you think that was controversial, when sperm land on the female parts of flowers, three of them get their undulipodia going and they go down to the womb, and rather than have one sperm like we do with one egg, they have three at a time. And the first one goes into the egg and fertilizes it, but then the second one that comes down, sometimes two come down, they go to the sister cell in the womb and they fertilize it together and create the seed and all the food for the sister cell and surround it so that when you break open a seed you see the little part that's going to grow into the flower and like on a bean you'll see all that food, which is to help it grow. Well, that's three different sperm that are acting together with the first one that got there and made the fertilization. Sometimes there's even a fourth whose job it is just to get down there, kind of to do all the drilling. So what you have here is one of the more amazing creative acts on the planet.

This is the second part of the act. This is really controversial and hasn't been proven yet. Maybe Lynn, myself, and a few others of the Maniacal Naturalist Society are the only ones that believe it. Here we have the same thing happen. A spirochete got through the cell wall and its head got lost inside a bacteria. And when it did, what happened was a nucleus formed to take shelter from this invading spirochete. So the whole evolution of the nucleus of the cell came as a reaction to this new symbiosis that's going to again form by another spirochete.

This is having so much trouble because there's been such an era of central control starting with the Communists, Fascists, everybody. And that ideology really got into science. And in getting into science what it said was there has to be central control for life to happen, and it all happens inside the nucleus of the cell, that's the nut where it all happens. No one wanted to believe there was DNA in the other parts of the cell.

Well, when this second spirochete came in, it kind of blew up, and in doing so it kind of created a thick texture of tubes inside the cell and partly went into the nucleus, which again wasn't complete, and created this matrix. This is the original matrix, forget the movie. This matrix said that when a cell got too big and came apart that, rather than just sloshing apart, the pieces of the cell followed the pattern of configuration created by this other spirochete. What it did was it took two pieces of its tail and the technical names are citriole and kinetestone, and these pieces of its tail sent out the information to grow the rest of the tail. But instead of just growing the rest of the tail it directed the chromosomes to follow in that dance choreography. So the whole dance of chromosomes, the whole reproduction of chromosomes, follows these paths created by two pieces of the spirochete. What did this allow? It allowed one cell to turn into many cells because you could now split yourself in half. It was the first real conglomerate on the planet.

The problem is, it's the Cheshire Cat problem, since it happened two billion years ago all the other stuff that's not so important to this process has slowly disappeared and as it has disappeared what you are left with is the smile of the cat. What the scientific community is arguing about is, is that smile indicative of an invading spirochete or did it come from somewhere else? For me there's no other way of explaining how the inner cell got so creative and mobile and why it's that way, except to say it's another act of symbiosis.

Well, now we're ready to get out of the chthonian. We're ready to go away from that sulfurous time. The reason is that as you got bigger, with many cells, you wanted more energy.

Oxygen is sixteen times better than sulfur to create a life metabolism. So about two billion years ago, once again, we had an invasion. This invasion was really weird though, because this invasion started by eating the bacteria, and some of the bacteria didn't get digested. In other words, after eating a billion of these purple-black things, we've switched staff colors, we're into purple staffs of life instead of black staffs of life.

This is bedella vibres, which is really a great name. The *bedilleum* is the Greek word for a plant, it's like myrrh that's very gummy, it's a gum plant you use for making glue. *Vibros,* of course, comes from vibrator. What you have here is a gummy vibrator. What this thing did is it got in there, and it does shake, but it stuck, it stuck to the outside of the cell. Here it is stuck to the outside of the cell and what it's doing is putting all its different pieces into the cell. Gradually it moves into the cell. Hundreds of them just blew up. But one of them got in there and somehow its genetic makeup or how it worked allowed it to live inside.

So inside there we have these purple bacteria that evolve into this thing called a mitochondria. Mitochondria was always considered just part of the cell. But this also has its own DNA, this also supplies oxygen to the cell. It allowed the whole cell not only to multiply and become multicelled but powered it around so that it could take all those spirochete mouths it had and spin around and eat a lot more. It was really a great move.

So we suddenly developed this big new creature on the planet. The creatures that made us. And it's called a eukaryote.

That is a whole new part of what happened over the last two billion years. Suddenly out of that comes this whole new group of creatures they never teach you about in school called protists. These protists are not great looking things, certainly, like slime molds, amoebas, that are no longer a single creature but are literally a combination with one creature for mobility, another creature for power, another creature for splitting and growing and becoming multicelled and another creature, well the same creature for making a ciliated bowel for hairy mouth. But that wasn't the end of it.

This is a protist and inside is living a kind of algae. So it's a double creature again. In a third one, a kind of dervish creature of a protist, again is a kind of combination of three different earlier beings. We're getting complicated. At one point then we've thwarted cannibalism. We've moved into the oxygen. Everybody's eating everybody else. In one of those cases when everybody's eating everybody else, hunger, which is the prime mover on the planet, if you haven't figured that out, hunger, leads to one creature eating another. And now that little staff changes. You no longer have a purple staff, we no longer have a black staff, we have a green staff. It comes in the form of a cyanobacteria. *Cyan* meaning "blue-green." Or it comes in the form of a red bacteria called a rotoplast that you see in red seaweed. Or it will come in the form of a brown plast, *plast* just means "molded," form, like you see in brown algae.

And so all of a sudden inside one creature became these green creatures and that led to every plant on the planet. And this was pretty interesting, because this was cannibalism leading to a love affair. From there everything on the planet was no higher than this. As soon as the chloroplast cannibalism worked out, everything could grow. You can look at trees as just candelabras to hold blue-green algae to the sun. And you'd be pretty accurate. And you can look at ferns as just fancy ways to hold blue-green algae to the solar radiation.

This is cannibalism. We have one big protist engulf another. It went on and on. Once you got inside you could keep the chloroplast from being digested. Here it is again. These are cyanobacteria that got eaten and became the chloroplasts of all of our plants.

As these things became bigger and bigger, and they ate each other, they started to absorb each other. Soon they were so big, and they had so much information from their DNA that they couldn't deal with it. This is called too much information, redundancy, however you want to do it. It slowed life down and literally bloated it. It became so bloated it literally couldn't move around. This led to the introduction of the first editing job in evolution. And what it did was at times when life was really good you only had half the number of chromosomes in your cell and when life got bad and hunger moved you, you fused again so you'd have twice the amount of ability of body mass to get through the drought. Well, this got very refined. Now it can be done on cue, and it can be done without fail, and we call it sexual reproduction. In fact the word *miosis* means "an understatement" in Greek. It was a way of taking less, dividing yourself in half, to get to greater esteem. It was literally an editing job. To write less to get a greater prose.

Actually some plants don't do it. Some animals don't do it. They kept on bloating and getting bigger and bigger, and this was the beginning of the rose that you give out at the wedding because the rose is really only five petals but because humans like things extravagant, they wanted hundreds of petals. The way you did that was you chemically dosed these poor roses, to domesticate them, with mustard gas or with x-rays, and they kept their own chromosomes and became doubles and triples and octuples, whatever you want to call them, and they got hundreds and hundreds of petals, which is what you buy when you buy a red rose. Similarly some people went off again and dosed them with mustard gas and x-rays and got what was a very mild perfume to be those very stenchy perfumes you get when you buy the commercial roses. Or if you look at lilies, the same thing happened.

This was the beginning of the understanding of domestication. What you did was you took and you devolved the creature back to another time and then you played with it until it fit what your ideas were. But notice this happened a long time ago. I mean the fungus domesticated the bacteria to make the lichen. Nature was domesticating nature way before humans were domesticating nature.

But with the invention of miosis in this section we notice two things happening: sex and symbiosis have brought our plots together. Sex becomes the cyclical fusion through symbiosis of single-celled beings that come together and then separate. It's more predictable, it's seasonal. It's actually less creative than the things I've shown you and it's much more casual. And overlaid on top of that is a symbiosis that happens rarely, maybe once every billion years, which is a huge leap in an invasion. Once it happens it's totally reliable, and as we said, it's more like a braided river, it comes back to make creativity that will change huge life forms.

From this point of view gender isn't that interesting. There's one protist that has seventeen genders. The protists just bump into each other all the time, if you watch them under a microscope, and they say, "Oh no, wrong gender," bump, wrong gender, bump, wrong gender. If you try to separate them out, you get seventeen genders. I don't know what you call that, Male 1, Male 2, Male 3, Female 4, I don't know how you do that.

In fact, the group I'm studying is an all-female lizard group. This is a really lovely story. For all these years these guys at the Museum of Natural History have collected all these lizards. And every one of them was a female and they kept thinking, "Well, the males are just hiding." So they sent out more and more students, tens of thousands of dollars to find, where are these males, we've got to find them. They must be under this rock or that rock. You know, climbing to the top of the tree. They sent their students all over the place. Finally someone figured out that the female lizards split into halves and re-fertilize each other right into their own body. And so they're what's called parthenogenic. There are no males. The advantage of that for the females is that if you don't sing like a bird it's hard to find a mate. So if you're going into new land and you can't sing like a dinosaur or sing like a bird, what do you do? You have to go wandering around and wandering around looking for the nearest rock and hoping that on the top of the rock is some sunning male you can finally mate with. These are grassland lizards. There are no rocks where the guys can show their blue dewlaps, show off, do little push-ups. So they just gave up the males, went in, and took over the grasslands. So most major grassland lizards of the southwest are all female lizards.

I don't want to give the impression that once there was an egg and once there was a sperm it all got resolved and everybody knew what that led to, two genders. No one even knows how to deal with protist genders.

So we wind up here with five kingdoms. With bacteria, the ones we saw. With protists, the multiconglomerant shimmerers. And then with the animals, plants, and fungus that went off in different ways. The interesting thing is that there's a rhythm created here, and it's a real aesthetic rhythm. It's the rhythm of being receptive and being creative. Both can be difficult, the receptive part is getting that fusion and the creative part is what you do after you get it. But the receptive part is equally important. That the spirochete can get in the cell, that the undigested purple bacteria becomes your mitochondria, is as important as the final result, which is this burst of creation. That's one of the lessons of symbiosis.

Another lesson, it sounds kind of Buddhist, it's meant to be only Naturalist, is that all composite beings are temporary. And since we are all composite beings, and we are multicelled, and we put ourselves together, we are not like the bacteria. You could say that the bacteria are noncomposite beings and have never fallen apart. They have just exchanged delightfully their genes back and forth for 3.8 billion years and they are just the same creature they started out to be. They are just little variations on the uni-cell, the ur-cell. The other thing we notice is that in sex you always dissolve back to the bacterial state, the uni-cell state.

The biggest great symbiotes on the planet are termites. You have to think about what vegetarians have to do. I mean it's hard to eat leaves. They're slippery, they're exposed to sunlight so if you go out and try to chew on them casually, you dry out, they usually have big wax layers on them you have to get through, they're not really very nutritious, so you have to eat a lot of them, and many of them have toxins in them like tannins that make them really distasteful. So the big idea was how do you eat wood, eat leaves, and get away with it. Termites did it with this great thing. In their stomachs is one of the greatest microbial communities on the planet.

There might be a half million critters living just in any one of those little tiny termite stomachs. Each one of them has their own job. You have the same old ciliated protist wandering around finding little particles of wood, then they kind of dissolve the wood and when it comes out you get another protist that's going ahead and eating the waste product and turning it into something else. No one to this day has ever figured out the total number of kinds of things living in termites. It's another little job, if you want one.

Cows are the same way. Cows have a half million little bacteria living in their four stomachs. Each one of the four stomach is the chthonian world, it ferments, it's hot, it's sulfurous. They belch. Most people think methane comes out of their farts, actually it comes out of their belches. The first thing the mother cow will do for its young is have the little calf lick its own mouth. The reason is not just that they're kissing each other, but they're exchanging bacteria. The calf is getting all the bacteria into its four stomachs. About a fifth of all the food that goes through a cow, because grass isn't that nutritious, comes made by bacteria in those stomachs. I don't know if I said, but there's about a half million of those bacteria in that length, about a half millimeter of space inside it.

What's really interesting is that in societies, human societies that did not have cattle, like Native Americans on this continent, or the Chinese, who never domesticated cattle, they did not develop a tolerance for milk, because our own bacterial colonies, in our own stomachs, also had to take care of lactose. Lactose is not one of the milk sugars found in women's breast milk, it's a special cow milk. And so, if you give milk to Japanese, or to Apaches, they will pretty much not do anything with it but get the runs. Certain groups of Jews in Eastern Europe who probably came from the Caucasian Mountains, or areas that again did not domesticate cattle, because it was too dry, that tribe is also not lactose tolerant. As you know, you go into stores now and you actually get lactose-free milk, the first time it's happened is in the last five years. The basis of that is that the bacterial colonies in your stomach are still in the process of developing a symbiosis. They're mutualists in training, that's what I call them.

Leaf-cutting ants run into the same problem as the termite, but it's probably the most elaborate agriculture on the planet. The queen cultivates her own fungus. She carries that fungus with her to a new colony. She uses her own manure to grow the fungus for the first time. She weeds the garden of any bacterial colonies that might grow in it. She'll weed it of other fungus. She starts growing these huge colonies. A typical colony will have 2,000 chambers, each is a growing chamber, like 2,000 fields, and each one is about ten inches big. This is probably the most elaborate agriculture on the planet, this combination and domestication with the fungus. Again, the ant can't eat the leaf so they shred the leaf and have the fungus eat the leaf for them. Complete symbiosis. Without one, the other wouldn't exist.

The perfection of symbiosis is where a flower, in this case, an orchid, actually evolves to look like the female. It's kind of the Marilyn Monroe of the bee family. The guys can't resist, they come in and in trying to mate with this flower thinking it's the female bee. They pollinate it. It's not a bee, that's the flower and you get a symbiosis. The orchid can't survive without the bee and the bee without the orchid.

I want to say that this symbiosis is so direct. I don't know if you've ever read about it, but in 1971 a guy named David Vetter was born, and he was born without an immune system. It was a weird genetic thing, he had no immune system, and his brother had already died because he had no immune system. So in order to save his life they had him taken, immediately as he came out into a plastic bubble, a sterile plastic bubble. He lived in that bubble, at $100,000 a day, making bigger and bigger bubbles, until the age of twelve. I would just love to know what he was thinking about. He had no ability to tolerate bacteria. It really shows the difference between being sterile and being pure, I mean this man was sterile.

Our bodies have 500 species of bacteria and protists in it that are necessary for us to live. If we don't have them we die. So we have them on our eyelashes, we have them on our eyeballs, we have a lot of them in our intestines. This just shows you that we too are symbiants. That we too cannot survive without our bacterial colonies inside us. And in fact most recently, one of the causes of asthma has been shown to be that people are brought up in too sterile an environment. When you're kids, and it has to be really young, I mean like between one and two, you have to be in the dirt. And one of the reasons you have to be in the dirt is so that this guy can get inside you. This is a mixococcus, a kind of branch tree bacteria, and when that gets inside you, it's kind of a training ground. This mixococcus trains the body to accept all kinds of things later which will be dander and cat hair and pollen, and if it doesn't develop in that early stage, between one and two years old, then your body doesn't learn how to do it, that's its learning time. So not only do we have a symbiosis, but perhaps a lot of asthma has come because of the separation and the sterilization of babies from dirt. So if you're going to have kids, make sure they're in dirt.

The main conclusion is that everything is in transition. There's nothing settled in here, and it's not by "tooth and claw," but by the creation of mutualists in training. Some of these mutualists just don't work out. Here we have a cowbird baby that was laid in a bird's nest, the cowbird is a complete parasite, it doesn't ever bring up its own kids. It just lays it in some other bird's nest. The cowbird baby hatches out real quick, throws everybody else out of the nest, and the mother is so fixated that anything in its nest must be its own, that it feeds the cowbird's young until it grows up. So one of the main problems now in the United States is that cowbirds like destroyed or fragmented habitat, and so they're moving in on all the wood warblers, and the wood warblers have never had a long time, they're mutualists in training, and this egg that they're getting is not their own egg. Cowbirds should be called buffalo birds, actually, they used to live with buffalo, not cows. But some birds have gotten used to it actually, and can tell color, they can look into the color and tell, that is not the color of my egg, and they throw them out. But because we fragmented the habitat, and again the configuration is different, we have a new kind of evolution occurring.

An interesting side on it, it's just been discovered that birds see into the ultraviolet. Cowbirds get fixated on one kind of bird and they'll lay an egg that looks just like the other bird's egg. No one knows just how they learn to do that. Anyhow they'll do that and sometimes they'll get thrown out and sometimes they don't. And it turns out that they actually differ their beauty or their coloration differs in the ultraviolet, so the egg we're looking at is not the egg the bird is seeing.

So here's a typical other one, this turtle got its tongue to look like a little good waving food that attracts the fish and the fish has yet to learn that this is not a good food. Again a complete parasite situation. A mutualist in early training. There are by the way fish, like the ones that clean sharks, where the shark will not eat the fish, because it has learned, or however that evolved, that the fish can actually go into the shark's mouth, clean off its teeth, take all the bacteria, and go out.

We are of course in the same position. We are trying in developing our symbiosis, we are so scared of germs and bacteria that we now experiment with monkeys, we haven't figured out what to do, so we're in a sense parasitic on monkeys to heal ourselves in a very direct way. It's an incomplete symbiosis, really unfair to the monkey. Monkeys have tried revenge by spreading Ebola virus all over the United States, and chimps probably gave us AIDS, so there is a conflict there that has yet to be symbiotic.

This is another really interesting human symbiosis. In order to do falconry, the Arabs need to catch the birds out of the wild. You cannot train a falcon to be a good hunter. You have to catch a wild one that's already learned how to hunt and then make him come back to you as you're hunting. These are all falcons with hoods on in the airplane flying, I have a friend Marvinus who does this, he works in Saudi Arabia and he's a pilot for one of the princes. He flew these guys to Afghanistan right before the war and they landed in this weird airport with all their falcons and there's a red silk rug they lay out and the guys get out with their falcons and then he comes back, takes another prince to Europe, flies back and picks them up, so that he can then take him and the falcons back. So this is the beginning of domestication of falcons who refuse to be domesticated, and so who can only be trained rather than domesticated to work for human beings in the way they want.

A similar thing is happening with condors in the United States. They've let condors go. It's really fun, I actually enjoy it thoroughly. The condors were trained by a glove that looks like a mother condor, because everyone was afraid they'd get attached to human beings, as if the condor couldn't look past that little puppet and see who was at the other end. So finally they let all the condors go in the Verde cliffs up in Arizona and the first thing all the condors did was fly to this one point called Madison

Point where every evening the sun sets to the sound of a thousand clicks of cameras as all the Japanese come. They all come just two minutes before the sun sets, everybody gets out, you hear the cameras going, click, click, and the sun sets, right? Well, the condors saw all those people and remembering who was on the other end of the puppet, now fly to the same point in order to beg from the Japanese to get food. And so we have a kind of weird thing where maybe we're domesticating the Japanese tourists, or maybe the condors are domesticating the . . . but it's a really great sight. These giant birds. I used to fly with condors in the sixties in gliders and you get in the same air bubble and you go around with them and they have a twelve- to fourteen-foot wingspan. But you can't get a glider to go as slow as that condor, so eventually you're going to overtake the condor which looks back at you right in the face and then drops down and then you just glide over it. You can actually hear them squawk at times, and then you come back again around them. That was when there were only eighteen condors left in the United States and now they've bred close to 200. Maybe this week, we won't know, the first three to hatch may have hatched in the United States in the Mesa Verde, living off Japanese tourists.

One of the oldest symbiotic relations between human beings and animals is where elephants actually get totally attached to a human being for their whole life. Should I tell this story? I'll tell this story. It's a horrible story. 1964, I was working in Kenya and John Wayne was making a movie. At one point he has to shoot an elephant. Well, they obviously weren't going to shoot a real elephant, and you can't train African elephants, so they brought over an Indian elephant with a young kid, about fourteen who had brought up this elephant. And of course John Wayne was going to get out there, and with the sound of the gun the elephant had learned, been trained to, fall, look like he had dropped dead.

John Wayne was very alcoholic at that time. He got up there, the elephant charged, and he shot him. He killed it. And this fourteen-year-old boy went crazy. And I was sitting there in the camp with John Wayne sitting around looking at a triptych mirror being shaved by his assistant, this woman, literally drinking out of the bottle of bourbon saying buuuullll-shhhitt, buuuulllshhhitt. And all of the vultures coming in to try and start eating the elephant. It was a pretty sad story, not a symbiotic one.

And then one other aspect of mutualism on the planet is that everything goes back to light. And in order to see light a circular receptor called the eye began to evolve. And the internal bodily eye, this kind of circular thing started ripples aesthetically throughout the planet. And in doing that everyone began to notice, for instance, that eyes are at the front of the head, that eyes were round. And that became a big detriment in life because the predator knew which way you were going to go because your eyes were always at the front of your head. Fish evolved this new way of making a more level playing field, which was to put the eyes at the back of their body so that the other fish might think they were going in the other direction.

Other animals decided instead to get rid of the eye. And you'll see a lot of the coloration of animals on the planet is to disguise the eye, stripes of all kinds, or to create both false eyes and get rid of that notion. In Buddhism when you're trying to be quiet, you close the eye partway, you don't show that complete circuit. That circle is too advertising. It advertises to the world that you are awake and that you are good food. A small owl wanting to scare its predator gets large eyes in the back of its head so the big owl will be more wary of attacking it, maybe. So in Buddhism when you want to get scary you just go in the other direction, you get as big eyes, as circular eyes as you want. This is true for all iconography. Artists may think they're doing something special, but they're just part of this big symbiotic mass that's covering the world. We have much more in common, it overwhelms that we differ. It's as old as the first eyed creatures of fish, probably 265 million years old. My favorite artist in that is Klee, Paul Klee who really understood all that and who used the eye form really subtly in his paintings.

So we see that the symbiosis cannot only take place physiologically, but can take place by this thing called memes, kind of a little idea that gets frozen, or a little circle form that gets frozen and then everybody in the world has to react to it, or deal with it. And it becomes how do you create a mutual understanding, really a commonality of an aesthetic.

In doing this I come to the final woman in this talk, which is Gaia the Earth Goddess. Because we are bathed in the same air and the same water on the whole planet, the symbiosis is planetary wide. In your breath today, some of those molecules probably went through the lungs of Jesus, or maybe the lungs of Marlene Dietrich, or maybe the lungs of Hitler, but you're recycling their breath at this moment. The same would be happening with water on a longer scale of time. At some time in your life you are probably drinking the urine of some gorilla. This is the physiology of Gaia, and the understanding that the planet itself incessantly creates new environments and new forms by this kind of connection, or bathing in the air and water. This is what I mean when I say that symbiosis is a propelling creation, a self-propelling creation. That all we can really do is understand and look at it in some way. The Gaia hypothesis, again it was a science literary connection. James Lovelock lived next door to William Golding, he walked next door and said to Bill, as they used to take walks in the afternoon, he said, look, I got this whole idea going that the planet may have a geophysiology. That all these bacteria have been exhaling oxygen, because

I'm looking at Mars, and Mars doesn't have the same atmosphere, why doesn't Mars have the same atmosphere? Well, this is in the 1970s. Why could it be that we have so much oxygen? Where did that oxygen come from? How come we don't have more methane when there should be a lot of methane on the planet if we're just like Mars? How do I talk about this? Golding went home and came back the next day for dinner and said, "I think you should call it the Gaia hypothesis." So the Gaia hypothesis started to spread. It was added to by Lynn Margulis who then joined because she knew all the creatures who were making this physiology, and became a very interesting word I haven't yet seen in the literary world. And that word was autopoesis. And autopoesis has become for this group of the Maniacal Natural History Society our mythopoetic. Autopoesis: *poesis* means creation, *auto* just means it was done by itself, and so it describes the self-creating possibility of what the earth is about. It's about, you have to understand that since the Archean, about three billion years ago, all creatures exuded love compounds, compounds to attract other creatures, and so there's been a long, long history of this atmosphere and perfumes of love going all around the planet that's gotten very perfected. This is not ever seen on Mars. When people try to make an alternative community, like Biosphere II, they found they couldn't do it, it collapsed. I was one of the designers of it. There's some really great stories there. The bacteria just kept exhaling and exhaling and exhaling and because, it's really interesting, there was an Old Testament overlay to the directors of Biosphere II, so they wanted to repeat Noah and put everything in all at once. That meant for us little ditty scientists, that we had to create a soil that was so rich that it would last for a hundred years. So everybody did that because we were told, nothing new is ever going to come to Biosphere II, it's sealed. And of course, that was so rich that the bacteria really had a great time. Here we had one of the richest soils on earth, they started to chew it up, eat it, and exhale carbon dioxide, soon the carbon dioxide was just incredible. But it was oddly not as incredible as we thought it might be once we figured out the problem. And it was figured out by a construction worker, who in meeting with a graduate student at dinner said, "When did you finish building this?" We finished days before it closed, and he said, "You know, the cement hasn't hardened yet. It takes a long time to age. And when it ages, it eats carbon dioxide."

And so we had created this new world, this alternative community, where the cement was regulating the amount of CO_2 inside the Biosphere. Meanwhile, they had gone crazy in my area, which was the savannah, and said, "Oh, we've got to get the grasses to grow more so they'll eat more, we'll stabilize. . . ." So they cut all the grasses and all the frogs living in it disappeared, it was a big holocaust.

What's really bad about Star Trek, and I know your generation lives Star Trek, I think it's one of the worst kind of cartoons I've ever seen. No one ever eats food, there's no understanding about how you live, there's no sense of community that's wider than this little kind of melodrama on the spaceship, you know. And when you think about landing on Mars, the first thing that's ever going to happen is that they're going to take out a fungus and they're going to mix it with the dirt and rocks of Mars and they're going to look for some water and they'll take the fungus and the algae and they'll put it in a sealed container and they'll come back in 20 years to see if they've actually gotten life to live on Mars. I mean it's the first thing you could possibly ever do to create a living alternative community.

What's interesting is that in attraction, in this love, whatever the difference between attraction, lust, love, I don't want to get into this, is that it created a species recognition. That the species all want to recognize each other just like the fungus wants to recognize the algae. And that may be a very deep evolution of hubris, of pride, of thinking that we're special. And the worst of it is that we think we can take care of the planet. The Gaia hypothesis says, no, no matter what we do, the planet takes care of us. Not we it. And that's the major truth we see in watching how this bacterial microcosmos keeps on trying to readjust the earth to allow life in it. Humans can come and go. Most species live one to ten million years, we're about halfway through that, we're about five million years. Life will stay here in some form or another. Remember the Maniacal Naturalist view is that we're all equally evolved beings. The hubris is that the planet needs to only keep us forever, for eternity. We have to drop that one. We have to understand that since the planet is taking care of us, our job is to protect ourselves from ourselves. And once that change is made, that we are protecting ourselves from ourselves inside a symbiosis, then we can go on and create a politics that is different from the politics we have now, which is the politics that we can somehow manage the earth. It's the ultimate antiglobalization statement. And it leads to what I'll call the Frame of Reference Blues. I've given you a frame today. It's one way to look at this exuberance of the earth and the symbiosis, to get out of the despair and the grief caused by people who are looking at the Bush administration for the next eight years. That's very impermanent. It's not going to be there. It's not that you shouldn't fight or try to change it, but the grief that's being caused, and I see the grief perhaps more than anybody, every day on my e-mail another endangered species bites the dust, has to be nested inside these other frames of reference. I'm going to end with a little poem by Emily Dickinson, to understand that this is this long Gaian physiology, she wrote in 1896.

This World is not Conclusion.
A Species stands beyond—
Invisible, as Music—
But positive, as Sound—
It beckons, and it baffles—
Philosophy—don't know—
And through a Riddle, at the last—
Sagacity, must go—
To guess it, puzzles scholars—
To gain it, Men have borne
Contempt of Generations
And Crucifixion, shown—
Faith slips – and laughs, and rallies—
Blushes, if any see—
Plucks at a twig of Evidence—
And asks a Vane, the way—
Much Gesture, from the Pulpit—
Strong Hallelujahs roll—
Narcotics cannot still the Tooth
That nibbles at the soul—

A Tribute to Sappho

EDWARD SANDERS
2001

* * *

1. SHREDS OF INFINITY

I think of Sappho often
Her life on little tattered papyrus shreds
or snippets in critics—
Longinus, or Dionysius of Halicarnassus

I love her songs of longing
—the one in the meters known as
the 2nd paean, and the Ionic a majore

$$\cup \stackrel{-}{} \cup\cup \qquad --\cup\cup$$

δέδυκε μεν ἀ σελάννα
καὶ Πληϊαδες μέσαι δὲ
νύκτες, παρὰ δ' ἔρχετ' ὤρα,
ἔγω δὲ μόνα κατεύδω.

Something like
   Selanna (the moon) has dipped
   And the Pleiades too
   Ahh midnight darkens
     & I sleep alone. . . .

but, you know, there's so much more
in her sequences of sound

O Sappho! Sappho!
Shreds! Shreds!

They may have heated the baths with your verse
But I think of you every day
Because you are a helpmate to those of us who are

Thirsting for Peace in a Raging Century
Thirsting for Peace in a Raging Century

2. TIME EATS POETRY

and Sappho sorely suffered from that devoration.
Her poetry survives in a number of forms:

> • on ostraca or pieces of pottery
> • on pieces of 6th or 7th century parchment
> • on papyrus fragments from a place in Upper Egypt
>   called Oxyrhynchus, where many ancient writings
>   were found in the late 19th early 20th centuries.
> • in brief quotes of her poetry by ancient writers
> • on lists of her words and lines in ancient glossaries
>   & dictionaries

> and, the only two surviving full poems of Sappho
> were saved by two literary writers; one by Dionysius of
> Halicarnassus, and the other by the writer named Longinus
>   in their books

What happened to the ancient poems?
Well, you'll recall that Akhenaton's name was chipped
away from his monuments deliberately
by those who later opposed his religious innovations.

What the Taliban did
to the rock statues of Buddha recently
the Christians, as they rose to power,
& the so-called Barbarian invaders that sacked the
                            Roman empire
and later the Muslims, as they too grabbed hegemony,
tended to do to the ancient manuscripts.

They got rid of as much of the multi-deity past as they
could get away with.

There were many libraries in the ancient world
and libraries are often the victims of war
& the ancient libraries were virtually all rubbed out of the
                                        tracks of time

When Caesar set fire to the fleet in Alexandria's harbor
the flames accidentally destroyed one of the big libraries

Around 391 AD, Christians destroyed the books in the Serapeum,
another big library in Alexandria

It is alleged that when the Muslims seized Egypt
the ancient manuscripts were used to heat the
                                        water in the baths

        They're not sure today exactly where
        the Great Library at Alexandria was located.

Though war hates books, poets are sometimes fascinated with it
but you won't find any talk of war in the
                        shreds of Sappho,
                but rather the melodies of love, tenderness, family,
                partying, arousal, longing, sadness and fun.

An example of this is in the papyrus that begins

> οἰ μὲν ἰππήων στρότον οἰ δε πεσδων
> οἰ δε ναων φαισ' επι γαν μέλαιναν
> εμμεναι κάλλιστον, εγω δε κῆν' οτ-
> τω τις εραται

whose meaning is something like this:

        Some say that the most beautiful thing
                        on the darkling earth
        is a stroton of horsemen, others a stroton of troops
        and yet others a stroton of ships
        but to me the most beautiful
                is the one whom someone loves.

Later in the same tattered papyrus she
sings of her friend Anactoria

τὰς κε βολλοίμαν ἐρατόν τε βᾶμα
κἀμάρυχμα λάμπρον ἴδην προσώπω
ἠ τὰ Λύδων ἄρματα κἀν ὄπλοισι
πεσδομάχεντας

which is:

   I would rather look at her erotic walk &
     the shiny sparkle of her face
  than gaze at the chariots & soldiers
       of the Lydians
       fighting on foot

3. SAPPHO'S LEGACY

Greek scholars in the 19th & early 20th Century
were of course very learned
& tried to fill in the lacunae of her shredded fragments

Some of the fill-ins were quite clever
but, in the end, just guesses.

The Loeb Classical Library published an edition
of Sappho in 1921 which contained many of these
fragments with the filled-in additions.
That's the edition I learned Sappho on in college

A updated edition of Sappho was published by Loeb
in 1982, translated by David Campbell

& reveals more starkly how shredded the Sappho legacy actually is,
for gone now are the fill-ins

   and the fragments stand for what they are—
   pieces of a brilliant mind
   & they are sometimes frustrating & maddening
   because you hunger for someone somewhere

in an ancient desert
to dig up a jar with all nine of her books intact
so as to savor her entirety!

4. HER LIFE

Sappho was born on the island of Lesbos, near Asia Minor, around 650 BC
She was a contemporary of the poet Alcaeus

Like many controversial humans, you have to sift through the allegations
to isolate the possible truth.

She apparently was born to a family of means
She had a brother named Larichus
She apparently had a child named Cleis
whom she apparently took with her into exile in Sicily
                              during one of those Greek times of unrest

There are a lot of "apparently"s when you speak of Sappho's life

She may have run a kind of finishing school
for upper class young women of Mytilene, the Asia Minor coast, and
    nearby islands

Her fragments show clear passion for close women friends,
with names such as Gongyla, Atthis, Anactoria, and others.

All in all, there is a Shakespeare-level mystery about the facts of her life.

What's true is that she was thought of as "The Tenth Muse"
& she was so well known in Greek civilization that
the city of Mytilene put her likeness on its coins

5. THE SPECIFICS OF EROS

The Greeks did not talk much
about the vagina, or genitals in general
                              in their literature

There are, however, a number of examples of erotic activity
in ancient Greek vases.

and of course there's an erotic mystery
                                        about Sappho
but you will not find much in her extant verse
of a specifically erotic nature

The word for clitoris, for instance, ἡ κλειτορίς is not found in Sappho

nor is the Greek verb, κλειτοριάζω, to touch or rub the clit.

The word vagina, ὁ κτείς, is not found in her verse,

nor the olisbos, ὄλισβος, the Greek for dildo.

There was even a Greek word, ὀλισβοκόλλιξ for penis-shaped bread
but it is not found in the complicated lines of the Tenth Muse

The poet Archilochus was known to use the word ἀηδονιδεύς
the Greek for nestling nightingale, as slang for vagina.

There is a fragment of Sappho
which uses the word βρενθείω denoting a young waterbird,
which, in its context perhaps could be interpreted as the
same usage as Archilocus.
        Or maybe not.

In another of her fragments is a word ὄρπετον "orpeton"
which seems to be appropriately translated as "hot-bottomed"

The text was saved in Hephaestion's *Handbook on Meters*
(It's written in anapests, ⏑⏑⏤ ⏑⏑⏤ ⏑⏑⏤, a meter not used much in
modern times.)

Ἔρος δηὖτέ μ' ὁ λυσιμέλης δόνει,
    γλυκύπικρον ἀμάχανον ὄρπετον
Ἄτθι, σὺ δ' ἐμέθεν μὲν ἀπήχθετο
    φροντίσδην, ἐπὶ δ' Ἀνδρομέδαν πότῃ

        which is translated as:

Limb-loosening Eros
                    shakes me
sweet-&-bitter, helpless, hot-bottomed
Oh Atthis! It is hateful to you
to think of me,
but instead you
            flutter after Andromeda.

What you get from Sappho are the delicate combinations of
feelings of desire, erotic fascination and longing.

One of her singly saved lines is

$$\text{Καὶ ποθήω καὶ μάομαι}$$

for "I hunger and I am longing"

or the fragment saved by Maximus of Tyre

$$\text{Ἔρος δ' ἐτίναξέ μοι}$$
$$\text{φρένας, ὡς ἄνεμος κὰτ' ὄρος δρύσιν ἐμπετων.}$$

which can be translated as:

>   Eros shook my being
>   as a wind
>   down a mountain
>   shakes the oak trees

   There was probably as great a percentage of
           puritans in ancient times as there is now.
           & other Greek poets who wrote poems of Eros
           such as Archilochus & Hipponax
           suffered the same shreddy fate as the great poet of Lesbos

who, for all the centuries since her life has been controversial.
The Greek comedy-writers took her up—
at least six comedies titled *Sappho* were produced in ancient times.

6. POETRY & MUSIC

Sappho wrote in a wide variety of meters
                       in the Aeolian dialect of Greek
                       with its interesting verb-endings & variations
                       on words
Her lines have exquisite flows
               of metrical patterns.

The specifics of ancient metrics & pronunciation,
as well as those regarding stress or accent, and duration of syllables,
remain somewhat mysterious and controversial

but there's enough believable information
to make some educated approximations of the sound of
                                        ancient poems

Basically there were three accents: acute, grave, and circumflex.
and the syllables of verse were held for different durations
        according to fairly specific rules
                    to create complicated systems of metrics

Long syllables were to be held about twice as long as short syllables—
not as easy to accomplish when singing or reciting, say, Sappho
                                        as you might think.

Sappho's verse was written to be sung to a lyre
She's depicted on vases playing it.
& she calls out to her lyre in a famous two-line fragment
(in the Glyconic meter: $-\cup -\cup\cup- \cup- \cup-$
                         $-\cup -\cup\cup- \cup-$)

ἄγι δὴ χέλυ δῖα μοι λέγε
φωνάεσσα δε γίνεο

            Come o sacred lyre of mine
            make yourself sing!

Sappho also writes of singing her poems beautifully
            to delight her companions,
                        such as in the fragment:

            Τάδε νῦν ἐταίραις
    ταὶς ἔμαις τέρπνα κάλως

    translated as:
            I now shall sing
                these poems w/ beauty
        for the pleasure of my female friends.

Sappho wrote 9 books of odes, epithalamia (wedding poems), elegies &
    hymns

    (These 9 books were arranged by a scholar in the Alexandrian era, a
    time of literary classification & scholarship after the time of
    Alexander the Conqueror)

She created her own mode, the Mixo-Lydian, according to Plutarch.
& she realized her genius in a great variety of meters
which are astounding today to analyze

They're difficult—some of her meters
        remain elusive to me
                even after years of study

        but there's something that only the word exquisite
        can define, about the mystery
        and the smooth symmetry
        of her fragments

        Even in her single-word fragments
        you can see her
                genius with words.

Her most well-known metrical creation is the Sapphic stanza
which is the metrical form of the two poems that have survived
more or less intact.

The pattern is this:
$$— \cup — \cup — \cup\cup — \cup — \cup$$
$$— \cup — \cup — \cup\cup — \cup — \cup$$
$$— \cup — \cup — \cup\cup — \cup — \cup$$
$$— \cup \cup — \cup$$

7. THE HYMN TO APHRODITE

Here is the "Hymn to Aphrodite" saved for us by Dionysius
    of Halicarnassus
a Greek writer born around the time of Christ.

The poem is utterly remarkable in that it contains
a conversation between Sappho and the goddess Aphrodite.
It reveals that Sappho was a Fundamentalist Aphroditean
in her sense of the real-world presence of Aphrodite
whom she summoned in her longing
                to come from afar to help her:

Splendor-throned, deathless
love-ploy-plotting Aphrodite,
Daughter of Zeus, I pray to thee.

Do not overwhelm my heart
with cares and griefs, my Queen.

But, come to me now, if ever now and
again in the past, listening from afar,
you heard my prayers, and harnessed
your golden chariot to leave
your father's realm, the chariot
drawn by two swift swans with
thickly flashing wings from heaven
through the middle of the upper sky
down upon the darkling earth.

The swift swans brought thee
quickly near, o Aphrodite,
and you asked me,
with a smile on your deathless face,
what it was that
made me suffer so, and why
was I crying out, what
did I want most specially
to assuage my raging heart?

"Whom shall I persuade,"
you asked, "to bring you
the treasure of torrid love?
Who, o Sappho,
    who wrongs thee?

                    If she flees thee
                    swiftly shall
                    she dance at
                    thy heels

                    If she does not
                    take thy gifts
                    swiftly shall she
                    give

                    If she loves thee not,
                    swiftly shall
                    she glide in

the beams of desire,
even be she unwilling
at first," you said
to me Aphrodite.

O come to me at once, o
Aphrodite, and free me
from this harsh love pain!

That which my soul craves to be done
do it! o do it!
You yourself, in living person
be thou my ally!

ποικιλόθρον' ἀθάνατ' Ἀφροδίτα
παῖ Δίος δολόπλοκα, λίσσομαί σε
μή μ' ἄσαισι μηδ' ὀνίαισι δάμνα,
πότνια θῦμον

ἀλλὰ τυίδ' ἔλθ', αἴ ποτα κἀτέροττα
τᾶς ἔμας αὔδως ἀίοισα πήλυι
ἔκλυες, πάτρος δὲ δόμον λίποισα
χρύσιον ἦλθες

ἄρμ' ὑπασδεύξαισα, κάλω δὲ σ' ἄγον
ὤκεες στροῦθω προτὶ γᾶν μέλαιναν
πύκνα δίννεντε πτέρ' ἀπ' ὀρράνω αἴθε-
ρος διὰ μέσσω,

αἶψα δ' ἐξίκοντο· σὺ δ' ὦ μάκαιρα,
μειδιάσαισ' ἀθανάτω προσώπω
ἦρε' ὄττι δηὖτε πέπονθα, κὤττι
δηὖτε κάλημι

κὤττ' ἔμω μάλιστα θέλω γένεσθαι
μαινόλα θύμω· "τίνα δηὖτε πείθω
κἀὶ σ' ἄγην ἐς Ϝὰν φιλότατα; τίς τ', ὦ
Ψάπφ', ἀδικήει?

κἀὶ γὰρ αἰ φεύγει, ταχέως διώξει,
αἰ δὲ δῶρα μὴ δέκετ', ἀλλὰ δώσει
αἰ δε μὴ φίλει, ταχέως φιλήσει
κὠυκ ἐθέλοισα."

ἔλθε μοι καὶ νῦν, χαλέπαν δε λῦσον
ἐκ μερίμναν, ὄσσα δέ μοι τέλεσσαι
θῦμος ἰμμέρρει, τέλεσον, σὺ δ' αὔτα
σύμμαχος ἔσσο

CIVIL DISOBEDIENCES

8. THE "PHAINETAI MOI . . ."

The second full poem was saved for us by the writer, Longinus, in his book
On the Sublime, written sometime in the 1st or 2nd century AD.
This 4-quatrain poem has been translated by Catullus (into Latin), by
    Byron,
by William Carlos Williams, and by many other poets,
                                   including Edward Sanders.

My translation is:

> Equal to the gods
> is the man who sits
> in front of you leaning closely
> and hears you sweetly speaking
> and the lust-licking laughter
> of your mouth, oh it makes my
> heart beat in flutters!
>
> When I look at you
> Brochea, not a part of my
> voice comes out,
> but my tongue breaks,
> and right away
> a delicate fire runs just beneath
> my skin,
>
> I see a dizzy nothing,
> my ears ring with noise,
> the sweat runs down
> upon me, and a trembling
> that I cannot stop
> seizes me limb and loin,
> o I am greener than grass, and
> death seems so near. . . .

And here is the text, which I have set to music
in honor of the Mixo-Lydian original:

Φαίνεταί μοι κῆνος ἴσος θέοισιν
ἔμμεν ὤνηρ ὄττις ἐνάντιός τοι
ἰζάνει καὶ πλάσιον ἆδυ φωνεί-
σας ὑπακούει

καὶ γελαίσας ἰμμέροεν τό μ᾽ἦ μὰν
κάρζαν ἐν στήθεσσιν ἐπεπτόασεν
ὡς γὰρ ἔς τ᾽ἴδω, βρόχε᾽, ὥς με φώνας
οὐδεν ἔτ᾽ ἴκει

Sa a a a pho   I yearn for you
across the centuries

ἀλλὰ κὰμ μὲν γλῶσσα ϝέαγε λέπτον
δ᾽αὐτίκα χρῷ πῦρ ὑπαδεδρόμακεν
ὀππάτεσσι δ᾽οὐδεν ὄρημ᾽ ἐπιρρόμ-
βεισι δ᾽ἄκουαι

ἀ δέ μ᾽ἴδρως κακχέεται, τρόμος δὲ
παῖσαν ἄγρη, χλωροτέρα δὲ ποίας
ἔμμι, τεθνάκην δ᾽ὀλίγω 'πιδεύϝην
φαίνομαι -- ἀλλὰ ....

Sa a a a pho   I yearn for you
across the centuries

—Thus have I shared with you
some of my feelings for the great poet Sappho

NOTES
The "phainetai moi ..."

Melody by Edward Sanders
Transcribed by Steven Taylor

On the whole I believe that there is fairly wide agreement about the nature of the acute and circumflex accents, but not about the grave. The acute accentuation seems to have been an upward glide of the voice within a gamut of approximately a fifth (say, C to G or *doh* to *soh*). Probably—but this is not attested in the evidence—only the higher tones of this upward glide were clearly audible, and the peak note, *soh,* was probably the salient one, i.e., the point of maximum audibility. The circumflex apparently consisted in an upward glide similar to the acute on the first part of the vowel—which was always long—and a downward glide, also within the gamut of about a fifth, on the second part. Probably—but here again there is no evidence—the falling tone did not audibly descend all the way from *soh* to *doh.* Perhaps it reached its salient tone round about *mi* or E in the range C-G....We use approximation to these pitch-variations in our interrogative 'Yés?' and dubious 'Yé-ès.'

The vowels which are left without any pitch-mark in a modern Greek text, e.g., the first two in αρετη , were apparently pronounced at a pitch-level approximating to the low note of the *doh-soh* gamut.

—W. B. STANFORD, from *The Sound of Greek,* "Remarks on the Pronunciation of the Greek Pitch Accent," University of California Press, 1967.

The grave is a problem. What did the grave accent actually indicate, as it applies to the chanting or singing of Greek poetry?

Stanford believes that the grave is probably a "modification of the oxytone" or acute. It can be explained, he believes, "if the grave-accent mark was used loosely to mean both 'keep the pitch of your voice down' and 'bring the pitch of your voice down (from the normal high tone.)'"

Even so, Stanford admits, "there is no certain evidence at all" as to how the grave was actually pronounced. He thinks it may be pronounced as a "falling tone within the gamut *soh-doh* . . . "

On the Ballad

ALLEN GINSBERG AND HELEN ADAM
June 11, 1976

★　★　★

ALLEN GINSBERG: Where do ballads come from, where do songs come from? There aren't enough books in the library to get it out, and to lay out the origins. But fortunately, Helen Adam is still here. So I thought it would be interesting to ask Helen to lay the ballad on us, the history of the ballad, right—the classic ballad. Because she grew up in Scotland with Scotch border ballads—are they border ballads? Who collected them, Sir Walter? Childe, it's the Childe ballads I'm talking about, then. Let's work with Helen and find out about ballads, because I don't know very much about the history of the ballad, I'm just getting into it myself and learning about it, and producing some, so I'm interested in finding out more background than I know, and it might be an interesting thing for a class scene, for us to do, whip out a little music this week, and everybody write a ballad, which is something that probably most people here aren't into, because we're all writing crazy beatnik free verse. So I'm going to try and write a ballad this week, and so the class assignment for, I guess Monday, over the weekend, write up a ballad. Anything, sex ballad, sex blues—blues or ballad. Blues form is iambic pentameter 3-line stanzas rhymed A-A-A and the second line can repeat the first. But better still if we did a ballad, like a formal ballad like Helen is doing, because she's going to present some samples. Want to sit up here with me?

HELEN ADAM: Yes, that's fine. Ballads of course are story poems. Just before I begin, I spent a glorious afternoon up at the very top of Estes Park, on the tundra, and it's pure ballad country, the great fierce mountains and the beautiful things, like the tiny little alpine flowers, and the adorably tame birds, you know there's a lot of birds in ballads usually, talking birds, and there was this fantastic girl who was standing on the very edge of a great drop holding out her arms like this, with peanuts in them, and those enchanting birds would come flying and somersaulting in the air and snatch the peanuts and suddenly stay on the back of her hand, with this wonderful cold wind blowing. It was just absolutely gorgeous. And then on the way back in the car, Michael Castro (who gave me the ride) sang some of his songs to me, lovely ballad-y songs and a marvelous line in one of them that seemed to come straight out of the old ballads, about how when you're very happy or in love you could look up at the great sun—what was that line exactly, Michael?—and hear it hum on high—that's it, and *feel* the song he hums about. I think that's a marvelous line about the sun. And it's straight out of the old ballads, because the feeling of elemental nature was always so near, and it is still, in Scotland. I was back about six years ago—unlike America, and the gorgeous places I've seen in America, but none of them have this strange feeling of the supernatural. I once slept out alone in the High Sierras, and it was just beautiful and lovely, but when I slept out alone in the Isle of Skye, it was absolutely unearthly. Blazing bright full moonlight, and these terrific black mountains, and I had even gone out to the wrong mountain, at least I had told my friend I would be on one mountain, I changed my mind and went up another, so it was madness, because if you broke a leg or anything you'd be stuck, but this feeling of supernatural, unearthly beauty there was just overwhelming. But anyway, this is a lovely old one, which you may know, called "Lord Randall."

AG: Bob Dylan copied this.

HA: Did he?

AG: That's "Hard Rain," what's the first line of "Hard Rain"?—"Where have you been my blue eyed—"

HA: Yes, yes, of course, why it's true, I never realized that, well . . .

AG: "What did you see my blue-eyed son, Well what did you see my darling young one?"—So it goes back to "Lord Randall" obviously. Does anybody know "Lord Randall"? How many of those who have not heard "Lord Randall" have heard the Dylan? And how many knew that Dylan took it from "Lord Randall"? Raise your hands if you really did, really, really, oh great.

HA: (sings "Lord Randall").

> "O where ha you been, Lord Randall, my son?
> And where ha you been, my handsome young man?"
> "I ha been at the greenwood; mother, mak my bed soon,
> For I'm wearied wi hunting, and fain wad lie down."
>
> "An wha met ye there, Lord Randall, my son?
> An wha met you there, my handsome young man?"
> "O I met wi my true-love; mother, mak my bed soon,
> For I'm wearied wi huntin, an fain wad lie down."
>
> "And what did she give you, Lord Randall, my son?
> And what did she give you, my handsome young man?"

"Eels fried in a pan; mother, mak my bed soon,
  For I'm wearied with huntin, and fain wad lie down."

"And wha gat your leavins, Lord Randall, my son?
  And what gat your leavins, my handsom young man?"
"My hawks and my hounds; mother, mak my bed soon,
  For I'm wearied wi huntin, and fain wad lie down."

"And what became of them, Lord Randall, my son?
  And what became of them, my handsome young man?"
"They stretched their legs out an died; mother, mak my bed soon,
  For I'm wearied wi huntin, and fain wad lie down."

"O I fear you are poisoned, Lord Randall, my son!
  I fear you are poisoned, my handsome young man!"
"O yes, I am poisoned; mother, mak my bed soon,
  For I'm sick at the heart, and I fain wad lie down."

"What d'ye leave to your mother, Lord Randall, my son?
  What d'ye leave to your mother, my handsome young man?"
"Four and twenty milk kye; mother, mak my bed soon,
  For I'm sick at the heart, and I fain wad lie down."

"What d'ye leave to your sister, Lord Randall, my son?
  What d'ye leave to your sister, my handsome young man?"
"My gold and my silver; mother, mak my bed soon,
  For I'm sick at the heart, an I fain wad lie down."

"What d'ye leave to your brother, Lord Randall, my son?
  What d'ye leave to your brother, my handsome young man?"
"My house and my lands; mother, mak my bed soon,
  For I'm sick at the heart, and I fain wad lie down."

"What d'ye leave to your true-love, Lord Randall, my son?
  What d'ye leave to your true-love, my handsome young man?"
"I leave her hell and fire; mother, mak my bed soon,
  For I'm sick at the heart, and I fain was lie down."

AG: One thing I wanted to say, just as he's got, "Where have you been, Lord Randall, my son," so it's Cincinnatta—Where have you been, it's dialect. It's just that this is classic. But the American is classic, too, except people don't realize it's classic. But in like a hundred years, it'll sound classic. Kerouac, or anything written in that style, making use of a particular vernacular, like from Ann Arbor or St. Louis, or New Jersey, Brooklynese is classic, and Bruce Springteen is probably making Jerseyese classic. So it's not really ancient classic, it's just the classic local particular dialect of our own times. Here it looks terrific, because he's used to it. In America it doesn't yet look terrific to professors, because they're not used to it. But there's no reason why it can't be terrific, why your own tongue can't be terrific. If you stick to your own tongue. What is a ballad now?

HA: It's just a story poem, usually chanted, by wandering minstrels, who go from town to town, and often the audience would join in, or add a verse of their own, and that's why there's so many different versions. This is a different version of "Lord Randall" than I've known before. Very often improvised, the whole thing was almost a group thing, you know, they knew the basic story like, say, Cinderella or fairy tales, they usually knew the basic stories of the ballads, and then they change. In this country too, you'll find versions in the Smoky Mountains of old Scottish ballads, but it was different. I usually have chosen my own favorite verses out of the ballads and put them together. This is an eerie little one, which is really more of a psalm than a ballad, a warning to a soul just while it's dying, rather like the Bardo. It's the nightwatch, you know, when the person was dead, everybody, like a wake, in Ireland, would come to, sort of would watch, because the soul wasn't supposed to leave the body right away, it sort of hovered—

The Wife of Usher's Well

There lived a wife at Usher's well,
And a wealthy wife was she;
She had three stout and stalwart sons,
And sent them o'er the sea.

They hadna been a week from her,
A week but barely ane,
When word came to the carline wife
That her three sons were gane.

They hadna been a week from her,
A week but barely three,
When word came to the carline wife
That her sons she'd never see.

"I wish the wind may never cease.
Nor fashes in the flood,
Till my three sons come hame to me,
In earthly flesh and blood!"

It fell about the Martinmas,
When nights are lang and mirk,
The carline wife's three sons came hame,
And their hats were o' the birk.

It neither grew in syke nor ditch,
Nor yet in ony sheugh;
But at the gates o' Paradise
That birk grew fair eneugh.

"Blow up the fire, my maidens!
Bring water from the well!
For a' my house shall feast this night,
Since my three sons are well."

And she has made to them a bed,
She's made it large and wide;
And she's ta'en her mantle her about,
Sat down at the bedside.

Up then crew the red, red cock,
And up and crew the gray;
The eldest to the youngest said.
"'Tis time we were away."

The cock he hadna craw'd but once,
And clapp'd his wings at a',
When the youngest to the eldest said,
"Brother, we must awa."

"The cock doth craw, the day doth daw,
The channerin' worm doth chide;
Gin we be miss'd out o' our place,
A sair pain we maun bide."

"Lie still, lie still but a little wee while,
Lie still but if we may;

Gin my mother should miss us when she wakes,
She'll go mad ere it be day"

"Fare ye weel, my mother dear!
Fareweel to barn and byre!
And fare ye weel, the bonny lass
That kindles my mother's fire!"

AG: That's terrific, I've never heard it done that way. Is it supposed to be responsive?

HA: I don't know, it's just the way I've always done it. It's very eerie.

AG: Wait a minute, what do you mean by eerie?

HA: Eerie is uncanny, you know.

AG: Is that a characteristic of ballads?

HA: Not all of them, some of them are very practical, but they are in and out of the supernatural world all the time, and this one is eerie because it hints the moral of the story.

AG: One other thing you said the other day was that the ballads were, no conscience or mercy—

HA: No conscience, oh absolutely merciless, yes, nobody is going to let anybody off and as for giving people sins, Christians are absolutely pagan, you know, nobody ever turns the other cheek, or anything. Just swipe their heads off with one blow, if they're your enemy.

AG: They're definitely realistic that way, aren't they? It would be empty of any kind of attachment.

HA: Here is "The Fair Young Wife." This is a werewolf poem. It seems to me sort of appropriate for this part of the countryside, the lovely dark woods around and the great hills (sings "The Fair Young Wife").

This is a tale for a night of snow.
It was lived in the north land long ago.
An old man, nearing the end of life,
Took to his arms a fair young wife.

A wife to keep his house in the woods.
His house of echoes and solitudes,
'Mid forests gloomy and unexplored,
Hunting ground of the wolves abhorred.

Through miles of forest the wolves ran light.
She heard them running at dead of night.
She heard them running, though far away,
And her heart leapt up like a beast of prey.

"Lie still, my lady, lie still and sleep.
Though the north wind blows and the snow drifts deep.
My timid love, in our curtained bed,
The whine of the wolves you need not dread."

Hunger, when the north wind blows.
Starving wolves on the winter snows.
When old age sags in a sleep profound,
The rush of the wolves is the only sound.

She dreamt she walked in the forest shade,
Alone, and naked, and unafraid.
The bonds of being dissolved and broke.
Her body she dropped like a cast-off cloak.

Her shackled soul to its kindred sped.
In devouring lust with the wolves she fled.
But woke at dawn in a curtained bed.
By an old, grey man, in an airless bed.

She dreamt she walked where the wolf eyes gleam.
And soon she walked, and it was no dream.
She fell on fours from the world of man,
And howled her bliss when the rank beasts ran.

The morning life, and the mid-night life.
The sun and moon of the fair young wife.
The moon in the north land rules the sky.
She prays to it as it rises high.

"Moon in glory, shining so cold.
Oh! moon at my window big and bold.
On fields near the forest the snow lies white,
Will it show our tracks when we run tonight?

For fifty leagues on the frozen snow,
I'll feel through my fur the north wind blow,

As I run to drink of a bounding flood,
With the mighty pack on its quest for blood.

Strong, free, furions, swift to slay,
But back to his bed by the break of day!
Can I lie down at a husband's will,
When wild love runs, and my heart cries, Kill!"

"Wife, are you ready to come to bed?"
Her husband calls from the room overhead.
"The lights are out in the distant town.
And I can't sleep until you lie down."

Softly panting, she climbs the stair.
The moon lights the bed with a livid glare.
"I'll draw the curtains, and hug you near.
And we'll lie hid from the moon, my dear."

Curtains drawn in the deep of night.
Through smothering velvet no glimmer of light.
He turns to his love, lying warm in the dark.
In her eyes, shining near him, he sees a red spark.

A spark as bright as the break of day.
She tosses him down in ravenous play.
To the edge of the forest ring his cries.
"A beast! A beast! on my body lies!"

The wolf pack howls in the waste of snow.
She howls to answer them long and low.
But she will not run with the wolves tonight
Though the full moon shines with a blinding light.

Behind the curtains her jaws drip red.
She has found her prey in her own dark bed;
The man, who nearing the end of his life,
Took to his arms a fair young wife.

AG: And that poem was 4-beat 4-beat 4-beat, rhymed AABB. So that's another form you can use. If you have trouble getting into it, if you notice the way she was mouthing her language, mouthing her vowels, so you got blooood and hoooowl, so that it's somewhere in between speech, very conscious speech, with the consonants and the vowels really there, consciously pronounced, mindfully pronounced, so it's like a *vipassana* approach to vowels and consonants. *Vipassana* means mindfulness of your insight, you have to pronounce, just when you're breathing. When you pronounce your vowels you know you've got a vowel in your mouth, and you know you've got a "t" at the end of your tongue, or a "p" on your lips. So it's useful to have that in mind auditorially, silently or aloud when you're composing, so you can actually use that, it kind of brings inspiration—because that's what it is, actually, inspiration, breath, so it's conscious breath, formed in the mouth, it's a breath being consciousness not dissimilar to meditation practice. But this is mouthing speech practice, using your breath formulating vowels and consonants. And if you listen to Dylan or any great singer, you'll hear everything sung exactly to a "t." The consonants are really there, pronounced, dead, exaggerated, even, so you can hear it, clear, as you hear Helen saying, rrrrready. Be prepared to pronounce things aloud, in your head. Be corny with it in that sense.

HA: Yes, you oughtn't be afraid to be corny, with any ballad.

The Wang River Sequence, A Prospectus

ARTHUR SZE
June 1998

★　★　★

Wang Wei (701-761) is by now acknowledged as a great poet of T'ang dynasty China. In 1972, Wai-lim Yip published *Hiding the Universe: Poems by Wang Wei;* in 1982, François Cheng's *Chinese Poetic Writing* appeared in English; in 1987, Eliot Weinberger published *19 Ways of Looking at Wang Wei.* These are just three notable examples. Yet, despite these fine works, I believe the magnitude of Wang Wei's accomplishment has not been fully appreciated. He is generally regarded as a poet who created miniature masterpieces. Although François Cheng has made provocative and astonishing readings of individual poems, including "Hsin-yi Village," a reader does not learn the full context for such a miniature masterpiece. Although Eliot Weinberger does a fine job in presenting and discussing nineteen different translations of the same poem, "Deer Enclosure," it is not in the scope of his book to discuss its precise location and meaning in the larger sequence of poems. Of the three books mentioned, Wai-lim Yip is the only one to present these two poems in their proper context, as part of a much larger sequence.

I believe "The Wang River Sequence," written near the end of Wang Wei's life (roughly 756-761), is a monumental work and has not received the recognition it deserves. It is comprised of forty poems: each poem is formally a *chueh-chu,* or quatrain, with five characters to a line. Each poem of twenty characters can be considered a compressed lyric. In addition, "The Wang River Sequence" also incorporates the dramatic. Each poem by Wang Wei is always followed by a poem by P'ei Ti so that there are twenty pairs. It is important to know that in the T'ang dynasty poems were chanted, but, here, each of P'ei Ti's poems has the instruction or phrase *tong yong,* which means "together chant." A sequence of poems, chanted back and forth by two respective speakers, is a remarkable innovation. In addition to the lyric and dramatic elements, "The Wang River Sequence" incorporates the symbolic. Each pair of poems has the title of a place near where Wang Wei lived. The twenty place names incorporate the symbolic and act as markers for an interior journey. Here it is important to realize

Wang Wei was a great painter as well as a poet; he is supposed to have invented the form of the horizontal landscape scroll. This fact becomes very significant when one realizes that Wang Wei painted a "Wang River Scroll" which depicted all twenty places named in "The Wang River Sequence." We know that Wang Wei prized this scroll and that he kept it for himself. When he died, the scroll was passed on but was eventually lost. Nevertheless, a paraphrase, a "Wang River Scroll, after Wang Wei," attributed to Chao Meng-fu, 1309, in the British Museum survives. This scroll is nearly seventeen feet long and depicts a journey through one continuous unfolding landscape which uses the Wang River as a unifying thread. I believe "The Wang River Sequence" thus contains an interior narrative or journey that links all twenty pairs of poems together. If this is true, "The Wang River Sequence" combines lyrical, dramatic, narrative, and symbolic elements in a remarkable and monumental work of art.

Let's begin by looking at the overall structure. "The Wang River Sequence" consists of a pair of poems for each of the following twenty places. For the sake of convenience, I am using Wai-lim Yip's titles:

1: Cove of the Walls of Meng
2: Hua-tzu Hill
3: Grainy Apricot Heights
4: Frost-Bamboo Ranges
5: Deer Enclosure
6: Magnolia Enclosure
7: Dogwood Bay
8: Ashtree Path
9: Lakeside Pavilion
10: South Hillock
11: Lake Yi
12: Willow Waves
13: Rill of the House of the Luans
14: Gold-Dust Spring
15: White-Rock Rapids
16: North Hillock
17: Bamboo Grove
18: Hsin-yi Village
19: Lacquer-Tree Garden
20: Pepper-Plant Garden

I want to look carefully at poems #17, #18, and #5. My translation of Wang Wei's poem #17, "Bamboo Grove," follows:

> I sit alone in the secluded bamboo grove
> and play the zither and whistle along.
> In the deep forest no one knows,
> the bright moon comes to shine on me.

A five character line has a caesura between the second and third characters, 1-2 / 3-4-5. If I use a word or words in English to approximate the motion of each Chinese character, the first line is:

> alone sit / secluded, dark bamboo grove in

This poem is about revelation and, like so many of Wang Wei's poems, is a drama and a mystery. The first two characters, "alone sit," set the scene for sitting meditation, and a secluded bamboo grove is an appropriate setting. The third character, *yu,* is particularly rich. (The concept, *yugen,* in later Japanese literary theory, which can be described as "veiled, dark, mysterious, almost disappearing" stems from this Chinese character.) So, there may be an actual bamboo grove, or, the bamboo grove may be emblematical of the speaker's state of mind. Both. The poem will go on to show that the imagination and the external world are mutually responsive and equally shine. In line two, the speaker plays the zither: that one element of music might be sufficient, but, no, the speaker also whistles along. According to some studies, whistling is a Taoist practice connected with meditation. There's a kind of mutual counterpoint, then, in playing the zither *and* whistling along. In the third line, the "deep forest" picks up on the "secluded bamboo grove." There's an increasing sense of darkness and mystery. With "in the deep forest no one knows," there's a tension between what the protagonist of the poem is experiencing and his recognition that other people are not aware this is happening. Finally, in the fourth line, the "bright moon comes to shine" so that the speaker becomes activated as a source of illumination.

I believe this pivotal moment leads into Wang Wei's poem #18, "Hsin-yi Village," the crucial poem to the entire "Wang River Sequence." Here's my translation:

> At the tips of branches,
> > hibiscus
> opening red calyxes
> > deep in the mountains.
> A stream, hut:
> > yet no one.
> The flowers bloom
> > and fall, bloom and fall.

If one looks at the first five characters, one is astonished to see:

branch tip / hibiscus flower
(two characters for hibiscus)

In the first two characters, the area of visual focus narrows from tree branch to tip, then a hibiscus flower is presented. There's an allusion to a line in the *Ch'u Tz'u,* or *Songs of the South,* where the image of a lotus growing at the tip of a tree is used as an image of the miraculous. Here, the hibiscus at a point and moment of flowering is an emblem for the process of revelation. In the second line, the point and moment of flowering is moved into a larger perspective, "deep in the mountains." In that landscape, one sees a stream and hut, yet, there's no one around. "The flowers bloom and fall, bloom and fall." Here is the motion of nature, of life, without the interference of man—with man, in fact, dissolved into the landscape and into that process. By aligning the first five characters, Wang Wei is showing man moving into the process of unfolding so that he participates in the transformation of all life.

If we look now at Wang Wei's poem #5, "Deer Enclosure," we can see an earlier moment of revelation that counterpoints with #17, "Bamboo Grove." Here's "Deer Enclosure":

The mountain is empty, no man can be seen,
but the echo of human sounds is heard.
Returning sunlight, entering the deep forest,
shines again on green moss, above.

What is an empty mountain? A superb use of the caesura puts it in tension with "no man can be seen." The second line then contrasts *hearing* with *not seeing.* Yet, one does not hear human sounds but their resonance or echo, so there is a further distancing. In the third line, it is late afternoon. My sensation of the line in Chinese is that the sunlight is fading even as it enters the deep forest. The character I've translated as sunlight is particularly rich: it could be taken as "shadow, light, glow." In the last line, where, and even what, is the "green moss"? It is interesting to note that the poem begins on a vast scale, *empty mountain,* and ends with the minute, *shining on green moss.*

In looking now at the forty poems, what can be said about them? After several readings, it is clear that the work is meticulously crafted. P'ei Ti's poems, always coming after Wang Wei's, are like a bass line. In P'ei Ti's poem #2, he writes, "the mountain green touches one's clothes." He will pick this up in his final poem #20 with "scarlet thorns catch one's clothes."

A more remarkable act of balancing is Wang Wei's poem #5, "Deer Enclosure" and his later poem #17, "Bamboo Grove." Here are two key moments of revelation, balanced, near the beginning and toward the end, that use the image of sunlight and moonlight, respectively, as sources of illumination. In the forty poems, phrases also go back and forth between Wang Wei and Pei T'i. In #9, Wang Wei writes, "hibiscus blooms on all four sides." The *si mian*, "four sides," is emblemmatical of the world at large. P'ei Ti picks this up in his poem #11, "from all four sides, clear winds come." Furthermore, the image of the hibiscus leads to the crucial Wang Wei #18, where man finally enters and participates in the universal process of transformation.

Without translating all forty poems, it is difficult to give a reader a sense of the magnitude of Wang Wei's accomplishment. If one looks at the sequencing, one can point to a few highlights. In the beginning, poem #1, "Cove of the Walls of Meng," Wang Wei sets the place and begins with a meditation on time. The house Wang Wei purchased had previously belonged to another poet, Sung Chih-wen, who died in 712. Thus, the opening alludes to him as well as to Wang Wei. Poem #1 raises the issue of what decays and what survives. Pei T'i picks this up with, "Ancient walls, men come and go." In poem #5, "Deer Enclosure," Wang Wei makes a brilliant drama and moment of revelation out of sunlight shining on green moss. In a sense, the green moss may be the poet's mind. The sunlight is returning because there is a back and forth, morning and afternoon, recurring motion to the flux of existence. It is the green moss, the poet's mind, that begins to shine. In poem #14, "Gold-Dust Spring," there's the allusion to the Taoist practice of elixirs and search for immortality, but drugs and elixirs are ultimately of no help. In poem #17, "Bamboo Grove," the poet, in the heart of darkness, as it were, finds the music that is *his*. Nature responds, and he becomes a source of illumination. In #18, man passes into the very processes of transformation of all life. Poem #19 then turns to Taoist master, Chuangtzu, as a source of inspiration. In #20, Wang Wei's poem alludes to the *Ch'u Tz'u* and one reaches the very limits of time and space. Here, there's an invocation, as one might see in the earlier shamanistic *Nine Songs* which are part of the *Ch'u Tz'u*, for the divine spirit to descend.

Let's look, finally, at the remarkable use of empty space throughout "The Wang River Sequence." In many of the *chueh-chu*, Wang Wei exploits the conventional caesura between characters two and three, 1-2 / 3-4-5, to brilliant effect. There's also the empty space between each of his poems and P'ei Ti's which allows each pair to form a polarized unity. In addition, there's the empty space between each pair of poems and the other nineteen. The twenty pairs of poems, following twenty symbolic place markers, help mark crucial moments of revelation in an interior journey. Although there is no overt first-person linear narrative, the self is dissolved in the very progression. The interior journey through twenty symbolic places coalesces in #18 to unification of inner and outer, nature and man, space and time.

Much work needs to be done. There need to be more insightful readings of individual poems as well as how they fit into the larger structure. Others need to further illuminate the whole. I hope this essay, then, is not an end but a beginning.

A Brief History
of the Early Prose Poem

COLE SWENSEN
June 1997

"Who among us has not, in his ambitious moments,
dreamed of the miracle of a poetic prose . . . "
——CHARLES BAUDELAIRE

1.

Early prose poems show strong similarities in theme and method as well as in form—the following chart perhaps makes these connections more visible: [1]

WRITER	WORK	THEMES
Louis Bertrand a.k.a Aloysius (1807–1841)	*Gaspard de la nuit* (published 1842) (written 1828–40)	the visual (paintings) identity (self/other, doubling, alter-ego) binary fusion (good/evil; day/night)
Charles Baudelaire (1821–1867)	*Petits poèmes en prose* (*Spleen de Paris*) (1862)	the visual (painting/photography) identity (sub/unconscious; anonymity) binary fusion (day/night; good/evil; privilege/poverty)
Isidore Ducasse a.k.a Comte de Lautréamont (1846–1870)	*Les Chants de Maldoror* (1868)	the visual (cinematic) identity ("If I exist, I am not another.") binary fusion (good/evil; day/night)
Arthur Rimbaud (1854–1867)	*Illuminations* (1886) (written 1871–75) *A Season in Hell* (1872)	the visual (engravings, illuminations) identity ("I is an other.") binary fusion (day/night; good/evil; known/unknown)

The prose poem was a brand-new form in 1828, and it emerged in connection with the social, political, and physical transformation of Paris during the 19th century. This transformation was so extensive that it engendered—if not necessitated—several new forms of expression to absorb the tensions and other emotions that it occasioned.

There are other, earlier examples of poetic prose; the Bible, for instance; the Old Testament in particular is often given as an example—however, the prose poem as an intentional form is a product of modern, urban society. It had an interesting quasi-precursor in some early 19th-century translations by Huber, Chateaubriand, Prosper Mérimée, and others. Rather than violate the rhythmic and sound qualities of the source language through a doomed attempt to create their equal in the target language, poems were sometimes translated into prose blocks. This method was both truly sensitive to the delicacy of language and shrewdly aware of the contemporary value of the exotic and of ways to emphasize it.

All that aside, the practice gave us, after a fashion, the first prose poems. Prosper Mérimée's are particularly interesting because they're forgeries; in other words, they are not really translations, but original compositions in which he imitated other literary traditions and passed them off as translations—a kind of inverted plagiarism.

This approach to translation remained popular throughout the century; many of Gerard de Nerval's translations from the German are in prose as are Baudelaire's and Mallarmé's translations of Poe. However, such translations are not true prose poems because the form was chosen for what it would *not* do (violate the sounds and rhythms of an original), and not in recognition and exploitation of the particular properties it offered.

The four writers in the genealogical list above, however, did intentionally search out a hybrid form that incorporated aspects of both poetry and prose. And though they did not know each other personally, they were, in cases, directly influenced by each others' work. Rimbaud, for instance, is said to have written his first poem "Les Deserts de l'Amour" after reading Baudelaire's prose poems. And Baudelaire, in a letter to a friend, stated very plainly that it was " . . . in reading for at least the twentieth time, the famous *Gaspard de la nuit* by Aloysius Bertrand (and a book known to you and me and several of our friends has the right to be called famous, no?) that the idea came to me to try something like them, and to apply to the description of modern life, or rather of *a* life modern and more abstract, the process that he had applied to the painting of an ancient life, so strangely picturesque."[2]

That "a book known to you and me and several of our friends has the right to be called famous" says much about the development of the genre—it had the marginal, word-of-mouth quality of things that emerge just before the general social mind is expecting them, and that therefore function to foreshadow an imminent future. And Baudelaire, being Baudelaire, was not impeded by awe from making adjustments to his model: "to apply to the description of modern life, or rather of *a* life modern and more abstract, the process that . . . " Baudelaire recognized that Bertrand had invented not so much a form as a process, a method of perception in which the emphasis remains as much on the looking as on what is seen. Bertrand's work offered a deviation from the norm, and yet resisted establishing another set of norms, another stable form. Furthermore, his prose poetry would resist another stable form, which made it oddly appropriate for responding to mid-19th-century life as it began to deviate from patterns that were centuries old.

2.

Throughout the 19th century, Paris went through a transformation that demanded a reassessment of the relationship between private and public space. Fairly early in the century, renovation projects began changing the medieval network of interconnected alleys into a more regimented system of expansive avenues and regular streets; tenements in the city were replaced with new, uniform buildings, and practical improvements, such as the sidewalks introduced in 1781, became widespread. Much of this renovation was at least partially politically motivated, for while offering the populace more fresh air and sunlight, the changes also flaunted progress and prosperity (thus advertising the sponsoring regime) on the one hand, while displaying power and discouraging the erection of barricades on the other. This transformation is generally referred to as the Haussmannization of Paris, and though it began before Haussmann's reign as Prefect of the Seine (1853-70), it was during Haussmann's time that the greatest changes took place. Over 20,000 buildings were torn down to allow construction of avenues and boulevards; 600 kilometers of sewers were constructed; gas lighting was installed along all major streets, and 2,000 hectares of park and woodland were opened up to public access.[3]

Haussmann's program, along with spreading industrialization, also altered views and horizons, transportation, air quality, and ambient sound. I. A. Richards, writing of the midcentury, emphasized the effect that ambient sound has on poetry: "No one at all sensitive to rhythm, for example, will doubt that the new pervasive, almost ceaseless, mutter or roar of modern transport, replacing the rhythm of the footstep or of the horses' hoofs, is capable of interfering in many ways with our reading of verse. Thus it is not a matter of surprise if we find ourselves often unable to respond in any relevant or coherent fashion."[4] Richards's comment finds a potential solution in the prose poem, which established a new rhythm, less regular, less formally structured; it was poetry adapted precisely to the changes in ambient sound. The rhythms of the popular arts of any age develop to aestheticize ambient sound, and in this case, the rhythms of the prose poem reflect an overall atmosphere of expansion, improvisation, and adaptability—socially, economically, stylistically.

And despite Richards's assertion, the predominant rhythm of the prose poem is linked to that of walking. As opposed to the strict twelve-syllable Alexandrine, more analogous to a formal dance step, which had dominated French poetry from the middle of the 17th century, the prose poem's rhythms are rolling and variable. They can take on an ambulatory gait, reinforced by the extended line, or become compressed with either regular or irregular syllabification. With this flexibility, the new genre offered, perhaps for the first time, a poetry that could be in a hurry, and thus a poetry well-adapted to modern life.

It was also the poetry of the *flaneur*—that 19th-century urban type theorized and epitomized by Baudelaire. A young man of fashion with time on his hands, the *flaneur* was obsessed with observing others, and yet refused to be moved by what he saw. His observation, while publicly presented as disdainful, was in fact deeply engaged in an attempt to unravel or to solve, puzzle-fashion, the modern life he saw before him. In his essay, *The Painter of Modern Life,* Baudelaire claims that the work of certain artists, particularly Constantin Guys, translates *flaneurie* into visual art; his own poems in prose are its translation into words. Looked at the other way around, the *flaneur* was the embodiment of innovations in various arts—the urban sketches of Guys or Daumier, the fleeting quality of much Impressionist work, the action-caught-in-flight of photography, and the scanning eye and ambulatory pace of the prose poem.

The *flaneur* was a marginal character, more so literally than figuratively, for while he often held a solid social position, he spent his time on the edge of the crowd, standing back and watching, somehow always outside it even when caught up in its flow. A similar stance haunts the prose poem—not only in form but also in content: the writer's eye is often observing, scanning a scene and recording detail, without becoming a part of it himself. The lives of the early prose poets reinforce the theme of marginality—all were outside the social mainstream to some degree; some, such as Rimbaud, chose, even cultivated, the distance, while others, such as Bertrand, tried to bridge it.

The *flaneur* and the prose poem also had a common social purpose—to reappropriate surveillance. Much of the period's urban renovation had as a secondary, if not primary, purpose the surveillance and regulation of the increasingly large and dense population. Streetlights, broader streets and fewer alleys, and—beginning midcentury—the numbering of houses, all enabled the increasingly anonymous individual to be tracked. The *flaneur* parodied this surveillance by acting it out but not using the information. Similarly, the prose poem kept a parodic report—a report that would be put to the service of the individual for affective and aesthetic reasons rather than to the service of the public, like the reports generated by the recently formed police force.

On the less ominous side, broader streets and new streetlighting, new parks and the benches that lined the avenues all implied an invitation to know the new city in a new way. The nature of the crowds that strolled these streets gradually altered—no longer were they composed entirely of those who had to be there; from Haussmann's period on, they included a sizable number of aristocrats and bourgeois who were there simply for the pleasure of strolling, a pastime that rapidly became fashionable. Like the *flaneur,* these strollers were visually oriented—there to see who else was there and to be seen themselves as part of fashionable society. An additional, and by no means secondary, visual attraction was the shopwindow. In addition to the shopping arcades or *passages,* which had formed genteel gathering places and commercial centers since the 1830s, shops with impressive *vitrines,* or shopwindows began to line the boulevards.

This emphasis on the visual is reflected in early prose poetry; many examples echo paintings, immediately and simplistically in their rectangular shape, but more importantly in their continued reliance on the "so strangely picturesque." The pictoral emphasis was ideal for negotiating urban change; being two-dimensional, all right there on the surface, it could capture the complex of emotional repercussions simultaneously. On the one hand, these repercussions included spontaneity, energy, and visual delight; on the other, anonymity oddly blended with lack of privacy and increased commodification, both of goods and human relationships. In its pictorial emphasis, the prose poem followed Baudelaire's dictum that art, to be relevant, had to concern itself with modernity, or, "the ephemeral, the fugitive, the contingent."[5] Such art worked two ways—it honored the fleeting and the tumultuous, but it also framed them as intentional compositions, making them more assimilable.

Another bi-product of urban renovation was stark contrast; by mid-19th century, Paris was composed of opposites, politically, economically, and visually. At times one extreme would vie for dominance, but frequently, and more disconcertingly, they seemed to co-exist. The tension and resolution of opposites that dominates the prose poem thematically was only partially rooted here, for it also reflected, and rejected, the dualism inherited from Enlightenment thinking. Repeatedly in these poems, binary oppositions are resolved, not by choosing one pole or the other, but by developing their discrepancy into a third term independent of the initial two, but not in turn part of another pair. The prose poem itself is a primary example—it is neither poem nor prose, or, as Baudelaire put it, ". . . it has neither head nor tail, for, on the contrary, it is both head and tail at once, alternatively and reciprocally . . . "[6]

3.

Though Baudelaire's name dominates any discussion of early prose poetry because of his valuable analytic and critical work, it was Aloysius Bertrand, with his volume *Gaspard de la nuit,* who first intentionally used the form, and he was fully aware that he was not only using it, but inventing it: *"Gaspard de la nuit,* the book in which I tried to create a new genre of prose . . . " he wrote in an 1837 letter to a good friend.[7] With Bertrand and *Gaspard* came the principal thematic preoccupations that dominated the "new genre of prose" throughout the 19th century: identity/subjectivity; good/evil; pictoriality, and darkness.

Aloysius Bertrand was the perfect "poet maudit"—he was poor, literally lived in a garret, and died young of tuberculosis. Born in Italy and raised in Dijon, he was marginal not only in relation to the dominant Parisian society, but also in relation to literary subculture. This second alienation was due in part to his coming from the provinces—in itself enough to engender feelings of inferiority in the susceptible—but was compounded by his personality, which has been described as shadowy, difficult, and melancholy. In his brother's words, he was "of an excessive sensibility, unable to tolerate contradiction, easily irritated, and susceptible to rages without reason."[8] A few lines further on, the same brother records that he was "dissatisfied with himself in general and unjust toward others." Perhaps it was a combination of this social marginality and his ornery nature that allowed him to deviate from the entrenched poetic patterns and do something formally new.

He began his writing career quite young, and though his early work is strongly influenced by the formally and stylistically progressive writers of his day, even some of his early pieces veered toward an unusual use of prose. He began presenting his work publicly while still living in Dijon; one piece from this period that attracted comment was an Orientalist piece, which was in itself nothing new, in fact it was right in line with the prevailing Romantic aesthetic, but it was written in a prose that foregrounded intentional rhythms and sound relationships more commonly associated with verse. His work, both then and later when presented in Paris, was very well received. Once in Paris, he was accepted into Hugo's and Nodier's salons, where he presented pieces and participated in the discussions of the day. Saint-Beuve remarked upon his work's "almost geometric precision . . . exquisite, picturesque curiosity of the vocabulary . . . like daguerreotypes in literature."[9]

As this comment indicates, Bertrand's interest lay in the spatial and the visual. In his "geometric precision," he attempted a spatial extension of the page, augmenting the strict linearity of the text. Precision too lay behind the "daguerreotype" quality noticed by Saint-Beuve. Bertrand was interested in art history, and filled notebooks with precise descriptions and analyses of Flemish, Italian, and French paintings, but he also had a lively interest in the emerging field of photography, and had his own daguerreotype equipment. His confusion or fusion of the disparate modes of the visual and the verbal was entirely conscious; by 1828, he was reading and publishing selections from a collection titled *Bambochades,* a word that means "rustic genre paintings," and the full title of his only extended work is *Gaspard de la nuit. Fantaisies à la manière de Rembrandt et de Callot.* This affiliation with painting has implications for the construction and use of space within the pieces as well as for the arrangement of their content, both of which are, in ways, more painterly than they are writerly.

Bertrand put unprecedented emphasis on the space of the page, orchestrating the interior use of space through detailed directions to the typesetter: "Monsieur the typesetter . . . should insert large white spaces between the blocks of text as if they were stanzas of verse."[10] In terms of content, the reader is offered series of images that occur, it seems, simultaneously, for the order implied by the necessary linearity of language is presented as just that—arbitrary and only due to necessity. It is up to the reader to wander this territory and establish (or not) its true order.

Though it has been suggested that Bertrand developed the prose poem in an attempt to render paint and visual composition in words, he was more than a failed painter; he seems to have known just what he was doing in playing with the peculiar tension achieved by using a medium against itself. Théophile Gautier referred to this intermingling of media as the "transportation of art," thereby downplaying its contradictory qualities and focusing on the added dimensions that could be achieved by fusing language's need to unfold in time with visual art's need to extend in space. One way to resolve this conflict is through motion, in which these two modes merge. A signature element of the prose poem, the attempt to capture emotion also begins with Bertrand, who attempted to record his scenes *"sur le vif"*—in mid-flight, mid-gesture, and with an on-the-spot feeling that foreshadowed the Impressionist painters.

Throughout the early development of the prose poem, space-related anxiety continues to be resolved through a pictorial emphasis. Like Bertrand's works, Rimbaud's *Illuminations* also approaches the visual directly, beginning with the title, which depending on whether it's read as a French or an English word, refers either to colored engravings or to the miniature paintings in medieval and Renaissance manuscripts. As there's some evidence that parts of the collection were written in England, both possibilities seem legitimate, and the ambiguity may well have been intentional. A more abstract and mystical interpretation can also be claimed; however, Verlaine, to whom Rimbaud entrusted the manuscript in 1875, claimed that Rimbaud intended its subtitle to be "painted plates." That aside, the collection is marked by an acute visual attention and a heightened sense of landscape. Yet they are impossible landscapes, with cathedrals that fall and lakes that rise, landscapes without frames and thus without constraint; these "tableaux" expand and overflow, blurring the line between their worlds and the natural world. Rimbaud is using the form, in part, to extend and complicate the natural world.

The pictorial is equally present in Baudelaire's *Petits poèmes en prose,* with their minute observation of daily urban life. His own daily life was immersed in the visual arts through his critical writings, in which he critiqued the works of painters such as Delacroix and Ingres, events such as the annual salons, and developments such as photography. He was a friend of one of the first commercial photographers, Félix Nadar, and he capitalized on something stark, almost brutal, that is native to photography in its early stages. The questions raised by photography, acutely felt in its early years—questions of impending perceptual change, the introduction of a new degree of realism, etc.—are implicitly explored in Baudelaire's urban scenes.

Isidore Ducasse's work, too, has a strong visual component, though, oddly, it's closer to film. Like a movie camera, his attention follows relentlessly, moving swiftly and untraceably, changing perspective and angle self-consciously. We can feel the frames going by, with the result that the *Chants de Maldoror* has an overall narrative fluidity even though it is constructed of small, self-contained prose poems.

The fragmentation that forms an important structural element of *Maldoror* is also apparent throughout the genre, and is another symptom of the painterly approach: each prose poem is a discrete unit, composed of discrete units within itself, again removing it from a temporal continuum and beginning to spatialize it. This aspect, too, addressed the disruption of social space, and in a way similar to another 19th-century literary genre, the feuilleton, in which extended works, usually popular novels, were published in installments in newspapers and magazines. The format had obvious commercial advantages, but less overtly, it said, "though this seems to be in pieces, with a bit of patience, you'll see that it really is a cohesive whole."

The relationship of the individual to society was in upheaval through-out the 19th century in France. The 1789 revolution had released many people from long-standing affiliation with estates, guilds, and other forms of community, and the migration to Paris in search of the work supplied by industrialization had separated many people from their families in the provinces. These trends demanded new modes of social organization, which often included a more direct relationship between the individual and the various powers bearing on his or her life. A reassessment of personal identity and the role of individualism is reflected in prose poetry by a focus on the "I" and on the proper name that began with Bertrand. Born Louis Bertrand, he adopted the pseudonym Aloysius before he began publishing, indicating a slight slip in the constancy of identity between man and writer; they are, somehow, not entirely congruent. His character, Gaspard, complicates the issue further. There is a strong but ambiguous link between writer and character, and the physical description of Gaspard is an accurate description of Bertrand, but the two characters that frame the tableaux are opposing rather than parallel, and the "I" that questions Gaspard is never named.

Isidore Ducasse made use of a similar layering and sliding in his work. He too wrote under a pseudonym, adopting that of the Comte de Lautréamont from the title of a novel by the popular writer, Eugene Sue. And he, too, at times gets confused with his character, Maldoror. Throughout the text, pronouns and other allusions get increasingly ambiguous, and to further complicate matters, Ducasse brings the reader into it, using a direct address that forces the question, "Who is *you?*" The text records the increasing instability of identity prevalent at the time.

Ducasse also addressed the issue of identity directly in comments: "If I exist, I am not another. I do not acknowledge this ambiguous plurality in myself. I wish to reside alone in my inner deliberations." There's a touch of "protesting too much" to this comment; clearly the issue was a live one for him.

Rimbaud took a very different approach in his famous statement, "I is an other." The two statements are not refutations or inversions of each other; they instead address entirely different territories. Rimbaud's I is other; it has no interior, no intimacy, no necessary connection to the speaker. It is an agent, almost always in action: "I climbed . . . ," "I churned," "Friends, I want her to be queen!" This is less true in the "Deserts of Love," but by the time he wrote the *Illuminations,* the I has become third person, and for pages at a time, doesn't appear at all. In such passages, the I is over-taken by the eye, which is flooded by the world, consumed by it.

Baudelaire doesn't deal as directly with identity and subjectivity issues; instead, they comprise a shadow presence behind and around his work, infusing it with a psychological weight that directs his explorations of what we would now call "the dark side" of the personality. This dark side is one of the sources of the general darkness—variously presented as night and as evil—which is one of the genre's signatures. These works all prowl the night, often, implicitly or explicitly searching, perhaps for the security and intimacy of an earlier social order, but more likely, for its replacement. Such nocturnal wandering is also a way of constructing a new inner space, as if walking, pacing, strolling, etc., all established within the individual psyche a territory corresponding to that covered in the outside world.

The nocturnal emphasis constitutes an inversion (thereby contributing to the legitimation of inversion per se) in that night is presented as the default condition; these texts imply that things—like most of these texts, for instance—naturally occur at night. Emphasis is also placed on the moment of shift from day to night, the gray zone of evening. In fact, the gray zones—whether between day and night, good and evil, monarchy and republicanism, the old world and the new, handwork and machine work, etc.—are the true field of action for the prose poem, as if its intention were to surprise an entity at the instant of change and thereby dispel the illusion of stability, of stasis itself.

Though the prose poem has become an increasingly popular form and is no longer regarded as marginal, it remains an unsettled form, inviting mutations and innovations, and resisting the stagnation of precise definition just as well as it did in the 19th century.

★

Notes:

[1] The following list does not include Stéphane Mallarmé, which is a grievous omission in one sense, as some of his earliest published texts were in the form of prose poems written around 1864 and therefore contemporaneous with those of Baudelaire. He is not treated here only because his contribution, while having its place in the initial development of the prose poem, is more properly seen as the beginning of the second stage of its history. Moreover, it cannot accurately be dealt with outside of the larger context of his reassessment of page space and his considerable work on the nature of the book. Rather than present a too-brief and therefore misleading treatment of the issues, I have decided to leave them out entirely and instead recommend the reader to the many available sources of this information.

[2] Baudelaire, Charles. *Petits Poèmes en Prose*. Paris: Gallimard, 1973. 21-22.

[3] de Moncan, Patrice. *Les Jardins du Baron Haussmann*. Paris: Le Louvre des Antiquaires, 1992. passim.

[4] Richards, I. A. Quoted in *Paris and the Nineteenth Century*, Christopher Prendergast. Oxford: Basil Blackwell, 1995. 129.

[5] Baudelaire, Charles. "The Painter of Modern Life." In *Selected Writings on Art and Literature*. Trans. P. E. Charvet, 403. London: Penguin Books, 1972.

6   Ibid.

7   Milner, Max. Introduction to *Gaspard de la Nuit*, by Aloysius Bertrand. Paris: Gallimard, 1980. 12.

8   Rude, Fernand. *Aloysius Bertrand*. Paris: Seghers; Poètes d'aujourd'hui, 1971. 9

9   Ibid. 19

10   Milner, Max. Introduction to *Gaspard de la Nuit*, by Aloysius Bertrand, 1980. 27.

Dharma
Poetics

Comment, Dharma Poetics Panel

GARY SNYDER
1994

★   ★   ★

GARY SNYDER: Several people here have commented on the contradictory attitudes found in the Buddhist tradition toward poetry and the arts. This has been a fruitful, ongoing contradiction. Not everybody in our practice wants to write poetry anyway, and those who do are not seeking gain. Dharma students and monks were told from long ago, as in the Zen tradition, and as I was told—that the lowest sort of Zen student is the one who writes poetry. That having been said, it is still up to you to see if you want to write poetry. If you do, give it your best energy.

Gelek Rinpoche pointed out how the initial austere Theravadin position toward literary expression gradually softened. I'm not sure if that list of "unprofitable talk" that he mentioned even includes poetry. The cautionary roster of unprofitable topics sounds more like chatter of television talk shows, which are without the silences. Right? No silent time on television.

AUDIENCE MEMBER: Dead time!

GS: Exactly, dead time. Whereas, we all know in poetry *silence is live.* And it may be that they weren't even talking about poetry at that point. Certainly in the later Indian and Tibetan—and very much in the Japanese and Chinese traditions—poetry became one part of advanced Dharma practice. There's a Noh play, the name eludes me at the moment, which has a dialogue between two priests in which one says, "Does not the Buddha forbid these frivolous activities such as music, dance, and poetry?" And the response is, "When coming from the true self, all music, poetry, and dance is an offering to the Buddha." That's indeed the way that Japanese culture took it. This view was reinforced by Kobo Daishi in the 8th century, who affirmed that the arts should be seen as part of a *puja,* the offering, that one makes to teachers, to the Buddha, to the Dharma. Kobo Daishi, the bringer of esoteric Buddhism to Japan, was a remarkable artist, a great calligrapher, a fine poet, and an extraordinary teacher. He was also the founder of the great temples on Mount Koya.

Poetry itself, we might think, by the virtue of its intuitive and imaginative openness is a Dharma exercise. Maybe some people think that?

Maybe it's true? In 1956 I found myself in a Zen temple in Kyoto. I finally timorously managed to say to my Roshi (he knew nothing about me)— "I also write poetry. Is that OK?" He answered, "As long as it comes from your true self." That gave me something to work on. I didn't write a poem for three years.

Dôgen Zenji is most precise when he says, "We study the self to forget the self, when you forget the self you become one with the ten thousand things." I think that many of us are now telling our students in poetry workshops: if you have come here to express yourself in poetry, think twice. Poetry is not self-expression. Students might say, well, what is it then? It is something that is slightly beyond the expression of yourself. So study yourself so you can forget it. And then, maybe you can freely play with reality. I once asked my professor in classical Chinese poetry at U.C.-Berkeley, Dr. Chen Shih-hsiang, who did he consider to be the greatest Chinese Buddhist poet. He thought for a while and said, "Du Fu."

I thought, "Du Fu? Du Fu wasn't even Buddhist." Chen said, "That's why he's so good." The doctrinal metric poems (of which there are many) in the Buddhist tradition have their use—they are a help in remembering points. But they aren't exactly poetry. Du Fu is deep. He didn't need to mention Buddhism. He didn't even have to be Buddhist. His work is the complexly clearest (rich in multiple meanings but never gratuitously difficult) poetry in the *shih*, lyric, tradition.

Gelek Rinpoche told us, "The folk song says,

> The moon is out, the wind is warm,
> The air is sweet, where's my girlfriend?"

A folk song belongs to an even older meaning of "classic," as in the "Classic of Poetry" compiled in 5th century BC China. It has a number of folk songs from as much as a thousand years before. Maybe these are the teachings of the Ancient Buddha.

Ki-no-Tsurayuki, a medieval Japanese poet commenting on poetry said, "All that lives loves to sing." Poetry is originally song. This past spring I've been paying attention to bird song. Each songbird has an extraordinary little phrase or two that it makes with variations. There is a robin who will not let up every morning for an hour and a half up in the top of a pine. The very pine woods themselves would not be what they are without the call of the red-breasted nuthatch—that is a key part, like the sound of the breeze, in the song of a forest. My wife Carole is a practiced birder. I asked her, "What do all the birds sing?"—she said, "His song is,

Where is my sweetheart? I am here.
Where is my sweetheart? I am here"

That's a *really* old song. It becomes a kind of kôan for the Dharma student who has to ponder, then, who am *I?* What is *Here? Sweetheart??*—in a dialogue with the Ancient Buddha.

Revised September 27, 2003.

Burroughs and Dharma

JAMES GRAUERHOLZ
June 24, 1999

★   ★   ★

Greetings, and thank you all for coming to my lecture today. I would like to dedicate my presentation to the loving memory of Rick Fields, who died recently after a long illness. Rick was a writer and historian whose masterful book, *How the Swans Came to the Lake*, is required reading for anyone who is interested in the historical underpinnings of American Dharma.[1] Rick knew William for many years, and he edited and published William's writing, so the links of that chain are unbroken.

In this talk I hope to illustrate the role that Eastern philosophy played in the life and work of William S. Burroughs, who—as you know—died peacefully almost two years ago at age eighty-three, on August 2, 1997. As you probably also know, I was William's companion and collaborator for the last twenty-three years of his life, beginning soon after he moved back to the United States in early 1974—the same year that Naropa Institute was founded, which of course is why we are celebrating the twenty-fifth anniversary of Naropa this year.

William Burroughs was not a Buddhist: he never sought or found a "Teacher," he never took Refuge, and he never undertook any Boddhisattva vows. He did not consider himself a Buddhist, nor—for that matter—did he ever declare himself a follower of any one faith or practice. But he did have an awareness of the essentials of Buddhism, and in his own way, he was affected by bodhidharma. Because of this, and because many of his closest friends—such as Jack Kerouac and Allen Ginsberg—were Buddhists (often considering him as one of their Teachers), Burroughs and his work can be explored within a Buddhist setting. So, since we are all here at a learning institution founded by Buddhists, this is perhaps an interesting way for us to approach the life and work of William Burroughs.

William spent a great deal of time in Boulder and was effectively a resident of this town for two years, from 1976 to 1978. His first visit here was for two weeks in 1975, and after he set himself up in "The Bunker" (his New York loft) with the help of his close friend, the Buddhist poet John Giorno, in late 1978, he continued to make annual visits to Naropa until

1989. There are many people in Boulder—still living here, or visiting here this week—who knew William during those years.

Before I talk about William's life, I would like to say a few things about my own life, in particular the years before I met William, so that you will have some context for my observations.

I was born in southeast Kansas in 1952, and my first awareness of the existence of something called "Buddhism" was in my grade school days, when—reading selections from the work of Arthur Schopenhauer in the "Great Books" series—I encountered his remarks on Buddhism, as found in his 1818 work, *The World as Will and Idea*. Like Schopenhauer (and everybody else, probably), I had an unhappy childhood, and I gravitated naturally toward the work of classic writers and philosophers whose view of human nature and human existence was essentially pessimistic: Swift, Voltaire, de Sade, Sterne, the Book of Ecclesiastes . . . and Burroughs, of course. I was fourteen when I stumbled onto his best-known novel, *Naked Lunch,* and it was love at first sight.

Schopenhauer's intellectual embrace of Buddhist principles was based primarily on his impressions of the First Noble Truth, as Buddhists call it: the idea that the essence of life itself is suffering, dukkha, or "unsatisfactoriness"—the First Mark of all conditioned dharmas (the other two being impermanence and egolessness). If you will indulge me I'd like to quote from the Buddha's Sermon at Deer Park in Benares: "Now this, monks, is the noble truth of pain: birth is painful, old age is painful, sickness is painful, death is painful, sorrow, lamentation, dejection, and despair are painful. Contact with unpleasant things is painful, not getting what one wishes is painful. In short the five skandhas [the five "heaps" of human personality] are painful."[2] My first contact with this scripture was decisive for me; it had, as William would put it, the aspect of "surprised recognition."

I went to the University of Kansas in Lawrence at age sixteen and by my sophomore year I had begun taking Eastern philosophy classes from Dr. Alfonso Verdu. Dr. Verdu was a very interesting Catalonian who had studied in Germany under Husserl, the phenomenologist and a student of the dialectical materialism of Hegel. Verdu went on to study the history of Eastern philosophy at various places in Asia. He was also a friend of the late Dr. Agehananda Bharati, a German-born Tibetanist whom Verdu brought to K.U. for a one-semester class, which I was also fortunate to attend in 1971.

At K.U. Dr. Verdu was teaching a staged series of classes covering the development of Eastern thought from Hinduism to Zen, emphasizing the evolution of these beliefs according to the Hegelian dialectical model of "thesis-antithesis-synthesis." I followed Dr. Verdu's course of classes through my last three years at K.U., but I dropped out of college just before the end of his class on Zen Buddhism. By that time I personally had become "too Zen" to stay in school any longer—or so I thought, at that tender age. I considered myself then a pratyeka buddha, or "lone-wolf boddhisattva," with no Teacher and no sitting practice, as such.

I hung around Lawrence for another year or so, playing guitar in local bands, and so forth; then I went to New York and met William Burroughs. That meeting set the stage for the rest of my life.

So as you see, I was not drawn to the Dharma by any predisposition toward finding a Buddhist Teacher whom I could follow, and with whom I could take Refuge, nor by any fascination with Buddhist symbology or ritual . . . my inclination basically originated in an artistic and intellectual attraction to any doctrine that could explain why I was so unhappy and so disgusted by the world of the so-called "adults" all around me. Of course, in a broader sense you could say that at age twenty-one I found my "teacher" in William himself, and I could not deny that.

From his earliest childhood in St. Louis, Missouri in the 1920s, Burroughs was alienated and repulsed by the personal and social hypocrisy that he could not help but perceive around him, even at the age of eight or ten. He was terribly shy, and frightened of the other children, but at the same time defiant in his own beliefs and inclinations—including his homosexual attraction to some of his classmates. A sense of being fundamentally "different" from the others marked his childhood, and never left him, all his life.

The Burroughs family's economic circumstances, while never approaching the kind of wealth that is often wrongly associated with his family (thanks to Jack Kerouac's pseudo-biographical inventions about him), were certainly comfortable, and he grew up surrounded by the children of the upper classes of old St. Louis and their parents. A bit like Gautama Sakyamuni, in his childhood Burroughs was somewhat insulated from the phenomena of "old age, sickness, and death"—but his parents' domestic servants at that time showed him his first glimpses of the not-so-perfect world that lay beyond his family circle. For example, an Irish nanny and a Welsh governess taught him how to throw curses and how to "call the toads." The servants also exposed him to sordid scenes from their own personal lives as lower-class émigrés to America. Burroughs's governess had a veterinarian boyfriend, and she and the boyfriend took little Willie along on a picnic date one day when he was about four years old. Apparently there occurred a sexual situation involving little Willie, which traumatized him.

In his twenties Burroughs saw a series of psychoanalysts in the hope that recouping this early trauma would allow him to break free of the psychic constraints and self-defeating reflexes that he felt as a lifelong curse. Then when he was thirty, in New York, Burroughs met Kerouac and Ginsberg, and after a period of several months in which he was conducting his own "lay analyses" of his new friends, his recently developed addiction of morphine began to take the place of his analytic efforts. He had abandoned all faith in psychiatry by the age of forty-five, but long before that, he had concluded that the Freudian model of "cure of neurosis through recuperation of primordial trauma" was overrated.

Burroughs was also troubled by philosophical questions about the significance of language; in 1939 he had gone to Chicago to attend a series of lectures by Count Alfred Korzybski, the founder of a school of thought that he called "General Semantics." From these lectures Burroughs took away the insight that a word is not its referent—the word has no tangible existence—and that what William called "dualistic," or "either/or" thinking is an intellectual trap. Like Nagarjuna, Korzybski had postulated the solution: "both/and." It was an article of faith with William that the "either/or" concept was completely mistaken, and he very often cited the "both/and" concept in conversation and interviews.

Although William seems to have had an intuitive grasp of the First Noble Truth (in so many words), it was only toward the end of his life that he seemed to embrace the Second Noble Truth: that the cause of suffering is ignorance. That is, William always perceived suffering—and gross forms of ignorance—all around him, but his reaction was rooted in a strong sense of self, and self-preservation . . . so that whatever natural compassion he may have felt was usually over-balanced by his contempt for the stupidity of Mankind, and his hatred of everything that he took as personal oppression or anything threatening his self-control.

Jean-Paul Sartre said, "Hell is other people"; the young William Burroughs said: "Other people are different from me and I don't like them." His response was to develop an obsession with weapons and self-defense, which lasted all his life. William sometimes affected a self-image exemplified by the lyrics of a blues song of the 1920s, which he often quoted in later years: "I'm evil, evil as a man can be / I'm evil, evil-hearted me." But his heart wasn't really in it, all this evilness; there was within him some strain of bedrock decency that always stopped him from elaborating himself fully in that direction.

And this fertile inner ground for the growth of compassion is shown by his youthful embrace of the "alternative decency"—so to speak—of "the Johnson Family." This was a turn-of-the-century term among hobos and the criminal underworld, referring to their code of honor: a Johnson minds his own business, his word is his bond, he gives help when help is needed, and he never offers information to the police, etcetera. William encountered this alternative ethics in the memoirs of a reformed safe-cracker and highwayman of the old American West named Jack Black, called *You Can't Win* and published in 1927, when William was thirteen. Again, this was a decisive and formative encounter for him.

So William really did have, in some ways—as his friend Lucien Carr put it—"the morals of a Boy Scout, although he'd never want you to know that." It's just that William's "Boy Scout" was the flipside of Lord Baden-Powell's goody-goody English Scout boy: a "Revised Boy Scout"—that is to say, a "Wild Boy." As Burroughs wrote: "A wild boy is filthy, dreamy, treacherous, vicious and lustful." This wistful formulation confirms at least the second part of Carr's remark. But Burroughs himself, in person, impressed most people who knew him fairly well as a gentleman: well-mannered and well turned out. He could be wild and crazy in private, like most of us, but his social front was genteel and courtly. And this tension—between upper-class social manners and a thoroughly democratic, can I say Whitmanic, impulse within intimate (particularly underclass or "underground") society—is a defining faultline through all of his life and work, I think.

What distinguishes William's writing in *Wild Boys*—after *Naked Lunch* and the Cut-Up Trilogy—is the emergence of hope: for the first time, Burroughs is not just ridiculing the world he has observed, but going on to fantasize another world in which he thinks he might like to live. Then the Red Night Trilogy, which he wrote in his old age (1974–1987), moves steadily from the self-absorbed, sexually-obsessed adolescent flights of the *Wild Boys*'s narrator's persona toward an always-older and wiser protagonist's viewpoint; Burroughs was reverting at the end of his writing career to the self-description with which he had begun it, in *Junky* and *Queer*. And like Siddhartha, he was growing into an ever-deeper sense of compassion for the suffering of others.

But I am getting ahead of myself. Let's go back to William's early life. I'm going to quote from his letters to Kerouac and Ginsberg during 1953–1955, because they contain a clue as to where he first encountered any notion of Yoga, Zen, and Tibetan Buddhism: we know that, while still living with his parents, he loved to read the boys' adventure and science fiction magazines of the 1920s, and Sax Rohmer's "Dr. Fu-Manchu" novels. These goofy pop images of "yoga," etc., presented as an exotic form of self-control for the attainment of mystical "powers," must have prompted him to send away for booklets promising to convey these "ancient secrets of the East" to young men. And we know that in 1943-44, in New York, he took courses from an instructor in "Jiu-Jitsu," which was popularized as a self-defense technique in those days; no doubt these courses carried a simplified dose of—quote—"Eastern wisdom"—unquote—also.

Burroughs graduated Harvard in 1936 and was in Vienna, Chicago, St. Louis, and New York during the next eight years. He pursued his fascination with the criminal underworld during that time, and was probably almost always armed with a pistol. He volunteered for service during the early years of World War II, but was repeatedly turned down; then after Pearl Harbor, he was drafted, but was given a psychological discharge. In 1944 Burroughs was back in New York, and he met Kerouac and Ginsberg through a Columbia University student from St. Louis named Lucien Carr. He also became addicted to morphine around this time.

By 1949 Burroughs was living in Mexico City with Joan Vollmer, a bright young woman with whom he felt a deep kinship despite his essential homosexuality. But as you all know, he killed Joan accidentally in 1951 while firing one shot from a pistol at a glass she had placed on her head. Within three years he was living a life of squalid excess in Tangier, still struggling to understand how this had happened. Burroughs felt he was defending his Self not only from outer opponents, but also from an inner enemy: the Ugly Spirit, as he called it. He felt that he was literally "possessed" by an inimical, invading personality with its own will that was quite contrary to his best interests. He claimed to have felt this sense of "possession" from his early years. And in his efforts to understand his shooting of Joan, he could proceed no further than to see an eruption of the Ugly Spirit in that rash, drunken act.

His letters from Tangier to Kerouac and Ginsberg were a lifeline for Burroughs. Meanwhile, Ginsberg had been inspired to look into Zen Buddhism after seeing some Chinese paintings in the New York Public Library in April 1953, and Kerouac had found Dwight Goddard's *A Buddhist Bible* in the San Jose, California library while he was staying with Neal and Carolyn Cassady in February 1954. Although their letters to Burroughs are lost, we can see that his friends were enthusing about these Eastern beliefs as they wrote to him. (Kerouac was also going through a phase of ascetic celibacy.)

To Kerouac, May 24, 1954, from Lima, Peru:

> As you know I picked up on Yoga many years ago. Tibetan Buddhism, and Zen you should look into. Also Tao. Skip Confucius. He is [a] sententious old bore. Most of his sayings are about on the "Confucius say" level. My present orientation is diametrically opposed [to], therefore perhaps progression from, Buddhism. I say we are here in human form to learn by the human hieroglyphics of love and suffering. There is no intensity of love or feeling that does not involve the risk of crippling hurt. It is a duty to take this risk, to love and feel without defense or reserve. I speak only for myself. Your needs may be different. However, I am dubious of the wisdom of side-stepping sex.

To Ginsberg, July 15, 1954, from Tangier:

> Tibetan Buddhism is extremely interesting. Dig it if you have not done so. I had some mystic experiences and convictions when I was practicing Yoga. That was 15 years ago. Before I knew you.
>
> My final decision was that Yoga is no solution for a Westerner and I disapprove of all practice of Neo-Buddhism. [...] Yoga should be practiced, yes, but not as final, a solution, but rather as we study history and comparative cultures.
>
> The metaphysics of Jiu-Jitsu is interesting, and derives from Zen. If there is [a] Jiu-Jitsu club in Frisco, join. It is worthwhile and one of the best forms of exercise, because it is predicated on relaxation rather than straining.

To Kerouac, August 18, 1954, from Tangier:

> [M]y conclusion was that Buddhism is only for the West to study as history, that is a subject for understanding, and Yoga can profitably be practiced to that end. But it is not, for the West, An Answer, not A Solution. We must learn by acting, experiencing, and living; that is, above all, by Love and Suffering. A man who uses Buddhism or any other instrument to remove love from his being in order to avoid suffering, has committed, in my mind, a sacrilege comparable to castration. You were given the power to love in order to use it, no matter what pain it may cause you. Buddhism frequently amounts to a form of psychic junk ...
>
> I can not ally myself with such a purely negative goal as avoidance of suffering. Suffering is a chance you have to take by the fact of being alive.
>
> I repeat, Buddhism is not for the West. We must evolve our own solutions.

To Ginsberg and Kerouac, October 23, 1955, from Tangier:

> The metaphysic of interpersonal combat: Zen Buddhist straight-aheadedness applied to fencing and knife fighting; Jiu-Jitsu principle of "winning by giving in" and "Turning your opponent's strength against him," various techniques of knife fighting, a knife fight as a mystic contest, a discipline like Yoga—You must eliminate fear and anger—and see the fight as impersonal process.[3]

"Suffering is a chance you have to take by the fact of being alive."— Here we see a glimpse of the First Noble Truth, but from a distinctly Romantic / Heroic standpoint: for Burroughs, it is our duty to suffer, and to learn from suffering. But he was referring primarily to sexual or romantic love, in which he had suffered much; for example, in New York at age twenty-six he was overcome by jealousy and heartache over a boyfriend's infidelity and neglect, and he cut off the end of his own left little finger; in Mexico ten years later he fell painfully for a young American who never came close to mirroring the depth of his feelings; and after Joan's death he realized that he was in love with Ginsberg, but when they were reunited in New York in late 1953, Ginsberg rejected him as a lover.

But at the same time that Burroughs wore this emotional hairshirt, he also showed (in writings sent to Ginsberg) some insight into the self-inflicted quality of his suffering:

> [Lee's] face had the look of a superimposed photo, reflecting a fractured spirit that could never love man or woman with complete wholeness. Yet he was driven by an intense need to make his love real, to change fact. Usually he selected someone who could not reciprocate, so that he was able [. . .] to shift the burden of not loving, of being unable to love, onto the partner. [. . .] Basically the loved one was always and forever an Outsider, a Bystander, an Audience.[4]

As for the notion of Buddhism as "psychic junk," here is an irresistibly funny bit from *Naked Lunch*, the novel he was writing in Tangier:

> ["a vicious, fruity old Saint applying pancake from an alabaster bowl"]:
> "Buddha? A notorious metabolic junky . . . Makes his own you dig. In India, where they got no sense of time, The Man is often a month late. . . . 'Now let me see, is that the second or the third monsoon? I got like a meet in Ketchupore about more or less.'
> "And all them junkies sitting around in the lotus position spitting on the ground and waiting on The Man.
> "So Buddha says: 'I don't hafta take this sound. I'll by God metabolize my own junk.'
> "'Man, you can't do that. The Revenooers will swarm all over you.'
> "'Over me they won't swarm. I gotta gimmick, see? I'm a fuckin' Holy Man as of right now.'
> "'Jeez, boss, what an angle.'"[5]

These writings indicate that Burroughs misunderstood Buddhism. A straightforward motivation of "avoiding suffering" is merely another form of craving, after all. And in Mahayana Buddhism the boddhisattva vows not to seek the extinction of Nirvana, but to be reborn for as long as other sentient beings remain unliberated by enlightenment.

In Tangier in the late 1950s Burroughs had sunk into an abject stasis of severe addiction. As he wrote in a 1962 forward to *Naked Lunch*:

I lived in one room in the Native Quarter of Tangier. I had not taken a bath in a year nor changed my clothes or removed them except to stick a needle every hour in the fibrous grey wooden flesh of terminal addiction. I never cleaned or dusted the room. Empty ampule boxes and garbage piled to the ceiling. Light and water long since turned off for non-payment. I did absolutely nothing. I could look at the end of my shoe for eight hours.[6]

I am not trying to minimize the misguidedness of mistaking an opiate stupor for a transcendental state, but it is undeniable that narcosis facilitates detachment, and Burroughs saw a rough equivalence between the cellular apathy of the stoned junky and the transcendental stillness of the meditator. And in a way, he was sort of on target: "emptying the mind," which is a preliminary stage in sitting practice, was the goal he was eternally seeking. But the subjective effect of junk is more like "emptying the heart," that is, numbing painful emotions such as unrequited love, self-loathing, and remorse. So again there is a misunderstanding, and a serious contradiction: Burroughs claimed to reject the "purely negative goal" of avoidance of suffering—but what else was he doing, by using narcotics?

In Tangier and Paris in the late 1950s, Burroughs's great friend, the painter Brion Gysin, introduced him to some of L. Ron Hubbard's earliest disciples: John and Mary Cook, and John McMasters. Later, living in London in the mid-1960s, Burroughs stayed at Hubbard's Scientology headquarters in East Grinstead; he was trying to "go Clear." (He was a card-carrying Church member for less than one year.) Also at this time Burroughs was impressed by a cognitive system which its proponents called Vipassana, using the Sanskrit word for "mindfulness." This he understood not just in its simplest form, awareness of one's own mind, but with also his old tendency to approach enlightenment from his starting-place of self-defense techniques.

From his impressions of this "Vipassana technique" Burroughs evolved a mindfulness methodology of his own, tailored to his solitary life in London during those years: the "Discipline of D.E.," or "Do Easy." This was an elaborate (and unintentionally humorous) system for carrying out household chores with a minimum of physical effort. For example:

Colonel Sutton-Smith 65, retired not uncomfortably on a supplementary private income . . . flat in Bury Street St James . . . cottage in Wales . . .
   The Colonel Issues Beginners DE
   DE is a way of doing. It is a way of doing everything you do. DE simply means doing whatever you do in the easiest most relaxed way you can manage which is also the quickest and most efficient way as you will find as you advance in DE.
   [. . .]

CIVIL DISOBEDIENCES

Never let a poorly executed sequence pass. If you throw a match at a wastebasket and miss get right up and put that match in the wastebasket. If you have time repeat the cast that failed. There is always a reason for missing an easy toss. Repeat toss and you will find it.[7]

This can be considered Burroughs's urbane equivalent of "chop wood, carry water," I believe. It also reflects the tedious solitude of his life toward the end of his London years (1960–1973), and his queer bachelorhood after his love affair with Ian Somerville ended in 1966. By this point he was middle-aged, committed to his career as a writer, and mostly out of danger from the youthful obsessions of romantic love.

Burroughs often wrote about his belief in a "magical universe." He studied anthropology and comparative religions, at Harvard and at Mexico City College, and he developed a view of the world that was based primarily on Will: nothing happens unless someone wills it to happen. Curses are real, possession is real. This struck him as a better model for human experience and psychology than the neurosis theories of Freud, in the end. But it also fit neatly into his personal experience of "Self and Other." For him, the Other was a deadly challenge to the Self, and never worse than when it manifested as "the Other Half," an Other inside. Eventually he identified the invading entity as "the Word," and rather than try to explain the rest of that theory, I will just refer you to his books, in particular the Cut-Up Trilogy, *The Job,* and *The Adding Machine.*

As a self-described "Astronaut of Inner Space," Burroughs cannot be considered a purely spiritual seeker. He was busy with the world of imagination, of scenes and characters and voices and action. But he did pursue a lifelong quest for spiritual techniques by which to master his unruly thoughts and feelings, to gain a feeling of safety from oppression and assault from without, and from within. The list of liberational systems that he took up and tried is a long one, including: Korzybski's General Semantics; Freudian psychoanalysis, hypnoanalysis, and narcoanalysis; Wilhelm Reich's orgone box and vegetotherapy; Alexander's Posture Method; L. Ron Hubbard's Scientology; est; Silva Mind Control; Robert Monroe's "journeys out of the body"; Dion Fortune's Psychic Self-Defense; etc. (Trungpa Rinpoche wrote about "cutting through spiritual materialism," critiquing the American tendency to go on a shopping spree in the supermarket of spirituality, and in some ways this applies to William's quest.)

William Burroughs was an early and longstanding adjunct faculty member with the Jack Kerouac School of Disembodied Poetics, founded in 1974 by Allen Ginsberg and Anne Waldman. In 1975, at age sixty-one, William was asked by Allen and Anne to come to Naropa and give some classes and readings. William had encountered Trungpa in London in the

1960s, but it was in the summer of 1975 that he became personally acquainted with him. Burroughs had already met a number of advanced spiritual leaders of one kind or another, and I think he already saw himself as one of them, a "holy man" of sorts. So William's stance toward Trungpa was collegial, with the mutual professional respect accorded by one showman to another—a kind of show-biz camaraderie. And I saw that Trungpa seemed to regard William in a similar light.

Now, you should know that a lot of controversy was caused by some of Trungpa's behavior, and a lot of American poets and writers were offended by Ginsberg's embrace of Trungpa as his teacher and his establishment of the Kerouac School under the aegis of the Naropa Institute and the Nalanda Foundation, in Boulder. The fact that Trungpa smoked cigarettes and drank a lot of alcohol, that he created a force of personal bodyguards called "Vajra Guards" and outfitted them in special quasi-military uniforms, etc., didn't sit well with some people's idea of how a spiritual teacher should behave—at least, in America. There were some incidents of confrontation and misunderstandings, such as the notorious Snowmass episode; that story is not worth telling again, but it involved excesses of zealotry by some young "Vajra Guards," and a stubborn contest of wills between Trungpa and an American poet and his girlfriend, who were perhaps spiritual tourists . . . "Mistakes were made," as the saying goes.

But none of these things perturbed William in the slightest. He understood that holy men are eccentric by definition, and that showmanship and personal flair are standard tools in the shaman's medicine bag. He also had a sort of Taoist feeling that everything happens for its own reasons and one ought not to take such things personally. Trungpa's "crazy wisdom" appealed to Burroughs, and so did the concept of the "Shambhala Warrior"—after all, Burroughs's own path since childhood had been the way of the warrior. At this same time, the mid-1970s, William was drawn to the "Don Juan" books of Carlos Castaneda, with their emphasis on the "impeccable warrior" tradition. So there was a natural meeting-ground for the life-history and karma of William, and the vajradharma of Tibet.

Trungpa invited William to spend a few weeks in solitary retreat at his facility in Barnet, Vermont, called "Tail of the Tiger" (now Karme Choling). But when Trungpa told William he should leave his typewriter at home and do no writing while he was living alone in the little cabin, William rebelled and said that as a writer he could not afford to lose any ideas that might come to him during his retreat, and he would take along at least a notepad. This he did, and his notes from that period were published in 1976 as *The Retreat Diaries*. This decision shows that William did not subordinate himself in a teacher-student relationship with Trungpa; it also suggests that William did not understand the meditation purpose of a retreat, at least not in the Buddhist sense. Here is what he wrote in his introduction to *The Retreat Diaries*:

> ... I am more concerned with writing than I am with any sort of enlightenment, which is often an ever-retreating mirage like the fully analyzed or fully liberated person. I use meditation to get material for writing. I am not concerned with some abstract nirvana. It is exactly the visions and fireworks that are useful for me, exactly what all the masters tell us we should pay as little attention to as possible. [. . .] I sense an underlying dogma here to which I am not willing to submit. The purposes of a Boddhisattva and an artist are different and perhaps not reconcilable. Show me a good Buddhist novelist.
>
> [. . .] And so as far as any system goes, I prefer the open-ended, dangerous and unpredictable universe of Don Juan to the closed, predictable karma universe of the Buddhists.
>
> Indeed existence is the cause of suffering, and suffering may be good copy. Don Juan says he is an impeccable warrior and not a master; anyone who is looking for a master should look elsewhere. I am not looking for a master; I am looking for the books.[8]

As I have said, William was quite at home in the solitary state, and he spent countless hours alone, meditating in his own way, as a matter of course. Perhaps his two weeks in the Vermont cabin was more a change of scene than anything else. The simple life of a cabin retreat appealed to him in another way, too: his childhood memories of summertime visits with his family to primitive resort cabins at Harbor Beach, Michigan, and Missoula, Montana, stayed with him all his life, and you can find many scenes based on these experiences in his work, particularly in the Red Night Trilogy.

In *Cities of the Red Night,* which he wrote between 1974 and 1980, is a chapter called "I Can Take the Hut Set Anywhere," set in the 19th-century American West and depicting Burroughs's teen-aged protagonist and a friend setting up house in a remote location, going to the nearby general store and stocking up on basic survival goods, etc. This "Hut Set" chapter is the doorway to the next book in the trilogy, *The Place of Dead Roads,* written between 1977 and 1982. *Dead Roads* was originally called "The Gay Gun" and it is primarily set in the Old West. The Way of the Gunfighter is a chief preoccupation of the book, and when you know that William did read Herrigel's *Zen in the Art of Archery* and similar books in the 1960s, you can see how this examination of the dhyana of marksmanship was a natural evolution of his lifelong study of warriorship, and an organic refinement of his effort to attain "one-pointedness."

Dead Roads is also very influenced by William's experiences in Colorado during 1976–1978. For example, the book opens with a pistol duel at the Boulder Cemetery. Now, one of the things that William preferred about Boulder over New York City was that he could go just a little ways out of town and target-practice with pistols to his heart's content. He could—and did—buy pistols over the counter at a gun store near Pearl Street. William liked to go shooting at our friend Steven Lowe's cabin in Eldora, in the Foothills, and he was living with Cabell Lee Hardy at Apartment 415 in the old Varsity Manor (which he always called "the Varsity Ma-nór") at Marine Street and Broadway.

William resided in Boulder from June 1976 through October 1978, although he was only scheduled to spend a week or two in June at the outset. He stayed on because his twenty-nine-year-old son, Billy, came to town for Naropa in the summer of 1976 and immediately collapsed: his liver gave out, and this life-and-death crisis worsened for several weeks until Billy was given a new liver in a transplant operation at Denver General Hospital in August 1976. William was very close to everything happening to Billy, and he was with him through many horrific experiences. Anyone who thinks William Burroughs got away scot-free after Joan's death should have been around Boulder in the summer and fall of 1976, when Billy's physical, psychological, and spiritual collapse came down hard and right in William's sixty-two-year-old face.

After the fall of 1978 William began to divide his time more between Boulder and New York, and in August 1980 he gave up the Varsity Manor apartment and went back to the Bunker in New York. Billy, with his new liver failing, went to Florida in January, and he died there on March 3, 1981. William stayed in New York until Christmas 1981, when he moved to Kansas. He had built up a new heroin habit sometime in 1979 but now he was on methadone. William had visited my Kansas outpost several times, and he decided to retire to Lawrence, a Midwestern college town that was much like Boulder in the "golden age," when there were poetry readings at "Le Bar" in the Boulderado Hotel (where William and I lived in fall 1976) . . . the magical days of the mid-1970s in Boulder, before a tsunami of money swept most of that away and turned this town into Colorado's Santa Fe.

(Sorry! But I mean, even Trungpa left Boulder, in 1986 for Halifax, Nova Scotia—and in the Shambhala web site biography of Trungpa, no less, it says he did this "based on his desire to establish the center of his organization in a less aggressive and materialistic atmosphere"—! So I'm not alone in seeing a disadvantageous change in Boulder since the mid-1970s. But we were all much younger then, too. And since Boulder is the home of Naropa, that in itself is auspicious, and we must make the most of it.)

Billy Burroughs died at age thirty-three in March 1981, just as *Cities of the Red Night* was being published. William had begun as early as 1977 writing scenes that would end up in *Dead Roads,* but that novel took on a more somber tone as he worked on it after Billy's death. He finished it during his first year in Lawrence, and once again, there was in it a long passage that was a doorway letting onto the next and final novel, *The Western Lands,* which he was inspired to write after he read Norman Mailer's *Ancient Evenings* in the early 1980s.

In a two-story 19th-century stone house south of Lawrence, Kansas, William put the finishing touches on *Dead Roads.* He could shoot targets in the old barn right behind his house, and he began to make his first "shotgun paintings," but literarily he had already "done the gunslinger thing" in *Dead Roads* and now he focused directly on the question of immortality. Of course he made great sport of the "Egyptian immortality blueprint," as he called it—the Mummy Road:

> The most arbitrary, precarious and bureaucratic immortality blueprint was drafted by the ancient Egyptians. First you had to get yourself mummified, and that was very expensive, making immortality a monopoly of the truly rich. Then your continued immortality in the Western Lands was entirely dependent on the continued existence of your mummy. That is why they had their mummies guarded by demons and hid good.[9]

Burroughs's fascination with his personalized version of the Egyptian concept of "the Seven Souls" demonstrates his deep-seated theism (a universe not of One God but many Gods) and the literalness with which he imagined these deities. His "many gods" have meta-human motivations, like the Lords and Ladies of Mount Olympus—and a similar kind of control over the actions of mortals. One of William's favorite quotes was from Fitzgerald's translation of Khayyam: "On this checkerboard of nights and days / Hither and thither moves and checks and slays / And one by one back in the closet lays."

The "he" in these lines is Death himself, whom William studied as one of the gods—and one with particularly inscrutable motives. "Why does Death want to kill me?" he asked himself. One of William's great strengths as a writer was closely allied to one of his spiritual weaknesses: a deep strain of solipsism. By taking Death's onslaught personally, he was distracted from considering the broader approach, that all things pass away—lakshana, the Second Mark of all conditioned dharmas. That is, William understood this phenomenon intellectually, but not in his heart; at least, not until his final years.

Burroughs did instinctively believe in reincarnation; as he wrote in a key passage of *Dead Roads:* "Kim has never doubted the possibility of an afterlife or the existence of gods. In fact he intends to become a god, to shoot his way to immortality, to invent his way, to write his way."[10]

In *Cities* William wrote about the "Transmigrants," adepts who underwent ritual suicide at a young age after careful training so they could select their next incarnation at will. "Death is a landing field," as he wrote in 1975 in the introduction to his novella, *Ah Pook Is Here* (Ah Pook incidentally being the Mayan God of Death):

> If you see reincarnation as a fact then the question arises: how does one orient oneself with regard to future lives? Consider death as a dangerous journey in which all past mistakes will count against you. If you are not orienting yourself on sound factual data, you will not arrive at your destination or in some cases you may arrive in fragments. What basic principles can be set forth? Perhaps the most important is relaxed alertness, and this is the point of the martial arts and other systems of spiritual training—to inculcate a psychic and physical stance of alert passivity and focused attention. Suspicion, fear, self-assertion, rigid preconceptions of right and wrong, shrinking and flinching from what may seem monstrous in human terms—such attitudes of mind and body are disastrous. See yourself as the pilot of an elaborate spacecraft in unfamiliar territory. If you freeze, tense up, refuse to look at what is in front of you, you will crack up the ship. On the other hand, credulity and uncritical receptivity are almost as dangerous.
>
> Your death is an organism which you yourself create. If you fear it or prostrate yourself before it, the organism becomes your master. Death is also a protean organism that never repeats itself word for word. It must always present the face of surprised recognition. For this reason I consider the Egyptian and Tibetan books of the dead, with their emphasis on ritual and knowing the right words, totally inadequate. There are no right words. Death is a forced landing, in many cases a parachute jump.[11]

But at that time, the 1970s, William visualized rebirth as a challenge, not a threat. His Transmigrants wanted to be reborn, so they could re-experience the magical period of childhood and the sexual intensity of adolescence. These youths are not exactly held up as a model, however, and we may observe that William had already spent a decade working with that sexual material in his writing, in *Wild Boys* for example—re-running sexually potent scenes over and over, as in a film loop or a Scientology auditing session, in an effort to neutralize the power he felt these scenes had over him. So again he was—after all—seeking the "cessation of suffering" (Third Noble Truth) by way of the extinction of craving. And in the 1980s he had the assistance of old age and methadone maintenance to help him leave behind the first of the Three Fires that are obstacles to enlightenment, i.e., lust.

When Burroughs returned to New York in 1974, he immediately renewed his friendship with the poet John Giorno, with whom he had been close friends since 1965 when Burroughs and Gysin spent a year in New York. As a Columbia undergraduate in the 1950s Giorno had minored in Oriental Studies, and by the mid-1960s he began serious Buddhist meditation practice, following the Nyingma school.

Burroughs spent countless hours alone with Giorno after 1973, especially in 1978–1981 and during John's numerous visits to William in Kansas after 1981. They often discussed Vajrayana concepts of death and dying, and John made an inquiry with his teacher Dudjom Rinpoche, on William's behalf about the fate of Bill, Jr.'s spirit after his death in 1981.

John Giorno arrived in Lawrence a day or two after William's death in 1997 and did sitting meditation with William's body at the funeral home and in William's bedroom, where John slept during that visit. John's essay, "The Death of William Burroughs," describes this period in detail. John Giorno was an important vector of dharma transmission in the life of William Burroughs.

Billy's death and William's move to the Midwest prepared the ground for William Burroughs's bodhi, the awakening of his tender heart to the limitless field of compassion, and the vector of this awakening in his life arrived in the form of . . . cats. By the time *Western Lands* was published in 1987, William had become a dedicated cat-lover, with a household full of animals. His cat-inspired meditations can be found in the last part of *Western Lands* and, of course, in *The Cat Inside,* where he wrote:

> My relationship with my cats has saved me from a deadly, pervasive ignorance. [...]
>
> I have said that cats serve as Familiars, psychic companions. [...] The Familiars of an old writer are his memories, scenes and characters from his past, real or imaginary. A psychoanalyst would say I am simply projecting these fantasies onto my cats. Yes, quite simply and quite literally cats serve as sensitive screens for quite precise attitudes when cast in appropriate roles. The roles can shift and one cat may take various parts: my mother; my wife, Joan; Jane Bowles; my son, Billy; my father; Kiki and other amigos; Denton Welch, who has influenced me more than any other writer, though we never met. Cats may be my last living link to a dying species. [...]
>
> This cat book is an allegory, in which the writer's past life is presented to him in a cat charade. Not that the cats are puppets. Far from it. They are living, breathing creatures, and when any other being is contacted, it is sad: because you see the limitations, the pain and fear and the final death. That is what contact means. That is what I see when I touch a cat and find that tears are flowing down my face.[12]

In the mid-1980s William went through a period of deep sadness and depression, reviewing a life's catalogue of mistakes and regrets, and this seems to have resulted in a kind of spiritual awakening, because by the end of his life ten years later he really had become enormously sweet and tender-hearted. I don't mean saccharine-sweet—William was salty and irreverent and funny to the end—but he was more patient, more kindly, more considerate, more grateful, and more gracious. I would say he was trying to extinguish the Second Fire, ill-will, and to stave off the onset of the Third, mental dullness or boredom. In *Western Lands,* and even more so in *My Education: A Book of Dreams* (which he assembled in the early 1990s), he encounters most of his old friends in the "L.O.D."—the Land of the Dead, which in turn is coterminous with the world of his dreams, meaning that his view of the afterlife is a life in dreams, or a bardo state, between lives.

As death approached, William was writing in what he knew would be his final journals. In these he wrestled with his anger at man's bottomless ignorance, and seems to have overcome it to a large extent, by the end. I think he never stopped believing that, in the words of Sri Aurobindo, which he often quoted: "This is a War Universe"—and he always saw himself in the warrior's role. But by some dispensation of his own curious karma, including all the social and historical baggage he was born with, and all the passions he felt and violent actions he took in his life, William Burroughs was given a final decade of old age in which to look back upon that life and study its lessons—and in this time, with the help of his beloved cats, he attained a state of ahimsa, compassion for the suffering that is everywhere.

I'd like to close with these lines from *The Place of Dead Roads:*

> "Whenever you use this bow I will be there," the Zen archery master tells his students. And he means there quite literally. He lives in his students and thus achieves a measure of immortality. And the immortality of a writer is to be taken literally. Whenever anyone reads his words the writer is there. He lives in his readers.[13]

*

Notes:

1   Fields, Rick. *How the Swans Came to the Lake: A Narrative History of Buddhism in America,* 3rd ed. (Shambhala Books, 1991).

2   Burtt, E. A., ed. *The Teachings of the Compassionate Buddha: Early Discourses, the Dhammapada, and Later Basic Writings.* (Mentor, 1955).

3   Harris, Oliver, ed. *The Letters of William S. Burroughs 1945–1959.* (Viking, 1993).

4   Burroughs, William S. "Lee's Journals." *Interzone.* (Viking, 1988).

5   ———. *Naked Lunch.* (Olympia Press, 1959).

6   Ibid.

7   Burroughs, William S. *Exterminator!* (Viking, 1972).

8   ———. *The Retreat Diaries.* (City Lights, 1989).

9   ———. *The Place of Dead Roads.* (Holt, Rinehart and Winston, 1983).

10 Ibid.

11 Burroughs, William S. *Ah Pook Is Here* (Calder, 1979).

12 ———. *The Cat Inside.* (Viking, 1992).

13 Ibid.

NO ONE SPOKE
Chögyam Trungpa's Teachings
of Dharma Art

REED BYE
2003

* * *

Is there ever a moment when mind is not both perceiving something and expressing that perception? Every experience, it seems, whether consciously noted or not, even the experience of "nothing happening," involves both perception and expression. Perception *is* expression. Watching a child with backpack walking to school; the feeling of being "late"; a squirrel flicking its tail; a whiff of bus exhaust; a basketball player shooting a free throw; "me" starring in a romantic fantasy in my mind: all phenomenal experience involves perception and perception is expressive. The self-expressiveness of perception lies at the heart of Chögyam Trungpa's teachings on dharma art. These teachings were presented in programs held at Naropa University and elsewhere in the nineteen seventies.[1]

The Sanskrit word "dharma," according to Trungpa, refers to the fundamental norm or "isness" of phenomena (whether "subjective or "objective"), as well as to traditional Buddhist teachings on how to perceive and relate to phenomena with openness and directness. The word "art" derives from the Latin *ars* meaning "skill," and is further derived from the Indo-European root *ar-*, to "fit together." Dharma art, then, refers to the ways in which the things we make and do fit together. Dharma art begins with perceiving openly and accurately and seeing the self-existing symbolism of phenomena in perception. "Self-existing symbolism" means that the things we experience are full of their own meaning, even if there is not *a* meaning that can be abstracted from the experience.

From this point of view, the realm of the aesthetic includes the entire range of human activity. We are in continuous engagement with the world through our impulse to look, listen, smell, touch, taste, and think about it. For this reason, "inquisitiveness," says Trungpa, "is the seed syllable of the artist." (*Calligraphy* 24).

Why do we look? ...Why do we listen? ...Why do we feel at all? The only answer is that there is such a thing as inquisitiveness in our makeup. The artist is interested in sight, sound, feelings, and touchable objects (24).

Trungpa characterizes dharma art as "genuine art" because it is based in the self-existing symbolism of phenomena, and because, at the moment of perception, there is no one manipulating or marketing it. He characterizes it as "without aggression" because, at the moment of composition, the sense consciousnesses in which phenomena arise in their self-existing symbolism are not obscured by a "holding back" through which we would like to "possess" our experience, "chew it, swallow it, and eat it up" (*DA* 63). "Aggression acts like a big veil preventing us from seeing the precision of the functioning of . . . symbolism (63)."

The source of sophistication that allows for us to be able to see messages coming here and there, ordinary symbolism, is some kind of gap—*that* which is free of *this*. Without that, we are unable to experience anything of that nature; everything is "me" all over the place, "I am" all over the place. Whatever you experience is only "me" talking back to you (*DA* 46-7).

Instead of viewing the world with an eye tethered to a stake of self-reference and expectation, the artist is willing to look into moments of phenomenal being or "isness" without holding back. Training this way sharpens awareness which, because it is sharpened, might be pleasing or irritating or both at once. But it is only by such direct looking at things as they are that we see their ordinary symbolism.

If you watch a beautiful rose or if you watch a dead dog bleeding with its innards out, the same experience of blankness takes place. That is where symbolism actually begins to occur in your state of mind. When you first perceive something, there is a shock of no conceptual mind operating at all. Then something begins to occur. You begin to perceive: [you feel] whether you like it or not, you begin to see colors and perceptions, to open your eyes. So that non-reference point mind can become highly powerful and extraordinarily sensitive.

. . . We are talking about the principles of perception. In order to realize unconditional symbolism, we have to appreciate the empty gap of our state of mind and how we begin to project ourselves into that non-reference point (*DA* 42–43).

MEDITATION

To practice sitting meditation is to train mind to relax into basic open awareness in which phenomena can be experienced simply and directly.

It generally takes training to stay in touch with this basic state of being. Through sitting, we give ourselves the opportunity to let mind's surface settle in order to be with its bigger nature, which is more or less indifferent to the wandering thoughts and emotional swells which occur, as entertaining or compelling as those might be. This expanded awareness is accomplished by placing attention on the breath as it comes in and goes out, as a continuous connection back to the openness of the present. Openness needs an ongoing groundedness to see itself, and this is the practice of *mindfulness*. Grounded in the present, we are not so susceptible to the seduction of momentary developments and gradually feel more and more familiarity with mind's naturally open state. We don't tune out thoughts and sense experience, but notice them in the space of larger awareness. Through this practice, attention becomes more active than reactive with respect to whatever arises; and sees it on its own terms.[2]

> How admirable,
> on seeing lightning
> *not* to think, "Life too is brief!"
>
> —BUSON

Trungpa encouraged meditation practice as a support for the practice of dharma art. But he was clear that the main point is the further encounter with the basic openness of mind. This kind of attention, he argued, whether any tradition of formal practice has been involved or not, is always present in the creation of genuine art.

> What do we mean by the practice of sitting meditation? For instance, Beethoven, El Greco, or my most favorite person in music, Mozart—I think they all sat. They actually sat in the sense that their minds became blank before they did what they were doing. Otherwise they couldn't possibly do it. . . . Some kind of mind-less-ness in the Buddhist sense has to take place (20).

When mind perceives something, for instance a crack of sound from the sky, there is a moment of mind-less openness, an "empty gap" before a thought-pattern kicks in and labels it: "thunder." That mind-*less* openness is actually mind-*full* at the same time and you can notice the sound at first as not separate from your mind. Energized form of some kind arises in the meeting of sense object, sense organ, and sense consciousness. And usually, quicker than we see it happening, the experience of the thing becomes lost in discursive naming, thinking, and emotional reactions (joy, fear, etc.). All of these reactive responses tend to overwhelm the original phenomenal experience. First there was a crack of perception.

> When you first perceive something, there is a shock of no conceptual mind operating at all. Then something begins to occur. You begin to perceive whether you like it or not, you begin to see colors and perceptions, to open your eyes (DA 42).

These teachings on dharma art recommend that we notice the first crack of perception. Why? Because such moments are in contact with "reality," defined in these talks as "the basic space in which we operate in our ordinary, everyday life." In meditation and in artistic practice, one can begin to feel the basic quality of this space and phenomenal experience arising together. The difference between active and reactive attention to immediate experiences is made clear by Gary Snyder with the following example:

> To see a wren in a bush, call it "wren" and go on is to have (self-importantly) seen nothing. To see a bird and stop, watch, feel, forget yourself a moment, be in the bushy shadows, maybe then feel "wren"—that is to have joined in a larger moment with the world (Space 179).

The practice of allowing awareness to extend instead of close down exposes the tendency of self-reflexive mind to view reality as essentially dualistic: a series of more or less problematic or joyful meetings between self and others. The dharma of things is actually experienced before one constructs a world out there and a singular mind in here. Our impulse toward knowing and naming *that* is not the problem, but attempting to fix it as a way of confirming *this* is. According to Trungpa, this impulse involves a kind of aggression toward our own experience, and the result for art, is deadly.

> When you project toward an object, you want to capture it, as a spider captures a fly, and suck its blood. You may feel refreshed, but that is a big problem. The definition of dharma art . . . is the personal experience of nonaggression (DA 62).

> In a lot of art there is a tendency to try to capture a glimpse of one moment of experience and make it into a solid eternity. We have some brilliant idea and we try to make it into a piece of art. But that is captured art. We try to capture our artistic talent in a particular work of art. . . . It seems that such an attempt to solidify one's work of art, instead of giving birth to artistic talent, creates death for artistic talent (DA 70).

In contrast, training attention through meditation to the space before subject and object separate, wakens every sense organ to the expressiveness of its immediate perceptions, and to their self-existing symbolism.

THE "PRESENT MOMENT"

This term tends to become jargon in places like Naropa University where sitting meditation is practiced and discussed. It can become an annoyance to those unfamiliar with what it points to experientially because it seems to suggest something vaguely spiritual and immaterial, a "touchy-feely" term. For those with some familiarity with sitting practice, however, the "present moment" indicates a particular order of experience in which the natural awareness of mind is highlighted. In this way, our attention becomes mindful. Mindful awareness is related to what Suzuki Roshi has called "big mind,"

> If your mind is related to something outside itself, that mind is small mind, a limited mind. If your mind is not related to anything else, then there is no dualistic understanding in the activity of your mind. You understand activity as just waves of your mind. Big mind experiences everything within itself. Do you understand the difference between the two minds: the mind which includes everything, and the mind which is related to something? Actually they are the same thing, but the understanding is different, and your attitude towards your life will be diferent according to which understanding you have *(Zen Mind* 35).

Big mind experiences the distinctiveness and impermanence of phenomena in the present moment.

> Midfield,
> attached to nothing
> the skylark singing

—BASHO

The present moment is obviously not Buddhist or anything else, but traditional Buddhist meditation practice is designed to draw attention to it. The present moment may not be a moment at all but is the environment in which moments of perception occur. Big mind is our awareness before I-and-you, body-and-mind, past-and-future split apart.

Traditional Buddhist epistemology and pedagogy works from the present moment as the basis for knowing oneself and phenomena. The "three prajnas" (knowledges) of *hearing, contemplating,* and *meditating* are the disciplines by which we gain this knowledge. *Hearing* refers to unbiased listening and study, *contemplating* to mixing what one studies with daily life, and *meditating* to the practice of opening to undistracted awareness.

Far from being a vaguely spiritual or psychological tag, the present moment is regarded as profound personal experience; where reality actually takes place, in totally open space. "There is some kind of complete, open space, ground that has never been messed up by plowing or by sowing seeds—complete virgin territory" (DA 67). The present moment is what we tend to ignore in thinking that we comprise a "me" wandering in a world of "others." The following comment on our ordinary relation to the present by the Tibetan Buddhist teacher Ponlop Rinpoche may seem extreme, but it is worth contemplating:

> We have never, ever lived in all these years. We think we are living. We believe we are living. We are either in the state of having lived or will be living, but we have never lived; we are never living. That's how our mind functions in our basic world, in our samsaric world.... Our mind has never been free to live in the present. It has always been under the dictatorship of our memories of the past or living as a service for the future (*Bodhi* 3).

The term "samsaric" here refers to the world of attachment to past and future and to the notion of a permanent self existing as the subject of that attachment. "We have never lived" because that samsaric world is an imagined one; there is no reality outside of the present. This does not mean we can ignore the past and future, but we can see that we only can meet them in the present and must deal with them *here*. We cannot see realistically when holding the view that we are independent agents vying for pieces of the phenomenal pie. When we look with big mind at the world, it is a fabulous, complex game of charades. We are all acting ourselves. Keeping one's big mind, one can work with "real world" situations in ways that expose self-referential mind as the cause of unnecessary confusion for ourselves and others. Perception and expression only happen now. And art, everyone knows, can open mind to vivid insight, and blow away self-referential fixation, at least momentarily.

The things we perceive and the things we do and make are vivid when they are viewed with active attention. Phenomena are alive because they arise momentarily; they are not other than the mind perceiving them. Many poets have made similar observations:

William Blake:

> If the Spectator could Enter into these Images in his Imagination approaching them on the Fiery Chariot of his Contemplative Thought if he could

Enter into Noah's rainbow, or into his bosom or could make a Friend & Companion of one of these Images of wonder which always intreats him to leave mortal things as he must know then would he arise from his Grave then would he meet the Lord in the Air & then he would be happy General Knowledge is Remote Knowledge it is in Particulars that wisdom consists and Happiness too.

("Vision of the Last Judgement")

John Keats:

> If a sparrow come before my Window I take part in its
>   Existence and pick about the Gravel.

(letter, November 22, 1817)

Emily Dickinson:

> I had no portrait, now, but am small, like the Wren, and my Hair is bold, Like the Chestnut Bur—and my eyes, like the Sherry in the Glass, that the Guest leaves. . . .
> When I state myself, as the Representative of the Verse—it does not mean —me—but a supposed person

(letter, June 7, 1862)

Matsuo Basho:

> However well-phrased your poetry may be, if your feeling is not natural— if the object and yourself are separate—then your poetry is not true poetry but merely your subjective counterfeit.

Gertrude Stein:

> The thing one gradually comes to find out is that one has no identity, that is when one is in the act of doing anything. Identity is recognition, you know who you are because you and others remember anything about yourself but essentially you are not that when you are doing anything.

("What Are Master-peices and Why Are There So Few of Them")

Gerard Manley Hopkins:

> There lives the dearest freshness deep down things.
>
> ("God's Grandeur")

George Oppen:

> Surely infiniteness is the most evident thing in the world.
> . . .
> One must not come to feel that he has a thousand threads in his hands,
> He must somehow see the one thing:
> This is the level of art. . . .
>
> ("Of Being Numerous")

James Schuyler:

> Open the laundry door. Press your face into the
> Wet April chill: a life mask. Attune yourself to what is happening
> Now, the little wet things, like washing the lunch dishes.
>
> ("Hymn to Life")

Allen Ginsberg:

> A thought like a poem begins you can't tell where then it gets
>   big in the mind's eye an imaginary universe and then
> Disappears like a white elephant into the blue or "as a bird
>   leaves the imprint of its flight in the sky"
>
> ("Meditation and Poetics")

"FIRST THOUGHT BEST THOUGHT"

Trungpa and Allen Ginsberg came up with the slogan "first thought-best thought" while composing a poem together in the early years at Naropa University. "First thought" refers to that which comes out of the blue, from a gap in reflexive thinking ("that thought which is fresh and free" DA II). It is not necessarily the first thing you come up with, which could be merely discursive commentary. First thought is free of reactive manipulation or oversight.

When open attention allows space into a situation, lively, fitting, and surprising things may occur. This is what Ginsberg and Trungpa called first thought and, for Ginsberg, it was a quality he associated with good writing in general, and with the work and teaching of his friend Jack Kerouac, whose inclination toward spontaneous composition made an important bridge between Ginsberg's poetics and the spirit and principles of dharma art.

> Perfect moonlit night
> marred
> by family squabbles
>
> —KEROUAC

Haiku is a poetic form focusing on immediate perception and its extension into a minimal verse form. Unlike longer literary forms, haiku aim at momentary presence with perception and extending engagement with that perception's symbolism.

> A salted sea-bream
> showing its teeth
> lies chilly at the fish shop
>
> —BUSON

Haiku, in translation at least, are usually displayed in a three-line visual form as in the above example. This presentation may emulate or reflect a three-fold movement which, according to Buddhist psychology, is inherent in perception itself. This three-fold movement happens in increments so small they are not normally seen. First, it is said, there is a simple sense of being; then comes a "flicker" or projecting of attention toward something in our thought or sense-fields. And third, there is communication between the the sense of being and the sense object (DA 56).

This threefold process of perception can be explored in relation to artistic creation by a) simply noticing one's sense of being at any given moment, b) noticing as attention goes out to something arising in mind, and c) making a gesture to communicate with or from that thing. In the above haiku by Buson, for example, we can feel a) the space in which the event is noticed (the fish shop), b) the focal object of attention (the teeth of the sea-bream), and c) the feeling quality of the two together (chilliness) as further communication. The poet's attention is given over to the object of perception in order to feel its self-existing symbolism. Trungpa speaks of this kind of perceptual giving-over in terms of relaxation:

> If we are able to relax—relax to a cloud by looking at it, relax to a drop of rain and experience its genuineness—we see the unconditionality of reality, which remains very simply in things as they are. . . . When we are able to look at things without saying "It is for me or against me," "I can go along with this," or "I cannot go along with this," but when we can simply look at things very thoroughly and directly, just simply on the dot, we begin to develop some sense of awareness and precision. We are not moved by hope and fear; therefore we do not run away from things and we do not cultivate them either (*Shambhala* 101).

In one of his talks on perception, Trungpa emphasizes a distinction between the activities of *looking* and of *seeing*. In this contrast, *looking* takes place without any bias in its view. One looks out of open curiosity, as at the moon or the teeth of the chilled sea-bream. *Seeing*, on the other hand, implies a more developed view of this thing in relation to others. "First we look and then we see." (*Calligraphy* 23). We see the relation between the moon and the tension of the family squabbles, the fish's teeth and the chilliness of the fish shop. Looking involves surrender or relaxation into perception; seeing has a sense of expansion that comes from looking.

> When sense objects and sense perceptions and sense organs meet, and they begin to be synchronized, you let yourself go a little further; you open yourself. It is like a camera aperture: your lens is open at that point. Then you see things and they reflect your state of mind (*Calligraphy 25*).

The point is to relate to the phenomena of our experience directly, with openness and without trying to make something out of them.

> The phenomenal world is not all that pliable. Each time we try to grasp it, we lose it, and sometimes we miss it altogether. We might be trying to hold on to the wrong end of the stick. It's very funny, but it's very sad too (*Calligraphy* 23).

First thought gets in touch with the "humor [that] exists within the cosmic world. With that kind of humor, we begin to see through the separateness of me and others, others and me" (*DA* 67). First thought could come as a word, a wave, a honk, a spontaneous song. However it arises, it remains in touch with a nondualistic moment of perception and communication, and we can notice and speak from that.

There has to be a sense of vision taking place in one's state of mind. Such vision comes from a state of mind that has no beginning and no end. We could call that vision first thought-best thought. First thought does not come from subconscious gossip, it comes from before you think anything. In other words there's always the possibility of freshness (DA 104).

The following haiku by Issa is a good example of first thought, best thought:

No one spoke—
the host, the guest,
the white chrysanthemum.

—ISSA

Is the dharma or isness of a particular moment rendered here? Is there freshness, humor, and a feel of open vision? The three non-speakers of the poem seem to agree that there is. And the threefold process of perception mentioned above—sense of being, flicker of noticing, communication—is apparent in the poem's perception, execution, and form. In Trungpa's teachings on dharma art, these three joints of perception correspond to the three-part universe of classical Taoist philosophy and aesthetics: Heaven, Earth, and Human. This dynamic relationship inherent in any experience is central to Trungpa's teachings on how to make and perceive artistically.

HEAVEN, EARTH, AND HUMAN

Since dharma art comes from the live space of eternal possibility and from the uncertainty, apprehensiveness, and upliftedness encountered at its threshold, we don't know what will occur as we execute. This not knowing is the artist's state of mind.

As Basho said of haiku, "the composing must be done in an instant, like felling a massive tree, like leaping at a formidable enemy, like cutting a watermelon, or biting into a pear."

In traditional Chinese Taoist terms, that live space of possibility is called *heaven* and it provokes both vision and apprehension. Vision needs to make contact with *earth,* the ground on which its potential might be realized. Heaven and earth are joined by the *human,* which actualizes vision through art. The basic movement of perception itself and its expression of self-existing symbolism are analogous to the artistic gesture that brings heaven, earth, and human together. A passage from the *Tao Teh Ching* may help to give a feel for the dynamic of the heaven-earth-human relation:

Between Heaven and Earth
There seems to be a Bellows:
It is empty, and yet it is inexhaustible;
The more it works, the more comes out of it.
No amount of words can fathom it:
Better look for it within you. (*Wu* 11)

The heaven-earth-human relationship in artistic creation is a central principle in the practice of *ikebana*, traditional Japanese flower arranging. In this tradition, the artist comes from "big mind" or *heaven* with the placement of one branch or flower, makes a relation between that and *earth* with placement of a second stem, and "joins heaven and earth" with a third placement, the *human*, so that the whole communicates vision and practicality at once. Trungpa, who studied ikebana in England before coming to the U.S., felt that these relations also describe the process of poetic composition, as epitomized in haiku poetry. The poet begins with empty mind and a simple sense of being. From that something comes up, a "flicker" of thought or perception. Having noticed it, one extends to the thing and writes. Then, having written, one feels the play between original empty space, still present, and the thing noticed. And then, perhaps, there is one thing more to say.

> It is a question of writing your own mind on a piece of paper. Through poetry, you could find your own state of mind. You learn how to express that. Of course to begin with you have to be familiar with the language, but beyond that poetry is writing your own state of mind.... People shouldn't be too dilettantish or artistic, but they should write their own state of mind on a piece of paper. That's why we say, "first thought, best thought." We have to be very careful that we don't put too many cosmetics on our thinking. Thoughts don't need lipstick or powder (Chögyam Trungpa, Interview).

With heaven, earth, and man naturally collaborating in composition, the communication within the work and from the work out will have the chance to be lively and open. The work will hold its own intelligence and humor, even if focused on the most mundane experience.

The bottom of my shoes
are wet
from walking in the rain

—KEROUAC

Trungpa distinguished the heaven, earth, and human experience of the viewer of a work of art from that of the creator. For the creator, as mentioned, heaven is the space of uncertainty and potential, the blank page. For the viewer, heaven occurs in the first glimpse or moment of perceptual connection with the work. So here, in this Kerouac haiku, is a moment of *that,* in which the "initial perception breaks through your subconscious gossip" (*Calligraphy* 25). The dharma of the moment is presented and fitted together by the artist who noticed the condition of his shoes.

Heaven, earth, and human are undifferentiated in essence, but felt as a three-fold process, they offer an explanation of poetic composition that includes space, particularity of momentary perceptions, and the natural impulse to communicate their symbolism truthfully.

RELATED VIEWS OF ART

There are many aesthetic crossovers between dharma art and established Western theories of art and aesthetics. The poetics of the modernist and postmodernist periods especially seems to have many basic points of agreement with the premises of dharma art. This is not a surprising historical coincidence given the past century's intense curiosity and investigations into time, space, consciousness, and identity. An example of such a crossover aesthetic principle is that of *ostranenie,* the "defamiliarizing" or "making strange" power and purpose of art: its way of interrupting habituated responses and bringing attention back to actual experience. *Ostranenie* was a central point in the poetics of Russian "formalism" in the early twentieth century and the classic statement on it is Victor Shklovsky's:

> Habitualization devours works, clothes, one's wife, and the fear of war. . . . Art exists that one may recover the sensation of life; it exists to make one feel things, to make the stone *stony.* The purpose of art is to impart the sensation of things as they are perceived and not as they are known. The technique of art is to make objects "unfamiliar" ("Art as Technique" 751).

The defamiliarization Shklovsky is speaking of is an effect of experience momentarily left unguarded by our habit of reflexive self-referencing. We could compare this statement to Basho's classic one on the need for the poet to meet phenomena directly:

> Your poetry issues of its own accord when you and the object have become one—when you have plunged deep enough into the object to see something like a hidden glimmering there. However well-phrased your poetry may be, if your feeling is not natural—if the object and yourself are

separate—then your poetry is not true poetry but merely your subjective counterfeit (from notes; source unfound at time of this writing).

Another Russian modernist literary theorist and linguist, Roman Jakobson, drew attention to the natural semantic ambiguity of language functioning poetically. In performing this function, he argued, the linguistic sign draws attention to its own phenomenal event, relegating its referential implications to a lesser importance. This, I think, makes a linguistic corollary to the notion of the self-existing symbolism of phenomena experienced directly, when, as discussed, they are sensed and seen in their primary being or "isness." The experience of meaning is then immediate and ambiguous rather than determined.

> Ambiguity is an intrinsic, inalienable character of any self-focused message.... a corollary feature of poetry. Let us repeat with [William] Empson: "The machinations of ambiguity are among the very roots of poetry." Not only message but also its addresser and addressee become ambiguous (*Language* 85).

Many of the Anglo-American modernist poetic credos of the twentieth century also suggest a dharma poetics-like emphasis of perceptual immediacy: William Carlos Williams's "No ideas but in things"; Ezra Pound's definition of the image as "that which presents an intellectual or emotional 'complex' in an instant of time; Marianne Moore's poetic mandate for "imaginary gardens with real toads in them"; Gertrude Stein: "the business of Art is to live in the actual present"; and, more recently, Robert Creeley: "A poem denies its end in any 'descriptive' act, I mean any act which leaves the attention outside the poem."

In his poetics statement called "Hunting is not those Heads on the Wall," Amiri Baraka (then Leroi Jones) writes of the "doing, the coming into being, the at-the-time-of . . . Contemplating the artifact as it arrives, listening to it emerge. *There* it is. And *there*." Baraka is also distinguishing art arising through active attention from that made out of subjective processing.

SELF-EXPRESSION

Art is often spoken of as "self-expression." For dharma art, a question is, What self is expressing/being expressed in a work? To what extent does the experience of *stony*-ness that Shklovsky mentions require an independent self to experience its phenomenality and make art out of the experience? As Gertrude Stein wrote, "Identity is recognition, you know who you are because you and others remember anything about yourself but essentially you are not that when you are doing anything." Robert

Creeley likewise, "I want to give witness not to the thought of myself—that specious concept of identity—but rather, to what I am as simple agency, a thing evidently alive by virtue of such activity." Does the self of self-expression exist before, after, and/or during perception? What does the practice of meditation have to do with such questions? Poet and meditator Gary Snyder writes,

> Meditation is the problematic art of deliberately staying open as the myriad things experience themselves. Another one of the ways phenomena 'experience themselves' is in poetry. Poetry steers between nonverbal states of mind and the intricacies of our gift of language (a wild system born with us.) ("Language" 113).

Here "selves" would seem to be only self-reflexive moments in the general space of awareness. The notion of a singular self as perceiver of phenomena might be just a habit of discursive thought. From the point of view of the practice of meditation, this is not so much a tangled metaphysical problem as a matter of direct experience, investigated by simply sitting and observing the ongoing processes of mind and our tendency to identify with them. Returning attention to the breath and space into which it goes, we come back to the open present with a loosened sense of self.

> When we practice zazen our mind always follows our breathing. When we inhale, the air comes into the inner world. The inner world is limitless, and the outer world is also limitless. We say "inner world" or "outer world" but actually there is just one whole world. In this limitless world, our throat is like a swinging door. The air comes in and goes out like someone passing through a swinging door. If you think, "I breathe," the "I" is extra (Suzuki 29).

When attention is trained in this way, we begin to see that all experience—vocal patterns on the telephone, leaves swirling in the street, someone gassing up a car in the rain, a tree in a field with a broken limb, a broken heart—have self-existing vividness that needs no embellishment. "Things are symbols of themselves," Trungpa says. And things "experience themselves," Gary Snyder says, both in meditation and in art.

Chögyam Trungpa's teachings on dharma art have many correlations with views of others who have looked into the artistic process with a practitioner's mind. The basis of these views can be said to be a nondualistic attitude toward experience. With confidence in the powerful "isness" of things as they are, all activity is dharma art. Trungpa was not interested in promoting an aesthetic theory with these teachings; but was concerned about the role of art and artist in the world. His view was that genuine art is free of the aggression which comes from neurotically holding ourselves back from encounters with the phenomenal world, and he passionately wanted to discuss this problem and ways through it with his students in these talks.

✲

Bibliography:

Jakobson, Roman. "Linguistics and Poetics." In *Language and Literature.* Cambridge: Harvard University Press, 1987.

Ponlop Rinpoche, Dzogchen. "The Four Foundations of Mindfulness." In *Bodhi* magazine. Issue number 3.

Snyder, Gary. "Language Goes Two Ways." In *A Place in Space.* Washington, DC: Counterpoint, 1995.

———. "A Single Breath." In *A Place in Space.* Washington, DC: Counterpoint, 1995.

Shklovsky, Victor. "Art as Technique." In *Critical Theory Since Plato.* Hazard Adams, ed. Fort Worth: Harcourt Brace, 1992.

Suzuki, Shunryu. *Zen Mind, Beginner's Mind.* New York: Weatherhill, 1980.

Trungpa, Chögyam. *The Art of Calligraphy.* Boston: Shambhala, 1994.

———. *Dharma Art.* Boston: Shambhala, 1996.

———. "Reflections on the Cosmic Mirror." In *Shambhala Sun,* July 1995.

Notes:

[1] Although only one of these programs was entitled Dharma Art, the name serves as a useful overall title for the ideas and practices presented in all of them. These talks have in common a general focus on art and the artistic impulse from the viewpoint of Buddhist perceptual psychology. Since they have been gathered from a variety of programs and seminars, the talks in the book, while thematically arranged, were not progressively sequential in their original presentation. Dharma Art is the obvious overall title for the collection but the talks actually come from programs with titles such as Mudra Theatre Intensive, Art in Everyday Life, Milarepa Film Workshop, Iconography of Buddhist Tantra, and Visual Dharma. Many of these talks have been edited and collected in the volume *Dharma Art.* Boston: Shambhala, 1996.

[2] I take the term in sense of "active attention" from Ken Mcleod in his book *Wake Up to Your Life: Discovering the Buddhist Path of Attention.* HarperSanFrancisco, 2002. Mcleod contrasts *active* with *passive* attention in a similar way to "active" and "reactive" here.

Revolutionary
Poetics

Revolutionary Poetics

ALLEN GINSBERG
July 4, 1989

★   ★   ★

ALLEN GINSBERG: It was the idea today, being Independence Day, fireworks, politics, Neruda, Whitman, Blake, John Sinclair, Ho Chi Minh, Williams, Akhmatova, Mayakovsky—the gamut of political poetry— since today is Independence Day and since the Supreme Court is on people's minds. Or just wide open, no particular subject, and just talk and anything that I know we haven't gone through ever, or any questions, we might begin with that, any inquisitiveness, or any ideas that should be filled out that are blank areas over the last couple of years . . .

KIMI SUGIOKA: The Supreme Court ruling is definitely on my mind and then, in relation to that, I'm curious about whatever poetic ventures you've had or experienced or participated in, that have helped to bind communities, and to make a stand, make a statement—what works? I feel like we're all these individual voices and it's difficult to be heard, to be reckoned with. I'm really curious about that because I feel like that's got to be a direction of poetry—to become more integrated—

AG: Yeah, I keep thinking I would like to be able to write another "Howl." You know like taking the problems of the eighties, like ecology and the Moral Majority, and all that. But you know you can't do that deliberately, it has to come accidentally almost. The experience I've had, well historically, Neruda has written a lot of poetry that bound together Latin American poetry and got people very excited about the United Fruit Company, for instance. Are you familiar with *Residence on Earth?* Things that come to mind that united people politically—there is the [Anna] Akhmatova "Requiem." Under Stalin she was persecuted, and Mandelshtam, another great Russian poet, was persecuted. A lot of the great Russian poets had to commit suicide. So, how did they survive, and what did they write during that long period of Stalinism when twenty to thirty million people were killed and sent off to concentration camps, and there was, like in China now, a total brainwash, intimidation and doublethink, and people scared to open their mouths lest their neighbors hear them and report them to the police. Sisters turning in their brothers and things like that. That was a consideration—Yeah? The big one that she was dealing with was a crisis in '37. Her friend, Mandelshtam, was arrested. One thing I would recommend is *Hope Against Hope,* which is an account of literary civilian life in the times of the purges. One of the opening chapters is a description of a visit that Anna Akhmatova, one of the greatest Russian poets of the century . . . The three greats incidentally, for those of you interested, are Akhmatova, [Maria] Tsvetayeva, Bella Achmadullina. Then among the men who had to suffer through it, Pasternak and Mandelshtam are of interest.

When I thought of the topic I thought of Neruda, Whitman—the Neruda I'll read a little bit of—Whitman has got this great line: "Vivas to those who have fail'd." You know that part? The part of "Song of Myself"? And "To a Foil'd European Revolutionaire." And in "Song of Myself" he's also got this long section about "vivas" or, you know, salutations to those who have failed. To those who fell in the battle and didn't win, to those whose ships sunk in the sea—like an ode to failure. I followed it up with "Ode to Failure," you know, thinking of the revolutions that didn't make it. And yet they were right, or the situation was right, but they just couldn't make it—like: vivas to the students who got shot in Tiananmen Square. Vivas to those who have failed, rather than to those who have won. The winner is not really the winner in the long run. But that's sort of like trying to console yourself for losing. But that Whitman springs to mind.

Also, Whitman opened up a lot of political space, simply by changing the poetry from a very fixed and classical form, to an open form that anybody could participate in. He changed the poetry of all countries of the world. Like 1919 in China, Ai Quing introduced Whitman. And it was Ai Quing working with Mao Tse Tung that organized the Yenan Conference on Art and Literature in 1942. Though Ai Quing caught it in the neck and was exiled by Mao Tse Tung from '58 to '78 as part of the antirightist campaign. Although he had been the liberator of poetry and official poet of the revolution until 1958.

Anyway, Whitman opened up Chinese poetry and he also opened up Russian poetry. It was Whitman that kind of inspired the Symbolists and the Acmeists. The Symbolists in 1890–1910 in Russia. And Whitman is behind Mayakovsky and some of Yesenin. And a lot of the turn-of-the-century, prerevolutionary poetry, that led to the revolution—the Futurists, the Russian Futurists. And in America, I think Whitman through myself and Kerouac and Snyder and Williams, and all those people and Pound, originating with Whitman, opened up the San Francisco Renaissance and Beat generation, which did have some kind of socio-political fallout. Liberating the mind or deconstructing the rigid authority of the military in the state and the sexual stasis of the fifties, and the nuclear stasis, and the social stasis of blacks and women and gays and whatnot.

Auden had a line: "Poetry makes nothing happen." You know, it's not supposed to, then there's the other ivory tower view that it's just sort of like meditation—it's not supposed to make anything happen, just clarify. Clarification makes things happen maybe. Clearing your head might put you in a position to make things happen.

LELAND BARTHOLOW: Well, oftentimes you have to become a personality or well-known, which is, I think, addressing Kimi's anxiety a little bit. That you have to become well-known and you have to—

AG: I don't think that's the key. I think if you write something strong enough, then you become well-known. That the flag of the poem precedes the person that comes through. You know it's the poem—

LB: But you can't always count on that.

AG: Well, no, like Blake was completely obscure, Van Gogh was obscure, and Whitman to some extent—though I think he was pretty well-known. Rimbaud was obscure until later. But they all had this effect on people's minds. Blake certainly, was totally obscure, and yet he has tremendous impact over long range. You know, some of the impact isn't immediate. Some of the impact is immortal in the sense that—the image I had was that of a radio station that broadcasts permanently through the centuries.

In Stalin's time, a number of the greatest poets were either forced to commit suicide or literally died in Kolyma. So I was saying, Madam Mandelshtam wrote a book called *Hope Against Hope,* and a second volume, *Hope Abandoned.* And another great book on the subject is by Madam Ginsbourg, who is the mother of Aksyonov, the Russian novelist living in America now. Aksyonov was the Kerouac of Russia, and a friend of Achmadullina and Yevtushenko and Voznesensky, the contemporary (sort of) radical poets—middle radical poets—were able to survive. The political radical liberal poets. But then Achmadullina says Yevtushenko and Voznesensky are "nothing but business men"—"they're not poets." They were on top of the bureaucracy—they did nothing to get into real trouble. They didn't get sent off to camp or imprisoned, like Solzhenitsyn, like many other poets and dissidents and writers [who] did get sent to jail because they were not able to play it adroitly, you know, on the fence. Yevtushenko's view, he said, was . . . talking in Nicaragua once, we had this conversation: I said, "You're an official—how can you be an official in a police state?" He said, "Because I am official, everything I say is official, and if I can say one thing that moves a whole country a millimeter to the left, toward liberation—like 'Babii Yar' bringing up the Jewish question, or antibureaucratic, or friendship with hippies or something—that moves the entire country just one inch to the left, and that's my role." Somebody's got to be in the middle of the CIA, so to speak, somebody's got to be in there in the middle of the bureaucracy. Somebody has to play that role, and it's a very difficult role, and you see it on his face: this pain, anxiety, constant worry. You know, is he going to get hit in the neck by the police or is he going to get hit in the neck by the radicals? And at this point, now that there's Glasnost, he and Voznesensky are considered second-rate, because they wasted their time—not writing pure poetry, but doing political satire on the bureaucracy and transitory stuff.

In Madam Mandelshtam's *Hope Against Hope,* in the opening chapter, you see the greatest Russian poet, Mandelshtam, sitting with his wife. He's in exile in a little town, Voronezh, outside of Moscow, and there's very little food, and there's no jobs for them, and they're practically starving living hand to mouth, with Madam Mandelshtam. And Akhmatova comes in the middle of the night off the railroad station, on a sort of daring trip to see him—to connect. And the police are not quite sure—or have the police followed her? And they have one egg between them—the three of them—and a little bit of vodka, and it's three in the morning, and they're talking, and all of a sudden there's a knock on the door. In come the police, followed by the local janitor who fingered them. Every block had a janitor that kept watch—sort of the block warden—like they have now in Cuba. You know, there's supposed to be a democratic organization—every block you got a representative of the people? Who turns you in and keeps a dossier? So he's led away because he had written a sonnet about Stalin, which somehow somebody showed Stalin, and Stalin got really pissed, and called up Pasternak on the phone. Said, "This guy Mandelshtam—can he write?" Well, it so happened that Pasternak and Mandelshtam had a feud. So Pasternak got a little finicky—wanted to give a pure literary judgment—said, "Yes, he can write. I think he writes wrong, but he can write and is a great writer." So, the first time, in 1934, Stalin let him alone. But then Mandelshtam wrote this sonnet, and that really, sort of pissed Stalin off. So finally Stalin said, "Well I wash my hands of this, the local cops can take care of him." So in '37 they busted into this room in the middle of the night and took him off, and he was sent to Siberia, to Kolyma, which was way out toward Vladivostok, in the arctic area—a concentration camp where several million people died, as bad as any German concentration camp. And from then on it's legends/rumors, what happened to Mandelshtam—nobody quite knows.

It's a monumental work, and it's all the literary gossip of Russia under the repression, and how people survived, and what they wrote. And the amazing thing is, that they wrote fantastic works which were circulated, either in manuscripts, or the manuscripts [were] burned and committed to memory, and passed from head to head, under most extreme situations—like we have in China now. And we may have it yet in America before it's all over. As the polarization gets greater, and the quasi-fascist neoconservatives begin to feel their powers.

We go to Akhmatova. This is an excerpt from her poem, "Requiem," which is maybe, the greatest poem of the 20th century written in Russia. 1935–1940—so in the worst years, up through the years of terror. I've got about three pages of it—the highlights of it. So, 1961, she added a little epigraph:

> No foreign sky protected me,

(she didn't leave Russia)

> no stranger's wing shielded my face.
> I stand as witness to the common lot,
> survivor of that time, that place.

Then there's a section: "Instead of a Preface." Yezhov was the bureaucrat in charge of the secret police.

> In the terrible years of the Yezhov terror I spent seventeen
> months waiting in line outside the prison in Leningrad.

Her son had been arrested as a way of keeping her on a leash—and they threatened to kill him or torture him if she didn't behave and shut up. So she took in laundry or something like that. So every week she would go to receive a package, or to send a package of food, or a letter, to her son. The conditions were like a bureaucratic office, like a welfare office, or a train station office, but there was one little slot that you opened up to hand in your letter or to get a letter out, and there were all these people, waiting on line, hours and hours and hours. So you didn't want to waste their time by arguing, and if you argued you got treated even worse. So it was the ultimate of pitiless, mechanical bureaucracy—and you didn't see the person you were arguing with—they were all loathsome bureaucrats.

> One day somebody in the crowd identified me. Standing
> behind me was a woman, with lips blue from the cold, who had,
> of course, never heard me called by name before. Now she
> started out of the torpor common to us all and asked me in a
> whisper (everyone whispered there):

Can you describe this?"
And I said: "I can."
Then something like a smile passed fleetingly
over what had once been her face.

That's a recollection—1957—and then there are different pieces from 1935 on: "Dedication"

Such grief might make the mountains stoop,
reverse the waters where they flow,
but cannot burst these ponderous bolts
that block us from the prison cells
crowded with the mortal woe . . .
For some the wind can freshly blow,
for some the sunlight fade at ease,
but we, made partners in our dread,
hear but the grating of the keys,
and heavy-booted soldiers' tread.
As if for early mass, we rose
and each day walked the wilderness,
trudging through silent street and square,
to congregate, less live than dead.
The sun declined, the Neva blurred,
and hope sang always from afar.
Whose sentence is decreed? . . . That moan,
that sudden spurt of woman's tears,
shows one distinguished from the rest,
as if they'd knocked her to the ground
and wrenched the heart out of her breast,
then let her go, reeling, alone.
Where they are now, my nameless friends
from those two years I spent in hell?
What spectators mock them now, amid
the fury of Siberian snows,
or in the blighted circle of the moon?
To them I cry, Hail and Farewell!

That's for the women and the families on line. Then the "Prologue":

That was a time when only the dead
could smile, delivered from their wars,
and the sign, the soul, of Leningrad
dangled outside its prison-house;

(the hanged men)

> and the regiments of the condemned,
> herded in the railroad-yards,
> shrank from the engine's whistle-song
> whose burden went, "Away, pariahs!"
> The stars of death stood over us.
> And Russia, guiltless, beloved, writhed
> under the crunch of bloodstained boots,
> under the wheels of Black Marias.

(the black trucks that came to take prisoners away—then to her son:)

> At dawn they came and took you away. ·
> You were my dead: I walked behind.
> In the dark room children cried,
> the holy candle gasped for air.
> Your lips were chill from the ikon's kiss,
> sweat bloomed on your brow—those deathly flowers!
> Like the wives of Peter's troopers in Red Square
> I'll stand and howl under the Kremlin towers.

I think at some point or other, Peter the Great killed a whole bunch of his troops and the wives stood outside the Kremlin and howled. So, "Like the wives of Peter's troopers in Red Square / I'll stand and howl under the Kremlin towers." Then, "To Death"—1939:

> You will come in any case—so why not now?
> How long I wait and wait. The bad times fall.
> I have put out the light and opened the door
> for you, because you are simple and magical.
> Assume, then, any form that suits your wish,
> take aim, and blast me with poisoned shot,
> or strangle me like an efficient mugger,
> or else infect me—typhus be my lot—
> or spring out of the fairytale you wrote,
> the one we're sick of hearing, day and night,
> where the blue hatband marches up the stairs,
> led by the janitor, pale with fright.

(The secret police had a hat with a little blue hatband. And it was the janitor that would finger the local people.)

(Then the conclusion, the "Epilogue," is very strong also)

I have learned how faces fall to bone,
how under the eyelids terror lurks,
how suffering inscribes on cheeks
the hard lines of its cuneiform texts,
how glossy black or ash-fair locks
turn overnight to tarnished silver,
how smiles fade on submissive lips,
and fear quavers in a dry titter.
And I pray not for myself alone . . .
for all who stood outside the jail,
in bitter cold or summer's blaze
with me under that blind red wall.

 . . .

Remembrance hour returns with the turning year.
I see, I hear, I touch you drawing near:

the one we tried to help to the sentry's booth,
and who no longer walks this precious earth,

and that one who would toss her pretty mane
and say, "It's just like coming home again."

I want to name the names of all that host,
but they snatched up the list, and now it's lost.

I've woven them a garment that's prepared
out of poor words, those that I overheard,

and will hold fast to every word and glance
all of my days, even in new mischance,

and if a gag should blind my tortured mouth,
through which a hundred million people shout,

then let them pray for me, as I do pray
for them, this eve of my remembrance day.

And if my country ever should assent
to casting in my name a monument,

I should be proud to have my memory graced,
but only if the monument be placed

not near the sea on which my eyes first opened—
my last link with the sea has long been broken—

nor in the Tsar's garden near the sacred stump,

(where she grew up as a kid)

where a grieved shadow hunts my body's warmth,

but here, where I endured three hundred hours
in line before the implacable iron bars.

Because even in blissful death I fear
to lose the clangor of the Black Marias,

to lose the banging of that odious gate
and the old crone howling like a wounded beast.

And from my motionless bronze-lidded sockets
may the melting snow, like teardrops, slowly trickle,

and a prison dove coo somewhere, over and over,
as the ships sail softly down the flowing Neva.

—March 1940

It's like iron. That was like a moment of remission, because the war had begun, Stalin had to mobilize everyone in Russia, including the ex-prisoners and the people who were persecuted, to fight the Germans.

GARY ALLEN: The only thing that could give you relief was World War II.

AG: Yeah, and then it closed down again. The bastard closed it down again and began killing people again, immediately after the war. But this is so amazing! So the question, "What can you do?" "And if a gag should blind my tortured mouth, / through which a hundred million people shout." Well, can you write and bespeak what nobody else can say? Can you formulate the situation to break through mass consciousness and media consciousness so that it's a proclamation of a common consciousness—common understanding, common grief, common suffering—that will wake people up to their own suffering or their own hidden consciousness? Or the silent consciousness that's known and not hidden but only spoken to each other, or the self, because it's too scary to speak it abroad, because of either secret police or common conditioning and repression, or just sort of buried under television news or something. But the basic human grief and feeling or passion that everyone has within, that's hidden. In the extreme case here, you can see the total extremity of it—total repression, total paranoia, and yet by herself, she was able to formulate. The poem was read and passed around in samizdat, and then most of it burned, and people memorized it—as most of the poems I read by Mandelshtam, were burned, and only remembered by his wife, who wrote them down afterwards.

Because the way Russians compose is, they don't write on the paper, they do it in their heads, with rhyme, very often, and they walk up and down, and think it out, and accumulate rhyme by rhyme, line by line, and then when they've got it all down, then they write it down. So the very nature of the method of composition is, sort of, secret police-proof. Foolproof in the sense, like the Australian Aborigines, it sort of sticks in the memory rather than having to be externalized on the paper. And so it's preservable, in passing mouth to ear—whispered transmission, so to speak—in times of extreme repression and distress. But this, come to think of it, has anybody written anything that's this powerful? This is like Sappho and Emily Dickinson, it's really amazing.

This thing about "and will hold fast to every word and glance / all of my days, even in new mischance, / and even if a gag should blind my tortured mouth, / through which a hundred million people shout"—now there's a passage in Whitman that's similar, which should be related, where he's also breaking out of the repression and pronouncing his own soul, or his own private understanding. In "Song of Myself":

> Walt Whitman, a kosmos, of Manhattan the son
> Turbulent, fleshy, sensual, eating, drinking and breeding,
> No sentimentalist, no stander above men and women or apart from them,
> No more modest than immodest.
>
> Unscrew the locks from the doors!
> Unscrew the doors themselves from their jambs!
>
> Whoever degrades another degrades me,
> And whatever is done or said returns at last to me.
>
> Through me the afflatus surging and surging, through me the current and
>   index.

I speak the pass-word primeval, I give the sign of democracy,
By God! I will accept nothing which all cannot have their counterpart of on
　　the same terms.

Through me many long dumb voices,
Voices of the interminable generations of prisoners and slaves,
Voices of the diseas'd and despairing and of thieves and dwarfs,
Voices of cycles of preparation and accretion,
And of the threads that connect the stars, and of wombs, and of the father-
　　stuff,
And of the rights of them the others are down upon,
Of the deform'd trivial, flat, foolish, despised,
Fog in the air, beetles rolling balls of dung.

Through me forbidden voices,
Voices of sexes and lusts, voices veil'd and I remove the veil,
Voices indecent by me clarified and transfigur'd.

I do not press my fingers across my mouth,
I keep as delicate around the bowels as around the head and heart,
Copulation is no more rank to me than death is.

I believe in the flesh and the appetites,
Seeing, hearing, feeling, are miracles, and each part and tag of me is a miracle.

Divine am I inside and out, and I make holy whatever I touch or am touch'd
　　from,
The scent of these arm-pits aroma finer than prayer,
This head more than churches, bibles, and all the creeds.

And then he goes through an enumeration of his own body:

Winds whose soft-tickling genitals rub against me it shall be you!
Broad muscular fields, branches of live oak, loving lounger in my winding
　　paths, it shall be you!
Hands I have taken, face I have kiss'd, mortal I have ever touch'd! it shall be
　　you.

Whitman broke out of centuries of formalistic speech and repression of consciousness, repression of erotic consciousness, sensory consciousness, and
centuries of authoritarian dominance over individual perception in favor of:
the state, or authority, or the social system, or morality, or religion, or

whatever coverings there were that prevented people from noticing their own minds and their own perceptions and their own emotions. And so Whitman is the great breakthrough. Course he's not dealing with the immediate, paranoiacal police state repression—the Yehzov terror—he's not dealing with that, but on the other hand he is uncovering centuries of unnoticed repression, which is also another aspect. The poet proclaiming the private truth above and beyond the conscious repression, subliminal repression, pointing out where the repression in a prison-house is. That may be somewhat the situation now. Here. If you were in El Salvador, you might have to take the Akhmatova role. If you were in Beijing now, you would have to take the Akhmatova role. And God knows what would happen if you were in Sudan, where there's not only repression and civil war, but ultimate starvation; where you're just sitting, a skeleton in a camp—what are you going to write about then? And who's going to hear you? And would you even have the energy to write? Burroughs has this line: "Human beings cannot be expected to behave like human beings under inhuman circumstances." You shouldn't feel guilty. If you're put in a vat of molten iron, you're not going to write a haiku necessarily. Or you're not going to write a sonnet. On the other hand, who knows? It might turn to bliss.

The breakthrough thing. I experienced that with "Howl"—very similar—a breakthrough, not of the universal consciousness or the social consciousness, but a discovery of my own consciousness, and then a proclamation of that. I'm trying to lay it out on the page: what is it I really desire, instead of what I'm told I should know, or desire.

And so, the question is really, what is it you really desire? What social order, or what specific deal, or event, do you really desire, that is now forbidden, either by the court of the culture, or by television, or by the media, or by the common understanding of American conditioning? What breakthrough are you looking for? Can you formulate, can you focus on, your cause, so to speak? It has to be a genuine cause of the difference between what you know with your senses and your feelings and your friends, as distinct from what the common consciousness is in the newspapers, in the government, in congress, in the White House, in *Time* magazine, in the newspapers, even in the neighbor's . . . Where is the difference between your life, and life as it is described almost universally, that runs the country and makes the budget appropriations and the schoolteaching . . .

GA: That's what I think about a lot of bad poetry. You hear a lot of these poems protesting nuclear war which somehow is what you're supposed to be thinking, and I immediately shut it off everytime.

AG: Yeah. But in the depths, what are your genuine thoughts as distinct from the official thought? In the readings at Penny Lane, do you get a genuine expression of what the inner desire is, or do you get rebellious stereotypes and generalizations against generalizations? Do you get a genuine formulation of your real inner perceptions—you know: what you really know with your friends, when you're being serious and you're not just being mean, and you're not just complaining, and you're not just being political, or angry, like—this morning . . . Where is the difference between your soul and the soul of the nation? And could you focus on it, define it, formulate it for other people? Because if that schizophrenia exists between you (your soul and the soul of the nation) it exists within everybody's soul and the soul of the nation. And it takes somebody to name it. Like Whitman named it. There. Right in that spot, I think he really named it. Akhmatova named it. I named it, maybe, almost: "Moloch," or particularly for my circle of friends: "The best minds of my generation destroyed by madness." I formulated it with detail.

It's not naming what's wrong, it's naming what's right. Can you name what you desire? I took one key—I don't know if you looked at that big "Howl" book (The Annotated "Howl")—from one line in Williams: "Unworldly love, that has no hope of the world, and cannot change the world to its delight." Certainly, in Akhmatova, there's an impractical love in those circumstances, you can't say it aloud even! Unworldly meaning, not out of this world, not meaning unreal, just meaning not fitting into the present world scene. But still springing forth from your heart, and from all hearts over and over through the centuries. Some unextinguishable nobility and passion and tenderness and sense of goodness and idealism and desire. You know it's most easily focused on in the tenderness of sexual desire—and the repression of it.

I got it from my mother. My mother was crazy, she died in the bughouse. I had to give up on her, but nonetheless there was still this kid desire for mommy! See, so that's the key: "unworldly love that has no hope of this world and cannot change the world to its delight." Cannot persuade the world to its delight.

So what eternal spring of feeling do you have in you, that you feel sure of, or that you feel unsure of, but returns over and over again, in dreams, and in waking moments of longing? What object of love, or what desire, or what delight, returns over and over despite the appearances, despite discouragement, and despite all rational calculation—even trying to repress it, it still comes through. What freshness of feeling, and what freshness of perception, comes through anyway, even despite blocking it, even despite, either the condition of not noticing it, or thinking you better not do it (you better go straight, you better get a job)—what comes through anyway? What unworldly love, that has no hope of the world, and cannot change the world to its delight, persists, and breaks through always, if only in dreams? Because in dreams you get these great baths of eroticism or liberation or recognition. You know, your mother recognizes you, Kissinger recognizes you.

BARBARA MEIER: Did you ever have any dreams about Kissinger?

AG: Yes, I had this great dream about Kissinger! It has to do with this actually. We were having a conversation. (This is an example, because the background is A.A., low self-esteem, and then discovery of self-esteem.) So this dream I had of Kissinger was: "The trouble with you is," I said, "your voice. You may have a reason and a rational thing, but your voice is very heavy, and intimidating, and it's almost as if you're saying you know everything and everybody else knows nothing—you have this authority in your voice. And so it's intimidation, and in that sense it isn't a conversation, it's your domination. And it's an S&M trip, and it's violence. It's violence through the voice. And if you're talking about making peace, you can't make peace with violence. You're trying to force people to follow your mind. And just as war is an extension of politics by other means, or politics is just an extension of war by other means, so your voice is an extension of war by other means. And war does not bring peace. And you've got to finally recognize that. It's the tone of your voice that's all wrong. And you can't get away from that." So, he said, "Well, but I have a secret plan." So, I said, "What is your secret plan?" He said, "My plan, was to have everybody on earth, exactly at the age of two (when they began individuating from the mother), receive an empowerment, from the mother or from some guardian spirit, so that they would go forth into the world with their trusts intact, and their self-esteem turned up." You know, like the mommy says, "You're a nice little boy, you got a good cock, you go out in the world, women will love you, you're good. Go out there. Be there. You're born. You have my approval. You are my best friend. Go out there and don't be afraid of anyone. Girls'll love you." No, but he didn't say that. He just said that, everyone at the age of two, when they began individuating from the mother, would be empowered. He was trying to create this condition on the planet. And I said, "Oh, well why didn't you say so! Why don't you write some little essay about this, and some declaration, and I'll write a preface to give it a little bit of, you know, credibility. And we'll publish it!" And then I woke up.

So that was: "unworldly love, that has no hope of the world, and cannot change the world to its delight." That's absolutely on the mark and on target. Or in waking life, as you have here, in Akhmatova, or as you have in a more embittered form: "Hillocks of human heads in the horizon," which everybody was afraid to say. Or you have in Whitman: "Through me voices of centuries of interminable repression and lust."

So the point is, OK, can you make a clarion call? It can't be just a state-ment of feeling feelings, it's got to be focused and located and embodied in something with which others have contact too. A grand example, which I've been brooding on all spring, is the case of W. E. B. DuBois, the great black writer, who wrote a book in 1903 called, *The Souls of Black Folk*. This was the origin of the regaining of self-esteem among blacks as a mass phenomenon. It was the beginning of a vocalization, like Whitman, of black pride. The realization that it was OK to be black, that black had its own power and its own beauty and its own history and, above all, its own enor-mous grief and suffering and ostracism that had become so internalized that blacks no longer recognized their human selves, and thought of themselves as dumb and degraded and dopey. The white ostracism of blacks had been so internalized that both blacks and whites had grown up deformed, mentally, in relation to each other. And it's the commonest thing, even in me, that blacks are, you know, slightly inferior socially. They don't have my power and they can't get my power. They can always be questioned. No matter what they say, somebody will always be notic-ing that they're black while saying it. I carry that now, and blacks carry that too. So, he said, after 200 years of being knocked on the head with slavery, how could blacks be other than stupid and dumb and lazy and shiftless and fucked up socially—except in individual cases. But his phrase was: "after being knocked on the head for 250 years." He said it so down-home—and a lot of other insights. It's an absolutely monumental work of redeeming the souls of black folk, or reminding, or remembering—remembering the repressed humanity. And the enormous weight behind it, ultimately, is the weight of grief, more than anything else, not anger; the enormous grief of the blacks at how they've been treated. Like a kid who is constantly being abused by the parents. And the grief of the parents in having lost love, and having realized what they've done to themselves. They had to cut off feelings in order to maintain this distorted relation-ship, and exploit—use the blacks—for cleaning latrines, for doing the hard labor . . .

BM: That really creates some kind of breakthrough experience, I mean, if you're so conditioned . . . It reminds me of that Lew Welch poem about searching for supreme, perfect enlightenment. It's like looking for a flash-light when what you need the flashlight for is to find the flashlight.

AG: So, actually reading all this stuff, and then reading the subsidiary lit-erature too, has enormously changed my view of black people. And just physically, on the street, I look at them and I talk to them now, because I always used to be afraid of them, because I didn't know where they were coming from or where I was coming from. I didn't recognize the exact situation. I thought: oh they're equal so I don't have to face them. I don't have to relate to them because they're already equal. But then I realized hardly any whites relate to any blacks. They have their own world and the whites have their own mental world. The word that DuBois used was the "veil" of consciousness—beautiful word for that—the veil between blacks and whites. Like a great veil of consciousness and nonrecognition, "mis-noticing," as Kerouac wrote.

LB: In some sense that's what you're talking about now in terms of our own relationship with ourselves—is breaking through some kind of veil so that we recognize . . .

AG: Right. OK, so Yeats says the great poetry is not between a quarrel with the world, but a quarrel with oneself, or a breakthrough of one's own integral feelings that had been repressed. So, if you want to attack the Supreme Court, it probably won't do—it's like the bull attacking the red flag in the matador's hand. The Supreme Court is sort of like the rag bearer to distract you. What is it that you have internalized from the culture that, on realizing (not so much rebelling against but realizing) and going beyond into the fresh springs of your own feeling and perception, would allow you to make a statement of self-liberation?—like Whitman or Akhmatova—which would ring a sympathetic vibration in other people who have not had the same realization. So that you then have to formulate your own cause, so to speak. You couldn't do it by flashing it on the screen of the external world—it would be a matter of self-discovery. So you'd have to find out what in yourself has been conditioned wrong. What are the sources of your own low self-esteem, which we all have.

But I've been looking for the, sort of, alchemical philosopher's stone. How do you write another "Howl"? I keep looking for the breakthrough—what do I have to break through in myself? I keep looking for the material on the outside, rather than trying to figure what it is in myself that needs breaking through. More likely, I'm too comfortable. I have a nice job, I got money and I'm too comfortable. There's all those people homeless on the street, but it ain't me! So now, how would you approach that? You can't approach it through describing them only (making believe you're suffering for them). So then the way would be: what feelings do I have to repress in order to walk through Tompkins Park and see the homeless and break away from them? What is it in myself that I have to be afraid of or repress or—what extension of myself do I have to hold back—to pass three blocks away and lock my door behind me and have my nice cool neat rooms (sixty-three years of experience of how-to-keep-the-house). Full refrigerator with artichokes, a little caviar—while those guys are out there starving, in plastic. What distortion do I have to go through to limit my sympathy, to preserve my comfort, to preserve my vulnerability, my life, my health.

The black thing I was blind to. The women's thing I was blind to. The Jewish thing I am blind to I'm sure. A lot of the American thing I'm blind to. The art thing I'm blind to.

GA: Is this the source of your low self-esteem?

AG: The homosexual thing—I still haven't really come on as a gay lib type. I'm maintaining my masculine dignity as, you know, whatever.

So then you read books on nicotine, sugar, coffee, and alcohol, and suddenly you realize that you've been subjected to all these poisons. Then you read a book on ecology and you realize you're living in a dream world that's destroying the whole planet. There's a lot of areas . . . and then you begin getting into animal rights, which I'm afraid to even look at for fear . . . In fact that was the thing, as a white man I was afraid to seriously investigate the black situation for fear of having to look into the pit of grief, and having to recognize how much grief there was around, and that I was involved with. Same with animal rights, same with meat, same with coffee, tea, sugar. Same with women, same with gay lib, same with military—in every direction. Finally the whole planet! What are we doing to the planet? The grief and the pit of that. We're afraid to look at it because it's so . . . heavy.

WARREN KARLENZIG: Because they're involved—I mean they're causing all this.

AG: So it's we, we, WE, not they! So it may be that "human beings can't be expected to act like human beings under inhuman circumstances." We may be, for all our richness, at this point, subjected to nonhuman conditioning; hardly any human can break through. The thing I like about Blake is, he made one big fucking breakthrough from religion. He removed that dark satanic church, satanic factories and the churches, the "Nobodaddy" in heaven, the Judge that everybody was scared of. They had to compare their human tinyness to this big, permanent, power-father-figure that was always there. He removed the fear of the lord. So Blake did that. That was like a big thing. Imagine having this demonic god on top of you all the time. You know, the monotheistic cancer in Western civilization. And Blake's whole image is of 5,000 years of delusion, 5,000 years of mental slavery. Now, since Blake, you could say you have a couple hundred years of displaced slavery—the state, to communism, to Stalin, to Mao, to masculine, to the white man, Western culture, to science. All these authorities that have enslaved us.

You know they said, over a hundred million people stolen from Africa, forty percent or more died on the slave ships. And they were treated worse than anyone when they got to America and were put on those slave blocks, families were separated immediately, so they wouldn't be able to conspire. And men were separated, from the same village or town, so they wouldn't be able to talk and get to any kind of underground political network. So they deliberately split people up and alienated them, and knocked them on the head so they couldn't get anywhere. They weren't allowed to learn to read, their ears would be clipped.

WK: They weren't allowed to dance or sing or do any of the things—

AG: Yeah, everything was taken. They were total aliens—just like here—total dispossession, alienation, and driven into the ground mentally, and stupefied, purposefully, in order to keep them as slaves. And then when you think of it—they're slaves? The idea of a human slave? Nowadays, when you think they actually had this S&M thing where you had this economic slave? You could fuck 'em—that's why they have all these mulattoes around, and yellows. You could fuck 'em—you own them? Women feel bad in our culture?! Think what happened to the blacks. And the Jews didn't get it as bad as the blacks did. And then there's the Armenians, and then there's the Irish, and the Palestinians, and the Amazon Indians.

So OK how to look into the pit. One is the problem of looking into the pit and realizing the full suffering and horror. Then the other one is looking into the pit of oneself, I guess, and how do you discover what's inside yourself that's soft and tender and humane and classic and old, as being shat on—that you're shitting on yourself. Because otherwise what you have is anger at the outside. And it may be cleansing to some extent, but it still doesn't recognize the ultimate self or non-self or whatever it is—the ultimate feeling. So the real poetry that would move would be poetry or feelings—like here is lots of feeling. Feelings with cases. Feeling in cases—minute particulars filled with feeling. OK so what is your particular grievance; your source of grief. Finally getting down to answer your question, what is *your* particular grievance and grief (not generic)? Are you even allowed to say that in this close company? Would one even want to begin speaking about it—it's hard.

BM: To integrate all that shadow material too?

AG: No no—just what's on your mind. It doesn't have to be everybody. What is your case of grief or grievance? What is it in yourself that you've had to deny? Not generically, but specifically in relation to your mommy, your daddy, me, the tent, Naropa, Gary Allen, Anne Waldman, yourself—you know, the whole scene? What have you lost that you're just glimmering with, what do you want to reclaim? Then, the way to reclaim it is to make a model of it. What is this unworldly love that has no hope of the world and that cannot change the world to its delight? What is your love? What is your unworldly love? Could you define it? Could you make a model of it to begin? That would be one path—to show what's missing—even if you have to imagine it. As Blake says, it's in the imagination—where the world of poetry lies. In a sense, the lost world that is still retained in the imagination and in memory and in dream. Or, generically, poetic imagination. The unworldly love that has no hope in this world, that has disappeared from this world, but only remains within you in your imagination. I think that's what they mean when they say: All Power to the Imagination! That's what Williams means when he said, "only the imagination is real." William Carlos Williams says that over and over and over. He doesn't mean only the never-never land is real, only the fantasy is real. He means what remains in us of our original nature but can only be imagined, but is missing, because we don't see it, because we've repressed it or been conditioned out of it.

LB: I take issue with that. I mean I feel that actual imagination is perception of the ordinary world. Just what we see, in such a way, that we can participate with it in a transformation or a transmutation, which maybe is what the imagination is.

AG: Well, certainly—it's only a word. There's a way Williams is using it is what I meant. I think what he means is, only our imagination and guessing and dream of what we are missing—only by reclaiming that, recognizing it, taking it seriously (when you take it seriously you give it credibility other than ironically dismissing it as being "idealistic")—only then can you apply it to the everyday world and say, this is what's missing and I want to introduce this new element. Of course Blake also says, everything we see is imagination. But that also means, everything we see is our conditioned social imagination, or our conditioned family social imagination, but there still is a remnant of saving grace somewhere that has to be accounted for. Like the little kid that's brought up beaten by his parents all the time and doesn't know parental love, has yearning and responds to some authority that gives him tenderness, even though he's never had experience with it. Then he realizes, oh, that's what I was missing with my mommy and daddy. Then, that's when he starts giving to the world or trying to contribute or to see, in every situation and contribute, or uncover, in every situation.

But as a practical thing, since this is a poetry workshop, not just theory, how could you yourself formulate your desire or your unworldly love, in a way that makes it a contrast with what is available in the world. And thereby show the potential that's being missed.

WK: Do you think it enables a poetic community to be built or envisioned easier if you're successful at that?

AG: Sure, that makes a community, but the common thing is the reclaiming of lost insight. You know, whether it's women's lib or black lib or Mandelshtam lib, prison lib. It's the realization that there's a hidden world that you don't know when you're in high school or grammar school. And maybe you have glimpses of, in your secret longings and then at some point or other, it precipitates and you become conscious of it. From some experience of opening up, or acid or a teacher or meditation or some way or other, the sensory world opens up, the mind-world opens up. For me it was from reading Blake. But again, this is all generalization, so I'm saying the area to look for is, where in yourself do you find a difference between what you can say to yourself and others and what you really feel. It may not be women's lib toughness, it may be something else, it may be feeling hurt and not wanting to acknowledge it and be that vulnerable. Generally that's what it is. Acknowledging all the hurt and vulnerability then puts into profile all the sadism and the harshness and the inhumanity that's in the social form that's created this situation. So it's only by the lamb bleating that you realize the ultimate nature of soul. The ultimate nature of sensibility, compassion. Soul: compassionate awareness to oneself, of oneself.

But getting back to politics. Do most of you know some of Neruda? Why don't I just read part of one poem by Neruda, "Let the Rail-Splitter Awake." It's the really interesting part of this poem—he turns around and begins looking at his own feelings.

> Here I say farewell, I return
> to my house, in my dreams
> I return to Patagonia where
> the wind rattles the barns
> and the ocean spatters ice.
> I am nothing more than a poet: I love all of you,
> I wander about the world I love;
> in my country they jail miners
> and soldiers give orders to judges.
> But I love even the roots
> in my small cold country,
> if I had to die a thousand times over
> it is there I would die,
> if I had to be born a thousand times over
> it is there I would be born
> near the tall wild pines
> the tempestuous south wind
> the newly-purchased bells.

Let none think of me.
Let us think of the entire earth
and pound the table with love.
I don't want blood again
to saturate bread, beans, music:
I wish they would come with me:
the miner, the little girl,
the lawyer, the seaman,
the doll-maker,
to go into a movie and come out
to drink the reddest wine.
I did not come to solve anything.
I came here to sing
and for you to sing with me.

From *Somewhere in the Americas,* May 1948
(translated by Waldeen)

That's great—you know he had to give up—he couldn't be angry. So what he did however, was he hit the core of feeling that was beyond anger and beyond exploitation and beyond retribution. You know, "I don't want blood to be covering the bread, the wine, the music." A great line—"I didn't come here to solve anything." So that failure, really, to invoke a revolution, was really a success in invoking an emotional revolution in himself, tender heart.

He had to name all the things that were bugging him, too. So I think the ultimate question is: How do you make poetry that will make people cry? How do you reduce Kissinger to tears? How do you make all the generals and diplomats cry? How do you invoke the feeling itself that's lost? The vulnerability, tenderness . . . how do you invoke tender heart? And the other question is, is tender heart enough? Will that define the problems? If you have tender heart, will you have clear enough vision to define the problem?

Bleeding heart won't do it . . . there's a question of "idiot compassion." But I can't get over some of these poems—it just makes me cry. Somehow they've broken through all their own defenses and the world's defenses and they've said something that's so clear, so true, that it reminds you that you're human and that somewhere there is some sense of emotional reality which gives you a glimpse of the emotional delusion we all live in all the time. Not having access to all our feelings, which is what Amiri Baraka is always complaining about, that he doesn't have access to his own feelings, as a human being, as a black man—that he was driven out. "Moloch that frightened me out of my natural ecstasy!" that same notion.

So how do you get to that? Well, first of all, there's the question—because it's got to do with weeping, it has to do with rhythm, breathing rhythm. You know, the long haul of exposition of your feeling. So it has a lot to do with a litany quality: peace to this, peace to that; I'm a shaman woman, I'm a diseased woman, I'm an Anne Waldman woman; "Moloch whose eyes are a thousand blind windows! Moloch who frightened me out of my natural ecstasy! Moloch whom I abandon!" It has to do with the build-up of a heroic emotional rhythm—to get a great breakthrough.

A poem of Williams that I always thought was great was "To Elsie." [It's] just precisely definitive for America: no one in control, "no one to drive the car." But that great line: "as if the earth under our feet / were / an excrement of some sky // and we degraded prisoners / destined / to hunger until we eat filth." Like everybody turning on the television, eating McDonald's, or whatever, you know, take what you can get. You can't get anything, you can't get much, so go suck off some sailor in a urinal under the Brooklyn Bridge. Whatever love you can get, whatever way you can get it. Or get with some mean football player who'll beat you up and fuck you good. But just the whole cultural situation—what have we got for public communication: total mass media propaganda p.r.; "destined to hunger [for language] until we eat filth."

So Williams says, "The government is of language," ultimately. The poets who control the language will outlast the temporary politics. He's pointing out that, as Akhmatova did—Akhmatova's emotion and that solid gold of her perception; "the hat with the blue band led forward by the trembling janitor"—she had the details of the terror. Or the woman howling like a beast before the iron gate clanged shut. She embodied the suffering in these details so they were visible. And she embodied her feeling in the poem. A great phrase of Zukofsky and Pound: "only emotion endures." The iron gates dissolve and rust, the sphinx loses its face, the Acropolis' walls tumble, the forum in Rome's in rubble, but feelings, set forth in those days by Sappho and Catullus, survive brass and monument. Or as Horace said, "I have built myself a monument stronger than brass or stone." So Pound says, "only emotion endures." Zukofsky says, "Only emotion objectified endures." By "objectified" he means, concretized into the iron gate, the woman howling like a dog, waiting for a hundred hours in front of the line, the doves above the statue cooing—specific detail. When the woman says to her, "can you describe this?" And she says, "I can." So can you describe this? For yourself? Can you describe *your* suffering? Or your delight? Either way or both at once, you know, one taste: bittersweet. The ideal would be to weep while writing. I do when I write something that I know is the truth. So I'm sure Keats and Shelley and many people wept while they wrote—for the realization.

BM: Not for the sentiment?

AG: Well, it's all the same: realization, nostalgia, sentiment. Sentiment at realizing you've arrived at the thing that will penetrate through your own core to other people's core, and do it through the real world. Describing the real world in such a way as to find the pattern of the real world. So I conclude, the only way to do it is to stick with the real world one way or the other and hope that, in describing the real world, you'll stumble on your feelings. Rather than just try and describe your feelings, without any details of the real world. But then that could lead to a mechanical description.

GA: Well like "the hillock of human heads" was not literally something he saw, but metaphorically . . .

AG: Yeah, so I think it requires, in order to be a really good poet, noble ambition, heroic ambition. Not just be witty and not just be smart and not just to write something pretty, but to break through to your own truth first, and to others that way. You got to have that bodhisattva heart going out of yourself into the world and giving yourself to the world. Here in America, we have a great source of opportunity because America's the source of all this clanging machinery and earth destruction, and the rest of the world is imitating us, so we're in the belly of the leviathan. If we could only break through ourselves, and make a proclamation that would be serviceable in America, and try and form a wakened feeling in America.

You know Blake's version of that for England, it's great. Back in '65 we had this big poetry reading in London, in Albert Hall, and in the program, in the p.r., we voted Blake as the keynote speaker. From "Jerusalem":

> England! awake! awake! awake!
> Jerusalem thy sister calls!
> Why wilt thou sleep the sleep of death?
> And close her from thy ancient walls?
>
> Thy hills and valleys felt her feet,
> Gently upon their bosoms move:
> Thy gates beheld sweet Zion's ways:
> Then was a time of joy and love.
>
> And now the time returns again:
> Our souls exult and London's towers,

Receive the Lamb of God to dwell
In England's green and pleasant bowers.

It would be great to start a poem: "America! Awake! Awake! Awake!"
And then list all the things it could actually awake to.

There's a great line in Kerouac, "I'm writing this because we're all going
to die." You know the breakthrough of his feeling in writing. From *Visions
of Cody:*

> I'm writing this book because we're all going to die—In the loneliness of
> my life, my father dead, my brother dead, my mother faraway, my sister and
> wife faraway, nothing here but my own tragic hands ... that now are left to
> guide and disappear their own way into the common dark of all our death,
> sleeping in me raw bed, alone and stupid: with just this one pride and con-
> solation: my heart broke in the general despair and opened up inwards to
> the Lord. I made a supplication in this dream.

Like coming out of the dream into realization and addressing all the
universe. That was his mode for writing. And that was a key passage for
him I think to explain how he arrived at the superhuman energy and perception necessary to encompass all of his life in a series of novels in realization of mortality. And I guess it's that mortal realization that a lama was
talking about last night, the compassionate . . . On Chögyam Rinpoche's
death, really struck me as a great formulation:

> The passing experience of the profound sorrow characteristic of compas-
> sionate awareness of the suffering pervading cyclic existence ...

So maybe it even goes deeper than the social. Like with the Neruda, "I didn't
come here to solve anything, I only came here to sing and for you to sing
with me."

Transcribed by Kimi Sugioka.
Edited by Anne Waldman.

Hieroglyphics and Money

PETER LAMBORN WILSON
June 30, 1998

★   ★   ★

You probably know that real Egyptian hieroglyphics were first deciphered by a man named Champollion, a brilliant French scholar who had the good luck to study the Rosetta Stone, which had been stolen from Egypt by Napoleon. It was one of the souvenirs he brought back. (Napoleon was the first modern tourist. Conquered Egypt in order to collect antiquities.) Around about 1821, Champollion cracked Egyptian hieroglyphics. Because the Rosetta Stone had both Greek and hieroglyphics on it, he was able to do this.

At that point, a whole world of research into the hieroglyphs fell into oblivion. The hieroglyphs had been discovered, rediscovered, during the Renaissance and were of immediate interest to the Hermeticists. The Hermeticists were basically alchemists, astrologers, ceremonial magicians, and in fact natural scientists. The important thing to remember about Hermeticism is that when we look at it now, it looks like crackpot pseudoscience; but when it was new and exciting during the Renaissance it was one of the paradigms for science that could have emerged. There was a kind of paradigm war at this period—and the Hermeticists were in a struggle against, you might say, the Cartesians and the Baconian/ Newtonian crowd, the Royal Society in London. They all had their different views of material reality. But as it turned out, the Baconian/ Newtonian faction had much better success in the laboratory; they actually got hold of some workable, technological, scientific ideas, and this was of great interest to the ruling class. So the paradigm war was won by the paradigm that provided hard science as we know it: real laboratory science with real mathematical provability. So Hermeticism lost the paradigm war and went underground and became the Western occult tradition. It still survives today in many ways, including your horoscope in the daily paper. This is basically Hermeticism. The irrational, if you want to call it that, doesn't go away. We're very much still living in a world in which the ghost of Hermeticism, the specter of Hermeticism, is haunting Europe and European culture.

The Renaissance sages discovered the Egyptian hieroglyphs as they rediscovered late antiquity. In other words, when you're an archeologist, you begin digging down through layers of dirt. The first layer you come to is the most recent, and then they get later as you go down. When the Renaissance began to dig into the past, the first past that they met was not early antiquity—not Plato, Aristotle, Aeschylus, and Sophocles—it was late antiquity, Hellenistic antiquity, post-Alexander-the-Great: a world which had been unified by Alexander's conquests and synthesis of all the cultures of the middle world, the classical old world from Spain to India, really. So Hellenistic culture was a great syncretistic period and very much the first real modern period. All kinds of ideas flowed together, especially in the city of Alexandria, founded by Alexander himself, where Egyptian magic and religion met up with Greek neo-Platonic philosophy and science, where Buddhists came from India—and possibly even Hindus. And a great melting together of ideas took place. There were Jewish intellectuals; Christianity was emerging during this period and establishing its claim on the consciousness of the world. Paganism was still thriving and the different pagan religions and philosophical schools were being brought together politically and therefore also economically and also therefore intellectually.

Hermeticism, which is named after the Greek god Hermes, was conflated together with the Egyptian tradition to produce the phenomenon which we call Hermeticism. Hermes began his career as a pile of rocks in the Greek landscape, and these *herms,* so called, were border markers. You would erect a cairn of stones on the border of your farm. Hermes was first of all the god of boundaries, of the in-between. He became the god of all transactions. You could say anything in the nature of a transaction falls under the Hermetic sign; that includes language and writing. Hermes is communication, transposition of information from one place to another and its reception. He also became the god of crossroads, places where roads come together and form an in-between space; and the god of language, the god of writing, which he was supposed to have invented; and also the god of thieves and merchants who have transactions of their own, having to do with wealth. Hermes also comes out as, not only the god of occult science—those borderland sciences, you might say—but also the god of money. He's been appearing on coins ever since. Not long ago, he was on the American dime, the ten-cent piece, the mercury dime. He was identified with the Egyptian god Thoth who was the inventor of hieroglyphics. In Greco-Egyptian Hermeticism, Hermes is very closely connected with hieroglyphic writing in the minds of the Hellenistic magicians or scientists.

However, around about the 3rd or 4th century, it's clear that the actual knowledge of hieroglyphics is lost. The Egyptian tradition had fallen into complete decadence as a result of the Roman conquest, even though it lasted a long time and had a lot of prestige. Christianity had a deleterious effect here. It was the Christians who really burned the library of

Alexandria, not the Moslims. By the time the Moslims got there, there was almost nothing left to burn. The Christians had done away with it all. As they came more and more into power, they took a very anti-intellectual stance. They killed Hypatia, the last neo-Platonic philosopher, a very interesting woman. Stoned to death by the Christians in 415 AD. So the knowledge of the hieroglyphs was lost. There was one fascinating manuscript from the 5th century called the *Horapollo,* the Horos-Apollo. Horos being an Egyptian god and Apollo being a Greek god; so you can see how syncretistic it was. It was written in Greek. It was discovered during the Renaissance. The last surviving manuscript was found in Crete, an interesting place, because it is halfway in between Greece and Egypt. It seems that a Greek speaker had learned some fragments of ancient Egyptian lore about the hieroglyphs and had written them down. There are a few nuggets of actual hieroglyphic information in the book but distorted, useless for actually reading hieroglyphic text. But, when it was rediscovered in the Renaissance, it was thought to be a real, actual explanation of the hieroglyphs. An attempt was made to crack the hieroglyphs already from about 1450 onward. People were interested in this phenomenon. In ancient times, the Romans had brought some booty with them from Egypt to Rome, including obelisks and other objects that had hieroglyphic writing on them. As the Italian intellectuals began their archeological work, if you can put it that way, the first layer that they discovered was ancient Rome and among the ruins of ancient Rome were bits and pieces of Egypt which intrigued the hell out of them. The book, the *Horapollo,* encouraged them to believe that they had a form of magic writing such that if they could learn how to read it they would discover the magical mysteries of Egypt which, of course, even in the Bible is known as the homeland of magic. The very word alchemy is actually the old name of Egypt. *Khem* means "black earth," which was the old Egyptian name for Egypt, and was transferred to the science of alchemy, *the* Egyptian science in other words. Moses and the Egyptian magicians and so forth and so on. Everybody knew that Egypt was the source of real magical knowledge. And if only we could read these texts, this power would be ours. The power of a culture, of a dynasty in a sense, that had lasted for 3,000 years. Real power. Very, very tempting. Not only political power but spiritual power, spiritual, magical power, the ability to manipulate the world through writing.

Of course writing itself always begins as a form of magic. It performs action at a distance. This is very easy to understand. Before writing, if you owed me money, I had to chase you down and get it. Later on, with writing I could send you a bill and you would have to pay. That's action at a distance. That's magic. Writing in both Mesopotamia and Egypt, we now know, began around 3100 BC. It appears very suddenly in the archeological record. It was a brilliant invention of a small group of people in the city of Uruk in Sumeria. The idea floated over to Egypt very quickly. Although they didn't use any of the same signs, they developed a similar pictographic form of writing. It was developed in the temples, because the temples were also the banks. Economy and religion were one and the same. Well, they still are you might say. You'll notice that banks were built to look like Greek temples until quite recently. Now, they look like McDonald's outlets. I guess that pretty much shows where our idea of the sacred has migrated. But in the old days, there was a distinct connection between religion and economics. You could see it on any street corner, and you still can if you look at an old bank.

The bank and the temple were one and the same thing. They ran the show for the master class who were the priests and kings. The kings were the representatives of the gods, and the priests were the representatives of the kings. They were the ones who expropriated the surplus labor, to use Marxian terms, sometime during the late Neolithic or early Bronze Age period. So when writing appears, we already see a completely evolved hegemonic, hierarchic state symbolized by the pyramid. They built these buildings in the shape of their own society as they conceptualized it. This is an ideological symbol. A very Hermetic idea: to use an image to express ideology. Nowadays you might think of ideology as primarily a textual affair. It was a textual affair in that the writing itself was full of images. If you look at Egyptian hieroglyphs, you'll see them very clearly. They're not so easy to see when you look at the Mesopotamian writing. The Renaissance magicians believed that these pictures were meant to "be" the things that they showed in some way. There was a real connection between the thing and its image. Using neo-Platonic philosophy, applying a neo-Platonic flashlight on this problem, they came to feel that this was a direct form of magic, that you could write and change the world magically by writing these things. Each hieroglyph was like a Platonic archetype. It was not only a symbol of the thing, but it was in some sense identified with the thing in a magical way.

Now we think we know, thanks to Champollion, that this was a completely wrong theory of the hieroglyphs. In fact these animals or other recognizable symbols were not being used in any overtly magical or Platonic way; they were being used for the sound. If the Egyptian word for hawk, for example, begins with the sound "k" (I don't know if it does), then the hawk is actually the letter "k" or the sound *kah*. That's probably not right; I'm just guessing. I don't really know hieroglyphics. I've only studied Renaissance hieroglyphs which is wrong, actually a wrong reading of the hieroglyphs. I'll explain why I wasted my time this way. The fact is that all the work that was done on the hieroglyphs during the

Renaissance was proven to be wrong. It was considered to be a total waste of time. So all this work was thrown out of the academic world, much more so than even the other Hermetic sciences. Alchemy and astrology had their popular followings. The hieroglyphic science was so completely discredited by Champollion that 300-400 years of serious work by brilliant people was totally forgotten. In fact of all the books which deal with it, not one of them has had a modern edition or modern translation. You can go to the library and still see the first editions of these books. They really knew how to make books in those days, not like now. These 15th, 16th century books are in perfect shape. No one ever reads them also; that's another point. So they're really pristine.

As a result, I feel a whole lot of extremely useful work actually got thrown out the window. Because if you have a semiotic understanding of a semiotic system, it really doesn't matter whether you get the actual meaning or not. You have a semiotic system. That in itself is a powerful tool. We now believe that all signs are really arbitrary; quite the reverse of what the magicians believed, that there was a nonarbitrary relation between the sign and the thing that the sign signifies. We supposedly know better. We know that signs are arbitrary. Any system of signs is a semiotic system. It doesn't matter what values you assign to the signs. It's a system. It communicates something. It has meaning. Each of these Renaissance magicians, as they attempted to read the hieroglyphs, developed (through sheer force of the imagination) semiotic systems, sign systems. Some of these have extreme interest in their own right. They didn't deserve to be thrown out just because they happened not to work as means of deciphering real Egyptian writing. And yet they were; they were totally forgotten.

It was mere curiosity that drove me into looking at what little literature exists in modern scholarship to find out what all those brilliant people thought they were doing. Some of them wrote in other fields and that work survives. We have Marsilio Ficino and Pico della Mirandola and the great Platonic Academy of Florence. The real high-brow, brilliant guys of the Renaissance were working on this. We still know who they were.

It struck me that there must be something of value to be salvaged from this wreckage. I believe I'm right. I think that there's really something very important at stake here. What it is is not semiotics in the modern sense of the word, which I call "passive semiotics," just the analysis of signs. What is at stake here is what I call "projective semiotics." What they were really trying to learn ultimately was not so much how to *read* hieroglyphics as how to *write* hieroglyphics. Because that's where the real power would be, would come into play. If you could manipulate these signs with full knowledge of their meaning, then you would have the secret of the ancient Egyptians and you would share in their mysterious power.

All of these systems were not just passive semiotic studies in the modern Saussurian linguistic sense. They were actually attempting to learn how to project those semiotics—either reflected into their own souls for the work on the self or else reflected outward for work on the world. Potentially that could involve, in their minds, real political power. Some of this work was of interest to the rulers. And the rulers paid for this work because they thought that a secret of power would come out of it.

There are characters like Giordano Bruno, for example, who are clearly playing both sides of the coin here. They are on one hand spiritual seekers on their own behalf, trying to achieve enlightenment through magic as a spiritual path. On the other hand, they're quite willing and ready to sell their services to the highest bidder. We know that Bruno worked as a spy for Queen Elizabeth through the first great spy master Sir Francis Walsingham. And John Dee, also at the same time, who is Prospero in *The Tempest* basically, was Queen Elizabeth's court astrologer and wizard. The reason that these people were valuable, among other reasons, was that they knew about codes, secret ways of writing.

Modern cryptography and cryptanalysis comes out of Hermeticism. It is one of the Hermetic sciences that is still with us, in a sense. John Dee and Bruno knew how to write in lemon juice and hold it over a candle and all that kind of stuff which is just kid's play now. Then it seemed very, very important. In fact it is the beginning of modern intelligence. That's another very important reason to study these things, because intelligence, which is a hidden science, a Hermetic science, is very much still with us. If we want to try to understand the CIA by delving into the history of intelligence back to at least the Elizabethan period or the Renaissance, if not further, then we have to study Hermeticism. Very few scholars have done this actually.

It's interesting that John Dee had a secret cipher that he signed his most secret papers with. It was "007." I think that Ian Fleming knew that. I don't think that was a coincidence. Sir Francis Walsingham was obviously "M" from the Bond novels. The spymaster. The original spymaster. The magician, the *magus* at the center of the web of secret knowledge and power. During this period few means existed to separate these two worlds. They "murked" into each other. Christopher Marlowe, who also worked for this outfit, ended up the victim of a little wet-work operation, because he was getting out of hand and giving away too many secrets. One of the secrets he gave away, as one of my students reminded me this morning, was . . . he said: "I have as good a right to coin money as the Queen of England." That's true. Who's to say he's wrong? You just have to have the power to get away with it and you can coin money.

Paracelsus, the great alchemist of the 15th–16th century, was wandering through Germany and was asked to have an interview with one of the petty rulers. This king says to Paracelsus, "We hear that you're very good at transmuting base metals into gold. We would like to set you up with your own private laboratory here in the palace, OK? We're going to pay for your research." And Paracelsus says, "Your majesty, I think you're laboring under a misapprehension. I'm not really an alchemist; I'm just a puffer, someone who works the bellows in the alchemical lab. Kings are the real alchemists." The king says, "Oh, really? How's that?" Paracelsus says, "I'll tell you a great Hermetic secret: All you have to do is set up a national bank, give it a monopoly on coining money and then borrow it. Then you'll have created something out of nothing. You'll have created gold out of nothing." The king says, "Fabulous idea! Thanks so much!" Paracelsus is free to go on his way. In my view, the king takes his advice and sets up a national bank and starts borrowing money. In a few years he finds out Paracelsus' joke, which is that he's now in debt to the bank. So now we have the modern world where national debt comes into being—where in fact it's not kings who rule anymore, it's bankers. That was indeed a Hermetic secret. It's just that Paracelsus didn't tell him the other half of the secret.

We see that in the idea of creating gold, there's a very strong connection between Hermetic science and money, which is the theme that I want to eventually get to here.

The idea of projective hieroglyphics was broken down and reassembled into the idea of the emblem. The emblem is a picture with words. During the 16th and 17th century, a whole delightful genre comes into being called "the emblem books." Some of them are Hermetic; some of them are just aphoristic and moralistic, allegorical. Walter Benjamin has discussed the emblem books in his work on German Baroque drama in a very interesting way, showing how they become more and more abstract, less and less connected with anything real. A sort of "air of melancholy," as he puts it, enters into this genre. Melancholy, moralistic meditations on death and decay. Earlier in the Renaissance, it has a much livelier and more engaged aspect to it, because the emblem is essentially a hieroglyph. Or the hieroglyph is essentially an emblem.

If you break down the hieroglyph which is a word that is an image, you get a word and an image. If you can't read or write hieroglyphs, at least you can construct emblems. Some of the emblems are based on misinterpretations of the hieroglyphs. You can see fake hieroglyphs in a lot of these emblem works. This was an early experimental period when emblems were considered to have magical power. Not just to be allegorical—that A stands for B in a crude allegoristic sense. There is an existential connection between the emblem and the word, and between your experience of that emblem and the reality that the emblem is supposedly representing, re-presenting. In other words, it isn't just plain re-presentation; it's presentation on some level. The reality of the thing is being presented, not just re-presented. That was the idea. It didn't work any better than laboratory alchemy worked, really.

The whole reason why Hermeticism turned out to be a failure is because these sciences didn't work in the quantitative, modern sense of the word "work." Bacon and Newton, by the way and secretly unbeknownst to most modern people, were themselves Hermeticists. Newton wrote far more about alchemy than he wrote about anything else; but his manuscripts weren't published until the 20th century. Then everybody discovered that Newton was in fact a Hermeticist. And the whole idea of gravity being action at a distance was a Hermetic idea that he had smuggled into modern science through the back door. Because he was able to quantify it, then it was acceptable. It's basically your old magic again, your old action at a distance. To this day nobody knows what gravity is. You can make a mathematical formula to describe it but you can't tell me what it is.

There was this attempt to use hieroglyphs for power. On the quantitative level, on the laboratory level, this power was not forthcoming. However, what we should remember is that there was an aspect to this science which does actually work. If we just think of it as old dusty mumbo-jumbo from the Renaissance, we'll laugh at it and we'll say that this doesn't work. But if you think of the emblem, for example, as propaganda or advertising or brainwashing, and you compare it, let's say, with modern advertising which is always made up of words and images; then you'll begin to see that the Hermeticists do have descendants in the modern world. The spin doctors. The propaganda masters. Madison Avenue advertising, the psychological science of advertising. Again, nobody understands how this works, but it works. Or at least so we believe, because the entire system of global capital is based upon this idea of the creation of need through advertising.

Let's just take advertising and stay away from the other aspects of this. An advertisement is an image. There are words with the image that tell you how to interpret it. Then it creates in you a desire for the product, and you (zombie-like) go out and buy it. That's the way it's supposed to work. And far as we know, like I say, it does work. It shouldn't work, but it does. It's never really studied very seriously by social scientists and certainly not by hard scientists. It's a murky Hermetic little world of its own with its own secret laws. I'm sure all those people on Madison Avenue were reading McLuhan at least if not the Situationists and possibly the Hermeticists. Hermeticism didn't entirely disappear from the world of power. We don't think of all this as Hermeticism anymore but it really is.

To get back to the hieroglyphs per se, it struck me that there was a key here to understanding this whole business. I didn't come up with this idea on my own. It derives from a professor of comparative religion named Ioan Couliano, a Romanian who was working with Mircea Eliade at the University of Chicago. In his book *Eros and Magic in the Renaissance*, this is an idea he just throws away in passing very quickly, this idea about modern advertising being a continuation of ancient Hermeticism. He does so by analyzing a little text by Giordano Bruno, you remember the spy, who was, by the way, burned at the stake in Rome in 1600. He had the bad sense to return to Rome after having worked as a spy for Queen Elizabeth. He's the great Hermetic martyr. There's a statue of him in the spot where they burned him in Rome. They apologized, you know, three or four hundred years later and put up a statue. A very Clinton-like idea. So sorry Galileo, so sorry Bruno. We were wrong, you were right.

He's analyzing a little text by Bruno called *De Vinculis*, "About Chains," on the subject of chains. Bruno is giving the game away in this text. He's telling exactly how magic works. He's saying that the image creates an invisible chain that makes a link between you and it. This is a very clear way of thinking from the Renaissance point of view, because they didn't think that sight was a passive thing. Sight was a projective potency. There was a beam that came out of the eye, an active beam according to ancient science that would rub itself over the image and convey the information back to the brain. It was a very active interpretation of looking and seeing. Sight was the most important and noble of the senses for these philosophers. This chain which Bruno speaks of is the chain of desire, the desire which moves the world. This is an ancient cosmic idea; it goes back to the deepest religious ideas of humanity. He gives it a new spin. The ancient Greeks believed that Chaos was the first god and Eros was the second god. Originally we have formless, shapeless Chaos and then Desire which brings it into shape. So the third deity is Gaia, the earth, the shape which comes out of that marriage between Chaos and Desire. According to the Hermetic philosophers, matter desires form. There's something inherent in matter that forms itself into form. An idea which has been resurrected again in Chaos science. What they're really talking about in modern mathematical terms is the strange attractor. The strange attractor here plays the role of desire. You find modern scientists without even knowing what they're doing repeating old Hermetic slogans like "matter desires form." I've actually come across that in a work by a modern mathematician. He says, "This chaos science is so amazing. It's as if matter desires form." Accidentally rediscovering a whole field of ancient wisdom and magical mumbo-jumbo and applying it to the most up-to-date and hard scientific mathematical work in the latest form of modern science. This is the basic idea that Bruno was working on: that inchoate matter desires form.

The formlessness which is within you as a psychic chaos will form itself out of desire around this image and it will project itself out over this chain of vision, and a connection will be set up. It is desire which is the actual power of magic. This chain can work in two different ways. It can be a ladder like Jacob's ladder leading up to Heaven, up to spiritual realization for the individual magician who is contemplating this image. Or it can be projected outward onto the masses, so to speak. They are enchained by the desire for this image. The image can be any image, actually, so long as it is a coherent image. But if it is a powerful image or an image of power, then you are enchained into this complex of power. And you will do the bidding of the magician.

Where did Bruno get this idea? Possibly from the obelisks which were among the objects brought from ancient Egypt to ancient Rome as symbols of kingly power, of royal power. The ancient Romans obviously thought that they could steal the magic of the Egyptian pharaohs by stealing the obelisks and bringing them back to Rome. I think Bruno and his fellow magicians had some similar idea in mind—that there could be a public broadcasting antenna. Think of the obelisk as a magic antenna broadcasting hieroglyphic messages to anyone within eyeshot of the object. And I think you'll get something of the idea of the powerful power that Bruno was envisioning here. As I say, he really gave the game away, because he didn't make any metaphysical claims. These were all psychological claims. They could be interpreted on a purely psychological level. You don't have to believe in the literal existence of spirits or gods or magic in the usual, crude sense of the word. This actually works on the psychological level. It's a psychological form of magic. There's no doubt in my mind that, among the many things that the Hermeticists did, they pre-discovered modern psychology.

It was Bruno's outspokenness on these kinds of things which led him to be burned at the stake, of course. One doesn't speak of these things. These are public secrets, as Michael Taussig, the anthropologist, calls them. These are things everybody knows but nobody can speak about or even really articulate. Everyone knows this: that they're slaves of desire, that they're chained to the image. But no one can really speak of it. It's a public secret. A very Hermetic concept.

Out of this meaningless mumbo-jumbo and dusty old failures to achieve cracking the code of the hieroglyphs, a very interesting critical tool might emerge. I call it "Hermetic criticism" or the "hieroglyphic theory." We could use this Hermetic metaphor. I think of it as far more powerful than a mere metaphor. We could use this Hermetic model and apply it to all sorts of things going on in the modern world. Professor Couliano didn't manage to do this and there's a very interesting reason why he failed to go on from this point.

I'll make just a little parenthesis here to tell you what happened to this man. Mircea Eliade, who was the dean of modern comparative religion and the history of religions, had a murky past of his own which he hid away from his American postwar admirers. Before the war, he was a member of the Iron Guard in Romania, the most fascist outfit in the world. They were so far to the right that the Nazis had to wipe them out when they conquered Romania. Eliade had written vicious anti-Semitic tracts during his youth. Later when he fled from Communism and came to America and became the great professor of religion at Chicago, he suppressed this information. He didn't mention it at all in his famous autobiography. In his three-volume autobiography there's not a whisper of this. And Couliano was also a Romanian who would escape from Communism, but he was not a fascist. He was just simply anti-Communist. In fact his anti-Communism led him to a fairly libertarian position. Not capital "L" libertarian; I mean simply a freedom-loving position. He loved freedom because he had escaped from the slavery (as he saw it) of Ceausescu's Romania. Couliano's dream was to study religion with Eliade, and he achieved this dream, moved to Chicago, and became his disciple. Later on when Eliade came to trust him, he let him into the archive to work on his papers. There he discovered some of Eliade's old Romanian texts, the anti-Semitic texts. Couliano was devastated. This was his master who turned out to be this monster instead. Just at the point he was bringing himself to discuss this with Eliade (you can imagine how painful that would have been) Eliade died and left him with this agony totally unresolved in his personal life.

At this point the so-called revolution in Romania broke out in 1989. If you happen to be lucky enough to have been here years ago, it must have been in 1990, when Andrei Codrescu came back from Romania and gave a talk here at Naropa which later became his book *The Hole in the Flag,* then you will know that the Romanian Revolution was a media event. What was really going on was that an element of Romanian intelligence, called Securitate, had decided to overthrow Ceausescu and join the modern world under the aegis of being make-believe democrats so that they could get in on all the global goodies. So they pretended that a revolution had broken out, and they took over the television station. They tricked a few young idealists into running the television station, and they fed them false information about the revolution that was supposedly breaking out all over Romania. In this way, they were able to achieve power. They overthrew Ceausescu. They came into power as the New Patriotic Front or some bullshit title like that and they won. Andrei had to go to Romania to discover this. He went there and was extremely disillusioned and he came back and told us about it here.

Couliano, however, didn't even have to visit Romania, because he was a student of Hermeticism. He had already figured out that the whole of modern media is nothing but a Hermetic scam. He was able to analyze instantly what was going on in Romania from Chicago. He wrote an article in Romanian. He had rarely written in Romanian before; it was always Italian or English. He blew the whistle on the Romanian Revolution. A few weeks later, someone shot him through the head in the men's room of the University of Chicago Department of Religion with a .22 while he was taking a crap. This crime was never solved. Nobody was ever caught for this. Research has been done into it, and it seems fairly clear that the hit was carried out by old members of the Iron Guard. Chicago was a place where a lot of Romanians went immediately after the war. A lot of the fascisti went there and they were still there. They were working for Securitate. We have a Stalinist/fascist link here.

It's apparent that the hit was put on Couliano from Romania and it was carried out by old Iron Guardists in Chicago. Incidentally, Andrei received death threats at the same time. They were trying to shut him up as well. He refused to shut up, and thank God he's still with us.

There's something really at stake here. These are life-and-death matters we're talking about. This is not just a hobby of mine. I'm not interested in Hermeticism because it's weird, because it was a failure, because it's dusty, because it's underground. Yeah, I like all those things. Those things are great; I don't put them down. There's something more at stake than just my pleasure here. There's something far more at stake here, and Couliano paid the price. I want you to know if you read his book, that you're reading a book of another Hermetic martyr like Giordano Bruno. These words are written in fire and blood for me.

I'm not a scholar at all. I'm a populizer or, as the French say, a vulgarizer. I thought that since nobody else seemed willing to take up this work that I had to do it, I had to keep on working on this fabulous insight Couliano had expressed on Bruno's little piece *De Vinculis*.

George Washington of course was the Grand Master of the Free Masons of Virginia and later on probably of the entire United States. The American Revolution was a Free Masonic revolution. The city of Washington is laid out like a Hermetic mandala deliberately by Masonic initiates. In the middle of it, there's an obelisk. It doesn't have words on it, it doesn't have any hieroglyphics on it, but it's there. It's doing its job as a magic wand of power at the middle of this Masonic mandala. The Constitution is a Masonic document. Ben Franklin, head of the Philadelphia Masons. Thomas Jefferson belonged to a rival outfit, the Grand Order of the Orient. He didn't like the English Masons. The reason Jeffersonians and Madisonians were at odds was actually a quarrel within Masonry. I'm giving you the crackpot conspiracy view of early American history here. I just want to put a label on it before you do. If you read most histories of the American Revolution and look in the index, you won't even find a listing under Free Masonry. It's kind of embarrassing. If you go to the Masonic Museum in Washington, DC, you'll see a portrait of George Washington in his Masonic regalia, including an apron with magical symbols on it, presiding over the secret inauguration, the Masonic inauguration which was held in the Masonic lodge where his true accession to power as the Masonic messiah, almost, was enacted.

Look at the U.S. one-dollar bill. In the upper right corner of the dollar bill, if you look at the shield that surrounds the numeral one and has olive leaves around it, and then you look at the upper left hand curve of the escutcheon, you'll see that there's a little tiny white blip in there. It's not part of the design. You've probably not noticed it before. If you've got really good eyesight, you'll see that it's an owl. This is the owl of Athena which was the emblem on the Athenian drachma, probably the first real international currency. It was used all over the Mediterranean.

The economic and political prestige of Athens made it the first "Yankee dollar," you might say. So the Yankee dollar appropriated that Hermetic image.

On the reverse of the one-dollar bill, things really get exciting. Here we have the great seal of the United States which, of course, was designed by Free Masons. This is the reverse, the pyramid with the eye is the reverse, the hidden occult side of the great seal. The one that we're much more familiar with, the eagle and the shield, is the front. However, through a strange method of labeling, the words "great seal" appear underneath the reverse. On the other side, it says "of the United States." In fact, that's the great seal and this is the reverse. A little psychological trick is being played on you here. The reverse is being turned into the outward, and the outward is being turned into the inward. A very typical Hermetic trick. The one you're actually going to think of as the great seal is this pyramid with the eye—which brings us back to the Egyptian pyramid and the ideological architecture of the hierarchical state. At the bottom you have the *fellahin,* the peasants slogging away in whatever shit fields are available. At the top is where the king goes up and meets the descending God. If this were a Mesopotamian pyramid, this would be much clearer. The explanation that they gave is that this is supposed to be the great pyramid of Cheops, the biggest one in Giza. But it's unfinished. It's missing the pyramidion which was the thing that goes on top of a pyramid. They made a deliberate leveling off to show that the great work of the Masonic conspiracy was not yet finished. The official explanation is that the work of achieving democratic freedom in the world is not yet finished. What they really meant was that their Masonic program was just getting started, so the pyramid was not yet finished. In place of the pyramidion, you see the eye. This is the eye of Horus. The single eye which sees the One. The image of the single eye has positive and negative symbolism. The negative symbolism is Polyphemus, the one-eyed giant in the *Odyssey* who captures Odysseus. Polyphemus is stupid. He doesn't have binocular vision. He doesn't see depth. At the same time, the single eye has positive symbolism in that the single eye sees the One, the true unified reality beyond the multiplicity of illusion or the illusion of multiplicity. That's the single eye of Horus, the single eye of insight and wisdom. In the official explanation of the great seal, it says that this is the eye of the lovers of freedom who are watching out for your benefit, keeping eternal vigil. Sort of like Bentham's "Panopticon."

Let's do the Latin words. First of all, there's *annuit coeptis*. It's bloody hard to find out what *annuit coeptis* means. "He approves the undertaking." Who is this he who approves the undertaking of the building of this unfinished pyramid? I guess it's God. "In God we trust," after all. It's obviously God as an architect, as the Masons call him, "the grand architect of the universe." That's Masonic talk for God. The He in the *-it* ending of *annuit* is the Masonic deity who approves the undertaking. What is the undertaking? The undertaking is the *novus ordo seclorum,* the new order of the centuries. History has now taken on a new meaning. The precise date is given below the pyramid: 1776. In 1776 there's a new order of the centuries. The world changes. That's the Masonic order, the Masonic revolution.

Having said all this about the reverse, it's almost banal to go to the face of the emblem. But that has a lot of interesting things to say about it too. The shield is the family coat of arms of the Washington family. You wondered where the American flag came from. Betsy Ross didn't dream it up out of nothing. It's George Washington's coat of arms. Stars and stripes and red, white, and blue. I saw it myself in the house where the Washington family originated in England. They'll show it to you quite proudly. [In English accent:] "Here's your flag, you see the origin of your flag. You didn't know that I suppose." And indeed I didn't. It was quite a revelation. Then you have the thirteen stars and thirteen arrows which is the fascine (we don't like to use that word around America anymore because the fascists took it as their symbol). The fascine is one of the oldest stories in the world; you'll find it in every culture. Genghis Khan supposedly gave his son an arrow and said, "Here, break this." He broke it. He gave him two arrows and he broke them. Then he gave him five. Then he gave him thirteen and he couldn't break them. The lesson is from Genghis Khan, one of the great power mongers of all time: stick together in adversity. "You, sons of my sons, if you work against each other, you will be broken. But if you stick together, the empire will hold together."

The eagle: one of the oldest emblematic or heraldic animals in the world, you find it in the very earliest art in which we can tell one animal from another. Even amongst the Native Americans here, the eagle or its supernatural cousin, the thunderbird, is the prime symbol of power. Certainly, the eagle has always been a symbol of power in nomadic, barbarian tribes. That's why the eagle is in the coat of arms of most of the royal houses of Europe who are descended from barbarian hordes. The eagle is the bird that the shaman turns into very frequently to make the ascent into the sky. The eagle is the bird that Indra, the great Indian patriarchal god of the sky, uses to rescue the soma, the magic mushroom if you like, the sacred drug of the Vedas which has been sequestered by an evil one-eyed giant named Vritra. The eagle rescues the soma and brings it back to earth. In Scandinavian mythology, the eagle rescues mead which has been stolen by the trolls. The mead of poetry. Thor and Odin send an eagle to rescue the mead of poetry. Etc., etc., etc. The double-headed eagle of the Austrian-Hungarian empire symbolizes the dual rule of church and state, of Caesar and Pope. The eagle is one of the most overdetermined Hermetic emblems you can think of.

This is the latest incarnation of a very old story, because money itself as we know begins with the science of emblems. I'm talking of coinage, money as we know it now, which begins with coinage in the 7th century BC in Lydia, a kingdom in Asia Minor which is now called Turkey. Coins were invented by or at least under the aegis of the famous King Croesus, the archetype of the wealthy king. Why not? He invented coins. The coins were made out of electrum, a mixture of gold and silver. Gold symbolizes the sun; silver symbolizes the moon. Electrum is the meeting of the two opposites, the marriage between male and female, red and white, yin and yang, night and day, etc. What we have here is a magical metal and a magical medal. The coin starts out as a single slug of electrum, a shapeless blob. What makes it a coin and not just a piece of precious metal that you could trade as a commodity currency—what makes it real money is the emblem which is sealed, stamped, in that bit of electrum.

For a long time this symbol is a religious symbol. Secular symbols take a long time to appear on coins and even then they're associated with royal families or ruling governments, and therefore have a religious significance—because all ancient governments rule by some form of divine right. The picture of the king is also a religious icon. This is true up to the Roman empire, where you're supposed to worship the emperor. This is why Jesus says, "Render unto Caesar those things which are Caesar's and unto God those things which are God's." He's talking about the actual coin that has a picture of Caesar as God on it. He's saying money is shit. Money is the devil's shit, as an Italian grandmother of a friend of mine says. (I'm sure it sounds really good in Italian.)

The symbols are frequently animals and these are the animals which were offered in sacrifice at the temples which made the coins. These coins are issued by temples. In fact they're probably temple souvenirs to begin with. It's only later on that they become used as a symbolic means for exchange. First and foremost they're a symbol of a symbolic exchange, the sacrifice itself. This is your portion of the sacrifice which you bring away from the temple as a souvenir. It's full of *mana*, the anthropological term that comes from Polynesia. It's really impossible to translate. In Arabic we say *baraka*, the blessing or magic aura that surrounds an object that makes it more than itself. That's *mana*. Kings have *mana*, certain individuals have *mana*, sacred objects have *mana*, anything which is sacrificed has *mana*. These are the temple souvenirs.

Very quickly they invent the double-sided coin which is fascinating, because money faces both ways. It faces into the material world and into the imaginary world, the world of pure image. How do we know that? I'm not saying anything very esoteric here. The coin can have more or less value than the metal which is in it. That's what makes it a coin, money in the modern sense of the word. The value is floating free from the actual cost of the metal. It doesn't have to be metal; they could have used wood or clay. In fact, in ancient Mesopotamia, they did use clay. Money has a prehistory. It doesn't spring out of nothing in the 7th century BC. First there's commodity money, where a cow is worth ten bushels of wheat which is worth a shekel of silver which is worth etc. Commodity money was used in the early 1700s, when there was not enough coin coming over from England and they had to have an economy in Virginia. What did they use? Tobacco was money in America. There's a great story from colonial Canada where the only thing they had was playing cards. For some reason the French government had sent a whole shipload of playing cards to Canada. They didn't have any money so they used the playing cards as money. Anything that is believed to be money is money. Money can be anything you want.

It just happens that precious metals have a very interesting magical symbolism, which I explained to you. Incidentally, the ratio between silver and gold has nothing to do with their rarity in the world. Gold is more valuable than silver because the sun is more important than the moon. Gold doesn't tarnish and the sun doesn't diminish. Silver does tarnish and the moon is diminished. That's why gold is more valuable than silver. And the ratio for centuries has hovered around fourteen to one, which in fact is the solar-lunar ratio. If you know these things, maybe you can play the stock market with some success. I myself am completely penniless; I've never made a cent from all this knowledge but I'm passing it on to you. I expect if it works for you that you'll be grateful and remember me.

Money faces both ways. It's very logical for it to acquire two faces. On one face you now have the ruler and the symbol of his rule on the other. It didn't take a long time to work out that neat flip-the-coin. Coins were probably used in divination for this very reason which is why we still flip coins to make a decision. That's why we use coins when we're throwing the *I Ching* in the simple method. The Chinese invented paper money. They tried it out in the 9th century and it was such a total disaster they stopped. They didn't quite understand how to make it work then and they went back to a metallic standard. Paper money didn't reappear again until very recently, 16th century maybe. Hard to say. It's hard to tell the difference between a letter of credit and a bill. Letters of credit are often discounted and passed around as currency. That goes back to ancient Mesopotamian times.

If you read works on Sumerian economics, you'll find them fascinating. Long before the 7th century BC, there are references to lending and interest. Even though the temples were trying to control the economy, there were already money lenders. There are references in these early texts somewhere to a bazaar of money lenders as early as the second millennium BC.

With commodity currency, you can almost do everything that money does. The one step, the brilliant step, that Croesus took was to put the image onto the commodity currency. Taking the precious metal which was used in exchange and making that into means for symbolic exchange. Now, because this token comes from the temple with a superabundance of *mana*, of magical power, over and above its metallic value, the coin can now circulate at a value different than that commodity value. In this way, capitalism can take off.

Before there was usury, now there is capitalism. Usury is lending at interest; we know this already began in the Neolithic. The first hierarchicalization of society is based on interest, probably. Maybe, tribute in the sense that I hit you over the head and take your money and say this is tribute. Oh, thank you for paying your taxes. That's how the state arises. Then it gets sophisticated later on, and it's all done with mumbo-jumbo with taxes and money. Pretty soon you don't really have to have taxes, because debt is built into the money.

Money is not wealth. This is tender for debt. This is not wealth. Wealth is something you can eat or build your house with. Wealth is something real. This is not wealth. This is debt. Your pocket is full of your debt. You are in debt to the extent that you have money in your pocket because you're going to spend it to pay your debts. It's future debt already; it's not wealth. It's only wealth for that small percentage of people who make money, who create something out of nothing like Paracelsus' German king or rather the bank he set up with the monopoly. Money itself is expropriation of surplus labor. I don't know if Marx would agree with me there. I had a real problem understanding that part of *Das Kapital*. I got bogged down there. I'm not sure whether Marx said this or not but it seems clear to me that historically money is nothing but the absence of wealth. If wealth weren't absent, there wouldn't be money. You only have money because you don't have the thing that makes you wealthy. Money is the absence of wealth, not the presence of wealth, except for those who are coining the money. They do it by fiat (we even have in economics the expression "fiat currency"). God said, *"Fiat lux,* let there be light." The king said, *"Fiat pecunia,* let there be money." By the way, numismatics comes from the word *numina, numen,* meaning a deity. It's related to the English word numinous.

What makes money numismatic is its numen, its aura, its mana. Money is mana. It's nothing else. Almost as soon as coins appear, coins begin to be degraded. Put a little bronze in there; nobody will notice. Pretty soon the coin is not worth its weight in gold, because the gold has been debased. The currency inflates. It apparently changes in value. You need more money to pay your debts now. A very clever arrangement. It's not the price of something that changes. Money is what changes. Pull the wool over your own eyes, as the Church of the Subgenius says. We're all agreeing to a consensual hallucination. The only consensual hallucination. None of the other ones work. Money accomplished what God could never do. God was supposed to be all powerful and yet purely spiritual, but only ended up being purely spiritual. Money, however, is purely spiritual and is all powerful. What is God? God is money, money is God. Money is our God. These are the thoughts which began to flow through my mind as I applied the flashlight of the hieroglyphs to the idea of money.

There's a lot to be said about this. We could analyze the early Greek coins which got to be exceedingly beautiful—just as gorgeous as the painted vases in many ways. There's an encyclopedia of religious and royal symbolism and magic on these coins. Each one we could analyze for its own message. The basic message is always the same. The very first coins didn't have words, but even before the double-sided coin appeared, they were putting words under the image. This is very interesting because the 7th century BC is also the period when the Greeks developed the alphabet, when they inherited the clumsy pictographic writing from the Phoenicians, who had gotten it from the Mesopotamians, and by adding vowels had turned it into the modern alphabet. Our alphabet is basically the Greek alphabet, which is basically the Phoenician alphabet, which is picture writing from ancient Mesopotamia and Egypt. If you look at it, you'll still see it's full of pictures. The "A" is actually the bull's horns turned upside down. The bull, the sacrificial bull. The "P" is actually a picture of a foot turned upside down. In Indo-European languages, the word for foot always begins with a "f" or "p." It's either *pedes* or foot or some such sound. With the Greeks it began with a "P." That's a picture of a foot. Our alphabet is not abstract at all; it's very rooted in imagery.

It wasn't really an alphabet until the Greeks got hold of it. They did that by adding vowels. What are vowels? Vowels are actually sounds. Consonants are only ways of stopping sounds. In Mesopotamian writing and in Arabic to this day, if you don't put the little dots and dashes over the words, all you're getting is the consonants, the stopping of the sounds. This is why it's actually impossible to pronounce ancient Sumerian, for example. There are many ways people have guessed, pretty good ways to pronounce ancient Egyptian or Sumerian. But we don't know for sure really how they were pronounced. We can only base it on later linguistic developments. We read backwards. All you have is the consonants. There is no sound there.

Sound enters only with the Greeks. They invent the alphabet where each word is not to be confused with any other word. In Semitic forms of writing, because all you have is consonants, you can read those letters in different ways. In Greek writing there is no ambiguity. Writing loses its ambiguity, its fuzzy edges, its nonexistent outlines. Each word acquires a sharp, crisp outline, because it has both sound and the stoppage of sound within it. This gives rise to pre-Socratic philosophy. The first so-called scientific way of viewing the universe would have been impossible without this alphabetic tool, this new way of thinking, this new paradigm.

Each word is also like each coin. We even use the word *coinage* when we come up with a new word. We coin a word. A word is a coin and a coin is a word. It's a discrete unit of value that cannot be confused with any other discrete unit of value. Alphabetical literacy and money in the true modern sense of the word emerged from the same complex of thought which also includes lyric poetry, the modern drama, pre-Socratic philosophy, and therefore Socratic and Platonic philosophy, Aristotle. All arises from this one brilliant insight of King Croesus, let's say, or whoever. There is a legendary Greek figure who supposedly invented the alphabet but I can't remember his name. He might have been a real person. Croesus was a real person and he really did invent coins. There really was a real set of clever little temple scribes who invented writing in 3100 BC in Sumer. We don't know their names. It would be interesting to have a few portraits of these people and meditate on how they could be so damn smart.

Each coin is a Hermetic emblem. When you get to paper money, you can really spread out and see a whole text, a whole book, in images and writing. The image, we know from Bruno, is what causes the invisible chain of desire. The word is what defines that desire for us. Otherwise, we might not be able to focus in with just an image. Benjamin and Brecht talked about this. They said that the photograph itself is just a whorehouse without walls. But a photograph with writing underneath it is a dialectical operation, because you're actually defining the image for the observer. You have strong dialectics at work when you combine image and word.

That's what money is par excellence. As I said, the combination of image and word appears almost immediately on the coins. From then on there's no such thing as a coin without words. There are coins without images. The Islamic world makes them, beautiful coins with nothing but writing on them. But the writing itself becomes imagistic there. The beautiful calligraphy. The grace and exquisiteness in which the king's name is written is itself a kind of image.

We are the real money mongers par excellence, we citizens of a globe where money really comes into its own; and for us, money is always an image, a hieroglyphic image, a Hermetic image. In fact, sometimes, it's

Hermes. Hermes makes his appearance on coins right away obviously, because Hermes is the god of thieves and merchants. He's a very good god to preside over coins. He's the god of writing, the alphabet. He's the god of the hidden sciences, of secrets which are hidden. Money is in essence an outward form behind which there's a hidden something, a hidden imaginal image, the image of wealth. The image we can see on the early coins is the sheaf of wheat; the image of the cow or bull that was on a lot of Greek coins and also Persian coins; the image of the tripod. If you've ever read Homer carefully, you'll notice they're always trading these metallic tripods around, almost as if they're using them for money. Those tripods appear on coins as well right away. There's a whole universe of discourse and imagery waiting to appear on coins, lurking in the wings, waiting for their chance on stage. One by one they come out and do their turn.

The study of numismatics, numens, allows us to trace a psychological portrait of money. We can do what Gaston Bachelard did for fire or for the house. We could do for money what he did in *The Psychoanalysis of Fire*. We could psychoanalyze money by studying these emblems. We're only ever going to come up with the same old story. There's not going to be any surprises here, really. The basic thing that is going on is a trick, a coin trick. Now you see it, now you don't. The original coin trick is the coin. What you don't see is the trick by which you've been tricked into thinking that this coin is wealth instead of the absence of wealth. That's the original coin trick.

In other words, applying the Hermetic critique just to coins as images allows us to come up with a whole economic theory that stands alongside of, for example, the Marxist or anarchist analysis of money. Different kinds of analyses could help each other, throw light on each other. We could get a synergistic thing going on here, put a whole lot of stuff together and stir it up like broken eggs and see if a chicken comes out. This is not so much a psychological analysis but a magical analysis.

This is action at a distance again. Money works over a distance. It's easy to send over distances. We know that now because we've invented electronic banking. Now we don't even need paper money anymore. Money itself will become the image of money. It will be nothing but image. Now the image will absent itself from money. This is why I'm not sure if it's going to work incidentally. I don't advise you to invest in any electronic currency schemes yet. I'm not sure if it's going to work, because money is what people believe money is. So far I see no evidence of widespread desire to believe in the disembodiment of money, money as a disembodied image. An image with no image. We're still very attached to images, to emblems, even though they're such ancient, dusty, meaningless things. Somehow or another we can't seem to do without them. And advertising again would be a prime example there. Imagine if advertising decided to make itself entirely electronic. What would that mean exactly? I suppose you could have an implant in the back of your head and it would just beam desire for commodities directly to the skull. By the way, if it could be accomplished, it would be right here in Boulder, world center of the chip implant industry. I'm not sure if you should invest in that either, unless you want to be a complete immoralist.

Maybe money has reached its final form or maybe there will be a later development which will be called electronic currency. Debit cards. They're not called credit cards. You don't have any credit. All you've got is debt, so it makes perfect sense for you to have a debit card.

Then the question arises: So what? What does this mean? Who cares? Why should I care? Is there anything I can do about this? I don't really know what's to be done. If I knew, I'd do it. Then I would be fabulously wealthy, or I would be able to start the revolution. As I say, I didn't get any clues or hints out of this on how to be wealthy. I don't know how to manipulate this imaginal system for myself. Like Kit Marlowe, I have as good a right to coin money as the Queen of England, but I don't have the power to. I can't orchestrate belief in my currency the way the United States government can orchestrate belief in its currency. I can't do that. That's out. That's called counterfeiting and that's how they got Kit. They got Kit Marlowe partially on counterfeiting charges. When you're counterfeiting, you're striking at the heart of the system. It's the ultimate crime. You can kill, you can rob, you can be a pirate, you can get away with lots of stuff. But counterfeiting is the sin against the holy spirit. It's a sin against money which is God, as I explained before.

I don't know what to do with this. I don't see how to overthrow money by simply understanding it and how it works. I'm not the first person to realize that money was a scam. Good heavens. It was probably known as soon as King Croesus did it. I'm sure some witty fellow or woman in Lydia probably made some jokes about King Croesus and the bullshit scam he was pulling on everybody. Knowledge of the mechanism has been there right from the start. Knowledge by itself apparently doesn't do anybody any good—except maybe George Soros, who claims to be a magician. He claims that there is an intuitive leap that he makes when he's got all the information about the world market. There's a moment, just a moment where his reason goes out the window and his intuition comes in and he makes a decision where to put himself vis à vis the gold market or southeast Asian currencies. He admits to the irrational element in the secret of how to become fabulously, obscenely wealthy.

Lokapala: Interview

JOANNE KYGER

Interviewed by Anne Waldman
January, 2000

ANNE WALDMAN: Since we have been staying and working together here in the Mexican city of Patzcuaro, a place you know, it would be interesting to ask about your recent book, *Patzcuaro* [Blue Millenium Press, 1999]. Were the pieces and poems in here extracted from or embellished upon an earlier journal? What was the time frame?

JOANNE KYGER: My first trip to Patzcuaro in 1986 with Donald Guravich was so pleasing we've returned many times since—this is our fifth visit. We stayed for three months during the winter of 1990-91. I wanted to feel what it was like to really live there, shop, cook, settle in. I always kept a journal but not a lot of "poems" arrived.

So on our visit to Patzcuaro from December 17, 1997, to January 26, 1998, I wanted to attempt to compose some words that were more "precise." I approached this formally at a certain time every day, and excerpted journal entries I had written over the past weeks—a collage portrait of events, including dreams that seemed prescient. I gave myself lots of space on the page using a 9" x 12" watercolor sketchbook. I did this periodically over our forty-day stay and the poems in the book resulted.

December is a time of celebration for the local Virgin of Health, de la Salud, who is much revered all over the state of Michoacán. This is followed by the celebration for the Virgin of Guadalupe, the Empress of Mexico. The outpouring of worship and petitioning given to these two deities moved me deeply. Worshippers cared in a deep and fundamental spiritual way, they *believed*.

So there were these currents of worship running along with the everyday necessities of buying and selling food, clothing, local handicrafts, all happening in the same location at the cathedral. And then there was me, the writer trying to connect, with daily living, the weather, dreams. Margaret Drabble popped up in a dream soon after I had arrived. I was unfamiliar with her work but read it after I returned to California. Humorous, wry, domestic, English. I took what dreams presented as information.

Then I found what sketchy historical pieces that were available of preconquest Patzcuaro and added those. The destruction of the culture and libraries during the conquest of Mexico leaves much of the history conjectural. But the Purepecha, the native speakers of the area have survived and live there today in villages around Lake Patzcuaro.

AW: Perhaps you could speak about your long relationship to Mexico—as a writer. What drew you here initially? What was the occasion?

JK: Over the past thirty years I have visited Mexico ten times. My first trip was to San Cristobal de las Casas in 1972 where I saw Mayan tribal living, Ladino culture and some of the many different geographies of which Mexico is comprised. On a subsequent trip to San Cristobal I wrote a series of poems called "News from Maya Land," published in *The Wonderful Focus Of You* [Z Press, 1980]. The ancestral spirits of the Mayan people have never left and one sees how lightly and with what a delicious scramble conquest Christianity lays over their religion.

Visiting the Yucatan Peninsula in 1985 I kept a journal which was published as a part of Charles Olson's Curriculum of the Soul Series, titled *Phenomenological* [The Institute of Further Studies, 1989]. This amazing country of pyramids and civilizations of antiquity showed me how little we of this hemisphere understood our own geographical history. Trips to Oaxaca revealed further monumental pyramids, ruins, and culture.

Before 1972 in order to understand where my "roots" were as an "American" human being I had thought "east" and "west." Living in Japan for four years, from 1960-64 with a six-month trip to India [*The Japan and India Journals,* North Atlantic Press, 2000] I got some sense of the religion and culture of the "east." Then realizing I needed to know my "old world" origins, my Atlantic crossing roots, I spent nine months visiting the cities and museums of Europe in 1966-67, ending with a year in New York City.

When I moved to Bolinas in 1969, a small town on the coast north of San Francisco, where I still live, I experienced the cultural emptiness of the place. The Coast Miwok were no longer inhabitants, as a result of the gold invasion of the last century, and had left no edifices. I realized that everything in the small cottage in which I lived, had been brought there from somewhere else. But where was *here?* I knew that at one time in California's early and short history it had been part of Mexico. I started to think "north" and "south," *this* hemisphere.

After that first trip to Mexico I understood how little "Americans" actually know about what lies south of the border, the United States of Mexico. How in terms of the history of indigenous tribal movement, there is no border. How a sense of who I am culturally, geographically, has to do with the heritage of this continent.

AW: You have strong political feelings concerning NAFTA, the tense situation in Chiapas, the fate of the indigenous people here in Michoacán. What is your current view of these endangered cultures?

JK: There is no denying there is striking poverty in Mexico and NAFTA seems to add to it. Simply put, NAFTA has had horrible consequences for a vast majority of Mexicans—the working poor, small farmers, etc. It is an organization that is the brainchild of the multinationals and corporate government under the guise of "free trade." What little was left of the positive results of the Mexican Revolution has been seriously undermined. Safety, environmental, and wage laws have been eroded. An easy example would be the exponential growth of maquiladoras along the Mexican border, and the subsequent rise in pollution and union-busting that accompanied that growth. Farther south, in poor states like Oaxaca and Chiapas, it is the dumping of cheap corn on the market by U.S. agricultural business that is one of the biggest threats. The small farmer simply cannot compete with a product that results from mega use of pesticides, herbicides, and chemical fertilizers, that is highly mechanized and grown on huge tracts of land. Corn, for tortillas, is a major staple in the Mexican diet. Corn and coffee-growing are one of the main triggers for the Zapatista uprising in Chiapas. That and the opening up of Ejido or communal land to privatization. First NAFTA pushes farmers into a position where they cannot compete, then it gives them the opportunity to sell out when they are desperate. Ejido land was common land owned by indigenous villages and tribes which could not be sold, was handed down through generations. Now big business, big landowners are buying up these small farms and the small farmer is where he was before the revolution—working for the wealthy. About ten percent of the population of Mexico owns over forty-one percent of the wealth. The army in Chiapas seems to support that wealthy but powerful minority. Unions are basically wiped out when large companies impose their wage scale. And it is the indigenous people, the humans on the lowest scale of the economy who continually suffer.

Today in downtown Patzcuaro we passed a group of farmers who had closed the Banco Serfin on the main plaza with a sign draped across it saying in effect that the farmers of Patzcuaro should be helped, but the bankers are only interested in helping themselves. The small farmers of Michoacan are losing their land in much the same way the small farms of the U.S. lost theirs to "big business" and the banks.

Along the same lines, "globalization" is a real threat to the support of "endangered cultures" as it means competitive prices, which in turn means going to countries where goods can be produced at the lowest wages and natural resources harvested at the lowest prices. Which is what the bottom scale of Mexican wages are all about as an "emerging economy." The current President, Ernesto Zedillo, in the continuing political rhetoric of his party stresses the "right" of Mexico to develop a competitive global economy and lauds "the inhabitants of old Mayan towns working in the new garment factories established in the Yucatan; rural migrants from southern Mexico finding jobs in the gigantic maquiladora plants of Tijuana and Juarez." Etc. Yuck.

AW: How do you see the "economics" of poetry in the current Distraction Culture?

JK: When I was a young poet in the late fifties and studying informally with Jack Spicer and Robert Duncan and reading the Beat writers like Kerouac, Ginsberg, Snyder, Whalen, etc., I was aware that these writers and poets were outside the then-current university or academy scene. The "New American Poets" as Don Allen called the collection that introduced them to the public at large, were not beholden to the university for their living and were therefore able to write as they wished. They were part of a generation that made their livelihood by working often at "blue collar" jobs—merchant seaman, forestry service, post office, warehouses, etc. (Robert Duncan typed manuscripts.) This style of earning income allowed freedom from the establishment's "man in the gray flannel suit." One could save money and take time off to write, paint, and live a modest existence, but with the company of others in small groups and communities of like-minded people. I worked variously as a secretary in a bookstore and as a part-time office person.

Poets were always poor in income but hopefully great in spirit and were published by the small presses that came into being in order to print them.

I haven't seen that "outlaw" tradition in some time. More poets now seem to be published by university presses, speak at "conferences," earn attractive incomes, have "high" standards of living, seem rather bland and formulaic, get stuck in graduate programs writing about poets that were "rebels." There is nothing "wrong" with this, one needs to make a living, but it is often a dependent relationship. The whole approach to "right livelihood" is a constant consideration. Poets who actually make a decent livable income from just writing are probably nil these days, and fortunately there are some teaching jobs that are free from academic restraints. The whole occupation of poet, if it does exist as an identity in the current society, is one that has to do with a spiritual, cultural practice of words, and can't be "bought."

AW: I've noticed you always carry a small notebook noting the exact times and locations of particular incidents and events, great and small. You spoke of your journal practice in our "Luminous Details" workshop here. Could you reiterate some of that?

JK: I keep a small daily notebook for jotting down the endless "things to do" list. The day's date at the top of the page. This is the notebook that accompanies me wherever I go during the day. When traveling I find it especially useful to jot down any information, names, phrases, directions, thoughts that enter the mind. Otherwise they're gone, whether trivial or important. It solidifies all the ephemera of daily interaction, observations.

My larger spiral-bound notebook, when traveling especially, is my writing home. Where I check in, locate, take account. It's the interaction/ intersection of the physical hand, in time and in location and space. One locates oneself. And this act produces words which may or may not be "luminous" but are "there" in black on a white space. And it's an absolutely free space. Writing about past time, and present time, but always writing *in* time, now time. I always begin with the date and the time. This is a record of entering into history, and however one writes, one *is,* writing one's history. One day happens after another.

One needn't write much. Three or five lines a day can tell a lot. The famous journals of pioneer women crossing the west by wagon train marked by progress of miles, hunting for food, sickness, burial, birth give a spare and eloquent history. No worry about literary style.

And it's that nonjudgmental condition of writing that is so appealing. You are writing for yourself, and if *you* can't read your own writing back, it's time to find out what or how you want to write things. "Confessional" writing can be a very unburdening act, and is useful for clarifying confusing emotional situations. But if that is *all* you write down, it can become repetitious and tiresome.

Usually the more specific and detailed the writing is, the more grounded it feels later on, when memory has faded. Memory of the immediate present lasts only a few days before the selection process sets in, so get it while it's hot.

Try and be specifically responsive to your environment. Ask questions. Give the dignity of names to the generic plant, tree, bird, animal, etc. It takes the blur out. Find the nuances in your emotions so it's not love, hate, like, dislike, etc. Try writing in the third person to give some distance and space to a crowded "I."

Journal writing is often quick and notational, often like poetry. Gertrude Stein says, "A diary should be instantly like recording a telegram. A diary should simple be."

So it's your book and it's not plugged in to anything but you, and it's *portable.*

Lecture

AMIRI BARAKA
July 7, 2000

★   ★   ★

AMIRI BARAKA: A socio-aesthetic, a geo-socio-aesthetic portrait of the world would be the top of the world which is a frown and the bottom of the world which is a smile. So that when you see for instance, the masks of theater, you're hip to those right? The theater. One of them is smiling, and one of them is frowning. You have actually, a geo-social aesthetic. Why do I say that because . . . for instance, I went to college. Most of you all went to college and you know in college they taught us that the highest form of art was what? What did they tell you the highest form of art was?

AUDIENCE MEMBER: Tragicomedy.

AB: Tragedy, tragedy. If you went to comedy you were in Africa, no, no, no, no. They said the highest form of art is tragedy. Meaning what? Aeschylus, Sophocles, you know the dude that, you know, killed his father. You know, slept with his momma. Put out his own eyes. And searched the world for mediocrity. You know that dude. It's the first crazy Eddie, Eddie-puss. And what does Oedipus mean? Oedipus means—come on Greek scholars, I know if you haven't had any Greek scholarship you haven't been to school! What does Oedipus mean?

AUDIENCE: Lame foot.

AB: Lame, right. Club foot. Which is what? Even today in urban America. People we call what? Lames. See? "Ya lame motherfucker." Now are we talking about Oedipus? When we say that, when we say lame mother-fucker, are we talking about language, we talking about imagery, we talking about history? Now, for instance, when the Afro-Americans or "Urban People," because as quiet as it's kept, in the opinion of Jesse Helms and the rest of the people who want to make the world safe for nobody, the world is *mixed*. Unalterably, inevitably mixed. I mean if the Africans were the first persons here, if you don't have some African trace in you, you must be from beyond—what is that?—the Van Allen Belt. In which case we would have to bring you in and spray you for some kind of weird disease which we don't know nothing about. But the point is this, that language which began with one base, wherever that was, and spread wherever the conditions had changed, is the oldest record of human life.

For instance, these things were once what? Paws, right. They were all shaped the same way. And everybody, everybody read the same information down there on the ground, there wasn't much to see on the ground. Then the monkey, the ape who had to leap off the ground and therefore break his thumb, break his hand. Toop. Pop. Turn it this way, "opposing thumb," so therefore I can pick up a stick and beat you to death. Or, like they say, the tool-making instrument.

At the same time if you read Engels. Is anybody here not addicted to imperialism that would read Engels? If you read Engels. Solid. And he talks about the development of the hand as a form of labor, you know the development of society as a form of labor and that labor, this hand is created by labor.

Why? We keep jumping up, we keep jumping up, you can't jump up with a paw. Well you keep jumping up, you keep jumping up, you go B-whap! The woman did it actually. The woman said, "Why are you down here on the ground with these big teeth animals? Why don't you get up off the ground? Get your lazy ass up off the ground. Get up!"

And so, you know, belatedly, we stood up and said, "Uh-huh, I can't get that . . . my paw won't get it." Engels talks about the development of the *vowels* at the same time that the fingers develop. The development of A, E, I, O, U—the vowels. At the same time that the five, that's the trace to the pentatonic scale, we're talking about music, talking about language, talking about a lot of things, talking about anthropology. So that at the same time it becomes possible for you then to, not be cheetah, to pick it up. With that kind of articulation, it becomes possible for you also to say "A, E, I, O, U"—that is the beginning of language.

What does it mean? It means a lot of things. If you read Paul Robeson. Does anybody know Paul Robeson's work? I don't mean as a singer. His work on aesthetics. He's a great singer, a great artist, but he was also an *aesthetic theorist*. His work on backgrounds of Afro-American music—very interesting, very important. You can see that in his *Selected Works*. He talks about first the pentatonic scale, which is the blues, the *black notes*. That's why the blues singers could play and sing that easy because there were the black notes. They could hear they were their notes, right? . . . This is my notes, they're black.

Well then it turns out that the piano was not *segregated* until the 15th century—ah ha, now we getting to that. That before that there is a transition instrument called what, lovers of Mozart? A harpsichord. Solid! And those levers on the harpsichord are to do what? To transition the old pentatonic scale into a modern, that is capitalist emergent diatonic scale, that is the "tempered scale."

I know some of you look like this is over your head. Hey, what can I do? So you understand what I'm saying now, this is interesting, and this I thought was pretty, they got a picture (Sistine Chapel Rock and Roll) of my man there, actually . . . my woman, I guess her hand is pointing down there for the man, "Get up off the ground, dude." She got one hand up there, women they get that one hand up and they say, "Why don't you get your ass off the ground and get your paw up on this . . . limb." That's what she's talking about.

But what Robeson said is that you can trace the development of the pentatonic, whether you're listening to the Volga Boatmen in Russia, in the Ukraine, or whether you're listening to "Deep River," in the South. You understand, [mouths out "Deep River" tune], that's essentially the same scale, the same chords. Now Robeson goes through the whole musical technical thing.

The Bösendorfer is a huge piano, but what distinguishes it is that it has black notes down in the bottom too. And of course the sharps and the flats, we figure we have to do, two jobs, you know . . . you got to be sharp and you got to be flat. But the Bösendorfer has the black keys on the bottom and has the sharps and flats—to suggest what? To suggest the motion of the piano itself, so that when, for instance, Europe became sure enough of itself, via emerging capitalism, etcetera, then the harpsichord is left in the background, except for the purists, and you begin to get a segregated instrument, which is clearly much like modern-day imperialism.

What does that all have to do with what I'm talking about? Well a lot actually. We talk about *griot,* you know, "six o'clock, six o'clock all is well." Griot, the town crier. Well *djali* had a different function. D - J - A - L - I. Djali, djali. Djali was literally to make you jolly. We get the term glee, glee man, glee club. When Louis Armstrong, for instance, used to sing, "Just because my hair is curly / Just because my teeth are pearly / Just because I wear a smile on my face all the time / that's why they call me shine." We're talking about history that is not understood by those which it has shaped. Do you understand what I'm saying? That we're walking around full of "you square motherfuckers." Why do we say that? Square. Well the Egyptians said square was what? The angle of failure. The pyramid was the angle of success. Who knows that on the street yet walks around saying "you're a square lame-ass motherfucker." I mean, we don't know that. But the anthropological, the whole historical, the whole history and language itself is with us all the time.

We talk about the griot verses. What is djali's function? How do you think the griot was supposed to function? "Griot" is a word that comes into use through colonialism. How does this work? If you go to Senegal, Mali, any of those places, which are great places to go to. My second son Ras and I went there to visit the old slave castles, that's a hell of an experience. It's like the Jews when they go back to those concentration camps. It's something that just breaks you down. You're just sitting there without saying anything weeping. I think I confounded them a little bit, I wrote my name inside an old castle, so they said, "Oh you mean there was a Baraka in here many years ago."

But when you go to the French possessions nobody's there outside the cities. You travel for miles and there's nobody there, there's nobody in rural Senegal. You drive for miles, there's nobody there. You see the Baobab trees, empty villages. Where are the people? Right here in Denver. They're in Los Angeles. They're in Oakland.

But the strength of that French/African connection meant that the words coming out of Africa, like Djali, would become Creole. But what is the job of the Djali, then? Somebody told me. Storyteller. Ok. Storyteller makes it abstract a little bit. Historian, storyteller, poet, musician. Historian. Storyteller. Because if it's not a story, that is, if it hasn't stored something. That's what a story is. A story's what? A story is a storage place. You store stuff in there. Right? Then if it's not really interesting, it's "historian." Charlie Olson was the person that introduced that to some of us.

So what the Djali is supposed to do is go into each place and tell the history of the joint. Djali comes the first thing they do is say, "Well you know the world began this way and then this happened and then this happened, you know, we used to be this, this, blah blah blah blah," . . . to get to the point and "now this is the case."

Also, when Djali gets down you call that what? Jelly-ya. D-J-E-L-I-Y-A. What is that? Why is that significant? Well what do we say? Billy Eckstine's most famous hit was what? "Jelly, Jelly, Jelly"—that's right. What was the great pianist's name from New Orleans? Jelly Roll Morton. We always hook up Jelly with, of course, sex. Why? Well, you'll have to reason that out, yourself. But Jelly must be jelly because jam don't sound like that, don't shake like that actually.

"Jam," actually, is another word, we could go on with this association thing. Jam comes from Jamaa, Jamaa, Jamaa—which means *family*. The whole Jamaa, which ultimately means a *cooperative*. But the point is, it must be jelly because jam don't shake like that. So when he says, "Jelly, jelly, jelly drove my old man crazy." Right. "Made my momma wild." I guess, he was one of those entrepreneurs—of the social life. But the point of this is that the Djali's job was to light up the mind, to make the mind shine, to make the mind smile, to make the mind laugh, to make the mind laugh with what? Understanding. Recognition. *To understand history as a revelationary story.* So that the poet, or at least the poet, per, my own self, like I say, DOC-I-MEANT. Doesn't talk about what you might'a meant, doesn't talk about what I might've meant, which is why I say doc-I-meant. So the poet that I meant, that is Djali, has the first function to light up peoples' minds, to make them understand the world.

Why music? Because it is an expression of the word itself. When, for instance, the Greeks and Romans always used to say the Ethiopians, Africans smile too much, which is a hell of a put-down, I guess because you down there with the sun and everything picking stuff off the trees and whatnot. Which has a down side to it, I mean these other people who risk their life from the snow, who tend to be a little stricter and harder with this. You know what I mean? There's an upside and a downside. There's an upside to the frown and there's a downside to the smile. You understand, together it's infinity, right? That's what it is. You keep doing that, you just keep going on, it's infinite—infinity. What we're trying to do is, as human beings, hopefully, is somehow make a circle rather than that which is always fluctuating. You understand, because it's bound to have a dialectic to it. If there's an up there's a down, if there's a slow there's a fast, if there's a hot there's a cold. You understand what I'm saying? So where there were once the masters of the universe, so-called—"Egypt, the light of the world," the people called themselves, who now must push bags for fat aging business men. So there's an upside and a downside to everything.

The task of humans—and I don't know that the Earth is ready for them yet, we're struggling to make the Earth habitable for human beings. You understand that, can you understand that? Because anybody who thinks that only a few people have the right to live, something to eat, you know, so forth. When this world is full of infinitely more than you could ever use or even conceive of what exists. So anybody who thinks that we've got to have this. It's mad in the first place.

But why music? Well, music is the motion of rising and changing, as thought given form, feeling as an object, delivering reflection of material life, the thoughts I see, I hear, what we call sonoideographs, graphs, grams, sounds, sign, so forth, drama itself.

Now, in terms of word music, the African, when we arrived here, and now Afro-American, Black-American. People who think Africans remain Africans in the United States are unrealistic. You know, Duke Ellington, Thelonious Monk—those are Western musicians. You know, when I taught at Yale with a guy named Bill Ferris who's now the head of the NEH, we taught a team-taught course. And he showed this film, which is an incredible film, a drummer named Tony Williams, who used to play with Miles Davis, they took him to Africa to the shore. He comes to the shore of Africa and sets up his drum set and goes "boom-boom, etc; pow-pow, etc," so a minute later they hear from across the, you know, [sounds of pounding, imitating drum beats], and the people are saying, "We heard you but we don't understand what you're saying." And not only they say they heard you, they say we heard you, *plural*. Why plural? Because we play an industrial instrument. Not African hand drums. It's got levers, and a little motor there, they thought it was ten, fifteen people. When it was actually Tony Williams, you know, young Max Roach. And they thought it was a whole battalion of people. Why? Because that's an industrial, a Western instrument created by who? The one-man bands after the Civil War. The guys who used to stand out there, they didn't want to go do the work, the cotton whatnot, so they put everything, harmonicas, drums, everything, banjos, and they were playing [drum beat/music sounds], that's where that comes from, that is: to play it all.

Now, the point is, the African (and this has not got to do with just the African qua-Nationality) culture now is imbedded in the United States—if you don't think American culture is African, European, and Native, you don't know what you're talking about. Standard English? Hey Americans never spoke English. Or about U-bonics, Ebonics, all of those are off-the-wall. The language is created by people together.

You cannot be on the East Coast, or let's say you cannot be on the West Coast and not speak Spanish, you know that. You start talking about I want to go where—where you want to go, Los Angeles? What are you going to say? You want to go to San Diego, what you going to call it? You can't be in the Midwest unless you speak Native American. You can't be in the South unless you speak Bantu. There are more Bantu names, African names in South Carolina, which is why they're trying to keep the Confederate flag up. Because they figure all those Bantu names are going to rise above the ground. And get them. But you cannot speak an American sentence without going from Europe to Native America to Africa and Afro-America, you can't do that. Because we're one people, even though the social-political-economic oppression keeps us separated and sometimes hateful and not understanding of each other. But still we're one people—wild, wild thing—who have the history to kill each other off. To kill each other off or to learn to be human beings, now that's the way that is. Somebody told me that a long, long, long time ago and I said, "Pshaw, nonsense, fiddlesticks." I didn't understand that then.

So, the question of this word music. We want to use the words and the music to extend the words and to extend the music. Music is a strictly abstract function. But, music as an actual form of telling. For instance, the thing about slavery that was critical was at the point where the ability was lost to say [banging is heard, like on drums] "Meet me tomorrow at seven o'clock, bring your largest knife and do not be late." At that point, where that is stopped, that is when the slave owners "take the drums away." (Why do you take the drums away? Because you don't like percussion in your symphony orchestras? Why isn't there percussion in Europe? Well, we have to ask, why is the piano segregated? The question of history and art, that's the same thing. What happens in social history happens in aesthetic history, i.e. in the arts.)

So, if Crouch says, "Look boss, if you take that piece of wood away from them slaves there, you see that wood they keep beating on, if you take that piece of wood, all that, all that bullshit about them rising up in the middle of the night, that would be over with."

"Pshaw, fiddlesticks, certainly that can't be true? How can that piece of wood be related to slave uprisings?"

"Watch them and for three more pork chops I will tell you."

Sure enough, that night, there he goes again, [banging is heard, like drumming]. He hears it and says, "Uh-huh—there is some kind of relationship. What is it? They're speaking to each other, boss."

"You mean it's code?"

"No it's not a code, it's language."

"How can there be language? They're just beating on the drum."

Because it's a tonal language and they're using the drum under their arm. What do you call that? The Dun-Dun, d-u-n, d-u-n, Dun-Dun or "talking drum." You know the drum shaped like the hourglass with the strings around it, with the cords around it, you hold it under your arm like that so that you can make it function like a stringed instrument. Tight, high. Loose, low. [Baraka makes sounds like the instrument with his mouth.] It's a tonal language, they're actually *speaking*. So the question is, why is that so important? Because, actually, as great a drummer as the greatest drummers now are playing a form of *abstract expressionism*. Old folks say, "We hear you, but we no longer understand what you're talking about and neither do you." You understand the emotion which drives you and makes you do certain things, but to actually be able to say, "Meet me tomorrow." You see, and then in periods of backwardness, such as the one we're in today, notice for instance how the music has changed in a decade . . . in terms of words, in the revolutionary sixties, *crystal clear*. Listen to Stevie Wonder, you hear everything, everything he says. Marvin Gaye, very clear. But then commercial rap, I defy you to understand most of that, I mean just right off the thing [makes music melodies with his mouth].

Take reggae, remember nobody is clearer than Bob Marley. "Redemption songs, help me sing these redemption songs," very clear. Tell me what they're singing now? [Makes melodies with his mouth.] Why is that? Why is that? Because it is the society itself that no longer wants that clarity, you see. When rap began, now they call it hip-hop, but when rap and I say rap because rap relates to what, rap [bangs on something to make drum sounds], that's what they used to do on a *log*, that's what the sailors did, you remember, they kept the *log*. What did the log do? A tale, what happened, that's the same thing [bangs something to make drum sound/rap sound]. So the question of language as a means of communication, as a history, and as poetry is very, very important.

Panel: Politics of Identity

CHAIRED BY COLE SWENSEN

Panelists: Robin Blaser, Samuel R. Delany,
Michael du Plessis, Akilah Oliver, Eileen Myles,
kari edwards, and Roberto Tejada

June 25, 2001

COLE SWENSEN: We're here today, this week, this month, for political reasons. Not to talk about politics but to enact it. As we all know, to write is a political act, and to write in ways that operate upon, that alter, that enlarge language is perhaps the most important political gesture anyone can make. And it's one that today's panelists are both uncommonly qualified to make and are uncommonly gifted at making.

Language in this country is under attack, the insidious and paralyzing attack of homogeneity. When we consider the language that we experience each day and then consider how much of that language is literally mediated—by radio, newspaper, film, magazine, cliche, etc.— and then reflect that American media is owned by an incredibly small and ever-shrinking number of people, we realize we have reason to be alarmed.

To dedicate yourself to a labor in language is to combat this. It's to focus your life on the precise point at which perception turns to thought. Which is also the site of a principal and constant life choice—to affirm existing modes of expression, to strengthen and solidify them, or to open them out, taking on all the risks that go along with that.

The panelists speaking today have all chosen unequivocally to open out language, which often also means risking their individual circumstances. Theirs are not vague gestures toward the notion of expanded social possibility, but are specific and concrete contributions to a more articulate and articulated world. In making these, they form an active stand against the paralysis of thought encouraged by homogeneous language. For homogeneous is a misleading term—it in fact signals a language structured along a hierarchical model whose controlling base is like a seductive English garden path, always just slipping out of sight—an abstract concept with curious practical echoes.

We get a perfect example of it in a phone tree. Just think of the last time you tried to phone a bank, a library, a government office, a hospital, etc. and tried to ask a question that wasn't on the multiple-choice menu. That recording is your voice being taken and molded into a limited series of multiple expressions. These writers refuse that arboreal model.

Instead, to borrow a term from Gilles Deleuze, their work follows a rhizomatic model, in which constant proliferation insures a decentering that will never find equilibrium, that will never reach the paralysis of stability. Their work, with its myriad presentations of difference, its fractures and fissures, splinters into ever-smaller and more particular vectors that infiltrate mass media and mass language, that break it up like frost in the cracks of stone force that stone to open. It's a force as elemental, as natural, as patient, and as relentless as weather.

In this way, their varied works exemplify another Deleuzian concept, that of a minor literature, a literature that undermines the dominant by enacting a difference within it. "Conquer the major language in order to delineate in it as yet unknown minor languages"—this is literature that puts the major language to flight, that is the flight of language, for it is precisely the minorizing of our common language, our language made into a flying machine, that these writers perform.

The people here today represent the two most important assets this country has at the moment. One, an unprecedented variety of racial, religious, gender, linguistic, economic, ideological, and cultural input, and, two, the courage to refuse. To refuse to speak in and with a unified voice. For unification is another misleading term. It's a euphemism for conformity. We must resist that conformity even among ourselves. We must continue to differ, even to disagree. But a la George Lakoff we must change the metaphor presiding over disagreement, from one of conflict to one of expansion.

In view of the topic and spirit of today's panel, it seems more appropriate to let the participants identify themselves than to have me do so, and this way they can use their own terms, their own words, but I will give you their names. Robin Blaser, Sam Delany, Michael duPlessis, Akilah Oliver, Eileen Myles, kari edwards, and Roberto Tejada.

SAMUEL R. DELANY: A forebear who supports our being here is Paul Goodman. A meeting held a long time ago, put together by the Mattachine Society, had the distinction of being among the first times homosexual literature was publicly and sympathetically discussed. Held in 1952 or 1953, the meeting focused on the topic, "What is the greatest problem facing the homosexual novelist at this time?"

In 1952 they had a problem finding homosexual novelists who would indeed admit that they were gay. Sanford Friedman was one of the writers who agreed to appear. Another of the volunteers was Paul Goodman.

The meeting began, and the moderator posed the question, "What do you feel is the biggest problem facing the homosexual writer today?" He turned to Goodman. "Mr. Goodman, what do you have to say?"

Goodman answered, "I believe the biggest problem facing the homosexual novelist today is the hydrogen bomb."

Whenever we are asked a local question, we must never forget the larger questions and principles that surround our local concerns, without which those local questions don't make a lot of sense or are insolvable.

I want to mention two larger principles today, which I believe are terribly important for any real progress in discussions of such topics as we undertake here. First is a problematic that raised its head somewhere between the *Communist Manifesto* of 1848 and, after the 1848 revolution in France, the more focused analysis of the 1851's the *18th Brumaire of Louis Bonaparte,* after which time it becomes a regularly expressed bit of Marxist distress: "Why do the working classes, especially the poorest and most depressed groups among the working classes, always vote in the most politically conservative manner?"

The answer is one Marx never formulated. Yet it's so simple that we lose sight of it. If we are going to make any progress in racial or gay problems, we have to bear it in mind. The answer involves a principle any eighteen-year-old sweep-up boy or counter girl can formulate for him- or herself. "In a money economy, where my whole salary comes from X, it's lunatic for me to vote against X's best interests." It's that simple. As a principle this works to stabilize the society at a fairly conservative level, as it keeps the class war from ceasing to be just a Marxist metaphor and becoming an honest-to-goodness armed encounter.

It's the political reason why money economies are more stable social institutions than barter economies. As soon as monetary trajectories establish themselves within a society, and people's livelihoods depend on them, the general political task becomes their preservation well before it becomes their reformation.

Left or progressive, we must be aware that this principle is always operating.

A second principle it's good to be aware of has to do with the family. The idea of the family and what are called family values are a bulwark of conservatism, against which topics having to do with gay matters, or racial oppression, or sexism always find themselves at odds. Progress on any of these fronts is seen as something that will pollute the family.

The historical research of Philippe Ariés in the fifties, published in the sixties in books such as *Centuries of Childhood,* teaches us that the family is not a transcultural Arcadian unit that has existed for all time. Specifically it's a bourgeois institution first established in the upper tiers of society and that only then spreads down through the social fabric toward the lower classes.

In good economic times, it spreads toward the bottom through the process of people who have less, wanting to emulate people who are better off from them and have more. In bad economic times, it crumbles from the bottom up. The family is a site for the control and administration of food, money, shelter, reproduction, but it is only one of the sites where reproduction takes place, not the only site. Even Engels, in *The Holy Family*, loses himself in this notion of family-as-Arcadian-absolute, instead of an upper-class bourgeois model for controlling money, food, reproduction, and shelter.

Its fallout ideology—patriarchy—really is not the only way to live; nor is its assumed opposite, matriarchy.

Keeping both of these major facts, principles, models in mind can yield a variety of ways to make progress with more local problems that arise in dealing with matters of our own sexuality, of gender problems, or of racial and class conflicts. I throw these out as two large but important models to keep in mind as we go on through some of these things we will no doubt discuss here.

MICHAEL DU PLESSIS: I'm going to read a piece called "Wrong Body Politics."

In the wrong body, sex with the wrong body, wrong time, wrong place, trapped in the wrong body. Utopia: The right body in the right place at the right time. Utopia: No place. I identify as transgender and bisexual, which means the configurations of sex gender and sexuality, as it seems to make sense to most other people, have never made the same sense to me. Having said that, I should qualify identity immediately by saying that I don't believe in identity politics. I don't think that the politics based in identity can take one very much further than politically expedient forms of self-congratulation.

Gay lib in the 1970s offered the promise of alliances, with the antiwar movement in the U.S., with feminist and workers' struggles, with militant antiracist organizations, with worldwide battles against colonialism. Queerness in 2001 lures us, lulls us, with partnership benefits.

Back in 1991, we knew we were in trouble when the chant, "We're here, we're queer, we're fabulous, get used to it," was edited down to the more acceptably in-your-face, "We're here, we're queer, get used to it."

A friend calls me to say that yesterday's Gay Pride in Denver seemed like a two-hour Coors commercial—"We're here, we're beer, get sick of it." Identity politics and niche marketing cozy up to one another. Have you puked up your rainbow pride yet?

Having said that I'm skeptical of identity politics, I should qualify that immediately by saying that I also write in a way that is autobiographical, that comes from my wrong body, my wrong sex, and it does dream of utopia. Perhaps, contradiction is not the worst way to think about queerness and identity. Having said that my art dreams of utopia, I should qualify that by saying that I have very few illusions about the socially transformative power of cultural production.

Some of what I have to say may seem mean, but it's intended to be provocative. Growing up in South Africa, I learned that bombs do more to bring down oppressive regimes than many generations of well-intentioned artwork can, or so I learned growing up.

Nevertheless, I believe that art can and should achieve a transformation of the *everyday,* and that the *everyday* can and should transform art. I'm interested in the politics of "mundanity"—a poetics of banality. What cultural production does for queerness is insist on the rightness of our supposedly wrong transgender or transexual bodies of coexistences.

Art can claim our right to live in the world. But, more than affirm, art can criticize, can open up the internal dissidence, the crucial critical distance that queer once promised.

Several years ago, I dreamt that adding and including "transgender" "bisexual" to "gay and lesbian" would transform the latter. A decade ago, I thought that "queer" signaled a break with the way in which gay and lesbian identities were arranged at that time. Little did I realize that we would all be marching in the big gay pride parade.

Regardless of what we thought we named ourselves, we've all been lockstepped with rainbow consumerism, taking HIV cocktails that don't work, thinking of sex reassignment surgery as something on demand, something like cosmetic surgery, freely available to those with the money to pay. But then, what can we expect when even the right of self-naming has become a matter of picking a letter out of the alphabet soup of GLBTQ?

Identity politics. What can we expect when "diversity" as a word has become so calcified as to mean virtually its opposite? We must dream of utopia, but with our eyes open and clear. Thinking critically. Dreaming critically.

AKILAH OLIVER: I'm thinking about what both Sam and Michael just said. In many ways I think you both touched on, in terms of family and identity, how we construct community out of individual identities, and how that works in conjunction with economic and social structures. One determines the other to the degree there's insurgency which allows individuals to reshape society and institutions.

I'm into a utopian idealism ideal, that individuals can, by reshaping how we play with identity, bodies, language, and how that becomes historicized, reshape society, and structures. I've been thinking particularly about which gendered bodies historically and currently have invited a type of fear that seeks to destroy and mutilate those bodies, and why those bodies have become the multiple sites of a kind of a homophobic and racist fantasy that's enacted upon those bodies. I was thinking particularly about black male bodies during the historical period of probably the late 1800s till the early mid-forties of the U.S.

When you think about ritualized lynching acts, and black women were lynched as well, but when you think about lynching as ritual—and they were very ritualized, they weren't necessarily spontaneous or unplanned, but even when they were, there was a ritual to it, as in it was a community gathering—then we can begin to think about the role of ritual in the queering of the body and in the denial of the queered body. Lynching was a ritual that enforced certain codes and structures, and why was the black male body the primary site of attack, as opposed to other bodies that could have been on the margins that were a part of the suppressed class?

The implications seem to be that one part of the lynching ritual was to castrate the penis of black men. So clearly, this was the act of a gender attack, much in the way that gay and lesbian or trans-people are attacked today, because what their body signifies, what that site signifies.

So what was it about the black male body and particularly about the genital signifier of masculinity that had to be disrupted? What was the lesson for the witnesses who were there who were often communities of whiteness? What was the lesson for that community? We pretty much know what the lesson was for, or was supposed to be the applied lesson for the black community, that is fear, etc. But, what were the applied lessons for the white gaze? What did that create in the white gaze? What was it intended to create in the white gaze if we're looking at genitals as representations of masculinity or femininity? Which, of course, in the new queer age, we're not anymore, but if in fact the penis is a representation of masculinity, then the cutting off of the penis is obviously the act of emasculation of that image, of that body.

What I'm thinking about in terms of the Queer Movement, now, is how did that queer black masculinity, and what was the internalized reaction of black males in community structures to that queering of black masculinity?

I think when it's a choice, when queering of the body is a choice, and I'm using that term to mean anything from gender play to gender bending to any kind of surgery, reconstructive surgery, but when it is a choice, whatever that word *choice* means, then it is an act of subjectivity. When I as subject decide that my body is mine, then I can reconstruct it to fit whatever I need it to fit. But, when the choice is taken away, then the body is robbed of its subjectivity and acts of queering the body become historically problematic.

So clearly, the black man didn't say, "You know while you're lynching me, could you cut off my dick, while you're at it." So it clearly wasn't a choice in that way. So when the body is queered in that way, when what represents masculinity (since genitals are still so tied into identity, who we are, how we form notions of being a man or a woman) is still so biologically connected to our genitals, how did that play out in terms of expressions of black masculinity, in communities and individual bodies, in the mass imagination and the black imagination?

I'm asking that as a rhetorical question, as a question that I'd like for people to look for answers to when we have the dialogue part.

I often hear people saying, "Well, you know, because the black community is so homophobic," or, "You know, there's more homophobia in the black community." I never have any idea what they're talking about. As opposed to what, the Boulder community? Or rural Iowa community? I haven't the slightest idea. I know that *gayness,* as an act, is contextualized in different ways in all kinds of communities, and the black community is just one of those. I'm not saying that there is a direct correlation between penis castration lynchings and how black queered identities might be suppressed or expressed, but I do think there is something about the performative aspect of gender, the performance of lynchings, and contemporary expressions of black queer identities.

So, I think that one impact that this forced queering of the black male site in terms of how it has played out historically, has been in a kind of dual opposite of performing masculinity and queerness. One performance is a hyper-masculinity, that you might see in pop culture, in terms of rap stances, posturing, etc., that I find quite cute and sexy, and very gay actually, but that type of hyper-masculinity exploits white imagination as it relates to perceptions of the "big dick" or virility of the black male genital. The other thing, is a different contextualizing of homosexuality and homosexual bodies in the black community (and perhaps this is where the notion of black communities being more homophobic might enter), where queer identities are often very subsumed in historically strong black communal sites, like the church, and a kind of passing or not revealing occurs that is protective in its gesture. It's interesting that there is an often-heard rumor that you'll find many gay men and women in the choir in church, and that this has been a place of queer expression, within black cultural communities, which links us to the ideal of the spirit.

How does the spirit continue to express itself in bodies that are attacked, in bodies that are continually destroyed physically or spiritually, or attempted to be? I think it's ironic then, that, when we look at expressions of black masculinity and the queering of it, we have both the public, hyper-masculinized, in some cases—and then we have also this private, within spiritual communities, no matter how contested, how negotiated that relationship might be within those communities. Of course there is a broad range of gay, queer, and homosexual performative sites for black folks that is not limited to these two and that is obviously not only within the real or imaginary borders of blackness or black communities as well. But that we have these paradoxes between the public performative of black masculinity that by focusing on gender/genitals is a kind of queering of the body, and that we have the hidden queered identity within traditional black communal sacred sites reiterates that we don't have these neat little categories of identities or expressions of gender or masculinity or femininity. I do think that Westernized identity expressions are still so loaded that we are all still performing in dialogue with, in reaction to, colonialism and the concurrent acts of violence within that. History and how the body has been deformed, formed, reformed, or claimed does have something to do with performances of black queerness. History calls everything into question.

EILEEN MYLES: I'm totally glad that Akilah had the balls to talk about masculinity, I feel like that's what Chip was talking about in the Paul Goodman moment—in response to that whole dumb ploy of being asked, "Well what *do* homosexuals face today?" And you say the bomb. You say the fact that the presidency was stolen. You know? And to always kind of replace and disrupt the order. That's my sense of what it's like to be a female homosexual today, having this disruptive job—and my view of gender and genders, and all that is this. And we're in a weird place because of the fact that, yes kids in the Midwest still can't safely come out in junior high today, and things haven't changed that much outside of more urban liberal sophisticated places.

By and large, I think the real danger to any dissemination of new language and values and ways of thinking around gender are these kind of tolerance ghettos we live in that are giving us some toehold in the culture and then start producing these kinds of categories that we're all sort of obediently supposed to stay in.

I had a weird experience this year where I had a new book come out, and so back in October a friend of mine who writes for the *Times* and is gay says "I'll write a piece about you." So fabulous, you know?

So, he interviewed me. The book was coming out in November. He interviewed me in October, and then, luckily it was fun—because we were good-enough friends, so happily I could hound him once a month and say, "Is it coming out? Is it coming out?" and for him not to feel pushed.

He was, you know, "Eileen, it's coming, it's coming," and then a few months down the line, he told me this thing he was so embarrassed to tell me, but, but, it was so great to get the information which was that he thought the paper was waiting for gay pride weekend. And, the article wasn't about me being, you know, a dyke, the article was about my book and about this female writer, and that I had been around some and my entire career, and yet they did allow a few pearls of lesbianity in the article, and that was enough. I always think it's sort of like, just a few drops of lavender ink in the fish tank makes all the water go, you know, bad, and then we've just got to wait for the gay month. And it's like the new invisibility. It's sort of like a very rhetorical device—it's a corporate device, to take the safe place and, put it in an even safer place, so you vanish into the light, you know?

And I think there's an epidemic of that, at this point in time—like gay day, gay month, gay week, black month, black day. It suggests that we should all kind of run to our corners and sit there and eat our porridge and feel tolerated.

They are tolerance ghettos—that's what we get offered, and it seems to be the most insulting form of censorship—it's the infantilizing of power, and freedom, because the whole range of a phenomenon is important in transgressive ways of being, and you know, it's just a million illustrations of them, but it's interesting that a lot of them have to do with time.

Like there was a really infuriating article that came out, I guess a year ago, last spring in the *Times* magazine section, and there was an article by Andrew Sullivan, you know, the conservative, well-educated, Republican gay poster-boy. It's sort of like—when they need a queer, Andrew usually gets the job, because he's not going to upset the apple cart. You know? And so, he is taking testosterone and that's interesting. That's what this article was about. Though, really, to approach the issue of hormones, which are so important at this point in time for trannies, for women in menopause—hormones are really where it's at right now, and yet, the only interesting hormones for the *Times* is testosterone. I mean I think it's fine that a guy who is HIV positive gets this opportunity to write about the hormones *he's* using. I mean, of course, but the fact that that is all that is interesting, and so we will go and track Andrew's emotions and feelings—turns out he feels a little angry, you know. There was just something deeply indulgent about the article and maddening.

And the most maddening part was that, finally, Andrew announced that it was time for a new assessment of masculinity—after the Feminist Century. I was like—Wait a second! How could we have all missed the Feminist Century? How come I didn't know about this? Where was I? I don't think I know a single woman who was there. It's over now, though. Or, it's like your mother loved you. She *is* dead, but she loved you. Didn't you know that? Again, it was like an incredible hijacking of power. It wasn't Andrew giving us the 21st century, which might be nice, but the one that already passed—he was there, he knew.

Again and again it's this same kind of fraud, this kind of rhetorical fraud, that same kind of "How do you do?" "Good-bye!" You know? So, I think that's the problem. I think so. The face of gayness today, many people I know have a variety of ways of looking back on the closet fondly you know? Because there was a certain kind of coterie freedom, a certain kind of gay culture flourished freely without being marketed and cordoned off and ultimately ignored.

So, there was a big Gay Shame weekend this June in NY. A bunch of younger queers were doing it. People I know weren't exactly going but we were so happy it was happening, you know?

My own version was just a little realization that in my heyday of female camaraderie, like when I was younger, when I first came out, people would say, you know, if they liked me, if they thought I had some actual female value, they would say, "What a waste." You know? "She's a dyke, what a waste!" You know, I thought, how great at fifty-one . . . I am a truly wasted lesbian, I am entirely and truly wasted, you know, and I feel like it is what I want next to "lesbian" from now on—for that to be my moniker.

And, I'm all for falling apart, I just think that's the way I feel about it, there's more distribution possibilities in falling apart as *anything*, but certainly as a dyke today, you know? It's sort of like just let the holes be there, add some new things on. I think we see ourselves more in other people. I think there's more communal value in falling apart, and there are certainly for female homosexuals. There's always a right kind of woman to be. If it's a hip woman, it's a right kind of hip woman. And certainly lesbians are always looking over their shoulder—like who's doing it right?

Girlfriends are quick to slap each other down and say that's wrong . . . in the seventies there was a wrong kind of sex, in the eighties there were the wrong kind of clothes, and on and on, there were always a lot of opportunities to be the wrong lesbian, and you know, it made it less possible for women to exist as a group and support each other, because, the way it plays out in mainstream publishing, for example, is that there are a lot of lesbians in power in mainstream publishing, and they're not publishing dykes. They don't want to be associated with us. When I was looking for someone to publish my book, it was difficult because my work is so poor and complaining and whining and lower class. This was certainly not the lesbian you want to put up there and say . . . it couldn't be sold . . . The falling down, falling apart, adding on, is the way to go . . . You start to discover surprising lineages in who might make common cause with you and your mess, and I mean a wrecked ship falls apart and flies all over the place. Shipwrecks are distributed forever.

Finally, it hooks into one of my favorite people; I've been thinking about a visual artist Robert Smithson for a few years and he was around in the sixties and seventies, rumor has it, he was queer . . . but . . . his whole thing was taking art out of the galleries, or finding fragments in nature and bringing them in, taking from the fringe, and bringing the fringe, pieces of nature to the center and then bringing this center out. He called it "sites" and "non-sites." It was bringing a language function into visual art.

Smithson was very interested in this philosopher, Anton Ehrenreich. Smithson was really impressed because Ehrenreich talked about art and culture in terms of the sacred. He said that generally there was the buried god and the strewn god and that cultures could be divided into either of those two, and I think the buried god, maybe, means the hidden sacred and the hidden power, and the strewn god was about taking the pieces of god and dropping it everywhere.

I feel like there's so much more value for me in being a lesbian where lesbians are not. Allen [Ginsberg] was the master of it. If the great poet Allen Ginsberg came to Russia, he would announce suddenly that he was a queer. They'd be like trying to get him out fast.

I think, finally, this closure serves much more . . . I want to wrap it up in some final way . . . just tear it up, fall apart, go toward the unlike rather than the like . . . there's much more . . . making common cause with unlikely compadres really works and it flies faster.

We learned that from the web, too . . . get attached to something and then move out from the center and to not expect much there. I think it's true for poetry too.

Poets in a circle talking to each other is poets in a circle talking to each other and it doesn't advance poetry or queerness . . . so you know? [Shrugs.]

KARI EDWARDS: i hold the unique position of a gender voyeur, disidentifying with the system, but still very much a part of the system which gives me a unique vision of the world inaccessible to insiders.

we live in a gender-segregated society where we are given only a choice between two of something[s] . . . [that] is not a choice at all, but rather the opportunity to subscribe to a value system, that is enforced with its courts, its tribunals, its body of laws . . . its tortures, . . . its executions, [and] its police. last year more than thirteen individuals were murdered for not meeting society's gender requirement.

as a writer i attempt to disidentify from the narrative and use it at the same time to test the limits of its intelligibility, truth, and reality of societal taboos. i write from the fringes of what is seen as recognizable, not where gender and sexuality are defined in a neat bipolar package.

where language has become mc-speak, simple classification for everything, so you're a number two with a side order of fries.

these classifications where one (never names . . . [but] one classes some-one else) is bound up with force and violence . . . severing the connections between different genders and sexualites, placing one in set of relation-ship[s] structured through sanctions and taboos, including the sameness taboo that is ever-present in a gendercentric society, especially when the difference between women and men starts to blur.

we continue to believe in the myth that "men" and "women" have always existed and will always exist, and that the categories of male and female are based on anatomical criteria—which are neither universal nor valid concepts.

are you then amazed that the history books have excluded or "newly" discovered as parentheticals to human development, the hijras of india who exist outside the gender binary, the first nation's two spirit people, the castrated gallaes (who date back to the stone age). the gender trans-formations in ovid's *metamorphoses?* pope joan? the sapphist and mollys were considered a third and fourth gender. or the drag queens at stonewall.

whenever there are two [genders], a third cannot be far behind, and where there is a third, there can be a fourth and a fifth and so on. we want to think gender is solid, and that there is an absolute segregation between genders, but then that would deny the existence of those who are inter-sexed, and the numerous types of chromosome configurations. if we con-tinue to insist on this segregation by personal pronouns, we will continue to perpetrate a reliance on the slave master relationship.

we might say, one is not born a woman [or man, but] becomes one . . . [one then could say,] if one chooses, [one could choose to] become neither female or male, woman or man. if human beings have constructed and used gender—human beings can deconstruct and stop using gender. the most obvious way would be to deliberately and self-consciously not use gender.

what i am suggesting is that we call into question the structure . . . [in] which we recognize each other as human[s].

we are living in a historical discursive moment in which our language has run out, maybe it's so beyond our words that we don't know how to talk about it. we need to recognize that there is no longer a stable binary, when men have vaginas and women have penises. when we can surgically alter, strapped-on theme and variation genitalia beyond most people's imagination and where sexual encounters are no longer held tightly in categories of gay, lesbian, straight, bisexual, transgender, but become mul-tilocations of desire.

gender then can become an action that requires a new vocabulary.

if each person has their own individual perception to time and space which is based on relationships to the objects, then could this not also be said of a person's relationship to gender or sexuality?

if [we] continue to speak of ourselves and conceive of ourselves as women and men, we deny each and every person their individual relationship to space, time, and gender.

we need to imagine another body, capable of living beyond the incompleteness of what we designate as real . . . alive in its own name, in its own words, where everyone exists as an individual, as well as a member of a community.

[Text collaged from the following text: Jamake Highwater, *The Mythology of Transgression: Homosexuality as Metaphor*; Kate Bornstein, *Gender Outlaw: On Men, Women and the Rest of Us*; Monique Wittig, *The Straight Mind*; Jacques Derrida, *Of Grammatology*; Sarah Cooper, *Relating to Queer Theory: Rereading Sexual Self-Definition with Irigaray, Kristeva, Wittig and Cixous*; Judith Butler, *Gender Trouble: Feminism and the Subversion of Identity*; Gilbert Herdt, *Third Sex Third Gender: Beyond Sexual Dimorphism in Culture and History*; Alluquère Roseanne Stone, *The War of Desire and Technology at the Close of the Mechanical Age*; Judith Lorber, *Paradoxes of Gender*; C. Jacob Hale, "Consuming the Living Dis(re)membering the Dead in the Butch/FTM Borderlands"; Jason Cromwell, *Transmen & FTMs: Identities, Bodies, Genders, and Sexualities*; Antonio Porta, *Dream & Other Infidelities*; Elizabeth Grosz, *Space, Time and Perversion*; Will Roscoe, *Changing Ones: Third and Fourth Genders in Native North America*.]

ROBERTO TEJADA: I will eventually read something very short. I also wanted to say that . . . it may be rendered completely obsolete . . . given what's been said at the table already. I think one thing I want to concentrate on is that we're talking about identity and like Michael and others on the table, I think I'm less interested in identity politics, although I don't want to give it up entirely. I'm interested in identity, but I'm also nervous as to how identity is often rendered and circulated through institutions. There are all kinds of institutions.

Eileen was mentioning the newspaper for example, and the publishing world, and universities and even a gathering like this—may be thought of, in one sense an institutional setting. At best, it's probably a community of desire. I guess, I would be interested in the sense of identity or talking of the *notion* of identity. If and always, we think of identity in terms of not . . . what I want to say is that . . . I'm less interested in my identity.

I'm interested in how other identities shape and conform my identity, and where my sexual identity overlaps, or is traversed, or intruded by, or caressed by cultural difference and other cultural identities.

I love this word Eileen used about the unlikely. I think I'm interested in the unpredictability of identities that intersect in my life as well as the fluidity—the unpredictability of my own identity, sexual or cultural. In part, because I can't . . . overall what we're talking about here, as writers, is this very powerful tool called representation. Whether it be by writing or by visual representation, that's the means by which we can express the notions that are being debated today at the table.

But, I can never be 100 percent representative of myself; there's always going to be a residue or the *minus one*. Something left out of the way I represent myself, in which I need a community of readers, or I need a community of any kind of established community, to make up for that *minus one* that I will never be able to entirely represent. So, that being said, I would like to read briefly about the kind of representation, and let's call it writing, for the sake of shorthand today, that I'm interested in.

I'm interested not in a right, in a poetry based on a brand of identity, often legitimated by, and shelved under, the theoretical architecture of certain discourses and cultural criticism. Where, in a typically condescending fashion, it can be dubbed, quote, "marginalized performative agency." As I understand it, rendered experience, especially as it pertains to the possibilities of poetry, to speak only of poetry, should it best be considered in the sense of a subject involved in active invention, employing all forms of knowledge and direct interaction with visible and invisible powers—be the cannons, traditions, legacies, so as to forge renewed artifices in which the self can be publicly engaged.

I want to see work in which border crossing and displaced identities are expressed in disruptive languages. A poetry that claims the recognition of meaning, but in a speech that in no way lends itself to accommodation. I want my mind changed by poetics or sexualized subjectivity, so I can overcome what often seems to be closed in relation to language, and to see a refusal to comply to conventions of inherited style.

In short, the registers in scope made available by knowledges, other than the modern and postmodern poetic practice, are not *only* in English.

I'd like to read a poetry that engages a public beyond the poetry of the art world, or poetry world, or the margin of the margin of it claimed by the "smaller marginalized of advanced poetic writing."

I want to see writing that makes available the anxiety and ambivalence of representing personal, cultural, or historical narratives. Avoiding preconstructive essences, modalities, and effects. So as to reinvent certain processes of resistance, of poetics of the entire keyboard, where urgency and immediacy impose themselves to wake me to the intrinsic importance of what *needs* me to exist. And that's a difficult, but joyous place to begin.

ROBIN BLASER: It seems to me that two great cultural movements have been underway for the last half of my lifetime. One is the women's movement, and the other one is the sexual liberation movement. Those are both incomplete and ongoing and have an enormous job to do.

I have been interested in those who found me here before, watched me move through this concern with community. We have social worries and social concerns, but also community is that sense of belonging together. And it is community that we broadly lack, and it is now, of course, very endangered by globalization. It is also in danger, particularly in the U.S., by democracy under great attack.

Now, the source of this attack first appears in religious movements toward, not the sacred toll, but toward power. Their intentions are very clear. When I began working on the issue of the irreparable, in our sense of community. I began by doing a big research job on television-vision-channels. I listened to more religious muck than I really could bear. I think it has damaged my mind. I've barely escaped an enormous hatred.

One example that I will not forget was in the very height of the AIDS epidemic. The AIDS epidemic is still at a height, but now it takes longer to die so we hear less about it. At the very beginning of it, it was a horror. So, a minister came on vision-TV with the young brother of a gay man who had died of AIDS. A detailed version of his death. The horror of what could happen to an AIDS patient. And then, we have the minister turn to the young brother. Much younger than the man who had died, and have him explain to the television audience that this was God's judgment.

Now, this is even in their terms, and I'm never kind to *their,* any kind of *their,* in *their* terms—is blasphemy. It is historical blasphemy. It is religious blasphemy. It is sexual blasphemy. It is social blasphemy. It is taught. It is also of course, given money to keep this going.

I don't know whether you have ever watched when Reverend Van Impe and his wife, Rexella. I have not made this up. The Reverend and Rexella are treated as women have been treated for centuries. She doesn't know much, but she reads *Time* magazine. This is a television program.

And she reads *Time* magazine and then she says, "Oh Jack, what does this mean?" We have some example of Israel or something and she says, "Book of Daniel. It's all coming to an end. Every bit of it. If you're very good, lean forward and I will bless you," and the way you do that is put your hand on the television screen.

I have felt very good ever since. I turned it off. Those fuckers. They fuck our minds. They fuck our society and so on. My next move in response to all this conversation and wanting so much for those two great revolutions to continue. There is something irreparable. And I have worked from Giorgio Agamben's book *The Coming Community* in which the recognition of the irreparable is an accessed necessary condition of love. I have then worked from Jean-Luc Nancy's book, translated as the *Inoperative Community,* in which he talks about the business in this context that God is dead.

Now, look at the word *God*. That's Nietzsche in his brilliant incisive philosophical mind, which is not well read in philosophy so often because he wrote dithyrambically. The kind of poetry in ancient Greece, they wrote, that doesn't keep the regular rhythm, it's irregular.

The God is Dead thing . . . what is pointed out in anybody, as I have thought about this over so long, having been brought up a Roman Catholic, and so on . . . I knew that the word *God* is the most loaded word in our language. Nietzsche and no one of us could say "God is dead" and mean that the word *God* is gone.

Melville, as I have put it in a poem—quoting Melville's letter to Hawthorne, "the first time you mention the word God you hang yourself." It's powerful. What we must imagine is this word to which we've attached our sense of sacred . . . and it is such that we must think that if there is a God, we do not yet know who a God is. We do not know of course the gender of that God. We do not know, but there would be always the possibility of an appearance of a God in the condition when God is gone. And going faster than you can imagine. He runs all the red lights in contemporary culture.

This, as much as I wish to say . . . the two great movements . . . and historically all great movements run into trouble. Marx in particular didn't know what the nature of the state was. He grew up in the period . . . the state was a monarchy . . . an absolute . . . and if I had any message to give to anybody before I go off into some other realm, I would like to say beware of absolutes . . . every fucking one.

Beware beware beware. That means that when one tries to move to think with a freedom of definition of what one is . . . and what one perhaps will be . . . and what society . . . community could be. . . our writing suffers considerably. Not just because we all read to one another, I love that too, on top of the fact that that's where it always is . . . it suffers because we're also pushed into that spot that will not answer to that constant run of globalization of a renewal of religion that isn't there anymore anyway, it's all power, and in my view, the terror of absolutes is out of that traditional absolute, the paradigm of that. It's out of that that our fascisms come, it's very interesting, the fascists of Italy, they destroyed all the philosophy of poetry, though the poets went on, and they're still there.

They destroyed in Germany poets, etc. etc. etc, all of this, on top of what they did racially, these are irreparables, forgiveness isn't an issue here. Forgiveness works for me only when I've decided it's awfully good to be alive and go on. You don't forgive what you can't witness.

Well, I'll just close with . . . Giorgio Agamben has a recent book translated into English and published by Northwestern called *Remnants of Auschwitz* . . . it's a very complicated read . . . marvelous . . . but it is there that you look at what can be witnessed. I just read Julia Kristeva's book on Hannah Arendt, in which she argues that the next century belongs to the Women's Movement. But in Hannah Arendt's section, she also goes into great care with this issue of what can be forgiven and what can be a promise—that is at issue in the work of Hannah Arendt from the beginning of her first work, published in 1951, the origins of totalitarians.

CS: Thanks to everyone for their comments. Perhaps we should give a moment for panelists to respond to each other and then open it up to the room at large.

EM: I wanted to jump in just for a second, because I know that I inadvertently dissed the moment and the importance of poets talking to one another and also I mean that . . . we're all bashing identity politics . . . yet I'm all for a huddle . . . and I think there's a huge need for people as a group and a specific, even defined, group to know one another and have there be places . . . I guess I'm just always looking for the door too. And think that I need to know that it's there, but, certainly among poets there's nothing wrong with poets talking to poets and novelists too.

SD: I'm interested in identity politics. I'm interested in them from the position of one who believes they don't actually exist. I don't think "identity" refers to anything substantive in the actual world. Nevertheless, we spend a lot of time talking about things that do not exist . . . you know . . . like God: a wonderfully convenient conceptual instrument that makes us aware of how instruments are used, because we posit it as the source and origin of all instrumentality and conceptualization. More to the point, great progress and real reform have been accomplished by people who did and do believe in identity politics—and we must not lose the advances they have made.

Like Newtonian physics vs. Einsteinian physics, in lots of situations, where activism is called for, identity politics, despite the fine points, will do very nicely, thank you, even though it's got some theoretical holes.

Now what *about* those holes, those fine points? Well: The "I" never *has* an identity. We all know "I" is never at one with the identity it's assigned for more than a little while—days, weeks, maybe a few years if we're lucky. Probably this is part of what Robert was trying to say. "I" is always in excess of or inadequate to my identity . . . we all experience that as we move day through night to day.

What keeps the notion of identity circulating through society, I believe, is the fact of desire. Identity is what we desire in someone else. You know: "I want a man." "I want a woman." I want a particular *type* of man or woman. That's the thing that keeps identity out there moving as a social force.

Language coheres through desire. Language is the tool for talking about what we want. "Pass the salt." "I demand to live in a better world!" "I'm cold and hungry and need a blanket." "Spare change?" "Stop—stop—stop—stop *hitting* me!"

What I think we have all begun to learn is that what we want in spite of what we're told is changeable. One learns it is changeable.

I learned it was changeable three nights ago. Watching a live pornography show on *Dirk Yeats Live,* on the web . . . there I am, fifty-nine years old. Certainly by *now* I should know what I enjoy sexually. Well, I saw something that had never struck me as sexually interesting before. But there it was. And there I was, having a sexual response to something that, if you'd asked me about it twenty minutes before, I would have said: "Oh, no. Not *me* . . ." So, now, I have to revise the *whole* thing . . . once again. It's endless! As desire changes, so language changes—and "lived experience" (what happens) changes, as well. The point is, people who have begun to question identity politics have also begun to set in place a vocabulary that allows this requestioning to happen a little more easily, especially for people who are sixty. Or, I don't know, twenty, or three—

RB: Seventy-six.

SD: Seventy-six—there you go!

[laughing]

As long as desire is articulated in language in such a way that we can say, "I'm looking for . . . whatever it is I'm looking for," identities are going to remain in circulation, but they are also going to be mobile, malleable, and changeable—anabsolutes.

Identity is category—it's another word, a synonym, for category. Here's the big contradiction I find in identity politics: the notion of identity—such a rough notion—was that we should all find an identity and cleave to it. "You haven't accepted your identity . . ." Well "I," whoever "I" is—the subject—*never* wholly accepts his or her identity.

The really powerful people, the people who belong to the unmarked category (the categories in power), are precisely those who don't have to define their identity. That's what their power means. Nevertheless, as long as we have to talk about others, and as long as we have this tool, language, which talks about dogs, trees, flowers, poems, wars, men, women, and mosquitoes (as each is a word, it's a category, an identity), you're going to have all the problems that identity imposes. As soon as you not only talk about them, but talk about them in some *relation* of the sort "I like that one, but I don't like this one," desire is at work: the notion is kept stable, because we want to recognize the desired object. But the truth is, most of what these people get done of worth in the world is done through their transcending any notion of identity, of their going beyond the categories assigned them.

If we want to get anything of real worth done, we have to do the same.

To recognize an identity is to look for what is *similar* in it to the last example seen, rather than what is *different* in it. Thus, I don't think it's a problem that will go away any time soon. But while those similarities will tell you of a group strength (always important), what is different alone constitutes individual value with the greatest chance of responding creatively to change.

MDP: I just wanted to mention one thing to pick up on what Samuel has just said, Akilah said, and what Robin said. I think it's very important that we think about and I agree with . . . in terms of identity . . . but I think the critical conjunction is identity *in* politics and I think that's the point Robin was making and Akilah was making as well . . . it's through the ritual, the reinforcement of social rituals, and the kinds of institutions of identity that problems arise.

Right? I very much like your description of desires, as a kind of ongoing opening "personal ad" to the world . . . "I am, I like, I desire," you know? So on and so forth. Changeable. But, it's . . . I think, the issue is the institutions through which those identities are historically mediated at any point . . . what Cole said in the beginning . . . for example . . . simply thinking about media . . . the controls and limits on media . . . and so on and so forth.

I think thinking about the institutions instead of focusing so much on identity *as* identity politics and how we might respond . . . of course it's critically important at various points to respond to identity politics to institutions *in* institutionalized forms, also what's really important in what Akilah was suggesting is the way in which social rituals of reinforcement aren't always necessarily a good thing. I think the very significant historical reminder of the rituals of lynching is that they did reinforce identity and that they did reinforce identity politics for white people in very particular ways in very violent acts against particular kinds of bodies.

That's my way of qualifying identity politics. . . . It's thinking about the institutions.

RT: I would like to add to both what Michael and Samuel Delany were saying—that one thing Samuel brought up was this idea of the fact that those in power, those who potentially can be my oppressors, don't have an identity. And that's very often true, because it's the identity that is made invisible. Right?

It's identity that doesn't have to question itself. But, I guess I'm interested, or my task as I see it, is to make that identity visible. I'm interested in the normative identities and what I can bring to those identities. Male heterosexuality for example. I think that's an identity I'm interested in shaping as well, even though it's not an identity that I can assign to myself.

We can also bring out aspects of identities that are the norm and color them or shape them in ways that were invisible to themselves and make them visible.

SD: Michael and Akilah were talking about lynchings a bit ago, and I was reminded of something unsettling. When I was, oh, thirteen or fourteen, my family had a book edited by Paul Robeson, along with a group of his fellow activists, *We Charge Genocide*. It was filled with case histories of lynchings, including photographs. They were unsettling pictures. That book was the document that first made lynchings real for me. Now members of my family had been lynched—

My father had grown up on a small black college campus, and one of the anecdotes he first told me when I was five or six years old is how some cousins of his had been lynched. A husband and wife; she was a fairly light-skinned black woman; she had been eight or so months pregnant. A bunch of white men had come across her and her husband, who was notably darker than she was, and they had lynched both of them. Her belly had been split open and her baby's body had fallen out onto the ground.

Those are the same words he used to tell me about it with, when I was five, when I was six. He told me how their bodies had been brought back to the campus in a buckboard wagon in the evening. Remembering it, he became very angry. I was pretty upset by it, and I cried. Well, some years later, when I looked through *We Charge Genocide,* one particular photograph and the case history along with it struck me. It was the case where a white Jewish man had been lynched. His name was Mr. Frank, and it was around 1917. It was a charge of rape—the same thing that had been done to so many black people.

Akilah has talked about castration of the lynched black man. But other bodily deformations were common at lynchings. Frequently the victim's tongue was cut out. With the mouth that mutilated, there was much less noise—and lynchings involved burning the victims alive almost as frequently as they did hangings. Another common practice was cutting the ears off the still-living victim and sewing them—or, more frequently, nailing them—to the victim's buttocks. Several of the pictures in *We Charge Genocide* showed white children, boys and girls, seven, eight, ten, and thirteen, standing in front of the charred black corpses roped to the stakes in the background, smiling.

Here I am, forty years away from that book, and almost fifty-five years away from my dad's personal account of lynchings. Right now, the only three lynchings that I know about, that I can tell you about specifically, is the case of a white Jew being lynched and the case of my two relatives being lynched and all lynchings reported by Robeson and his researchers. I know they existed. I know they were there. While I can think of some of those photographs, I don't have names to connect them to; so somehow, my model of the lynching has become somewhat odd—what would you call it?—as though it's the corrective for a general notion.

I remember the white man being lynched. I remember the lynching of my black relatives. This median place, which was the one you were talking about, although I absolutely know it's there—know it's there intellectually—it's not the one that I go to, when you say lynching. I go to the ones I've told you about. I go to ones my family spoke of. I go to the pictures I've seen.

There's something wrong with a larger process that forgets that, yes, black men were lynched; but also that black women, like my cousin, were lynched; white men, like Mr. Frank, were lynched; white women were lynched; white children were lynched—a twelve-year-old white girl was beaten unconscious and then hung by her father, while his neighbors watched, because she had played with a mentally retarded adult black man and there was the possibility he had touched her sexually; black children were lynched—a fourteen-year-old black boy was burned alive because he looked at a white woman in an inappropriate manner.

No one was one-hundred-percent free of all possibility of being lynched, because he or she belonged or did not belong to a particular group. That means you, and you, and you, and me, and you.

In terms of statistics, yes, the victims were overwhelmingly black men. We must know that—as we must know many of them were castrated. But we must also know about the Native Americans and the Chinese railroad workers who were lynched. We must know that there are recorded cases for *all* these, as we must know about those tongues and ears. We must know what the permeability of those margins, what those smiling children, say about the violence of the process, if we are to start to know what, truly, lynchings were.

ROXY POWELL HAMILTON: This is a question that's going to try to address what Eileen said about shipwrecks are always distributed, what Akilah said about queering the body, and, hopefully, what Samuel said about the biggest problem facing the homosexual novelist today and that is . . . I'm interested in the notion of queering a body of literature by choice.

So, taking a second example of Akilah's queering of the body, the one that is involved with choice as opposed to exhibition, or being made a spectacle of, in order to reify another culture's power over you, I'm wondering whether or not you guys have anything to say about an alternative model that is something other than this problem, of what I think of as the ship-wreck model of queer literature, which is that we're constantly diving into the wreck?

Sorry, to excavate great models of, or historical examples of, experiences that are basically tragic, that are basically examples of queer memoir, one way or another, experience retold from the position of a life that was wrecked and retold endlessly. I think about repetition as both a problem and a solution, because I think that the problem with lynching is that you have to repeat the act of lynching over and over against many different bodies.

You can't make one final statement, although they're *trying* to make a final statement that this *is* the significance of the black male body and you restate that over and over again.

To summarize: I think that it's necessary to find a different form other than the shipwreck or the myth or what Nietzsche talks about as monumental literature that tries to make some kind of final statement about who we are and that could be related to identity politics or gay pride day or ghettos of tolerance or—whatever, but, how do we queer writing? How do we queer by inventing new narrative forms beyond the long historical narrative that tries to tell the story in some ways. And, I know that none of us believe *that* here on this panel, but I'm wondering if the three of you have any approaches to queering the body of our community writing?

SD: I think there are two ways to do it. One, is to talk about the things that you have seen in your own life, the things you have heard other people talk about in their own lives. Do that accurately and you will start to accomplish that queering. The other way is to talk about what *you* want. Talk about what you would like to have in your own life. Both of these, I think, are scary because frequently they go outside all sorts of approved group agendas. But if you write about (one) some reality you've actually seen, and (two) what you would like to be your reality (not what you've been *told* is there, or what you've been told you *should* want; or what you think other people will approve of you if you say is there or what they'll approve of your wanting), you're going to move toward accomplishing some of that queering.

The truth is always queer.

EM: I do, I guess, I feel, seriously, that all lives are wrecks and decomposition is where it's at, and that's where we're all going—sooner, quicker, later, and to embrace it. Because I really think that the biggest danger to literature at this moment is the clean story. Either swift and clean and direct or . . . but women to be dirty sloppy crazy falling apart rich women, is something I really aspire to be aesthetically, and personally, and I think it's eminently attractive and widely distributed—earnest. I was saying that with humor, that shipwrecked thing, I was like—yeah—yeah. I am a shipwreck.

I'm all for it. You know? I just think that it's sort of like women are continually pushed into some kind of ineffectual position of striving to be in charge. I mean to reclaim female masochism—but be the pathetic woman, because, again the female narrative is über-woman, clean and winning top top top. And you know, it's sort of like, who wants to be there, it's not a human deep winning rich place, and I'm sure it's the same for men as well.

I just think there's an absence of female—there was a ceding of some of the prizes of feminism and into Pathetic Masculinity in the nineties. Yeah, there actually was an art movement called Pathetic Masculinity and all it was was a retooling of feminism in the art world and it's like—no— let's take it back, Girls—let's be a mess. I think late feminism was creating a faux female which I think is a mistake.

SD: I think that's one side of a dialectical process. Yes, my heart leaps up when I behold you free to fall apart, to let it all hang out.

But you achieve a certain power when you're of a group traditionally felt never to have it together—always falling apart—and you present yourself as relatively and articulately together. You take on power when you can talk about your situation in a together way. The dialectic moves back and forth—between falling apart and getting it together.

EM: Any given work of art . . . at a certain part we fall apart, you can regroup and get going.

RT: I was just going to tie into what Eileen was saying as well, which was, I think what was at stake here was this idea of wellness and pathology. As Samuel was saying . . .because of certain advances that have been made we have the privilege of going back and looking at pathology as opposed to wellness.

I think we do go back to the legacies to look at that. The first thing that came to my mind when you brought the question up was looking at Hart Crane, who I'm fascinated by, and particularly not his homosexuality, I don't want to call him a misogynist, but let's say he had problems with women. Particularly, his relationship with Katherine M. Porter in Mexico. The pathology of that relationship to me is as productive looking at it, to read Crane's life, than to look at some positivity or the wellness of how he dealt with his homosexuality. So, I think that's the doubleness we want to look at, that which is destructive or self-destructive and that which arises out of those ashes.

KE: i'm not sure if, in response, creating new forms means speaking outside or apart from history, and i'm not sure if i misunderstood part of the question in terms of historical references or re-narrating even those references.

i even heard the lynching narrative be heard as a queering process, but the re-telling for me in that way, that for me is a new form, is creating a new form, how that would look in terms of literature, in terms of text, is very open, it is endless in terms of what we can do with form. i'm still kind of musing over the outside of history if I misunderstood that or not, or that i don't desire to exist outside of history; i don't find subjectivity outside of historical context.

DAN TURNBULL: This question has nothing to do with literature, it has nothing to do with politics, it's sort of open to everyone, it's directed to Robin a little bit specifically, because it comes from a statement you make: don't forgive what you can't witness, and this has a few parts. Are you implying not to have absolute forgiveness and just true forgiveness and an open heart to everything that happens, because that in itself is an absolute and are you also implying that forgiveness is something that can be given to most things, but it's something that like anything else takes work and understanding, you can't just do it like that, and in the interim, if we don't forgive, then what are you suggesting remains thereafter?

Because when people don't forgive, there's always a lot of anger and hatred that just perpetuates the negative ideas and energies of what was created in the past and that in itself creates not just an absolute, but a negative absolute, which forms again, and then is going to try and stomp out the past thing that was not forgiven.

RB: Well I hope my syntax didn't get confused there, my point was that there are certain things that are beyond forgiveness, and I think it's best if we don't forget them. As a consequence, you replace that your way of forgiving is to go on living among others—that would be my point in that, not to build any kind of absolute of hatred of something or be unhistorical, not remember.

Burning at the stake continued until 1748 in Europe. Now, are we going to forgive burning at the stake, providing you know what it was like to be burned at the stake? Joan of Arc had a slow fire that would make the skin fall off before she passed out. And then she didn't pass out, so they made it a little hotter. You see, this isn't an issue of forgiveness, this is a matter of awareness.

And, here we are with the Buddha all around us, and my sense is, to remember in terms of those things, those terrible things, the Buddha refused immortality in order to come back and be among us, to help. That comes to mind, because I'm here at Naropa, but it's also important to me—that sense. Certain things are beyond forgiveness, like the Nazi camps.

DT: My question is—when it's not forgiveness, what's there instead of that?

RB: Your memory and awareness of what it was and what aspect of your social world allowed that to come out. That's the reason I was trying to warn about the dangers of democracies, as fumbling as they all are, is something very much like an absolute.

You begin to get the power systems. And as soon as you get those, they begin to do these unforgivables. I think somewhere in you as there is in me, forgiveness is one of the highest values I could think of, but not for the unforgivable.

SD: The young are better at forgiving than the old. That's one of the great strengths of youth. As Robin said, forgiveness is the highest thing—one of the highest things—one can do. I hear in what you're saying, Robin, that forgiveness is closely allied with forgetting. Certain things should not be forgotten, because, if you forget them, they'll happen again.

God, remember, eventually forgets everything. It's called entropy and the second law of thermodynamics. That's *how* He forgives. More than once I've written: "We are at our most human when we remember—and at our most godlike when we forget."

Even things like torture, like lynchings, at some point, have to be forgiven. But they have to be remembered, too, and people have to change the world in ways such that they will not happen again; or at least not happen for a long, long time. Making those changes requires energy and anger. If you lose that anger, you're not likely to make the changes. Now forgiveness is a great action—remembering the pain, the suffering, and saying, as one remembers, I forgive. But the people who *can't* forgive also have their place in society. They are the ones who are going to make society different. It's the ones who can't forgive, but who nevertheless recognize the necessity *for* forgiveness, who are most likely to change the world in beneficial ways.

Another dialectic.

Femanifestos

ANNE WALDMAN

* * *

FROM *FEMINAFESTO*

Summer Writing Program, July 1992

Do you have to be circumscribed? Do you really have to be circumsized? Women are considered *sebel,* unclean, in Hindu Bali. You are forbidden to enter temples if you are menstruating, or you wear the chador which covers all but the eyes, but even they must be lowered, averted, in narrow Arab streets. Your power, your nakedness, would cause men to go mad, commit unspeakable deeds. Would change the world! Would paint it scarlet! Would seize and restore the night with sweet ancient control. Check out the Levite laws in the Bible, the destruction of the Astoreth goddess temples. Your passion would run amok, make riot. Your multiple orgasms, your oceans of bliss, your cum would flood the world. Coming into power as a writer had to do with becoming a mother as well. I could say outrageous things, could proclaim my "endometrium shedding." Could manifest the "crack in the world." I shouted, "You men who came out of my belly, BACK OFF!" I could literally stomp and walk on the "periphery of the world." I might—as Sumerian Inanna did—get the male poets (my "fathers") intoxicated on alcohol, methedrine, ecstasy, charm them with my wit, my piety, then steal their secrets. Cast a discerning eye at the progressive anthologies of poetry. Are we still having to count the men versus women, and is the canon a lost cause or is it the battleground? Look at the scarcity of women in any institution, sacred or secular. Keep counting. How many pinks to so many blues? Is language phallogocentric? Is writing a political act? Do you women writers I'm speaking to feel marginalized? Do you agree, you'd almost have to, dear scholarly sisters, that the experiences of women in and with literature are different from those of men? Much feminist criticism has centered on the misogyny of literary practice—women as angels or monsters, mothers or nuns, daughters or whores—harassment of women in classic and popular male literature and text. You know it: James Joyce, Freud, Jack Kerouac, Norman Mailer, Henry Miller, Homer, the Bible, the Koran, the Vinaya. But I want here to declare an enlightened poetics, an androgynous poetics, a poetics defined by your primal energy, not by a heterosexist world that must measure every word, every act against itself. Not by a norm that assumes a dominant note subordinating, mistreating, excluding any other possibility. In fact you could be a man with a "lesbian" consciousness in you, a woman with a "gay" consciousness inside. I propose a utopian creative field where we are defined by our energy, not by gender. I propose a transexual literature, a transgendered literature, a hermaphroditic literature, a transvestite literature, and finally a poetics of transformation beyond gender. That sings its wisdom. That the body be an extension of energy, that we are not defined by our sexual positions as men or women in bed or on the page. That the page not be empty female awaiting penetration by dark phallic ink-juice. That masculine and feminine energies be comprehended in the Buddhist sense of *prajna* and *upaya,* wisdom and skillful means, which exist in all sentient beings. That these energies coexist and are essential one to the other. That poetry is perceived as a kind of *siddhi,* or magical accomplishment that understands these fundamental energies.

Perhaps women have the advantage of producing a radically disruptive and subversive kind of writing right now because they are experiencing the current imbalances and contradictions that drive them to it. They are turning to skillful means in figuring how to combat assaults on their intelligence and time. She—the practitioner—wishes to explore and dance with everything in the culture which is unsung, mute, and controversial so that she may subvert the existing systems that repress and misunderstand feminine "difference." She'll take on the subjects of censorship and abortion and sexual harassment. She'll challenge her fathers, her husband(s), lovers, male companions, warmongers, micromanagers, spiritual teachers. Turn the language body upside down. What does it look like?

CAUTIONARY THOUGHTS MANIFESTO
RE: The American War on Terrorism, September 26, 1992

I touched down in Florence, Italy the moment the first airplane hit the World Trade Center. There was no way to get "home" to New York for days and I settled in with an international community at the Civitella Ranieri Center in Umbria for a five-week work and study retreat.

This piece and the next are immediate responses and pleas written in the heat of the moment and are dedicated here to Nicaraguan poet, priest, revolutionary Ernesto Cardenal whose presence at Civitella provided both inspiration and solace.

>   Sunday night, and on Wall Street a foul wind blows
>   newspapers along the empty sidewalk. Wall St. with stars
>   eerie and empty. The bank windows dark
>   though not all. A few rows lit up
>   in the black monstrosities. They can be identified:

the foreign departments of the big banks.
The iron doors barred and padlocked.
But by back doors some people have entered
the foreign departments. The lights—secret meetings,
decisions we're unaware of (and their cigar smoke
rising like shares) but they affect us all.
Devaluation sparks off a riot in Malaysia, buses burned
and blood flows in the streets like water from a hydrant.
At the hour that the stars shine over Wall Street
and the hour the banks open in London.

— ERNESTO CARDENAL, from *Cosmic Canticle*

Umberto Eco, semiologist-philosopher, reminds us of the three ways cultures clash: the members of Culture A cannot recognize the members of Culture B as human beings (and vice versa), seeing them as "barbarians" to civilize or destroy, which is the Conquest Model. In the Cultural Pillage Model, Culture A must steal from B and colonize or subjugate politically or militarily and in that way undermine and usurp the invaded culture. The Exchange Model is a two-way process of reciprocal support, often "influence" in the best sense and respect.

*Always invoke Model Three.

It is a fact, woefully, that Western culture (European civilization) has been most engaged with the first model—and, as just one example, subjugated African and Amerindian cultures with unmerciful acts of cruelty. And that now, more particularly America—the richest and most powerful country in the world—the "cop of the world"—acts and has acted with unmitigated and brutal economic self-interest in many parts of the globe.

Because of media control (particularly since the American War in Vietnam) Americans do not fully comprehend the damage we have inflicted on Iraq. And now do not understand the "karma" of that conflict which galvanized so much hatred of the U.S. Or how the indignities that the Palestinians have suffered in Israel/Palestine have led to such loathing and call for "jihad." I was working in Germany during the Gulf War and was shocked by the contrast in media coverage between the States and abroad. I only heard Ramsey Clark speak live of the devastation of Basra (bodies in the streets, no water to drink) via transmitted reports from Cuban radio.

*Demand comprehensive, intelligent, reliable, and mature media coverage from television (where most of America & a lot of the world gets its news). Support alternative media. Does it only take a tragedy to subsist from constant pushing of the Market? It seems shameful that only a week after the terrorist attacks in the U.S. we were back to business as usual, slick advertising pushing the American Economic Way, theme music for the American War in Afghanistan, sentimental ads to hike cell phone biz to communicate with tearful "loved ones." And endless repetition/assault of images that invoke patriotism and fear and revenge. The inane flicker of media and war. *Be scared, buy more.*

After Operation Desert Storm, a United Nations mission to Iraq reported that the Gulf conflict "wrought near-apocalyptic results" by destroying "most means of modern life support," relegating Iraq to a "pre-industrial age." Again, is it any wonder that citizens of that country, as much as they might be under the iron rule of a tyrant, abhor America and everything it stands for? As we know, as has been proven, they are not alone in this.

Or, historically, the instability we brought to South & Central America, Indonesia, and the Caribbean in support of corrupt governments out of self-interest. In a recent conversation with Ernesto Cardenal, Nicaraguan Catholic priest, poet, and former Minister of Culture under the Sandinistas—the suggestion was that karmically the U.S. helped create Osama Bin Laden (& others like him) through a variety of actions, but most particularly the U.S. covert (CIA) support against Russia in Afghanistan on which side Bin Laden fought. Bin Laden also later saw arrogant U.S. presence in Saudi Arabia, which he resented. His call for jihad, his heinous words against Americans and Jews are the product of a sick and twisted yet ideology-based seemingly "righteous" mentality. Ernesto also noted that Bin Laden helped support the Contra movement against the Sandinistas, who had overthrown the brutal dictatorship of Somoza, who was supported by the U.S.! (This is documented in an Oliver North biography, although Bin Laden has said he didn't know what he was funding.)

*Invoke Investigative and Documentary Poetics. Know the score! Know the history!

The TV pundits and media cannot keep mindlessly repeating the simplistic notion that these recent horrific disasters are merely an attack on America's "freedom" in light of such demented, albeit complex history and the grinding truth of cause and effect. It is insulting to our dignity as free-thinking individuals. Bin Laden—if he is the mastermind—is another hardened player in the big "game." He can play both sides in his agenda. Glamorizing him as a "holy warrior" would be idiotic as well. His agenda, presumably, is to rid the Middle East of U.S. capitalist presence, which is understandable. Any ends—to that goal—justify the means. And he's got the money!

*Study the nature of power-politics!

In Buddhist psychology one of the Six Realms of Existence includes the Warring God Realm, a super-intelligent paranoid realm of energetic activity in which enemies have to be created and maintained in order for the neurotic mind to function and thrive. It operates on the notion of revenge. This state manifests in an endless cycle of balance and checks around power and perpetuates suffering, and yet its strategies, to some, are fascinating, compelling even, and may suck one in.

*Check out the Warring God Realm of everyday existence! U.S. Military budget could go as high as $400 billion this year and higher in the future. Weapons in space? Drilling on Mars? You know where your dollars are?

Meanwhile, an innocent victim of the Warring God Realm could be anyone of us. We can empathize now with innocents who have died & suffered while the Masters of War carry out their agendas. Writing this text from Europe, one hears countless stories of the suffering of innocent victims during times of war still within memory. Czech friend/writer/translator/scholar lost an aunt to U.S. bombing during WWII, the U.S. never apologized. Of course Hitler had to be stopped. The U.S. was late in that conflict and was responsible for the deaths of thousands of Japanese civilians. We know governments do not always serve the best interests of their citizens.

The situation in Afghanistan is extremely complex. The Taliban in power represent only a minority of the Pashto-speaking Afghanis who border Pakistan. The nation has been described as a "pre-modern warlord state." The Pashto speakers are mostly Sunni Muslims, the Persian (Farsi) speakers are those who look to Iran. The underclass Shiite Heraras speak an archaic Persian and resemble in physiognomy Tibetans or Nepalis. Residents of Bamiyan were evidently enraged when the Taliban destroyed the magnificent large twin statues of Buddha there (in Gary Snyder's phrase, they took "refuge in the dust"). How irresponsible for the U.S. to portray Afghanistan as a united front to the American public, dehumanizing the situation. William Blake implores us to "observe the minute particulars" and to "look to the little ones."

*Discriminating Awareness Wisdom (*prajna*) Now! Poetics adages are useful here: "No ideas but in things" (Williams); "Go in fear of abstractions" (Ezra Pound). Poets & artists: make your own lists of sane trustworthy language measures. . . .

Aren't there sane models for mutual coexistence on this precious planet? Aren't there any wise leaders (with clout) who may be allowed to speak sagely & effectively at this crucial time? And speak with historical/cultural/ philosophical/religious perspective? Why don't governments have such council in place? The U.S. presidential cabinets are made up primarily of partisan lackeys, often not even trained in their supposed arenas of expertise. And they too can be bought. Are the Muslim clerics the only "body of elders" to weigh in on this? Isn't there a way of invoking and developing (through U.N. auspices) a body of mediating enlightened human beings from all nations and cultures and communities that aren't simply representing and reflecting their own government's national interests? Who hold the whole of existence sacred? Cannot we have, also, a body of folk going in just to help (as witnessed powerfully in the aftermath of the attack in NYC?) Not aid groups of religious groups with ideologies or strings attached, but . . .

*Form cadres of "bodhisattvas" for mediation, for true compassionate (not self-serving) action. And bands of articulate poet-warriors!

The U.S.'s questionably legitimate presidential leadership, its government's rejection of the Kyoto Accords, its boycott of the U.N. conference on racism (related to the situation in Israel/Palestine), its undoing of sane and sensible legislation that protects its own citizens (standards for arsenic levels in water, etc.) has been most troubling, depressing. Does not the current scenario, at the brink of a consuming war in the Middle East— simply benefit this country's hegemonic interest, economy? Will it root out terrorism or create more terrorism? Does the U.S. not showcase its most advanced weaponry once again, which will lead to support of Star Wars and other scary outer-space death machines? Is it not true that the U.S. wants an oil pipeline through Afghanistan? And won't we be paying a heavy price for an "us versus them" mentality, for invoking a sense of righteous "crusade" and revenge? Where are the women critiquing the use of patriarchal language now when we need them? Where are the responses of women leaders in general as we see unfolding before us another macho drama? What are the five wives of Osama Bin Laden thinking? Where is Hillary Clinton in articulation of the suffering of the Palestinian people now, at the eleventh hour? Should we not examine our language with perspicacity at this time? Should we not explore other less devastating methods for uprooting terrorism and its causes before we inflict more suffering on already desperate and suffering peoples?

*Stay vigilant. Be a guardian of "right speech"!

Consider the deals that are being made to insure support of U.S. policy planet-wide! Will Russia now even have more permission to persecute its "terrorists" in Chechnya, will China in Tibet and Taiwan etc., etc....

As patriotic U.S. citizen who has always strived to "save America from herself" and one (with many) who mourns her country's loss, & who feels tremendous assault on her native city, and as writer defending creative expression and the right to dissent and as denizen of the world who aspires to know the world (& the cosmos)—understand it, witness it in all its richness & complexity—I take a vow for an aspiration of *vipashyana* or clear-seeing (insight). The world does not need more war. Pursue the path of least suffering . . .

Umberto Eco also invokes the Tower of Babel collapsing as a result of humanity's hubris in a salient essay that examines the search for the original language of man. The plurality of tongues should hardly be seen as a tragic consequence and yet there is something to be said for an image of restoration and communication. Is it really too late?

By this merit may all obtain omniscience
May it defeat the enemy wrong-doing . . .

Sarva mangalam.

IS THERE ANYONE UNDER THAT BURQA?
Sisters Arise & Vocalize
Full Moon Over Umbria and Afghanistan, October 2, 2001

Language has been on the feminist political agenda for years. It can't just go away meekly now. It is agonizingly evident as of September 11 that there has been a paucity of women's voices from the political arena (the world over) as well as in the arena of high public culture and discourse. Something is missing. Is there anyone, metaphorically speaking, under that burqa?

One observes the endless parade of presidents, mullahs, generals, prime ministers, cabinet members, diplomats, politicians of all kinds, pundits, experts, czars, etc. flash across the screen and surface in the daily massive missives of newsprint. But so few women. Where are the boddhisattvas like Aung San Suu Kyi? The talking head female folk on TV are a relief. Susan Sontag, Arundhati Roy, and Maureen Dowd are hardly a relief, but there has got to be more female leadership and articulation and input allowed into the public discourse and decision-making apparatuses. More mainstream illumination from the hidden *dakinis* and *durgas!* & more

Amy Goodmans! Some alternative/corrective recourse to power of VOICE. How things are expressed, stated, conveyed whether it be condolence, dissent, opinion—whatever the form or genre—needs attention. U.S. nationwide surveys show a marked difference of opinion when it comes to issues of "war" "education" "literacy." We need more THINKING by women aired and expressed on urgent issues. It is not good for the civic psyche that we are so deprived.

SISTERS—SPEAK OUT YOURSELVES & DEMAND MORE DISCUSSION OF THE CURRENT STATE OF THE WORLD AND THE WAR ON TERRORISM NOW. INSIST THAT YOUR FEMALE ELECTED LEADERS GET MORE VOICE & INK!

A feminist critique of language calls into question our assumptions about who is speaking. And for whom? And to what purpose? Who is the language representing and what kind of ideology? Whose interest? How does language attempt to manipulate us? We've had in the not-too-distant past genteel tyrannies of custom and practice. It was a crime under slavery for African Americans to read and write. Remember when a woman couldn't vote? When saying a liturgy or a public oratory by women was forbidden? A certain ilk of males have had a monopoly on NAMING WHAT COUNTS AS REALITY. This seems more and more insane in a universe with infinite possibilities. It doesn't need to be this way. Of course we understand that gender is a social construct and that the possibilities of "difference" are endless and all beings who are not just representing the dominant male constructs are also welcome here!

RECLAIM NAMING. CHECK OUT WHAT LEADERS ARE SAYING AS WE ENTER INTO ANOTHER WARRING PATRIARCAL GOD MENTALITY. DECONSTRUCT OLD GRAMMARS, METAPHORS, IMPERIALIST IMPERATIVES. POETS: STAY ON THE CASE!

We know that the privileged and powerful have had a vested interest in shaping the world through language. Tailoring the world to suit their ends, constructing a world in which they are the central "players." Structures, categories, meanings have been shaped by the dominant white man. Capitalism thrives on a political discourse that marginalizes alternative thinking and exploits those without a "voice." Our modern state emerged from the ashes of the feudal state and was built on a class and patriarchal model. Political representation began as the right of property owning MEN. Now the capitalist state addresses itself to a generalized citizen/consumer, presumably classless, sexless, a hip citizen of the increasingly troubled world. It's not working! Look at the mess we are in. Also to protect this version of reality the capital-driven state constructs its weapons of mass destruction with impunity and threatens the very planet we dwell on by its greed for wealth and power. We also see so many women suffering (unable to drive, get an education, bare their faces in public, etc.) under other (in some cases less subtle) regimes that are also constructing their weaponry and so on . . . the victims of strife are also women.

But I ask of the discourse in general: where are the women? I ask it of women writers: what are your boundaries, the liminal demilatarized zones? How far will you go crossing the line? How many wailing images do we see every day after day of women mourners? Is their role only to keen at the death of their husband and child martyrs, to howl at the skies? And symbolically I use this again: burqa, chador, cloth, cowl, death shroud—perhaps in the sense of "hiddenness," of safety. Who is completely safe in this ozone? Under the cloth? Or standing under the tits-and-ass male gaze billboards of buy-this-sex-object imagery (whatever the product) now.

What is hidden, what is revealed and why? The guise and guile of language? Why do women and others continue to be disempowered in their version of reality—version of gender—version of the body politic—version of language? Particularly in America—where you would expect a modicum of acknowledged liberation. Is there no remnant of a public intelligentsia? Did we ever have one, as citizens do in many parts of Europe? Or as people do in many oral cultures that wouldn't exist, wouldn't feel they have a right to without their art. The human realm must chant and tell stories & put its handprints on the cave walls & cavort with the animals, imitate their animalized spirit & intensity.

Images:

The male terrorist disguised as a woman on the Israeli bus . . .

The immortalized character (in William Burroughs's Titanic) dressed as a woman jumping into the lifeboat. What does it signify? codify? The guise of the feminine? Is she a coward? It's reclamation time!

Cross-dressing as ploy . . .

The skilled Balinese performer—now in her nineties—playing in the ritual drama Colan Arung—leading participants to the graveyard at dawn in a rite of passage to look death in the eye.

Maria Sabina, Mexican transducer-Shaman. Crossing the line through language and song in an all-night *velada*—or "watch"—so that one travels mentally helped by the saintchildren, the *hongos* (mushrooms), on the phones and phonemes of language into other states of being—empathies or the Boddhisattva's return. *Wisdom is language,* she says.

Arundhati Roy, salt on her tongue, diminutive of body, chiding at the gates.

This is a question as a woman, as a writer. Reclamation of that power, that a gaze might kill, which is why you must avert your eyes, women, in some cultures. Reclamation—that's what I try to do, *not* avert that gaze.

To exist in one's own eyes, that is the praxis. And in the working of our writing. To exist in its eyes.

The revolutionary potential of everyday life as a writer—that seems to be the order of the day, & tithing our time. "Entertain 6 impossible ideas before breakfast"—The Red Queen's admonition to Alice-in-Wonderland. Invoke Negative Capability. Or be "incapably positive."

Sisters, we can shake off the burqa, come out of the cocoon, or rest comfortably inside it. Isn't it getting hot in here?

POETRY IS NEWS
A Counter-Intelligence Symposium, February 1, 2003

Welcome. It's 2 p.m., Saturday, February 1, 2003, Manhattan, NYC, planet Earth, do you know where the U.S. government is?

It is wonderful to be able to host this investigative event at historic St. Mark's Church, which houses the Poetry Project—an activity zone that investigates language and imagination—among other many worthy venues over the years. I am reminded these days of the American/Vietnam War years for obvious reasons as we convene today—and thinking of how this site has always welcomed the work and industry of countercultural artists and activists. I've been in this room not only with the deceased and ongoing bastions of poetry and performance—all the lineages of the New American Poetry, Black Arts, Nuyorican and several generations beyond as well as poets from many other countries and cultures—but also with the likes of Pete Seeger, Dennis Banks, Dave Dellinger, Carlos Feliciano, Allen Ginsberg (in role as gadfly/peacenik), Abbie Hoffman, to name a few . . .

As all of us recognize, these are extremely grave and dangerous times—hair trigger to WWIII, also times that were they NOT so scary could be characterized as absurdist, and incredibly so with the fare we confront daily:

India seeking cheetahs from Iran to clone, the Vatican banning transexuals, Iraq taking over as Chair of the Disarmament Conference in Geneva for four weeks, Nelson Mandela rightly calling Bush a president who has no foresight who cannot think properly who is wanting to plunge the world into a holocaust & you'd think that kind of moral authority would ECHO through the land & reverse the course of history, a desolate slum friendly to Americans in Iraq yet will fight to the teeth for its honor, a tax break for drivers of SUVs, U.S. investigators able to enter the country from Mexico, Canada, Jamaica with fake names and false I.D.s, Bush's "Clear Skies" initiative, Cheney's "Bioshield," weird proposals for the World Trade site, ad absurdum, the European *Time* magazine conducting a poll asking "Which country in the world poses the greatest danger to world peace?" and with 318,000 votes, the responses being North Korea, seven percent; Iraq, eight percent; the United States, eighty-four percent.

So we live in a bifurcated realm, and we have the rule of Euphemism from the junta team in DC. Thus we are stretched in many ways—linguistically, psychically, emotionally (not to mention economically), facing yet again an aggression that will bring deeper harm, suffering, further destabilization worldwide. Hard to laugh about. But remember we will be held accountable by future generations. Where were we as human beings? Isolated, self-serving? Or guarding the repercussions for the actions of a very few crazy evildoers, our own terrorists in DC will be endless—like the Eternal War. The Warring God Realm hallucinates its enemy with great zeal, we know this. We have to break into that hallucination with our cultural interventions, with our subtler language, and with convictions and actions that might ultimately put our comfort on the line. This is a *war for the imagination,* in the words of Diane di Prima.

Because of this cognitive dissonance of the language—in word and in deed—we are called out as writers and performers and artists. We may all resound as magnificent groaning Cassandras here, prophets of doom but we might also reclaim our world. I think my patriotic coconspirator—Ammiel Alcalay—and I launched the Poetry Is News coalition because we were troubled by the on-again, off-again nature of the discourse. Curious about the disjunct. It wasn't about the content—that one needed to hear specifically "political" writing, "preaching to the converted" work, but about the contexts we found ourselves in that seemed so bizarre, "in denial" as it were.

That one could walk into readings, events and be in situations like a Modern Language Association convention or other academic setting where it was as if nothing strange were happening out there—in the body politic. A kind of eviscerated vocal/verbal lockdown. And that there wasn't enough mix with the rich poetic legacies of other cultures, the very cultures who were being subjected to such invasion, manipulation, and risk under u.s. hegemony and New World Order and Imperialism. What about the founding statement of the Project for the New American Century, that advocates threat and force for projecting u.s. influence anywhere in the world. This is not a hidden agenda.

Aren't we all on the same threatened planet together?

And it was also hard to take the hackneyed generalizing rhetoric heard at the various demonstrations mounting in the land. More identity politics, the same slogans, inflamed hectoring.

It seemed several months ago—and the tide is shifting as it were—there was a pandemic somnambulism in the art/culture world in this country as if a response to the infantilizing job the government and the media were doing on us. Never underestimate the intelligence of land. So we wanted to start a coalition that would empower others as well. Encourage the intervention. *Poetry is news that stays news. The eye altering alters all. Look to the little ones.* We can be legislators, antennae, guardians. And so we put together a program of engaged and extraordinary individuals who could report from the various "fronts"— from Afghanistan, Iraq, the occupied territories, to inner-city schools—just as they do on real TV! But with more compassion and perspicacity. And also those who might comment on where we are going—with their considerable wisdom, insight, interpretation and suggestions for action. Responses helped create the program today and we hope there will be more gatherings such as this one. You are all invited to create such events yourselves. Please do. Onward.

How to See through Poetry:
Myth Perception and History

LORENZO THOMAS
July 2, 2002

* * *

The title of my talk is "How to See through Poetry." Or rather "How to *See* through Poetry: Myth Perception and History." And that is essentially what I plan to talk about. Myth Perception and History and Poetry. I'd like to begin with the question that Kevin Killian addressed briefly on yesterday's panel. "When is poetry efficacious? When does it need to be superceded by action?" is the question that was asked. I think that we could even widen the discussion a bit by asking, "When is poetry or the word, itself, action?" So that we do not have two distinct categories of "When does poetry work?" and "When do we need to take action?" but, more directly, "When does the word itself become action?" And in order to approach that, I'll discuss three poems, and a speech that is considered to be one of the classics of American oratory.

The first poem is more than two thousand years old. A beautiful and shockingly violent poem.

By the Rivers of Babylon

By the rivers of Babylon, there we sat down, yea, we wept, when we remembered Zion.

We hanged our harps upon the willows in the midst thereof.

For there they that carried us away captive required of us a song; and they that wasted us required of us mirth, saying, Sing us one of the songs of Zion.

How shall we sing the LORD'S song in a strange land?

If I forget thee, O Jerusalem, let my right hand forget her cunning.

If I do not remember thee, let my tongue cleave to the roof of my mouth; if I prefer not Jerusalem above my chief joy.

Remember, O LORD, the children of Edom in the day of Jerusalem; who said, Raze it, raze it, even to the foundation thereof.

O daughter of Babylon, who art to be destroyed; happy shall he be, that rewardeth thee as thou hast served us.

Happy shall he be, that taketh and dasheth thy little ones against the stones.

Anyone know the story behind that poem? What it refers to? That's Psalm 137 and it dates to what is called the Babylonian captivity of the Israelites in exile. And that song became a favorite text of the African American preacher and congregations who found some way of relating the experience of the Hebrew children and Israelites, ancient Israelites, to their own plight as people exiled in a strange land. Of course, the first part of the poem, the longing for home and the loneliness of being among strangers who mock you as saying, "Oh yeah, you all got rhythm so, you know, do a little folk song for us" is tempered on the other side by the last part of the poem which is the part that says, "Happy is he who will take your babies and bash them on the stones."

You know, the first time I heard the poem and paid attention to what the words were, I said, *"That's* in the Bible?" Well, yes. Actually, if you think carefully about that particular Psalm—Psalm 137—though it is written for an ancient period of time it has great relevance to events at this very moment. What has been going on in what we call the Middle East is the continuation of the same situation that that poem refers to. If you believe in mythological reality, then the people who currently call themselves Israel are the same people that the song refers to. If you believe in modern political science, then you have a whole other kettle of fish to deal with. And then exiles on different sides there, you know, you can be exiled in your own land. If you watch the evening news, you'll see that some people are going into exile every moment of every day as the Israeli government builds walls, stretches barbed wire, and demolishes buildings in the West Bank and Gaza and the rest of it.

The whole idea of poetry that, indeed, speaks to events that might require action—as the question was posed yesterday—is not simply a matter of contemporary writings of this moment or the critical situations that we find ourselves in. I think we might find something very interesting if we look at poetry in any era, if you go and look back at it in its historical context—as you would, for example, examining Psalm 137 for what it meant when it was written—and then considering the use that it had 1,800 years later, thereabouts, when it falls into the hands of African slaves in America, and then noting whatever relevance it might have today. I point to Psalm 137 because that text runs through American literature as an often-quoted text for many, many reasons. Right? Well, one of the reasons it is an often-quoted text is that it's also a magnificent poem. A very beautiful and effective poem.

I also wanted to talk about a work of oratory. 1852 was the seventy-sixth anniversary of the founding of the United States of America, right? That is, considering the founding of this country in terms of the Declaration of Independence signed July 4, 1776, in Philadelphia. Here's a text written by

Thomas Jefferson, at the behest of the Congress. They said, "This is what we want to do, Tom. Go home, draft it. You can write. You're good with words. And bring it back tomorrow." And Jefferson did that and incorporated into it the basic idea that he phrased, "We hold these truths to be self-evident, that all men are created equal, that they are endowed by their Creator with certain unalienable Rights, that among these are Life, Liberty, and the pursuit of Happiness." And everybody went, "Yeah, that sounds good to me" and voted for it and signed it. Of course, signing it also immediately made them criminals because they were declaring that they were no longer legal loyal subjects of the King of England. I learned about that in elementary school and I imagine that many of you did, too.

Lately, recently, I thought about it. And thought about 1776. And I got a brand new shiny quarter the other day. On the back of it was the state of Virginia and they're fixing to celebrate the quatro-centennial? 1607-2007, right? *Quadricentennial?* Well, the United States is only just a bit over 225 years old. But if you're in Virginia, that's not what counts. What is being commemorated is Jamestown, Virginia. Jamestown Colony. So Virginia considers themselves to be the foundation of this place. And they date it from 1607 when the Englishmen landed in Jamestown.

So, I said, 1607. Jefferson and Washington are from Virginia. 1776. The British Colony of Virginia wasn't like a makeshift thing. It was more than a hundred years old! They were abdicating—if that's the word—from a country that was more than a hundred years old. It wasn't something that was put up three weeks ago and was still in process, you know? So, "Hey, it ain't goin' right, so we can just leave."

And nobody ever explained that to me in elementary school—why the King might have considered these people traitors. Native-born English citizens of Virginia, which had been a British colony for more than a century. Think about the boldness of their act and the boldness of their words. All based on this principle that "all men are created equal" and have rights that can't be *given* to you by anyone. That can't be taken away from you. That you cannot sell or lease out or time-share. Right? Interesting.

So, in 1852, seventy-six years after that, people are celebrating all over the country. The founding fathers won the war, the United States of America was established, successfully defended in 1812 and, now seventy-six years later, is a viable nation in the world. And people celebrate happily with fireworks and parades and everything. And they were all happy. Well, not everyone was happy.

In Rochester, New York, the Ladies Anti-Slavery Society organized a program for the fifth of July and they asked Frederick Douglass if he would give the speech. Frederick Douglass was a former slave. He was born in 1817 in Maryland. He escaped from slavery to New England and his first book written in 1845—*The Narrative of Frederick Douglass: An American Slave, Written by Himself*—explains his growing up; recounts his childhood and how he learns to read and write by bribing little white boys to teach him what they learned that day in school, and tells us how he eventually escapes to the North. His new Northern friends, the Abolitionists, send him to England and they raise money to buy his freedom, so that he's no longer a fugitive when he comes back from England. In the meantime, his book is published and he comes back from England not only no longer a fugitive, but actually a celebrity, right? The author of this auto-biography.

So, he was asked to speak and his text was, "What to the American Slave is the Fourth of July?" And it was a bold statement. It was a dramatic state-ment. Afterwards it was published as a pamphlet, which you can see he included in his second autobiography, *My Bondage and My Freedom,* which came out in 1855. He also wrote a third autobiography in 1893, two years before he died. Almost wrote as many as Maya Angelou. Douglass started his speech to the Ladies Anti-Slavery group in Rochester by saying, "With little experience and with less learning, I have been able to throw my thoughts hastily and imperfectly together." In fact, he spent three weeks working on this speech, composing a text that would become one of the landmarks of American oratory. He said that the continued existence of slavery in the "Land of the Free" made the Fourth of July celebrations "a sham." "Your boasted liberty," he said, becomes "an unholy license; your national greatness, swelling vanity; your sounds of rejoicing are empty and heartless; your denunciation of tyrants, brass-fronted impudence; your shouts of liberty and equality, hollow mockery." In the face of this irony—that the "Land of the Free" was the home of the slaves—the only scripture that Frederick Douglass could think of to quote on this momen-tous occasion—and you know, you always have to find some scripture to quote to decorate your speech—was "By the rivers of Babylon, where we sat down. Yes! We wept when we remembered Zion." And *that,* he thought, was the appropriate text. While his neighbors were celebrating the nation's independence, Douglass was constrained to be a witness to the crime of American slavery.

When I first encountered the excerpt of this speech included in *My Bondage and My Freedom,* I was amazed at the demeanor of Frederick Douglass in addressing the Fourth of July this way. And I was astonished that his indictment of American self-satisfaction seems so absolutely con-temporary. We live in a country that today goes around denouncing tyranny all over the globe. Turn the page in the newspaper and you can only wonder on what basis do we stand to tell folks in this part or that other part of the world what they should be doing. We tell them they should have democracy and then we try to oust elected leaders.

But the message that Frederick Douglass brought across in this speech that was even more impressive to me is his insistence that we must ever strive to live up to the principles upon which this nation is founded. A good deal of the speech is criticism, but the other part of the speech puts Frederick Douglass in a place where he differed from the other Abolitionists. There were leaders such as William Lloyd Garrison, who said Massachusetts ought to secede from the Union, that New York ought to secede from the Union. These were states that had abolished slavery decades ago! But states like Virginia and South Carolina still insisted on their "right" to have slaves and sell people. William Lloyd Garrison and his people reasoned that if the United States supported that so-called right, then they could not support the United States. They said, "We ought to secede from the Union."

They are saying this in the 1830s and '40s. Somebody also said, "When you put out ideas, you know, you don't know who might get the idea. And act on it." That's worth thinking about. There were also people like Henry Allen Garnett, right? And John B. Russworm. Free African Abolitionists. They advocated a different position. "Yeah, slavery should be abolished and all of us ought to get up outta here 'cause you all gonna make us lose our minds up in here. And there's nothing here for us after the treatment we've received for now two centuries here."

Of course, they didn't say it quite that way. But Douglass didn't stand with them either. Douglass insisted that the Declaration of Independence that Thomas Jefferson had written was the truth. That was *it!* For Douglass, the United States Constitution that follows the Declaration and is based upon it—with the ten Amendments that Thomas Jefferson's law professor George Mason drafted—are, in fact, the principles on which this country was founded, upon which we should act, and what we should live up to. And none of that has become obsolete.

This was a speech that I really liked. You can look at it yourself, by the way, because the whole thing is on the web at www.douglassarchives.org. In its entirety, it takes about ninety minutes. In 1852 people expected when they went to hear a lecture that it was going to last for ninety minutes or more. And if it didn't, they were going to say, "Give me my money back. I came out here to learn something. To be entertained. To have my intellect invigorated. To have a tear come to my eye and a pang in my heart and leave here with something to tell people."

I remember one time when I worked for the Juneteenth Blues Festival—and you remember Percy Mayfield, who did that wonderful "Please Send Me Someone to Love," right? You know, great song. And he says in that song something like, "The world is in turmoil and if there is one thing I can ask for from God, you know . . . God, I know you can't solve poverty and racism and religious hatred, but please send me someone to love." That's what it's about. Great song. One of the greatest songs ever written. Ray Charles does a beautiful recording of it but Percy Mayfield wrote it.

So, I said to my boss at the blues festival, "We've got to have Percy Mayfield on this show." But Percy Mayfield won't answer any mail. He doesn't answer phone calls. You can't get in touch with him. Nevertheless, I persisted with this and finally we got Percy Mayfield to say, "Yeah, OK, I'll appear." Signed the contract. Sent the plane tickets and everything. I gave him this great introduction and he came out on stage. Sharp, you know, like the old-time bluesmen. The band was *there* and they hit it. And he sang one of his great songs. You know he also wrote "Hit the Road, Jack" and a whole bunch of songs. So he sang one or two of his songs and then he did "Please Send Me Someone to Love." That was the third number. And the people went crazy, "Oh man, *Percy Mayfield!*" Plus, he's from Houston anyway, right? And then he bowed, said "Thank ya" and walked off. And the band said, "Huh?" And I said, "Oh shhh . . ." And my boss said, "Yeah?" Percy Mayfield had done what he had thought we had paid for. We wanted to hear him sing "Please Send Me Someone to Love" and he did that.

But in the 1850s if you went to a concert—well, they didn't have concerts in the 1850s, they had lectures and debates and speeches. And if you went to one and you spent your twelve-and-a-half cents. Right? One bit, right? Two bits is a quarter. You expected a show. You expected an evening. So, Frederick Douglass spoke for ninety minutes and it's a marvelous speech.

One year everybody on the staff at KPFT, the Pacifica station in Houston, decided that they were going to Willie Nelson's Fourth of July Picnic. Lawrence Jones had this jazz show at night and I was a volunteer and member of the local board. But we said, "Well, no man, we ain't into the Willie Nelson Cosmic Cowboys. We're soul brothers, man. We don't go for that kind of music. So, we're not going." So, they said, "Well, OK, you run the station." Lawrence and I decided that we would broadcast Frederick Douglass's Fourth of July speech, "What to the American Slave is the Fourth of July?" Now, we understood that nobody—even in Houston— would listen to a speech for ninety minutes. In Houston I listen to *All Things Considered* every day in my car, right? That takes two hours, but I find somewhere to drive to.

Anyway, we said, "Well, nobody's going to listen to this," you know. So we came up with the idea that we'll play music—sort of alternate music, speech, music, speech. We chose music that would be appropriate and we played Ian Hamilton Finlay, off of John Giorno's *Dial-a-Poem* recording, reciting "Why I Will Not Pay Taxes." Right? It was an antinuclear demonstration poem. But Finlay's reciting it in a British accent, right? So, you could imagine it was like John Adams or George Mason might have sounded when they said, "Why I will not pay taxes." And we played Gil Scott-Heron's "The Revolution Will Not Be Televised." And we played the reggae version of "By the Rivers of Babylon." [sings] "Where we sat down and there we wept."

We played the Beatles' "Revolution #9." Then we did some Frederick Douglass. We came back and we played a little "Search for New Land," right? Freddie Hubbard's beautiful music. Dinah Washington's "What a Difference a Day Makes." Well, people started calling up saying, "Wow, man! You're blowing my mind, man! This is so cool. This is beautiful, man. But who's this dude who keeps interrupting the music?" "What's all this freedom he's talking about?"

But in 1852, Frederick Douglass understood that it was his business to interrupt the music. That he could not have his neighbors parading up and down the street talking about how great this country is. How wonderful we are . . . while there were hundreds of thousands of people born into lifetime bondage and being sold in marketplaces like cattle. Or automobiles. Well, they didn't have any automobiles. In other words, Lawrence Jones and I felt that we had done precisely what we needed to do—to once again underscore the meaning of the words that Frederick Douglass had carefully chosen to celebrate the Declaration of Independence.

Much of Douglass's speech talks about the Fugitive Slave Act, which had been passed in 1850 and required that even in Free States, like Massachusetts, people who managed to escape slavery in the South, there in Massachusetts, would be apprehended by the sheriff, the police, and returned to the flesh peddlers. Douglass says this law has made the entire nation a slave market. The Fugitive Slave Act effectively superceded the will of the people of Massachusetts. John Greenleaf Whittier wrote a whole series of poems about the same thing. He was a Quaker and much of John Greenleaf Whittier's poetry is about the slave issue. He had some very eloquent poems, including one called "Massachusetts to Virginia," specifically denouncing the Fugitive Slave Act.

I want to say something here about the United States Constitution. Douglass says, "The u.s. Constitution inaugurated to form a more perfect union, establish justice, ensure domestic tranquility, provide for the common defense, promote the general welfare, and secure the blessings of liberty, could not well have been designed at the same time to maintain and perpetuate a system of raping and murder-like slavery, especially as not one word can be found in the Constitution to authorize such a belief." And that statement was directed at anybody who thought that the Constitution somehow endorsed slavery. Douglass insisted that it did no such thing and among the Black Abolitionists he remained adamant on that fact.

That position is also the basis of the Civil Rights Movement a century later in the 1950s. Kalamu ya Salaam has said that "the great American secret is that we have made America a democracy." And by "we," he means all those people who marched and picketed and sat in and wrote letters and did whatever else was needed during the Civil Rights struggle. He said, "Their efforts made the rhetoric of the American Revolution become closer to the reality of American life," which is what should have happened in 1789 in the first place. And it should have happened again, if it didn't happen then, in 1866 after the Civil War, but it took until 1964 and '65, the Civil Rights Act and the Voters Right Act, for what was written in 1776 to actually become feasible in Virginia and South Carolina and Mississippi, Oklahoma, etc., etc., right?

Kalamu ya Salaam says, "We forced America to be America." Again the idea of action and words are so closely entangled there that it becomes an interesting exercise to try to figure out. If, in fact, the words of the Declaration are empty or in fact the words of the Declaration are true. Let's think of it as, you know, how you can dehydrate soups and teas and whatnot and all you need to do is add a drop of water and it is reconstituted into its real substance. Maybe, that's what those words in those great documents are. You can still see the document—at least, they claim it's the document—if you go to Washington. This glass-encased treasure.

What becomes clear to me when I read or reread Douglass's speech is the struggle. He talks about the Jim Crow cars in his autobiography. How he's rousted out of his seat on the railroad and put in another car when he was traveling. Henry Highland Garnett, for example, the abolitionist preacher, black preacher, was taken out of his seat on a train going to the Canadian border. Nowhere near slavery. And when he protested he was beaten up and thrown off the train. 1850s and 1840s is when that happened, right?

But that's not what the struggle was about. It wasn't about drinking fountains or separate bathrooms or anything like that. The struggles, as now, have always been how to make the self-evident truths of the Declaration of Independence a permanent reality in our life and applicable to everyone. And that is what Douglass presented in his speech in Rochester in 1852.

Let's get to the other two poems. Fifty-one years after Douglass made this bold speech in Rochester Corinthian Hall, Paul Laurence Dunbar wrote a sonnet in praise of Frederick Douglass. Dunbar, of course, was the best-known black poet of the late 19th/early 20th century. He was very famous. He wrote hit songs for Broadway musicals. Of course, those songs were kind of racially offensive then and they are now, too. And he traveled around. He had the prominence of a rock star. He was a poet, though; and he was discovered, in a way, by Frederick Douglass.

At the 1892 World's Fair Columbian Exhibition in Chicago they didn't have a black pavilion or anything celebrating African Americans. But they did have a Haitian pavilion and Frederick Douglass, having been the United States consul to Haiti, was in charge of that when he heard about this young man. This young poet from Dayton, Ohio. Douglass met Dunbar and probably said, "This kid is bright" and he gave him a job working there at the World's Fair in his pavilion. Later he got Dunbar a job working for the Library of Congress in Washington DC, so he would have some time for writing some poems.

This poem is *not* one of Dunbar's better poems. But it's a painfully honest poem in registering the mood of despair that engulfed the black community in the wake of mob violence in Illinois, North Carolina, Indiana, and a rising number of lynchings all over the country.

Douglass

Ah, Douglass, we have fall'n on evil days,
Such days as thou, not even thou didst know,
When thee, the eyes of that harsh long ago
Saw, salient, at the cross of devious ways,
And all the country heard thee with amaze.
Not ended then, the passionate ebb and flow,
The awful tide that battled to and fro;
We ride amid a tempest of dispraise.
Now, when the waves of swift dissension swarm,
And Honour, the strong pilot, lieth stark,
Oh, for thy voice high-sounding o'er the storm,
For thy strong arm to guide the shivering bark,
The blast-defying power of thy form,
To give us comfort through the lonely dark.

Now that's a terrible poem. "The country heard thee with amaze . . . ment." Yes? But that doesn't rhyme. Right? It is my opinion that the alarm that Dunbar the citizen felt overwhelmed the poet and undermined the poem. What he wants to say has to fight its way through clichés and fake Shakespearean language. But what he's talking about is that as the era of racial segregation began to be put in place, it was enforced by the gun, the local law, the rope, and the torch. So, the poem is bad because it is not a "tempest of dispraise" that Black America is facing. It's the likely possibility of being murdered for believing that the Declaration of Independence applies to you. Somehow, Dunbar was not able to put that in his sonnet.

He was able to put it in an op/ed article for the *New York Times* published the same year as that sonnet, July 1903. The essay was called "The Fourth of July and Race Outrages." It begins "Bellville, Wilmington, Evansville, the Fourth of July and Kishinev. A curious combination." Now, Kishinev was the city in Russia, Moldova, where there was a pogrom in 1903. A slaughter of the Jewish residents of the town reached the headlines around the world. There is, by the way, a great poem about that by Chaim Nachman Bialik who was a year younger than Dunbar. He was born in 1873. Dunbar died in 1906 after spending time in Denver where he thought the high thin air would cure his tuberculosis. Chaim Nachman Bialik eventually retired to Tel-Aviv, Palestine, his promised land, where he lived till 1934. There is a paragraph about him in the *Princeton Encyclopedia of Poetry and Poetics,* but not too much. But Bialik wrote about Kishinev in a magnificent poem. He wrote in Hebrew.

Anyway, the *New York Times* piece that Dunbar wrote says, "Bellville, Wilmington, Evansville, the Fourth of July and Kishinev. A curious combination and yet one replete with a ghastly humor. Sitting with closed lips over our own bloody deeds, we accomplished a fine irony to a protest to Russia." It reminds me of recent news broadcasts. "Contemplating with placid eyes of destruction of all the Declaration of Independence and the Constitution stood for, we celebrate the thing, which our own action proclaims we do not believe in."

He goes on later in the essay to talk about those "who sit silent in their closed rooms and hear us from afar the dinner of joy comes muffled to their ears as on some later day their children and their children's sons shall hear a nation's cry for supper in her need. Aye, there be some, who on this festive day, kneel in their private closets and with hands appraised and bleeding hearts cry out to God. If there still lives a God. How long, oh God? How long?"

It's an impressive piece of writing and it says what the poem could not say. It says, How dare you celebrate freedom in the United States when every law and every mob is taking away the citizenship of the black people who became citizens under the 13th and 14th Amendments? As you know, it takes until the 1950s and 1964 and '65 for us to get back to where we were supposed to be. But Dunbar is writing in 1903. Douglass had just died in 1893 and what Dunbar is saying when he writes that poem is, essentially, Frederick Douglass spoke the truth in 1852 and we have no one here to say it now.

POETICS AND POLITICS IN ACTION   347

And then it dawns upon him: "Oh yeah, the *New York Times*." What he could not do in the sonnet Dunbar did by finding the words for the *New York Times* op/ed page that would express the extreme crisis that the country was in at that moment.

Here's the third poem and the last one. By the way, that essay and the 1903 poem are in the *Norton Anthology of African American Literature*, which is in your library. Paul Laurence Dunbar. This week will be the 150th anniversary of Frederick Douglass's Fourth of July or Fifth of July Rochester speech. It's a century ago, minus one year, when Dunbar wrote his poem for Douglass and his *New York Times* essay.

It was clear in 1903 that the Fugitive Slave Act—Douglass's primary concern—was irrelevant, but so was the promise of Reconstruction, which had been spoiled by local ordinances and the United States Supreme Court. For Dunbar, it wasn't a question of singing in a strange land. Born in Ohio in 1872, Dunbar was a native-born American citizen, he was at the top of his high school class, and could've been the President of the United States—had black people been able to vote, maybe.

Now, at the beginning of the 21st century in a nation at war, I have heard people speak seriously about the possibility that Dr. Condoleeza Rice might become in this new millennium the first woman President of the United States. You know who Dr. Rice is? She is an African-American political scientist and head of the National Security Council.

I have also heard people seriously propose that in the interest of national security, now that we are a nation at war, we should all think about whether or not we can afford the Bill of Rights.

So, let me end here as Frederick Douglass and the great orators of the past have always ended by reciting a poem. This one was written in 1962. Robert Hayden wrote with passion and with a timely optimism. This poem is also a sonnet, but a 1962 type sonnet. Doesn't rhyme.

Frederick Douglass

When it is finally ours, this freedom, this liberty, this beautiful
and terrible thing, needful to man as air,
usable as earth; when it belongs at last to all,
when it is truly instinct, brain matter, diastole, systole,
reflex action; when it is finally won; when it is more
than the gaudy mumbo jumbo of politicians:
this man, this Douglass, this former slave, this Negro
beaten to his knees, exiled, visioning a world
where none is lonely, none hunted, alien,
this man, superb in love and logic, this man

shall be remembered. Oh, not with statues' rhetoric,
not with legends and poems and wreaths of bronze alone,
but with the lives grown out of his life, the lives
fleshing his dream of the beautiful, needful thing.

We have time for some questions or comments.

ALEXANDRA HIDALGO: I was wondering how did people react to Douglass's speech in 1852 when he gave it? What did his audience do?

LT: Well, the audience he spoke to originally, the Ladies Anti-Slavery Society, were delighted to hear what he was saying because they too wanted to mobilize people against the Fugitive Slave Act. Not all of his fellow Abolitionists were delighted with it because, again, many of them were of the opinion that the Constitution and the nation itself was flawed. And Douglass spends a good deal of time in his speech praising the founding fathers. Pointing out that he says rather sarcastically George Washington couldn't die until he freed his slaves, which he left in his will. You know: "When I'm dead and my wife is dead, then all these people should have their freedom."

Well, I liked the way that Douglass put it. There was a lot of controversy about people who agreed that slavery was wrong but did not agree that the United States was not a viable and living thing. And I think that you still find such controversy now. Would you agree? That there are people who don't think that the 1776 principles are up to date with the 21st century?

JENNIFER FOERSTER: Yeah, that's what I wanted to talk about. I just wanted to add that with poetry or with things that are spoken really well, like this speech, I find ways to relate to it because I think we all do. And that's where my question comes in about my experience, for example, "What is the Fourth of July to the Native American?" and this is just a larger question of our responsibilities in our writing and our representation. It was striking me when I read this that all these things are connected that are happening to peoples. At the time I was looking at the end of his speech. And he said, talking about the hypocrisy, he said, "A thin veil to cover up crimes that would disgrace a nation of savages." Now, I don't know what context he's writing that in at the time—"a nation of savages." Hopefully, he was not referring to the Native Americans with the savage, but at the time that's what was happening, of course. So, I was reading and thinking that's ironic that when I read this speech I can really relate to it thinking that, at exactly the time that this celebration was happening, members of my family were, you know, their houses were burned down and they were going to Oklahoma. So, all of this was happening throughout the country at the time that the Independence was being celebrated, so I can relate to what he's talking about. As probably we all can in our own ways. And yet at the same time, "A thin veil to cover up crimes which would disgrace . . ." as if this is not actually happening whether or not he was aware of what was happening to other peoples at this time. And whether or not that was his responsibility. This is just a question that I'm putting out mostly for myself. All of these things are related. And in our poetries, whether I'm even intending it or not, I'm just focusing on the song. And if it carries a message, I mean, I don't see how the politics can be separated from it. So, it's my responsibility to just speak what's true for me and that can come from all sorts of different political standpoints and that can't be stereotyped either. But what is our responsibility as poets or as artists or as anyone to also be attuned to all those things that are happening simultaneously if you're given the microphone and you're standing in a group of people? And you have that opportunity to bring that awareness out?

LT: I think your reading is perfectly accurate. The term "savages," as he uses it there, would have had the resonance with his audience as a reference to the Native Americans. The Anti-Slavery and Temperance evenings paralleled the Lyceum Movement, which starts in the 1820s all across the country in town halls and church auditoriums. People go out on the evenings for speeches. Some of the topics in the 1830s and '40s were, for example, one topic I recall was "Is it fair for a civilized nation to dispossess a savage nation?" On the other hand, there's another topic of the Lyceum's, "Which is the group that contributes most to progress: the male or the female?" And this was a debate. Of course, there were no women on the platform for that particular program, so, you wonder a little about that. The limitations people have. Certainly, people like Douglass—Douglass was also involved in the Suffrage Movement for women. That was, in his view, the same as the Abolition movement and once slavery was abolished at the end of the Civil War, Douglass then put all his energy into Suffrage for women. And so all of these things. And I'm looking now at the word, *poetry,* beyond just genre such as a sonnet. Douglass, too, when Douglass stands on the platform and presents this magnificent oration. That's the word I'm talking about. The poetic word. Yes, you must start where you are, so Douglass starts by saying quite clearly, "I am a slave. I escaped from slavery and now I'm a free man because I have escaped from the slave territory. But my friends had to come with the American money to pay this guy, so I'm legal. But yes, I start from there, but then I can talk about the injustices that are residual among other people because I know something about it."

So, if I may continue to put words in their mouths, Dunbar says: "Yes, I'm outraged by Wilmington, North Carolina, where the government puts into motion forces that eventually burn down the entire black community in their city." But Kishinev in Russia is the same thing to Dunbar and he sees it's the same thing. And he *has* to say in the *New York Times,* "Yeah, Indiana, Illinois, North Carolina, and Kishinev—and now the Fourth of July we're celebrating?" Think! Because it moves further than just you or just your own situation. And there, I think, is when the word becomes powerful. If it's just my situation, I might plead eloquently for myself, but the true power of the word would be when it can then expand.

JF: Yeah, and I think it's a tricky question for all of us. I know for me I can only speak from where I stand. If I hear someone else not from where they stand, but from an idea of something that they haven't experienced then that doesn't reach as far.

LT: But I thank you for bringing up that point because Douglass is making a rhetorical gesture that everyone in his audience would have understood. He is saying, in effect, "We claim that we are superior to a nation of savages, you know what I mean? Now, let's examine our own behavior." Right. What does the word "savage" really mean? You see what I'm talking about?

JF: And I'm reading this essay. I'm just so curious in the context that was given if it was even taken that far.

LT: It was.

JF: How could it have been?

LT: All right, this is what I'm saying. This is how it could have been. The same well-meaning people who saw advertised, "Who contributes most to progress: the male or the female?" apparently didn't see anything wrong with not engaging a woman to be included in the debate. We have limitations even when we are meaning well. And sometimes people actually see them and say, "Oh, wait a minute, we can't do that." Sometimes you wonder, "How could they miss that?" It's not as if there weren't women able to speak. There were. You know what I'm saying? But somebody dropped the ball somewhere along that way and apparently nobody else noticed this. So, if we grasp what Douglass is saying here . . . he used a coded word. A *charged* word that his audience would certainly have related to and so that's one more thing for them to think about as they get up and go home. And he knows he's planting that next seed.

JF: Yeah, it strikes me that communication is really powerful, every word.

LT: Thank you for bringing that up.

QUESTION: Thank you so much for bringing Frederick Douglass into this hall. You mention in your talk that Douglass believed about the founding documents of this country that we have to breathe new meaning into them.

LT: Or merely exist, live up to them.

Q: Right, right. This is an ongoing dilemma for me and I want to know where you stand. Do you see yourself more with Douglass? The reason it's a dilemma for me is that while I see it in a pragmatic way, that it's really important to assert that. To be able to talk about rights in the context of America and the nation. But then, so much of political rants in the contemporary moment, to me, needs to get beyond the rhetoric of the nation. So, I'm just curious where you stand and how do you see reconciling that tension. You know, there's American exceptionalism that is like, "Only in America could all these people come together and live together." As a daughter of immigrants, my parents believed that to a certain degree. A lot of immigrants believe that. It's a tension for me because I see behind that and part of what Jennifer was saying in terms of the necessity for American nationalist myth to have created this "nation of savages." Basically, they had to sort of empty out the landscape of who was living here. And so, it's a part of that driving force of "the new" and I feel that it's still really powerful in what's driving us.

LT: I think I understand. I am an immigrant, too, and when I was in sixth grade, I had to go see a judge in Brooklyn and he asked me, "Do you fully understand what you're getting yourself into?" And I said, "Yes." And I believed it. I believed all that stuff, right? I also find it very troubling when in the wake of September 11th I listened to a talk show on the radio and someone says, "What we need is an I.D. card for everybody. One color for the citizens, one color for the naturalized citizens, and one color for the aliens." And I said, "Well, I thought I *was* a citizen. That's what I thought I was raising my hand for, you know. I didn't think I got another color now." I also find it troubling that we have to go all the way to the Supreme Court over and over again before somebody decides that it is not fair to execute imbeciles. Every day I find some reason to be very upset. What counters that is my belief that those founding principles are, in fact, sound. And that what we're supposed to be doing is making sure that we do, in fact, follow those principles. And when we find that our course is veering away from it that somehow we marshal the energy or get the help to bring it back into line. But right now, we have a Justice Department that is attempting to do now what the Justice Department did in the beginning of the 20th century and that is to trample upon the First Amendment under the guise of National Security. That's what A. Mitchell Palmer did under Woodrow

Wilson and that's what I'm afraid Attorney General John Ashcroft seems to be wanting to do when he starts talking about sending people to trials that will be held in secret without any evidence being presented. That, to me, is the most frightening thing I've ever heard. And I can't understand how a lawyer, Senator, Attorney General . . .

So yeah, I agree with you very much. I think the principles have to be defended with all the energy that we have because even well-meaning people can lose sight of what this is supposed to be about.

ANNE WALDMAN: Maybe you can comment on the last Presidential election and whether you felt that was a legitimate election that then had to go to the Supreme Court and so on. I went to DC with poets trying to make poetry action in some way. We went to support a lot of the African American community coming from all over the East Coast mainly and Florida, and were impressed with the range of speeches that day, feeling that people had actually been dissed in that election. So, could you just comment on that—on how to turn that around.

LT: Yeah, I wonder if *any* of our elections are legitimate when we have . . . compared to a country like Switzerland where you have ninety percent of people voting in everything. We have, what? Twenty percent of the people voting in off-year elections sometimes. We have a brand-new stadium in Houston that was voted on a referendum in an off-year election and they said fifty-one percent of the people voted *for* the stadium. It's there now. They're actually playing in it. It's now called "Minute Maid Park." Used to be Enron Field.

I don't think that everything really depends on the business of adding computer machines as opposed to the ones they have in New York with the little latches, or the ones you have in Texas where there is the little pin that you stick in the ballot card . . .

AW: Are they going to make a difference?

LT: That's not the point. The point is either people are going to say that they are into the *issues* or they are into the personalities and, "Well, I like his hairdo." Otherwise, it doesn't matter what the figures are or who tabulates them because the public is not into making these decisions. Someone somewhere else in this system is doing it. And in this last case, the 2000 election was the most blatant example of the people having abdicated their own power . . . and those who tried to express it were stymied by political forces. Shenanigans that have gone on since the 19th century, but, apparently, not enough public pressure to shout it down. And so that's another aspect of it too. That's the other aspect of words in action, right? If there's enough hue and cry, things change. The last two administrations the President would always . . . well, the last three or four! The President would announce something. Public reaction would come back positive and they'd do it. Public reaction came back, "Hey, what?!" "Well, the President misspoke." And that's what happens.

If everybody says, you know . . . Right now in Houston they said, "Well, because you have so much pollution here, the law saying that the speed limit goes back to seventy doesn't apply to you all. And so we're taking down all the seventy signs and we're putting back up all the fifty-five signs." Yeah, right! Well, somehow they made a deal with the state of Texas and the EPA and they figured out they could shut down a factory or two and in Houston we'll go back to seventy miles an hour. Because it was clear that it was unenforceable. The police would make more money, $20,000 a month more, for writing tickets, but the public wasn't going for it. So they found a way, politely, for everybody to save face. EPA, state of Texas, city of Houston, police department. It's going back to seventy because that's what the people want. Apparently though, people are not as much interested in who's in the White House.

Gnosis &
Aesthetics

★ ★ ★ ★ ★ ★

★ ★ ★ ★ ★ ★

Courting the Muse

ROBERT HUNTER
November 1992

FREEDOM AND THE METAPHOR OF FAME

We don't know what we want. We want to want something, and believe to the sky we really want this want fulfilled. We fill our bellies, our veins, our lungs, and our minds only to find we still touch on emptiness. I'm going to argue for the value of this emptiness because I believe it to be our first and last freedom, and all freedom between.

Nine out of ten and possibly more would rather be flayed than forced to be free. But we all get sentimental about it sometimes, and sometimes we write about it. If the lines don't cover the whole page and we manage to get to the point with less reason than rhyme, we call it poetry. Poetry maintains that once we were free and so shall we be again: in the so-called eternal moment, perhaps, that fictitious creation of language known as *present time.* But time itself is a trick of perception, is it not? We know about that by now. So how shall we do the trick within a trick? Can it be done?

Well I think it could be done. But I think we also expect too much of it and therefore tend to miss what it is when it actually presents. Freedom is a small thing. Lack of freedom would seem to be the real problem, not some overwhelming presence of it. The balance point, where freedom would seem to be just possible though unmanifest . . . that may be the target worth sharpening our pencils to pierce.

Of course, these are just words, but this is a lecture after all, something to bind and create time. Any model would be a metaphor, I won't say *only* a metaphor, but a metaphor nevertheless . . . but it's a pleasant pond to skate around and the idea of motion is not that distant from mobility itself. In the beginning was nonspecific continuity and in the meantime there is poetry.

Wanting is emptiness. The luster of what we want is a fiction of hunger. *Fame* is an example that falls easily to hand. We think we want fame only to discover fame annuls life and fruitful change according to its degree, wanting only completeness to approximate death.

Nevertheless, once tasted, we seek greater or more comprehensive fame, perhaps to find out why whatever renown we manage to accumulate fails to fulfill those childhood fantasies of receiving utter and unconditional admiration from people we don't even know. A good splattering of this gilded vomit arouses in us contempt for the reality of such fantastical and treacherous transference. Yet the wanting remains even as we touch the emptiness at the metaphoric center.

Those with vast quantities of dubious recognition conceive a lust for a higher quality of renown, unable to understand that fame itself is simply a pernicious metaphoric condition. They think maybe they just need a different brand. Those with more modest portions of arguably respectable fame come to crave broader areas of acknowledgment. It is analogous to the psychological disturbance in which the sufferer feels compelled to devour parts of his own body.

The newly famous are like the newly rich who do not yet understand what money can and cannot buy. Identity itself undergoes a sea change. Fame has ideas and designs of its own concerning who may wear it and under what conditions. None wear it lightly, none wear it unchanged. None wear it unscathed. Very few set it aside willingly nor fail to set too great a store by it. Those with the greatest fame are at long last famous simply for being famous. What else they are famous for becomes largely irrelevant. They are walking metaphors for success.

Living life under the auspices of the trope of fame depletes the capacity for joy—it distances the bearer from any but over-conditioned human contact, making of one an object in the eyes of others, inciting envy and undertones of resentment, a state only a psychotic would embrace knowingly. The only thing worse than gaining it is losing it after it has done its irreversible damage.

If one were to pursue the path of the poet, it were better to avoid the occasion of fame and rest content with the metaphor as it engages the poem instead of becoming one yourself. Unfortunately, this stance is one that the Muse finds so attractive it can hardly resist visiting you—and whom the Muse frequents can hardly avoid the laurel which attracts recognition. Besides, which of us is so holy as to abjure appreciation for our efforts? I doubt that many write poetry these days simply to squirrel it away in little packets wrapped in ribbon as did Emily Dickinson . . . and even she made some token effort to publish, much as the desire scandalized her. Poetry is, after all, a communicating art.

There is, however, a sly way both to gain fame and continue to grow as an artist and a human soul, which is one and the same thing: to court the Muse with diligence and, once won, never to forsake it.

> Bring me my Bow of burning gold:
> Bring me my Arrows of desire:
> Bring me my Spear: O clouds unfold!
> Bring me my Chariot of fire!
>
> —BLAKE, from *Milton*

THE TROPE OF DARKNESS

I thought I'd talk about the motivating power of the ego in the act of erotic excitation of the mind as articulated by the tongue. What may be called the Muse.

On a less criminal level, it is a love affair with the mystery of articulation itself I want to address—as well as touching upon the crisis to which the art of words eventually leads the practitioner—and the nature of the words that will resolve the crisis if chosen in a decisive act of freedom and spontaneous design.

I intend to deconstruct a particular trope which I assert is not a trope at all, though it masquerades as one. A trope is like a crochet stitch, a method of making a sweater out of a ball of yarn. The tropes are legion: image and metaphor, simile, comparison and contrast, flavor of address such as irony, which is thought by many to be a leading trope; enthusiasm, alarm, transcendence, Orphic descent, opulence, decadence, sensuality, and desire, the part standing for the whole or the whole standing for the part. To name but a handful . . . in short, whatever turns a handful of nouns, verbs, adjectives, and what have you into shape and texture of thought or description, coherent or otherwise. A trope literally means a turning—a stance, an approach. Just to get that straight before we commence. You'll notice I've used the trope of the plural pronoun "we" to indicate community of endeavor here. It could be misleading. On to my thesis.

Poetry is not a path of doubt. Though doubt is its sign and signet, even the mangled tropes of hell themselves manage to twist and transform to paradoxical extremities of affirmation in the service of the Muse if only because doubt arrests action. Without action, time collapses. Lives are lost rather than spent. There is no specific trope of doubt as such, only of failure to affirm which is a state of static absence portending no poem at all. As black is the absence of color, doubt is the absence of trope.

There, I've just stated something that has not, to my knowledge, been said before; something that makes me understandably nervous to articulate, since it would seem that, were it consistent and palpably apprehensible, someone would have noticed and said it before. So where do I get off saying something quite as categorical as "doubt is the absence of trope?"

I'll tell you where I get off. The reason it hasn't been said before is because it partakes of a category not heretofore isolated. Granted such a category, the statement that *doubt is the absence of trope* is not such a farfetched thing to assert. But if you admit the statement, you must also admit the hypothetical category, of which it is a representative remark, into the conscious light of day. In asking you to swallow a fly, the spider, the bird, the cat, dog, goat and horse are waiting anxiously in the wings, each primed to swallow the other.

What I choose to say in such a manner, what could be called the critical stance (a trope in itself) is as true as, and no truer than, my ability to isolate and expound it within the framework I build for myself from materials of my choosing for the specific purpose of discovery and exposition. Should you wish to refute my proposition, you must choose a framework of your own to embody your challenge and between us we would generate dialogue. I trust it would not be merely the accepted say-so of someone else that would motivate you, but a recognition, by your own lights of the probable error or shortcoming of my assertion. This would be very fine. This would be very fine indeed. It's what a critical stance is for. Stir things up; get the dialogue going. Invent new ways to look at things. It would be a state of dynamism engaging minds in poetic discourse, with subsidiary discoveries popping up all over the place. That's what it's all about, so far as I know. Why we came here and what we may take with us when we go. Broader, dare I say it, horizons. Enhanced capability. New scales for new music and new tropes for rhyme.

Allow me your suspended disbelief and I will tell you the secret of squeezing water from air with the aid of a stone at the conclusion of this monologue. Then we'll question some of what was said and you can point out where I'm wrong or ill-advised . . . and I'll defend my point of view or attempt to batter yours into submission. Or maybe we'll just agree to disagree. That is the format of these things. But given one chance in life to say something truly worthwhile at long last, what would *you* say? This is a serious try to answer that question.

Muse of the Lectern
guide me to phrases
revealing the tricks of trope;
to formulations that justify
excess of words to hide
the poverty of language.
Blow horns in the silent places,
melodious invention
heralding each luxuriant
insight into the what
and wherefore of creation.
Inform irony with pathos
and logic with alarm;
hold nothing from my reach
that's fitting to my arm.
Let there be a speech such
as fathers give when

sons go off to war, or as
mothers give to daughters
behind closed doors
concerning things not meant
for the tender ears of men.
Let poetry and prose stay
their ancient rivalry and
approach with solemn spirit
and irreverent humor
the bright unspoken mystery:
how any may communicate
the size and scope of anything
that others have not seen
and let them see and taste of it
as though it were their own.

TO SEE IS TO BELIEVE

We never see the same red wheelbarrow twice, but one glance can be
enough to split the subject/object complex down the middle. What's well
seen is seen forever. Though absent, it is not dead. This does not mean it is
alive: that would presume too much in the name of art, as artists are
known to do, requiring yards of credibility to justify inches of achievement. It is enough that the rare act of relatively unconditioned seeing is
marked by a brief notation and left to shine among moss-backed lines like
a crown jewel of discrimination.

True service, which is to say *useful* service, rearranges the ground of
definition against the dominant perceptions of one's own culture and
contemporaries. Specifically against these. What they believe is to be dis-
mantled and the timber burned. Nothing new is to be made of the old
parts, regardless of the quality of materials.

It is particularly rewarding to offend and annoy your own contemporaries, speaking less of individuals than of movements and tendencies.
Anything more than one person unequivocally subscribes to can be called
a movement or a tendency. Rejection of this creature comfort calls for
equal measures of insolence and faith.

It must be admitted that some degree of consensus is harmless and not
unpleasant, but too much out and out agreement among contemporaries
diminishes the ability to make individual truth and make it stick. This is
the only kind that actually takes root and grows into edible fruits for the
soul. Artistic truth resides in the edified presumption of the individual; in
the act of invention of and for the moment; in the actual creation of the
moment, which otherwise cannot be said to truly exist, no more than the

past and glimmers of the future which likewise have no existence outside the crucible of spontaneous creation. All truth deemed self-evident above and beyond the witness of a specific individual makes mock of the Muse who is fluid, capable of assuming any shape and stance inside, outside, and tangential to eternity, whatever or whoever that is.

It might be surmised I am advocating anarchy, but that is an old term for old ideas. I am advocating a keen awareness of the shifting lights of unguarded perception; the transorbital leukotomy of established rhetoric and the refusal to willingly aid in the establishment of a new one. I am talking poetics, not politics. There are too many posters on the kiosk for events already closed. They make it difficult to see what is scheduled for the days to come.

Were I a teacher able to teach what I believe, I would take pains not to teach others to believe as I do. I hope I could cheerfully accept the opposite of what I'm maintaining and see no contradiction. I have my heart set on doing so as a sort of personal notion of salvation. Some misguided soul may wish to believe it too, but that would be a mistake. Better to keep your own counsel and confront such issues in your own terms by your own lights. The test question for me is: does it summon the Muse? If so, all is well—and all manner of things were well if that were well.

No one could ever manipulate my peculiar set of beliefs as well as I. So why preach it at all? Only to illustrate the mechanics of belief. To provide a reference point and a well-marked target. It is a public service. Self-definition is self-sacrifice, but it is not suicidal if it sets greater store by belief itself than by the shifting contents of what is accessible to be believed at any given point in the process of continuous transformation. One sets aside the partial error of solipsism in such a situation by refusing to seriously consider that others are somehow less real than one's own self, such as it is. There is, I think, a clue here for the art of serious trans-structural criticism. A foundation of inklings. Does it facilitate or becloud the Muse?

What is it speaks when something speaks clearly? Why is a mouse when it spins? Who put the ram in the ramalamading? Answers are amusing but I think there can be no teaching of the subject, only object lessons: the actual poem of the poet. Meat, muscle, and movement.

Poetry is the antagonist of common sense. To name and defame are one and the same for the Muse-attentive poet who praises only what lies beneath the name, honoring it with the eyes of love. Plato correctly understood there could be no place for poets in the perfected Republic. Poetry plows the sea and sails on city streets. It is the enemy of dominant thought; is, in point of romantic fact, the impulse to thought innocent of thought's by-products. It does not build so much as clears ground where building might occur, visiting destruction upon whoever lays personal claim to ground consecrated to Minerva. That space must be kept unencumbered. What can be named must be changed and only what is beyond naming let stand in its place. Poetry does not play the game. Whatever the game, poetry does not play it. Whatever personal or political hell words conspire to provide, poetry is not to blame. It is rather the pure use of language for the love of words. The flamboyant gesture of articulated breath.

A generation of poets is informed by a common ideal, or they would not be a generation of poets but an aggregate of onanists holding nothing in common over which to differ. The differing is all-important, but the conception from which departure is made or exception taken must be clearly stated. Let me propose an example: *In this time of crisis, poetry must lever the world of thought away from rhetoric by the use of rhetoric.*

That would be a happy way to go, though a lot of brain power would need to be expended defining what it means lest it succumb to its own paradoxicality. All propositions regarding language must prove paradoxical, though a self-referential language attempting to sidestep such paradox is even now being attempted in the field of linguistics, that conglomerate of quiet rabble rousers who seek to deny the sole preeminence of poetry in the service of the word.

If you break down a word, you have a broken word. It is not meanings poetry is concerned with, nor even so much relationships. It is rather more properly concerned with the athletic ability of words in concert to overstep assigned meanings and touch eternity. What cannot be defined can nevertheless be clearly seen, with the eyes of love and in no other way, outside the transformations of the so-called moment—and spoken of in tropes and signs, in signal codes relating to a common presence, the perplexion of the personal, the Yucatán of what it is to be, the Cape Horn of consciousness.

No ideal is the highest; it must evolve or the earth would cease its trope of spinning and the sun go dark. It is a hateful fact that the hard-won paradigm of the master maker is required to shift at the very moment of its greatest creative tension and possibility, but entropy insists. The moment a masterpiece is created, the art that created it is dead. It has said all it has to say and another art must intervene, though both arts bear the name of poetry. The field becomes more comprehensive. Elder poets decline before the growing crush of fresh iconoclasts. Disarmed by honor, the world's acknowledgment of their sad and venial merit is their downfall.

Total commitment to the new is a prime necessity for the living trajectory of art, and it is lamentably true that the elders cannot fully partake of any new dispensation since they are honor-bound to hold true to the ideal that first gave them its decisive and tangible light, which of course no longer applies. We have learned from them all they have to teach and move on advised. It is the very essence of their vision and for them it must remain true and central. Let us hope, even choose to believe, that the Muse provides some private compensation within the soul of the rebel poet who tries to perform faithfully poetry's major task: to record and to remain as true as might be possible to received personal vision, at whatever cost, regardless of the vagaries of critical recognition or public indifference. It says that it does, but can we believe it? Exhort! Exhort! Incite to rebelliousness. In some circumstances peace is not a good thing.

Others do well to deny what is past, however pitiably the blood of the poet calls from the slippery pavement, reject and move on in search of their own burial ground. Nor must the brave new poets protest too much when they are confounded at the height of their own powers by an emergent point of view which decisively excludes them from contemporary consideration. All glory is dawning; sunsets are redundant. And noontide is terminally innocent of the ecstasis of extremities.

On a practical level, we set out to do something, but what can we do? We can pay attention. We can inspect with the attitude of rebellion appropriate to our time and so develop a clear and present ideal of our own. We are currently in the throes of Ideal formation. The old has been disavowed and the new is not yet made apparent. It is, after all, a creation, not a discovery, though it will seem to be a discovery by the time it is evident to all. At that point the paradigm will shift again. Simple as that.

Will your poetry be better than ours? Almost certainly not, nor very much worse. But it will have the benefit of innocence which an older poet may not profess unless that poet is a liar or an unteachable fool. Innocence tells all, what whiter heads know better to conceal. The confessions of elders have all the effulgence of faded flowers pressed in musty books. Nevertheless, if their communion with the Muse remains sweet to them, they have the better part of the bargain and can leave the sordid slopes of incipient fame to those with wind and will to climb them.

THE POETIC IMPULSE

The first song ever sung, *sleep, baby, sleep,* seeded all song to come. Out of the seeds of lullaby came poetry. Poetry cannot return to the seed, though seed may come of it which is also song. Minerva collected the fruits of poetry and preserved them in structures of rhyme, which became her body, the flesh of the Muse. This is how it happened, though it happened so long ago the details are forgotten.

The Muse confers power to seduce others to believe as the poet believes. The poet becomes a believer by believing in the power of belief.

The spells and tropes reveal a common core. What the poet believes in is the Muse.

The Muse of Poetry is different from the Muse of Song, which is primordial. Poetry's Muse is young and seductive—seduces others to believe as the poet believes with its hints of immortality. By contrast, the Muse of Song peers through curtains of mortality and is consequently melancholy, a necessary attribute of all truly sublime beauty. Poetry is less concerned with beauty than with truth. I don't take issue with Keats here, his formulation was appropriate to his context, but nothing in this domain must be allowed to remain static and unquestioned.

Poetry has greater powers of persuasion than the common sense of speech due to breath and cadence. The breath of the Muse. The rhythms of the flesh of Minerva. When it sings of Arms and of Men all we really know of history, how it felt, is truly conveyed.

All grounds, exact or inexact, are plunder for poetry, our common core expressed in personality. There is no poem without its person, named or not. One of the main strategies of poetry is to disguise this. Not to deny, but to disguise. A preliminary slight of hand demonstrating the possible conditions of actual magic. No magician truly dematerializes, but invisibility is witnessed nevertheless by those who watch and see no one where someone in fact stands.

Abstraction obscures the poet's persona. The more the poet vanishes, the more the poem is permeated by another presence which is the poet writ large. In this state, things come out of words not put there by design alone. They come out from between the words of their own accord and are shapely.

There is nothing to distinguish the operation from other forms of magic but the presence of a poem. This is an entire difference. Magic disappears but poetry endures. No poem is lost and none goes unwritten. The poem that never was never could have been. The poem of which there is no such poem remains only to be written. Any could write it if dream provided pen and paper.

The poetic impulse, being mad, is radically different from the strictly sane impulse. Sanity desires to impose order over chaos by enforcing structured belief. Poetic desire examines, discards, or rearranges belief to allow breathing room for the organisms of chaos, thereby enriching and redefining notions of sanity. The reward of truly eventful poetry is ostracism from the society of the sane, an uneventful place good for funding grants and little else.

The problem is how to get from A to B by way of words to produce something worthwhile, avoiding stylistic blind alleys. When styles change, mere mannerism becomes painfully evident. Thus it is written that should one encounter the Buddha by the side of the road, one should kill him. This applies to Buddhas of the clouds and sky as well, should you be able to shoot so high. Stylistics are a residue of poetics, never a proper leading thrust.

Do not seek your voice, rather be true and your voice will seek you. Order the chaos and move on. Of what use is it to you once laid out in lines? Boil it down to essences then expand within. Write big and cut hard. Never mind the identity lost in the abandonment of the residue of stylistics. You must continually kill the poet you are, to erect the poet you've yet to be.

A Reverie on the Making of a Poem

BARBARA GUEST
June 1998

★   ★   ★

Arrived at the terrain of her sensibility

—a stasis and

pull in the composition physical—
      remember, a contradictory tug phantom-like—
           upon the environs if the poem—;

---

think of poem going through these stages
struggle
balance and non-movement
preparation
always an inert force in poem to try to bring it back and force this on the
surface of poem

        darkening of the page and then withdrawal
of darkening;   gradually the page lightens,
the invisible heaviness   lifted itself.

Perhaps—cinematic—

        this elevation.

With no warning (from inside the text,

mind attached to the text.)

_____

method to elevate poem from surface

and attacked by dizziness of atmosphere!

In the attack of suspense; a masterful

    development of plot and erasure.

The echo the words grant *us* on page and off!
          sound of the last few words—;
they will be abolished and this new movement
embracing an echo,

only discovered *here the poem*
     sustains *marginality*—

---

destructiveness

the *timing* of this substitution one   idea for another
  Countdown!   knuckle on the hand
illustrates itself   tames—

               the sentence covering it

          with a fist, held loftily—

          muscular control . . . fastidious

          continual restiveness, also

---

timing supplant strong attack

struggle necessary—but not to let go

risk

                    a blissful discontinuity
              orders this estrangement of each

              available word and the disinclination to advance   (at
that point in time)   or   desire to hurry toward an abrupt
              ending—

              rushing or spectacular jumps over the hurdles—

---

as in conversation
or
do not hurry poem

but take chances

motion, movement in poem

an advanced punctuation bursting from vases

                                     into an arena of sound
the aroma continue as a cloud of invisibility   shelters

                         ghost exiting

          there from center right: solid objects merciless.

---

mood

what else can poem perform in its arena

of possibilities

the phantom of possible ideas

(maneuvering inside a volume)

a *force majeure* to *shred the atmosphere*
        this fist its imprint almost
observable!

---

poet in charge

and all the while   movement coalescing
with the strict *idea*—.

Startling these maneuvers!

       of idea and erasure.

---

not to lose sight of the ideas, and movement they must meet

not to tell all possible choices in poem

Death, Shivers, and the Tick of Poetic Stress

DOUGLAS OLIVER
1999

★   ★   ★

It's peculiar to start upon the subject of prosody by talking anecdotally about death. I don't mean the somber hooded figure; rather a sense more basic than our mere individual fear of dying, however powerful and necessary that may be. My interest is in the form that death gives to our lives and in certain odd feelings it gives rise to.

Many years ago, I had an apparent premonition concerning the death of my son, who was mentally handicapped. Let me leave the tragic aspects of that quite aside. Even if it was a premonition and I failed to understand it, even if I now look straight-eyed at the very moment of the baby's death, I have come to find in it grounds for a happiness that isn't simply anodyne.

At the moment when an older person dies or at the funeral something grave and complete may be given to us, more than just our normal memory of a person's life. I am now talking of the deaths of my father, my sister, and the poet John Riley, and of my mother's coma before she died. What appeared to be the unity of the life across time appeared to me, summed up by the bedside or coffin-side. For an imaginative mind, and therefore properly for the poetic mind, it can be an almost literal vision of that life, a shaky sense that one is about to see something. I think of it as halfway toward the premonitory voice or vision someone near to the person seems quite often to hear, like a literal whisper, or to see like a shining gray possibility, as the loved one dies. In another analogy, that almost-vision is like a figural vision of a personage in a novel, created in words, but nearly fleshed out by his or her adventures. Probably the whisper, at least, can be sensed even when the death occurs at a distance; it is a serious voice with no voicebox behind it, rather like a voice we hear as we fall asleep. My mother heard such a voice before my father died. I'm talking about experiencing the life and its death as experienced from the *outside,* by people emotionally involved in it. I believe such phenomena are well documented and have spoken to others with similar experiences; but I don't have any occult or religious opinions about them and am unconcerned here whether they're considered psychological disturbance, telepathy, projected superstitious fears, or anything else.

And I should add that I hate indulgence in spookiness, flatlining and so forth.

So, as I say, I'm talking about the moment of death, and gladly. By "moment," I refer to the death as though it happened at a given instant (and leave to one side whether this is ever physically possible). That is, deathbed and funeral, however actually drawn out in time are envisioned as containers of an instantaneous event, the precise end of a life. In the case I've just mentioned of the unintelligent baby, we may conceive of the death-instant as a blessed unachievement, a mere pinprick along the forward-pointing of time, a moment containing very little of its own but glistening with unrealized potential like a young baby itself whose movements are jerky but whose face is radiant. Or in that other example of the elderly person, we may think of the death-instant as richly stored with the past, a summing up of the past in the present.

And now, I am imagining the death of an honorable old man or woman seen from the *inside* of it, when time may stand still and in that hackneyed, so possibly true, legend we have about dying, a past life flashes before the eyes so speedily its events are almost simultaneous. Perhaps our nearest knowledge of such awareness comes in acute danger, as when we risk a car crash and time slows down; we have all the time in the world to deal with the situation and take avoiding action. The past and the future of our actions seem to bend into a present awareness which is slowed down and wide. Once, skidding broadside in snow toward an oncoming truck, I swerved the car around it calmly in this way; most of us have friends who recount parallel experiences, so this apparent time warping may be commonplace. But it doesn't have to be danger: other emotional tensions open us up to time anomalies. Again, I should not elevate private, personal experiences to the status of evidence, but I am concerned that, because of the prevailing scientism of our culture, and because of an over-reliance among philosophers on Wittgenstein's outlawing of private evidence from public discussion, so much of ordinary beliefs is excluded from critical discussion.

Those funeral moments are profoundly sensed as impregnated with goodness and not-harming. Contrasted in my mind is our encounter with swift cruelty and harm. To take some examples from my work: a policeman murdered at a dance; a rail crash or the car crash I've mentioned; an assault in the streets; a boxing match; police in Uruguay rounding up Tupamaro guerrillas in horrid, bundling movements and behaving very sadistically. These are precise swift cruelties. As we observe such quick events, either really or in the imagination, there may appear in the mind's eye a slow knowledge akin to a trick of certain modern films where, when they portray people being shot, they wind down into slow motion or into a frozen still. It's not accidental, that technique. I have a poem in *The*

Diagram Poems ("The Diagonal is Diagonal") in which imagining such swift, cruel events as Uruguayan police savagely rounding up Tupamaro guerrillas is compared to staring fixedly at a waterfall: what we see is swift waters in constant destruction of fluid forms; but gazing intensely we see the unity of the falling water—that moment by moment it has an overall form which isn't exactly still, in time, but changes in a slow-stately way compared with the furious changes of the events themselves. So, too, in the swiftness of cruelty we may see the slower, sad forms of sadism almost holding still:

> Slowness of gaze, the slowness behind fear
> perception
> calm thoughts staying in the mist
> above a waterfall from the left: but what of the speed
> of calmness, since it doesn't stay still?
> The wavering of lights doesn't
> but moves in remote consequence to
> foam at its fastest . . .

To take another example, two boxers in a ring—this from prose fiction and some poetry—two boxers jab and hurl their punches in clusters; but we, the spectators, and the boxers too, know that one of them is losing, that his face has become pasty gray and dourly sad, his limbs leaden with hopelessness; a gradual, sad awareness tells us that the unifying principle of his movements is defeat; within the still-energetic fighter a grave and defeated man is already bowing out; it's almost a vision we have. His body postures begin to hint at it too, as if he were unable to avoid patterning his movements to fit a similar vision of himself. Again, I mean a vision almost literal but half-escaping from the literal because it is formal, yet unwilled by us. It makes obvious what's wrong in the most exciting cruelties, whether those are sexual, sporting, or political.

These semi-visions have a characteristic time dynamic. There are manifold events happening across time; perception of them is accompanied by mounting emotional suspense (I really mean "suspense"—it's *suspended*); then suddenly, "immediately," a vision comes to us unwilled. It seems to come out of some kind of mental unity and its immediacy bears witness to that: I just say "seems."

When the visions come, they share another characteristic: we have apparent certainty that between what we see and what we feel is a relationship of truth. I don't mean that the vision itself is "true," but that the relationship between it and the emotional tension is true: it is this truth of relation that we are certain about.

The best poetry gives me through its music a closely similar sense of incipient vision: the verbal music goes into a time-glide in my mind as if there were no distinction between the stresses or beats and the flow of sound, although the stresses are still sensed.

So when I look at the prosody, or music, of most English-language poetry I look at the stresses first. I search for relationships of truth between sound, meaning, and emotion arising through the "slowed instant" of time (the stress) passing into movement. The purpose is to find a way of relating the stroke of it—the apparent instant of it—to the flow of the melody. That is, to see how a single "instant" glides into time. When I most vividly sense this in relation to the whole meaning of the poem, the words sometimes give up a near-vision. This can be gained only from performing the poem, not from judging it as a text. So I look at performances only; and when I lecture on this topic I usually choose performances of blues songs. Conveniently, in a blues the first line of the couplet is repeated but varied in the repetition to draw out diverse features.

By now, I've played blues songs and read poems to some 1,000 people in fifteen or so lectures, asking them what factors cause them to think a syllable carries a main stress (usually I consider the tonic accent, the main information focus). I'll take the example of Bessie Smith's two versions of the line: "Backwater Blues done caused me to pack my things and go" in which (audiences say), the first time it's sung, "Blues" carries the main stress, and, the second time, "caused." From close examination, there is wide agreement that the following factors may affect our sense of how heavily a syllable is stressed:

A. SOUND. Difference of (a) loudness; (b) duration of syllable; (c) pitch up or down; (d) a complex of factors called "voice quality" (timbre, sharpening or flattening of pitch, etc.); plus (e) silence or pauses in the immediate vicinity of the syllable; (f) tempo (to which duration is related). Any individual stress only has meaning if considered in relation to what's happening in the rest of the sound *within the syllable,* or *further away* in the past or future of the poetic line. Influences from past or future sound may therefore be prospective or retrospective.

B. LINGUISTIC SYSTEM. (a) syntax, grammar, word position, punctuation, etc.; (b) metrical pattern, especially if abstract and conventional (iambic pentameter, etc. The Blues genre, etc.), the pattern laid down by James P. Johnson's piano, for example; (c) semantic and other kinds of difference, textual and intertextual, spatial and temporal.

C. BODY. (a) pacing of the line by breath—if a reader is pacing by breath (actually, measure is mostly conceptual); (b) how the sound happens in the mouth and chest; (c) our bodily memory of this (perhaps even what happens in brain physiology if it could ever be measured). Again, for any particular stressed syllable, these factors are relative to what happens in a poetic line's past and future.

D. EMOTIONAL SIGNIFICANCE AND OTHER "EXTRA-LINGUISTIC" FACTORS. The stressed syllable's (or word's) emotional significance to us within the Blues and within our own real lives influences how much we think the syllable was stressed. Virtual proof of this is given by Bessie Smith's second rendition of the line, where she sings: "Backwater Blues done caused me to pack my things aaaaand go."

The "and" slides down in pitch, is slightly loud, and has quite unusual duration—all these factors would normally mark it to the ear as a "stress." Audiences agree that because "and" has little semantic or emotional significance it is not, in fact, sensed as stressed but creates suspense before "go."

E. NONE of these factors is necessarily determinant but a single factor or combinations of some of them make us think a syllable has been stressed.

In this definition, the paradoxical element is "duration." We are judging that an instant of time, a stress, is heavier or lighter according to its duration. And an "instant," of course, has no duration. It's more complex, because "duration" is a necessary element of all the other factors too, including pitch, loudness, voice quality, meaning, and emotional significance. None of these have any meaning without duration. An instant of pitch considered in isolation is no pitch at all. An instant of loudness is neither sound nor silence. And so on. So no wonder we have duration in the list: duration is the paradoxical partner of the instant of stress: its functioning here is evidence that somehow, by a mental trick, we set the instant of stress moving in time and cannot experience it without that movement and small duration.

Our minds seem to judge a pretended present instant, the stress, only from information and feelings extending on either side of the instant. At the stress itself nothing much seems to happen. I don't think we can escape this paradox by metaphor, by saying, for example, that the moment of stress has a "thickness." Nor can we postulate that the stress has an infinitesimal duration which we don't notice—we've seen that the durations which actually come into play are often broad and obvious. If you sing the line to yourself, mentally clapping the moment when the stress falls precisely on the word, "Blues," you may see that the stress itself is soundless, colorless, a sort of spasm in your sense of time, like the merest twitch of a spermatozoa.

This is a space-time conundrum. A scarcely perceptible instant passes in the music, and it creates an almost meaningless spasm which nevertheless implies that quite a lot "happened" at that instant. All the meaning in that spasm is donated to it by duration—that is by the sounds, silences, meanings, and emotional significances that lie in the *past* and in the *future* of that moment since during an instant there is no time for anything to happen.

Even the precise positioning of the stress *within the syllable* varies infinitesimally from performance to performance, as it is not too hard to show by making people clap as they read.

To complete the picture: the weight of importance we ascribe to the stressed syllable is constructed not in the actual tick of the stress but in our memory as we reconstruct what we think we heard. This is because, clearly, we can't bring a present moment into conscious mind: it always goes past too quickly. We add the durations to the instant by thinking of the stress as just past, but also as something we heard in a present moment.

To sum up what I'm saying: A poetic stress is an apparent instant, perhaps real though we could never be sure, that unites some of the sound, some of the meaning, and some of the emotional significance from the immediate past and future on either side of it in a line of poetry. Influence upon it may also come from farther away in the poem than the line. I would put it another way: a poetic stress is the smallest example of artistic form in a poem. It unites meaning, emotion, and sound into a form that is paradoxically diverse in its content, yet seems, miraculously, to be unified in a way that defies our normal sense of space and time. It is also a premonition of the overall form that is being shaped.

Most poetry organized by stress has this for its principal craft: it relates the instant of time—represented by the "beat" or "stress"—to the whole form of the poem's own "life."

Accordingly, because of an implicit and hardly noticed space-time bending the mental instant of stress and mental durations of sounds, meanings, and emotions enter an ambiguous relationship. The point of time is made to slide into flow.

An idealized description can now be created for how point of sound and overall music are united in a poem. Each stress becomes a notional instant in which the immediate past and future are made to concenter. Since the stress glides in time, we need to anchor it down; so we site it inside a syllable, a little container of duration. Then the gliding of time from one stress to the next flows seamlessly from syllable into the *melodic stretches* of the line (where the voice box sounds). The melody, as in song, can therefore be carried along united with meaning and "emotion." (Voiceless consonants and gaps in sound set up secondary effects.) The short stretches of continuous melody interact with the form of the verse *line* and set up *cadences;* the cadences interact with *stanza* and may overflow it; the stanzas or comparable units form into the poem; and so the *instant*—the stress—is united eventually with the remembered *whole music* of the poem as we finish it. At the end of the poem the finished form bends the whole flow of it *back,* as if into a formal "point" or "instantaneous" perception—like an instant but a very full one, from which the poem seems to radiate. That's what it feels like, even if the formal point also seems to be an illusion.

It would be pretentious to relate these workings of poetic art too directly to the life and death events I began by describing. Yet a funeral, to return to that example, may give us the presentiment of unity I've mentioned, as if the person's life were suddenly a poem, formally ending at that moment but radiating from some "central" formal principle. And you may have picked up an analogy—it's no more than that—between poetic stress and the little tick of my baby's death as I have described it, a potential that the whole life would have had, a premonition of its worth. Anyone who has suffered the death of a baby knows that, for the rest of the parents' days, their baby's life keeps playing on in the imagination, as if trying to complete its music. And still, poetry is a particularly adequate medium for portrayal of such presentiments because the form of a poem bears a relationship to the various events of a poem similar to the relationship that a person's whole life—envisioned as a form at a funeral—bears to the various events of that life. In all our formation of mind-acts, whether considering the small circumstance of a poetic stress or whether summing up a whole poem or a whole life, a similar trick occurs: that a notional instant in our memory seems a present moment brimming over with a mental content. A notional instant of death brims over with past life. The instant glides into duration, almost seems to have a future, as if a dead person could have a future—or at the very least, as if the meaning and emotional significance of that life could have. This is still the dynamic we were looking for in a definition of stress.

Note:

I have tried to keep most technicalities out of the prosodic discussion. The tougher detail is gone through in my studies of vocal recordings described in my *Poetry and Narrative in Performance*, London and New York: Macmillan and St. Martin's, 1989.

Beauty Trouble: Identity and Difference in the Tradition of the Aesthetic

STEVEN TAYLOR
1998

*   *   *

The following is an edited version of a talk given at Naropa in the fall of 1998. The venue was the lunchtime lecture series curated by Rabbi Zalman Schachter-Shalomi. The lectures were open to students, Naropa staff, and interested persons from the Boulder community. The topic, beauty, was designated by Rabbi Schachter.

> some say men on horses, some say
> men on foot, some say men in ships
> are most beautiful o[n] this dark
> earth; but I say it is what one
> loves[1]

While I was thinking over what I would say about beauty I heard a radio report about a new kind of brain-scanning-machine that gives doctors a more detailed picture than the old brain-scanning machines. The reporter said that with the new machine, Dr. X can see "exactly what is going on in a patient's mind," and that this might enable scientists to "finally establish what consciousness is." It occurred to me that the assumption that we can arrive at exactly what's going on and finally establish things has very much to do with beauty. That's what I want to talk about.

Well, what's it going to be? Consciousness is all salts and magnetics? Beauty is a charge to the pineal gland? You laugh because it's frightening. That's where terror comes from—an absurd, fixed position. And beauty is implicated in this absurdity and in its unmasking. So that's what this will be about.

This is beauty trouble and it has two aspects and each aspect has an effect. I will call the first aspect identity, and say that its effect is death, and oppose it to difference, the effect of which is life, and beauty is in between.[2] It is the third term that mediates the opposition. This is what I want to say about beauty.

So there are three terms. Now we'll do a kind of algebra, substitute terms, and try to see the problem in the context of a larger system. I'll begin with identity and difference, and wind up with beauty, which is the synthesis. I'll situate these terms via some English words that share a common Greek root. Ecology: eco-: from *oikos,* house, -logy: from *logos,* word or reason, so ecology is the sense or logic of our house. Economics: eco- and *nemein,* to manage, so economics is household management. When what we learn from the study of our house does not inform the management of our household, the result is *ecocide,* eco- and *cidium,* a slaying, so demolition.

Now what do I mean by equating identity with death? Identity comes from *idem,* the same, and means sameness. So to take an example from ecology: environments change, and organisms that adapt to difference live, and organisms that endlessly replicate sameness don't.

Here's a more complicated example from economics. The dominant mode of economics in our world centers on commodities—movable goods valuable by a common measure which is money. Commodities are objects that, for purposes of exchange, are rendered equivalent. For example, let's say that at the level of exchange, two pounds of gold equal two tons of coffee, which equal a luxury automobile, which equals a down payment on a small house in an unfashionable Boulder neighborhood, and so on. Commodification forces sameness or identity on things. This also applies to persons. Under commodity economics, difference is downplayed, and irreducible difference may be violently despised.

The modern notion of identity in the sense of that which supposedly makes a person unique is a mistake. We might say it is a 180-degree error: the opposite is the case. Identity does not mean difference, it means sameness. Here we have a *paradox,* from *para,* beyond, and *doxon,* belief: a paradox is a self-contradictory statement, an absurdity. It is a rule of thumb for analysis of power structures that if you locate the paradox, you've found the source of power. In George Orwell's novel *1984,* the government agency that fabricates a history of lies is called the Ministry of Truth, and the slogan of the ruling party is "freedom is slavery." Remember I said terror comes from an absurdity? This is one application of that.

Identity, the paradox that says sameness is difference, is the mechanism for the commodification of persons, and it works through what Theodor Adorno calls "the culture industry" which sells identity via cars, music, clothes, etc., which are superficially different reproductions of the same. In the social realm, just as in the ecological realm, sameness is a dangerous maladaption. One of the more obvious examples of the nightmare of the same has been racism. The idea that all persons of a particular ethnicity are essentially the same makes people into objects of increasingly limiting definition, until they are defined out of existence.

This phenomenon has been linked by some critics to the quest for universal law through rational method that got its start among the philosopher scientists of ancient Greece, and which, in 18th-century Europe, became a major trend. We call this period and its project the Enlightenment. Adorno portrays the Enlightenment as a noble effort gone wrong. The Enlightenment sought liberation through knowledge. All the darkness was to be illuminated, and everyone was to be free. We see the major political manifestations of this in the American and French revolutions. But the method was valued above its consequences, and the outcome was the opposite of the purported goal, slavery and slaughter on an unprecedented scale. This is what is meant by equating identity with death. Another way of saying this is that the eternal explanation, finally establishing what's going on, monumental truth, is a con game, a false god, an idol. It is interesting to note here that the religions of Abraham—Judaism, Christianity, and Islam—associate idol worship with the most disastrous consequences.

Now, where does beauty figure in this? Well I said beauty has two opposing aspects, and beauty trouble is of two kinds. On the one hand, beauty is troublesome because the idea of beauty can be a vehicle for the imposition of identity, absolutes, universals, or final solutions; and on the other hand, beauty troubles identity because it embodies difference.

A recent article in the *Chronicle of Higher Education* says that in the academic world beauty has had some problems in the last few decades.[3] The article describes an opposition between on the one hand, aesthetics, which is defined in this context as the study of beauty, and on the other hand cultural studies, a broad interdisciplinary field that draws upon literary criticism, philosophy, and the social sciences. Now as a student of cultural studies I have personally never had any difficulty embracing beauty. But there is trouble in the academy on this, the *Chronicle of Higher Education* is right.

The problem is like so: beginning in the late 1700s, there was an increasing tendency to regard art as a thing above worldly circumstances, something that must be kept apart from material concerns. This view, which was eventually popularized by a small circle of scholars at Oxford in the 1880s, became the conventional wisdom, something taken for granted. This aesthetic attitude holds that a work of art must be judged purely on the basis of formal criteria or emotional response. Beauty is seen as an absolute value above historical or cultural context.

For cultural studies, on the other hand, the question is not how art invokes the transcendental, or whether a particular artifact is or is not beautiful. The question is what are the historical circumstances that gave rise to the idea of transcendent beauty in the first place, and what have been the consequences of this way of thinking. The assumption that there are universal standards for beauty has forced aestheticians into uncomfortably close company with those who confuse culturally determined values with monumental truth. As professor Allan Bloom, a leading academic exponent of the superiority of Western culture has it, "The fact that there have been different opinions about good and bad in different times and places in no way proves that none is true or superior to others."[4] The problem with this view is that the criteria of truth and superiority are themselves culturally determined. Once and future presidential candidate Patrick Buchanan puts the position more bluntly: "Multiculturalism is an across-the-board assault on our Anglo-Saxon heritage. . . . Our culture is superior to others."[5] This is a view that first came under attack in European philosophical literature in the 1780s when the German theologian Johann Gottfried von Herder wrote that "the very thought of a superior European culture is a blatant insult to the majesty of Nature."[6]

In 5th-century BCE Athens, where Professor Bloom gets his groceries, the idea that the Athenian citizen was a higher order of human was unlikely to be challenged. It's a small-town mentality. Herder notwithstanding, a similar situation applied in 19th-century Europe, because science was the mouth of truth and evolution was all the rage. Everything had to be a science and everything had to be evolving. So you've got the science of child rearing and the science of swatting flies and the science of canning peaches and the scientific ladder of social evolution with savages on the bottom, barbarians in the middle, and civilized people on top. The middle-class European male is the pinnacle of biological evolution and his values are the pinnacle of social evolution; and since values are among the least examined aspects of a worldview, they've outlived the scientific racism paradigm. Prejudices always outlast their rationale.

Back in the 1780s, Herder advised that we regard our culture as one among many, but when you actually get down to comparing cultures, you come up with a lot of troubling questions. For example, if in a certain milieu, beauty requires that a girl have her feet bound so that they grow deformed, are the foot-binders mistaken about the nature of the beautiful? Are they not yet evolved to our level so they don't see *true* beauty? Why does their notion of beauty require that women be unable to walk? And haven't our notions of the beautiful also been connected to oppressive agendas? Why, for example, do we associate feminine beauty with shoes that limit women's mobility, and why did we, for centuries, associate beauty with clothing that limited women's ability to breathe? The belief in universals avoids such questions, but what if universals persist precisely because they are connected to coercive agendas?

Friedrich Nietzsche pioneered the critique of universal categories. He was schooled in philology, which means he was by training a linguist. In 1887

Nietzsche published *On the Genealogy of Morals* in which he points out that the words in Indo-European languages that mean good and bad can be traced to historical root-words meaning things like high-born and low-born, light-skinned and dark-skinned.[7] Nietzsche's method was, as the book's title suggests, genealogy, the study of historical descent. You hire a genealogist to find out about your ancestors, about the origin of your name. Nietzsche turned this method to investigating the origins of the taken-for-granted, in this case, European bourgeois morality. He did what many innovators in philosophy and science do. He asked a question that had never been asked before. Everybody had asked whether this or that was good or bad, and many people had asked what is the meaning of good and bad, but nobody had asked what is the history of the idea of good and bad. Suddenly good and bad appear to have been tied up from the start with issues of social advantage. Things like "the truth" look different after that.

Adorno says, "Only those thoughts are true which fail to understand themselves."[8] The truth that doesn't understand itself, the manipulative universal category, is called ideology. Ideology tends to avoid or discount history because it can only operate if we are ignorant of history. It's like a con artist. Suddenly, one day, there he is, one of those guys you feel you've always known. Where did he come from? It's impolite to ask. His past is not discussed, ideally it is just continually erased, that's how he stays in business. A concept or value or category can only pose as the truth by obscuring its origins, by hiding the fact that it was invented by particular persons with particular interests. This is why knowledge of history is essential; it's basic survival equipment. A society in which history is increasingly obscured or regarded as irrelevant, is a society in which people are increasingly powerless.

Literature provides a good example of something that appears to embody eternal values, but if we look at history we find that "literature" has meant different things at different times. Up until the 18th century, it meant what we now call literacy, both the ability to read and the quality of being well-read. It was said of a person who could read and write or of someone who had read a lot that he or she has literature. Literary theorist Terry Eagleton says that in the 18th century literature came to mean "the whole body of valued writing in society: philosophy, history, essays, and letters as well as poems" and that the novel and the drama were of dubious status.[9] In the 19th century, with the need of the old aristocracy to form alliances with the increasingly powerful middle class, the goal became cultivation of noble values, and literature featured sermons and manuals on morals and etiquette. Then, with the increasing dominance of industrial capitalism, the focus shifts to fiction and poetry. Eagleton cites several reasons for this. First, the new ruling class prioritizes things that make a profit, so art is distanced from real life. Secondly, the shift of the majority of people from farming and small-scale tradesmanship to wage slavery creates widespread poverty, massive unrest, and brutal repression. At this point the educated classes increasingly favor escapist art and literature. Finally, it becomes necessary to educate the lower classes so that they are able and willing to participate in modern industry and empire. You can't educate the underclass in the same way as the upper classes; you can't have them reading essays and social treatises and learning that truth is negotiable. At this point literature is novels and poetry and art is now a transcendent thing, divorced from social reality.

So this is one kind of beauty trouble, beauty as something apart from real conditions, it's supposed to be somehow more important than the real, more real than the real. The trouble with beauty in this sense is the part it can play in the avoidance or downplaying of the suffering of real beings in the interest of some vaguely defined, imaginary realm whose real effect is the maintenance of oppressive relations.

I began in a Greek outpost in the 6th century BCE with Sappho. In her poem, Sappho connects beauty with love, as might be expected of a devotee of Aphrodite, the ultimate beauty and the goddess of love. For Sappho, Aphrodite stood for a kind of cultural ideal, life devoted to youthful beauty and lovemaking. But a century later, in the city of Athens, this is all a bit steamy for Plato who, after his teacher Socrates, associates beauty with goodness. The beautiful is seen as a means to the good, where goodness is conceived in terms of what is good for the state.

Desirous love, says Plato, is the soul aspiring to a good which it has not yet reached, just as the philosopher reaches after wisdom but is not yet in possession of it. That which awakens desirous love is beauty. At the lowest level, the love of a beautiful person, desire is really a passion to attain immortality by producing children. A higher form of desire is the urge to combine with a kindred spirit to produce stable institutions. Still higher is the desire to join in dialogue with worthy companions to make a contribution to philosophy and science. Then, if one follows the quest far enough, one becomes aware of the supreme beauty, the ideal form of the good, the principle of order that harmonizes the relations and institutions of the state which, in the Athens of Plato's student years, was not a democracy but an oligarchy, a dictatorship by committee.

Plato was a member of a noble family line believed to be descended from the god Poseidon, and he was related to the oligarchy that ruled Athens until democracy was restored when Plato was twenty-four years old. It was under the democracy that Plato's teacher, Socrates, was condemned and executed on trumped-up charges, which did nothing to improve Plato's estimation of democratic government. In his great treatise on the ideal society, the *Republic,* Plato characterizes democrats as flighty and selfish, given to indulging their desires, neglecting their duties, and flip-flopping on issues.[10] Sound familiar? Plato's political ideal was an enlightened despotism, rule by a philosopher king and an educated elite. Membership in the ruling class is by birth and by merit. Marriages are arranged by a lottery, which is secretly rigged by the rulers so that persons born into the lower class don't get to enter the ruling class. Sound familiar? A philosophical system invented by someone who advocates a dictatorship of an elite minority could be expected to subscribe to a system of fixed truths and transcendental values.

Now I want to discuss the other kind of beauty trouble, which is beauty that troubles identity, or ideological fixation, by embodying difference. Beauty can be complicit in the imposition of abstract universals and manipulative ideologies, but it can also trouble unquestioned categories, values, and generalized truth because beauty embodies the particular. Beauty troubles sameness because it embodies difference.

One way of saying it is that having a powerful impression from an artwork, something that is frankly artificial, makes everything appear artificial and therefore subject to change. The Russian Formalist linguists called this poetic estrangement. When we get a message that calls attention to itself as message, everything, even ourselves, appears strange.[11] Adorno applied this idea to painting. It's not that a picture of a vase creates the illusion of a real vase, but that the painting makes the real vase appear strange. Art can make reality appear constructed, which it is. Adorno says genuine art shows us the world as it could be. Art hints at alternatives to our situation. We don't realize that we're in a constructed situation, and suddenly there's Matisse's *Celestial Jerusalem* and the world looks like it's made out of colored paper with a pair of scissors.

It's a matter of the universal versus the particular. Universals, completion, wholeness, fixed, immutable values are fetishism, the sin of idolatry that licenses abusive relations, the god of fire to whom we sacrifice our children, Molech. God told Moses: And thou shalt not let any of thy seed pass through the fire to Molech.[12] In his poem "Howl," Allen Ginsberg made Molech synonymous with the inhuman madness of modern civilization.

> What sphinx of cement and aluminum bashed open their skulls
> > and ate up their brains and imagination? . . .
> Moloch whose fate is a cloud of sexless hydrogen![13]

Genuine art supersedes sacrifice. We could say that the golden calf, the last word, monolithic truth itself becomes the sacrificial offering. In art, the idols die. The work of art could never come into being without moments of apparent discreet wholeness, but the work continually undoes itself. Adorno likens this to Penelope's unraveling of her weaving each night.[14] Odysseus has been away so long at the war that the local bullies want to take over his house and his wife and she's afraid to refuse them, so she says, "OK, you can take over when I finish my weaving," but she never finishes it because she weaves during the day and unravels the work at night. This is a metaphor for art's defiance of the illusion of finality that allows the bullies to take over. There is no permanence or discreet wholeness. Identity is a selective remembering, a mistake. As psychoanalyst Jacques Lacan says, there is no "identity" except in "misrecognition."[15]

Poet Gregory Corso, who has been an occasional guest here over the years, used to say something that is a key to this whole issue of aesthetics. What he said was, "Given a choice between two things, take both." Now it seems to me that the academic argument between aesthetics and cultural studies comes about because of a certain stiffness, a lack of humor, a lack of willingness to take both, an inability to embrace ambiguity. Beauty is tricky. The middle ground is always tricky. Humor is of course tricky, that's its agency.

The middle ground is the place of art and the place of myth. Anthropologist Claude Lévi-Strauss says that the purpose of myth is to overcome a paradox.[16] Myth does this through characters who mediate the contradiction. All myths feature at least one character who in some way lives in two worlds. Sometimes it's a coyote, or a raven, or a clown, or a blind man. The trickster characters, like raven and coyote are the obvious ones, the characters who can never be nailed down. You never know what they're going to do next. Ambivalence, ambiguity is their way of being. We can't reconcile life and death. But the trickster exists half in the death world and half in the life world. He or she mediates paradox by embodying it. The trickster is the third term that breaks the deadlock and keeps things moving. Another character who has this mediating function is the god or goddess who is both good and bad at the same time, like Aphrodite, who is beauty. Beauty is both good and bad. Beauty defies identity.

Beauty incites regeneration through ecstasy —ex stasis—out of place, not static, moving. We are moved by beauty and so are human communities. Participating in ecstatic ritual or what we call art has been seen by many theorists as the very engine of social regeneration and change. Those who wish to resist social change always intrude into the realm of ecstasy, via censorship, criminalization, regulation, or dogma, because ecstasy defies domination and invokes change. Beauty is between worlds; it is double-edged. It can both serve and challenge dominant ideological forms because it invokes the universal and the particular. As Allen

Ginsberg wrote in his ecstatic poem "Wales Visitation": "The great secret is no secret. . . . What did I notice? Particulars! The vision of the great One is myriad."[17]

Particularity, at the level of human relations, demands respect for difference and uncertainty against the drive to sameness and fixity. We have to occupy two worlds at once. We must be lovers of beauty *and* cultural critics. Art does not occur in a vacuum. We have to appreciate beauty and take responsibility for its social implications. We must be able to embrace uncertainty, because generalized certainty kills. And it's OK to invoke the gods, especially the ones that are good and bad at the same time. I'll close with another fragment from Sappho:

> Deathless Aphrodite, child of Zeus, seated
> upon a dazzling throne, setting love traps; please,
> goddess, don't pour more sorrow into my heart [18]

✭

Notes:

[1] Sappho fragment translated by Karen Van Dyck and Eleni Sikelianos.

[2] "Identity equals death" is Theodor W. Adorno's formulation from his book *Negative Dialectics* (New York: Continuum, 1992). He opposes this with "non-identity," which he equates with freedom. I have adapted this basic opposition but am calling "non-identity" difference. The idea of beauty as a mediating term comes in part from Adorno's *Aesthetic Theory* (London: Routledge, 1984).

[3] See the *Chronicle of Higher Education*, December 4, 1998.

[4] Bloom, Allan. *The Closing of the American Mind.* New York: Simon and Schuster, 1987. 39.

[5] Braun, Aurel and Scheinberg, Stephen, eds. *The Extreme Right: Freedom and Security at Risk.* Boulder, CO: Westview Press, 1997. 69.

[6] Herder quoted in Raymond Williams, *Keywords.* New York: Oxford University Press, 1983. 89.

[7] See *On the Genealogy of Morals,* Essay 1, parts 4 and 5.

[8] Adorno quoted in Martin Jay, *Adorno.* Cambridge MA: Harvard University Press, 1984. 164.

[9] Eagleton, Terry. *Literary Theory: An Introduction.* Minneapolis, MN: University of Minnesota Press, 1983. 17.

[10] See Plato, *Republic.* 561 c-d. Also Bloom. 87–88.

[11] See Roman Jakobson, "Linguistics and Poetics," in *Language and Literature.* Cambridge, MA: Harvard University Press, 1987. See also Julia Kristeva, "Revolution in Poetic Language" in *The Portable Kristeva.* New York: Columbia University Press, 1997.

[12] Leviticus 18:21.

[13] Ginsberg, Allen, "Howl." In *Collected Poems 1947–1980.* New York: Harper and Row, 1984. 131.

[14] Adorno. 267.

[15] Lacan, Jacques. *Écrits*. New York: W. W. Norton and Company, 1971. 172.

[16] See Claude Lévi-Strauss, "The Structural Study of Myth," in *Structural Anthropology.* New York: Basic Books, 1963. 229.

[17] Ginsberg. *Collected Poems*. 482.

[18] Sappho translation by Karen Van Dyck and Eleni Sikelianos.

The Art of Melancholy

LAIRD HUNT
June 22, 2000

★　★　★

1) W. G. Sebald, a German writer who made his home in southeast England for some thirty years, wrote four works of fiction that had been published in English at the time of his death in 2001, *The Emigrants, The Rings of Saturn, Vertigo,* and *Austerlitz.* 2) In each of the books, a shadowy narrator, whose identity cleaves, in the dual sense of the word, to that of Sebald himself, and who is deeply preoccupied with memory and history, relates a series of incidents that may or may not have befallen him or others. 3) At the heart of the works then is a shimmer of uncertainty, amplified by an acknowledgment that memory is an imaginative act, and that, for various reasons, attributed "facts" are not always credible. 4) This state of affairs, with which it can be said that the narrator is far from happy, is calipered by an overarching desire, that often slips over into desperation, to get at something solid, something real, something that, when leaned on, won't come crashing to the floor. 5) The implied conflict fuels the four narratives, helping chart their melancholy course, adding to their air of tragedy.

1) W. G. Sebald, a German writer who made his home in southeast England for some thirty years, wrote four works of fiction that had been published in English at the time of his death in 2001, *The Emigrants, The Rings of Saturn, Vertigo,* and *Austerlitz.*

Sebald left his native Germany and went to England as a young professor of literature some thirty years ago. He wrote four books about emigrants, wanderers, and unhappy voyagers, in which a sense of profound dislocation prevails. Sebald's characters are always going somewhere from somewhere else, or feel as if they are. Even when they seem to have arrived, their condition as emigrants and refugees ensures that they are neither quite here nor there. Historical figures like Nabokov, sometimes known only as the butterfly man, Swinburne, Joseph Conrad, Edward Fitzgerald, Henri Beyle, Kafka, and Wittgenstein flit through the books like ghosts. The narrator himself, particularly in *The Emigrants* and *The Rings of Saturn,* seems to be haunting his own books. He is a curious character, rather somber, a journeyman of sorts, the kind of gently-mad, deeply melancholy intellectual you might have expected to find wandering the heaths and country lanes of a 19th-century German novel. He listens and observes and takes copious notes, chronicling lives caught like his in powerful webs of memory and absence.

Sebald's books were published to acclaim in Germany, and over the past half-decade have been translated with great success into English, first by Michael Hulse and then, for *Austerlitz,* by Anthea Bell. Part of that success can, apparently, be attributed to the collaborative nature of the project— Sebald reviewed the translations before they went to the publishers, often laying his own English into that of Hulse's and Bell's. The resultant texture is remarkable. It is not quite like Beckett's translations of himself, but not too far off. There is something, characteristically, uncanny in this.

The *sui generis* nature of Sebald's writing has been much discussed, and there has been considerable debate on what exactly to call them. Treatise, memoir, travelogue, elegy, novel, dance of the dead . . . the books seem built of elements of all of these and of none. Near the beginnings of *The Rings of Saturn,* in taking up the subject of Sir Thomas Browne, 17th-century physician and philosopher, Sebald says that he, Browne, left behind a number of writings that defy all comparison. There is probably no better way to put it than to say that Sebald achieved the same.

2) In each of the books, a shadowy narrator, whose identity cleaves, in the dual sense of the word, to that of Sebald himself, and who is deeply preoccupied with memory and history, relates a series of incidents that may or may not have befallen him or others.

An important part of the fictionality of Sebald's four works is the distance between Sebald and his narrator. The narrator, who seems to differ from book to book only by degrees of presence, clearly shares many of Sebald's experiences and characteristics (he is a friend of the poet and translator Michael Hamburger, for example), and yet one registers divergences at times. Over the course of the works, once you've become aware of this—it's quite interesting—you start to doubt constantly, almost everything, so that, unlike in the case of the standard realist novel, where suspension of disbelief is encouraged, a suspension of belief is brought about. Nowhere did I feel this more strongly than in *Austerlitz.* This was probably in part the case because there is absolutely no way of knowing whether the eponymous character whose tale "Sebald" relates over the course of the book's 300 pages is a product of Sebald's imagination or not.

In a fascinating interview that can be found on Dalkey Archive's web site, Raymond Queneau, another writer of strange, hybrid works, talks about a theory of Michel Butor's, in which the history of the novel can be divided into two general strains: Those that are constructed like the *Iliad,* i.e., in which character is subsidiary to historical context (and you could place *War and Peace* and the novels of Zola, for example, in this line); and those that are constructed like the *Odyssey,* in which history, in a sense, is subsidiary to character development (here you can find any number of examples: Flaubert, Dostoyevsky, Brontë). Queneau then suggests that 20th-century literature saw, in its signal instances, a fusion of those tendencies: in this regard he pays special tribute to Gertrude Stein, who, in her *Making of the Americans,* made history itself a character.

And I think Sebald, albeit differently, does something similar. History and its active ingredients—time, event, memory, imagination . . . —are taken up on almost every page, almost every sentence. What emerges at the end of the four volumes is a vision of history as a vast, dark entity ravaged by loss and erasure, bolstered by partial and dubious recreation.

There is an element of paranoia here, one most explicitly addressed in the aptly titled *Vertigo,* in which the narrator imagines he is being followed across Europe and hallucinates the literary characters he is preoccupied with. But in all the books we are dealing with care-worn, to say the least, individuals who are not apt to imagine that what's lurking around the corner wants to make friends with them. This reminds me of Kafka's great story, "The Burrow," in which one of those amazing, frightening animal characters spends all its time preparing its burrow for defense. The creature lives in a state of awareness of its condition as doomed, at some level recognizing, as it does, that its foe is in fact the future it can't help moving to meet. Its preparations—turning its burrow into a labyrinth, patrolling the subterranean corridors, lying in wait, killing all the small animals it comes across—can be seen in this light as a form of biding time. And there is no shortage of characters in Sebald's writings who have set themselves up with curious, perhaps futile or even doomed tasks. Jacques Austerlitz, for example, spends years taking notes for an enormous history of architecture, only to end up, one desperate day, taking the stacks and stacks of notebooks he has accumulated out to the burning pile. It is little wonder that one of the central images in the books is that of Dürer's famous engraving, *Melancholia,* in which an angel sits waiting, as Sebald writes, "steadfast among the instruments of its destruction."

3) At the heart of the works then is a shimmer of uncertainty, amplified by an acknowledgment that memory is an imaginative act, and that, for various reasons, attributed "facts" are not always credible.

The 20th century did tremendous damage to certainty. Massive social and political upheaval, revolution, failure of revolution, counter-revolution, war after war after war, globalization, enormous economic imbalance, mass demographic shifts, famine, war, deconstructionist pyrotechnics, the creation and use of atomic weapons, war, massive exploitation of natural resources, war—all these elements, whose tendrils, of course, reach far back into the past, have contributed to pulling the rug out from under a worldview, intellectual and otherwise, in which it was possible to proceed from a set of assumptions, in which the grounds for the argument were always already there.

Almost everything Sebald gives us comes through a filter of adjectives, slight exaggerations, qualified observation of unverifiable fact. Occasionally he is explicit. As his narrator travels in space and time, displaying, as he goes, a constantly astonishing erudition (reminiscent of Montaigne, who, it is interesting to note, frequently bemoaned his faulty memory), he acknowledges that like weavers, who have much in common with writers and scholars, insofar as they spend long hours bent over their work, and are susceptible to melancholy, he may, in the creation of his intricate design, have gotten hold of the wrong thread.

While Sebald made clear his distrust for the kind of writing that proceeds from some presumed mastery of fact and overarching comprehension of the world (in other words most strains of realist fiction), it would be erroneous to conclude that he advocated some kind of artlessness in writing: clearly his works, so carefully structured, would belie this. I think it's a question of tone and of stance—Sebald, or rather his narrator, is deeply drawn to this world of beauties and horrors, but like the traveler, he contents himself with exploration and hypothesis, fully aware that he might be misreading everything around him. For an example, we need look no farther than the first chapter of *Vertigo,* in which, in a kind of dreamer's biography, we follow along with Henri Beyle, a.k.a. Stendahl, as he lays in experiences during the Napoleonic campaigns, and then beautifully, with a kind of instructive acceptance, misremembers them.

4) This state of affairs, with which it can be said that the narrator is far from happy, is calipered by an overarching desire, it seems, to get at something solid, something real, something that, when leaned on, won't come crashing to the floor.

One of my favorite sections of *The Rings of Saturn* is the chapter that deals with the history of the exploitation of herring in the North Sea. Sebald gives a sort of Melvillean rundown of human/herring interaction since the middle ages, which as you can imagine has been mostly a pretty good thing for humans and nothing but bad for the herring. One of the more interesting anecdotes relates to the curious phenomenon that herring glow for a certain period of time after they die. Around 1870, a pair of scientists who were eagerly competing in the race to establish a viable form of artificial illumination, and who were named, Sebald raises an eyebrow at this, Herrington and Lightbown, investigated the phenomenon in hopes that it would lead to a formula for an organic source of light that had the capacity to regenerate itself. Having related this, Sebald then writes with characteristic understatement and more than a touch of gallows humor, "The failure of this eccentric undertaking, as I read some time ago in a history of artificial light, constituted no more than a negligible setback in the relentless conquest of darkness." Another herring-related curiosity, this time legend, not scientific phenomenon, was the belief that herring died the instant they left the water, in other words not by suffocation but by some kind of implosion or other. Scientists got so interested in this that any number of experiments were carried out on them, usually involving, as is often the case when scientists and animals meet in the laboratory, some kind of mutilation. We tend to imagine, however, that fish are somehow immune to pain and fear, unlike the warm-blooded species. But the truth is, as Sebald writes, "We do not know what the herring feels. All we know is that its internal structure is extremely intricate, and consists of more than two hundred bones and cartilages."

Unlike the herring, however, we do know something about what the narrator feels. He feels, as he writes, "far from happy" and he suffers from bouts of paranoia, and nausea and a kind of spiritual vertigo. And within that or out of that he feels, which at times brings him to the point of panic, a need to get at something solid, something composed of more than after-shock and shadows. His endless reference to the historical record, his concern with and unmasking of various incidences of deliberate falsification, his use of framing devices (the narrator is constantly stepping aside to let the record, however potentially flawed, take center stage), his love of the visual and his wariness, even tenderness with respect to it all, and the fact that he does travel, does move, even if at times rather than seeking out he is running away, that he doesn't spend his life pottering about the garden or hiding among his papers in the back shed, all point to this.

5) The implied conflict fuels the four narratives, helping plot their melancholy course, adding to their air of tragedy.

Sebald is drawn, again and again, to instances of partial or complete obliteration. (Sebald's meditation on the firebombing of Dresden, along with other essays, has been published in English under the title *A Natural History of Destruction*.) Certainly the Holocaust, perhaps the 20th century's greatest vortex of insanity and erasure, casts a pall over all four books, although it is interesting to note that Sebald always treats the subject obliquely. As a native of a country that spawned a regime that tried, during his lifetime, to annihilate a people, and having grown up in an environment in which that awful fact was almost never spoken of, and in which heinous acts, if not forgotten, were too often denied, it is perhaps no great surprise that memory and oblivion came to so obsess Sebald, and that he might, having time and again encountered chilling gaps in the record, and having all but given up on himself, long for something that hadn't, even as he at last approached it, already slipped away.

Form and Culture

ALAN GILBERT
July 6, 2000

★　★　★

—Dedicated to the documentary spirit of Harry Smith

What follows is an outline of four different concerns I think it might be useful for contemporary poetry to continue to address: documentary, hybridity, localism, and culture. This essay is both descriptive and theoretical, and it draws on a wide variety of cultural objects and materials. Its primary concern is with the relation of these cultural objects to the contexts in which they are produced and experienced.

I. DOCUMENTARY
THESIS: All art is site specific.

In 1975, two very different documentary projects depicting New York City's Bowery Street were produced. At the time, the Bowery was home to some of the most famous "bums" in the world. The first project is Michael Zettler's book, *The Bowery,* which contains both photographs and text that portray men living on the sidewalks and in the flophouses of the Bowery. The second is Martha Rosler's more conceptually-oriented photograph and text installation entitled *The Bowery in two inadequate descriptive systems.* In Zettler's book, sympathetic close-up photographs of faces signifying poverty, homelessness, and alcoholism are juxtaposed with statements made by many of the photographer's subjects. One pictured denizen of the Bowery declares: "I'm here by choice . . . That's right . . . Gotta make the choice, the wine or the job . . ." Another declares: "You must learn the art. The art of staying alive and staying drunk . . . " (1975: 4, 24). The photographs in Rosler's piece are primarily of storefronts, and don't contain a single human figure. The accompanying text consists of a list of slang words for alcoholics and inebriation: "tipsy," "loopy," "sottish," "shit-faced," "fried to the hat," "sloshed," "wino," "barrelhouse bum," etc. (1981: 11-57).

Though these are obviously two distinct approaches to similar subject matter, their roots can be traced back to Depression-era Farm Security Administration photographs taken by Walker Evans, Dorothea Lange,

Ben Shahn, and many others. There's some evidence that Lange's photo-graph *Migrant Mother*, from 1936, is the most reproduced photograph ever (1981a: 75). But clearly, Zettler and Rosler have diverged from a shared source. Specifically, while Zettler trusts the forms of conventional documentary to fully represent the destitute men of the Bowery, Rosler's project is as much about investigating documentary forms as it is about the subject matter it presents. In Rosler's project, context becomes a form of representation, as opposed to functioning as either an explanatory back-drop to a cultural object or an element that can be separated from a work's self-reflexive questioning of its representational qualities.

Rosler's images of storefronts emphasize the social and economic contexts for the experience of a particular kind of poverty and marginalization. Her piece also comments on the tradition of social documentary. In this sense, it might be useful to compare it with a couple different photographs by Walker Evans. The first is almost as famous as Dorothea Lange's *Migrant Mother*. Evans's *Alabama Tenant Farmer Wife [Allie Mae Burroughs]* was taken in 1936 while Evans and the writer James Agee spent a year in Alabama with three indigent tenant farmer families, which resulted in the book *Let Us Now Praise Famous Men* (2000). A slightly earlier Evans photograph I'd like briefly to focus on is somewhat different, and more connected with his larger body of work. Taken in 1935, it's entitled *West Virginia Living Room*. It shows a young boy sitting on the left-hand side of a room furnished with the basics: chair, armoire, and table. On the right-hand side of the photograph is a wall that has been patched and insulated with advertisements for various commercial products, along with a large cut-out image of Santa Claus. These details amplify and contextualize the information about poverty contained in the more well-known *Alabama Tenant Farmer Wife*. The contrast between the poverty of the room and the images of material abundance on the walls signals the economic and cultural conditions that produce class stratifications in North American society. As Karl Marx argues, the fetishistic quality to the commodity form disguises the under-lying labor exploitation used to produce it (1976: 163–177). In Evans's *West Virginia Living Room,* the advertisements *literally* fill the holes in human life that commodities *symbolically* both fabricate and then try to satisfy.

The photograph also suggests that the production and reception of cultural objects is inseparable from their social, historical, political, and eco-nomic conditions. The problem with presenting the face of poverty stripped of any contextual information is that it assumes an equally timeless response on the part of the viewer. This is the classic bourgeois response to art, which isn't to say it's the classical view of art, since for centuries religious art posit-ed the viewer in time, if only to differentiate this state from an eternal one. There are no nonideological responses to art, and this is important to remember, particularly in regard to poetry, which has always been tempted to enact experiences of internal and external eternities. This is why Langston Hughes writes in his short early poem "Johannesburg Mines":

> In the Johannesburg mines
> There are 240,000
> Native Africans working.
> What kind of poem
> Would you
> Make out of that?
> 240,000 natives
> Working in the
> Johannesburg mines. (1994: 43)

The question here, as in Rosler's *The Bowery in two inadequate descriptive systems*, is as much about the form a cultural object takes as it is about its subject matter. It's a question Hughes asks of himself, fellow Harlem Renaissance artists, and other writers of the period. In other words, Hughes is proposing a historically-based, site-specific poetry that examines the material conditions of class, ethnicity, and culture. He makes this request in a language approximating everyday speech, with its frequent repetitions and rephrasings. I think there's still plenty of work for contemporary poetry to do in this regard. Documentary is one approach, as long as we don't ascribe to documentary universal values in either its form or content.

In keeping with the themes of documentary, the American South, poverty, and mining, I'd like to mention one of the more well-known songs performed by the old-time folk musician Dock Boggs. It's entitled "Down South Blues" (1997). A coal miner for most of his life, Boggs lived primarily in Norton, Virginia, in the heart of Appalachia. Boggs recorded twelve songs between 1927–1929, two of which appeared on Harry Smith's groundbreaking *Anthology of American Folk Music* (1997). Boggs 1927 version of "Down South Blues" contains a common trope in folk, blues, and country music of returning to the South. It's a complex metaphor with both reactionary and progressive connotations: the South as a region where people know and accept more rigidly delineated social roles, but also as a place where one's relationship to the land and traditional, stable communities provide the potential for a degree of autonomy and economic self-sufficiency unavailable in the industrialized North. It's a desire to live within what E. P. Thompson describes as a more supportive "moral economy" (1993: 185-258), which in reality is just an earlier, less sophisticated version of capitalism.

Boggs learned this song in 1923 from a record he heard by an African American blues singer named Rosa Henderson (1995). He rearranged the verses and changed the musical structure slightly. Of significance in Boggs's version are the alterations he made in order to document social conditions around him. Henderson does this in her own way by focusing on gender dynamics in the song. Equally important, is how Boggs's rendition of Henderson's original elucidates the hybrid and cross-cultural aspects of a folk tradition that is frequently seen as mono-cultural, ethnically one-dimensional, and quaintly archaic. Instead, folk music is a genre informed by a wide variety of traditions that are flexible in their responses to changing cultural and technological conditions.

II. HYBRIDITY
THESIS: All cultures are hybrid.

As Cecelia Conway describes in her book *African Banjo Echoes in Appalachia,* instead of adopting the more strumming "knock-down" or "clawhammer" style that other members of his family used—a style that itself has roots in African music—Boggs took the "two-finger 'picking' style" of the African American banjo players that he mentions and "made up his own style—an unorthodox three-finger style" (1995: 23, 148). Conway's *African Banjo Echoes* tries to dispel the myth that the banjo in particular and old-time folk music in general are the product of white rural America. In fact, the African influences on folk music are in certain places at least as strong as its more widely acknowledged Celtic inheritance.

This isn't to deny there are indigenous traditions that develop with a degree of independence and according to their own internal logics. As Conway writes: "The banjo symbolized the black musical tradition that resulted from an African instrument in the care of an enslaved people. The banjo and the griots who played it at the crossroads in this foreign land helped African Americans preserve their historical African identity, cultural continuity, and community" (1995: 83). The attempts by different cultures to preserve what they consider valuable aspects of their heritages are necessary in a global economy where cultural exchange is frequently a one-way street, as North American postmodern capitalism seeks to culturally and economically colonize all areas of the globe, including those pockets within itself which are resistant to this process.

For contemporary poetry, a "cross-cultural poetics"—a phrase found in the writings of the Caribbean author Edouard Glissant—entails a contextualizing approach to subject matter (1989). Take, for instance, the first section of a poem in six parts entitled "high plains drifting" by Anselm Hollo.

high plains drifting

on the high plains,
when we meet
the inspector
we say, "buenas tardes, inspectór" (1983: 44)

I've been a fan of this very short poem for almost a decade, though I'm still not certain I fully understand it. What it represents to me in four short lines is a poem concerned with its larger cultural and social contexts, both in what it articulates and in its mode of direct address to the poet Robert Grenier. The poem points out that these contexts are always multiple, always interacting (in this case, respectfully), even if they don't speak the same language.

Furthermore, Clint Eastwood's movie *High Plains Drifter* (1973), which the poem's title references, is concerned with the ways in which a community polices itself (1973). This ties directly into the appearance of the "inspector," who seems to be causing the speaker/poet to keep a close eye on his use of language, both in responding to the inspector and in writing the poem. That one of the sets of speaker and spoken to are Hollo and Grenier in retrospect tempts me to read the poem as commenting on a policing or disciplining of and even within a writing community, which certainly would be applicable to the controversies Grenier became embroiled in a few years later during the San Francisco "Poetry Wars." But more importantly, in its brevity, and in the vernacular quality to the form and language of the poem, I read "high plains drifting" as a kind of late-20th-century multilinguistic and multicultural version of William Carlos Williams's "the red wheelbarrow."

XXII

so much depends
upon

a red wheel
barrow

glazed with rain
water

beside the white
chickens. (1986: 224)

One way of reading Williams's poem is to argue that it's an example of Modernist phenomenological bracketing, theorized most notably by Edmund Husserl as a way of lifting material phenomena out of their social and cultural circumstances in order to obtain a more objective and scientific knowledge of them (1931). At the same time, "the red wheelbarrow" is a very different poem when read within the book *Spring and All* in which it originally appeared before it began to be published as a separate poem in various poetry anthologies and selected writings by Williams. In *Spring and All*, Williams contextualizes his short imagistic poems with extensive prose commentary on the aesthetics and literature surrounding their composition. Both Hollo and Williams's poems are similar in that they eschew rhetoric and conventional poetic forms in order to rely on careful observation rendered in an everyday language that places their poems within a particular set of historical circumstances.

As should be clear from the above discussion of old-time folk music, music is perhaps the cultural form wherein hybridity most readily occurs. As one of the major figures in the "Asian Underground" music movement, Talvin Singh's work is an excellent example of this hybridity on a more global scale. Moving along trade routes that existed between countries formerly colonized by the British Empire, Singh consciously blends music from India, Jamaica, the United States, and England. In other words, it's not an arbitrary sampling and appropriation of world music sounds. In a piece entitled "Traveller"—a reference to economic, ethnic, and cultural migrations—Indian woodwinds and tablas combine with London drum 'n' bass, Detroit techno, Jamaican dub, and European classical music. The phrase "the world is sound" which opens the song doesn't refer to a collapsing of the world into one uniform music, but instead is a reference to cross-cultural sharing.

Despite the ongoing political tensions between India and Pakistan, Muslim singers have historically been among the most acclaimed performers of Hindu religious songs; and as Andrew Schelling points out in the introduction to his selected translations of the Indian poet and singer Mirabai, Hindus, Muslims, and Sikhs all sing her songs honoring the Hindu god Krishna (1993: 14). Singh taps into this history of music leaping over national boundaries that primarily serve the interests of political and corporate plutocracies. Referencing both the regional and the global, Singh's work travels along routes originally created for economic purposes, but which quickly became conduits for cultural transmissions as well. Thus, it might be useful for a cultural poetics to keep in mind a few proposals Lawrence Grossberg makes for the conducting of historical research: "Appreciation of difference; understanding of context; and ability to make critical comparative judgements on the basis of empathy and evidence" (Lippard 1997: 20). Pluralism means not making everyone conform to your own ideological viewpoint, aesthetic or otherwise.

III. LOCALISM
THESIS: Different works of art have different effects in different contexts.

However much postmodernism may boast of free-floating signifiers and the tenuousness of the relation between signifier and signified, signification and representation always arise out of particular social conditions. Language gains meaning in its specific usage, and this meaning and usage shift in relation to changing contexts. Rosalyn Deutsche refers to this when she writes of "meaning understood to be geographically, historically, and socially situated, rather than guaranteed by an underlying and stable reality" (1991: 52). For instance, the innovative appeal of Walker Evans's photographic work is in the near seamless fusion he creates between its social and formal aspects, what John Palattella describes as the "pursuit of a realism trued by abstraction" (2000: 8). This relation between form and content must be constantly re-interrogated, because there's no inherent political content in any aesthetic form outside of its employment within a specific context.

At the same time, the groundbreaking quality to Evans's compositional methods should not solely be attributed to "artistic genius." Instead, it may be more helpful to understand the ways in which Evans's signature framing style was arrived at within the New York City economy of the 1920s and '30s. In other words, the seamless blend of form and content in Evans's photography is as much a product of the historical conditions in which he was working as it is the result of his own creative inspiration. Evans's compositional methods are a response to changes in the design of commercial signs; the rise of the automobile, which cleared the city's streets just enough to emphasize a formal quality to Manhattan's gridded layout; and the geometric application of steel in architecture, including a more widespread construction of skyscrapers. All of these urban elements influenced Evans's development of his distinctive method for framing photographic subjects, an approach Evans applied for the rest of his life to different settings, as have countless photographers after him.

When moves toward the local are made by less prominent figures, they tend to slip beneath the radar, which isn't necessarily a bad thing, because there are also positive aspects to being off the map. When this vanishing act occurs, it may indicate a cultural moment that hasn't yet found its way into the mainstream media or university system. However, it will continue to illuminate connections and tensions between the local and the global, and within the local itself. This is the case with a CD of contemporary Vietnamese street music entitled *Hò! #1: Roady Music from Viêtnam 2000,* recorded by a group of Austrians in Saigon as part of a cultural exchange program. All of the songs point to a complex set of relations that exist between the performers and a variety of internal and external cultures. Take, for instance, a Vietnamese folk song found on a multiple CD anthology entitled *The Secret Museum of Mankind,* which is a kind of international folk music version of Smith's *Anthology of American Folk Music.* The song "Lô'i Sông Nui (Voice of the Mountain and Stream)" was recorded in the first half of the 20th century and is played by a small group of musicians called a *ban nhac,* who use homemade stringed instruments to accompany the singing of traditional songs (Hoang-Vúy 1995). Then compare it with a composition by the "Dead Men's Orchestra" entitled "Totencombo" on *Hò! #1* (obviously, both the name of the song and the group were coined by the CD's producers [1998]).

The ethnomusicologist Gisa Jähnichen's frequently patronizing liner notes for *Hò! #1* are nevertheless helpful in elucidating "Totencombo": "This music is only played at funerals and only in Saigon—all the instruments have no tradition in Vietnam (with this climate brass instruments are permanently out of tune). It started when the liberation forces wanted to bury their soldiers like great heros [sic] (see French/American/Soviet examples)" (1998: n.p.). In other words, add brass instruments not indigenous to Vietnam but brought by invading French and United States armies; add more than a century of French colonial presence, along with a couple years of Japanese political control during the latter half of World War II; add military funerals by the French and U.S.; add decades of devastating war with the French, U.S., and Cambodia; add French and U.S. martial and pop music influences; combine these with local musical forms and religious ritual, and it might be possible to begin to understand "Totencombo," recorded on the streets of Saigon in the early morning.

IV. CULTURE
THESIS: Form is never more than an extension of culture.

Every Labor Day in New York City since 1967, the West Indian community—based primarily in the Flatbush section of Brooklyn—has held its West Indian American Day Carnival, which some years draws nearly a million spectators and participants. Until 1996, organized labor in New York City used to hold its annual Labor Day Parade, also on Labor Day. But as a result of changing economic conditions in New York City, the loss of political power by unions in the city, workers leaving town for the long weekend, media disinterest, and the popularity of Carnival, organized labor was forced to move its parade to the following weekend. The story, however, is more complicated than one of a decline in working-class politics. As Joshua Freeman writes in *Working-Class New York: Life and Labor Since World War II*: "Many participants in Carnival themselves were active unionists, not surprising since many unions in the city . . . had large Caribbean memberships" (2000: 329). He goes on to point out that the changing of the traditional day for the Labor Day Parade occurred during organized labor's resurgence both in New York City and across the United States (2000: 330). These relationships between culture and politics increase the sites of resistance to socio-economic oppression—sites that can be documented and interposed locally in hybrid cultural forms.

The local, all the way down to the particular usages of individual linguistic signs, is the place where representation and meaning are contested most immediately. This is echoed by Rosler's description of the primary task of documentary: "[I]n producing counterrepresentations, the specificity of a locale and its histories becomes critical. Documentary, rethought and redeployed, provides an essential tool, though certainly not the only one" (Rosler 1991: 32). There is no prescriptive form these "counterrepresentations" should take if they are to remain in dialogue with the communities and institutions that help to generate them. At the same time, I think it's important that the notions of oppositional culture and institutional critique remain significant elements in any radical cultural practice, however easily this practice is oftentimes absorbed into consumer capitalism and its advertising branch.

As the art critic Katy Siegel points out in her review of the 2000 Whitney Biennial: "The curators at the Whitney want to challenge the in and out lists that seem to have replaced the modernist dialectic of avant-garde and mainstream" (2000: 173). I would argue that at this particular moment in contemporary poetry, these "in and out lists" are as prominent as ever, and are given added weight through institutional sanctioning. While it's true that current cultural conditions have made the categories of "mainstream" and "avant-garde" nearly obsolete, or at least blended them together in a way that renders them mostly meaningless, this has to do partly with the institutionalization of the avant-garde and the co-optation of many of its methods by the mainstream media and corporate advertising. For poetry to continue to build on significant avant-garde lineages, while always rigorously examining them, it will have to remain committed to the creation and support of oppositional cultures, not simply academic ones. Yes, I am making a distinction between institutionalized avant-gardes and oppositional cultures, though not an absolutely rigid one. Walter Kalaidjian ends his study of progressive political poetries in the u.s. during the 20th century by saying:

> As we pass beyond the twentieth-century scene into the new millennium, it will surely be in the collaborative aesthetic praxes of such new social movements—articulated as they are to class, environmental, racial, feminist, gay rights, and public health issues—that America's avant-garde legacy of cultural critique will live on, its political edge cutting through the semiosis of everyday life and going to the heart of the postmodern spectacle. (1993: 262-263).

Poetry needs to remain focused on the pluralism and heterogeneity of contemporary North American society, and they need to be addressed more thoroughly than they have been by certain tendencies within post-World War II avant-garde and mainstream literature in the u.s. Critiques of representation, necessary to any social art, will have to incorporate an awareness of this pluralism.

Otherwise, the avant-garde is reduced to an unending dialectical pushing and shoving match with the language of an increasingly imagined—i.e., early 20th century French—bourgeoisie. Roland Barthes pointed this out over forty years ago: "What the avant-garde does not tolerate about the bourgeoisie is its language, not its status" (1972: 139). Self-reflexive critiques of representation are academic exercises without being articulated to larger social and cultural formations. A sign begins to lose its social quality when it loses its meaning, and isn't this exactly how the sign is ideally meant to function within postmodern capitalism? And in postmodernist discourse and consumerism doesn't the subject then become a fragmentary product of these signs? And in the process, hasn't indeterminacy become just another determinacy? If we begin to think of language as contingent upon its usage in specific social contexts, then we begin to see alternatives to isolated personal expression or language and discourse as totalizing systems. Instead, a dialogical poetics shares certain key characteristics with a politics of alliance that honors differences in experience and understanding.

At a recent show at Feigen Contemporary gallery in New York City, Gregory Green exhibited a restored 1967 Volkswagen Westfalia Campmobile that contains fully functional television and radio stations, along with providing access to the Web. The project is called "M.I.T.A.R.B.U. (Mobile Internet, Television and Radio Broadcast Unit)." When poetry really gets going, it can be a kind of roving information analysis and production unit, documenting and helping to facilitate cross-cultural connections and ideological interventions, all the while remaining flexible in its responses to local environments. This poetry can take as many forms as there are cultural producers and environments in which to create work.

Unfortunately, Green's vw bus is beyond most people's means (it was selling for $30,000, which in today's art market is remarkably low). Nevertheless, it taps into a long underground tradition within oppositional art: "What signals cultural power in the 1930s is a work's localized and contentious interpretive productivity, rather than any idealized 'literary' merit we may assign to it" (Kalaidjian 1993: 161). This includes both the production and the reception of this work. Thus, I think it might be necessary to update Robert Creeley and Charles Olson's axiom: "FORM IS NEVER MORE THAN AN EXTENSION OF CONTENT" (1997: 240), and instead propose: form is never more than an extension of culture. It's somewhat articulating the same idea, but subsumes content within culture, which almost goes without saying, but still needs to be said—especially if we're to continue examining the relationships between poetries and their surrounding contexts.

✶

Bibliography:

Agee, James and Evans, Walker (2000) *Let Us Now Praise Famous Men*. Houghton Mifflin Company, Boston and New York.

Barthes, Roland (1972) *Mythologies*. Trans. Annette Lavers. The Noonday Press, New York.

Boggs, Dock (1997) "Down South Blues." On *Dock Boggs: Country Blues: Complete Early Recordings (1927–1929)*. Revenant.

Conway, Cecelia (1995) *African Banjo Echoes in Appalachia: A Study of Folk Traditions*. University of Tennessee Press, Knoxville.

Dead Men's Orchestra (1998) "Totencombo." On *Hò! #1: Roady Music from Viêtnam 2000*. Trikont.

Deutsche, Rosalyn (1991) "Alternative Space." In *If You Lived Here: The City in Art, Theory, and Social Activism. A Project by Martha Rosler*, ed. Brian Wallis. The New Press, New York. 45-66.

Eastwood, Clint (1973) *High Plains Drifter*. Directed by Clint Eastwood. Produced by Robert Daley. Universal Pictures.

Freeman, Joshua (2000) *Working-Class New York: Life and Labor Since World War II*. The New Press, New York.

Glissant, Edouard (1989) "Cross-Cultural Poetics." In *Caribbean Discourse: Selected Essays*. Trans. J. Michael Dash. University Press of Virginia, Charlottesville. 134–144.

Green, Gregory (2000) "M.I.T.A.R.B.U. (Mobile Internet, Television and Radio Broadcast Unit)." April 22-June 3, 2000. Feigen Contemporary, New York.

Henderson, Rosa (1995) "Down South Blues." On *Rosa Henderson: Complete Recorded Works in Chronological Order, Volume 1 (1923)*. Document Records.

Hoang-Vúy (1995) "Ló'i Sông Nui (Voice of the Mountain and Stream)." On *The Secret*

Museum of Mankind, Vol. 1: Ethnic Music Classics: 1925-48, ed. Pat Conte. Yazoo.

Hollo, Anselm (1983) "high plains drifting." In *No Complaints.* The Toothpaste Press, West Branch, Iowa. 44.

Hughes, Langston (1994) "Johannesburg Mines." In *The Collected Poems of Langston Hughes*, ed. Arnold Rampersad and David Roessel. Vintage Books, New York. 43.

Husserl, Edmund (1931) *Ideas: General Introduction to Pure Phenomenology*. Trans. W. R. Boyce Gibson. The Macmillan Company, New York.

Jähnichen, Gisa (1998) Liner notes to *Hò! #1: Roady Music from Viêtnam 2000.* Trikont.

Kalaidjian, Walter (1993) *American Culture Between the Wars: Revisionary Modernism & Postmodern Critique*. Columbia University Press, New York.

Lange, Dorothea (1982) *Dorothea Lange: Photographs of a Lifetime*. Aperture, Millerton, New York.

Lippard, Lucy (1997) *The Lure of the Local: Senses of Place in a Multicentered Society*. The New Press, New York.

Marx, Karl (1976) *Capital: A Critique of Political Economy, Vol. 1*. Trans. Ben Fowkes. Penguin Books, London and New York.

Olson, Charles (1997) "Projective Verse." In *Collected Prose,* ed. Donald Allen and Benjamin Friedlander. University of California Press, Berkeley, Los Angeles, and London. 239-249.

Palattella, John (2000) "The Patina of Circumstance." In *FYI.* Vol. 16, No. 2, Summer 2000: 8.

Rosler, Martha (1991) "Fragments of a Metropolitan Viewpoint." In *If You Lived Here: The City in Art, Theory, and Social Activism. A Project by Martha Rosler*, ed. Brian Wallis. The New Press, New York. 15-43.

———. (1981) *The Bowery in two inadequate descriptive systems*. In *3 Works*. The Press of the Nova Scotia College of Art and Design, Halifax. 11-57.

———. (1981a) "In, Around, and Afterthoughts (On Documentary Photography)." In *3 Works*. The Press of the Nova Scotia College of Art and Design, Halifax. 59-86.

Schelling, Andrew (1993) "Introduction." *For Love of the Dark One: Songs of Mirabai*. Trans. Andrew Schelling. Shambhala, Boston and London. 13-34.

Siegel, Katy (2000) "Biennial 2000." In *Artforum*. May 2000: 171–173.

Singh, Talvin (1998) "Traveller." On *OK*. Island Records.

Smith, Harry (1997) *Anthology of American Folk Music*. Compiled by Harry Smith. Smithsonian Folkways Recordings.

Thompson, E. P. (1993) "The Moral Economy of the English Crowd in the Eighteenth Century." In *Customs in Common: Studies in Traditional Popular Culture*. The New Press, New York. 185-258.

Williams, William Carlos (1986) *Spring and All*. In *The Collected Poems of William Carlos Williams: Volume I, 1909–1939*, ed. A. Walton Litz and Christopher MacGowan. New Directions, New York. 175-236.

Zettler, Michael (1975) *The Bowery*. Drake Publishers, New York.

Documents

Statement for Panel
on Robert Duncan

BEVERLY DAHLEN
June 1996

✳ ✳ ✳

I think of *Bending the Bow* as Robert Duncan's antiwar book, though it is much more than that, of course. The evocation of the Vietnam War in poems such as "Up Rising: Passages 25" or in "Earth's Winter Song" is nearly as shocking today as it was when these poems were first published almost thirty years ago. They are shocking as testimony, as prophecy, and as prophecy they carry a sense of curse, of calling down a just retribution for the wickedness of one's own people. The violence of the war is reflected in the violence of the damnation of the war. The war was obscene and Duncan's imagery is sometimes also obscene. In the second part of "Earth's Winter Song," for instance, Duncan writes:

> In the great storm of feer and rage
>
> the heds of evil appeer and disappeer,
>
> heds of state, lords of the cold war,
> the old dragon whose scales are corpses of men
> and whose breth blasts crops and burns villages
> demands again his hecatomb,
> our lives and outrage going up into his powr
> over us. Wearing the unctuous mask of Johnson,
> from his ass-hole emerging the hed of Humphrey,
> he bellows and begins over Asia and America
> his slaughter of the innocents and the reign of wrath.

The incantatory effect is awesome. As Duncan so often invokes the spirit of primal Eros, here he calls up the opposing power, primal Evil, personified by the images of bobbing heads, empty puppet-heads one imagines, superimposed on the figure of the ancient dragon, the "Midgard Serpent whose scales are the corpses of men. . . ." (*Rites of Partic.*)

Seen on the page, this passage has the quality of a primitive text; with its phonetically rendered spellings, it seems to be "off-English," touched with that northern sense of *grue,* that word itself a survival from Middle English, its definition "to shiver" reminding one of Duncan's frequent allusions to the shaking or trembling that accompanies a state of passion.

Why is it that the word "head" spelled here "h-e-d" suggests to me "knob," a lifeless, thoughtless thing; the spelling of "appeer" and "disappeer" (double "e" instead of the standard "e-a") yields the uncanny visual pun on "peer," so that there is a kind of hallucinatory scene at which one peers, as through dense smoke, the "heds" themselves peering blindly. Indeed, Duncan forces the "rime" here, catches ore in the spell of these spellings as if one were in the presence of an archaic and obscene ritual.

An object of taboo, the person of the president, has been shown forth stripped and reduced to a "simulacrum" (as Duncan calls him in "Up Rising"), an empty form. Perhaps what is so helplessly fascinating is his "powr / over us." In an essay called "Man's Fulfillment in Order and Strife," Duncan writes: "I saw Johnson as the demotic leader, unleashing into action and moved by the secret evil of American karma as Hitler or Stalin had impersonated the evil karma of Germany or Russia. These leaders gather their will and power from the popular craving to be led into ways of reprisal and repression." That emanation of the unconscious will of the people is the true source of the power, the "powr / over us."

"We do not mean an empire"; Duncan has written in the "Introduction" to *Bending the Bow,* "a war then, as if to hold all China or the ancient sea at bay, breaks out at a boundary we name *ours.* It is a boundary beyond our understanding."

It is this confusion, this disorder which is one of the terms of *Bending the Bow,* that sweeps us into the glitter of apocalyptic fury. But a central concept of the book, from which its title is derived, is quoted from a fragment of Heraclitus: "They do not apprehend how being at variance it agrees with itself. There is a connexion working in both directions, as in the bow and the lyre." Or in the spare, plain translation by Guy Davenport: "We do not notice how opposing forces agree. Look at the bow and the lyre." The literal tension of the strings against the curved frames that hold them account for the usefulness of these instruments. The bend of the bow becomes a trope, then, for the unity of oppositions. It is not a simple or sentimental unity, but an order of being that includes every detail of that being, even, as Duncan conceives it, unto a cosmic order. Let these lines from "Orders: Passages 24" stand for a credo, as Ian Reid calls them in his essay in *Scales of the Marvelous:*

                    There is no
good a man has in his own things except
it be in the community of every thing;
            no nature he has
but in his nature hidden in the heart of the living,
in the great household.
                    The cosmos will not
dissolve its orders at man's evil.

In a commentary on these lines, Duncan has written: "The dialectic of this Sentence in which every happening informs all other parts of the structure appears in history as a poetry of events" *(Tr & Life of Myth)*. It is a faith iterated again and again, that the actual world we inhabit from moment to moment, the ground of history, is the same as the ground of poetry. "Williams is right in his *no ideas but in things*", Duncan tells us, "for It has only the actual universe in which to realize Itself. We ourselves in our actuality, as the poem in its actuality, its thingness, are facts, factors, in which It makes Itself real. Having only these actual words, these actual imaginations that come to us as we work" (Intro, *B.B.*).

The poem from which the title of the book is drawn, "Bending the Bow," is such an instance of a work sprung out of the actualities of immediate domestic life (the life of the household—so important in Duncan's work) and flowing toward the imagination of an other. The poem, as Denise Levertov reveals in her memoir of Duncan, was begun in the midst of a letter to her.

Bending the Bow

We've our business to attend Day's duties,
bend back the bow in dreams as we may
til the end rimes in the taut string
with the sending. Reveries are rivers and flow
where the cold light gleams reflecting the window upon the
            surface of the table,
the presst-glass creamer, the pewter sugar bowl, the litter
            of coffee cups and saucers,
carnations painted growing upon whose surfaces. The whole
composition of surfaces leads into the other
            current disturbing
what I would take hold of. I'd been

in the course of a letter—I am still
in the course of a letter—to a friend,
who comes close in to my thought so that
the day is hers. My hand writing here
there shakes in the currents of . . . of air?
of an inner anticipation of . . . ? reaching to touch
ghostly exhilarations in the thought of her.

    At the extremity of this
    design
"there is a connexion working in both directions, as in
    the bow and the lyre"—
only in that swift fulfillment of the wish
    that sleep
  can illustrate my hand
 sweeps the string.

You stand behind the where-I-am.
The deep tones and shadows I will call a woman.
The quick high notes . . . You are a girl there too,
having something of sister and of wife,
    inconsolate,
and I would play Orpheus for you again,

    recall the arrow or song
    to the trembling daylight
    from which it sprang.

It is a poem of correspondences, in many senses of that word, and including the sense of the medieval doctrine of correspondences in which any object or person is potentially significant, the bearer or harbinger of signs of cosmic import. The woman who stands "behind the where-I-am" has become such a figure, Euridyce perhaps, "inconsolate" in the other world.

Often in Duncan's work we find this evocation of a scene or figure "behind" the one presently being enacted or observed. Here, it is the imagination of memory at play: she (the "you" addressed) is both there and not there, a felt presence in the mind, but also an absence, a figure made of "deep tones and shadows . . ."

It is a poem of doubleness, of surfaces and depths, of dream and tangible reality, of persons who are at once mundane and incarnations of mythological beings.

Duncan "would play Orpheus . . . ": play the part/play the lyre and "recall the arrow or song": recollect (the dream) but also bring back (from history, from story?) from a dark past (the night of the dream/the night of history) "the arrow or song" into the "daylight," which can only be the light of our own day.

The recollection is the "connexion working in both directions," the bow is strung across immensities of time and space. The arrow or song is seen or heard in a future as well as a past which is recalled to us by the presentness of the poem. The "end rimes," as Duncan writes, "in the taut string / with the sending."

Notes on Intention and Editing

BEVERLY DAHLEN
June 1996

★   ★   ★

"I like rigor and even clarity as a quality of a work—" quoth Robert Duncan, "that is, as I like muddle and floaty vagaries. It is the intensity of the conception that moves me. This intensity may be that it is all of a fervent marshmallow dandy lion fluff. In cloudy art I admire boldness. . . . And certainly I like intensely evasive art. . . ." *(Fictive Certainties)*.

I begin to wonder what Duncan means by "intensity" (how can we judge "the intensity of the conception"?) and then I wonder if "intensity" isn't sprung from the same root as "intention." (A Duncanesque gesture: to search back to the root—) So looking up the words, I find they *are* related: the root is *intendere,* to stretch toward. Often, the root definition consists of a concrete image, as it does here. "Intense" and "intent" both have to do with the direction of attention (same root again); I imagine the egret at the edge of the marsh, its exquisite intention revealed in the sudden swift stretch of its elegant neck, the quick thrust of its beak into the water—I imagine myself at some distance, watching with fixed intensity.

And who is this watcher watching? The stranger, the other, the writer, the one Jack Spicer might have called a Martian or a ghost; she is perhaps not to be trusted, or trusted implicitly. One waits for her arrival.

She is the "third person," signifying an empty set, the unlimited potential of the new: the void, let's say, as an aspect of consciousness. Or the *un*conscious. The presence within consciousness of the alien on whom we wait.

It is this oscillating presence/absence that makes intention difficult. Do we not intend her? Where is she?

(Here's something: the third person is gender-marked. Do I mean "she"? But it's also possible to speak of "it," a nonspecific, nongendered, nonperson. Do I mean "it"? And what do I mean by using the third person plural? It's as if I wanted to implicate my reader in my thoughts, weighting (him/her) with extra numbers so as to make my thoughts appear to be common property. "We" assumes agreement.)

The editor is this one in parentheses, interrogating, asking why. This one is analytic.

The editor intends something, intends these details of meaning, as usage means conventionally, in order to focus on what does actually appear.

The editor may or may not be overly hasty to correct "errors." Errors may point beyond themselves to something meant, another meaning, latent. What's latent here is the question of the possible identity or identities of the author.

I do not know the ground of my intention. I begin in this place that lacks definition. Stretching toward it, I imagine the feathered tip of a wing stretching.

The "intensity of the conception": is that something we can know?

It is true that my writing is marked by doubt. Some would say (have said) that it "fills its reader with infinite doubt. . . . " Indeterminacy always shadows its beginning, and it is always beginning.

One does intend a beginning, a writing, a work in progress.

Beginning again and again; is that an evasion? (One might even hope to have been "intensely evasive.") What does one (he, she, it) evade in this constant beginning? The censor, the editor; one intends a kind of promiscuity, faithless, that is, to a standard of "rigor and even clarity." Evading closure, what comes into doubt is the sense of boundary. Yet, as Denise Levertov quotes Emerson: "The health of the eye demands a horizon." This horizon is always implied, indeed one's evasiveness is in a dialectical relation with boundary, line, definition, and other measures of rigor and clarity.

Ending without concluding: open-ended, then, and in place of another beginning.

Statement for Panel on Gender

BEVERLY DAHLEN
June 8, 1996

*   *   *

In *Writing Beyond the Ending*, the feminist poet and critic Rachel Blau DuPlessis analyzes the work of a number of 20th-century women writers, specifically focusing on what she calls "narrative strategies" of interrogation, revision, displacement, or disruption of traditionally given and culturally sanctioned texts.

DuPlessis cites several poets (H.D. prominently among them) who "turn again and again to rewrite, reinterpret, or reenvision classical myths and other culturally resonant materials, such as biblical stories or folk tales. They are reformulating a special kind of persistent narrative that is the repository of many dimensions of representation."

The chapter from which these lines were drawn is titled: "'Perceiving the other-side of everything': Tactics of Revisionary Mythopoesis." The first part of this heading is quoted from a poem of H.D.'s; its use here calls attention to her multifaceted imagination and her powerful reinventions of mythological materials.

At a certain point H.D.'s work became especially relevant to me; her influence hovers throughout the latter part of the first volume of *A Reading*. Another disturbing power in that book is the voice of Robert Duncan, who was an early and lifelong devotee of H.D.'s poetry.

The double influence of the work of these two writers, both serious scholars of classical mythology, but also of Christian theology, particularly heretical, apocryphal, mystical, or dissenting texts, has suggested a kind of investigative, but also a contemplative practice, and a willful revisionism.

I will cite one example. Sometime in the spring of 1979, I was rereading "Three Pages from a Birthday Book" in Duncan's *The Opening of the Field*. I was struck by this passage:

> In the passion of the Unicorn, believing, he laid himself down to the White Lady's lap. The Butcher's men came then and slaughterd the heavy beast, Whose near-sighted eyes held to the Lady's dreamy eyes, fixd without flicker, most foreign. Because of the blood, the flayd flesh, the brutality, we picture (instead of the true monoceros, occult and impure) the white innocence of a fairy horse, of the crownd animal hero.

Now this is itself a revision of the myth of the unicorn; Duncan was a Freudian and I think he recognized what Freud would have called a sublimated figure in the image of the "fairy horse." He reminds us that the unicorn is a sacrificial animal, but also that the precipitating agent of its sacrifice is the figure he names here the "White Lady." Here is the traditional story as given in a 12th-century bestiary:

> He is a very small animal like a kid, excessively swift, with one horn in the middle of his forehead, and no hunter can catch him. But he can be trapped by the following stratagem.
>
> "A virgin girl is led to where he lurks, and there she is sent off by herself into the wood. He soon leaps into her lap when he sees her, and embraces her, and hence he gets caught." (T. H. White, trans.)

There follows an entry beginning: "Our Lord Jesus Christ is also a Unicorn spiritually . . ." then lists half a page of allegorical details supporting this statement.

What was the meaning of this little myth? Duncan's version had been troubling, with its glimpse of the bloody execution of the beast. But it was the part played by the Lady that set me meditating. This is the record of that meditation, as it appears in *A Reading,* Part 6:

> in the myth of the unicorn the Lady collaborates. she, lovely, is working for the enemy, a spy, a trap, a snare. a man's lady. she comes on the scene. of course the unicorn is innocent, the child's body, slain. for her sake. lovely lady. our mother. lay your head in my lap. the seductive virgin. no wonder she is sentimentalized, her rolling eyes, as she bears the son. the dead son.
>
> her part. that is not you, he said. but it was. it was some part of me disowned, disavowed. to reclaim it is to see that she was not first one and then another but the same. she is involved in it, implicated, silent, it is her silence we cannot bear, she is lovely.
>
> he paws the ground, snuffles before her, what does he think she is? how does he know she is beautiful. strange, illiterate beast. who taught him beauty?
>
> and what does she think, what does she think she is doing there, sitting under the trees, her blonde hair, her downflowing milky, her eyes, what does she see. when he is captive at last does she look away in horror, "O god, I cannot save my child from death." how does she fare, pretty lady, in this world, captive, a maiden in both camps, nothing but beauty, illusory. a reclamation of the 'occult and impure.' jagged.
>
> . . . .
>
> foreign, her foreign eyes. one would be exiled. I would sing you one-o. the river of the lady. the sound the trees make when she is spring, the sound of insect hum. we both loved her, swore allegiance to her. I a child and you

a man. 'I a child and you a lamb.' we have been innocent after great difficulty, after wars among powers, fought out early and secretly, then we begin our lives. as innocent children. all it masks, little lamb who made thee. and Blake, who saw so many things upside-down and so shook the truth out, partly, still had the songs of innocence precede experience.

Let me conclude by observing that "the other-side of everything" is likely to be many-sided. H.D.'s vision of the lady in "Tribute to the Angels" valorizes her as a figure of the open, limitless potential life of the future—virgin indeed. She is the "other-side" of the icon of the Madonna and Child.

But the nodular myth of the virgin and the unicorn, with its themes of seduction, betrayal, and murder, casts the lady in a lurid light. Her passivity masks her complicity; her beauty masks her duplicity. This tiny story is a knot of contradictory impulses sprung from medieval lore: the cult of the virgin which coexists with, is the other-side of, a deep core of misogyny.

And what of the unicorn, the child, the martyred Christ, the "crownd animal hero"? He is a figure of unacknowledged longing and desire, perhaps of forbidden incestuous desire. His attraction to the maiden is an allegory of the incarnation of the Christ child, but also of incarnation generally. It is the child's passion for its mother that is played out in this miniature Oedipal tragedy.

I spoke of "reclamation," and perhaps that is what one seeks in unraveling myths of innocence and betrayal. One wants to bring into the light the "occult and impure," in all its "jaggedness," to make it "part of the picture," in H.D.'s phrase. Here it is the mother/child dyad, the original couple, that is part of the occulted picture, the carnal experience from which we emerge, as if we had been innocent children. And it is then that the animal becomes the hero, the symbol of one's achieved innocence.

But there is a double fate here, the fate of the lady as well as the child. Her passage through patriarchal culture continues to be problematic. The lady has been revised again and again, and now we know we are on the ground of history rather than myth. Perhaps that *is* her fate: to enter history as a woman of flesh and blood, stripped of both her idealization and her victimization. Let her, in that sense, go. Myth has been oppressive as well as expressive.

Still, I am bereft without her (my identity as the child speaks here) insofar as she is a figure of the mother and everything that is lovely in the natural world.

Let the dyad be set in the center again in prehistoric time, the child's time before time began. And this time before time recurs in memory as an instance of eternity. It is the moment before the hunters, the "Butcher's men," enter with knives drawn. That, in this myth, is the beginning of history.

Yo, Self / Yo, Maximus

ELENI SIKELIANOS
June 17, 2002

Long ago, to put myself through the first years of college, I worked as a waitperson in a French restaurant in California, where everyone was French or spoke French or was getting their Ph.D. in French. Back in the kitchen, one of the waiters who was studying French and feminist theory made a list of all the waitresses' names on the wall in pencil and wrote above them, "*Vive la différence!*" The difference in this case is that you're a boy and I'm a girl, and there actually is a biological basis for this one—even now, my brain is probably telling my body to make more estrogen than yours is (if you're a boy, or something like it). But we humans have never felt ourselves to be very limited by biology. And despite any *différence,* we all took the same basic shape—footed, headed, armed stars; five-pointed starfish wheeling through human space, my arms fitting into the space yours leave as we whirl, with tiny snaggle-tooth differences here and there: I got little bigs and you got big littles and he got big bigs or bigs and littles—so? So the world says I'm a white gal—but somewhere in history there was an other-gendered Sappho with an afro! And when Plato's creatures embrace, any two halves can make up the whole (word): love.

Thinking is a shape the body makes. It starts with a little fire between neurons in the brain.

The poem is a shape the thinking body makes.

The poem arises from the body like a cloud.

A billow of electric activity.

And is itself a thinking body made of bodies: of knowledge, of linguistic and scientific thought, of the small (medium-sized) me-body sitting here and the big bad body out there that is our body politic.

Soon (as in evolutionarily soon) we may no longer need bodies, but the poem shall still arise.

For now, we live in temporal, spatial, cultural, bodied maps that are personal *and* political, and often these two collide. At the same time that we must be aware of material differences, it does not seem a time for us to be thinking solely along individual or national lines; we are involved in a global cross-species soup, and until we figure out a way to sustain all life forms that soup will be at the boiling point, and at that point or any, "identity ruptures."

> I too will wrestle with the human hurricane, hulking black storm

>> —Wait, what is
>> "the human"? : the will, & "I have a hand"
>> that disintegrates into darkness,
>> fate, false history, I cannot
>> make this list because
>> another it

> is "at it with a vengeance, and what [this]
> *it* is is Nature"

Our gendered captivity extends to a dangerous series of imprisoned, exploited ecosystems. The investigative nature writer Scott Weidensaul writes that the planet currently "loses 3 or 4 species an hour, 80 or more a day, 30,000 a year—the highest extinction rate in 65 million years. . . . the world is witnessing a major wave of extinctions caused by human beings."

Let us expand the notions of the body. Let these notions of the body include an area that can or can't be walked through, that can be annexed to the mind, but not as personal property. Name local plants and animals wherever you can, create a catalog of vanishing ecosystems, differences between places that can be acknowledged not to reinforce random borders, but to argue specifics back into existence. Get the black-footed ferrets out of Dante's limbo! When we begin to know precise things about a landscape or series of landscapes, we begin to find ourselves in the midst of an intimate knowledge that makes us feel "at home." We all know a woman's place is in the home—that is, our eco-home, and our task is to drag The Man out of his castle and bring him home to roost in a knowledge of what's around in his/her immediate rock and plant and animal, indigenous inhabitant, and history, weather pattern and power port surround-sound, with some sense of shepherding minus the paternalism. This gendered landscape is in need of a woman's touch—we should be touching it all over its infrastructure.

If, as Marx says, labor is the mediator between nature and culture, we must change our labor—and we are each implicated minute-by-minute—so that its fruits become less poisonous, i.e., get our queer and gendered, socially differentiated and species-specific shoulders to the wheel. Meanwhile, whatever a self is in public, in the private domain, it "sheers to abstract models."

Yo, self
Soy something but not a hill (beans)
Soy self
Self: say something (child killer) (little bird)

I say: Is is definition by division, or is
is definition by clumping

"No identity can any longer stand forth
which is only itself" Yo, thou thouest

      little bird in the earth black back
      of the car   —   Oh, what's this—the
      car is an earth! the bird is a self! the
      mask is human! & shows the
      insuperable nest next to the second
      ago, shattered, saying, "What, friend?" "What
      precision" "What art" in proper names we repeat
      tea habits over complex
      centuries in gold = discovery, gold =
      luminosity, gold = grief, greed, the
      killer at the back of the sea, say, says
      words do describe my aversion to drag rag-
      dolls down to the river, a river
      sibling over the middle waters

            It cleans "you"

      Now I'm planning on not being that person that I was

Yoyo, out of my hair! So you, so you go
      toward the music, human

★

Note:

The sections from The California Poem *included here were inspired by opening an edition of Charles Olson's* The Maximus Poems *in a Barcelona bookstore to discover the first line of that poem in Spanish ("Yo, Maximus"). The essay around the bits of poem was written for a panel in the 2002 Summer Writing Program's* Writing the Body/The Body Politic/Feminism & Gender *week. People quoted or borrowed from who are not directly mentioned in the text include Mei-mei Berssenbrugge, Lucy Lippard, John Keene, Aristotle, and Thomas Sayers Ellis.*

The Infinite Amount of Work to Be Done

JACK COLLOM
August 1999 & July 2003

—Title from Malinda Sanborn, poet and senior citizen

A HISTORY AND DESCRIPTION OF WRITING OUTREACH AT NAROPA

In 1985 a few nagging, beautiful ideas began to coalesce for Anne Waldman, cofounder and director of the writing program at the Naropa Institute (now Naropa University) in Boulder. Ideas of ramifying creative writing practice out into the local Real World.

In 1986 Mary Kean, poet and teacher at Naropa, "got sick of my students just writing about their roommates." She thought of sending writing students into community groups and brought the idea to Anne. Anne, "with burning eyes," showed Mary the file she'd been building up—and the program was born.

Mary began the methodology from scratch. She'd been teaching writing and had led Buddhist meditation groups, and she had access to a few books such as Kenneth Koch's famous *Wishes, Lies, and Dreams*. Along with Eleni Sikelianos, then a student, and others, she started in this manner: she would talk with the individual Naropa student and divine where the interest lay. Then she'd make some phone calls and hook the student up with a community group, usually "at risk" in some sense (though certainly all children, and perhaps all people, are "at risk").

Eleni and Mary went to Cañon City in southern Colorado, site of the state penitentiary, and worked with prisoners. Mary would accompany all her students, whatever group they worked with, into the field sites or meeting places and apply the human touch.

As Mary moved on to other things and places in her life, other people ran Outreach. Leland Bartholow and Chuck Pirtle each led the program for a spell. Near the beginning of the nineties I took over and have led the program since. I'd been doing a lot of poetry-in-the-schools since 1973, including a five-year stint in New York City. This experience was available to students in the form of two books of and about writing by children, both published by Teachers and Writers Collaborative. *Poetry Everywhere* (co-authored by Sheryl Noethe) contains descriptions of more than sixty writing ideas, with examples collected in the classroom, along with essays on such topics as working with different age groups and integrating creative writing with the curriculum.

Here's how Project Outreach has worked for the last few years: Students sign up for two or three credits. They meet once a week for an hour as a class, and at first the focus is logistics—getting the students together with groups. A coursebook is distributed containing a couple pages of names and phone numbers in the Boulder-Denver area. Schools, special schools, senior citizen organizations, groups for people with disabilities, homeless shelters, jails, safehouses, and others—any group we can find that is willing or eager to work at creative writing. Students are of course free to discover their own groups to work with, and often do. A floating library is brought to class each week: books on writing and on working with all conceivable sorts of people, as well as a large collection of essays and anthologies by previous Naropa students.

Along with the logistics of getting going, the early focus is on how to work with groups of actual folks (sometimes glowing idealism has to be pragmatically shaped) and how, in detail, to lead the various writing exercises. In addition, the Outreach class tries to practice an in-session writing idea at each meeting, to learn more about presentation and also just to do it—to get into the joys and facts of group writing and the sharing of same.

As students get aligned with groups and actually begin working with them, the focus of the class meetings shifts to recitations of how/what/why everybody's doing: approaches tried, in detail (so that we can all learn from each other), difficulties encountered (often plentiful, sometimes heartbreaking), solutions found (never final, frequently delightful).

There are a number of issues that seem to stand out in this, as it were, transfer of introverted writing ideals and senses out and into the "real world."

First of all, there's implementing actual contact with that real world. Sometimes students approach this topic with a moralistic (and minimalist) sense, as in, "If I make a phone call and they don't call back, well, it's not *my* fault!" All too often, "they" don't call back; then the student might be tempted to sit back with folded arms (as the semester trickles through the cracks in the floor). But the repetition of initiative typically involved in really setting something up "out there" is a wonderful lesson in Forgetting the Self and focusing on the work. It's also a necessary approach to writing itself. Outreach serves, in part, as Intro to The World 101.

Once in the room with the group, the Outreach student encounters many more transitions between the Self and the Great World. Introductory chitchat is the first. When I began working in the schools, I felt impelled to speak abstractly of Poetry's Beauties at the outset. "This is great! Beautiful! Don't you see?" I would implore, not having given any concrete demonstration of its greatness. I soon learned to apply the same rigor of show-don't-tell to my class talks as is de rigueur for a poem. Beyond that, human conversation is a good loosener-upper (which tends, however, to gobble time relentlessly, becoming its own end, if it isn't curbed).

How to talk about poems and get poetry going in ways that are satisfying both to the artistic sense and to the, perhaps, nonartist clientele? Different strokes for different folks, of course, but it's usually good to talk about poetry (or other creative writing) in a down-to-earth, brass-tacksy sort of way. "Mention colors and all sorts of details; then reading it is like walking into a picture." A free-and-easy manner encourages the many people who are shy of writing to just plunge in.

Beginning writers often expect they'll have to master some exotic technical skill, and tend to believe that's the main education it takes to be a poet. I think, though, that the two main lessons a poet learns are plain attention to detail (of language and of the world) and relative originality of image and syntax. These qualities are achieved simply in the practice and in exchanges with others (which includes reading their books). Both these qualities require a breaking-through, on the part of the poet, of conservative attitudes, which are simplistic and formulaic. Small children tend to have, on the surface, the most conservative attitude in the world, but their conservatism tends to be as breakable as thin ice; kids become quickly capable of the most radical imaginings. This kind of thought-capability, initiated in childhood, will tend to allow children to grow up with wide-ranging, livewire imaginations. With this basic faculty, they will be able to master practical things much better than otherwise, as well as interact more subtly and compassionately with other people and lead a rich life-of-the-spirit.

Out in the community, actually teaching poetry (or opening up a space for it), one wants to avoid the extremes of being a mere Ronald-McDonald-type on the one hand or being academic, obscure, or boring on the other. One must—not so much compromise as include the values one wants, in proportion. Energy, loud or quiet, is the secret of what happens in a group. Still, writing itself is the proper focus, not psychology. That is, to focus on the work (or play) of writing will tend to pull therapeutic values along with it. Psychology must be the servant (not the explicator) of the art of poetry. When poetry is worked at and achieved as much as possible, the psyche will smile too.

But hands-on poetry succeeds gloriously in most groups. At least for the moment—in the communal matrix of energy—authenticity and revelation and play roll and bounce through the rhythms and metaphors. Personal energy results, by written, verbal means! The session leader can always genuinely note something good to praise, and the praise, too, should be detailed. Speech rhythms and other music, unusual turns of phrase, feelings beyond the mere labels of the feelings—people often succeed. After all, they've been practicing speech their whole lives, and poetry is basically speech! Then, very carefully and in balance, criticism can be given and is valuable. It's true that there's no absolute right or wrong in writing, but neither is all writing of equal worth, like some idiot flood of pudding. "I really like this part, Jimmy—the colorful language gives a vivid sense of the street—jagged rhythms—but down here I think it loses energy, sounds too much like a lot of other things I've read." When a session leader gets to know the participants, he or she can get a friendly but at least semiobjective critical weather going. People can then truly feel they're working together at a craft, as well as, and intertwined with, at expression.

Here are just a few more tips on working in community groups. For one thing, the desired warm and kind projection of humanity may well include a little dart or two of sarcasm if things seem to be turning into goof-off time. I.e., the "opening up" that creative writing so wonderfully performs has its risks. On the other hand—be patient. Have a program and proceed with it, unquenched by any feelings of negativity (which may be real but temporary or may be your own projected anxiety). It's good not to insist on getting everyone totally involved at once; any recalcitrants will likely get pulled in eventually by the group energy. Publishing the writings, or selected writings—within the community group at least—is very important. By means of publication, the work is both honored and preserved. Also, many other follow-up activities—bulletin boards, public readings, festivals, etc., are great to do.

Several things happen when Naropa writers meet the public via the Institute's Outreach Program.

- The community group—schoolchildren, troubled teens, seniors, the homeless, disabled people, or any group whatever interested in creative writing workshops—tends to coalesce, gently and humanely, through the art of writing.

- Individuals *find* themselves, through verbalizing their experience and discussing the process with others doing the same.

- Paradoxically, people's ego problems dissolve in the act of putting the "self" into words.
- Client writers learn to handle the language more vividly, more accurately. Their gift of speech grows more subtle.
- People have fun, develop writing as a hobby, learn to understand others more thoroughly, exercise their mental agility and their compassion, deepen their cultural engagement.
- Student/leaders (Naropa writers) gain experience in writing, in teaching their ideas, in formulating their ideas, in working with various people, in dealing with the "real world"—altogether in extending and testing their sense of literature beyond the incubators of their minds.
- The Naropa student/leader turns in an essay—at least five to six pages for three credits but often more—detailing thought, approach, and experience. The student also presents an anthology of similar length (open-ended on the up side) and a letter from the client organization ratifying field-hours spent and giving some informal evaluation plus an indication whether further workshops are desired.
- Often, the student/leader and the group "fall in love" to the extent that they keep on meeting/writing/talking beyond the student's time of receiving credit for this participation!
- Naropa writing students heighten their sense of community with each other—beyond their writings and academics and recreations and personal lives, into this additional field, the spread of hands-on literature into the surrounding folk.
- And all of these good things spread further, and further.

For a Minor Art: Publishing & Poetry

STEVE DICKISON
July 4, 1998

* * *

PART ONE: That There Is Poetry

Poetry as an instrument of research, investigation, finding out, listening and telling; as a means of engaging and negotiating memory; an unfolding of "sight, sound, and intellection"; "the way the voice moves from person to person"; poetry tied up in its vocabulary with the vocabulary of love and desire, its needs and its search; poetry maybe always involved in a relationship with romance; its enactment of what's sometimes called vision—"this wind has a multiplicity of aliases." Can we say something like this: if somebody hasn't had the sense of being "taken up" on finding themselves inside a poem—in this strange place, unforeseen—can we say they know that poetry exists? Part of this strangeness, the daze or (Robin Blaser's word) *astonishment* of the fact of the poems returning us there is what keeps us attending this domain of what, for us, is writing marked by its incursion into and obsession with what we do not yet know. So Kristin Prevallet in her remarks on Bernadette Mayer's work, specifically, this place "is where I always want to be." Or, more famously, Allen Ginsberg's early "Song," where the place of love and very physical desire colludes and agrees with this place found by way of the poem:

> yes, yes,
> > that's what
> I wanted,
> > I always wanted,
> I always wanted,
> > to return
> to the body
> > where I was born.

Or as John Wieners, a decade later, writes:

> Oh my dreams are there
> and I pledge to fulfill them
> as they go by in smoke.

It's a question here of dream and pledge, and of our wants that drive us to and fro, after (and behind) the poem in its inherently inquisitive shapes—its questions and proportions—what's been called its *measure*. The poem proposes an unforeseen measure. It's unpresupposable—and also, according to Jack Spicer, reinscribing a favored word out of Edgar Allan Poe, it's *indefinite*. There's the stupendous book of instruction by Jack Spicer that warrants and bears repeated reading he called "A Textbook of Poetry," where failure is as much the provenance of the poem ("An argument between the dead and the living") as any effort otherwise:

> They won't come through. Nothing comes through. The
> death
>
> Of every poem in every line
>
> The argument con-
> tinues.

Can we put beside this Eileen Myles's suspicion of the poem as a kind of residue, and her turning away from the heavy emphasis and over-valuation of "the poem" per se:

> I've been haunted lately by the notion that the poem's not the thing at all, that the "performance of being" is what's real and we poets merely take notes in relation to that.

"I've been haunted" . . . that "we" "take notes in relation to" "what's real"—"in relation to" this so-called "performance of being"—that our "notes" more than "the poem" per se follow and attend to "the thing," they note "what's real" or else, maybe, (in Spicer's words) they're what "Descends to the real"—and (again Jack Spicer) "Not as a gesture of contempt for the scattered nature of reality."

PART TWO: Le Mépris

Odd, in a talk on "poetry and publishing"—the two conjoined—to end up on this sentence rejecting the "gesture of contempt." Because there was in Jack Spicer a kind of contempt for publishing which I think is an inheritance that poets live with. What's embraced in Spicer's rejection—specifically "the scattered nature of reality"—it's as if this "scattered nature," this "reality," were interrupted or betrayed by the poetry's being made too much public. Something like an encrypted message: that the gross activity of publishing holds reality in contempt. We can think of Spicer as an advocate for "private circulation." And that's one model various in itself, and a very real one for the publishing of poetry and writing close to it. Certainly there are countless examples and among these very famous ones (William Blake or Emily Dickinson, Franz Kafka or Charles Reznikoff, etc., etc.). Certainly, too, there are instances of a kind of degraded poetry written whose entire orientation seems bent on publication.

A factor in the former, Spicer's private circulation model, is the great amount of very specific hands-on *care* that could be given to the presentation of the poetry—a care that, in his case, extended even to a form of control exacted over its reception, a design regarding just whose hands the poetry might land in. Such care—and the term here wouldn't exclude apprehension, caution, hurt, fear, paranoia—also amounts to one of the most positive arguments for an autonomy surrounding the publication of poetry, and for this practice being as it is, in fact, so often one specifically of poets. If one could say there were an ethic involved or enacted in the publishing of poetry, it would have to be first of all an ethic of care.

PART THREE: "No Both"

Most of the words that we use to try to talk about publishing and poetry fall apart on us. The "independent" publisher, the "literary" publisher, the "small press," in the old days the "little magazine," all apparently opposed to or at least apposite—across the spectrum from—the "corporate" publisher. All the labels if pressed tend to dissolve into a kind of uselessness. The formerly or still nominally family-run house that's been swallowed by the shittiest of multinational conglomerates, though their agenda has shifted, still publishes occasionally the amazing book. The independent literary small press can and will publish the shitty book. Much as publishers might want it to be so, there's no value as such that automatically attaches to being "independent" or "literary" or "small"—while there is still I think an opportunity or possibility that's specific to the relatively more autonomous publisher, and there's also the risk this chance can be betrayed.

PART FOUR: "We Speak"

One throws a handful of questions out to several dozen publishers, and a jungle of answers come flying back. What's common if anything's common to their responses is the contention that publishing—this kind of publishing we've been talking about—comes from and is itself an act of conviction. It's an effort despite the flood of information, *the official words don't fit us, we're here to be read,* in these micro-economies of scrutiny and attention, unassimilables, entertainments suspended in print between one's pencil and another's ear, "communalism," publishings in the root sense of publicking—"lost in the crowd"—for the people who can find us in the blur, *what's clear above all is that decisions are based on what we want,* the broadcasting of rumors based on what we hear, heard, will have heard.

I don't want it to be idealized. I'm putting words into their mouths, our mouths. We are bringing things into the world that otherwise the world would be (almost) empty of.

PART FIVE: The Singular Multiplied

The word "autonomous" might not hold up entirely either, I apologize, but it points in its base form—*auto-nomos* = self-law—not just to insubordination to some outside rule, but also to this chance or risk one is enveloped in whenever the possibility of autonomy is opened up. When we say things like "publishing is an art," don't we mean that it exists under this rule of chance, that its risks exceed—though that's real enough—an economic failure?

One says "self" and says "one"—in the singular—when in fact every publisher is more than one, a collective entity *necessarily multiple.* So the risk of failure beyond economic comes maybe from this *collective enunciation,* even the smallest publisher is already made up of many, it doesn't take decades for what we mistake as the single thing to metamorphose into a multiplicity of singularities. It's not just the collision of the diversity of authors represented by a press, as a publisher helps make the multiple composition that is the press, but the whole vexed question of *community* that opens up and envelops the ones.

PART SIX: A Minor Art

"What in great literature goes on down below, constituting a not indispensable cellar of the structure, here takes place in the full light of day, what is there a matter of passing interest for a few, here absorbs everyone no less than as a matter of life and death."
—FRANZ KAFKA (*Diaries,* 1911)

If I say or suspect that poetry publishing can be thought of as a "minor art," it's because it exists in an economy that wouldn't exist at all except through its own collective self-determination. It's one that repeatedly has to *tear itself away* from those forces or institutions that through lack of regard or through incomprehension judge it insignificant or senseless. It's one that's constantly needing *to invent another way.*

Previously published in Crayon, *No. 2, 1999.*
Thanks to editors Andrew Levy and Bob Harrison.

Statement on the Events of September 11, 2001

AKILAH OLIVER & STUDENTS
2001

★ ★ ★

The events of September 11, 2001 will mark that day as one of incomprehensible tragedy. We grieve the lives lost in New York City, Washington, DC, and Pennsylvania. In this moment of grieving, we have been given an opportunity to understand and extend compassion for the pain that violence brings to people all over the world.

There is a rising sentiment of fear, confusion, a sense of loss, anger, and the need for confrontation. We are at a crossroads. We can choose war or we can choose peace. Our government's actions will set the course for what events are to follow. We have a collective responsibility to acknowledge that all our actions are interconnected. Out of this tragedy an opportunity has arisen. The public need for unity can create dialogue, reconciliation, and insight.

We stand behind a nonviolent solution that will lead to peace. This is a moment to develop and express deep empathy for people all over the globe for whom senseless violence has been a daily reality.

Particularly at this point, we should be cautious of acts of violence, hateful language and intolerance directed against Muslims, other non-Christians, and people of color.

This is a moment to look toward new models for peace. We have guides. We can look toward the words of Gandhi, Martin Luther King, Jr., the Dalai Lama, Mother Theresa, and many others. We have a choice to act in love and compassion in this incredibly complex moment, rather than in fear and anger.

Those responsible for the attacks on the Pentagon and the World Trade Center should be brought to justice, but without a vengeful spirit that harms innocent people. It is possible to envision compassionate models of justice. It is possible to be accountable and to hold one another accountable for individual and collective actions without demonizing nations, nationalities, religions, or groups of people.

We stand behind the courage of the possible, rather than behind the simplistic predictability of models of aggression. Let the violence stop with us.

Concerned students, friends, staff, and faculty of Naropa University.
This statement does not represent the views of the entire administration, student body, board of trustees, faculty, and staff at Naropa University.

→→ Nomad →→ Century →→ Ahead →→

PIERRE JORIS
1998

★　★　★

I am going towards a future that does not exist,
leaving every instant a new corpse behind me
—RENÉ DAUMAL

not because I could have been a wax archangel
or evening rain or car catalogue
—TRISTAN TZARA

1. CLOSING TIME: As this century draws to a close, here comes everybody's eerie feeling that we've been here before, or in the immortal words of Yogi Berra, "It's déjà vu all over again." So it would seem Joyce's man, Vico, may have been right after all, that it all is cyclical, that our end is in our beginning, & that the spiral draws tighter & tighter around our scruffy necks. Yet this century a certain kind of history was, if not abolished, at least brought up short & shown up for the con it is—(oh no, not by the official war artists, & not by the thinkerers & tinkerers of the Polit-Sphere, nor by the Hackademic watchdogs of kulchur)—namely, the linear soon-to-be-over, escha-teleo-logical time-machine. You know what/ who I mean: the various fascisms, the Vatican, the leagues of protestant ball-cutters, the myriad totalitarianisms, macro & micro, etc. *La condition humaine,* one man wrote, is revolution in a far-off country, & then went home & made the world over as state-subsidized museums.

Reality is not simply there, it must be searched for and won
—PAUL CELAN

I was very curious to see how they planned to bring me to life again.
—ISM-SORTER BY JEFIM GOLYCHEFF

It is strictly forbidden to touch objects in the collection I felt dizzy
—KURT SCHWITTERS

2. SNIP-SNAP: We go on or back, by nerve alone, on rafts made of the skin of our teeth, nostalgia always already being what it is, i.e., exactly that linguistic formula, we try to find ourselves in the old journals & magazines, flip the pages & all of a sudden discover that all the images have disappeared, have been cut out carefully, only the shadow of their absence, only the ragged edge of their contours giving a vague indication of who or what was here, I mean there. Snip, snap. They are over there, I mean here, now, rearranged, collaged & decollaged, montaged & demontaged, syntaxed & parataxed, but taxed for sure, cyber-mounted in the demonic-maniacal autobiography of this century "prewritten" by *Time-Life, The Saturday Evening Post, Paris Match, Die Welt, Popular Mechanics, El Moujahid, Rolling Stone, Pravda* & rewritten by the various collage & cut-up avant-gardes. Does this look familiar? It should—the century has come back to haunt you, to show itself (up) one last time for what it was, for what it stood for & against, from Tzara to Kitaj, from Duchamp to Kienholz, from Schwitters to Pélieu, from a to z: COLLAGE, its core innovation, foreseen by Lautréamont late in the previous one. It cut the time lines, taught us a new history, and yet is also graft, a rearrangement of arborescent structures, trees as always already roots I trunk I branches, even when cut and rearranged, say branches I trunk I roots, the heavenly tree grows downward in polarities we can no longer afford, if we ever could. No time left, neither ascent nor descent beckon. GO to the treeless planes of the Pleistocene, DO NOT turn back, DO NOT RECOLLECT, GO flat out at top speed across curve of earth is the only way. Get down on all fours & run, become fox, wolf, become animal once again.

> wandering creates the desert
> —EDMOND JABÈS

> I am a line which expands and I want to grow in an iron tin pipe
> I say that to amuse you.
> —TRISTAN TZARA

3. OPENING SPACE: What is needed now is a nomadic poetics. Its method will be *rhizomatic:* which is different from collage, i.e., a rhizomatics is not an aesthetics of the fragment, which has dominated poetics since the romantics even as transmogrified by modernism, high & low, & more recently retooled in the neoclassical form of the citation-ironic & or decorative-throughout what is called "postmodernism." Strawberry Fields Forever. A nomadic poetics will cross languages, not just translate, but write in all or any of them. If Pound, H.D., Joyce, Stein, Olson, & others have shown the way, it is essential now to push this matter further, again, not so much as "collage" (though we will keep those gains) but as a material flux of language matter. To try & think, then, this matter as even pre-language, proto-semantic, as starting from what Kristeva calls the *chora,* which she defines as "a temporary articulation, essentially mobile, constituted of movements and their ephemeral stases." And then to follow this flux of ruptures and articulations, of rhythm, moving in & out of semantic & non-semantic spaces, moving around & through the features accreting as poem, a lingo-cubism, no, a lingo-barocco that is no longer an "explosante fixe" (Breton) but an "explosante mouvante."

> The relations of poetry are, for our period, very close to the relations
> of science. It is not a matter of using the results of science, but of seeing
> that there is a meeting place between all the kinds of imagination.
> Poetry can provide that meeting place.
> —MURIEL RUKEYSER

> People wish to be settled: only so long as they are unsettled
> is there any hope for them.
> —RALPH WALDO EMERSON

4. STATE OF: The days of anything static, form, content, state are over. The past century has shown that anything not involved in continuous transformation hardens and dies. All revolutions have done just that: those that tried to deal with the state as much as those that tried to deal with the state of poetry.

> I lived in the first century of world wars.
> Most mornings I would be more or less insane.
> —MURIEL RUKEYSER

> I have never been able to tell a beginning from an end.
> —GEORGE BRAQUE

5. MEMORY BABE: From the 20th century we will retain everything—in memory. We will forget nothing and we will forgive nothing. We will also remember that the 20th century was the tail wagged by the 19th century dog.

> What I have tried to do is to inflect the French language, to transform it
> in order to express, let's say: "This me, this nigger-me, this Creole-me, this
> Martinican-me, this Caribbean-me." That's why I was much more interested
> in poetry than in prose—exactly because the poet is the one who creates
> his language, while the writer of prose, in the main, uses language.
> —AIMÉ CÉSAIRE

> Poetry is the promise of a language.
> —HÖLDERLIN

6. BAROCCO: We will write in foreign languages (real or made-up ones) in order to come to the realization that all languages are foreign. And those that are not are uninteresting in their self-reflecting egoism. All live languages are creolized by what Edouard Glissant has called the chaosworld. The first need thus is to have done with the prison-house of the mother tongue, i.e., why should one have to write in the mummy/daddy language, why should that oedipal choice be the only possible or legitimate one, why should it not be my own choice, that moment of one's discovery of the other, that moment when it is our body/mind that speaks and not that of our progenitors. The mother tongue will become the lover's tongue, the other's tongue. A nomadic language of effects, of free lines of erotic flight, that break the triangular (the strongest of shapes, as Bucky Fuller has shown us) strictures of the Freudian scene de famille and of its sociopolitical macroprojection, the nation-state.

> We stand in relationship with all the components of the universe,
> as well as with the hereafter and with antiquity. Which relationships we
> will cultivate, which for us is preeminently important, and which should be
> realized, depends only upon the course and duration of our watchfulness.
> —NOVALIS

> in the cerecloth of devious stratagems
> —DENNIS BRUTUS

7. WORLD: Here now to propose expanding Robin Blaser's beautiful saying It is an absent America whose presence is at stake to read. It is an absent World whose presence is at stake. A world yet to be invented. Déjà vu all over again must not win out. As I write this, March 1998, the Bible and the Sword (in the shape of that most reactionary of popes and that most pliant of U.S. presidents) are crisscrossing Africa, softening up the continent for the New Colonialism of the coming century. In the U.S. media the only voice I heard speak accurately to this condition was that of a poet—Dennis Brutus. Which brings to mind Helene Cixous's sense that "the twentieth century, in its violence, has brought about the marriage of Poetry and History." History not dead yet, imagination, imagine, not dead yet, history is yet to come, we are all in need of becoming archaeologists of the morning after.

> unmouthed lip, announce,
> that something's happening, still,
> not far from you.
> —PAUL CELAN

Torch Song
(Prose Is a Prose Is a Prose)

LAURA MULLEN
June 25, 2002

"That's the way fire does, it don't have no rules on it."
——ANONYMOUS FIREFIGHTER, SUMMER 2002

"I think her words were, 'You're going to be really mad at me.'
I don't think I was mad at her, I was just more shocked and saddened."
——FOREST SERVICE RANGER SARA MAYBEN,
DESCRIBING FORMER FOREST SERVICE TECHNICIAN TERRY BARTON'S
ADMISSION OF RESPONSIBILITY FOR THE HAYMAN FIRE

Story #1: She smelled smoke and discovered fire.
Proverb: *Where there's smoke there's fire.*

Perverbs
(homage to Harry Mathews)
All roads lead to fire
Where there's smoke there's a way
A rolling stone gathers no fire
Where there's smoke wait for no man
The road to hell is paved with fire
Where's there's smoke must come down
When the cat's away there's fire
What goes up must . . .
in flames

IT SPEAKS: A failure of belief is often figured as a problem of incorporation: *No one would swallow that,* we say, or, "it just doesn't smell right." It *stinks.* Sometimes that's as close as we can get to it. To "burn" is also to deceive. Given the distance and the wind direction . . . —this scent of smoke (clinging to cloth and skin, tangled in hair) vanishes into the air we insist is "thin." As any excuse.

Story #1a (her own words): "I saw the fire and tried to put it out."
Hayman Fire "at a glance" (updated from the *Coloradoan,* June 21, 2002)
Size: About 137,000 acres
Evacuations: About 8,200
Damage: 133 homes destroyed.
On scene: 2,508 personnel.
Cost: $29 million.

DISCUSSION TOPIC: TECHNOLOGIES AND GESTURES: In a transparent sentence the subject sees and comes to knowledge and then action, though the imbalance of verbs as well as the syntax (note the distance of the "I" from that final, failed effort) alerts us to her sense of powerlessness. Before she got there, the fire, before anything—before the speech it sparks, or the writing she'll later claim started it—"kindled by a person unknown." "I saw the fire": "I" is a shifter. Do you see her seeing (a face at the edge of the frame, registering—in slightly too-lurid color—shock and increasing dismay) or do you see yourself in her place? "I tried to put it out." "I tried." Repeat at least 2,500 times.

RE: VISION: "Tirelessly the process of thinking makes new beginnings, returning in a roundabout way to its original object" (Walter Benjamin: *The Origin of the German Tragic Drama*). "Mosaic": the term for the varied and broken patterns a fire traces, comprehending a landscape, "burning at different intensities in different places and . . . burning different places in different years" (Margaret Fuller: *Forest Fires*).

> **Story #2:** "She reported that she looked at a letter that she had received that morning from her estranged husband. She became angry and upset and tried to get rid of the letter." (court doc.)

ADVICE FROM A FICTION WRITER (DEAD): "You've got to sell your heart, your strongest reactions, not the little minor things that only touch you lightly. . . . This is especially true when you begin to write, when you have not yet developed the tricks of interesting people on paper, when you have none of the technique which it takes time to learn. When, in short, you have only your emotions to sell" (F. Scott Fitzgerald).

> **(Back) Story #2a:** At one point we're told that our heroine's two teenage daughters put a letter of their father's into their mother's day pack before she went off to work. Their goal: repairing the marriage; her job: protecting the wilderness.

RE: VISION: A woman enters a forest with a letter. The letter, a love letter, never mentions the forest but some people can look at a stand of trees and see nothing but paper. The sweet, rank, cloying stench of the pulp mill fills the air a thousand miles from here. Some people can look at a line of words and see nothing but reference—or the lack of it—most of the sentence seems like a by-product, a way to get there. The defendant declared she "stayed with the burning letter until it had burned completely." Most people, visiting the national parks, never go more than 250 feet away from their cars.

BACK DRAFT: *"Darling I can't live without you,"* etc. Before they fold the letter into their mother's day pack, the girls read the trite phrases over to each other in awed, hushed whispers punctuated by—on the part of the youngest—fits of uncomfortable giggles. In short they read it like teenage girls. They *are* teenage girls: we know what that means.

QUESTIONS FOR FURTHER STUDY:
- *What does that mean?*
- Are you thinking here of the book or the movie, the original or the remake of *The Parent Trap?*
- How did the girls get their hands on the letter?

AND THE WORD *WAS* LIGHT: Reread Jacques Lacan on Edgar Allan Poe's story "The Purloined Letter"? Reread Poe—the letter is set out in plain sight so it can't be seen; the letter must be recovered and can't be read, ever; the letter is replaced by another letter which *can* be read: but the words are not the words of the letter's author. Reread Walter Benjamin ("The reader warms his shivering life with a death he reads about": "The Story Teller"). "[S]he was so upset after reading the letter that she burned it inside a campfire ring but it escaped, accidentally igniting Colorado's largest wildfire" (Note from the *Coloradoan* [6/22/02]).

QUESTIONS FOR FURTHER STUDY:
- What work is "accidentally" doing in the above sentence? And, "largest wildfire"?
- In the phrase "burned it . . . but it escaped" is the pronoun's reference secure?

RE: VISION: As if made for a made-for-TV-movie the already tired scene played over and over: "She was so upset," etc. (Question: How upset do you need to be to burn 137,000 acres?) The print is grainy. Did you see her, "in your mind's eye," with matches, crying so her hand shook too much to strike a light at first? Or do you picture her standing there, resolute, raising a lighter aloft like a concert-goer during the encore? "The only

CIVIL DISOBEDIENCES

thing that is different from one time to another is what is seen and what is seen depends upon how everybody is doing everything," Gertrude Stein repeats ("Composition as Explanation"). The Russian filmmaker Andrei Tarkovsky dies in exile, his countrymen having refused his vision, even now some people say of his movies that there's not enough story there. In *The Mirror* a drenched woman appears in the charred room of a gone house, a dream or memory, haunting the narrator. *Homage,* as if the word had a home in it. All the elements the filmmaker loved and lovingly reassembled are here: the woman, the forest, the tears . . . a letter on fire.

OUT-TAKES, OR EVERYBODY'S EX: June 21, 2002: The stuff of the event burns so fast—there's no time to establish or absorb any single story, or to see a previous version be fully replaced by another, so that all the possible truths seem still to be in play, though only able uneasily to acknowledge each other. Remember the zero story? Something about a car spotted fleeing the scene. Was a male figure mentioned or did I make that up? Some guy . . . —boiling water for coffee, or noodles or? Ready in an instant, as if he were himself a reconstituted soup mix, this character: the beer in his hand, the car radio blaring "Smoke on the Water," the story he tells himself in half-phrases, "Shit, she used to love it here. . . ."—the way he roughly brushes at his eyes with the back of his fist, and tosses his cigarette butt at the campfire pit—"ah, goddamn it. . . ."

NOTES ON CRAFT (FICTION): A false line of dialogue can ruin an entire scene.
NOTES ON CRAFT (FORESTRY): Old burns tend to stop fires.

> **Story #2b** ("What's this paper doing here?"): Our heroine pulls her ex-husband's letter from her pack, alone in the forest, and breaks down, deciding to burn it at once, which we are meant to "understand" or be understanding about—although she is in fact on duty, in her role as a Forest Service Technician, enforcing a ban on fires, in her probationary year.

IT SPEAKS: A failure of understanding is often figured as a failure of grasp. We say, "I don't get it." We say, "The meaning completely escaped her." Anne Carson remarks Paul Celan's idea of language as net or grillwork—*Sprachgitter*—in whose limits and meshes we are "cleanse[d] of the illusion that we could talk" (*Economy of the Unlost,* 33).

> **Story #3** Her husband has "told investigators he never wrote her a letter. Prosecutors also said there was no evidence of burned paper at the scene, but they are still conducting tests on the debris."

DISCUSSION TOPIC: TECHNOLOGIES AND GESTURES (OR: THE COMPANY BAR-B-Q). Unquestioned understanding: of course you burn a *love* letter (historical and literary precedents: *The Wings of the Dove,* etc.), but—even as we imagine the tender words (had tears splotched the paper?) turning to ash—a question occurs. What if, as is so likely now, the letter was written on a computer? (Reread Benjamin, "The Work of Art in the Age of Mechanical Reproduction," etc.) Oh, not a *love* letter?! Our desire to allot specific technologies a certain range of emotional gestures is itself worth a paper. Discuss the differences in texture-of-event between burning a love letter and shredding documents. Why *don't* we shred love letters? If it comes out that Ollie North and Fawn Hall sat up late burning the Iran-Contra evidence together do we think they were in love? And if it turns out that employees at Arthur Andersen *burned* papers relating to the Enron account? What if the papers were used to help the coals catch beneath the stiff suckling pig on its spit, as full of righteous indignation as any accused executive?

Q. What would you save from a house on fire?
A. The fire (Cocteau).

BACK DRAFT: For days we'd been reading, beneath the dry news reports, the easy cliches this letter would have had to include, a fire beginning, "I love you"; a fire beginning, "I want to start over." The tears in the reader's eyes give the air a heat shimmer. Okay. Now you have two hours to go back in and bring out everything you want to save forever. As is so often the case, the words had a powerful effect, though not the one intended by their author!

WHAT WE TALK ABOUT WHEN WE TALK ABOUT CREATIVE WRITING: In those contemporary stories which still function, despite appearances, as instruction manuals for if not *good* then at least *better* behavior our heroine brusquely crumples the letter, thinks for a minute, unfolds it again and, putting the offending document on the seat beside her, drives home. If she doesn't have the almost requisite fender bender (late-20th-century epiphany territory: a chance for some sudden intersubjectivity and necessary soul searching), she arrives home—lowers the blinds, pours herself a drink and plays something like "Smoke Gets in Your Eyes" over and over. It's as if what she's read has seared itself into her memory, the rhythm of those terse sentences with their focus on physical details, e.g.: The sound of the ice against the glass made a cool noise which soothed her.

ADVICE FROM THE TRIBE'S PIECE OF TALE: "Sometimes trying to rekindle an old flame works, but frequently the best advice we can give a woman who thinks she's still in love with her ex is *Next!*" *(The Rules II,* p. 25).

THE PLEA: Innocent.
THE SENTENCE: "We have yet to take our thinking about fiction to the level of the sentence." (Kass Fleisher)

> **Story #4** "In the custody," as Maurice Blanchot puts it, "of the third person," a report lists our protagonist's age (38) in the sentence describing her as "dry-eyed as she entered the plea." And continues, "But after Thursday's hearing got under way, she wiped away tears and reached for a tissue as one witness, u.s. Forest service special agent Brenda Schultz, said it appeared [the defendant] had moved rocks from a campfire to allow the fire to escape and ignite surrounding brush" *(Coloradoan).*

ADVICE FROM A POET (DEAD): "No tears for the writer, no tears for the reader" (Robert Frost).

DISCUSSION TOPIC: GESTURES AND TECHNOLOGIES. An acid trip allowed Anaïs Nin to discover that women weep because "IT IS THE QUICKEST WAY TO REJOIN THE OCEAN." Loyola's journal traced his spiritual progress by recording his degree of responsiveness to the act of worship, noting the absence or presence, while praying, of tears. Recall and discuss instances (from life or literature) in which this bodily function marks a "dissolve" between public (exterior) and private (interior). In your own experience, is this a gender specific technology? In the report above, why is the defendant crying? What do tears stand for here?
QUESTIONS FOR FURTHER STUDY:
- What are the social benefits of a legible body or a body perceived as legible?
- What costs might be involved in the production of such bodies, both presently and in the future?
- Who pays and how?

> **Story #4a? Or 5?:** She dreams of being a fire inspector, a debris-sifter, one of the experts called in after the whole thing's over. She can tell you everything that happened there, in order. Just one glance and she knows how this one began. She shakes her head. We can't see her eyes behind the sunglasses but her brow is furrowed and her lips are firmly pressed together. "You see what I see?" she asks, but we never do, not ever, not until she tells us what to see. She shakes the evidence into a carefully labeled plastic bag and we notice the tan line on her left hand's ringless third finger.

DEBRIS OR NOT DEBRIS: "It was expressing John's feelings for Terry that he loved her and wanted to get back together with her . . . " (Connie Work, family friend). These blank skies and astonishing, romantic sunsets. Static in the background heavily amplified to stand for the sound of the fire. Heavily overgrown forests, residential construction in so-called "red areas," an increase in the population of wood-eating beetles, and almost no snowpack: *Now you're getting warmer.* A friend—out west for the canceled family vacation—stays until the fire is over, to go through the ashes with his parents, looking at what his grandparents (who built the cabin) can't bear to see. Some people would say there's nothing to see here: a blackened rubble full of strange shapes it takes hard observation and sessions of guessing to remember, to place, to recall the use of, to restore to meaning. But that thin line of lead might be a pencil, those shards of metal the exploded lamp, maybe. What's left of the mirrors and windows these twisted, gleaming, stopped flows of melted glass: these frozen tears. "Fuck it," the poet's tattoo says, "burn everything." The problem of breathing in this atmosphere.

QUESTIONS FOR FURTHER STUDY:

• Do you think we could just start over?

Interview

AMMIEL ALCALAY

Interviewed by Marlowe Fawcett
April, 2003

★ ★ ★

MARLOWE FAWCETT: Comment on the following from Eliot Weinberger's talk at the Poetry Is News Conference at St. Mark's[1]: "In all the anthologies and magazines devoted to 9/11 and its aftermath, nearly every single writer resorted to first-person anecdote: 'It reminded me of the day my father died . . . ,' 'I took an herbal bath and decided to call an old boyfriend . . .' Most American writers have lost the ability to even think politically, or nationally, or internationally. . . . We are where we are in part because American writers—supposedly the most articulate members of society—have generally had nothing to say about the world for the last thirty years."

AMMIEL ALCALAY: I can think of a number of ways of responding to this. I could go on the offensive and say, I'm a writer, and I've been thinking and acting politically since I started publishing, which is about twenty-five of those thirty years, and a lot of my concerns and activities have been international. Or I could list a whole bunch of people who I think have been thinking politically and acting internationally, but they might not be the people this text was addressed to. In other words, I think Eliot was aiming this at a very specific part of the poetry world but with implications for American intellectual life in general. While I subscribe to its sentiments, more or less, I think the situation has to be looked at a lot more closely. First of all, it is crucial to create one's own reference points and intersection of people who share your concerns or impulses. Here's an example: sometime around 1990 I was asked to guest edit a special issue of the journal *Lusitania,* along with a friend, the Palestinian painter, Kamal Boullata. The issue was supposed to be on the quincentenary of 1492, on al-Andalus/Sepharad/Spain, but from the perspective of Arabs and Middle Eastern Jews. But when the siege of Sarajevo began, we realized that our issue had to be about that because the kind of culture that had once existed in Islamic Spain, in Andalucia, was now being destroyed in Bosnia. About half the issue was material from Bosnia, reportage, artworks, historical material, and so on. The second half was my own selection of writers that I wanted to see together between the same covers, and it was a very eclectic group, mixing foreign and American writers, from the great Arab poet Adonis to the Cherokee poet and artist Jimmie Durham. It was an attempt to create the kind of cultural space that is rarely achieved in this country, a true mix of people with different aesthetics, different disciplines, and different trajectories. My point is that there wasn't much happening on the poetry scene regarding Bosnia at the time, so my impulse was to create my own scene and provide a critique by example. Moreover, most of the anthologies or magazines coming out at the time were practicing their own versions of apartheid and it was very clear to me that my statement had to be not only about the divisions occurring over "there" but had to relate very closely to what was happening here. So calling upon people like Jimmie Durham, Alexis de Veaux, Rashida Ismaili, Juan Felipe Herrera, Enrique Fernandez, and others, was a very important element of the whole thing.

Going further, though, I would have to say that I think people have generally conceptualized their own roles as writers in an incredibly limited way. There was a rather vitriolic critique of Eliot's piece that went out on the Poetics List (which I look at every now and then to check the collective temperature of one segment of the poetry world), and it also mentioned how there were many politically conscious poets out there and various great readings. But I hadn't been at any of those events so my impression might be that people were not as politically conscious as I might have hoped they'd be. I was enormously disappointed by this on a number of counts. To begin with, the event at the Project had been conceived in a wider and more inclusive way than anything I've personally been witness to or involved in for many many years. I think that accounts without axes to grind will bear this out—we were addressed by one of the Arab world's foremost novelists and intellectuals, Elias Khoury; we had reports from a woman who'd ridden ambulances in Jenin as an International Solidarity Movement Activist; Paul Chan, a New York artist, reported on a recent trip to Baghdad; two artists who'd been doing actions centered around INS detention policies presented; two high school kids from Bushwick spoke about organizing against military recruitment; the cartoonist and journalist Ted Rall spoke about Afghanistan, and on and on and on. We really made an attempt to tie things together and get people to think beyond their narrow confines.

If one wants to engage with the public world, there are all kinds of venues and possibilities. The fact is that too many writers have closed in on themselves, working within various professionalized or guild-like structures and not getting their hands dirty by taking on the media or taking on the public arena in order to create new spaces and possibilities. Politics, at root, not only implies but signifies the public, the opposite of private. If art is not to participate publicly, why should it be displayed, published, or performed? If it has no part in public life, why not leave it in your drawer or your head? Living, as we are, in the heart of the empire, we must discover new ways to both renounce and take up power. Any politics of integrity must start at home, with how you spend your time and where you put your energy. Is it solely in service of yourself or in the service of others? Are the rewards tangible or intangible? As professionalization in all walks of life, perhaps most insidiously in the arts since the gains are so negligible, proceeds apace, and there is less and less public or amateur space to interact in and with, everyone must find different ways to cross borders, take risks, and make commitments. We must always be ready to question any privileges we might have and figure out ways to redirect those privileges. Public and cultural space, the space of politics and citizenship, cannot simply be allowed to disappear without a struggle.

MF: You say in *Poetry, Politics, and Translation* . . . that American texts almost declare their aloneness, and that your work has attempted to approach that and try and bridge the gaps between that "American aloneness" and the Old World's "collective memory," in an attempt to "challenge writers to try and find those places in themselves that they haven't gotten to." How do you go about this in your work? Do you notice a "coldness" in contemporary American writing? A blending of the personal and the ironic, a new look at postmodernism?

AA: I'd say I go about it partially out of necessity. That is, I'm a first generation person in this country, on this continent, and there are other things pulling me elsewhere. I am continually astonished at how much there is to learn about this country and how well hidden things are, though they seem to be in plain sight. I've been teaching a graduate seminar this year, for example, on Los Angeles and San Francisco, from 10,000 BC to the present. We're not exactly doing it chronologically, but simply trying to take that whole time span into account. I mean, if you were going to study about Iraq, you'd start in Ur and Mesopotamia; if you were going to study about Italy, some reference would be made to the Romans. We don't think that needs to be done here, and it's appalling. There are collective memories here but we've been made to think they don't matter. I find, for instance, that a lot of my work on Middle Eastern Jews resonates very deeply with African Americans because they sense deep similarities in terms of the kinds of experiences they've had in this country and the kinds of experiences Middle Eastern Jews have had in Israel. In fact, one of the most important Israeli political movements coming out of the mizrahi or Middle Eastern Jewish community called itself the Black Panthers. So I think a lot of things I've been doing have also been aimed at changing the makeup or the expectations of audiences here: in other words, there are direct relationships between the way I might approach prison literature by Palestinians or other political prisoners and the experiences of incarceration in this country. Those are connections that I don't see enough writers making and I think they are absolutely crucial to making people understand how things operate. It is no accident that the night Bush gave his speech announcing the war against Iraq, he also approved of the execution of a decorated African American Gulf War veteran who had murdered a cadet. So I don't think it's a "coldness" I see in a lot of American writing—it's more like a massive dose of denial, a kind of privatization and fetishization of the word that may translate into emotional distance. There is some kind of fear of being emotional—it was very significant at some of the discussions during the People's Poetry Gathering[2] that poets like Etel Adnan and the Moroccan, Abdellatif Laabi, spoke of the need for life to be at the very center of poetry's purpose. I think Americans are very scared of saying something like that.

To go further, I'd have to possibly question the context of the categories you bring up—the personal and the ironic, the postmodern. Any definition of the postmodern that I'd use would have to go back to Charles Olson, woefully unfashionable these days, who actually came up with the term as we know it in a series of letters to Robert Creeley in the early 1950s. In a letter to the anthropologist Ruth Benedict, Olson wrote: "The EXPANSION of peoples, materials and sensations that the AGE OF QUANTITY involves itself in, DEMAND a heightening of that servant of clarity, the CRITICAL FUNCTION, wherever: that is, the above increases in the quantity of experience is also an increase in the sources of confusion, and so, to cut them down requires more labor than previously . . . that the job now, is to be at once archaic and culture-wise—that they are indivisible." He went on to write, again to Ruth Benedict: "It is my feeling that *the record of fact* is become of first importance for us lost in a sea of question. . . . In New History, the act of the observer, if his personality is of count, is before, in the collection of the material. This is where we will cut the knot. . . . I think if you burn the facts long and hard enough in yourself as crucible, you'll come to the few facts that matter, and then fact can be fable again." The world we inhabit clearly has much less space to operate in; the kind of public space I remember being able to move in and through in the late 1960s or early 1970s is almost nonexistent. The motivation of experimental writing, in many cases, jettisoned anything that seemed conventional or had narrative content. Most crucial here, I think, is the excision of work by Vietnam veterans, suppressed people, political prisoners, and writers involved in popular movements around the world, from Central America to the Middle East, particularly Palestine, an issue central to maintaining U.S. domination over global narratives and realities. There are profound lessons to be learned from work like this, about the function and ethics of writing, the place writing can have as testimony, and the relationship between a writer and his or her potential or actual audience. Most importantly, though, is the fact that an unwillingness to deal with narrative allows dominant narratives more space to function and take hold. Writers and intellectuals bear great responsibility for this because if one gives up the right to narrate or intervene, both at home and in other parts of the world, that vacuum will be filled by the discourse of "experts."

MF: Talk about your process in *from the warring factions:* how did you select your sources; did you have an idea first and then search for the right words, or did the words speak to you about the idea? Also, in your use of multiple voices and "samples" you seem to be creating a "dub" version of the human voice, particularly the social/political voice, the voices of both power and powerlessness. Your samples are the reverb, fader, echoes, of a music dub, while your page and arrangement are the base/bass.

AA: I think the musical parallels you mention are quite apt. My pre-dub model remains someone like Albert Ayler, where the memory of the melody always lingers and is gone back to, kind of like the page or base/bass you refer to. There's no question that the text, and all of my work is very related to musical movement, to the relationship of a standard and the improvisational space that opens up around it. This is also true for Middle Eastern music, with its modes and moods. In terms of my actual methods of seeking source materials or words, I would have to say that the words chose me as much as I chose them. It simply became self evident as the process went on—at a certain point in the book, the form became more and more open and I realized that almost anything I could put my hands on would fit, or could be mobilized within the context I had created.

MF: What are your thoughts on "the authentic voice"; thinking of your work as translator and as "channel," a la Jack Spicer, for the voiceless.

AA: I think one has to be very careful with the term "authentic," though not exactly in the way people are usually careful about it. For me, the primary issue was about appropriation when working with documentary materials. I'd done enough work translating, transcribing court testimony or editing torture testimonies and that kind of thing that when I used that kind of material in an earlier book, *the cairo notebooks,* I became very conscious of differentiating the narrator's circumstances from the circumstances of the people whose words I'd appropriated to use in the book. I wanted to approach this problem differently in *from the warring factions,* and it was at that point that I realized the best way to do it would be if all the words were "appropriated." This, ironically, provided the kind of freedom that I think Spicer speaks of. All language is already translation anyway.

MF: Do you see a distinction between "Humanism" and humanity? I'm thinking of Humanism as presented in the *New York Times,* as taught at Oxford and Cambridge, etc.

AA: Of course, anytime we start talking about an "ism," we start to encounter problems. I think more and more that we need to approach things in a species specific way, so I'm drawing my parameters wider and wider, as in that approach to Los Angeles and San Francisco from 10,000 BC to the present.

MF: In your talk with Ben Hollander you ask if we, living in the cinematic and digital age, have renounced claims to stable memory[3]. What do you consider stable memory? And, if we answer your question in the affirmative, what is the result?

AA: The plan for Iraq can tell you a lot about this. The fact that the U.S. military stood guard in front of the Ministry of Oil and allowed the National Museum, the library, and dozens of ministries to be looted and destroyed can give you a fairly precise idea of what official American policy is toward historical memory. The criminal regime of Saddam Hussein cannot even be put on trial now, because most of the important records have been destroyed—so when Rumsfeld says, "The regime of Saddam Hussein is history," he is giving us a very precise definition, one that conforms very much to U.S. government archival policies. If you look for files in the FBI or the CIA, you will find many versions of the same document censored in different places. There is an absolute erasure of history in its documentary sense, and what we are left with is a record of subterfuge. You can go to Spain and look at records of the Inquisition and they will be absolutely accurate. That might be one definition of stable memory. Certainly what was represented in the National Museum of Iraq is a form of stable memory, a repository of artifacts relating to a very specific geographical space and historical time. Those same artifacts in the Metropolitan or the Louvre have completely different meaning. Now I don't mean stable memory in the totalitarian sense, that everyone is supposed to have the same narrative or remember the same things, but in the sense, say, that any Egyptian living through the Suez Crisis would have understood precisely the relationship of their family history—when their ancestors had been conscripted and died working on the Canal—to the actions against the colonial powers undertaken by Nasser. Stable memory then, I guess, has more to do with where we position ourselves in relation to events, and how deeply those events remain within us. I think the lengths to which American propaganda goes shows precisely, in an inverse fashion, how strong historical memory is. The lone gunman theory in the Kennedy assassination, for instance. The ridiculous zoom shot of Firdous Square and the toppling of the statue of Saddam which, when seen at a distance, shows you about 150 people in a space surrounded by U.S. tanks. The stable memory, the ethical memory that knows which image would corroborate most closely to the feelings of the time, that's the memory that has to be attacked by mass power.

★

Notes:

[1] Poetry Is News grew out of an increasing sense of astonishment that I shared with Anne Waldman as we saw the apparent ease with which people were able to divide their political and creative selves at public events in the months preceding the invasion of Iraq. We began circulating an e-mail statement/manifesto to this effect and it elicited a range of responses that led us to the idea of an event. We planned the event, along with Alan Gilbert, Kristin Prevallet, Rachel Levitsky, Maureen Owen, Gabrielle David, and many, many others, with the intention, not of creating an organization, but instigating thought and establishing a precedent for the kinds of things that ought to be considered by people in the heart of the empire engaged in any kind of public exposition, writing and poetry included. The free event, which took place over the course of a full day at the Poetry Project at St. Mark's Church (February 1, 2003), covered an enormous range of issues. We divided the day into four sections (Where Is Poetry? Responding to Crisis; Acting in Public: Expanding Cultural Space; Bringing Back the World; Being Censored, Censoring Ourselves). In between these sections (each represented by three to four speakers), we had "Reports from the Front." These "reports" included Paul Chan, a New York artist recently returned from Baghdad, showing slides of the city and its people; Rachel Murray speaking about riding in ambulances under fire in Jenin; the cartoonist and journalist Ted Rall speaking about Afghanistan; and Jesus Gonzalez and Angela Payano, two New York City high school students, on their efforts to organize against military recruitment in the schools. There were also people displaying and discussing other means of protest and communication, from art demonstrations organized in front of the INS building to urban pirate radio station operators. Amongst the writers and artists who addressed the packed hall were the Lebanese novelist and journalist Elias Khoury, one of the Arab world's foremost intellectuals; and poets, writers, and musicians David Henderson, Richard Hell, Karen Malpede, Michael Palmer, Eliot Weinberger, Samiya Bashir, and Moustafa Bayoumi. Despite expected criticism, some justified and some gratuitous, we felt that our Poetry Is News: Operation Counter-Intelligence, helped to focus and consolidate the attention of many individuals and groups in the struggle to determine how to best use our diverse energies and efforts to effect intellectual, social, and political change.

[2] The People's Poetry Gathering, sponsored by Poet's House, City Lore, and, this year, Arts International, asked me to be a consultant for a major component of the 2003 festival concentrating on the Arab and/or Islamic world; we invited the great Iraqi poet Saadi Youssef but his visa was denied. Other poets who did come included the Bosnian

Semezdin Mehmedinovic; Vénus Khoury-Ghata from Lebanon; Kishwar Naheed from Pakistan; Khaled Mattawa, originally from Libya; the Lebanese-American Etel Adnan, and the Moroccan Abdellatif Laâbi. At a remarkably moving reading of Iraqi poetry led by Elias Khoury and a group of graduate students, we also played a tape of Saadi Youssef greeting the gathering and reading his poetry in Arabic and English. One of the most distinct impressions I got at this year's gathering was that, despite the presence and participation of many prominent American poets, much greater attention was put on the poets who had come from abroad, and this added to the sense of an expanded vocabulary, a space where poets like Etel Adnan or Abdellatif Laâbi could speak of things not usually spoken about by many American poets.

3   This appears as "A Conversation with Benjamin Hollander," in my book *from the warring factions*. Los Angeles: Beyond Baroque, 2003. 171–203.

Diversityrap

MAX REGAN & LISA BIRMAN
2003

★　★　★

"I don't mind being in Boulder, I just pretend I'm in Sweden."
—JULIE PATTON

Boulder / 1974 / 1975 / 1985 / accreditation / 1990 / what we (have) seen / what we will never (see) / white bread capital of the world / diversity / 92% white / the people's republic of boulder / you must be kidding / where are all the real people? / they're in Denver / Naropa / Institute / Broadway, Pearl Street, Arapahoe / old schoolhouse / small cottages / wide expanse of green lawn / flatirons / curse of Chief Niwot / crouching statue on the bike path / Naropa in fall in winter in spring in summer / Naropa in pain / Naropa and white Buddhism / crazy wisdom / because we are founded on the controversial / summer institute / what can and cannot be transmitted / world wisdom chair / this being a place of lineage / writing students form SUEI / student union for ethnic inclusion / people begin to ask / diversity, what do you mean / aren't we all the same / summer writing program / 1992 Amendment 2 / 1993 Amendment 2 / Barbara in her office typing / 6 a.m. / we will refuse / we will refuse to comply with any amendment, law, ordinance that limits the full humanity of our students, staff / march to the band shell / Allen says we won't go back / skin and teeth skin and bone / Anne's rewrite of the Amendment / ecstasy of purpose / hate is not a family value / robin boycotts, my heart he says, breaking / (my birthplace) / 34 year old woman at bus stop in Denver beaten for wearing Overturn Amend. 2 button / while her children watch / so many / in pain / vision quests / warrior training / 84,000 ways to teach the dharma / U.S. Supreme Court ruling overturns Amendment 2 / we start over / religious right / focus on the family / tonglen / breathe in blackness / darkness? / breathe out whiteness / lightness? / he asks a question in class / says I left with a knot in my stomach / she gets a D on the quiz / white boys with dreadlocks / he writes on his eval: Langston Hughes, Howard Hughes: Not Related / Institute of American Indian Arts in Santa Fe / in a white town with a white teacher / people leaving say, I just couldn't take it / Racism / Ethnicity / Culture / Culture vultures / people leaving / in (pain) / she says, I now realize I have made a mistake, you didn't mean me / a taking / a dominant position / a delusion / a definition / budgetary issues / training and education / Buddhism as philosophy / as psychology /

as religion / suffering is not just metaphysical / in the class survey / American lit / 30 authors / 1 woman / 1 person of color / Ward says: to understand before we take / to give back if we take / to know what it means / to be the stolen generation / to be stolen / Diversity Awareness Working Group / Cheryl / a list on her wall / names of the ones who left / the ones who stayed / James / P. / The Color of Fear / Zora Neale Hurston scholarships / bake sales / rummage sales / auctions / restorative justice / student petitions / advisory board / shamanism / she says, does anyone else see the word sham? / he says, ultimately this is an accountability issue / and people are leaving / people are leaving / look at this systematically / long-range / touch the essence / get off your ass / at the mic she says, you have a gay dean / (cheers) / begin by accepting that the land you are standing on does not belong to you / as a matter of policy / who is entitled / who pays the bill / this is an accountability (issue) / last in first out / first in / first out / international students calling from the border / international students cannot work / when home is $1600 away / this is an issue of ability / this line u.s. citizens only / welcome home / community / dialogue / practice / committee / no action was formed at this time / Mission Statement / diversity awareness and inclusion / endless rounds of language / Slogans: / Naropa: I'm egoless but I'm a total asshole / Naropa: park somewhere else / Naropa: come join us in our weird little scene / Naropa: please don't fuck with me, I'm cultivating openness / Naropa in Boulder, California, London, Bali, Nepal, Prague, India / oppressions are connected / interlocked / a profound commitment to compassion / he says, I understood then / I could attend but not belong / malidoma: hospitality is inviting someone into your heart / pluralism / what it is to be a black swan / in a sea of white / listen (listen) listen / privilege = the choice not to see / because it is said to be not a problem / meaning ours / or look away / because it is not apparent / until mouth open / clothes removed / identifiable / Arapahoe road Arapahoe nation / they were merchants / they were the first to die in North America / this is not subject to intellectual conceit / not angst / this is pain / real lives / real people in real (time) / humility = maybe this isn't mine / 2001 / students of color sit-in outside president's office / no-uni-ver-si-ty without di-ver-sity / this being an institution / of learning / Sept 11 / Muslim woman with son in stroller / corner of Arapahoe and 16th / boy in jeep throws jam jar from car window / go the fuck home ragheads / aliens / we circle (protect) her, calm the baby / glass underfoot / pain and she's wailing / who are you / I work next door / at Naropa / pain and pain / we grieve the lives lost / should be brought to justice without the vengeful spirit that harms the innocent / Patriot Act / she writes from lower Manhattan / a world of smoke / birds in the gutters / fallen by the thousands / he says, we're a Buddhist college, right / can't we all hold hands and chant our way to oneness? / I-140-129 / renewal of documents / renewal of governments / 2003 / overthrow the regime / 5 million people march in 24 countries

/ it is no longer enough / it was never enough / and the bombs come / individual action / collective action / get a space / make something happen / bomb a mosque / bomb a hospital / west nile / SARS / exposure / target populations / if I don't have it, it doesn't exist / Baghdad falls / across the ocean across / the digital divide / human genome / this is an accounting issue / train to Vienna, she says, what good is contemplative education / these people have no clean water / no food / 2003 / breathing in Dachau / the killing wall at Terezin / bringing them back / transport / 1000 people, 0 survivors / back to themselves / this is an issue of counting / what are you willing to see / what are you willing to do about what you see / Operation Iron Eagle (again) / Department of Homeland Security / don't be afraid, be ready / biological threat / chemical threat / radiation threat / lawsuits / if I can't have it, I can't exist / ground rules / how it has worked to date / acts of meanness / individual systems conferring dominance / pain and (pain) / race class and gender on film / dances of Africa / stop, drop and process / learn to use the language / Special Asst. to the President for Diversity Affairs / personal racism vs. structural racism / she says, you can't do this work unless you get uncomfortable / pain and pain / it has to be mandatory / naming of classrooms / use the budget / Tendrel : A Journal of Diversity at Naropa / emphasize our commonality rather than our difference? / this of course, is a statement of privilege / recruitment and retention of students of color / a conference (and) a conference / the circles we talk / now we say interculturalism / meaning not just everyone who isn't us / meaning everyone / I always miss the revolution / your privilege / your pain / your privilege / our pain / our privilege / your pain / Faculty Training / ageism / he says, I've waited 40 years to take this class / push to discuss / sexism / Staff Training / White allies group / whiteness studies / if you let these issues stop with you, our work will take longer / our work will take / change will take longer / Columbus day / who was present at this meeting / Indigenous healers day / first they took our land / then our lives / then our culture / now they want our religion / nothing to report / faculty under fire / wildfires / Gill Foundation / 2003 / town hall / new president / draft of cultural appropriation policy / internalized racism / well after all, we're all middle class / this is my only pair of shoes / do you understand / homophobia / trans-gender / do we have to use the word appropriation? / it's so negative / let's just take that word out / we will refuse / are you listening? / what do you have permission (not) to see? / awareness (to be wary) / a crossing / a going beyond / Naropa in (fall) in spring / to embrace and extend identity / body as past the Binary / who we are / I say there is more than / He says / She says / after (all) let's just take that / (word out) / who we say we are / kari says no pronouns / Not Related / who are we? / our only strength is in difference / let the violence stop with us / pain and (pain) and people are (people) are leaving / (welcome home) / who we say / we are / let the violence / stop

Contributors

★   ★   ★

Helen Adam (1909–1992) was born in Glasgow, Scotland; she moved to the United States in 1939. She was a writer of Scottish ballads and has been associated with both the Beat literary movement and the San Francisco Renaissance. Her publications include *Selected Poems and Ballads, Ghosts and Grinning Shadows: Two Witch Stories, Turn Again to Me, Gone Sailing, The Bells of Dis, Stone Cold Gothic,* and the play *San Francisco's Burning!*

Ammiel Alcalay is a poet, translator, critic, and scholar who teaches at Queens College and the CUNY Graduate Center. His books include *the cairo notebooks, After Jews & Arabs: Remaking Levantine Culture, Memories of Our Future: Selected Essays* and *from the warring factions.* Some of his translations include a collection by Middle Eastern Jews, *Keys to the Garden,* and *Sarajevo Blues* by the Bosnian poet Semezdin Mehmedinovic. His work has appeared in big and little magazines including *Time, The Village Voice, The New York Times, Paper Air, Sulfur, Raddle Moon,* and numerous other venues.

Amiri Baraka, cultural-activist, poet & performer, published his first volume of poetry, *Preface to a Twenty-Volume Suicide Note,* in 1961 (this work was published under the name LeRoi Jones). Amiri Baraka's literary prizes and honors include fellowships from the Guggenheim and the NEA, the PEN/Faulkner Award, the Rockefeller Foundation Award for Drama, the Langston Hughes Award, and a lifetime achievement award from the Before Columbus Foundation. He is codirector, with his wife Amina Baraka, of Kimako's Blues People, a community arts space. Recent books include *The Leroi Jones/Amiri Baraka Reader, Wise Why's Y's: The Griot's Tale, Transbluesency: The Selected Poetry of Amiri Baraka/Leroi Jones (1961–1995), Funk Lore: New Poems (1984–1995), Jesse Jackson & Black People,* and *The Essence of Reparations.*

Ted Berrigan (1934–1983) was a central figure in the second generation of the New York School of Poets. He was the author of more than 20 books including *The Sonnets, Bean Spasms* (with Ron Padgett and Joe Brainard), *Poems, In Brief, Red Wagon,* and *A Certain Slant of Sunlight.* He edited and published *C* Magazine and C Press Books, wrote art criticism, and collaborated with many writers and artists. Berrigan taught at the St. Mark's Poetry Project and was Writer in Residence/Visiting Poet at The Writers' Workshop at the

University of Iowa, The University of Michigan at Ann Arbor, Yale University, SUNY Buffalo, University of Essex in England, Northeastern Illinois University, and Naropa University. Granary Books published *Ted Berrigan: An Annotated Checklist* (1998).

Lisa Birman is a poet and writer from Melbourne, Australia. Her chapbooks include *Some Things—Poems and Translations* and *deportation poems,* and her work has been published in the *Poetry Project Newsletter, FIR8, Bombay Gin, The Australian Writer,* and *The Melbourne Poets Union Anthology.* Her next chapbook, *possibly,* is forthcoming from Barefoot Books. Lisa is the cofounder of Movie Star Press and codirector of Naropa University's Summer Writing Program.

Robin Blaser was born in Denver, Colorado, in 1925. A seminal figure of the "San Francisco Renaissance," he was close to poets Jack Spicer and Robert Duncan. *The Holy Forest,* a collected poems, was published in 1993. *"The Recovery of the Public World": A Conference and Festival in Honour of Robin Blaser, His Poetry and Poetics,* was held in Vancouver, B.C. in 1995. The papers of the conference were published in 1999. Recent work includes *"Great Companion: Dante Alighieri,"* the keynote address for the international conference *"La presenza di Dante nella poesia nordamericane,"* in Pescara—Torre de' Passeri, Italy, 1997; and the libretto for Sir Harrison Birtwistle's opera *The Last Supper,* which premiered in German at the Berlin Staatsoper, April 2000, and then toured England. Blaser's 75th birthday was celebrated in San Francisco, hosted by the Poetry Center, May, 2000. His latest book is *Even on Sunday: Essays, Readings, and Archival Materials on the Poetry and Poetics of Robin Blaser,* 2002.

Reed Bye is the author of *Border Theme, Passing Freaks and Graces,* and *Gaspar Still in His Cage.* He has been a practitioner of Buddhist and Shambhala teachings for the past twenty years and served as Chair of Naropa University's Kerouac School Department of Writing and Poetics from 1996 to 2002, where he also teaches literature and creative writing.

Jack Collom is the author of numerous collections of poetry, including *Little Grand Island, Arguing with Something Plato Said, 8-Ball, Entering the City,* and *Red Car Goes By: Selected Poems 1955-2000.* His essays on teaching and collections of children's poetry appear in *Moving Windows* and *Poetry Everywhere.* Jack has produced two CDs of original work performed in collaboration with musician/composer, Ken Bernstein. He was awarded NEA fellowships in 1980 and 1990.

Robert Creeley has published more than sixty books of poetry, most recently *If I Were Writing This, Just in Time: Poems 1984–1994, Life & Death, Echoes*, and *Selected Poems 1945–1990*. His honors include a Lannan Lifetime Achievement Award, the Beyond Columbus Foundation's Lifetime Achievement Award, the Frost Medal, the Shelley Memorial Award, as well as Guggenheim, Rockefeller, and NEA Fellowships. He was New York State Poet from 1989 to 1991. He was a long-time faculty member at SUNY Buffalo, and is now on the faculty at Brown University.

Beverly Dahlen's ongoing work *A Reading* has appeared in three volumes, and excerpts from it continue to appear in periodicals (*Bombay Gin, Mirage #4/Period[ical], The Iowa Review*). Two selections from Dahlen's work were included in the anthology *Moving Borders: Three Decades of Innovative Writing by Women*, edited by Mary Margaret Sloan.

Samuel R. Delany is a critic and novelist, with essays and interviews so far collected in seven volumes, the most recent three of which are *Silent Interviews, Longer Views*, and *Shorter Views*. He has written a highly praised autobiography *The Motion of Light in Water*, the best-selling *Times Square Red, Times Square Blue*, and, among his fiction, *The Mad Man, Atlantis: Three Tales*, and *Dhalgren*. Over the last year some of his early science fiction—*Babel-17, Empire Star*, and *Nova* have come back into print. In 1999 a substantial book of his letters, *1984: Selected Letters* appeared. He teaches at Temple University, and is a frequent guest faculty at Naropa University's Summer Writing Program.

Steve Dickison is Executive Director of the Poetry Center and American Poetry Archives at San Francisco State. He is the editor and publisher of the award-winning press Listening Chamber, and coeditor of *Shuffle Boil*. Recent writing has appeared in *lyric&, Crayon, 26, Shuffle Boil*, and *The Recovery of the Public World: Essays in Poetics in Honour of Robin Blaser*.

Robert Duncan (1919–1988) was born in 1919 in Oakland, California. He is associated with the San Francisco Renaissance, and in particular with Jack Spicer and Robin Blaser. While teaching at Black Mountain College, Duncan composed most of the poems in his first major collection of poetry, *The Opening of the Field*. This collection, followed by *Roots and Branches* and *Bending the Bow* established Duncan as one of the most important poets of his time. His awards include the Harriet Monroe Memorial Prize, a Guggenheim Fellowship, the Levinson Prize, the National Poetry Award, and three fellowships from the NEA. His later works include *Ground Work: Before the War* and *Ground Work II: In the Dark*. The letters of Robert Duncan and Denise Levertov were published by Stanford University Press.

Michael du Plessis is the author of articles dealing with topics ranging from Brandon Teena to bisexuality. du Plessis is currently working on a manuscript for the University of Minnesota Press on transexual and transgender images, and has given readings at the Gay and Lesbian Center of Los Angeles and Highways Gallery in Santa Monica.

kari edwards is a poet, artist, and gender activist. Author of *a day in the life of p.*, *a diary of lies, Electric Spandex: anthology of writing the queer text,* and *post/(pink),* kari is also the recipient of the 2002 New Langton Art's Bay Area Award in literature. she is also the poetry editor of I.F.G.E's *Transgender Tapestry: An International Publication on Transgender Issues.*

Marlowe Fawcett, an MFA graduate of the Jack Kerouac School of Disembodied Poetics, is a freelance writer living and (sometimes) working in Boulder, Colorado. He is coeditor of the literary journal, 3.∴.2, and is currently in protracted negotiations with his first novel, a psycho-archeological thriller about the London underground.

Lawrence Ferlinghetti was a prominent voice of the Beat literary movement of the 1950s, proprietor of City Lights Bookstore, and is editor and publisher of the renowned City Lights Books press in San Francisco. His well-known text, *A Coney Island of the Mind* has been translated into nine languages, and there are nearly 1,000,000 copies in print. His most recent books are *These Are My Rivers: New and Selected Poems 1955–1993, A Far Rockaway of the Heart, How to Paint Sunlight, Love In The Days Of Rage,* and *Life Studies, Life Stories: Drawings.* He has been the recipient of numerous awards and was named San Francisco's Poet Laureate in 1998.

Alan Gilbert is a poet and critic currently living in Brooklyn, New York. Recent poems have appeared in *Sulfur, The Baffler,* and *First Intensity.* Recently published essays and reviews can be found in *The Chicago Review, The Poetry Project Newsletter,* and *XCP: Cross-Cultural Poetics.* In 1998, he received a Ph.D. in English Literature from SUNY Buffalo.

Allen Ginsberg (1926–1997) met William S. Burroughs, Neal Cassady, and Jack Kerouac, the core group of writers who later became associated with the Beat Movement, while he was a student at Columbia University in the 1940s. His first book of poems, *Howl!* published by City Lights, overcame censorship trials to become one of the most widely read poems of the 20th century. Ginsberg cofounded the Jack Kerouac School of Disembodied Poetics at Naropa University in Colorado with Anne Waldman, in 1974. In his later years he became a Distinguished Professor at Brooklyn College. Some of his later books include *White Shroud: Poems, 1980–1985, Cosmopolitan Greetings: Poems, 1986–1992, Journals Mid-Fifties 1954–1958, Selected Poems, 1947–1995,* and *Death and Fame: Last Poems, 1993–1997.* His honors include a National Book Award, the Woodbury Poetry Prize, a Guggenheim fellowship, the National Book Award for Poetry, NEA grants, and a Lifetime Achievement Award from the Before Columbus Foundation.

James Grauerholz lived and worked with William Burroughs for the last 23 years of his life. He is Burroughs's literary executor and has edited the Burroughs collection *Interzone* and *Word Virus: The William S. Burroughs Reader.* During the 1970s and 1980s Grauerholz often visited or resided in Boulder with Burroughs and participated in his Naropa-related events. He is working on a comprehensive biography of William Burroughs.

Barbara Guest is a major poet of The New York School. Her recent books include *If So, Tell Me, Miniatures and Other Poems, Forces of Imagination: Writing on Writing, The Altos* with artist Richard Tuttle, *Fair Realism,* and *Musicality* with artist June Felter. She published a biography, *Herself Defined: H.D. and Her World* in 1984 and has served as visiting lecturer at Bethlehem College, Brown University, SUNY Buffalo, University of California at San Diego, the H.D. Symposia at Bryn Mawr, and the Southbank Imagist Conference in London. Her awards include the Lawrence Lipton Award for Literature, the Longview Award, a Yaddo Fellowship, the San Francisco State Award for Poetry, and a grant from the NEA.

Bobbie Louise Hawkins was awarded a Fellowship in Literature from the NEA, and has to her credit fourteen books of fiction, nonfiction, poetry, and performance monologues. Her recording projects include *Live at the Great American Music Hall* and *Jaded Love* with Lee Christopher and jazz musicians. Her show, *Life As We Know It,* has been performed at the Summer Writing Program and BMoCA in Boulder and at Joe's Pub in New York. A new show, *Take Love For Instance . . .* was performed at BMoCA in 2003. She is a professor on the core faculty at the Jack Kerouac School's Department of Writing and Poetics and founded its prose fiction concentration.

Anselm Hollo, poet and literary translator, is a professor in the Jack Kerouac School of Disembodied Poetics at Naropa University. His recent collections include *Corvus, Rue Wilson Monday,* and *Caws and Causeries: Around Poetry and Poets.* His most recent book is *Notes on the Possibilities and Attractions of Existence: Selected Poems 1965-2000.* His work has been widely anthologized and he is a recipient of an NEA Fellowship in poetry, two grants from the Fund for Poetry, and the government of Finland's Distinguished Foreign Translator's Award. Authors whose works he has translated include Paul Klee, Bertolt Brecht, and Jean Genet.

Laird Hunt, Writing and Poetics core faculty member at Naropa University, is the author of a book of short stories, *mock parables and histories, The Paris Stories,* and two novels, *The Impossibly* and *Indiana, Indiana.* His writings have appeared in the United States and abroad in, among other places, *Ploughshares, Grand Street, Fence, Conjunctions, Brick, Mentor,* and *Zoum Zoum.*

Robert Hunter is a recording artist, poet and translator. He is best known as primary lyricist for the Grateful Dead. Hunter first contributed lyrics for the Grateful Dead in 1967, subsequently he became the group's major lyricist with his work appearing on all of the Grateful Dead's albums. His published works include *Sentinel, A Box Of Rain: Lyrics 1965–1993,* and *Night Cadre.*

Pierre Joris left Luxembourg at eighteen and has since lived in the U.S., Great Britain, North Africa, and France. Recent books include *Poasis: Selected Poems 1986–1999; 4 x 1, (translations of Rilke, Tzara, Duprey, and Tengour),* and books by Abdelwahab Meddeb, Celan, Blanchot, and Jabès. He coedited (with Jerome Rothenberg) the two-volume anthology of 20th century avant-garde writings, *Poems for the Millennium,* as well as books by Schwitters and Picasso. He often collaborates with Nicole Peyrafitte on performance work.

Joanne Kyger, a native California poet, often associated with the Beat literary movement and the San Francisco Renaissance, has taught at the Naropa Summer Writing Program and the New College of San Francisco. She is the author of over twenty books of poetry, including *Some Life, Strange Big Moon: The Japan and India Journals 1960-1964,* and *Again: Poems 1989-2000.* Her most recent book is *As Ever: Selected Poems.*

Laura Mullen is the author of two collections of poetry, *The Surface* and *After I Was Dead,* and a book-length "post-modern gothic," *The Tales of Horror.* Her work has recently appeared in *Chain, Facture, Ploughshares,* and on *Black Ice* at the AltX site.

Eileen Myles is a poet, performer, and politician (Myles conducted an openly female write-in campaign for President of the United States in 1992). Her books of poetry and fiction include *School of Fish, Maxfield Parrish:*

Early and New Poems, Chelsea Girls, Not Me, and *Cool for You.* She coedited *The New Fuck You, Adventures in Lesbian Reading,* winner of a Lambda Book Award. She currently teaches at University of California-San Diego.

Kai Nieminen is a Finnish poet, translator, and essayist. He has published fourteen volumes of poetry, most recently, *Serious Poems.* His translations from Japanese into Finnish include classics such as *Tale of Genji, Essays in Idleness, Ikkyu, Ihara Saikaku,* and Basho's prose and haiku. He also translates modern prose and poetry including the work of Soseki, Tanizaki, Mishima, Oe, Makoto Ooka, and Banana Yoshimoto. In 1999 he was awarded the Eino Leino Prize for his literary work.

Alice Notley's recent books include *The Descent of Alette,* a "feminist epic," and the book length poem, *Disobedience,* winner of the Griffin Poetry Prize. Her book, *Mysteries of Small Houses,* won the *Los Angeles Times* Book Award for Poetry and was a finalist for the Pulitzer Prize. A volume of essays, *Coming After,* is forthcoming from University of Michigan Press. She has been the recipient of an award from the Foundation for Contemporary Performance Arts, the San Francisco Poetry Center Book Award, and the Shelley Memorial Award. She lives and writes in Paris, France.

Akilah Oliver is a poet, performance artist, and teacher. She has read and performed experimental investigative performance art as a solo artist and in collaboration. She is the author of *the she said dialogues: flesh memory,* a book of experimental prose poetry. Oliver's poetry has been anthologized widely, including in *Chain, Kenning, Bombay Gin, Blood & Tears: Poems for Matthew Shepard, High Risk 2,* and *Blood Whispers: L.A. Writers on AIDS.*

Douglas Oliver's (1937-2000) books include *The Harmless Building* (nominated for the Booker Prize), *Three Variations on the Theme of Harm, A Salvo for Africa, Penniless Politics, Penguin Modern Poets 10,* and *Selected Poems.* He taught at the British Institute in Paris, and coedited the magazine *Gare du Nord* with the poet Alice Notley.

Michael Ondaatje was born in Colombo, Ceylon (now Sri Lanka), raised in London, and is now a Canadian citizen. He is the author of four collections of poetry including *The Cinnamon Peeler* and *Handwriting.* His works of prose include *Anil's Ghost, The English Patient* (later made into the Academy-Award-winning film), *In the Skin of the Lion, Coming Through Slaughter, The Collected Works of Billy the Kid,* and most recently, *The Conversations: Walter Murch & the Art of Editing Film.* His honors include the Kiriyama Pacific Rim Book Prize, the Prix Medicis, Canadian Governor-General's Award for

Literature, the Giller Prize for his novel *Anil's Ghost,* and the Booker McConnell Prize for *The English Patient.*

James Oughton's books include *Taking Tree Trains, Gearing of Love, Mata Hari's Last Words,* and most recently, *Counting Out the Millennium.* He studied writing at York University in Toronto, and at Naropa, where he worked closely with Robert Duncan and Anne Waldman. He is a community college teacher, literary journalist, and photographer.

Max Regan, MFA, is a poet, writer, and teacher. Max is the founder of Hollowdeck Press, and has served on the undergraduate faculty of Naropa University and the University of Colorado. Max has worked as a journalist, columnist, and guest lecturer. Max has worked at Naropa University in Boulder, Colorado since 1992 and currently serves as the codirector of the Summer Writing Program as well as the program director for Naropa's Study Abroad Program in Prague.

Sonia Sanchez is a writer, professor, cultural activist, and international human rights worker. She has authored over sixteen books, including *Wounded in the House of a Friend, Does Your House Have Lions?,* and *Shake Loose My Skin.* Sanchez's poetry celebrates the connection between social justice activism and the strength of human spirit. She has received numerous awards and fellowships, including the American Book Award, the Langston Hughes Award from City College of New York, the Peace and Freedom Award from the Women's International League for Peace and Freedom, a Pew Fellowship in the Arts, and a fellowship from the NEA. In 2001 she was awarded the Robert Frost Medal for Poetry.

Edward Sanders's recent books include *America, A History in Verse, Volume 1 (1900–1939), America, A History in Verse, Volume 2 (1940–1961),* and *America, A History in Verse, Volume 3 (1962–1970).* Also in print are *1968, A History in Verse; Chekhov;* and *The Poetry and Life of Allen Ginsberg,* all written in accordance with the principles of "Investigative Poetry." Another recent project, *The Fugs Final CD (Part 1)* has been released this year by Artemis Records. He is the founder and editor of the *Woodstock Journal,* a biweekly newspaper.

Eleni Sikelianos's most recent books are National Poetry Series winner, *The Monster Lives of Boys & Girls,* and *Earliest Worlds.* Forthcoming are a book-length poem, *The California Poem,* and a nonfiction work, *The Book of Jon.* She has been conferred a number of awards for her poetry, nonfiction, and translations. She currently teaches in the MFA program at Naropa, and at Denver University.

Gary Snyder was born in San Francisco in 1930. His recent publications include *The Gary Snyder Reader (1952–1998), Mountains and Rivers Without End,* and *No Nature: New and Selected Poems,* which was a finalist for the National Book Award. He has received the Pulitzer Prize for Poetry, an American Academy of Arts and Letters award, the Bollingen Prize, an American Book Award, a Guggenheim Foundation Fellowship, the Robert Kirsch Lifetime Achievement Award from the *Los Angeles Times,* and the Shelley Memorial Award. Snyder was elected a Chancellor of the Academy of American Poets in 2003. He is a professor of English at the University of California, Davis. Snyder was instrumental in founding The Art of the Wild, an annual writing conference on wilderness and creative writing, and Nature and Culture, an undergraduate program for students of society and the environment.

Cole Swensen's books include *Such Rich Hour, Oh,* and *Try,* which won the Iowa Poetry Prize and the San Francisco State Poetry Center Book Award, *Noon,* winner of Sun & Moon's New American Poetry Award, and *Numen,* finalist for the PEN West Award in Poetry. She also translates contemporary French poetry and has received grants from the French National Bureau du Livre and from Fondation Beaumarchais as well as residencies at the Camargo Foundation and the Atelier Cosmopolite at Royaumont.

Arthur Sze's most recent collection, *The Redshifting Web: Poems 1970–1998,* was a finalist for the 1999 Lenore Marshall Poetry Prize. His poems have also appeared in *American Poetry Review, The Paris Review, Mother Jones, Conjunctions,* and the *Bloomsbury Review.* His honors include a Lannan Literary Award for Poetry, an American Book Award, and Fellowships from the Witter Bynner Foundation, the Guggenheim, and the NEA. Sze currently directs the Creative Writing Program at the Institute of American Indian Arts in Santa Fe, New Mexico, where he has taught for more than a decade.

Steven Taylor is a composer, writer, and ethnomusicologist. From 1976 until 1997 he collaborated regularly on poetry and music projects with Allen Ginsberg. He has been a member of the seminal poetry-rock group the Fugs since 1984 and has collaborated on theater and concert works with Allen Ginsberg, Ed Sanders, Kenward Elmslie, and Anne Waldman. From 1988 until 1994 he toured and recorded with the New York hardcore band False Prophets. Works include poetry, essays, articles, theater, and concert music, orchestrations, songs, and more than a dozen records. His book, *False Prophet: Field notes from the punk underground,* was published in 2003 by Wesleyan University Press. He has taught full-time at Naropa since 1995 and served as chair of Naropa's Writing and Poetics Department from 2002-2004.

Roberto Tejada was executive editor at *Artes de Mexico* magazine and founding editor of *Mandorla: New Writing from the Americas,* both in Mexico City. He has curated exhibitions at the Museo de las Artes (Guadalajara, Mexico) and the Blue Star Art Space (San Antonio, Texas). He has published critical reviews and writings on contemporary Latin American artists and photographers in *Boletín de Curare, La jornada, Artes de México, Luna córnea* (Mexico), *Third Text* (UK), *Flash Art* (u.s.-Italy), *Arte Internacional,* and *Art Nexus* (Colombia). He is the author of *Gift & Verdict.*

Lorenzo Thomas is a professor of English at the University of Houston-Downtown. He is the author of several collections of poetry and has published many critical articles on African American culture, literature, and music. His latest books include *Sing the Sun Up: Creative Writing Ideas from African American Literature, Extraordinary Measures: Afrocentric Modernism and Twentieth-Century American Poetry,* and *Chances Are Few.* His most recent book is *Dancing on Main Street,* published by Coffee House Press in 2004.

Anne Waldman is the author of over thirty books of poetry including *Fast Speaking Woman, Kill or Cure, IOVIS, Books I* and *II, Marriage: A Sentence, Vow To Poetry: Essays, Interviews, and Manifestoes, Dark Arcana/Afterimage or Glow,* and *In the Room of Never Grieve, New and Selected Poems 1985-2003.* She is also the editor of numerous anthologies including *The Beat Book;* and coeditor of *Disembodied Poetics: Annals of The Jack Kerouac School,* and *The Angel Hair Anthology.* Her CDs include *Alchemical Elegy* and *Battery: Live at Naropa.* She is on the faculty of the New England College MFA Program in Poetry, and has recently read and participated in festivals in the U.K., Montreal, and Barcelona. She is an active member of the Naropa University Audio Archive Project. Anne is cofounder of the Kerouac School, and chair and artistic director of the Summer Writing Program.

Peter Warshall has served in public office as a contributor to environmental research, and been a consultant to the U.N. and to USAID on ecology and economic development. He edits *Whole Earth Catalog* and magazine. His articles have appeared in the *San Francisco Chronicle, American West, Animal Kingdom,* and in the book *Mind in the Waters.*

Peter Lamborn Wilson lived in Iran and India for ten years and has written extensively on Sufism, Persian literature, and Middle-Eastern religion. His books include *Ploughing the Clouds: The Search for Irish Soma, Avant Gardening* (with Bill Weinburg from Autonomedia), and *Drunken Universe: An Anthology of Persian Sufi Poetry* (with N. Pourjavady). He also has a spoken word CD with Bill Laswell, entitled *Hashisheen.*

Permissions

★ ★ ★

"In This Place Called America" has been used by permission of the author.

Ted Berrigan's Naropa Workshop Class, July 24, 1978 has been used by permission of the Estate of Ted Berrigan, Alice Notley executrix.

"A Little Endarkenment: and in my poetry you find me" has been used by permission of the authors.

"Irreparables, I: an essay-ode" has been used by permission of the author.

"The Poetics of Disobedience" has been used by permission of the author.

"On Translation" has been used by permission of the authors.

"From the Gone World" has been used by permission of the author.

"Personal Geography" has been used by permission of the authors.

"Symbiosis" has been used by permission of the author.

"A Tribute to Sappho" has been used by permission of the author.

"On the Ballad" has been used by permission of the Allen Ginsberg Trust, Bob Rosenthal, Trustee, and The Estate of Helen Adam.

"The Wang River Sequence, A Prospectus" has been used by permission of the author.

"A Brief History of the Early Prose Poem" has been used by permission of the author.

Gary Snyder comment, Dharma Poetics Panel © Gary Snyder 1994 – used with permission.

"Burroughs and Dharma" has been used by permission of the author.

"No One Spoke: Chögyam Trungpa's Teachings of Dharma Art" has been used by permission of the author.

"Revolutionary Poetics" has been used by permission of the Allen Ginberg Trust, Bob Rosenthal, Trustee.

"Hieroglyphics and Money" has been used by permission of the author.

"Lokapala Interview" has been used by permission of the authors.

Amiri Baraka's lecture has been used by permission of the author.

"Panel: Politics of Identity," June 25, 2001 has been used by permission of the authors.

"Femanifestos" has been used by permission of the author.

"How To See through Poetry: Myth Perception and History" has been used by permission of the author.

"Courting the Muse" has been used by permission of the author.

"A Reverie on the Making of a Poem" has been used by permission of the author.

Douglas Oliver's "Death, Shivers, and the Tick of Poetic Stress" has been used by the permission of the Estate of Douglas Oliver, Alice Notley executrix.

"Beauty Trouble: Identity and Difference in the Tradition of the Aesthetic" has been used by permission of the author.

Funder Acknowledgments

Coffee House Press is an independent nonprofit literary publisher. Our books are made possible through the generous support of grants and gifts from many foundations, corporate giving programs, individuals, and through state and federal support. This project received major funding from the Bush Foundation. Coffee House Press has received general operating support from the Minnesota State Arts Board, through an appropriation by the Minnesota State Legislature and by the National Endowment for the Arts, a federal agency; from the following private and corporate foundations; the Elmer and Eleanor Andersen Foundation; the Buuck Family Foundation; Consortium Book Sales and Distribution; the Grotto Foundation; the Lerner Family Foundation; the McKnight Foundation; the Outagamie Foundation; the John and Beverly Rollwagen Foundation; the law firm of Schwegman, Lundberg, Woessner & Kluth, P.A.; Target, Marshall Field's, and Mervyn's with support from the Target Foundation; James R. Thorpe Foundation; West Group; and the Woessner Freeman Foundation; and we have received significant contributions from the following individuals: E.T. Binger and Rebecca Rand; Stephen and Isabel Keating; Rena Kornblum and Joseph Schmitt; Seymour Kornblum and Gerry Lauter; Allan and Cinda Kornblum; Gail and Henry See; Jim Sitter; Charles Steffey and Suzannah Martin; and an anonymous donor.

This activity is made possible in part by a grant from the Minnesota State Arts Board, through an appropriation by the Minnesota State Legislature and a grant from the National Endowment for the Arts.

MINNESOTA
STATE ARTS BOARD

To you and our many readers across the country,
we send our thanks for your continuing support.

*Good books are brewing
at coffeehousepress.org*